Herzfeld's Guide to Closed-End Funds

Herzfeld's Guide to Closed-End Funds

Thomas J. Herzfeld

Chairman and President
Thomas J. Herzfeld & Co., Inc.
Thomas J. Herzfeld Advisors, Inc.

Edited by Cecilia L. Gondor

McGraw-Hill, Inc.

New York   San Francisco   Washington, D.C.   Auckland   Bogotá
Caracas   Lisbon   London   Madrid   Mexico City   Milan
Montreal   New Delhi   San Juan   Singapore
Sydney   Tokyo   Toronto

Library of Congress Cataloging-in-Publication Data

Herzfeld, Thomas J.
    Herzfeld's guide to closed-end funds / Thomas J. Herzfeld; edited
by Cecilia L. Gondor.
          p.   cm.
    Includes index.
    ISBN 0-07-028435-0
    1. Closed-end funds—United States.   2. Closed-end funds—United
States—Directories.   I. Gondor, Cecilia L.   II. Title.
III. Title: Guide to closed-end funds.
    HG4930.H47   1993
    332.63'27—dc20   93-7229
                                                  CIP

1 2 3 4 5 6 7 8 9 0 DOH/DOH 9 9 8 7 6 5 4 3

ISBN 0-07-028435-0

*The sponsoring editor for this book was David Conti, the editing supervisor
was Kimberly A. Goff, and the production supervisor was Donald F. Schmidt.
This book was set in Palatino. It was composed by McGraw-Hill's Professional
Book Group composition unit.*

Printed and bound by R. R. Donnelley & Sons Company.

To my loving wife, Rutli

Contents

List of Figures

Preface

At the height of the go-go years, in the 1960s, fresh out of the army, I went to Wall Street and took a job as a trainee with Reynolds & Co., with the intention of eventually trading glamour stocks. There, almost by accident, I stumbled across closed-end funds and became fascinated with the concept of being able to buy assets at a discount. Upon further study and evaluation, I became convinced that closed-end funds had the best risk/reward relationship the stock market had to offer and decided to specialize in the field. I worked very hard and within a few years bought a seat on the New York Stock Exchange, formed a member firm, and generally became acknowledged as the leading expert on the subject; but this honor was primarily by default, as virtually no one else in those heady days had any interest in such a boring group. In the 1960s closed-end funds had been out of favor for over three decades, ever since the 1929 crash. In the United States at that time there were only about 50 rather banal funds, and as recently as a decade ago, the industry was still composed of only 60 issues with $8 billion in assets. Then in the 1980s there was an explosion of interest, with closed-end funds becoming the most talked-about industry on Wall Street, with over $44 billion of new funds, vast diversity and complexity, and new opportunities. The 1990s continued the momentum, with 118 new funds so far this decade representing $27 billion of new growth in the industry.

After two decades of specializing in a group that was the stock market's understudy, I personally find it tremendously fulfilling that closed-end funds are now center stage and have become superstars. Indeed, the research departments of many prominent Wall Street firms are now devoting significant time and attention to the subject. The trading strategies and hedging and investment programs I pioneered, developed, and published in my books and research (which have yielded an average 20-percent annual return for our clients) are now being copied by investment management firms all over the world—I find this situation quite gratifying, for imitation is the sincerest form of flattery (and a profitable one, too)!

Great thanks are offered to everyone on my staff for their hard work and commitment to the creation of this book. Thanks to Robert F. Drach, Paul J. Petersen, Patrick J. Joyce, and Ted S. Williams, who analyze the portfolios of the equity funds; to my son, Erik M. Herzfeld, our newest research analyst; and to my devoted office staff, who keep our office running smoothly. And finally, but most importantly, words are insufficient to express my gratitude to my editor, Cecilia Gondor, for her unflagging efforts to produce a complete and comprehensive volume. This project could not have reached completion without her countless hours of research and coordination. Many thanks, Cecilia, for a job well done.

Thomas J. Herzfeld

Author's Note

The purpose of this book is to describe the opinions and investment techniques of the author.

Any investment is effectively a projection into the future, and certainty of the future is not within the ability of mankind. There is no way any investment strategy can be guaranteed to result in success.

No two investors have identical needs, goals, and resources. Individual investor needs, therefore, cannot be properly served by any book of this nature. Before embarking on any investment strategy, the investor should utilize expert, competent, professional services designed to fit individual needs, goals, and resources.

Portions of this book contain the actual results of the author's theories. Readers are advised not to assume any positions specified or techniques employed will be profitable or equal past performance.

The author and the publisher specifically disclaim any personal liability, loss, or risk incurred as a consequence of the use and application, either directly or indirectly, of any advice or information presented herein.

Herzfeld's Guide to Closed-End Funds

1

Description of Closed-End Funds, Charting, and Sources of Information

What Is a Closed-End Fund?

One of the best ways to define a closed-end fund is to state what it most definitely is not: A closed-end fund is not a mutual fund, which by its very nature is open-ended, continually offering new shares for sale to the investing public. In addition to being much more well known than closed-end funds—thanks to millions spent in sales promotion—mutual funds also operate differently. Their purchase price, for example, is based on the net asset value per share (NAV)—meaning the total net assets of the fund divided by the number of its outstanding shares, plus, for load funds, a sales charge that can run as high as 8 percent. In the case of the so-called no-load funds—those without a sales commission—shares are generally bought and redeemed at their net asset value.

Closed-end funds, on the other hand, do not continue to sell new shares endlessly, as the mutual funds strive to do. Closed-end funds issue—and this is essential to understand—a fixed amount of stock. In this respect, they are just like any industrial firm or utility, which, with the exception of splits or additional offerings of stock, essentially always has the same number of shares outstanding. Closed-end fund shares trade in the open market exactly like the shares of any publicly traded company.

There is generally only one way to buy or sell shares in a closed-end fund—in the open market. (Some exceptions are during the original offering, when shares are offered directly from underwriting brokerage firms, or during a rights offering—when current shareholders have the right to subscribe to [buy] additional shares from the fund.) This is another factor that differentiates the closed-end fund from the mutual fund. An investor purchases a mutual fund from the fund itself or through its sales agents, and when the investor sells his or her shares, they are redeemed by the fund. So trading in closed-end funds, either on the buy or sell side, is done in the open market—on the stock exchanges or in the over-the-counter markets. Shares in closed-end funds, it must be remembered constantly, are not redeemed at their net asset value, as are shares in open-end funds. Rather, they are bought and sold at the price the general market places on them. And that price could be at net asset value, above it, or, as is often the case, below it, meaning at *discounts*.

An additional difference between mutual funds and closed-end funds can be found in the way in which they are capitalized. Mutual funds' balance sheets consist only of common stock, while a closed-end fund can be capitalized with preferred stock and/or debt.

An Historical Perspective

Historically, with variations, the primary purpose of closed-end funds—diversification—has essentially stayed the same. Even the first closed-end fund created by King William I of the Netherlands in 1822 was designed to provide a means of capital diversification (as well as a way to invest in foreign government loans).

During the 1920s, closed-end funds experienced what can best be described as phenomenal growth in the United States. Among the hundreds of companies that were formed and thrived in the seemingly endless boom of the decade were Adams Express, International Securities Trust of America, and Tri-Continental Corporation.

When the stock market crashed on Black Thursday, October 24, 1929, among the biggest losers were holders of shares in highly leveraged closed-end funds. In fact, the fate of leveraged closed-end funds was drastically worse than the fate of nonleveraged companies. According to the SEC, "By the end of 1937, the average dollar which had been invested in July 1929 in the index of leverage investment company stocks was worth 5 cents, while the nonleverage dollar was worth 48 cents."[1]

Although they have been enjoying a resurgence in popularity in the past 10 years, closed-end investment companies never regained the elevated status they enjoyed in the 1920s before the Crash. Since the Depression, the overwhelming growth in investment trusts has been concentrated in open-end mutual funds.

Today, the basic guideline in the United States for both closed-end and

---

[1]*Report of the Securities and Exchange Commission,* Investment Trusts and Investment Companies, Part III, Chap. 1, p. 4.

mutual funds is the Investment Company Act of 1940. In many respects, it is a detailed code designed to provide individual investors in investment trusts with the kind of protection sorely lacking before the Great Depression. For example, the overly leveraged companies that fared so poorly during the Depression have been prohibited. Similarly, the capital structure and dividend policies of the funds are now strictly regulated. The funds may not issue any debt that is not adequately covered by their assets, and they are not permitted to pay dividends from profits realized on the sale of securities without disclosing the source of such distributions.

Another provision protects existing stockholders from new issues of stock at a price below current net asset value. Such transactions are closely scrutinized by the SEC, although a number of closed-end funds have been skirting this issue with aggressively priced rights offerings.

Despite the debacle of the Depression, the American investor of today has a wide variety of potentially profitable closed-end funds in which to invest. Some of these funds invest in common stocks, others in preferred stocks, municipal bonds, convertible bonds, foreign countries, or the bonds of foreign issuers. Some portfolios are diversified, reflecting a broad spectrum of American industry; others are concentrated in a single industry.

It is safe to say that for the vast majority of investors, closed-end funds generally remain a mystery. Certainly these funds, like all other investment vehicles, are not to be entered into lightly. Potential investors must be aware of their special language and qualities and, most of all, must have an understanding of how closed-end funds should and should not be traded in the all-important quest for profits.

Charting

A brief note about the charts used as examples in this book. In my trading, I have found that keeping charts of net asset value (NAV) and price is immensely helpful. I plot the NAV on a daily basis when possible, but at least weekly, and the price of the fund daily on charts using a semilogarithmic scale. On such a scale, the same vertical distance always corresponds to the same percentage change regardless of scale; i.e., the distance on the chart in a move from 3 to 5 will be the same as a move from 6 to 10, or from 12 to 20. The distance between the price of the fund and the NAV is, of course, the discount when the fund's NAV is higher than its price. The distance between the NAV and the price of the fund is the premium, if the price is higher than its NAV.

It is also useful to plot an appropriate established index on the chart as a comparison to performance of NAV (or perhaps indicator). For example, I chart the Dow Jones Industrial Average on the same page as diversified, large-cap, U.S. equity funds, and the Manila Composite Index on the same page as The First Philippine Fund, as that fund's NAV moves in close relation to that index (see Chapter 7). Since most closed-end funds publish their NAV on a weekly basis, using an index that is published daily gives me a daily indication of what the NAV is doing.

Sources of Information

The NAVs of most closed-end funds are published weekly. Figure 1.1 shows a reprint of the most complete listing, which appears weekly in *Barron's*. Similar lists are published in *The Wall Street Journal, The New York Times,* and several other papers. The closing prices of the funds are published daily under the appropriate stock exchange, alongside the listings for common stocks of operating companies.

The funds themselves will send you copies of their annual and quarterly reports upon request. At the time of the initial public offer, or subsequent offerings, a prospectus is also available. Unlike open-end funds, which continuously offer shares, closed-end funds are only required to make a prospectus available during public offerings.

CLOSED-END FUNDS

Closed-end mutual funds sell a limited number of shares and invest the proceeds in securities. Unlike open-end funds, closed-ends generally do not buy their shares back from investors who wish to cash in their holdings. Instead, fund shares trade on a stock exchange. The following list, provided by Lipper Analytical Services, gives each fund's exchange (American, ,NYSE, OTC, Toronto), the per-share or net-asset value of its portfolio; the closing price of its stock, and the difference between the NAV and share price (often called the premium or the discount).

Friday, November 6, 1992

Fund Name	Stock Exch.	N.A. Value	Stock Price	% Diff.
General Equity Funds				
Adams Express Co	NYSE	20.64	20⅛	− 2.50
Baker Fentress & Co	NYSE	21.72	18¼	−15.98
Bergstrom Cap Corp	AMEX	a98.23	121½	+23.69
Blue Chip Value Fund	NYSE	7.44	7¾	+ 4.17
Central Secur Corp	AMEX	13.49	11¼	−16.60
Charles Allmon Trust	NYSE	10.54	9⅞	− 6.31
Engex Inc	AMEX	10.65	8	−24.88
Gabelli Equity Trust	NYSE	10.13	9⅞	− 2.52
General Amer Investors	NYSE	29.22	28¾	− 1.61
Inefficient Mkt Fund	AMEX	10.65	9¼	−13.15
Jundt Growth Fund	NYSE	15.05	13½	−10.30
Liberty All-Star Eq	NYSE	10.61	10⅝	+ 0.14
Morgan Grenfell SmCap	NYSE	11.52	11½	− 0.17
NAIC Growth Fund	OTC	N/A	9	N/A
Royce Value Trust	NYSE	12.40	11⅞	− 4.23
Salomon Bros Fund	NYSE	15.12	14	− 7.41
Source Capital	NYSE	42.25	45⅛	+ 6.80
Spectra Fund	OTC	19.27	15	−22.16
Tri-Continental Corp	NYSE	27.99	25⅛	−10.24
Z-Seven Fund	OTC	13.78	15¼	+10.67
Zweig Fund	NYSE	11.01	12½	+13.53
Specialized Equity Funds				
ASA Limited	NYSE	cN/A	33⅜	N/A
Alliance Globl Env	NYSE	10.94	9½	−13.16
Anchor Gold & Currency	MSE	4.60	4⅝	+ 0.54
Central Fund of Canada	AMEX	c4.12	3 15/16	− 4.44
Counsellors Tandem Sec	NYSE	15.74	13⅜	−15.03
Dover Regl Finl Shs	OTC	6.56	5	−23.78
Duff & Phelps Util Inc	NYSE	9.50	9⅞	+ 3.95
Emerging Mkts Telecom	NYSE	13.02	13	− 0.15
First Financial Fund	NYSE	13.85	12	−13.36
Global Health Sciences	NYSE	12.69	11¼	−11.35
H&Q Healthcare Invstrs	NYSE	18.33	19⅛	+ 4.34
H&Q Life Sciences Inv	NYSE	14.18	13¾	− 3.03
Patriot Global Div	NYSE	a13.35	13⅞	+ 3.93
Patriot Prem Div II	NYSE	12.19	11½	− 5.66
Patriot Premium Div	NYSE	10.18	10	− 1.77
Patriot Select Div	NYSE	a15.76	17⅜	+10.25
Petroleum & Resources	NYSE	28.53	26⅞	− 5.80
Pilgrim Regional BkShs	NYSE	11.41	10¾	− 5.78
Preferred Income Fund	NYSE	18.67	19⅜	+ 3.78
Preferred Income Oppty	NYSE	12.77	13	+ 1.80

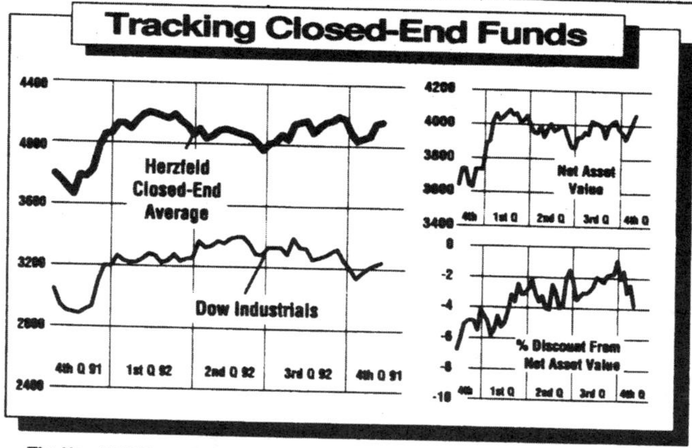

Tracking Closed-End Funds
Herzfeld
Closed-End
Average
Dow Industrials
Net Asset
Value
% Discount From
Net Asset Value
4th Q 91
1st Q 92
2nd Q 92
3rd Q 92
4th Q 91

The Herzfeld Closed-End Average measures 17 equally-weighted closed-end funds based in the U.S. that invest principally in American equities. The new asset value is a weighted average of the funds' NAVs. Source: Thomas J. Herzfeld Advisors Inc., Miami. 305-271-1900

Fund Name	Stock Exch.	N.A. Value	Stock Price	% Diff.
Ellsworth Conv Gr & In	AMEX	N/A	8⅜	N/A
Lincoln Natl Convert	NYSE	c18.61	17⅛	− 7.98
Putnam Hi Inco Conv	NYSE	8.54	8½	− 0.47
TCW Convertible Secs	NYSE	8.16	8¾	+ 7.23
Dual-Purpose Funds				
Convertible Hldgs Cap	NYSE	12.04	8¼	−31.48
Convertible Hldgs Inc	NYSE	9.44	11⅜	+20.50
Gemini II Fund Cap	NYSE	17.32	14⅛	−18.45
Gemini II Fund Inc	NYSE	9.79	12⅞	+31.51
Hampton Util Cap Shs	AMEX	c15.17	14⅛	− 6.89
Hampton Util Inc Shs	AMEX	c49.95	50½	+ 1.10
Quest for Value DP Cap	NYSE	28.11	25⅛	−10.62
Quest for Value DP Inc	NYSE	a11.52	13⅜	+16.10
Loan Participation Funds				
John Hancock Invest	NYSE	21.51	23⅝	+ 9.83
Kemper High Inco Tr	NYSE	a8.60	8¾	+ 1.74
Kemper Inter Govt Tr	NYSE	8.81	8¾	− 0.68
Kemper Multi Mkt Inc	NYSE	a10.83	10⅜	− 4.20
Liberty Tm Tr 1999	NYSE	9.16	10⅜	+13.26
Lincoln Natl Inco	NYSE	c29.84	29⅛	− 2.40
MFS Charter Inco	NYSE	10.33	10	− 3.19
MFS Govt Mkts Inco	NYSE	7.66	7½	− 2.09
MFS Intermed Inco Tr	NYSE	7.99	8	+ 0.13
MFS Multimkt Inco Tr	NYSE	7.62	7½	− 1.57
MFS Special Value Tr	NYSE	14.78	15⅛	+ 2.33
Montgomery Street	NYSE	19.23	20½	+ 6.60
Mutual Omaha Int Shs	NYSE	14.07	14⅛	+ 0.39
New America Hi Inco	NYSE	4.23	4	− 5.44

Fund Name	Stock Exch.	N.A. Value	Stock Price	% Diff.
Merrill High Inc Muni	N/A	10.58	N/A	N/A
MuniEnhanced Fund	NYSE	12.25	12⅝	+ 3.06
MuniInsured Fd Inc	AMEX	10.13	10⅜	+ 2.42
MuniVest Fund Inc	AMEX	9.97	10⅞	+ 9.08
MuniYield Fund	NYSE	14.91	15¼	+ 2.28
MuniYield Insured	NYSE	14.58	14⅞	+ 2.02
MuniYield Insured II	NYSE	14.32	15	+ 4.75
MuniYield Quality	NYSE	13.68	14⅜	+ 5.08
MuniYield Quality II	NYSE	13.93	14	+ 0.50
Municipal High Income	NYSE	9.55	9⅜	− 1.83
Nuveen Ins Muni Opp	NYSE	a14.51	14⅜	− 0.93
Nuveen Ins Quality Muni	NYSE	a15.15	15⅝	+ 3.14
Nuveen Inv Quality Muni	NYSE	a15.35	15⅝	+ 1.79
Nuveen Muni Adv	NYSE	a15.13	15½	+ 2.45
Nuveen Muni Inco	NYSE	a12.05	12⅞	+ 6.85
Nuveen Muni Mkt Opp	NYSE	a15.38	15⅝	+ 1.59
Nuveen Muni Value	NYSE	a10.51	11	+ 4.66
Nuveen Perf Plus	NYSE	a14.92	15⅛	+ 1.37
Nuveen Prem Inc Muni	NYSE	a15.73	16¼	+ 3.31
Nuveen Prem Inc Muni 2	NYSE	a13.54	13½	− 0.30
Nuveen Prem Inc Muni 3	NYSE	13.99	15	+ 7.22
Nuveen Prem Ins Muni	NYSE	a14.15	14⅛	− 0.18
Nuveen Prem Muni Inc	NYSE	a14.15	13⅞	− 1.94
Nuveen Qual Inco Muni	NYSE	a14.68	14⅝	− 0.37
Nuveen Sel Mat Muni	NYSE	11.20	11½	+ 2.68
Nuveen Sel Mat Muni 2	NYSE	11.12	12	+ 7.91
Nuveen Sel Qual Muni	NYSE	a14.93	15⅛	+ 1.31
Nuveen Sel Tx-Fr Inc	NYSE	a14.28	14½	+ 1.54
Nuveen Sel Tx-Fr Inc 2	NYSE	a14.13	13¾	− 2.69
Nuveen Sel Tx-Fr Inc 3	NYSE	a13.49	13⅝	+ 1.00
Nuveen Sel Tx-Fr Inc 4	NYSE	a13.80	14	+ 1.45
Putnam Hi Yld Muni	NYSE	9.24	9⅞	+ 6.87
Putnam Inv Grade Muni	NYSE	12.20	12⅜	+ 1.43
Putnam Mgd Mun Inco	NYSE	9.91	10⅛	+ 2.17
Putnam Tx-Fr Hlth Care	NYSE	14.17	14⅛	− 0.32
Seligman Quality Muni	NYSE	14.32	14	− 2.23
Seligman Select Muni	NYSE	12.19	12⅛	− 0.53
Smith Barney Int Mun	AMEX	10.30	10	− 2.91
Smith Barney Muni Fd	AMEX	14.68	14⅜	− 2.08
VanKamp Adv Muni Inc	NYSE	14.83	14⅜	− 3.07
VanKamp Inv Gr Muni	NYSE	11.24	11¾	+ 4.54
VanKamp Muni Inc Tr	NYSE	a10.62	11	+ 3.58
VanKamp Muni Oppty Tr	NYSE	a15.15	14⅜	− 5.12
VanKamp Muni Trust	NYSE	a15.77	15⅛	− [illegible]
VanKamo Tr For Ins Mun	NYSE	a15.49	14⅜	− [illegible]

Figure 1.1 Exerpt from Barron's weekly table of closed-end fund net asset values and discounts.

Putnam Dividend Inc	NYSE	11.46	12⅜	+ 7.98
Real Estate Securities	AMEX	7.54	7¾	+ 2.79
SthEastern Thrift & Bk	OTC	c14.09	11½	− 18.38
Templeton Global Util	AMEX	a12.96	13½	+ 4.17
Foreign Equity Funds				
Americas All Season	OTC	5.01	4¼	− 15.17
Argentina Fund	NYSE	8.92	9⅜	+ 5.10
Asia Pacific Fund	NYSE	14.34	14¼	− 0.63
Austria Fund	NYSE	8.01	7⅛	− 11.05
Brazil Fund	NYSE	c13.90	14⅞	+ 7.01
Brazilian Equity Fund	NYSE	c8.89	9⅛	+ 2.64
Chile Fund	NYSE	34.48	33⅛	− 3.93
China Fund	NYSE	14.26	14⅜	+ 0.81
Clemente Glbl Growth	NYSE	c10.16	8⅝	− 15.11
Emerging Germany Fund	NYSE	7.59	7	− 7.77
Emerging Markets Grow	N/A	N/A	N/A	N/A
Emerging Mexico Fund	NYSE	c19.86	19¼	− 3.07
Europe Fund	NYSE	11.31	11½	+ 1.68
European Warrant Fund	NYSE	cN/A	7¼	N/A
First Australia Fund	AMEX	8.46	7½	− 11.35
First Iberian Fund	AMEX	6.65	5⅞	− 11.65
First Israel Fund	NYSE	13.70	12½	− 8.76
First Philippine Fund	NYSE	14.50	11½	− 20.69
France Growth Fund	NYSE	10.43	9⅜	− 10.12
Future Germany Fund	NYSE	13.13	12	− 8.61
GT Greater Europe Fd	NYSE	10.31	9⅜	− 9.07
Germany Fund	NYSE	9.98	10⅞	+ 8.97
Greater China Fund	NYSE	13.91	13¾	− 1.15
Growth Fund of Spain	NYSE	8.56	7⅛	− 16.76
India Growth Fund	NYSE	d17.75	17⅛	− 3.52
Indonesia Fund	NYSE	8.97	9⅝	+ 7.30
Irish Investment Fund	NYSE	7.71	6⅞	− 10.83
Italy Fund	NYSE	8.03	7⅞	− 1.93
Jakarta Growth Fund	NYSE	6.88	7	+ 1.74
Japan Equity Fund	NYSE	9.85	9⅛	− 7.36
Japan OTC Equity	NYSE	6.85	8¼	+ 20.44
Jardine Fleming China	NYSE	15.30	13⅞	− 9.31
Korea Fund	NYSE	10.70	14½	+ 35.51
Korean Investment Fd	NYSE	9.44	11⅝	+ 23.15
Latin America Eq Fund	NYSE	14.98	14⅛	− 5.71
Latin America Inv	NYSE	23.90	25¼	+ 5.65
Latin American Disc	NYSE	13.27	11⅞	− 10.51
Malaysia Fund	NYSE	17.19	16⅝	− 3.29
Mexico Equity & Inc	NYSE	c16.42	15¼	− 7.13
Mexico Fund	NYSE	24.63	23¾	− 3.57
Morgan Stanly Emer Mkt	NYSE	16.91	17¾	+ 4.97
New Germany Fund	NYSE	11.17	10	− 10.47
New World Inv Fund	N/A	N/A	N/A	N/A
Portugal Fund	NYSE	9.32	8¼	− 11.48
ROC Taiwan Fund	NYSE	8.63	8¾	+ 1.39
Scudder New Asia Fund	NYSE	15.65	14¾	− 5.75
Scudder New Europe Fd	NYSE	8.98	8⅜	− 6.74
Singapore Fund	NYSE	c10.59	10½	− 0.85
Spain Fund	NYSE	7.97	8⅛	+ 1.94
Swiss Helvetia Fund	NYSE	14.21	14⅜	+ 1.16
Taiwan Fund	NYSE	c19.36	18¾	− 3.15
Templeton Emerging Mkt	NYSE	12.02	16¼	+ 35.19
Thai Capital Fund	NYSE	12.26	11⅛	− 9.26
Thai Fund	NYSE	20.96	19½	− 6.97
Turkish Investment Fd	NYSE	4.47	5¼	+ 17.45
United Kingdom Fund	NYSE	10.21	9⅛	− 10.63
Worldwide Value Fund	NYSE	13.91	12½	− 10.14
Convertible Sec's. Funds				
American Capital Conv	NYSE	22.52	19¾	− 12.30
Bancroft Conv Fund	NYSE	N/A	20⅞	N/A
Castle Conv Fund	AMEX	25.26	22¾	− 9.94

Allstate Prime Income	N/A	9.98	N/A	N/A
Eaton Vance Prime Rate	N/A	aN/A	N/A	N/A
Merrill Prime	N/A	9.99	N/A	N/A
Pilgrim Prime Rate Tr	NYSE	a9.97	9¼	− 7.22
VanKamp Prime Rate	N/A	10.00	N/A	N/A
Bond Funds				
1838 Bond-Deb Trading	NYSE	21.62	24	+ 11.01
ACM Govt Inco Fund	NYSE	a10.45	10⅞	+ 4.07
ACM Govt Oppor Fd	NYSE	a9.42	9⅜	− 0.48
ACM Govt Securities	NYSE	10.47	10½	+ 0.29
ACM Govt Spectrum	NYSE	a8.88	8⅞	− 0.06
ACM Mgd Inco Fd	NYSE	a8.93	9¾	+ 9.18
AIM Strategic Inco	AMEX	a9.34	9⅛	− 2.30
AMEV Securities	NYSE	9.97	11	+ 10.33
American Adj Rate '95	NYSE	ac9.83	10⅜	+ 5.54
American Adj Rate '96	NYSE	ac9.54	10⅛	+ 6.13
American Adj Rate '97	NYSE	ac9.53	10	+ 4.93
American Adj Rate '98	NYSE	ac9.56	9⅞	+ 3.29
American Adj Rate '99	NYSE	ac9.41	10	+ 6.27
American Capital Bond	NYSE	b19.84	20	+ 0.81
American Capital Inco	NYSE	7.82	7½	− 4.09
American Gov't Portf	NYSE	ac10.88	10⅝	− 2.34
American Govt Income	NYSE	ac8.31	8½	+ 2.29
American Govt Term	NYSE	ac9.49	10½	+ 10.64
American Opp Inco Fund	NYSE	ac11.25	11¼	+ 0.00
American Strat Inc	NYSE	ac14.99	15⅜	+ 2.57
American Strat Inc II	NYSE	a13.80	15	+ 8.70
Blackrock 1998 Term	NYSE	c10.26	9⅞	− 3.75
Blackrock 2001 Term	NYSE	c9.20	9⅝	+ 4.62
Blackrock Advtg Trm	NYSE	c10.19	10⅛	− 0.64
Blackrock Income	NYSE	c8.91	9⅛	+ 2.41
Blackrock Inv Qual Term	NYSE	c9.51	9¾	+ 2.52
Blackrock Strat Term	NYSE	c9.68	9⅝	− 0.57
Blackrock Target Term	NYSE	c10.23	10	− 2.25
Bunker Hill Income	NYSE	15.85	15	− 5.36
CIGNA High Income Shs	NYSE	7.02	7⅜	+ 5.06
CIM High Yld Sec	NYSE	7.59	7⅛	− 6.13
CNA Income Shares	NYSE	c10.46	12	+ 14.72
Circle Income Shares	OTC	cN/A	11⅜	N/A
Colonial Int High Inco	NYSE	6.45	6⅛	− 5.04
Colonial Intrmkt Inco I	NYSE	11.37	11⅛	− 2.15
Current Income Shares	NYSE	13.16	13	− 1.22
Dean Witter Govt Inco	NYSE	aN/A	9⅛	N/A
Dreyfus Strt Gov Inco	NYSE	a10.89	11¼	+ 3.31
Excelsior Inco Shares	NYSE	c18.52	17¾	− 4.16
First Boston Inco Fd	NYSE	8.38	8⅜	− 0.06
First Boston Strategic	NYSE	9.69	9⅜	− 3.25
Franklin Multi-Income	NYSE	c10.47	9¾	− 6.88
Franklin Prin Maturity	NYSE	c8.05	7½	− 6.83
Franklin Univ Trust	NYSE	ac8.67	8¼	− 4.84
Ft Dearborn Income	NYSE	a16.17	15⅝	− 3.37
Hatteras Income Secs	NYSE	a16.00	18⅛	+ 13.28
High Income Adv II	NYSE	a6.12	5⅞	− 4.00
High Income Adv III	NYSE	a6.68	6¼	− 6.44
High Income Adv Tr	NYSE	a5.56	5⅜	− 3.33
High Yield Income Fd	NYSE	7.29	7½	+ 2.88
High Yield Plus Fund	NYSE	7.95	7⅝	− 4.09
Hyperion 1997 Tm Tr	NYSE	9.52	10⅛	+ 6.36
Hyperion 1999 Tm Tr	NYSE	a8.73	10	+ 14.55
Hyperion 2002 Tm Tr	NYSE	9.43	10	+ 6.04
Hyperion Total Ret	NYSE	a10.76	11⅝	+ 8.04
INA Investments	NYSE	18.81	17⅝	− 6.30
Inc Opportunities 1999	NYSE	9.36	9¼	− 1.18
Independence Sq	OTC	17.72	17	− 4.06
Intercapital Income	NYSE	a18.05	19¼	+ 6.65
John Hancock Income	NYSE	16.21	16¼	+ 0.25

Oppenhmr Multi-Govt	NYSE	a8.49	8½	+ 0.12
Oppenhmr Multi-Sector	NYSE	a10.38	10⅞	+ 4.77
Pacific Amer Inco Shs	NYSE	bc16.30	16	− 1.84
Pilgrim Prime Rate Tr	NYSE	a9.97	9¼	− 7.22
Prospect St Hi Inco Fd	NYSE	4.06	3⅞	− 4.56
Putnam Int Govt Inco	NYSE	9.39	9⅛	− 2.82
Putnam Mstr Inco Tr	NYSE	8.52	8¾	+ 2.70
Putnam Mstr Int Inco	NYSE	8.60	8⅛	− 5.52
Putnam Prem Inco Tr	NYSE	8.52	8	− 6.10
RAC Income Fund	NYSE	c11.04	11	− 0.36
State Mutual Securities	NYSE	11.32	11⅛	− 1.72
Transamerica Income	NYSE	24.25	25	+ 3.09
Triple A & Govt '95	OTC	1002.14	1003	+ 0.09
Triple A & Govt '97	OTC	995.63	1003⅜	+ 0.78
Tyler Cabot Mort Sec	NYSE	10.96	13½	+ 23.18
USF&G Pacholder Fd	NYSE	19.05	18⅞	− 0.92
USLife Income Fund	NYSE	9.82	10	+ 1.83
VanKamp Intmdt Hi Inc	NYSE	a6.17	7⅜	+ 19.53
VanKamp Ltd Hi Inc	NYSE	a7.95	8½	+ 6.92
Vestaur Securities	NYSE	c14.83	14½	− 2.23
Zenix Income Fund	NYSE	6.26	6½	+ 3.83
Zweig Tot Rtn	NYSE	a8.93	9⅞	+ 10.58
World Income Funds				
ACM Mgd Multi-Market	NYSE	a9.72	9½	− 2.26
Blackrock No Am	NYSE	c12.94	13¾	+ 6.26
Dreyfus Strt Gov Inco	NYSE	a10.89	11¼	+ 3.31
First Australia Prime	AMEX	9.75	10⅜	+ 6.41
First Commonwealth	NYSE	12.94	13⅝	+ 5.29
Global Government	NYSE	7.63	7⅜	− 3.34
Global Income Plus	NYSE	9.36	9⅝	+ 2.83
Global Yield Fund	NYSE	8.28	8⅛	− 1.87
Kleinwort Benson Aust	NYSE	10.07	9¾	− 3.18
Latin Amer Dollar Inc	NYSE	13.41	14⅜	+ 7.20
Strat Global Income	NYSE	13.58	13¼	− 2.43
Templeton Global Govt	NYSE	8.53	8½	− 0.35
Templeton Global Inco	NYSE	a8.32	8⅞	+ 6.67
National Muni Bond Funds				
Allstate Mun Inc	NYSE	a10.55	10⅛	− 4.03
Allstate Mun Inc II	NYSE	a10.27	9⅞	− 3.85
Allstate Mun Inc III	NYSE	a9.60	9⅛	− 4.95
Allstate Mun Inc Op	NYSE	a8.74	7⅝	− 12.76
Allstate Mun Inc Op II	NYSE	a8.84	7¾	− 12.33
Allstate Mun Inc Op III	NYSE	a9.29	8⅜	− 9.85
Allstate Muni Pr Inco	NYSE	a10.11	10	− 1.09
Amer Muni Term Tr	NYSE	ac10.27	10½	+ 2.24
Amer Muni Term Tr II	NYSE	ac9.96	10⅛	+ 1.66
Apex Muni Fund	NYSE	10.10	9½	− 5.94
Blackrock Ins Mu	NYSE	9.65	9⅞	+ 2.33
Blackrock Ins Mu 2008	NYSE	14.15	15	+ 6.01
Blackrock Muni Tar Trm	NYSE	9.80	9⅞	+ 0.77
Colonial Hi Inco Muni	NYSE	8.78	8½	− 3.19
Colonial Inv Gr Muni	NYSE	10.88	11½	+ 5.70
Colonial Muni Inco Tr	NYSE	7.90	7⅞	− 0.32
Dreyfus Muni Inco	AMEX	a9.91	10½	+ 5.95
Dreyfus Strat Muni Bd	NYSE	a9.71	10¼	+ 5.56
Dreyfus Strat Munis	NYSE	a9.95	10¼	+ 3.02
Duff & Phelps Util T-F	NYSE	14.36	15	+ 4.46
InterCap Qual Muni Inc	NYSE	N/A	15	N/A
Intercap Ins Muni Bd	NYSE	a14.95	16⅜	+ 9.53
Intercap Ins Muni Tr	NYSE	a14.49	14¾	+ 1.79
Intercap Qual Muni	NYSE	a14.59	14¾	+ 1.10
Kemper Muni Inco Tr	NYSE	a12.26	12	− 2.12
Kemper Strategic Inco	NYSE	a11.70	11½	− 1.71
MFS Muni Inco Tr	NYSE	8.82	9	+ 2.04
Managed Muni Port 2	NYSE	11.86	11⅜	− 4.09
Managed Municipals	NYSE	12.06	11¾	− 2.57

VanKamp Tr Inv Gr Muni	NYSE	a15.68	15	− [illegible]
Single State Muni Bond				
Blackrock CA Ins 2008	NYSE	14.03	15	+ [illegible]
Blackrock FL Ins 2008	NYSE	14.13	15	+ 6.36
Blackrock NY Ins 2008	NYSE	14.14	15	+ 6.08
Dreyfus Cal Muni Inco	AMEX	a9.28	9⅛	− 1.67
Dreyfus NY Muni Inco	AMEX	a9.99	10⅛	+ 1.35
Minnesota Mun Term II	AMEX	ac9.43	10⅛	+ 7.37
Minnesota Muni Term Tr	NYSE	ac9.86	10⅜	+ 5.22
MuniYield CA	NYSE	14.33	14⅝	+ 2.06
MuniYield CA Ins	NYSE	13.64	14¾	+ 8.14
MuniYield CA Ins II	NYSE	14.32	15	+ 4.75
MuniYield FL	NYSE	14.48	15¼	+ 5.32
MuniYield MI	NYSE	14.48	15⅛	+ 4.45
MuniYield Michigan Ins	NYSE	14.34	15⅛	+ 5.47
MuniYield NJ	NYSE	14.14	14¼	+ 0.78
MuniYield NJ Ins	NYSE	14.29	15	+ 4.97
MuniYield NY Ins	NYSE	14.73	14⅝	− 0.71
MuniYield NY Ins II	NYSE	13.79	13⅞	+ 0.62
MuniYield PA	NYSE	14.22	15	+ 5.49
New York Tax-Exempt	AMEX	10.41	10⅜	− 0.34
Nuveen CA Inv Qual Muni	NYSE	a15.04	16⅛	+ 7.21
Nuveen CA Muni Inco	NYSE	a11.90	12	+ 0.84
Nuveen CA Muni Mkt Opp	NYSE	a15.24	15⅜	+ 0.89
Nuveen CA Muni Val	NYSE	a10.33	11	+ 6.49
Nuveen CA Perf Plus	NYSE	a15.25	15⅜	+ 0.82
Nuveen CA Qual Inc Muni	NYSE	a14.14	14	− 0.99
Nuveen CA Sel Qual Muni	NYSE	a14.60	14½	− 0.68
Nuveen FL Inv Qual Muni	NYSE	a14.85	15⅜	+ 3.54
Nuveen FL Qual Inc Muni	NYSE	a14.45	14½	+ 0.35
Nuveen Ins CA Select	NYSE	a13.66	15	+ 9.81
Nuveen Ins NY Select	NYSE	13.58	13½	− 0.59
Nuveen MI Qual Inc Muni	NYSE	a14.38	14¾	+ 2.57
Nuveen NJ Inv Qual Mun	NYSE	a14.60	14⅞	+ 1.88
Nuveen NJ Qual Inc Mun	NYSE	a14.29	14¾	+ 3.22
Nuveen NY Inv Qual Mun	NYSE	a15.47	15⅜	− 0.61
Nuveen NY Muni Inco	AMEX	a12.00	12⅜	+ 3.13
Nuveen NY Muni Mkt Opp	NYSE	a15.71	16½	+ 5.03
Nuveen NY Muni Val	NYSE	a10.59	11¼	+ 6.23
Nuveen NY Perf Plus	NYSE	a15.37	15⅞	+ 3.29
Nuveen NY Qual Inc Mun	NYSE	a14.38	14	− 2.64
Nuveen NY Sel Qual Mun	NYSE	a14.97	14½	− 3.14
Nuveen OH Qual Inc Mun	NYSE	a14.15	15	+ 6.01
Nuveen PA Inv Qual Muni	NYSE	a14.97	15¾	+ 5.21
Nuveen PA Qual Inc Mun	NYSE	a14.49	14⅞	+ 2.66
Nuveen TX Qual Inc Mun	NYSE	a14.31	14½	+ 1.33
Taurus Muni CA Hldgs	NYSE	11.68	12¾	+ 9.16
Taurus Muni NY Hldgs	NYSE	12.06	13	+ 7.79
VanKamp Adv PA Muni	NYSE	14.73	14⅛	− 4.11
VanKamp CA Muni Tr	AMEX	10.21	10⅛	− 0.83
VanKamp CA Qual Muni	NYSE	a15.40	14½	− 5.84
VanKamp FL Qual Muni	NYSE	a15.64	15⅛	− 3.29
VanKamp Inv Gr CA	NYSE	14.99	14⅜	− 4.10
VanKamp Inv Gr FL	NYSE	a15.10	14¾	− 2.32
VanKamp Inv Gr NJ	NYSE	a15.04	14⅝	− 2.76
VanKamp Inv Gr NY	NYSE	a14.98	15	+ 0.13
VanKamp Inv Gr PA	NYSE	a15.16	15⅛	− 0.23
VanKamp NY Qual Muni	NYSE	a15.85	15	− 5.36
VanKamp OH Qual Muni	NYSE	a15.57	15¼	− 2.06
VanKamp PA Qual Muni	NYSE	a15.99	15⅛	− 5.41
Voyageur MN Muni Inc	AMEX	a13.52	15	+ 10.95

a-Ex-dividend. b-Fully diluted. c-As of Thursday's Close. d-As of Wednesday's Close. N/A-Not available or not applicable. e-Assumes rights offering fully subscribed. Source:Lipper Analytical Services Inc.

Figure 1.1 (*Continued*) Exerpt from Barron's weekly table of closed-end fund net asset values and discounts.

2
The Discount, and the Other Variables of Closed-End Fund Trading and Analysis

Trading in closed-end funds requires a full-scale understanding of the discount and its causes and effects, as well as an evaluation of an assortment of other variables that affect closed-end funds. Unfortunately for the analyst, the degree of importance of the variables is not constant for the different types of funds (stock funds, bond funds, single-country funds, etc.). Also, the variables continually shift in relative importance to each other under various trading and market conditions.

The Discount

The discount from net asset value (NAV) per share is, by far, the most significant variable in all types of closed-end fund trading, regardless of the fact that funds may differ in scores of other aspects. The discount, by definition, is the difference by which the price of a fund is lower than its net asset value per share. Net asset value per share is the market value of the securities owned by a fund, plus cash etc., minus liabilities, divided by the number of shares outstanding.

A fund selling at a premium is one that is selling at a price higher than its NAV. The following table gives an example of the discount and the premium.

NAV	$10.00	$10.00
Price	8.00	12.00
	$2.00 discount,	$2.00 premium,
	or 20 percent	or 20 percent

Reasons for the Discount

Despite the many attempts and studies that have been made, I have never seen a complete and accurate explanation of why closed-end funds sell at discounts. I divide the reasons for the discount into two categories—those that apply to all funds, as a group, and those that apply to specific funds.

Reasons Applying to All Funds

Lack of Sponsorship.   Most stock brokerage firms tend to avoid recommending closed-end funds, primarily because other forms of investment trusts, such as mutual funds and fixed-unit investment trusts, generate higher sales compensation. The exception to this statement comes during the initial offering of a closed-end fund, when the underwriter or brokerage firm selling the new issue receives a fat underwriting fee often as high as 7 to 8 percent. In fact, in recent years Wall Street has discovered how lucrative launching new issues of closed-end funds can be, and has profited handsomely as a result.

For example, a customer buying a mutual fund with a NAV of $10 ordinarily pays an 8 percent sales charge for a total of $10.80 per share. The customer buying the fixed-unit investment trusts usually pays a sales charge of about 3 percent. (Ironically, since fixed-unit investment trusts are offered at a "net price," the customer often thinks he or she is saving the commission while actually paying a higher "built-in" commission.) A customer buying an existing closed-end fund with a NAV of $10—besides the opportunity to buy the shares at a discount from NAV, that is, at $8 or $9 a share—pays only a regular New York Stock Exchange commission, which has been negotiable since May 1975. His or her cost would be about 10 to 20 cents a share, versus about 80 cents in the mutual fund. However, if that customer bought a new issue of a similar fund at a price of $10 (incidentally, he or she would probably be quoted the initial offering price as $10 net with a "built-in" commission—just as the fixed-unit investment trust), because of the effect of the expenses to launch the fund (which include payment to the brokers), his or her initial NAV would typically be $9.30. The customer would, in effect, be buying the fund at a 7.5 percent premium!

Lack of *Continuing* Sponsorship.   For a few months after the initial offering of a closed-end fund, the underwriting firm generally maintains a "syndicate bid," or buys stock at the initial offering price to prevent selling pressure

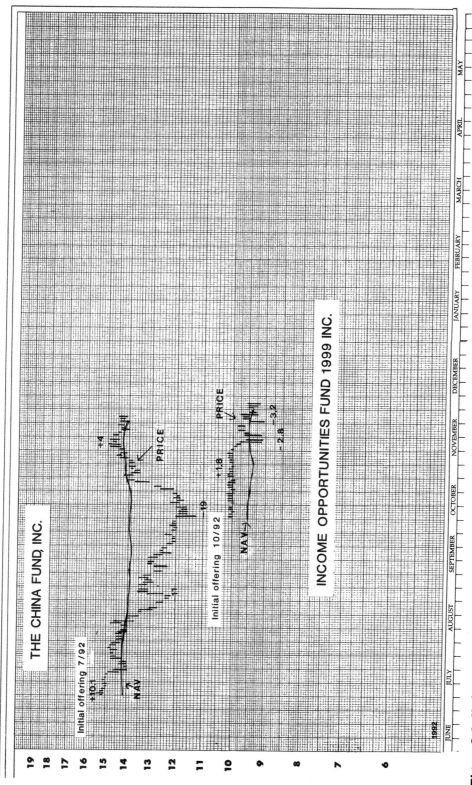

Figure 2.1 Underwriting support for the China Fund fizzled out just over a month after the fund began trading. Underwriters appear to have supported Income Opportunities Fund 1999 Inc. at $10 per share from its initial offering in September through late October, 1992.

from moving the fund to a discount. Of course it is in their best interest to prevent the fund from moving to a discount too quickly (which would mean a loss for the initial investors), if they intend to continue to launch new funds in the future. New funds are generally weaned after three months, at which time most tend to drift to a discount. (see Figure 2.1.)

Relatively Poor Yield. If an investor buys a portfolio of stocks on his or her own, the yield he or she receives will be the total dividends divided by the cost of the portfolio. When purchased at NAV, the yield on a closed-end fund compares unfavorably with the yield an investor would receive if he or she purchased the identical stocks held by the fund in the open market. This is due to the fact that there are expenses associated with the operations of an investment company, and the fund pays the expenses before distributing income to shareholders. If an investor buys a portfolio of stocks by taking a position in a closed-end fund, the yield will be reduced by the extent to which the expenses of the fund cut into its income. A fund drifting to a 10 percent discount may be compensating for a reduction of income due to 10 percent of operating expenses. What is generally overlooked is the fact that the funds get favored tax treatment and that, through its trading and long-term investments, a fund has an opportunity to make profits to offset expenses. Also overlooked is the fact that when the fund is selling at significant discounts to NAV, your dividend yield is significantly greater than you could obtain by buying the same stocks in the open market.

Domino Theory. If one or two similar funds go to a discount, investors tend to shy away from those funds in the group not selling at a discount. Eventually the lack of demand for the funds without the discount virtually forces those funds to gravitate to a discount. The domino theory, then, is the old law of supply and demand in action in the fund market.

Fear of a Larger Discount. Investors are naturally reluctant to buy a fund at a narrow discount if that fund has a historical pattern of selling at a wider discount. This fear of the discount being wider when an investor wants to sell adds fuel to the discount widening. In this regard, closed-end fund investors are like elephants: They have long memories when it comes to how wide the discounts have been.

If closed-end funds made regular tenders for their shares, this would solve the entire discount problem. Indeed, this is a concept now being considered by the SEC. Many funds have written into their Articles of Incorporation and Bylaws regular consideration of tender offers by their boards.

Tax Selling. Discounts almost always widen toward the end of the calendar year. In an effort to offset a realized capital gain in another security, an investor will sell a fund he or she is holding at a loss. Quite often the maneuver is unwise, because the funds tend to rebound in January and the investor therefore loses more by selling the fund than he or she gains in the tax savings.

General Level of Discounts/Premiums of the Entire Closed-End Fund Arena. In rising markets, the discounts tend to become less and premiums can exist. In declining markets, the discounts tend to be greater. The Herzfeld Closed-End Average, which is an average of the price movements of diversified U.S. equity funds, is published weekly in *Barron's*. The corresponding average discount of the group is also published, giving a good indication of this factor. (More about this in Chapter 3.)

Reasons Applying to Specific Funds

Capital Gains Tax Liabilities. This is a frequently mentioned reason that is not fully understood. Some of the older funds, as well as those that have been highly profitable, might very likely be holding positions that they purchased at prices substantially lower than their current market value. For example, a fund might own IBM at a fraction of its current market price. To qualify for favored tax treatment, most funds distribute to their shareholders at least 90 percent of any net realized capital gain (as well as dividend income). This means that if such a fund sold its IBM, thus realizing a substantial capital gain, the individual shareholder would be liable for his or her proportionate share of the capital gains tax—even if he or she owned the fund only for one day! Therefore, if an investor buys a fund with large unrealized capital gains, he or she is buying a potential tax liability. This is indeed a valid reason for a fund to sell at a discount. However, my studies have not been able to establish an obvious correlation between discounts and unrealized capital gains. I can only conclude that the reason for this is that some of the funds with large capital-gains-tax liabilities are also the funds with superior performance. One variable is therefore offsetting the effect of the other.

Poor Performance. Of course, if good performance is a reason for no discount, poor performance is certainly a reason for a wide discount. If a stock fund consistently underperforms relative to its area of investment, investors are obviously going to shy away from it in the kind of growing numbers that will quite naturally cause it to move to continually larger discounts.

High Management Fees and Fund Expenses. Very little discussion is needed on this point. It is self-evident that if the assets of a fund are drained by large expenses, it will and should sell at a sharp discount.

Illiquid Portfolios. Funds with high concentrations of illiquid holdings, that is, private placements or stocks with investment restrictions, more often than not sell at large discounts. The reasons for this are quite simple: Positions that are not readily marketable reduce the potential performance of the fund. Also, it makes those funds less desirable as takeover or open-ending candidates (see Chapter 10 on open-ending).

Leverage. At the time of this writing, 51 percent of all closed-end funds trading on U.S. exchanges are leveraged in one form or another. When the expenses associated with a fund's leverage are high, it can cause a drain on the fund's performance, and related widening of the discount. Also, poor NAV performance is magnified by leverage.

Rights Offerings. A popular way to increase the asset base of a closed-end fund is to allow current shareholders to buy additional shares of the fund at a specified price—a rights offering. When such rights offerings are aggressively priced, i.e., allowing shareholders to buy additional shares at a substantial discount to NAV, it can cause the fund to sell at a wider than normal discount during the subscription period.

Currency. A weak dollar can cause discounts on funds with overseas investments to widen. This also has a direct bearing on NAV performance. It can also deter foreign investors from investment in funds with portfolios of only U.S. shares.

Reputation of Management. This variable includes not only how well the management increases shareholder value through growth of NAV, but its sensitivity and responsiveness to large discounts. Some managements repeatedly ignore their fund's discount, rather than take measures to try to reduce it.

Advantages of the Discount

Now that we have given the warnings about discounts and their causes, let's move to the positive side—to the main advantages to the investor in buying closed-end funds selling at discounts from their NAV.

Leverage. When it comes to leverage, closed-end funds are of unique value to the investor. In all other forms of investing where leverage is used, the investor pays for the leverage. The reverse is true with closed-end funds where the investor receives leverage and, in addition, is being paid for it.

If an investor buys 1000 shares of a $10 stock, a $10,000 investment, he or she only needs to put up $5000, with the remainder provided by the broker in the form of margin. He or she would, therefore, be investing $5000 to control the market value of $10,000 worth of stock. As for the $5000 balance in his or her account, the investor would be charged monthly interest. In other words, in this case he or she is paying interest for the use of the leverage.

If the same investor bought 1000 shares of a closed-end fund with a NAV of $10 per share, at a 50 percent discount from NAV, or $5, he or she would also be getting $10,000 worth of securities and investing only $5000. However, he or she would be receiving the dividends and capital gains potential on the entire $10,000 worth of securities without incurring any interest expense. A closed-end fund is therefore, as previously mentioned, unique with respect to leverage and the absence of cost for the use of that leverage.

Higher Yield.   This is a matter of simple arithmetic. If a closed-end fund's dividend is 50 cents per year and the fund is selling at its NAV of $10 a share, the yield would be 5 percent. However, if the closed-end fund is selling at a 20 percent discount at $8 a share, the 50-cent dividend would then result in a $6\frac{1}{4}$ percent yield.

Larger Capital Gains Potential.   Closed-end funds bought at excessive discounts in declining markets tend to have narrowing discounts when the market turns higher. This causes a two-pronged force on the price of the closed-end fund: As the stock market moves higher, the closed-end fund's portfolio and thus its NAV move higher. This combination of a narrowing discount and a rising stock market creates a dramatic effect on the price of the closed-end fund.

Protection in Declining Markets.   Odd as it may at first seem, closed-end funds purchased at excessively wide discounts may provide the investor with a cushion in a declining market. As a closed-end fund's portfolio declines in market value and its NAV decreases, the closed-end fund's discount may begin to "normalize," or narrow, absorbing the erosion in the fund's portfolio.

Variables and Other Considerations Affecting Closed-End Funds

Broadly speaking, there are two categories of variables that influence the price of closed-end funds: those that generally relate to specific funds and those that apply to the overall stock market and economy.

Variables Relating to Specific Funds

Capital Gains Tax Liability.   This factor was discussed earlier as a reason for a discount. It bears repeating that a very large capital gains tax liability is a pressure for a wider discount.

Loss Carry-Forward.   Closed-end funds with loss carry-forwards merit positive consideration. This is quite simply because the loss carry-forward rules out any problem of capital gains tax liabilities. It also gives the fund added appeal as a merger target.

Past Performance.   The ability of a fund's management to consistently out-perform the appropriate indexes is a reason for a fund to sell at a narrower discount than similar funds with poor performance.

Volatility.   From a trading point of view, it is recommended that a trader look for funds that are relatively volatile, that do some "swinging." U.S. bond funds, for example, are significantly less volatile than single-country funds.

Leverage.   In rising markets, funds with highly leveraged capital structures have much more appeal than those without. Conversely, in declining markets, the buying of funds with leveraged capital structures should be avoided. (A leveraged capital structure means that the fund has a large proportion of preferred stock and/or debt in relation to its common stock.) Dual-purpose funds usually provide the highest leverage—2 to 1 (see Chapter 8).

Yield.   If it were possible for all other variables to be equal, then the investor would do well to seek funds offering the greatest yield. Yield will usually depend on the type of stocks in a fund's portfolio as well as the fund's discount and its operating expenses.

Management Fees and Expenses.   As funds with high yields are attractive, so too are funds with low management fees and expenses. Tri-Continental Corporation is a good illustration of a fund whose operating expenses are relatively low—its expense ratio is approximately 0.67 percent. Liberty All-Star Equity Fund, which has a similar portfolio, is on the high side, with an expense ratio of approximately 1.66 percent.

Where the Funds Trade.   It is advantageous to trade funds listed on the New York Stock Exchange or American Stock Exchange as opposed to the over-the-counter (OTC) market. This is primarily because funds traded on the major exchanges tend to have deeper, more liquid markets. Also, when it comes to funds that trade OTC, the investor has the spread between the bid and the asked price working against him or her. He or she is buying on the asked side and selling on the bid. On the other hand, with funds traded on an exchange, the investor has a better opportunity to buy on the bid and sell on the offer.

Relative Liquidity.   Funds with illiquid portfolios should be avoided, especially for short-term trading, unless the investor is quite certain that the discount more than compensates for this basic disadvantage.

Depth of the Market. A closed-end fund trader quickly learns which funds can be readily traded in any appreciable size and which cannot. As a general rule, the more largely capitalized closed-end funds can be traded in larger sizes at prices at or close to their last sale. An exception to this rule is a fund in which a single shareholder owns a large percentage of the stock.

Portfolio Composition. One must continually evaluate which industry groups are the strongest and weakest. For example, if oil and gas stocks are strong, Petroleum and Resources Corporation would most likely be a strong performer. Often the best values are found in out-of-favor groups, which usually offer the most attractive discounts.

Reputation of Management. Wide discounts in some funds often represent the investment community's appraisal of a fund's management. Very few officers and directors of closed-end funds have actually been censured by the Securities and Exchange Commission. More typically, some managements have consistently recommended against measures that would help to narrow discounts. The prime question one should ask is, "Are the officers and directors acting in the best interests of the shareholders?" Poor management reputation could prevent a fund's discount from narrowing to any appreciable degree. Many of the funds do, however, have capable, dedicated management.

Special Objectives. Some funds' premiums may be a reflection of their unique objectives. For example, when The Germany Fund was launched, it was the only way to buy a German portfolio without leaving the U.S. The fund traded at premiums until three similar funds were launched. Conversely, a fund whose investment objective is the same as 10 other funds will tend to sell at a relatively larger discount.

Quality. Funds that have high-grade portfolios should and usually do sell at relatively narrow discounts. This means that unless one of the other variables is far out of line, a closed-end fund with a very high grade portfolio that is trading at a large discount represents an unusually good buying opportunity.

Dividend Payment Schedule. Depending on the policy of the fund, dividends may be paid monthly, quarterly, or semiannually. Monthly dividends mean that the trader has the advantage of possibly catching a dividend on a short-term trade. On the other hand, if a fund pays an infrequent, but large, dividend or capital gains distribution, anticipation of such a payout usually touches off extra buying in the closed-end fund. As a result, the fund's price may tend to be more volatile at that time.

Dividend Policy. According to the tax laws, to qualify under the conduit theory, which is designed to eliminate double taxation of dividends to investment company shareholders, a fund must distribute substantially all of its net investment income. Most funds distribute their capital gains as well. However, some funds have adopted the strategy of making distributions from other sources (including return of capital). This may be confusing to shareholders. It appears that they are getting a higher yield, but actually they are only getting their own money back.

Takeover and Open-End Candidates. Funds with poor performance, relatively high expenses, and liquid portfolios may well be candidates for a takeover or for conversion to an open-end (mutual) fund. The trader is advised to be on the lookout for such funds. When a closed-end fund is converted to an open-end fund, it may be redeemed at NAV. This would, in most cases, mean an instant profit. Chapter 10 is devoted to this highly important variable.

Historical Discount. This variable is continually evaluated. The essence of my work involves trading at established deviations from a moving average of the fund's discount.

Maturity. This variable applies to bond funds, which are discussed in Chapter 5. Basically (assuming a normal yield curve), the longer the average maturity of a fund's portfolio, the deeper the discount should be; the shorter the maturity of the bonds in the portfolio, the narrower the discount should be. It is paradoxical that the opposite is usually true.

Convertibility. This variable applies to funds holding convertible bonds. Such bonds are convertible into the common stocks of their respective issues. Convertible bonds either have low interest rates and are selling close to their conversion price or high interest rates and less interesting convertibility features. A thorough discussion of this concept appears in Chapter 6 on convertible bond funds.

Termination. This usually applies to dual-purpose funds and is discussed in detail in Chapter 8. Briefly, a dual-purpose fund at a fixed date is either liquidated or converted to an open-end fund. The termination date is vital, because the discount will always be zero on that date. This variable can also apply to funds whose boards and/or shareholders have voted to liquidate. A third category is "term trusts," those funds that seek to return a fixed amount to shareholders at a fixed date and then terminate, e.g., BlackRock Strategic Term Trust.

External Variables Affecting Closed-End Funds

By my definition, the external variables are those that have no direct impact on closed-end funds individually or collectively. And yet, because they are "facts" of the economics of investing, their impact on the funds' prices is more often than not of crucial importance.

Market Direction.   In bull markets, one should buy undervalued funds, that is, ones that invest in out-of-favor industries that are at wide discounts. In bear markets, one should sell short overvalued funds—those at narrow discounts or premiums.

Interest Rates.   Rising interest rates usually mean a generally lower stock market, while declining interest rates usually point to a rising market. Interest rates have an even more direct effect on closed-end bond funds, because, not only are the prices of the bond funds caught in the general stock market weakness, but also their NAVs are falling due to declining bond prices.

Net Mutual Fund Redemptions and Sales.   There is an extremely high coefficient of correlation here. When mutual fund redemptions are high, discounts tend to be wide. During periods of net mutual fund sales, discounts are narrow.

The Herzfeld Closed-End Average (THCEA).   This external variable was invented by the author. It is an index that measures the general price trend of closed-end funds as a group. (The average is described in depth in Chapter 3.) The THCEA gives an excellent comparison of how closed-end funds, as a group, are moving compared to the Dow.

3

The Herzfeld Closed-End Average and The Herzfeld Single-Country Average

Why We Created the Averages

Mutual fund analyses focus on one variable as a measure of performance—percentage change in net asset value. Over the years this has generally been refined to show "total return"—i.e., percentage change in net asset value, adjusted for dividends and capital gains distributions. Most followers of closed-end funds, including ourselves, use this calculation in compiling our performance studies.

The weakness in using a mutual fund type of analysis in evaluating a closed-end fund is, of course, that it ignores the discount or premium to net asset value that a closed-end fund trades at, and, more importantly, it also does not take into consideration *share price.*

For many years we pondered this shortcoming, and that is why all of my research and writings devote much attention to "discount analysis." Additionally, in recent years, we have begun to publish total return for closed-end funds in terms of both NAV and share price. We have found that, from an investor's point of view, it is that second measure—share price—that is the prime consideration. After all, unlike a mutual fund, a closed-end fund does trade in the open market, and therefore most investors we talk to view performance not in NAV terms but as the profit or loss made on a trade or the unrealized gain or loss on current holdings.

Because of this increasing attention to share price analysis, I believed that the closed-end fund industry needed its own averages, that is, averages that measure changes in share price, not net asset value.

The Herzfeld Closed-End Average (THCEA)

This average measures the share price of seventeen U.S. closed-end funds that invest principally in U.S. equities. The following is a list of the funds in the average:

The Adams Express Company

Baker, Fentress and Company

Bergstrom Capital Corporation

Blue Chip Value Fund, Inc.

Central Securities Corporation

The Charles Allmon Trust, Inc.

Engex, Inc.

The Gabelli Equity Trust, Inc.

General American Investors Company, Inc.

The Inefficient-Market Fund, Inc.

Liberty All-Star Equity Fund

Morgan Grenfell SMALLCap Fund, Inc.

Royce Value Trust

The Salomon Brothers Fund, Inc.

Source Capital Inc.

Tri-Continental Corporation

The Zweig Fund, Inc.

The capitalizations of the funds range from about $9 million to $2 billion, with a total capitalization of approximately $8 billion. All of the funds are listed on either the New York or American Stock Exchanges. The average was established with all the funds weighted approximately equally. We commenced daily calculation of the average on December 31, 1987. At that time the Dow Jones Industrial Average stood at 1938.38; we pegged THCEA at the same level as the

Dow. The THCEA therefore gives an excellent comparison, at all times, of how closed-end funds as a group are moving, compared to the Dow (in their reports, most funds compare their own performance to the Dow, the S&P, or both).

The average is published weekly in the mutual fund/closed-end fund section of *Barron's* and monthly in my monthly research report, "The Investor's Guide to Closed-End Funds." Along with the average, a corresponding Herzfeld Closed-End Average by net asset value of the same group of funds, and the average discount from net asset value of the group, are also published, with the Dow Jones Industrial Average presented for purposes of comparison. (See Figures 3.1 and 3.2.)

The Herzfeld Single-Country Average (THSCA)

This average measures the share price of twenty-five U.S.-traded closed-end funds that invest principally in equity securities of foreign countries. The following is a list of the funds in the average:

ASA Limited

The Austria Fund, Inc.

The Brazil Fund, Inc.

The Chile Fund, Inc.

The Emerging Germany Fund Inc.

The First Australia Fund, Inc.

The First Philippine Fund, Inc.

The Germany Fund, Inc.

The Greater China Fund, Inc.

The India Growth Fund, Inc.

The Italy Fund, Inc.

Japan Equity Fund

Japan OTC Equity Fund, Inc.

Jardine Fleming China Region Fund, Inc.

The Korea Fund, Inc.

The Malaysia Fund, Inc.

The Mexico Fund, Inc.

The Portugal Fund, Inc.

The R.O.C. Taiwan Fund

The Spain Fund, Inc.

The Swiss Helvetia Fund, Inc.

The Taiwan Fund, Inc.

The Thai Fund, Inc.

The Turkish Investment Fund, Inc.

The United Kingdom Fund, Inc.

The capitalization of the funds ranges from about $35 million to $555 million, with a total capitalization of approximately $3½ billion. All of the funds are listed on either the New York or American Stock Exchanges. The average was established with all the funds weighted approximately equally. We commenced weekly calculation of the average on December 31, 1989, with 20 funds represented; at which time we pegged THSCA at 2000. On December 31, 1992, we added five funds to the average to adjust for global economic changes. The THSCA is designed to show how closed-end, single-country fund share prices are moving.

This average is also published monthly in my monthly research report, "The Investor's Guide to Closed-End Funds." (See Figure 3.3.)

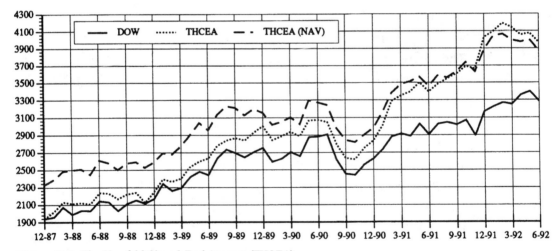

Figure 3.1 The Herzfeld Closed-End Average (THCEA).

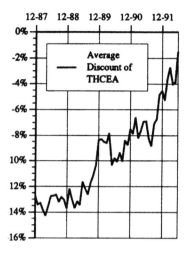

Figure 3.2 The Average Discount from Net Asset Value of the Funds in The Herzfeld Closed-End Average.

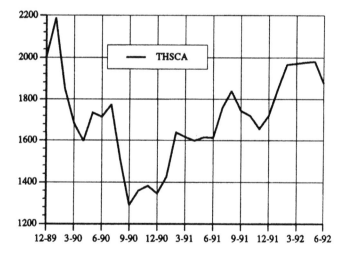

Figure 3.3 The Herzfeld Single-Country Average (THSCA).

4

Trading Closed-End Stock Funds and Specialty Funds

A list of the principal closed-end stock funds and specialized equity funds traded in the United States appears in Chapter 11.

Advantages of Closed-End Stock Funds and Specialized Equity Funds

Diversification. With such funds, an investor can buy a diversified portfolio of stocks through a single transaction. Some portfolios are speculative; others consist of blue-chip stocks. The prime objective of diversification is the spreading of risk. History has demonstrated that it is extremely unlikely that a fund's entire portfolio will fall out of bed—crumble—overnight. With the ownership of an individual stock, on the other hand, an investor may be vulnerable to a bad earnings report or some other form of negative news that could send the price down sharply.

Professional Management. A group of professional managers is working on behalf of the investor in a closed-end fund. The managers constantly monitor the portfolio, making buys and sells when they believe the timing is opportune to strengthen the fund's portfolio.

The Discount. Here is an advantage uniquely enjoyed by investors in closed-end funds. One can buy an entire portfolio at a discount from its market value.

A Basic Trading Approach
for Beginners

Trading closed-end funds need not be especially complicated. The approach I'm about to outline is relatively simple. I used it for many years before developing more refined techniques. The performance attained in using the basic approach is not, it should be noted, significantly different from performance attained in using more sophisticated methods. The primary advantage of the basic approach is that it requires less research time.

I start by making a chart of NAV and share price, as described at the end of Chapter 1.

The next step is to determine the average of the three widest discounts and the three narrowest discounts at which the fund traded over the previous year. For example, if a fund's three widest discounts in a year were 10, 12, and 14 percent, the average of these three discounts would be 12 percent. And if its three narrowest discounts over the course of the same year were 2, 0, and 4 percent, the average discount of the three would be 2 percent.

These percentage discounts become the buy and sell parameters for trading the fund. In the above example, one would be a buyer when the fund traded at a 12 percent or wider discount, and would sell when the fund traded at a 2 percent or narrower discount.

An example of the basic approach can be seen on the chart of Central Securities Corp (Figure 4.1). Over the six-month period from July, 1991 to December, 1991, the widest discounts were at 21 percent, 19 percent, and 21 percent; therefore we would look for buying opportunities when the fund approached a 20 percent discount. The three narrowest discounts of the fund were 16 percent, 15 percent and 17 percent; thus we would look to sell at approximately a 16 percent discount.

In the beginning of 1992, the fund hit a 20 percent discount at a price of $9⅜; point (A) would be a buy indication. The discount later narrowed, reaching 16 percent by the end of February, 1992, our selling level, at point (B) (at a price of $10¼). April presented another buying opportunity at point (C), at a price of $9¾, and we see a sell indication at the end of July, when the fund hit the 16 percent discount level again at $10¾, point (D).

Drawbacks of the Basic Trading
Approach

What are the drawbacks to the basic method? The most significant one is that it does not adjust to long-term continuous narrowing and widening of the dis-

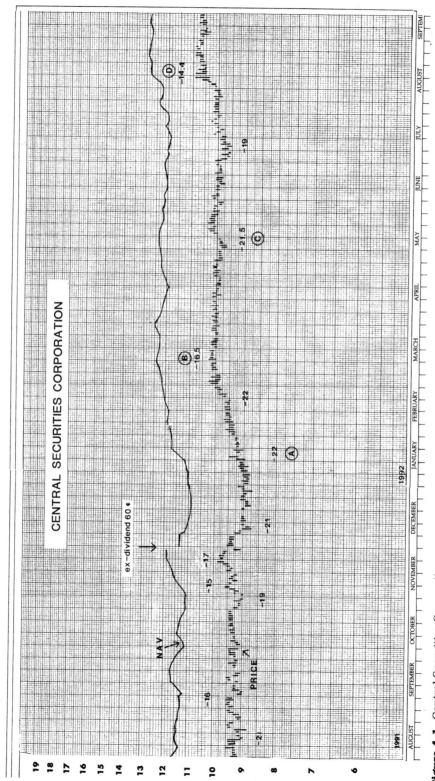

Figure 4.1 Central Securities Corporation.

count. The average discount of the funds in The Herzfeld Closed-End Average (described in Chapter 3) was approximately 16 percent at the end of 1987; by December, 1990, it was only 7.5 percent, and it currently stands at approximately a 3 percent discount.

The Advanced Approach

It is reasonably safe to say, therefore, that the basic approach will work for at least a one-year period with most funds. To overcome this flaw, I often use a moving average of the discount over a 12-month period, 6-month, or 3-month period, though I have found that for short-term trading a 3- or 6-month moving average is preferable. Generally, I try to buy a fund when it is trading at a discount to NAV that is at least five percentage points wider than its own average discount, based on the six-month moving average.

After constructing a chart and determining buy and sell levels, the balance of the decision-making process in the trading of closed-end stock funds becomes somewhat subjective, calling for a degree of investor judgment instead of trading based solely on mechanical methods. Here, buy and sell lines are adjusted based on some of the variables discussed in Chapter 2.

However, even after adjusting for all possible variables, the net effect ordinarily should not change a fund's buy or sell price by more than $\frac{1}{4}$ to $\frac{3}{8}$ of a point. (An exception to this rule occurs in a fund that is the subject of an open-ending attempt.) The following are the variables that bear particular watching:

1. The average discount of the funds in The Herzfeld Closed-End Average. If the average discount of this group narrows substantially at any given time, I become more aggressive in bidding for stocks. Conversely, when the index is widening, I drop my bid down $\frac{1}{8}$ or $\frac{1}{4}$, even though my mechanical method is giving me a buy signal at a higher price.

2. The average discount of similar funds. If several funds invest in a particular industry, i.e., the three closed-end funds that invest in banks are all trading near their buy indications based on discount, I will drop my bid for those funds by $\frac{1}{8}$ or $\frac{1}{4}$ of a point below their buy lines to adjust for the general weakness in the group.

3. Performance of the net asset value. If the funds that invest for similar objectives are all at their buy indications and I anticipate a rally in the group, I will buy the fund that historically has the best performance, bidding a little more aggressively for it than for other funds.

4. Liquidity. If I intend to trade in any size, I will avoid initiating trading positions in inactive funds, such as Z-Seven Fund or Dover Regional Financial Shares. I will look to the relatively more active funds like Salomon Brothers Fund and Tri-Continental.

5. Leverage. When looking to buy and feeling bullish on the market, I look more closely at funds with highly leveraged capital structures. In a nervous market, on the other hand, the highly leveraged funds are to be avoided.

6. Volatility. If all other factors are equal and if the general sentiment appears bullish, I seek out the more volatile funds and bid a bit more aggressively for them.

7. Currently strong groups. This is a variable with deep significance. As an example, if biotechnology and health care stocks are strong and several of the funds concentrating in them are at buying levels, I will bid more strongly for them than for funds whose portfolios are weakly represented in the biotech industry.

8. Quality. In rising markets, funds of comparatively lower quality often show better performance than those with top-grade portfolios. This phenomenon usually depends on the particular phase of a bull or bear market.

9. Overall market performance. For example, I generally use the Dow Jones Industrial Average as the leading daily indicator for the net asset value of the diversified U.S. stock funds that I chart. The net asset values themselves are published on Saturdays in *Barron's.* Then, by Tuesday or Wednesday of the following week, if the Dow should show a sharp rise, through interpolation I can accurately project the extent to which the next week's net asset value of a particular fund will be higher. Consequently, my bidding will become more aggressive.

Trading Techniques

I am convinced that the most profitable closed-end fund trading is for small profits with high turnover. A trader who can continually move in and out of funds, both buying and selling short, taking small profits, will have a total return at year-end that is much higher than he or she would have realized by holding any fund as a long-term investment.

With regard to bidding and offering, I suggest the following procedures. If a buy signal appears at $10, first I might adjust to $9\frac{7}{8}$ or $10\frac{1}{8}$ based on the variables above. Assuming my total objective is to accumulate 5000 or 6000 shares, I initially buy only 1000 at that point ($10). Then I bid for 2000 shares at $9\frac{7}{8}$ and 3000 at $9\frac{3}{4}$. With more expensive stocks, I may bid at $\frac{1}{4}$-of-a-point intervals rather than $\frac{1}{8}$-of-a-point intervals. The idea is to increase the size as we lower the price.

This is an extremely dangerous strategy in buying common stocks, because the stock may never reverse its downward movement, leaving the investor with a large loss from which there is no recovery. However, with a high degree of certainty it can be said that a closed-end fund will make a reversal when the discount becomes wide enough. If our method is correct, it will make that turn at a point extremely close to our projection. Even if we fail to pinpoint the exact ⅛ of a point where that turn is ultimately made, at the very least when the reversal occurs our average price will be near the reversal point—because we increased the size of our holdings at successively lower prices.

Dividends are also a factor in determining trading techniques. If a fund is about to go ex-dividend and it is not necessary to pay up to get that dividend, then it is definitely recommended that the investor try to buy a fund in which he or she can catch that dividend. If a fund has a sharp rise before a dividend, it usually should be regarded as a sale. Experience shows that more often than not, a stock falls off at least more than the amount of its dividend.

As for leverage, there is no reason why closed-end funds should not be traded on margin, especially in bull markets. In neutral or declining markets, one might not want to use margin, preferring to play a less than aggressive role. The proper way to adjust to such markets is to avoid trading solely on the long side and make short sales to establish a hedged position instead.

Quite often, a fund at an excessive discount will not decline as sharply in a down market as a fund at a narrow discount in a similar situation. The fund at the narrow discount will decline on a percentage basis that is greater than that of the fund at the excessive discount. Therefore, setting up the hedge position— being short in funds at narrow discounts and long in those at large discounts— often works to good advantage. (This technique is outlined in Chapter 9.)

Trading Specialized Equity Funds

There are very few hard-and-fast rules that can be applied to trading closed-end specialty funds as a group. Purely and simply, these funds confront the trader with decisions unlike those involved in other closed-end funds. As a result of this situation, a great deal of highly individual analysis is required to trade successfully in closed-end specialty funds. In general, I look for bargains by investing in closed-end funds concentrated in those industries that are out-of-favor.

For example, at the end of 1990 we were looking for bargains in the out-of-favor bank stocks. One such fund we took a large position in was Southeastern Thrift and Bank Fund (formerly Southeastern Savings Institutions Fund, Inc.) when it was trading below $5 per share at discounts approaching 25 percent. Eighteen months later, after bank stocks returned to favor, the fund was trading at its NAV of $12 per share.

5
Trading Closed-End
Bond Funds

Throughout my career, I have always put a great deal of emphasis on trading closed-end bond funds. This is primarily because the risks involved are, in many cases, lower than those of stock funds, while the rewards in many instances can be as high. A list of bond funds appears in Chapter 11.

Advantages and Disadvantages of Bond Funds

As with any kind of investment, bond funds have their advantages and disadvantages. Short-term considerations aside for the moment, a long-term investor in bond funds enjoys several advantages. First, by investing in a bond fund instead of individual bonds, the investor automatically derives the advantages of owning a portion of a diversified portfolio of investment-grade bonds—usually consisting of from 30 to 60 bonds selected and managed by professional bond specialists.

Another plus of bond funds is that they pay, depending on the fund, quarterly or monthly dividends, while individual bonds make interest payments semiannually.

Historically, most bond funds have traded at discounts from their net asset value per share. This means that the purchaser of a fund can buy an entire diversified bond portfolio at a discount from its true market value. Because of this, the yield is usually higher than that which could be obtained through direct purchase of the underlying bonds.

Yet another advantage of bond funds is that they provide opportunities for trading—probably more trading opportunities than are available in individual bonds.

There are two main disadvantages inherent in the bond fund concept. The first has to do with the management fee and the overall expenses of operating the fund, which usually will consume about 10 percent of a fund's income. The second concerns the discount. While one should always try to purchase at a substantially wide discount, there is absolutely no guarantee that when the fund is sold, the discount will not be wider than when it was purchased. Of course it could be smaller, as we shall see.

Variables Affecting Bond Funds

Apart from the above advantages and disadvantages, a number of variables must be weighed before any decision to buy a bond fund is made. Among these variables are:

1. What is the bond fund's discount from its net asset value? As in all forms of closed-end trading, this is a crucial variable. During the last part of the 1970s, the average discount from NAV for the group was about 5 percent, although discounts did tend to get larger in December because of traditional tax selling. During the 1980s, they gradually narrowed to 0 percent and even traded at an average premium a few times. At present, with many investors searching for any yield greater than the 3 percent they would get in CDs, the average closed-end bond fund is at a 4 percent premium. Assuming that other bond fund variables fall into place, a fund should be purchased only when it is selling at a discount larger than the average discount of its group. Conversely, a fund should be sold when it is trading at a narrower discount than this average (or if it begins trading at a premium).

2. What is the expense ratio? What are the management fees in relation to the income generated by the fund's portfolio? For instance, of the almost 200 bond funds that I trade, the average expenses of a fund are about 10 percent of income. If a fund's expense cost is 10 percent or higher, the fund cannot truly be regarded as a sound buy—unless it is selling at an attractive discount to offset the above-average expense ratio. An exception to this occurs in the case of bond funds that employ leverage (or borrowed money) in their trading. The interest expenses for the borrowed money should be deducted from the total expenses of the fund before computing the expense ratio (operating expense ratio). The reason for this is that interest expenses should be considered a trading cost of the fund, not an operating expense. Some of the bond funds with lower expense ratios are InterCapital Income Securities, Montgomery Street Income Securities, and State Mutual Securities Trust.

3. Where is the fund traded? Because of the depth of market, etc., assuming all other factors are equal, a fund traded on the New York Stock Exchange or American Stock Exchange will be preferred to one traded in the over-the-counter market.

4. What is the quality of the fund's portfolio? Several funds have relatively low-quality (junk bond) portfolios, with an emphasis on single-A, triple-B bonds or lower-quality bonds. Others stress triple-A or double-A holdings.

5. What is the average maturity of the fund's portfolio? If other variables are equal, a fund with bonds of relatively shorter maturity will have a comparatively more stable NAV during periods of rising interest rates than intermediate- or longer-term portfolios. Of course, their NAVs will also be less affected on the up side during periods of declining interest rates.

(Changes in maturity and quality can be used by the management of a closed-end bond fund to cause a fund's market value to rise or to increase the yield. For example, lowering the quality of a fund's portfolio and/or buying longer maturities will have the effect of increasing the fund's yield. Investors buying for yield may well move such a fund to a premium. Assume that five different funds of equal quality are all selling for $10 per share and paying 90-cent dividends—or a 9 percent yield. Then one of the funds shifts into buying lower-quality bonds and longer maturities. This could very well serve to increase the dividend to 95 cents, causing the price of the fund to rise to 10½. At a price of 10½, the fund would still be yielding 9 percent, remaining in line with the 9 percent yield of bond funds as a group. However, in a situation like this, the dividend increase is a result of a more speculative investment posture, and this should be noted and considered before investment.)

6. What is the degree of liquidity of a bond fund's portfolio? Some bond funds have portfolios that are relatively or even highly illiquid, primarily because they are heavily invested in privately placed bonds. Such bond funds usually sell at wider discounts than those with relatively liquid portfolios. The reason for this, of course, is that if a declining bond market is forecast, it is comparatively more difficult for fund managers to move into a cash position from privately placed bonds; they are not readily marketable. On the other hand, it must be noted that bond funds with a large percentage of privately placed securities usually have a higher yield than those with liquid portfolios. The result of this combination of factors is a bond fund selling at a larger discount and offering a much higher yield than many funds with relatively liquid holdings. This does not mean, however, that the shares of such a fund trading on a stock exchange are illiquid. They are indeed liquid, thereby giving the investor an opportunity to purchase an illiquid but high-yielding portfolio while enjoying the liquidity of a NYSE-listed common stock.

7. How does the fund pay its dividend? Those funds that pay monthly dividends are generally regarded as more attractive by investors, even though the yield—because of processing and mailing expenses—may be a touch lower than those that pay on a quarterly basis. Monthly dividend payments are most common at present.

8. What is the source of the dividend? Most investors assume that dividends are paid from the net investment income of the fund's underlying portfolio. In recent years, however, in an attempt to pay a stable monthly dividend, many funds have used other sources, i.e., net realized gains or paid-in capital—both of which reduce NAV. This can be as confusing as it would be for a depositor of $100 in a savings bank earning 5 percent interest, who withdraws the $5 in interest plus an additional $2 at the end of the year and mistakenly calculates his or her "yield" as 7 percent—ignoring the $2 reduction of his or her account balance to $98.

9. What is the size of the fund? The larger the fund, the greater the number of shares in the fund I will be willing to trade. In this regard, one should also determine whether or not the fund is actively traded. If a single individual or institution has an extremely large position in a fund, therefore causing the float to be thin, one should, of course, avoid taking large trading positions.

10. Does the fund utilize leverage? That is, does it borrow in order to make investments? A majority of the taxable and non-taxable bond fund groups now employ some sort of leverage. If we believe that interest rates are going to decline, then there is an advantage to buying a fund utilizing leverage. This is because in a general bond market rally, the fund using leverage will tend to outperform another that does not use that technique. Naturally, when the opposite situation occurs, when interest rates are rising and the bond market is falling, one should avoid funds utilizing leverage.

11. What type of leverage does the fund use? Many closed-end bond funds issue preferred shares that pay dividends based on short-term interest rates, while using the money raised from the issue to purchase long-term positions. When the interest rate available on short-term instruments is considerably lower than that obtainable on longer-term investments, this provides a benefit to common shareholders. However, when the opposite scenario exists and short-term rates exceed long-term rates, common shareholders can end up paying more for the leverage than the benefit derived.

Charting Bond Funds

In addition to the NAV and price, I often chart the Dow Jones 20-Bond Average with the closed-end bond fund group. As in earlier chapters where we compared the relationship of the Dow Jones Industrial Average or The Herzfeld Closed-End Average to the net asset value of stock funds, it should be readily apparent that there is an almost perfect correlation between movements of the Dow bond average and the movements of the net asset value of many of the bond funds.

Some of my charts have other elements that can be helpful in evaluation. For example, I recently started plotting the Fidelity Global Bond Fund (FGBDX), an open-end fund that publishes its NAV daily, on the same page as the Global Income Plus Fund, a closed-end fund that only publishes its NAV weekly (Figure 5.1). It has proved to be a good indicator of NAV.

Trading Bond Funds

There are two basic approaches to determining when to buy and sell a bond fund.

The first is to work solely from information provided by the chart, determining the moving average as we did for equity funds in Chapter 4. In the case of bond funds, however, I generally use a deviation of only two or three percentage points from the six-month moving average, rather than the average deviation of five percentage points I use with equity funds.

It is essential to look at what the discounts of all the bond funds are doing. If all bond fund discounts are narrowing, we may well buy the one with the greatest deviation beyond its normal discount from NAV, even if that deviation is only one or two percentage points. In other words, we always seek the most attractive fund in the group, relative to others with similar portfolios.

The ideal way to trade bond funds is to start by buying a fund that not only has the highest discount relative to its normal level, but the highest discount relative to the rest of its group.

Now let's discuss the actual trading of bond funds. In theory, we will buy Fund A at an 8 percent discount, if its normal discount is 5 percent. We will also try to catch the fund's monthly or quarterly dividend, but as soon as the discount narrows to 2 percent, we will sell Fund A. When we do, we will immediately switch into another fund selling at a discount 3 percent larger than the moving average of its discount. By leapfrogging, a trader may be able to increase his profitability dramatically—buying one fund, catching its dividend, selling that fund and buying another, catching its dividend, selling it when its discount narrows, etc.

The potential profit side, and the most intriguing consideration behind this method of trading bond funds, is that at no time during the trading cycle does the investor take any more risk than he or she would take if he or she bought a portfolio of investment-grade bonds at a substantial discount from their actual value.

To the uninitiated, the fact that we're actively trading may make it seem as if we're taking heavy risks. Actually, I believe the opposite is true. Through active trading, we're actually minimizing our risks. Why do I say minimizing? The fact is that by "scalping" (taking) a point here and a fraction of a point there, we are always putting away profits not for their own sake alone but to act as a potential cushion for the day when the bond market goes unexpectedly into a decline and a position goes against us. The importance of this trading concept with closed-end bond funds cannot be overemphasized.

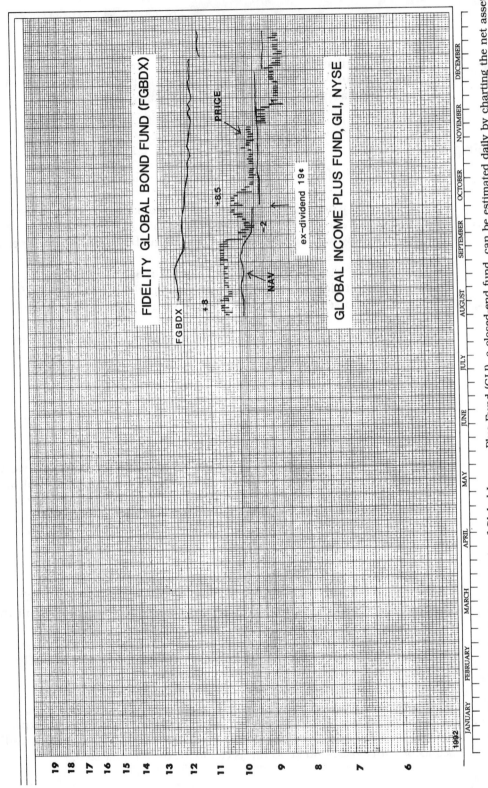

Figure 5.1 The net asset value movements of Global Income Plus Fund (GLI), a closed-end fund, can be estimated daily by charting the net asset value of Fidelity Global Bond Fund (FGBDX), an open-end fund with a similar portfolio, on the same page. FGBDX publishes its net asset value daily, while GLI only publishes weekly.

Compare it, if you will, to the individual investor or the institution seeking income through bonds in general. That investor will not, first of all, be getting his or her portfolio of bonds at a discount from their market value, as he or she would be by buying closed-end bond funds at a discount. He or she will be paying market value for each individual bond. And if the investor does, when interest rates rise, he or she is going to watch the value of his or her portfolio decline.

One might argue that the same unfortunate sequence could occur with a closed-end bond fund—rising interest rates serving to erode the portfolio value of the fund. However, there is a safety valve built into our system of buying closed-end bond funds—the fact that we buy the funds only when they are trading at prices that are wider than their average discounts. In this case, in a period of rising interest rates where bond prices generally are eroding, producing a decline in the fund's net asset value, the discount may tend to narrow, negating the downward pressure being exerted on the fund's net asset value by the declining bond market.

One further piece of advice, based on personal experience, should be kept in mind whenever trading closed-end bond funds. That is, average *down* when buying funds and do not average up, contrary to what most books about the financial market advise.

Traders who concentrate in growth stocks always seem to be saying, "Average up and cut your losses." As we advised with closed-end stock funds, this is precisely what *not* to do with closed-end bond funds. Rather, the trader should average down and, when doing this, increase the size of his or her orders. The result is that the investor's average price should be close to the reversal price at the bottom.

With common stocks, the ultimate danger in averaging down is that a company can indeed go out of business, thus causing a severe loss for an investor who has increased the size of his her orders while following a stock downward. To the best of my knowledge, no closed-end bond fund has ever been wiped out—even during the junk bond crisis. Therefore, excessive discounts should not be regarded as signs of internal weakness but rather as indications of unusually fine buying opportunities.

Before getting into specifics on why and how one should trade certain closed-end bond funds, I would like to return to the subject of timing for a moment. November and December have traditionally been attractive periods in which to purchase bond funds, and January is generally regarded as a profit-taking month. The buying opportunities in the last two months of the year are presented by investors selling to establish tax losses, usually to their misfortune, without considering what the future price performance of the fund may be. If tax-loss seekers would instead wait until January to liquidate their funds, they would very often find that the fund is a point or two higher than its November-December level. To put it bluntly, selling a fund in January will more often than not be a lot more profitable than the value of any tax loss established at the depressed prices of year-end.

In the current environment, the number of closed-end bond funds trading at discounts is very small. Investors searching for yield have bid up the prices of these funds to premiums to NAV. There is no reason to pay premiums for closed-end funds, since one can choose among hundreds of open-end bond funds at NAV. As interest rates have declined, closed-end bond funds have seen the yields of their portfolios decrease, thus causing them to reduce their monthly dividend payments. As mentioned earlier, in an effort to keep their dividend rates stable, some funds have resorted to paying a portion of their dividends from sources that reduce NAV, i.e., net realized gains or paid-in capital. However, eventually they have been forced to announce and institute dividend cuts to prevent further NAV erosion. A fund paying a large portion of its dividend from sources other than net investment income in a declining-interest-rate environment is a sitting duck for a dividend cut—and such cuts have created the majority of the best buying opportunities in the closed-end bond fund group in the past few years.

The chart of ACM Government Opportunity Fund, Inc. (Figure 5.2) shows two good examples of typical price movements following dividend announcements. In February, 1992, point (A), the fund announced that it would be forced to reduce its monthly dividend from 8.4 cents per share to 6.625 cents. Selling pressure from yield-oriented investors pushed the fund's price to a 4 percent discount the day of the announcement from a 7 percent premium. Within a few days the fund was trading at its NAV and soon moved to a premium. A trader could have sold at point (B) after catching the monthly dividend, with a profit of approximately 3.4 percent. Another opportunity to buy the fund at a 4 percent discount presented itself in October, 1992. A buyer at point (C), when the fund again hit a 4 percent discount at $9\frac{1}{8}$, would have been able to sell when the fund hit a premium of 2 percent a few weeks later at point (D), to "scalp" another 6 percent gain.

Tax-Exempt Bond Funds

As interest rates have steadily declined in recent years, and tax rates appear to be headed higher, the popularity of tax-exempt income funds has made it the largest sector of the closed-end fund industry as investors search for higher after-tax return.

As their name implies, municipal bond funds invest primarily in tax-exempt municipal obligations, and income on their portfolios are exempt from federal income tax. Further, income derived from a specific state's municipal securities is exempt from the income taxes of that state.

Another factor that has made the group popular in the early 1990s, as interest rates have declined, is that a majority of the municipal closed-end funds employ leverage to enhance yield. Of course, leverage can also work against you.

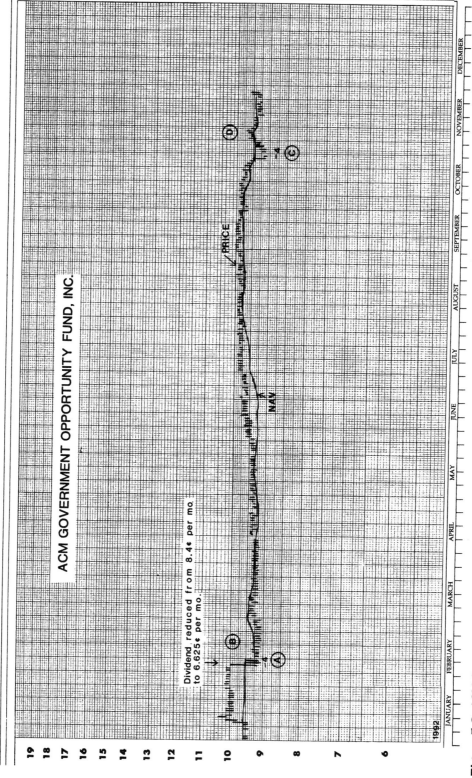

Figure 5.2 ACM Government Opportunity Fund, Inc.

Trading Municipal Bond Funds

Except for a few very small funds, this group was almost nonexistent before 1986, when MFS Municipal Income Trust was launched. Since then they have generally traded at premiums or small discounts, presenting only very few opportunities.

I trade the municipal bond fund group similarly to the bond fund group. Variables that require added attention, however, include the expense ratio, maturity, quality, and leverage.

I compare funds with similar portfolios; i.e., those invested in the same state, those with intermediate-term portfolios, those with leverage, etc. The recent weakness in the municipal bond market (third quarter, 1992), caused by defaults of underlying positions, has begun to put pressure on the municipal group, and opportunities are beginning to develop.

Allstate Municipal Income Opportunities Trust is a good illustration. (See Figure 5.3) In October, 1992 the fund announced that 11 of its portfolio issues, representing 9 percent of the fund's total assets, were now non-interest-bearing positions. A corresponding dividend cut was announced, moving the fund to an uncharacteristic 9.8 percent discount from NAV, point (A), and later to a 12.8 percent discount, point (B).

Many municipal bond funds have shown similar opportunities, prompting us, for the first time, to recommend selected buying across the group.

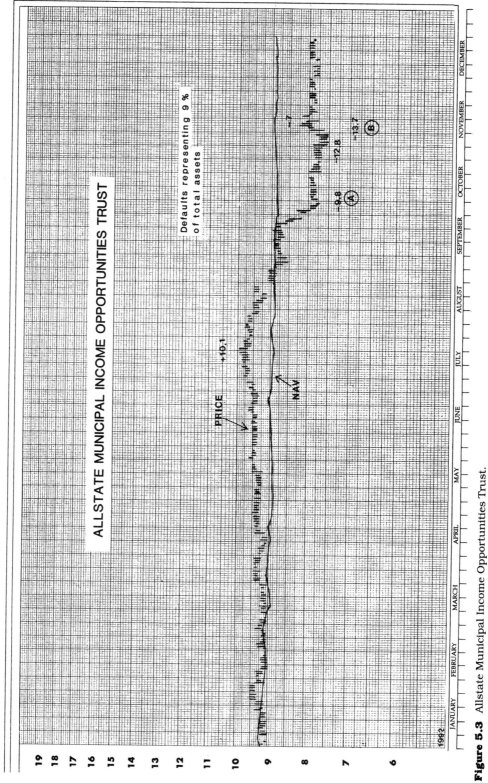

Figure 5.3 Allstate Municipal Income Opportunities Trust.

6

Trading Closed-End Convertible Bond Funds

Before getting into details, it should be pointed out that the term "convertible bond fund" is a bit of a misnomer. A better description would be "convertible funds." This is because these funds have a large percentage of convertible preferred stocks in their portfolios. An excellent example is the Castle Convertible Fund, which has a portfolio mix of about 62 percent convertible bonds and 22 percent convertible preferreds, with the remainder in common stocks and short-term instruments. As for the often-used term "convertible bond," it usually means a convertible debenture. A debenture is not backed by any specific asset of a company; rather, it is an unsecured debt obligation. In this book, the terms *debenture* and *bond* are used interchangeably.

Advantages of Convertible Bonds and Convertible Bond Funds

At this point, let us examine the general advantages of convertible bonds and convertible bond funds. Convertible bonds mature at a fixed date, assuring an investor that unless a company goes into bankruptcy, at maturity he or she will receive $1000 for each $1000 face value. Because a bond is a debt of the issuing company, bondholders have the right to force a company into insolvency if the interest and principal payments of the debt are not made.

Another plus lies in the fact that convertible bonds offer relatively high yields in comparison to other investments. In addition, these bonds have a potential capital gains factor. Since the bond is convertible into the common stock of a company, if the company's common stock rises, the bond's value will rise too.

All of the advantages of convertible bonds apply to the portfolios of convertible bond funds. In addition, the investor in a fund can often acquire a diversified portfolio at a discount from the value of the aggregate portfolio and at a yield, because of this discount, that is higher than if he or she had purchased the bonds separately.

A Review of Convertible Bond Analysis

In evaluating a convertible bond, priority should be given to a number of variables. These are the bond's maturity, its rating, its conversion ratio, investment value, and whether it is selling at a premium or discount or at parity with its conversion value. A bond's maturity and rating virtually speak for themselves: A shorter maturity will have a stabilizing influence on interest-rate fluctuations. As for ratings, it is obvious that high-rated bonds are preferable to low-rated ones.

A bond's conversion ratio should also be considered. This term refers to the number of shares of common stock that will be received by the investor through conversion of a bond. For instance, if a bond is convertible at $25 a share, for each $1000 bond the holder would be entitled to convert into 40 shares.

There are currently nine convertible bond funds trading on U.S. exchanges; eight are listed under the heading "Convertible Funds" in Chapter 11, and one, Convertible Holdings, Inc., is listed under the dual-purpose heading in Chapter 11. Their portfolios generally are composed of convertible bonds and convertible preferreds; however, several have an additional twist. For example, AIM Strategic Income Fund not only has the traditional mix of convertible securities, it also has a significant short position—46 percent of net assets as of December 31, 1991. So this is a fund whose NAV is hedged against market swings. Putnam High Income Convertible and Bond Fund holds a large portion of assets in high-yield junk bond funds, tying the fate of its NAV to the junk bond market—in good times and bad. Lincoln National Convertible Securities Fund includes direct placement securities in its list of holdings. And Convertible Holdings, Inc., which also falls into the dual-purpose-fund category, is a convertible play with the benefit of 2 to 1 leverage, thanks to its preferred shares.

Trading Convertible Bond Funds

In analyzing convertible bond funds, there are some general variables that affect them all: the quality of the fund, as indicated by ratings; the maturity of the portfolio, with shorter maturities providing a stabilizing influence against interest-rate fluctuations; yield and dividend changes; and whether the fund stresses conversion value or investment value when buying bonds. And of course the key variable, the discount from NAV.

Since many of these funds have similar portfolio compositions, their NAVs follow similar patterns. So in this group I look for the fund(s) trading at discounts wider than the average for the group, and wider than the average for the individual fund. Conversely, I sell when the discount narrows to less than the average for the group and less than the average for the individual fund, and look to rotate into another of the group.

7

Single-Country
and Foreign
Closed-End Funds

The single-country fund is the most efficient and best-designed investment vehicle to take advantage of opportunities in foreign markets. The fundamental advantages include: ease of investment and the use of U.S. dollars; diversification; liquidity and stock exchange listing; professional management with knowledge of local markets, at a relatively low cost; several layers of regulation; in certain cases, access to markets that are otherwise restricted to foreigners; simplified custody; and at times, the ability to buy assets at a discount.

There is now a wide selection of single-country and foreign funds—a list appears in Chapter 11. This group makes up, by far, the most volatile sector of the closed-end fund industry. When trading this group, one must not only use discount analysis, but also take into careful consideration some basic misperceptions and characteristics of the group:

1. One of the primary reasons for excessive valuations, and subsequent vulnerability, stems from the incorrect perception that single-country funds offer exclusive investment or have some type of monopoly on investment in a particular country. This, however, is the case only in a handful of country funds.

2. When a fund that is considered a unique avenue of investment in a certain country becomes very popular, thus trading at wide premiums, inevitably more funds will be formed with similar investment objectives. We saw this scenario with The Germany Fund, which traded at premiums to NAV as high as 100 percent in late 1989. By April, 1990 there were three more German closed-end funds, and the premium had evaporated. Therefore, eventually, rather than scarcity coupled with large demand, there is a glut of funds with satiated buyers—and naturally, discounts follow.

3. Another pitfall is the potential for manipulation. Single-country funds are misunderstood, trade thinly, and are basically a good story. These are the three fundamental requirements for a "short squeeze" or other type of manipulation—sophisticated groups acting together to push share prices up and down for their own gain.

4. Further complicating single-country fund analysis is the unpredictability of dramatic world events, which tend to bear heavily on the volatility of country funds.

Of course, any trader will tell you that volatility is the key ingredient for large profits. And herein lies my basic approach to trading single-country and foreign closed-end funds.

I established The Herzfeld Single-Country Average (THSCA) at the end of 1989 to keep an empirical measure of the price volatility of the single-country fund group. The average is composed of 25 single-country funds that principally invest in equity securities of 22 different foreign countries around the world. Each component was equally weighted at inception, and the index was pegged on that date at 2000. I use this index as a barometer of the overall valuation of the single-country group. (See Chapter 3 for a complete description and graph of this average.)

Trading Strategies for Single-Country and Foreign Closed-End Funds

My first question, when analyzing the group, is to consult The Herzfeld Single-Country Average. This measure helped me to predict the peak of popularity of the group in an article I wrote for *Barron's* in February, 1990, "What Goes Up...Is Country-Fund Crunch Near?", as well as its bottom in a publication in London in August, 1990, and its rebound in *Barron's* in February, 1991, "Way to Go—Country Funds are a Specialist's Favorite." And indeed, as The Herzfeld Single-Country Average indicated, there were bargains across the "world" at that time. In a published list of what I was buying at the time, there were 16 funds trading at wider than 20 percent discounts to their NAVs.

I also compare funds with similar portfolios, buying the one with the widest discount. For example, The European Warrant Fund (EWF), which seeks capital growth primarily through investments in equity warrants of Western European companies, was launched in July, 1990, when Europe was "hot." This fund invests in European warrants, which cost substantially less than their underlying securities, and have the potential for tremendous gains because warrants give the holder the right to purchase an equity issue at a fixed price on a certain date or within a prescribed period.

There were two other funds that concentrated their investments in Europe, The Europe Fund and Scudder New Europe Fund. By November, 1991, The European Warrant Fund's price had declined from the initial offering price of $12 to $6 (Figure 7.1) and was trading at discounts as wide as 28 percent, while the other two issues traded at discounts ranging from 10 percent to 15 percent. So, as the only leveraged play in that region, and offering twice the potential gain at half the risk, The European Warrant Fund was the logical choice as the promises of Europe 1992 filled the headlines. In January, 1992, EWF's discount had narrowed to less than 1 percent, and traded at $7\frac{3}{8}$. In the meantime, The Europe Fund had also narrowed to approximately a 3 percent discount, while Scudder New Europe still traded at a 12 percent discount.

I often employ a more aggressive strategy in trading the single-country group, but it is not for the faint of heart. When looking at individual issues, the most profitable approach is that of the contrarian: Buy on bad news, sell on good news. Here are a few examples:

■ *The Russian Coup.* Austria Fund's share price had been declining throughout 1991 and was down about 30 percent the day before the Russian coup was announced (Figure 7.2). Upon the announcement, the fund's price spiked down about 12 percent to a 19 percent discount, hitting $7\frac{7}{8}$, point (A). During the next four weeks, the fund gained 30 percent, moving from a 19 percent discount to an 8 percent discount, at a price of $10\frac{3}{8}$.

■ *Telefonos (Mexico's telephone company) announced that earnings were up 77 percent, point (A).* In January and February, 1992, bulls on Mexico and one of The Emerging Mexico Fund's largest positions, Telefonos de Mexico, abounded. Investors flocked to all the Mexican funds, including this fund (Figure 7.3). We sold the fund at a 13 percent premium, at $27\frac{1}{4}$, point (A). Four months later the price had declined by 43 percent to $15\frac{1}{2}$ on the back of some bad news.

■ *NAFTA in jeopardy, point (B).* News that the North American Free Trade Alliance was in jeopardy after presidential candidate Ross Perot announced opposition to the agreement, as well as the news that the Mexican unions might sell their shares of Telefonos, and bearish comments on Mexico in *Barron's*, caused the fund to move to a 20 percent discount in June. A buyer at point (B), at $15\frac{1}{2}$, could have sold three or four weeks later when Mr. Perot withdrew from the election, point (C), and the fund moved to a 4 percent discount in July, 1992, at $20\frac{1}{4}$. Similar trades were also possible with The Mexico Fund, which trades in a similar pattern.

Of course few country funds have offered more opportunities to trade on news than The First Philippine Fund (Figure 7.4), whose country made almost monthly headlines with political coup attempts, volcanic eruptions, the loss of the Subic Bay Naval Base, and a new government.

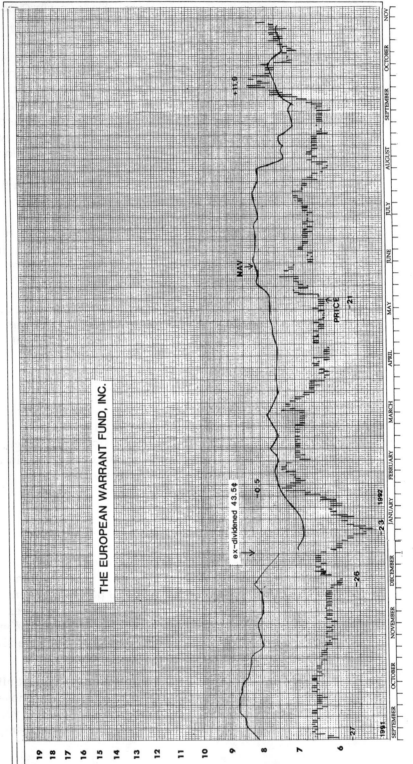

Figure 7.1 The European Warrant Fund.

48

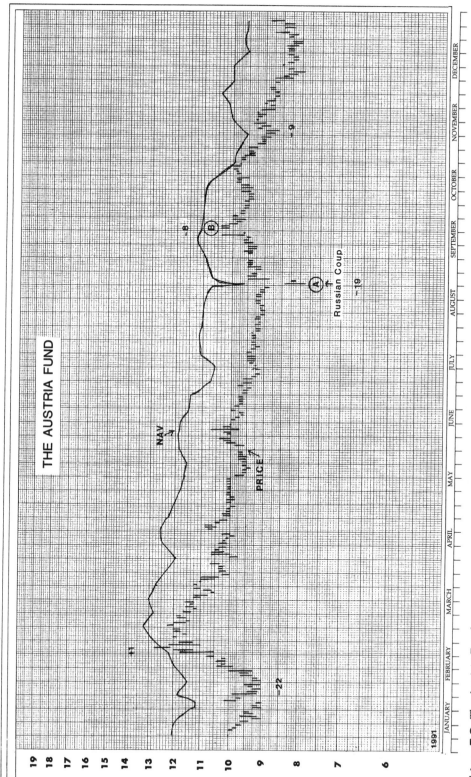

Figure 7.2 The Austria Fund.

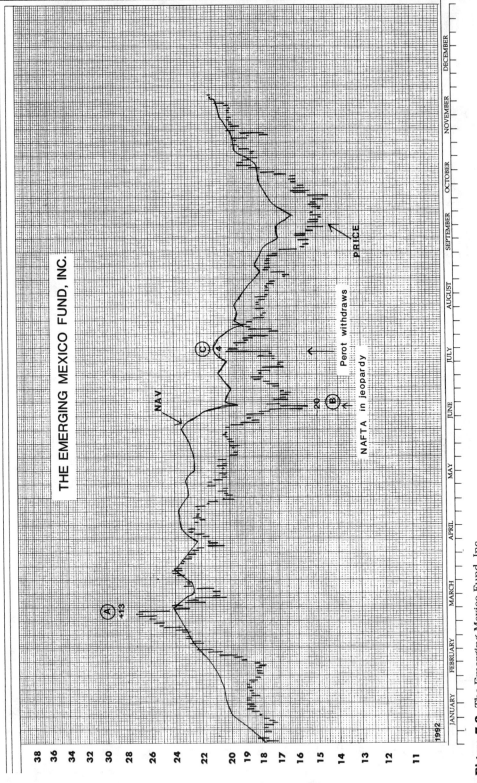

Figure 7.3 The Emerging Mexico Fund, Inc.

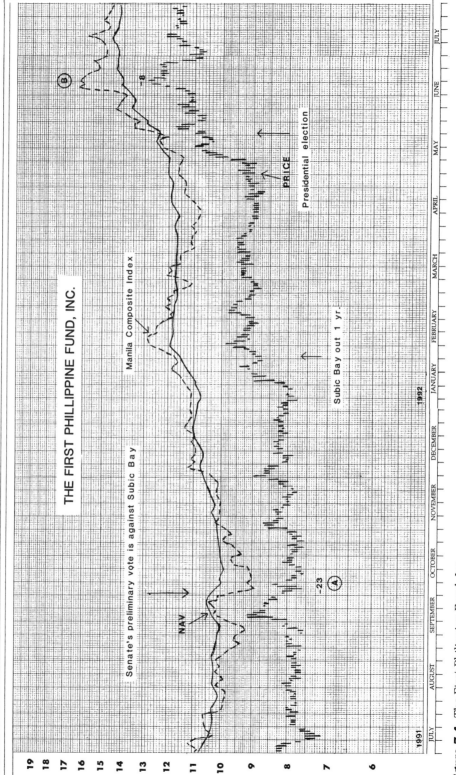

Figure 7.4 The First Philippine Fund, Inc.

■ *Loss of Subic Bay Naval Base/new government elected.*   The Philippine senate voted against extending the lease on Subic Bay in September, 1991, point (A). The fund was a buy on that news at $7¾, a 23 percent discount to NAV. The fund continued to trade at wide discounts in the following months, providing additional buying (and selling) opportunities. However, after Ramos's election in May, 1992, the euphoria over a new government and the promise of stability caused the discount to narrow to 8 percent and the price to rise to $13; a 90 percent gain in a 9-month period.

Other examples of crises that created trading opportunities include:

June, 1989, the collapse of the Hong Kong market. Asia Pacific Fund dropped 19 percent in two days. That same month, the Brazilian market was closed because a large investor could not meet his margin calls, and The Brazil Fund dropped 15 percent in one day (before the drop, it had been trading at a 40 percent discount to net asset value; one can only wonder what would have happened to the stock had it been trading at large premiums, as it did in 1990!). First Philippine Fund dropped approximately 32 percent from its November, 1989 peak, when the Philippine Stock Exchange reopened in December after an attempted coup. Interestingly, the portfolio was apparently in cash the entire time! Korea Fund dropped 11 percent in June, 1989, following the Tianamen Square incident; ROC Taiwan Fund declined by 15 percent that week, and Taiwan Fund by 13 percent. In 1988 the Taiwan government reimposed capital gains taxes; in the month that followed, shares of Taiwan Fund declined by over 30 percent.

Aside from political events, currency is a tricky issue. In the years that followed the launching of Mexico Fund in 1981, the peso underwent a series of large devaluations. The shares of Mexico Fund, which came to market at $12, eventually worked their way to $2 per share. The India Growth Fund came under pressure in July, 1991 after a currency devaluation was announced (this was compounded by the assassination of Gandhi a few months earlier). The stock price dropped to $9¾, from where it had been trading days earlier at $11½. By the end of that month, it had rebounded to a 13 percent premium, trading at $15¾.

Again I must emphasize that although the profit potential in the single-country and foreign fund group is the greatest of the closed-end fund industry, it also entails the highest level of risk, and many of the funds should be considered speculative.

8

Trading Dual-Purpose Funds

Dual-purpose funds, despite the special label the investment community has given to them, are surprisingly similar to the other closed-end stock funds we have been discussing in earlier chapters. The difference essentially boils down to (1) the way dual-purpose funds are capitalized, and (2) the fact that they have fixed expiration dates.

Specifically, dual-purpose funds are closed-end funds with two classes of stock—capital shares and preferred shares. Each of these two classes is designed to serve the aspirations and interests of two distinctly different breeds of investors:

1. The preferred shares are for investors seeking income.

2. The capital shares, as their name connotes, are for those investors in search of capital gains.

Dual-purpose funds issue equal amounts of common and preferred shares. Preferred shareholders are entitled to the income from the entire portfolio that the fund holds, and capital shareholders are entitled to the capital gains that the entire portfolio generates.

The investor's initial leverage is, therefore, 2 to 1. Here's how that leverage evolves. If 1 million shares of preferred stock are issued by a dual-purpose fund at $10 per share, and a million shares of common shares are issued at the same price, the fund would have $20 million in assets, less, of course, underwriting costs. With preferred shareholders receiving the dividends or income from the entire $20 million and the common shareholders receiving the capital gains, if any, from the $20-million portfolio, the result is a 2-to-1 leverage for each class of shareholder. A dual-purpose fund selling at a discount from net asset value would possess even greater leverage.

When a dual-purpose fund is formed, a specific date is established—usually 10 to 15 years in the future—when the fund's preferred shares are redeemed and the capital shareholders are entitled to divide the fund's remaining assets. This "divvying up" of the pot can be done in one of two ways:

1. The fund can be liquidated, with each shareholder receiving his or her proper portion of the assets.

2. Or, at the election of the common shareholders, the fund can be converted into an open-end operation, continuing as an investment company. Here, as in all open-end funds, the shareholders can redeem their individual shares at whatever their net asset value may be.

Before getting into some of the harsher realities of dual-purpose funds, it would be well to point out that their essential strategies are similar to those of the closed-end stock funds we discussed in Chapter 4. But dual-purpose funds, because of the leverage involved, tend to be a little more on the dramatic side in rising and falling markets.

However, and let's be candid about this, dual-purpose funds are a fine but sad example of jacks-of-all-trades who are masters of none. This is because they attempt to meet two distinctly diverse objectives, namely, income on the one side and capital gains on the other. And to be perfectly blunt about it, as their records affirm, dual-purpose funds do not meet either of their objectives very well. This double failure results in the complete negation of the advantage of leverage.

Trading rules for dual-purpose funds can be broken down into two categories:

1. Common shares should be traded like stock funds, as discussed in Chapter 4.

2. Preferred shares should be treated in the same manner as bond funds, as discussed in Chapter 5.

The only rule that can be revised has to do with timing. As each year passes and a dual-purpose fund gets closer to the point where its shares will be redeemed or the fund will be liquidated, its trading discount should, theoretically, be adjusted a notch narrower. But that's theoretical; in practice, I have found that this narrowing does not work over the long haul. Chances are it will work better in the last two or three years of the life of the fund.

It is true that when dual-purpose funds get to excessive discounts, their common shares will show dramatic increases in rising markets. The reason for this sort of action may lie in the fact that investors bid them up aggressively in the belief that their potential in rising markets is better than the potential of regular funds. As a result, in such rising markets, the discounts of dual-purpose funds tend to narrow faster than those of stock funds and, conversely, in declining markets they tend to widen faster.

In our discussion of the whys and wherefores of discounts in closed-end funds, we came up with a long list of reasons for them. In the case of dual-purpose funds, there is a highly valid reason why their common shares should sell at discounts. It is this: Since there is no yield on the fund's common shares, the investor is losing anywhere from 3 to 8 percent a year, income that he or she would have received by investing in closed-end stock or convertible bond funds.

A Trading Example

The capital shares of dual-purpose funds can often provide good trading vehicles. Using the methods described in Chapter 2, the chart of Quest for Value Dual-Purpose Fund's capital shares (Figure 8.1) shows the opportunities. At the beginning of 1992, the shares traded at discounts ranging between 21 and 26 percent at the wide end, and 18 to 20 percent at the narrow end. Buy indications would, therefore, be at approximately a 23 percent discount level and selling indications at approximately 19 percent. April, 1992, provided a buying point at (A), a 25 percent discount at a price of $18\frac{3}{4}$. By May, at point (B), the fund had reached our sell level of 19 percent, at a price of $20\frac{5}{8}$. It hit a discount of 23 percent again at point (C), where one could have bought at $21\frac{1}{4}$. Shortly thereafter, in November, one would have been a seller at $24\frac{5}{8}$, approximately a 12 percent discount from NAV.

There were actually about a half a dozen trades that could have been made during the year by more aggressive traders, buying at slightly narrower discounts as the time element of this sort of fund ticked away.

In recent years I have not taken any significant positions in the income shares of dual-purpose funds. Income shares' large premiums to NAV have made the bond fund group relatively more attractive.

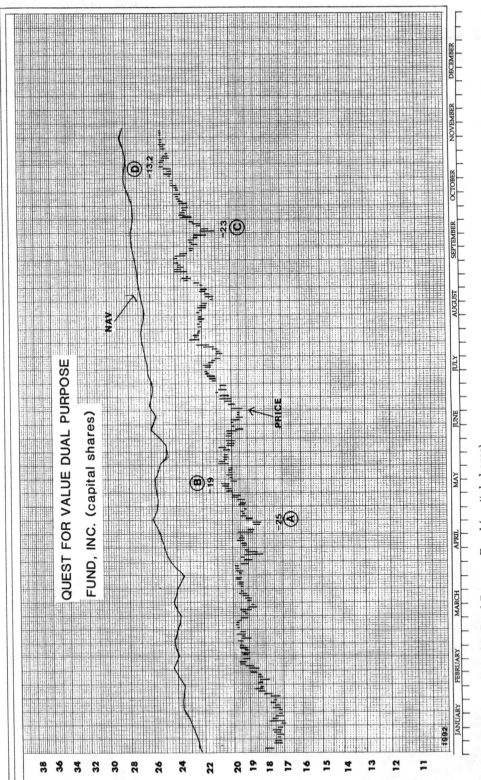

Figure 8.1 Quest for Value Dual-Purpose Fund (capital shares).

9

Closed-End Fund Hedging and Arbitrage (Including the Herzfeld Hedge)

The terms *hedging* and *arbitrage* seem to carry a mystique in the minds of a large percentage of investors. One of the principal reasons for this phenomenon is that very little has been written on the subject. Another is that arbitrageurs tend to be highly secretive about their work.

I would like to try to put an end to the mystique and the secrecy by showing that arbitrage can be little more than an exercise in high school-level mathematics.

A general-reference dictionary might define *arbitrage* as the buying and selling of the same securities at the same time but in two separate markets, so that a profit is made from the difference in price.

The New York Stock Exchange defines arbitrage as "a technique involved to take advantage of differences in prices."[1]

One of the better definitions that I have seen appears in *The Stock Market Handbook.* It says that arbitrage "is the simultaneous buying of securities on one market and selling in another market at a price advantage."[2] This same

---

[1]*The Language of Investing,* published by The New York Stock Exchange.

[2]Frank G. Zarb and Gabriel T. Kerekes, *The Stock Market Handbook: A Reference Manual for the Securities Industry.* Dow Jones-Irwin, Homewood, Ill. 1970.

[3]Ibid.

book offers another definition that is probably the best I have seen: "The buying of a security convertible into another one at a price advantage because the first one is selling for less than its converted equivalent."[3]

This definition begins to approach my own meaning of the term *arbitrage*, as it applies to closed-end funds. It must be emphasized that my definition of arbitrage, which follows, applies only to closed-end funds. That definition is this: "The simultaneous buying and selling of closed-end funds and the securities in their portfolios, or similar securities, or options on those securities, to take advantage of the temporary price difference between the market price of a fund and its net asset value per share."

Some hedging and arbitrage strategies I favor in trading closed-end funds are as follows:

1. Buy a closed-end fund selling at an excessive discount; at the same time sell short another closed-end fund that is priced at a premium. Result: If a down market carries the first fund's shares still lower, it will almost surely do greater damage to the premium-priced fund, enabling the short-seller to cover at a profit that more than offsets the loss.

2. Buy a closed-end fund at an excessive discount; meanwhile, go short on an equivalent amount of individual stocks in the same fund's portfolio. Result: During a rally, the NAV will rise in direct proportion to the rise in the short positions. However, the long position in the fund will outperform the rise in the fund's stocks as the discount narrows.

3. Buy a closed-end bond fund at an excessive discount; sell short U.S. treasury bond futures, or a combination of U.S. Treasury and corporate bonds. Result: As the bond market rallies and the excessive discount of the bond fund narrows, the long position should become more profitable than the short position. The loss in the short position will mirror the performance of the overall bond market, but because of the leverage factor in buying the bond market at a discount via the fund, it will produce a larger profit than the loss on the short position.

4. Buy a closed-end fund that is to be open-ended and is selling at a discount; sell short the stocks in the fund's portfolio. Result: This is a riskless arbitrage. As the closed-end fund approaches its self-destruct date, the discount will narrow. As an open-end fund, it will not sell at a discount—it is redeemable at NAV. The trader is locking in the discount as a profit. (An interesting note: This strategy was used in 1988 by a group that took a large stake in Financial News Composite Fund and then proposed an open-ending. The fund's portfolio was made up of the 30 common stocks that compose the Financial New Composite Index. The fund traded at discounts as wide as 21 percent during 1988, and was open-ended in September, 1989.)

5. Buy a closed-end fund at an excessive discount; sell naked call options against the fund's portfolio positions. Result: This strategy (which I developed

and is known as "The Herzfeld Hedge") may be summarized as follows: If the stock market declines, the diminishing time factor of the option, plus the probable erosion of the price of the underlying stock, exerts pressure on the excessive premium of the option. This probably will result in a greater gain on the short-option position than the resulting loss in the long position on the excessively discounted fund. If the market rises, in-the-money options will tend to lose their rich premiums and will probably not rise as fast as their underlying stocks. In addition, the diminishing time factor is working against the option. At the same time as the underlying stocks rise, the NAV of the fund should increase; combined with the probable narrowing of its discount, this may cause it to become more profitable than the loss developing in the options. The hedge may also result in dividends being received on the long positions in the fund.

6. Sell short a closed-end fund priced at a premium; write naked put options against the fund's portfolio positions (the so-called Reverse Herzfeld Hedge).

Of course the strategies described in this chapter, especially The Herzfeld Hedge, are intended for the sophisticated investor. I refuse to recommend that anyone attempt to employ any of the strategies of the hedge unless that individual has made himself or herself thoroughly familiar with option trading. And by this, I must stress that the individual be as aware as possible of the inherent risks involved in trading options, especially in the selling of naked options.

It is hoped that this chapter has taken much of the mystery out of hedging and arbitrage. My aim has been to give an overview of such techniques to prove that hedging and arbitrage are essentially straightforward strategies involving simple mathematics that can be used to reduce market risk.

10

Open-Ending, Takeovers, and Reorganizations

Since Wall Street appears to have an insatiable appetite for takeover and reorganization candidates, it was virtually inevitable that the closed-end fund group would become an item on the menu. It should be kept in mind, however, that the usual closed-end fund reorganization attempt or procedure is unlike the takeover of an industrial company in at least one very important respect: A closed-end fund reorganization is usually not attempted by an outsider group or a rival company, but rather by the shareholders of the closed-end fund itself through the process called open-ending.

To understand what is behind open-ending, one must remember the basic difference between a closed-end fund and a mutual (open-end) fund, which we discussed in depth in Chapter 1. That difference, which bears repeating here, lies in the fact that a mutual fund continually issues and redeems shares at a price based on its current net asset value, while a closed-end fund, on the other hand, has a fixed capitalization whose per share price is determined by supply and demand in the open market.

It also bears repeating that closed-end funds can trade at discounts from their net asset value. Given a hypothetical closed-end fund with a NAV of $10 per share and a market price of $8—that is, selling at a 20 percent discount—the shareholders could eliminate the discount by voting to convert the closed-end fund into an open-end fund. After the conversion is completed, the shares of the fund could be redeemed at their NAV, thus completely erasing the discount.

Here, in addition to discussing the concept of open-ending, I intend to show why some funds will probably be vulnerable to open-ending, and why most others may not.

One of the first questions asked by most novices in the closed-end fund field is usually, "Why don't the shareholders of all closed-end funds trading at discounts vote to convert them into open-ended mutual funds?" The fact is that many have: In the past 15 years, almost 70 closed-end funds have been open-ended, liquidated, or reorganized. The primary obstacle to conversion is, more often than not, a fund's management. Quite obviously, since the management fee is based on a percentage of a fund's assets, open-ending is fraught with danger for management, because it could very well be followed by large-scale redemptions that would shrink the asset base on which the management fee is based.

When a reorganization proposal is initiated not by management but by an outside stockholder, the odds are heavily against the adoption of the proposal on the first attempt. In addition, in many cases, management is aided by anti-takeover provisions in the funds' Articles of Incorporation or Bylaws, requiring supermajority votes to pass such measures.

(A personal note is necessary. With enthusiasm for open-ending seeming to be at a high in past years, I have been approached by individuals and institutions encouraging me to do one of three things: recommend steps that would narrow a fund's discount, invest for them, on a passive basis, in closed-end funds I believed were candidates for open-ending, or take an active role in forcing such funds to go open-end. I concede I have been involved in all three situations.)

Shareholder Positions

Of course, the most significant and cogent shareholder argument in favor of open-ending a fund is that the changeover would immediately eliminate the discount. This is because, quite simply, shares would be redeemable at NAV. In a similar vein, other proponents of open-ending argue that when a closed-end fund's shares are selling at a substantial discount from NAV, the fund is susceptible to what they themselves might be planning—a raid, only this time by "outsiders," whose goal is the management contract of the fund, not elimination of the discount. Open-ending, these individuals say, could prevent such an incursion.

Advocates of conversion to the open-end form assert that it provides not only increased values for stockholders, but also greatly increases liquidity, since shares are readily redeemable at NAV in unlimited quantity. They also assert that the directors of closed-end funds have a fiduciary duty to promote the interests of stockholders, in good faith, without regard to their own selfish interests. Here, they insist, the interests of stockholders cannot but be enhanced by the elimination of the discount and cannot but be damaged when they are unable to realize the full NAV of their investment.

In this regard, a fascinating point of view was expressed by a shareholder in a closed-end fund whose management performed the same functions for an open-end fund. He questioned why shareholders of the open-end fund were able to receive the full net asset value of their shares, while those owning the closed-end fund—operated by the same management—had to sell those shares at a discount. For him there was a bitter irony in the fact that in the case of these two funds, the quality of research and advice was the same for both the open-end fund and the closed-end fund.

Management Positions

The management positions in regard to open-ending are much lengthier and more comprehensive than those of shareholders. Closed-end fund managements in the early 1940s formed what is now known as the Association of Publicly Traded Funds to deal with the open-ending and other industry matters. From most of the shareholder proposals to open-end that I have studied in proxy statements, it appears that individual managements use virtually the same standard arguments to defend against open-ending attempts. The arguments or positions are essentially:

1. Redemptions could cause the asset base to shrink, thus hiking the expense ratio and slashing income to shareholders.

2. Large cash reserves for possible redemptions would have to be maintained. Such reserves could prevent a fund from making timely or less liquid investments.

3. It would become more dangerous for a fund to invest in less liquid securities, because to meet large-scale redemptions, the fund might have to sell these quickly, at less than fair prices.

4. It is typically more difficult for an open-end fund to borrow money than it would be for a closed-end fund.

5. Transfer costs would increase. This is because shares in closed-end funds are often held by brokers in "street name," while those in open-end funds are generally registered in the owners' names. In addition, conversion from closed-end to open-end status is costly, involving payments for new prospectuses and other expenditures that would have to be borne by shareholders.

6. The yield, in percentage terms, would be less attractive if a fund were open-ended. For example, a closed-end fund selling at $10, with a NAV of $12 paying an 80-cent dividend, yields 8 percent. If that fund were open-ended and selling at $12 a share, the dividend would represent only a 6.7 percent yield.

7. Sales efforts for open-end funds are costly.

8. An open-end fund would not be eligible for margin and would be disqualified for holding by some institutional investors.

9. A closed-end structure has been a significant element in the past success of a fund and therefore, by implication, would continue to be one in the future.

Managers' long litany of protests against open-ending also include the argument that moves in that direction usually are the work of a few people out for a quick profit and oblivious to the best long-term interest of other shareholders.

Managers also charge that open-ending hurts individuals participating in the fund's dividend reinvestment plan, because, under an open-ended structure, they would no longer be able to buy shares at a discount.

Sometimes, the arguments are unwittingly amusing or inane. One trust's management stated that it opposed conversion to an open-end structure because it might make it difficult for investors to find another suitable investment.

In any case, managers frequently note, many investors buy closed-end funds at a discount because they get more shares than they would if the discount did not exist and so are not disappointed when the shares continue to trade below net asset value. In line with this, managements often claim that if shareholders had wanted to invest in an open-end fund, they could have done so.

Some managements also defend the discount by saying it is merely a result of lack of information concerning closed-end funds. Here they seem to be implying that if the investing public were better informed on closed-end funds, their shares would no longer sell at discounts. Carrying this argument a step farther, managements have attempted to stop efforts to open-end by saying that their funds may sell at premiums in the future, as some have in various periods in the past. This argument is, of course, at odds with another management point—that the discount is an advantage to investors who wish to purchase more stock in a closed-end fund.

Then there is a kind of middle ground, with managements saying that over the long haul the discounts in their funds have decreased.

Another key management argument against open-ending is probably the most important. That argument holds that open-ending could cause adverse tax consequences. It is an argument worth dwelling on.

There are two tax considerations to bear in mind in a possible open-ending situation. The first concerns a closed-end fund that holds stocks in which there are large, unrealized capital gains. If those stocks are sold, the capital gains must be distributed to shareholders in order for the fund to continue to be eligible for favored tax treatment. Such a distribution creates a capital gains tax liability for all shareholders. If a fund were dissolved or liquidated, this type of capital gains tax liability would very likely occur in funds that are very old or have been very successful.

Such a situation occurred in Niagara Share Corporation. The fund was incorporated in 1929, and became a Regulated Investment Company in 1955. In 1991 the fund's board announced it would liquidate the fund, citing the inability of a closed-end fund to raise new capital as well as the expenses associated with running a relatively small, internationally managed fund. The fund also noted the average 16.3 percent discount of the fund for the twelve months preceding their decision. For reasons that included the tax impact of liquidating a fund with large unrealized capital gains, the fund later announced that it would explore other alternatives. The solution was to merge into a very large mutual fund, Scudder Growth and Income Fund, in a tax-free transaction that still gave shareholders the ability to redeem their shares at NAV.

The second aspect of the tax consideration appears when a closed-end fund is open-ended and some shareholders want to redeem their holdings. This could force the fund to sell stocks in which it would realize large capital gains, thereby subjecting all shareholders of the fund to the capital gains tax liability. Niagara Share averted this by merging into a very large open-end fund with many other positions to sell, if need be, to meet redemptions.

Another answer to the tax question is for the fund to distribute positions from its portfolio in lieu of cash, thereby not realizing a capital gain for the fund.

On the surface, management's arguments generally appear to be convincing; however, most of them do not hold up. When all their arguments fail, managements have some formidable advantages in fighting an attempt at open-ending. One is investor complacency; most shareholders tend to vote their shares the way management recommends. The second is money; dissident shareholders must spend their own money to initiate a takeover battle, whereas the management is spending the fund's money.

Additionally, various anti-takeover defenses have been introduced. A small sample: the requirement that a very large majority of shareholders approve any reorganization or liquidation; the use of various "poison pills," such as the flexibility to introduce a new class of stock with different rights; the conversion of a fund's structure from that of a corporation to that of a Massachusetts business trust (which makes open-ending considerably more difficult); and the acquisition of illiquid positions.

How to Spot a Candidate for Open-Ending or Liquidation

The following aspects of a fund make it more likely to become a reorganization candidate:

1. The fund consistently trades at a wide discount, and management is unresponsive in addressing ways to narrow the discount.
2. The expense ratio is high relative to similar funds.
3. Performance has been substandard.
4. The portfolio is liquid.
5. The portfolio can be easily hedged.
6. Management owns no shares, or just a relatively small number.
7. The yield is low.
8. There are shareholders with declared stakes in the fund who have, or

intend to acquire, strategic positions.

9. Automatic voting on open-ending is allowed under the charter or bylaws.

10. The fund is small and independently managed; or conversely, the fund is managed by a large organization that also manages similar open-end funds.

11. Trading in the shares is active.

On the other hand, a fund will probably remain a closed-end fund if:

1. The fund often trades at a premium.

2. The portfolio contains private placements.

3. A large majority of shareholders must approve changes such as open-ending (many funds have a 75 percent voting requirement for such proposals).

4. Board members serve staggered terms, or can't be replaced under normal circumstances.

5. The fund is a Massachusetts business trust.

6. The fund has a high payout—10 percent or more.

7. Directors are indemnified.

8. There are poison pills, such as the existence of two classes of stock, each with different voting rights.

9. Management has a large equity position.

10. The portfolio is highly illiquid, or has a large percentage of foreign securities (other than British or Japanese).

11. Performance has been strong.

Various Approaches to Open-Ending

The most common way to convert a closed-end fund to an open-end fund is by proxy solicitation. Another way to open-end a fund is through a tender offer. A group can make an offer for over 50 percent of a closed-end fund and, once it has effective control, it can take the necessary steps to open-end or liquidate the fund.

Examples of Reorganizations

Niagara Share Corporation, mentioned earlier in this chapter, is a good example of a mangement-initiated reorganization. The board first proposed a liquidation and dissolution that would, among other things, eliminate the fund's discount from NAV, which had run an average of 16 percent during the year preceding their announcement (Figure 10.1). We maintained a large position in this fund for several years, in anticipation of management's taking some sort of action to reduce the discount. That announcement came in July, 1991, point (A), which immediately caused the discount to narrow 10 percentage points, from $13½ to $15⅜. The fund later merged with an open-end fund, Scudder Growth and Income Fund, in a tax-free transaction.

The Japan Fund shows a shareholder-triggered reorganization (Figure 10.2). The Japan Fund, which had been trading at wide discounts during most of 1986, was the subject of a tender offer by a large shareholder group in early 1987. In response (and to retain control over the fund), the fund's board proposed an open-ending, which was passed by shareholders in mid-1987.

My firm and I were involved in a shareholder-initiated reorganization in 1986. As a major stockholder of The Growth Fund of Florida, I submitted a proposal to the fund to liquidate in order to eliminate the wide discount at which the fund had been trading. Management was in favor of the idea, and my proposal passed by an overwhelming 99 percent!

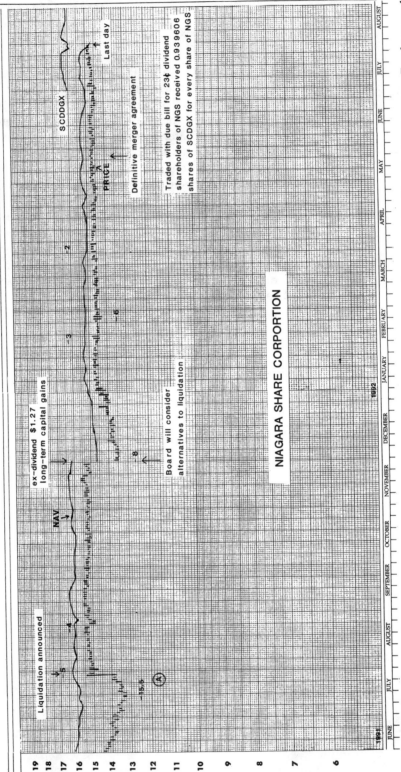

Figure 10.1 Niagara Share Corporation announced liquidation plans, then found merger with open-end Scudder Growth & Income Fund more advantageous to shareholders.

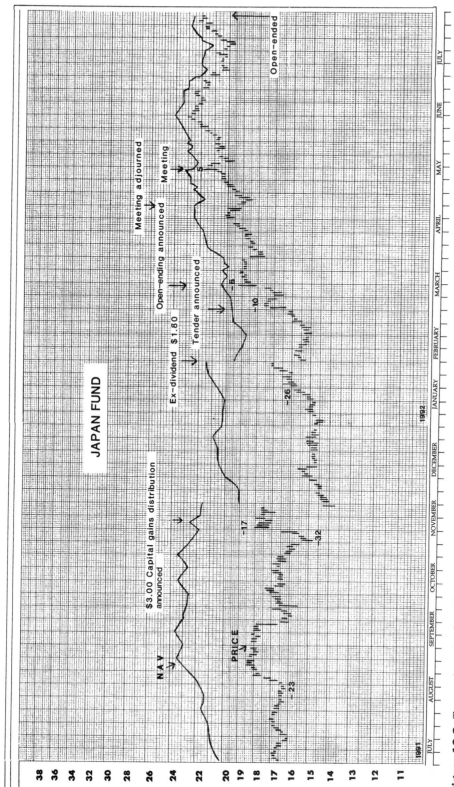

Figure 10.2 To counter a tender offer by dissident shareholders, The Japan Fund announced that the fund would open-end.

11
Industry Analysis

Now that you have an idea of what to look for in analyzing the various closed-end funds, this chapter provides statistical comparisons of funds by category.

Closed-End Funds Classified by Herzfeld Category groups funds with similar objectives or portfolios. These are general groupings. Chapter 12 gives a detailed description of the objective and portfolio composition of each individual issue. The exchange on which the fund is listed, and its ticker symbol, also appear.

Closed-End Funds Ranked by Size lists funds from largest capitalization to smallest capitalization, in the same groupings as above.

Closed-End Funds Listed by Investment Advisor lists each closed-end fund under its investment advisor, so one can see how many and which funds a particular advisor serves.

Expense Ratio Survey begins with the fund with the lowest expense ratio of its group and ends with the fund with the highest expense ratio of the group.

Income Ratio Survey arranges each group of funds from those with the highest income ratio to that with the lowest.

Performance Studies presents the performance rankings for calendar years 1991 and 1992. The 1992 study also includes a column listing the dividends and distributions paid in 1992. Both net asset value and price performance are presented.

New Issues gives some information about the funds that came to market too late to be included in Chapter 12 of this volume.

Closed-End Funds Classified by Herzfeld Category

EQUITY FUNDS

FUND	SYMBOL	PRIMARY EXCHANGE
Adams Express Company	ADX	NYSE
Baker, Fentress & Company	BKF	NYSE
Bergstrom Capital Corporation	BEM	ASE
Blue Chip Value Fund, Inc.	BLU	NYSE
Central Securities Corporation	CET	ASE
The Charles Allmon Trust, Inc.	GSO	NYSE
Engex, Inc.	EGX	ASE
The Gabelli Equity Trust Inc.	GAB	NYSE
General American Investors Company, Inc.	GAM	NYSE
The Inefficient-Market Fund, Inc.	IMF	ASE
Jundt Growth Fund, Inc.	JF	NYSE
Liberty All-Star Equity Fund	USA	NYSE
Niagara Share Corporation	NGS	NYSE
Royce Value Trust	RVT	NYSE
The Salomon Brothers Fund, Inc.	SBF	NYSE
Source Capital Inc.	SOR	NYSE
Tri-Continental Corporation	TY	NYSE

FOREIGN EQUITY FUNDS

FUND	SYMBOL	PRIMARY EXCHANGE
Alliance Global Environment Fund, Inc.	AEF	NYSE
The Argentina Fund, Inc.	AF	NYSE
The Asia Pacific Fund, Inc.	APB	NYSE
The Austria Fund, Inc.	OST	NYSE
The Brazil Fund, Inc.	BZF	NYSE
The Brazilian Equity Fund, Inc.	BZL	NYSE
The Chile Fund, Inc.	CH	NYSE
Clemente Global Growth Fund, Inc.	CLM	NYSE
The Emerging Germany Fund, Inc.	FRG	NYSE
The Emerging Mexico Fund, Inc.	MEF	NYSE
The Europe Fund, Inc.	EF	NYSE
The European Warrant Fund	EWF	NYSE
The First Australia Fund, Inc.	IAF	ASE
The First Iberian Fund, Inc.	IBF	ASE
The First Philippine Fund, Inc.	FPF	NYSE
The France Growth Fund, Inc.	FRF	NYSE
The Future Germany Fund, Inc.	FGF	NYSE
The Germany Fund, Inc.	GER	NYSE
The Global Health Sciences Fund	GHS	NYSE
The Growth Fund of Spain, Inc.	GSP	NYSE

FOREIGN EQUITY FUNDS (continued)

FUND	SYMBOL	PRIMARY EXCHANGE
GT Greater Europe Fund	GTF	NYSE
The India Growth Fund, Inc.	IGF	NYSE
The Indonesia Fund, Inc.	IF	NYSE
The Irish Investment Fund, Inc.	IRL	NYSE
The Italy Fund, Inc.	ITA	NYSE
Jakarta Growth Fund, Inc.	JGF	NYSE
Japan OTC Equity Fund, Inc.	JOF	NYSE
The Korea Fund, Inc.	KF	NYSE
The Korean Investment Fund	KIF	NYSE
The Latin American Discovery Fund, Inc.	LDF	NYSE
The Latin American Equity Fund, Inc.	LAQ	NYSE
The Latin American Investment Fund, Inc.	LAM	NYSE
The Malaysia Fund, Inc.	MF	NYSE
The Mexico Equity and Income Fund, Inc.	MXE	NYSE
The Mexico Fund, Inc.	MXF	NYSE
Morgan Stanley Emerging Markets	MSF	NYSE
The New Germany Fund, Inc.	GF	ASE
Pacific-European Growth Fund Inc.	PEF	NYSE
The Portugal Fund, Inc.	PGF	NYSE
The R.O.C. Taiwan Fund	ROC	NYSE
Scudder New Asia Fund, Inc.	SAF	NYSE
Scudder New Europe Fund, Inc.	NEF	NYSE
The Singapore Fund, Inc.	SGF	NYSE
The Spain Fund, Inc.	SNF	NYSE
The Swiss Helvetia Fund, Inc.	SWZ	NYSE
The Taiwan Fund, Inc.	TWN	ASE
Templeton Emerging Markets Fund, Inc.	EMF	NYSE
Templeton Global Utilities, Inc.	TGU	NYSE
The Thai Capital Fund, Inc.	TC	NYSE
The Thai Fund, Inc.	TTF	NYSE
The Turkish Investment Fund, Inc.	TKF	NYSE
The United Kingdom Fund, Inc.	UKM	NYSE
Worldwide Value Fund, Inc.	VLU	NYSE

SPECIALIZED EQUITY FUNDS

FUND	SYMBOL	PRIMARY EXCHANGE
ASA Limited	ASA	NYSE
Capital Southwest Corporation	CSWC	OTC
Combined Penny Stock Fund, Inc.		OTC
Dover Regional Financial Shares	DVRFS	OTC

SPECIALIZED EQUITY FUNDS (continued)

FUND	SYMBOL	PRIMARY EXCHANGE
Duff & Phelps Utilities Income, Inc.	DNP	NYSE
The Emerging Markets Telecommunications Fund, Inc.	ETF	NYSE
First Financial Fund, Inc.	FF	NYSE
H&Q Healthcare Investors	HQH	NYSE
H&Q Life Sciences Investors	HQL	NYSE
Morgan Grenfell SMALLCap Fund, Inc.	MGC	NYSE
Patriot Premium Dividend Fund I	PDF	NYSE
Patriot Premium Dividend Fund II	PDT	NYSE
Patriot Select Dividend Trust	DIV	NYSE
Petroleum & Resources Corporation	PEO	NYSE
Pilgrim Regional BankShares	PBS	NYSE
Preferred Income Fund Incorporated	PFD	NYSE
Preferred Income Opportunity Fund Incorporated	PFO	NYSE
Putnam Dividend Income Fund	PDI	NYSE
Real Estate Securities Income Fund	RIF	ASE
Redwood MicroCap Fund, Inc.		OTC
The Southeastern Thrift and Bank Fund, Inc.	STBF	OTC
Spectra Fund, Inc.		OTC
Sterling Capital Corporation	SPR	ASE
Z-Seven Fund, Inc.	ZSEV	OTC
The Zweig Fund, Inc.	ZF	NYSE

CONVERTIBLE FUNDS

FUND	SYMBOL	PRIMARY EXCHANGE
AIM Strategic Income Fund, Inc.	AST	ASE
American Capital Convertible Securities, Inc.	ACS	NYSE
Bancroft Convertible Fund, Inc.	BCV	ASE
Castle Convertible Fund, Inc.	CVF	ASE
Ellsworth Convertible Growth and Income Fund	ECF	ASE
Lincoln National Convertible Securities Fund, Inc.	LNV	NYSE
Putnam High Income Convertible and Bond Fund	PCF	NYSE
TCW Convertible Securities Fund, Inc.	CVT	NYSE

DUAL PURPOSE FUNDS

FUND	SYMBOL	PRIMARY EXCHANGE
Convertible Holdings, Inc. (capital shares)	CNV	NYSE
Convertible Holdings, Inc. (income shares)	CNVpr	NYSE
Counsellors Tandem Securities Fund, Inc. (common shares)	CTF	NYSE
Counsellors Tandem Securities Fund, Inc. (preferred shares)	CTFpr	NYSE
Gemini II (capital shares)	GMI	NYSE
Gemini II (income shares)	GMIpr	NYSE
Hampton Utilities Trust (capital shares)	HU	ASE
Hampton Utilities Trust (income shares)	HUpr	ASE
Quest For Value Dual Purpose Fund, Inc. (capital shares)	KFV	NYSE
Quest For Value Dual Purpose Fund, Inc. (income shares)	KFVpr	NYSE

BOND FUNDS

FUND	SYMBOL	PRIMARY EXCHANGE
ACM Government Income Fund, Inc.	ACG	NYSE
ACM Government Opportunity Fund, Inc.	AOF	NYSE
ACM Government Securities Fund, Inc.	GSF	NYSE
ACM Government Spectrum Fund, Inc.	SI	NYSE
ACM Managed Income Fund, Inc.	AMF	NYSE
American Adjustable Rate Term Trust Inc. --1995	ADJ	NYSE
American Adjustable Rate Term Trust Inc. --1996	BDJ	NYSE
American Adjustable Rate Term Trust Inc. --1997	CDJ	NYSE
American Adjustable Rate Term Trust Inc. --1998	DDJ	NYSE
American Capital Bond Fund, Inc.	ACB	NYSE
American Capital Income Trust	ACD	NYSE
American Government Income Fund Inc.	AGF	NYSE
American Government Income Portfolio, Inc.	AAF	NYSE
American Government Term Trust Inc.	AGT	NYSE
American Opportunity Income Fund Inc.	OIF	NYSE
American Strategic Income Portfolio Inc.	ASP	NYSE

BOND FUNDS (continued)

FUND	SYMBOL	PRIMARY EXCHANGE
AMEV Securities. Inc.	AMV	NYSE
The Blackrock Advantage Term Trust Inc.	BAT	NYSE
The Blackrock Income Trust Inc.	BKT	NYSE
The Blackrock Investment Quality Term Trust Inc.	BQT	NYSE
The Blackrock 1998 Term Trust Inc.	BBT	NYSE
The Blackrock Strategic Term Trust Inc.	BGT	NYSE
The Blackrock Target Term Trust Inc.	BTT	NYSE
Bunker Hill Income Securities, Inc.	BHL	NYSE
CIGNA High Income Shares	HIS	NYSE
CIM High Yield Securities	CIM	ASE
Circle Income Shares, Inc.	CINS	OTC
CNA Income Shares, Inc.	CNN	NYSE
Colonial InterMarket Income Trust I	CMK	NYSE
Colonial Intermediate High Income Fund	CIF	NYSE
Current Income Shares, Inc.	CUR	NYSE
Dean Witter Government Income Trust	GVT	NYSE
Dreyfus Strategic Governments Income, Inc.	DSI	NYSE
1838 Bond-Debenture Trading Fund	BDF	NYSE
Excelsior Income Shares, Inc.	EIS	NYSE
First Boston Income Fund, Inc.	FBF	NYSE
First Boston Strategic Income Fund, Inc.	FBI	NYSE
Fort Dearborn Income Securities, Inc.	FTD	NYSE
Franklin Principal Maturity Trust	FPT	NYSE
Franklin Universal Trust	FT	NYSE
Hatteras Income Securities, Inc.	HAT	NYSE
High Income Advantage Trust	YLD	NYSE
High Income Advantage Trust II	YLT	NYSE
High Income Advantage Trust III	YLH	NYSE
The High Yield Income Fund, Inc.	HYI	NYSE
The High Yield Plus Fund, Inc.	HYP	NYSE
Hyperion 1999 Term Trust, Inc.	HTT	NYSE
Hyperion Total Return Fund, Inc.	HTR	NYSE
INA Investment Securities, Inc.	IIS	NYSE
Independence Square Income Securities, Inc.	ISIS	OTC
InterCapital Income Securities, Inc.	ICB	NYSE
John Hancock Income Securities Trust	JHS	NYSE

BOND FUNDS (continued)

FUND	SYMBOL	PRIMARY EXCHANGE
John Hancock Investors Trust	JHI	NYSE
Kemper High Income Trust	KHI	NYSE
Kemper Intermediate Government Trust	KGT	NYSE
Kemper Multi-Market Income Trust	KMM	NYSE
Liberty Term Trust, Inc. --1999	LTT	NYSE
Lincoln National Income Fund, Inc.	LND	NYSE
MassMutual Corporate Investors	MCI	NYSE
MassMutual Participation Investors	MPV	NYSE
MFS Charter Income Trust	MCR	NYSE
MFS Government Markets Income Trust	MGF	NYSE
MFS Intermediate Income Trust	MIN	NYSE
MFS Multimarket Income Trust	MMT	NYSE
MFS Special Value Trust	MFV	NYSE
Montgomery Street Income Securities, Inc.	MTS	NYSE
Mutual of Omaha Interest Shares, Inc.	MUO	NYSE
The New America High Income Fund, Inc.	HYB	NYSE
Oppenheimer Multi-Government Trust	OGT	NYSE
Oppenheimer Multi-Sector Income Trust	OMS	NYSE
Pacific American Income Shares, Inc.	PAI	NYSE
Prospect Street High Income Portfolio Inc.	PHY	NYSE
Putnam Intermediate Government Income Trust	PGT	NYSE
Putnam Master Income Trust	PMT	NYSE
Putnam Master Intermediate Income Trust	PIM	NYSE
Putnam Premier Income Trust	PPT	NYSE
RAC Income Fund, Inc.	RMF	NYSE
State Mutual Securities Trust	SMS	NYSE
Transamerica Income Shares, Inc.	TAI	NYSE
Tyler Cabot Mortgage Securities	TMF	NYSE
USF&G Pacholder Fund, Inc.	PHF	ASE
USLife Income Fund, Inc.	UIF	NYSE
Van Kampen Merritt Intermediate Term High Income Trust	VIT	NYSE
Van Kampen Merritt Limited Term High Income Trust	VLT	NYSE
Vestaur Securities, Inc.	VES	NYSE
Zenix Income Fund, Inc.	ZIF	NYSE

MUNICIPAL BOND FUNDS

FUND	SYMBOL	PRIMARY EXCHANGE
Allstate Municipal Income Opportunities Trust	AMO	NYSE
Allstate Municipal Income Opportunities Trust II	AOT	NYSE
Allstate Municipal Income Opportunities Trust III	AIO	NYSE
Allstate Municipal Income Trust	ALM	NYSE
Allstate Municipal Income Trust II	ALT	NYSE
Allstate Municipal Income Trust III	ALL	NYSE
Allstate Municipal Premium Income Trust	ALI	NYSE
American Municipal Term Trust Inc.	AXT	NYSE
American Municipal Term Trust Inc. II	BXT	NYSE
Apex Municipal Fund, Inc.	APX	NYSE
The Blackrock Insured Municipal Term Trust Inc.	BMT	NYSE
The Blackrock Municipal Target Term Inc.	BMN	NYSE
Colonial High Income Municipal Trust	CXE	NYSE
Colonial Investment Grade Municipal Trust	CXH	NYSE
Colonial Municipal Income Trust	CMU	NYSE
Dreyfus California Municipal Income, Inc.	DCM	ASE
Dreyfus Municipal Income, Inc.	DMF	ASE
Dreyfus New York Municipal Income, Inc.	DNM	ASE
Dreyfus Strategic Municipal Bond Fund, Inc.	DSM	NYSE
Dreyfus Strategic Municipals, Inc.	LEO	NYSE
Duff & Phelps Utilities Tax-Free Income Inc.	DTF	NYSE
InterCapital Insured Municipal Bond Trust	IMB	NYSE
InterCapital Insured Municipal Trust	IMT	NYSE
InterCapital Quality Municipal Investment Trust	IQT	NYSE
Kemper Municipal Income Trust	KTF	NYSE
Kemper Strategic Municipal Income Trust	KSM	NYSE
MFS Municipal Income Trust	MFM	NYSE
Minnesota Municipal Term Trust Inc.	MNA	NYSE
Minnesota Municipal Term Trust Inc.--II	MNB	NYSE
Municipal High Income Fund, Inc.	MHF	NYSE
MuniEnhanced Fund, Inc.	MEN	NYSE
MuniInsured Fund, Inc.	MIF	ASE

MUNICIPAL BOND FUNDS (continued)

FUND	SYMBOL	PRIMARY EXCHANGE
MuniVest Fund, Inc.	MVF	ASE
MuniYield California Fund, Inc.	MYC	NYSE
MuniYield Florida Fund, Inc.	MYF	NYSE
MuniYield Fund, Inc.	MYD	NYSE
MuniYield Insured Fund, Inc.	MYI	NYSE
MuniYield Michigan Fund, Inc.	MYM	NYSE
MuniYield New Jersey Fund, Inc.	MYJ	NYSE
MuniYield New York Insured Fund, Inc.	MYN	NYSE
The New York Tax-Exempt Income Fund, Inc.	XTX	ASE
Nuveen California Investment Quality Municipal Fund	NQC	NYSE
Nuveen California Municipal Income Fund, Inc.	NCM	NYSE
Nuveen California Municipal Market Opportunity Fund, Inc.	NCO	NYSE
Nuveen California Municipal Value Fund, Inc.	NCA	NYSE
Nuveen California Performance Plus Municipal Fund, Inc.	NCP	NYSE
Nuveen California Quality Income Municipal Fund, Inc.	NUC	NYSE
Nuveen California Select Quality Municipal Fund, Inc.	NVC	NYSE
Nuveen Florida Investment Quality Municipal Fund, Inc.	NQF	NYSE
Nuveen Florida Quality Income Municipal Fund, Inc.	NUF	NYSE
Nuveen Insured California Select Tax-Free Income Port.	NXC	NYSE
Nuveen Insured Municipal Opportunity Fund, Inc.	NIO	NYSE
Nuveen Insured New York Select Tax-Free Income Portfolio	NXN	NYSE
Nuveen Insured Quality Municipal Fund, Inc.	NQI	NYSE
Nuveen Investment Quality Municipal Fund, Inc.	NQM	NYSE
Nuveen Michigan Quality Income Municipal Fund, Inc.	NUM	NYSE

MUNICIPAL BOND FUNDS (continued)

FUND	SYMBOL	PRIMARY EXCHANGE
Nuveen Municipal Advantage Fund, Inc.	NMA	NYSE
Nuveen Municipal Income Fund, Inc.	NMI	NYSE
Nuveen Municipal Market Opportunity Fund, Inc.	NMO	NYSE
Nuveen Municipal Value Fund, Inc.	NUV	NYSE
Nuveen New Jersey Investment Quality Municipal Fund, Inc.	NQJ	NYSE
Nuveen New Jersey Quality Income Municipal Fund, Inc.	NUJ	NYSE
Nuveen New York Investment Quality Municipal Fund, Inc.	NQN	NYSE
Nuveen New York Municipal Income Fund, Inc.	NNM	NYSE
Nuveen New York Municipal Market Opportunity Fund, Inc.	NNO	NYSE
Nuveen New York Municipal Value Fund, Inc.	NNY	NYSE
Nuveen New York Performance Plus Municipal Fund, Inc.	NNP	NYSE
Nuveen New York Quality Income Municipal Fund, Inc.	NUN	NYSE
Nuveen New York Select Quality Municipal Fund, Inc.	NVN	NYSE
Nuveen Ohio Quality Income Municipal Fund, Inc.	NUO	NYSE
Nuveen Pennsylvania Investment Quality Municipal Fund	NQP	NYSE
Nuveen Pennsylvania Quality Income Municipal Fund	NUP	NYSE
Nuveen Performance Plus Municipal Fund, Inc.	NPP	NYSE
Nuveen Premier Insured Municipal Income Fund, Inc.	NIF	NYSE
Nuveen Premier Municipal Income Fund, Inc.	NPF	NYSE
Nuveen Premium Income Municipal Fund, Inc.	NPI	NYSE

MUNICIPAL BOND FUNDS (continued)

FUND	SYMBOL	PRIMARY EXCHANGE
Nuveen Quality Income Municipal Fund, Inc.	NQU	NYSE
Nuveen Select Quality Municipal Fund, Inc.	NQS	NYSE
Nuveen Select Tax-Free Income Portfolio	NXP	NYSE
Nuveen Select Tax-Free Income Portfolio 2	NXQ	NYSE
Nuveen Texas Quality Income Municipal Fund, Inc.	NTX	NYSE
Putnam High Yield Municipal Trust	PYM	NYSE
Putnam Investment Grade Municipal Trust	PGM	NYSE
Putnam Managed Municipal Income Trust	PMM	NYSE
Putnam Tax-Free Health Care Fund	PMH	NYSE
Seligman Quality Municipal Fund, Inc.	SQF	NYSE
Seligman Select Municipal Fund, Inc.	SEL	NYSE
Smith Barney Intermediate Municipal Fund, Inc.	SBI	ASE
Taurus MuniCalifornia Holdings	MCF	NYSE
Taurus MuniNew York Holdings	MNY	NYSE
Van Kampen Merritt California Municipal Income Trust	VKC	ASE
Van Kampen Merritt California Quality Municipal Trust	VQC	NYSE
Van Kampen Merritt Florida Quality Municipal Trust	VFM	NYSE
Van Kampen Merritt Investment Grade Municipal Trust	VIG	NYSE
Van Kampen Merritt Municipal Income Trust	VMT	NYSE
Van Kampen Merritt Municipal Opportunity Trust	VMO	NYSE
Van Kampen Merritt Municipal Trust	VKQ	NYSE
Van Kampen Merritt New York Quality Municipal Trust	VNM	NYSE
Van Kampen Merritt Ohio Quality Municipal Trust	VOQ	NYSE
Van Kampen Merritt Pennsylvania Quality Municipal Trust	VPQ	NYSE

FUND	SYMBOL	PRIMARY EXCHANGE
MISCELLANEOUS & OTHER		
Allied Capital Corporation	ALLC	OTC
Allied Capital Corporation II	ALII	OTC
America's All Season Fund, Inc.	FUND	OTC
Bando McGlocklin Capital Corporation	BMCC	OTC
Capital Investments, Inc.		OTC
Franklin Multi-Income Trust	FMI	NYSE
Jupiter Industries, Inc.	JPI	ASE
Pilgrim Prime Rate Trust	PPR	NYSE
PMC Capital, Inc.	PMC	ASE
Rand Capital Corp.	RAND	OTC
The Zweig Total Return Fund	ZTR	NYSE

FUND	SYMBOL	PRIMARY EXCHANGE
MUNICIPAL BOND FUNDS (continued)		
Van Kampen Merritt Trust for Insured Municipals	VIM	NYSE
Van Kampen Merritt Trust for Investment Grade California Municipals	VIC	NYSE
Van Kampen Merritt Trust for Investment Grade Florida Municipals	VTF	NYSE
Van Kampen Merritt Trust for Investment Grade Municipal Trust	VGM	NYSE
Van Kampen Merritt Trust for Investment Grade New Jersey Municipals	VTJ	NYSE
Van Kampen Merritt Trust for Investment Grade New York Municipals	VTN	NYSE
Van Kampen Merritt Trust for Investment Grade Pennsylvania Municipals	VTP	NYSE
Voyageur Minnesota Municipal Income Fund, Inc.	VMN	ASE
FOREIGN BOND FUNDS		
ACM Managed Multi-Market Trust, Inc.	MMF	NYSE
The Blackrock North American Government Income Trust Inc.	BNA	NYSE
The First Australia Prime Income Fund, Inc.	FAX	ASE
The First Commonwealth Fund, Inc.	FCO	NYSE
The Global Government Plus Fund, Inc.	GOV	NYSE
Global Income Plus Fund	GLI	NYSE
The Global Yield Fund, Inc.	PGY	NYSE
Kleinwort Benson Australian Income Fund, Inc.	KBA	NYSE
Strategic Global Income Fund, Inc.	SGL	NYSE
Templeton Global Governments Income Trust	TGG	NYSE
Templeton Global Income Fund, Inc.	GIM	NYSE

Closed-End Funds Ranked by Size
(000)

FUND	NET ASSETS
EQUITY FUNDS	
Tri-Continental Corporation	$1,871,301
The Salomon Brothers Fund, Inc.	1,115,174
Adams Express Company	661,896
Liberty All-Star Equity Fund	601,219
The Gabelli Equity Trust Inc.	595,151
General American Investors Company, Inc.	587,213
Jundt Growth Fund, Inc.	499,319
Baker, Fentress & Company	417,355
Source Capital Inc.	317,715
Niagara Share Corporation	215,766
Royce Value Trust	166,550
Central Securities Corp.	131,640
The Charles Allmon Trust, Inc.	125,330
Bergstrom Capital Corporation	118,001
Blue Chip Value Fund	78,221
The Inefficient-Market Fund, Inc.	45,335
Engex, Inc.	9,201
FOREIGN EQUITY FUNDS	
The Mexico Fund, Inc.	555,348
The New Germany Fund, Inc.	344,569
The Global Health Sciences Fund	260,279
Templeton Emerging Markets Fund, Inc.	247,416
The R.O.C. Taiwan Fund	244,073
The Korea Fund, Inc.	235,917
The Growth Fund of Spain, Inc.	192,986
The Taiwan Fund, Inc.	185,061
GT Greater Europe Fund	175,074
The Brazil Fund, Inc.	166,719
The Future Germany Fund, Inc.	166,650
Scudder New Europe Fund, Inc.	162,117
The Chile Fund, Inc.	160,360
Morgan Stanley Emerging Markets	155,321
The Germany Fund, Inc.	144,175
The Thai Fund, Inc.	128,676

FUND	NET ASSETS
FOREIGN EQUITY FUNDS (continued)	
The Emerging Germany Fund, Inc.	124,069
The France Growth Fund, Inc.	123,757
The Asia Pacific Fund, Inc.	116,831
The Spain Fund, Inc.	116,665
The Swiss Helvetia Fund, Inc.	110,500
Scudder New Asia Fund, Inc.	105,517
The Europe Fund, Inc.	105,072
The Latin American Investment Fund, Inc.	104,435
The Mexico Equity and Income Fund, Inc.	102,481
The First Philippine Fund, Inc.	101,173
The Malaysia Fund, Inc.	98,338
The Latin American Equity Fund, Inc.	92,751
The Emerging Mexico Fund, Inc.	92,133
The Austria Fund, Inc.	85,899
The India Growth Fund	83,265
Japan OTC Equity Fund, Inc.	82,196
The Italy Fund, Inc.	70,186
The First Australia Fund, Inc.	66,374
Clemente Global Growth Fund, Inc.	63,783
The Argentina Fund, Inc.	63,290
The First Iberian Fund, Inc.	60,628
The Singapore Fund, Inc.	59,379
The Portugal Fund, Inc.	57,036
The Thai Capital Fund, Inc.	55,963
The Brazilian Equity Fund, Inc.	55,800
The Irish Investment Fund, Inc.	48,847
The Latin American Discovery Fund, Inc.	46,530
Worldwide Value Fund, Inc.	46,405
The Korean Investment Fund	46,309
The European Warrant Fund	45,741
The United Kingdom Fund, Inc.	39,823
The Turkish Investment Fund, Inc.	36,255
Pacific-European Growth Fund Inc.	35,680
The Indonesia Fund, Inc.	35,590
Jakarta Growth Fund, Inc.	32,533
Templeton Global Utilities, Inc.	28,785

SPECIALIZED EQUITY FUNDS

Fund	Net Assets
Duff & Phelps Utilities Income, Inc.	1,863,427
The Zweig Fund, Inc.	526,252
ASA Limited	429,168
Petroleum & Resources Corporation	343,919
Patriot Premium Dividend Fund II	270,701
Patriot Select Dividend Trust	231,180
Patriot Premium Dividend Fund I	205,169
Putnam Dividend Income Fund	194,779
Preferred Income Fund Incorporated	187,928
Preferred Income Opportunity Fund Incorporated	123,765
H&Q Healthcare Investors	112,284
Capital Southwest Corporation	107,522
The Emerging Markets Telecommunications Fund, Inc.	101,138
Pilgrim Regional BankShares	101,092
First Financial Fund, Inc.	99,067
Alliance Global Environment Fund	90,612
Morgan Grenfell SMALLCap Fund, Inc.	64,461
H&Q Life Sciences Investors	51,615
Z-Seven, Inc.	22,687
Real Estate Securities Income Fund	20,379
Sterling Capital Corporation	18,378
The Southeastern Thrift and Bank Fund, Inc.	17,623
Spectra Fund, Inc.	5,257
Dover Regional Financial Shares	4,136
Combined Penny Stock Fund, Inc.	863
Redwood MicroCap Fund, Inc.	739

CONVERTIBLE FUNDS

Fund	Net Assets
TCW Convertible Securities Fund, Inc.	172,331
Lincoln National Convertible Securities Fund, Inc.	113,398
Putnam High Income Convertible and Bond Fund	105,635
American Capital Convertible Securities, Inc.	72,079
AIM Strategic Income Fund, Inc.	63,068
Bancroft Convertible Fund, Inc.	54,915
Ellsworth Convertible Growth and Income Fund	54,680
Castle Convertible Fund, Inc.	52,138

DUAL PURPOSE FUNDS

Fund	Net Assets
Quest For Value Dual Purpose Fund, Inc.	615,727
Convertible Holdings, Inc.	275,045
Gemini II	279,862
Counsellors Tandem Securities Fund, Inc.	76,879
Hampton Utilities Trust	25,370

BOND FUNDS

Fund	Net Assets
MFS Intermediate Income Trust	1,643,701
Putnam Premier Income Trust	1,173,624
MFS Multimarket Income Trust	968,813
The Blackrock Target Term Trust Inc.	967,739
MFS Charter Income Trust	923,287
MFS Government Markets Income Trust	785,992
ACM Government Securities Fund, Inc.	707,043
The Blackrock 1998 Term Trust Inc.	595,698
Putnam Intermediate Government Income Trust	585,650
The Blackrock Income Trust Inc.	582,845
Dean Witter Government Income Trust	555,243
The Blackrock Strategic Term Trust Inc.	517,615
Hyperion 1999 Term Trust, Inc.	517,000
ACM Government Income Fund, Inc.	509,206
American Adjustable Rate Term Trust, Inc.--1997	485,325
Putnam Master Income Trust	468,234
American Adjustable Rate Term Trust, Inc.--1998	372,086
Tyler Cabot Mortgage Securities	331,976
Putnam Master Intermediate Income Trust	325,170
ACM Government Opportunity Fund, Inc.	113,386
Oppenheimer Multi-Sector Income Trust	301,568
Kemper Intermediate Government Trust	301,207
The Blackrock Investment Quality Term Trust Inc.	300,800
ACM Government Spectrum Fund, Inc.	288,664
Hyperion Total Return Fund, Inc.	281,898
American Adjustable Rate Term Trust, Inc.--1996	259,317
ACM Managed Income Fund, Inc.	254,865
American Government Income Portfolio, Inc.	234,479
InterCapital Income Securities, Inc.	224,071

FUND	NET ASSETS
BOND FUNDS (continued)	
High Income Advantage Trust II	223,132
Franklin Universal Trust	223,053
American Capital Bond Fund, Inc.	218,187
American Opportunity Income Fund, Inc.	216,197
Kemper Multi-Market Income Trust	204,509
First Boston Income Fund, Inc.	199,857
Kemper High Income Trust	178,145
High Income Advantage Trust	177,237
Franklin Principal Maturity Trust	164,994
Dreyfus Strategic Governments Income, Inc.	164,707
CIGNA High Income Shares	163,173
John Hancock Income Securities Trust	159,990
American Government Income Fund	159,116
Montgomery Street Income Securities, Inc.	157,060
John Hancock Investors Trust	156,026
Van Kampen Merritt Intermediate Term High Income Trust	140,025
The New America High Income Fund, Inc.	128,227
Transamerica Income Shares, Inc.	126,361
Colonial InterMarket Income Trust I	124,778
MassMutual Corporate Investors	122,326
RAC Income Fund, Inc.	120,051
AMEV Securities. Inc.	116,952
American Capital Income Trust	116,298
Fort Dearborn Income Securities, Inc.	110,609
American Adjustable Rate Term Trust, Inc.--1995	109,855
Van Kampen Merritt Limited Term High Income Trust	108,173
Pacific American Income Shares, Inc.	107,735
Zenix Income Fund, Inc.	105,842
The Blackrock Advantage Term Trust Inc.	104,210
Mutual of Omaha Interest Shares, Inc.	99,798
Vestaur Securities, Inc.	95,492
State Mutual Securities Trust	93,571
INA Investment Securities, Inc.	90,345
High Income Advantage Trust III	89,084
MFS Special Value Trust	85,978
The High Yield Plus Fund, Inc.	85,742
Colonial Intermediate High Income Fund	83,613
Prospect Street High Income Portfolio Inc.	83,040
CNA Income Shares, Inc.	81,151
First Boston Strategic Income Fund, Inc.	80,606

FUND	NET ASSETS
BOND FUNDS (continued)	
American Government Term Trust, Inc.	80,370
MassMutual Participation Investors	78,763
The High Yield Income Fund, Inc.	78,571
Lincoln National Income Fund, Inc.	72,752
American Strategic Income Portfolio Inc.	70,811
Oppenheimer Multi-Government Trust	57,208
1838 Bond-Debenture Trading Fund	56,163
Hatteras Income Securities, Inc.	50,964
USLife Income Fund, Inc.	50,552
Current Income Shares, Inc.	48,359
Liberty Term Trust, Inc. --1999	47,500
Bunker Hill Income Securities, Inc.	42,690
Excelsior Income Shares, Inc.	41,620
Circle Income Shares, Inc.	32,867
USF&G Pacholder Fund, Inc.	31,678
Independence Square Income Securities, Inc.	31,424
CIM High Yield Securities	28,015
MUNICIPAL BOND FUNDS	
Nuveen Municipal Value Fund, Inc.	1,686,936
Nuveen Performance Plus Municipal Fund, Inc.	1,229,035
Nuveen Insured Municipal Opportunity Fund, Inc.	1,116,736
Nuveen Premium Income Municipal Fund, Inc.	1,148,040
Nuveen Quality Income Municipal Fund, Inc.	1,146,962
Nuveen Municipal Market Opportunity Fund, Inc.	958,781
Nuveen Municipal Advantage Fund, Inc.	909,345
Van Kampen Merritt Municipal Trust	849,480
MuniVest Fund, Inc.	847,881
Nuveen Insured Quality Municipal Fund, Inc.	801,050
Nuveen Investment Quality Municipal Fund, Inc.	769,837
MuniYield Fund, Inc.	758,339
Nuveen Select Quality Municipal Fund, Inc.	713,377
Van Kampen Merritt Trust for Investment Grade Municipals	690,741
The Blackrock Municipal Target Term Inc.	659,166
Kemper Municipal Income Trust	649,924
Putnam Managed Municipal Income Trust	580,495
MuniYield Insured Fund, Inc.	542,815
Dreyfus Strategic Municipals, Inc.	516,412
InterCapital Insured Municipal Trust	509,286
Nuveen California Quality Income Municipal Fund, Inc.	496,925

MUNICIPAL BOND FUNDS (continued)

FUND	NET ASSETS
MuniEnhanced Fund, Inc.	485,268
Nuveen New York Select Quality Municipal Fund, Inc.	472,116
Nuveen California Select Quality Municipal Fund, Inc.	467,392
Van Kampen Merritt Municipal Income Trust	439,223
Dreyfus Strategic Municipal Bond Fund, Inc.	408,314
InterCapital Quality Municipal Investment Trust	405,696
Van Kampen Merritt Municipal Opportunity Trust	387,900
Allstate Municipal Premium Income Trust	380,657
The Blackrock Insured Municipal Term Trust Inc.	375,000
Nuveen New York Investment Quality Municipal Fund, Inc.	371,093
Putnam Investment Grade Municipal Trust	362,974
Allstate Municipal Income Trust	346,869
Nuveen Florida Investment Quality Municipal Fund, Inc.	337,834
Nuveen New York Quality Income Municipal Fund, Inc.	328,048
MFS Municipal Income Trust	325,077
Allstate Municipal Income Trust II	296,554
Nuveen Select Tax-Free Income Portfolio 2	296,239
Nuveen California Investment Quality Municipal Fund, Inc.	276,571
Nuveen Premier Municipal Income Fund, Inc.	274,709
Colonial High Income Municipal Trust	273,207
Nuveen California Performance Plus Municipal Fund, Inc.	269,890
Nuveen Premier Insured Municipal Income Fund, Inc.	267,940
Nuveen New Jersey Investment Quality Municipal Fund, Inc.	248,154
Van Kampen Merritt Trust for Insured Municipals	239,888
Putnam High Yield Municipal Trust	228,735
Nuveen Select Tax-Free Income Portfolio	229,793
Seligman Select Municipal Fund, Inc.	228,501
Van Kampen Merritt California Quality Municipal Trust	218,385
Colonial Municipal Income Trust	216,394
MuniYield California Fund, Inc.	208,991
Apex Municipal Fund, Inc.	204,904
Allstate Municipal Income Opportunities Trust	201,749
Allstate Municipal Income Opportunities Trust II	194,251
Nuveen California Municipal Value Fund, Inc.	191,430
Dreyfus Municipal Income, Inc.	189,453
Van Kampen Merritt Pennsylvania Quality Municipal Trust	187,754
Van Kampen Merritt Trust for Investment Grade Pennsylvania Municipals	182,432

MUNICIPAL BOND FUNDS (continued)

FUND	NET ASSETS
Nuveen Pennsylvania Investment Quality Municipal Fund	180,203
Putnam Tax-Free Health Care Fund	180,000
Municipal High Income Fund, Inc.	173,290
Nuveen California Municipal Market Opportunity Fund, Inc.	169,554
Nuveen Florida Quality Income Municipal Fund, Inc.	168,206
Van Kampen Merritt Trust for Investment Grade New York Municipals	153,801
Nuveen New York Performance Plus Municipal Fund, Inc.	153,147
Nuveen Michigan Quality Income Municipal Fund, Inc.	151,447
Van Kampen Merritt Florida Quality Municipal Trust	147,394
MuniYield New York Insured Fund, Inc.	145,156
Van Kampen Merritt New York Quality Municipal Trust	128,882
Colonial Investment Grade Municipal Trust	127,589
American Municipal Term Trust Inc.	126,987
Nuveen New York Municipal Market Opportunity Fund, Inc.	125,900
MuniYield New Jersey Fund, Inc.	119,542
Nuveen New York Municipal Value Fund, Inc.	118,926
Kemper Strategic Municipal Income Trust	118,864
InterCapital Insured Municipal Bond Trust	117,238
Van Kampen Merritt Trust for Investment Grade California Municipals	114,620
Allstate Municipal Income Opportunities Trust III	109,326
American Municipal Term Trust Inc. II	108,392
Taurus MuniNew York Holdings	103,721
Van Kampen Merritt Trust for Investment Grade Florida Municipals	102,887
Duff & Phelps Utilities Tax-Free Income Inc.	102,565
Nuveen Pennsylvania Quality Income Municipal Fund	100,406
Nuveen New Jersey Quality Income Municipal Fund, Inc.	99,859
Van Kampen Merritt Trust for Investment Grade New Jersey Municipals	99,252
MuniYield Florida Fund, Inc.	99,143
Nuveen Texas Quality Income Municipal Fund, Inc.	98,310
Seligman Quality Municipal Fund, Inc.	97,782
MuniYield Michigan Fund, Inc.	95,663
Van Kampen Merritt Ohio Quality Municipal Trust	97,328
Nuveen Municipal Income Fund, Inc.	89,912
Minnesota Municipal Term Trust Inc.	84,304

MISCELLANEOUS & OTHER

Fund	Net Assets
Pilgrim Prime Rate Trust	874,104
The Zweig Total Return Fund	648,118
Allied Capital Corporation II	90,387
Franklin Multi-Income Trust	59,470
America's All Season Fund, Inc.	52,540
Allied Capital Corporation	39,929
PMC Capital, Inc.	25,143
Jupiter Industries, Inc.	18,995
Bando McGlocklin Capital Corporation	11,554
Rand Capital Corp.	7,139
Capital Investments, Inc.	4,795

MUNICIPAL BOND FUNDS (continued)

Fund	Net Assets
Nuveen Insured California Select Tax-Free Income Portfolio	81,363
Van Kampen Merritt Investment Grade Municipal Trust	80,660
Taurus MuniCalifornia Holdings	78,543
MuniInsured Fund, Inc.	77,313
Smith Barney Intermediate Municipal Fund, Inc.	70,000
Allstate Municipal Income Trust III	63,086
Nuveen California Municipal Income Fund, Inc.	60,964
Nuveen Ohio Quality Income Municipal Fund, Inc.	60,882
Van Kampen Merritt California Municipal Income Trust	51,256
Nuveen Insured New York Select Tax-Free Income Portfolio	49,525
Dreyfus California Municipal Income, Inc.	41,141
Dreyfus New York Municipal Income, Inc.	35,104
Voyageur Minnesota Municipal Income Fund, Inc.	31,388
Nuveen New York Municipal Income Fund, Inc.	29,160
Minnesota Municipal Term Trust Inc.--II	28,362
The New York Tax-Exempt Income Fund, Inc.	23,839

FOREIGN BOND FUNDS

Fund	Net Assets
The First Australia Prime Income Fund, Inc.	1,272,569
Templeton Global Income Fund, Inc.	1,017,663
The Global Yield Fund, Inc.	593,376
The Blackrock North American Government Income Trust Inc.	451,200
The Global Government Plus Fund, Inc.	377,911
Strategic Global Income Fund, Inc.	266,570
Global Income Plus Fund	242,205
Templeton Global Governments Income Trust	193,740
ACM Managed Multi-Market Trust, Inc.	111,133
The First Commonwealth Fund, Inc.	110,293
Kleinwort Benson Australian Income Fund, Inc.	72,092

Closed-End Funds Listed by Investment Advisor

Accl Worldwide S.A. de C.V.
The Mexico Equity and Income Fund, Inc.

AIM Advisors, Inc.
AIM Strategic Income Fund, Inc.

Alliance Capital Management L.P.
ACM Government Income Fund, Inc.
ACM Government Opportunity Fund, Inc.
ACM Government Securities Fund, Inc.
ACM Government Spectrum Fund, Inc.
ACM Managed Income Fund, Inc.
ACM Managed Multi-Market Trust, Inc.
Alliance Global Environment Fund, Inc.
The Austria Fund, Inc.
The Korean Investment Fund, Inc.
The Spain Fund, Inc.

Allied Capital Advisors, Inc.
Allied Capital Corporation
Allied Capital Corporation II

Allstate Investment Management Company
Allstate Municipal Income Opportunities Trust
Allstate Municipal Income Opportunities Trust II
Allstate Municipal Income Opportunities Trust III
Allstate Municipal Income Trust
Allstate Municipal Income Trust II
Allstate Municipal Income Trust III
Allstate Municipal Premium Income Trust

American Capital Asset Management, Inc.
American Capital Bond Fund, Inc.
American Capital Convertible Securities, Inc.
American Capital Income Trust

Asset Management Advisors of Dresdner Bank
The Emerging Germany Fund, Inc.

Bank of Ireland Asset Management Limited
The Irish Investment Fund, Inc.

Bank One, Indianapolis, NA
Circle Income Shares, Inc.

Baring International Investment (Far East) Limited
The Asia Pacific Fund, Inc.

BEA Associates
The Brazilian Equity Fund, Inc.
The Chile Fund, Inc.
The Emerging Markets Telecommunications Fund, Inc.
The Indonesia Fund, Inc.
The Latin American Equity Fund, Inc.
The Latin American Investment Fund, Inc
Portugal Fund, Inc.

Bergstrom Advisers, Inc.
Bergstrom Capital Corporation

BlackRock Financial Management, L.P.
The BlackRock Advantage Term Trust Inc.
The BlackRock Income Trust Inc.
The BlackRock Insured Municipal Term Trust Inc.
The BlackRock Investment Quality Term Trust Inc.
The BlackRock Municipal Target Term Inc.
The BlackRock 1998 Term Trust Inc.
The BlackRock North American Government Income Trust Inc.
The BlackRock Strategic Term Trust Inc.
The BlackRock Target Term Trust Inc.

Brinson Partners, Inc.
Fort Dearborn Income Securities, Inc.

CIGNA Investments, Inc.
CIGNA High Income Shares
INA Investment Securities, Inc.

Chancellor Trust Company
CIM High Yield Securities

China Securities Investment Trust Corporation
The Taiwan Fund, Inc.

Clemente Capital Inc.
Clemente Global Growth Fund, Inc.
The First Philippine Fund, Inc.

Cohen & Steers Capital Management Inc.
Real Estate Securities Income Fund

Colonial Management Associates, Inc.
Colonial High Income Municipal Trust
Colonial InterMarket Income Trust I
Colonial Intermediate High Income Fund
Colonial Investment Grade Municipal Trust
Colonial Municipal Income Trust

Continental Assurance Company
CNA Income Shares, Inc.

CoreStates Investment Advisers, Inc.
Vestaur Securities, Inc.

D.H. Blair Advisors, Inc.
Engex, Inc.

Davis/Dinsmore Management Company
Bancroft Convertible Fund, Inc.
Ellsworth Convertible Growth and Income Fund

DBS Asset Management (United States) Pte. Ltd.
The Singapore Fund, Inc.

Dean Witter Reynolds, Inc.
Dean Witter Government Income Trust
High Income Advantage Trust
High Income Advantage Trust II
High Income Advantage Trust III

Dean Witter Reynolds, Inc. (continued)
InterCapital Income Securities, Inc.
InterCapital Insured Municipal Bond Trust
InterCapital Insured Municipal Trust
InterCapital Quality Municipal Investment Trust

Denver Investment Advisors, Inc.
Blue Chip Value Fund, Inc.

Deutsche Asset Management GmbH
The Future Germany Fund, Inc.
The Germany Fund, Inc.
The New Germany Fund, Inc.

Dover Financial Management Corporation
Dover Regional Financial Shares

The Dreyfus Corporation
Dreyfus California Municipal Income, Inc.
Dreyfus Municipal Income, Inc.
Dreyfus New York Municipal Income, Inc.
Dreyfus Strategic Governments Income, Inc.
Dreyfus Strategic Municipal Bond Fund, Inc.
Dreyfus Strategic Municipals, Inc.

Duff & Phelps Investment Management Co.
Duff & Phelps Utilities Income Inc.
Duff & Phelps Utilities Tax-Free Income Inc.

1838 Investment Advisors, L.P.
1838 Bond-Debenture Trading Fund

EquitiLink Australia Limited
The First Australia Fund, Inc.
The First Australia Prime Income Fund, Inc.

EquitiLink International Management Limited
The First Commonwealth Fund, Inc.

Federated Advisors
Liberty Term Trust, Inc.--1999

First Boston Asset Management Corporation
First Boston Income Fund, Inc.
First Boston Strategic Income Fund, Inc.

First Pacific Advisors, Inc.
Source Capital, Inc.

Flaherty & Crumrine Incorporated
Preferred Income Fund Incorporated
Preferred Income Opportunity Fund Incorporated

Fortis Advisors, Inc.
AMEV Securities, Inc.

Franklin Advisers, Inc.
Franklin Multi-Income Trust
Franklin Principal Maturity Trust
Franklin Universal Trust
Hampton Utilities Trust

Fred Alger Management, Inc.
Castle Convertible Fund, Inc.
Spectra Fund, Inc.

Fund Asset Management, Inc.
Apex Municipal Fund, Inc.
MuniEnhanced Fund, Inc.
MuniInsured Fund, Inc.
MuniVest Fund, Inc.
MuniYield California Fund, Inc
MuniYield Florida Fund, Inc.
MuniYield Fund, Inc.
MuniYield Insured Fund, Inc.
MuniYield Michigan Fund, Inc.
MuniYield New Jersey Fund, Inc.
MuniYield New York Insured Fund, Inc.
Taurus MuniCalifornia Holdings
Taurus MuniNew York Holdings

Gabelli Funds, Inc.
The Gabelli Equity Trust Inc.

Growth Stock Outlook, Inc.
Charles Allmon Trust, Inc.

G.T. Capital
G.T. Greater Europe Fund

Hambrecht & Quist Capital Management Incorporated
H&Q Healthcare Investors
H&Q Life Sciences Investors

Helvetia Capital Corp.
The Swiss Helvetia Fund, Inc.

Hyperion Capital Management, Inc.
Hyperion Total Return Fund, Inc.
Hyperion 1999 Term Trust, Inc.

Impulsora del Fondo Mexico, S.A. de C.V.
The Mexico Fund, Inc.

Indosuez International Investment Services
The France Growth Fund, Inc.

International Investment Trust Company, Limited
The R.O.C. Taiwan Fund

INVESCO Trust Company
The Global Health Sciences Fund

J. & W. Seligman & Co. Incorporated
Seligman Quality Municipal Fund, Inc.
Seligman Select Municipal Fund, Inc.
Tri-Continental Corporation

John Hancock Advisers, Inc.
John Hancock Income Securities Trust
John Hancock Investors Trust
Patriot Premium Dividend Fund I
Patriot Premium Dividend Fund II
Patriot Select Dividend Trust
The Southeastern Thrift and Bank Fund, Inc.

Julius Baer Securities, Inc.
The European Warrant Fund

Jundt Associates, Inc.
Jundt Growth Fund, Inc.

Kemper Financial Services, Inc.
The Growth Fund of Spain, Inc.
Kemper High Income Trust
Kemper Intermediate Government Trust
Kemper Multi-Market Income Trust
Kemper Municipal Income Trust
Kemper Strategic Municipal Income Trust

Kleinwort Benson International Investment, Limited
Kleinwort Benson Australian Income Fund, Inc.

Liberty Asset Management Company
Liberty All-Star Equity Fund

Lincoln National Investment Management Company
Lincoln National Convertible Securities Fund, Inc.
Lincoln National Income Fund, Inc.

Lombard Odier International Portfolio Management Limited
Worldwide Value Fund, Inc.

Massachusetts Financial Services Company
MFS Charter Income Trust
MFS Government Markets Income Trust

Massachusetts Financial Services Company (continued)
MFS Intermediate Income Trust
MFS Multimarket Income Trust
MFS Municipal Income Trust
MFS Special Value Trust

Massachusetts Mutual Life Insurance Company
MassMutual Corporate Investors
MassMutual Participation Investors

Merrill Lynch Asset Management, Inc.
Convertible Holdings, Inc.

Mitchell Hutchins Asset Management Inc.
Global Income Plus Fund, Inc.
Strategic Global Income Fund, Inc.

Morgan Grenfell Capital Management
Morgan Grenfell SMALLCap Fund, Inc.

Morgan Stanley Asset Management, Inc.
The Latin American Discovery Fund, Inc.
The Malaysia Fund, Inc.
Morgan Stanley Emerging Markets
The Thai Fund, Inc.
The Turkish Investment Fund, Inc.

The Mutual Fund Co., Ltd.
The Thai Capital Fund, Inc.

Mutual of Omaha Fund Management Company
Mutual of Omaha Interest Shares, Inc.

Mutual Management Corp.
Smith Barney Intermediate Municipal Fund, Inc.

NCNB National Bank of North Carolina
Hatteras Income Securities, Inc.

Nomura Capital Management, Inc.

Jakarta Growth Fund, Inc.
Japan OTC Equity Fund, Inc.

Nuveen Advisory Co.

Nuveen California Investment Quality Municipal Fund, Inc.
Nuveen California Municipal Income Fund, Inc.
Nuveen California Municipal Market Opportunity Fund, Inc.
Nuveen California Municipal Value Fund, Inc.
Nuveen California Performance Plus Municipal Fund, Inc.
Nuveen California Quality Income Municipal Fund, Inc.
Nuveen California Select Quality Municipal Fund, Inc.
Nuveen Florida Investment Quality Municipal Fund, Inc.
Nuveen Florida Quality Income Municipal Fund, Inc.
Nuveen Insured California Select Tax-Free Income Portfolio
Nuveen Insured Municipal Opportunity Fund, Inc.
Nuveen Insured New York Select Tax-Free Income Portfolio
Nuveen Insured Quality Municipal Fund, Inc.
Nuveen Investment Quality Municipal Fund, Inc.
Nuveen Michigan Quality Income Municipal Fund, Inc.
Nuveen Municipal Advantage Fund, Inc.
Nuveen Municipal Income Fund, Inc.
Nuveen Municipal Market Opportunity Fund, Inc.
Nuveen Municipal Value Fund, Inc.
Nuveen New Jersey Investment Quality Municipal Fund, Inc.
Nuveen New Jersey Quality Income Municipal Fund, Inc.
Nuveen New York Investment Quality Municipal Fund, Inc.
Nuveen New York Municipal Income Fund, Inc.
Nuveen New York Municipal Market Opportunity Fund, Inc.
Nuveen New York Municipal Value Fund, Inc.
Nuveen New York Performance Plus Municipal Fund, Inc.
Nuveen New York Quality Income Municipal Fund, Inc.
Nuveen New York Select Quality Municipal Fund, Inc.
Nuveen Ohio Quality Income Municipal Fund, Inc.
Nuveen Pennsylvania Investment Quality Municipal Fund
Nuveen Pennsylvania Quality Income Municipal Fund
Nuveen Performance Plus Municipal Fund, Inc.
Nuveen Premier Insured Municipal Income Fund, Inc.
Nuveen Premier Municipal Income Fund, Inc.
Nuveen Premium Income Municipal Fund, Inc.
Nuveen Quality Income Municipal Fund, Inc.

Nuveen Advisory Co. (continued)

Nuveen Select Quality Municipal Fund, Inc.
Nuveen Select Tax-Free Income Portfolio
Nuveen Select Tax-Free Income Portfolio 2
Nuveen Texas Quality Income Municipal Fund, Inc.

Oppenheimer Management Corporation

The New York Tax-Exempt Income Fund, Inc.
Oppenheimer Multi-Government Trust
Oppenheimer Multi-Sector Income Trust

Pacholder & Company

USF&G Pacholder Fund, Inc.

Pilgrim Management Corporation

Pilgrim Prime Rate Trust
Pilgrim Regional BankShares

Piper Capital Management Incorporated

American Adjustable Rate Term Trust Inc.--1995
American Adjustable Rate Term Trust Inc.--1996
American Adjustable Rate Term Trust Inc.--1997
American Adjustable Rate Term Trust Inc.--1998
American Government Income Fund Inc.
American Government Income Portfolio, Inc.
American Government Term Trust Inc.
American Municipal Term Trust Inc.
American Municipal Term Trust Inc. II
American Opportunity Income Fund Inc.
American Strategic Income Portfolio Inc.
Minnesota Municipal Term Trust Inc.
Minnesota Municipal Term Trust Inc.--II
Pacific-European Growth Fund Inc.

Prospect Street Investment Management Co., Inc.

Prospect Street High Income Portfolio Inc.

Provident Institutional Management Corporation

Independence Square Income Securities, Inc.

The Prudential Investment Corporation/ The Prudential Mutual Fund Management, Inc.
The Global Government Plus Fund, Inc.
The Global Yield Fund, Inc.
The High Yield Income Fund, Inc.

The Putnam Management Company, Inc.
Putnam Dividend Income Fund
Putnam High Income Convertible and Bond Fund
Putnam High Yield Municipal Trust
Putnam Intermediate Government Income Trust
Putnam Investment Grade Municipal Trust

The Putnam Management Company, Inc. (continued)
Putnam Managed Municipal Income Trust
Putnam Master Income Trust
Putnam Master Intermediate Income Trust
Putnam Premier Income Trust
Putnam Tax-Free Health Care Fund

Quest Advisory Corp.
Royce Value Trust

Quest for Value Advisors
Quest for Value Dual Purpose Fund, Inc.

Ryland Acceptance Advisers, Inc.
RAC Income Fund, Inc.

Salomon Brothers Asset Management, Inc.
The Salomon Brothers Fund, Inc.

Sandander Management Inc.
The Emerging Mexico Fund, Inc.

Scudder, Stevens & Clark Inc.
The Argentina Fund, Inc.
The Brazil Fund, Inc.
The First Iberian Fund, Inc.

Scudder, Stevens & Clark Inc. (continued)
The Korea Fund, Inc.
Montgomery Street Income Securities, Inc.
Scudder New Asia Fund, Inc.
Scudder New Europe Fund, Inc.

Security Pacific Investment Managers, Inc.
Bunker Hill Income Securities, Inc.

Shearson Lehman Advisors
Municipal High Income Fund, Inc.
Zenix Income Fund, Inc.

Shearson Lehman Global Asset Management Limited
The Italy Fund, Inc.

Smith Barney, Harris Upham & Co., Incorporated
The Inefficient-Market Fund, Inc.

State Mutual Life Assurance Company of America
State Mutual Securities Trust

TCW Funds Management, Inc.
TCW Convertible Securities Fund, Inc.

Templeton, Galbraith & Hansberger, Ltd.
Templeton Emerging Markets Fund, Inc.
Templeton Global Governments Income Trust
Templeton Global Income Fund, Inc.
Templeton Global Utilities, Inc.

TOP Fund Management, Inc.
Z-Seven Fund, Inc.

Transamerica Investment Services, Inc.
Transamerica Income Shares, Inc.

Tyler Cabot Securities Advisers, Inc.
Tyler Cabot Mortgage Securities

Union Bank
Current Income Shares, Inc.

Unit Trust of India Investment Advisory Services, Limited
The India Growth Fund, Inc.

United States Trust Company of New York
Excelsior Income Shares, Inc.

USLIFE Advisers, Inc.
USLife Income Fund, Inc.

Van Kampen Merritt Investment Advisory Corp.
Van Kampen Merritt California Municipal Income Trust
Van Kampen Merritt California Quality Municipal Trust
Van Kampen Merritt Florida Quality Municipal Trust
Van Kampen Merritt Intermediate Term High Income Trust
Van Kampen Merritt Investment Grade Municipal Trust
Van Kampen Merritt Limited Term High Income Trust
Van Kampen Merritt Municipal Income Trust
Van Kampen Merritt Municipal Opportunity Trust
Van Kampen Merritt Municipal Trust
Van Kampen Merritt New York Quality Municipal Trust
Van Kampen Merritt Ohio Quality Municipal Trust
Van Kampen Merritt Pennsylvania Quality Municipal Trust
Van Kampen Merritt Trust for Insured Municipals
Van Kampen Merritt Trust for Investment Grade California Municipals
Van Kampen Merritt Trust for Investment Grade Florida Municipals
Van Kampen Merritt Trust for Investment Grade Municipals
Van Kampen Merritt Trust for Investment Grade New Jersey Municipals
Van Kampen Merritt Trust for Investment Grade New York Municipals
Van Kampen Merritt Trust for Investment Grade Pennsylvania Municipals

Veitia & Assoc., Inc.
America's All Season Fund, Inc.

Voyageur Fund Managers
Voyageur Minnesota Municipal Income Fund, Inc.

Warburg Investment Management International (Jersey) Limited
The Europe Fund, Inc.
The United Kingdom Fund, Inc.

Warburg, Pincus Counsellors, Inc.
Counsellors Tandem Securities Fund, Inc.

Wellington Management Company
First Financial Fund, Inc.
Gemini II
The High Yield Plus Fund, Inc.
The New America High Income Fund, Inc.

Western Asset Management Company
Pacific American Income Shares, Inc.

Zweig Advisors, Inc.
The Zweig Fund, Inc.

Zweig Total Return Advisors, Inc.
The Zweig Total Return Fund

Internally Managed
Adams Express Company
ASA Limited
Baker, Fentress & Company
Bando McGlocklin Capital Corporation
Capital Southwest Corporation
Central Securities Corp.
General American Investors Company, Inc.
Niagara Share Corporation
Petroleum & Resources Corporation
Sterling Capital Corporation

Expense Ratio Survey
(expenses to average net asset)

Expense ratios continue to be one of the more important considerations in our closed-end fund analysis. There are a few technical points and comments to bear in mind when using the following table: Small funds tend to have higher expense ratios than larger funds; so do foreign funds. Leveraged funds have higher expense ratios because of interest costs (where available the operating expense ratio is presented). Funds whose advisory fees are based on performance tend to have more volatile expense ratios.

Please note that figures presented for the dual purpose funds show the ratio of expenses to average net assets of both capital and income shares combined, even though, in most cases, the income shares pay all of the fund's expenses.

FUND	EXPENSE RATIO	FOOTNOTE
EQUITY FUNDS		
The Salomon Brothers Fund, Inc.	0.43%	i
Adams Express Company	0.58%	i
Tri-Continental Corporation	0.67%	i
Royce Value Trust	0.79%	i
Baker, Fentress & Company	0.84%	i
Bergstrom Capital Corporation	0.88%	i
Central Securities Corporation	0.96%	i
Source Capital Inc.	0.97%	i
General American Investors Company, Inc.	1.02%	i
Niagara Share Corporation	1.22%	i
The Gabelli Equity Trust Inc.	1.24%	o,i
The Inefficient-Market Fund, Inc.	1.28%	i
Blue Chip Value Fund, Inc.	1.31%	o,i
The Charles Allmon Trust, Inc.	1.31%	i
Jundt Growth Fund, Inc.	1.43%	a,d,i
Liberty All-Star Equity Fund	1.66%	i
Engex, Inc.	2.66%	l
FOREIGN EQUITY FUNDS		
The New Germany Fund, Inc.	1.05%	o,i
The Future Germany Fund, Inc.	1.21%	o,k
The Mexico Fund, Inc.	1.22%	o,a,h
The Growth Fund of Spain, Inc.	1.23%	j
The Germany Fund, Inc.	1.39%	o,i
The Thai Fund, Inc.	1.44%	o,i
Templeton Global Utilities, Inc.	1.45%	a,b,g
Alliance Global Environment Fund, Inc.	1.49%	k
The Korea Fund, Inc.	1.50%	a,b,i
Japan OTC Equity Fund, Inc.	1.51%	g

FUND	EXPENSE RATIO	FOOTNOTE
FOREIGN EQUITY FUNDS (continued)		
The Italy Fund, Inc.	1.53%	o,h
The Europe Fund, Inc.	1.56%	o,i
The Mexico Equity and Income Fund, Inc.	1.57%	a,b,h
The Malaysia Fund, Inc.	1.70%	i
The Emerging Germany Fund, Inc.	1.70%	i
The United Kingdom Fund, Inc.	1.74%	g
The Chile Fund, Inc.	1.75%	i
The Emerging Mexico Fund, Inc.	1.78%	a,b,i
Scudder New Asia Fund, Inc.	1.79%	o,i
The India Growth Fund, Inc.	1.80%	a,b,i
The Austria Fund, Inc.	1.83%	a,b,g
Scudder New Europe Fund, Inc.	1.85%	o,k
The Swiss Helvetia Fund, Inc.	1.85%	i
Templeton Emerging Markets Fund, Inc.	1.85%	a,b,g
GT Greater Europe Fund	1.87%	k
The Asia Pacific Fund, Inc.	1.92%	o,f
Pacific-European Growth Fund Inc.	1.92%	g
The First Philippine Fund, Inc.	1.95%	a,b,i
The Portugal Fund, Inc.	1.96%	i
The Spain Fund, Inc.	1.98%	j
The Indonesia Fund, Inc.	2.00%	i
The Irish Investment Fund, Inc.	2.03%	k
The R.O.C. Taiwan Fund	2.11%	i
The France Growth Fund, Inc.	2.14%	i
Jakarta Growth Fund, Inc.	2.15%	f
The Brazil Fund, Inc.	2.15%	o,i
Morgan Stanley Emerging Markets	2.25%	a,d,i
The First Australia Fund, Inc.	2.25%	o,k
Worldwide Value Fund, Inc.	2.30%	i

FOREIGN EQUITY FUNDS (continued)

Fund	Expense Ratio	Footnote
The Latin American Investment Fund, Inc.	2.30%	i
The First Iberian Fund, Inc.	2.30%	o,l
The Latin American Equity Fund, Inc.	2.35%	a,d,i
The Turkish Investment Fund, Inc.	2.42%	k
The European Warrant Fund	2.44%	f
The Argentina Fund, Inc.	2.55%	a,d,k
The Singapore Fund, Inc.	2.56%	k
The Thai Capital Fund, Inc.	2.70%	i
Clemente Global Growth Fund, Inc.	2.74%	i
The Taiwan Fund, Inc.	3.10%	a,b,g

SPECIALIZED EQUITY FUNDS

Fund	Expense Ratio	Footnote
Petroleum & Resources Corporation	0.59%	i
ASA Limited	0.66%	j
Capital Southwest Corporation	1.10%	f
Duff & Phelps Utilities Income, Inc.	1.17%	i
First Financial Fund, Inc.	1.23%	f
The Zweig Fund, Inc.	1.28%	i
Pilgrim Regional BankShares	1.31%	i
Patriot Premium Dividend Fund II	1.38%	o,k
Patriot Premium Dividend Fund I	1.41%	o,a,b,f
Patriot Select Dividend Trust	1.46%	o,a,b,i
Putnam Dividend Income Fund	1.64%	a,b,i
Real Estate Securities Income Fund	1.66%	i
Preferred Income Fund Incorporated	1.67%	a,d,j
H&Q Healthcare Investors	1.71%	o,a,b,f
Morgan Grenfell SMALLCap Fund, Inc.	1.79%	i
The Southeastern Thrift and Bank Fund, Inc.	1.98%	a,b,i
Dover Regional Financial Shares	2.50%	i
Z-Seven Fund, Inc.	4.33%	i
Sterling Capital Corporation	4.70%	i

CONVERTIBLE FUNDS

Fund	Expense Ratio	Footnote
American Capital Convertible Securities, Inc.	0.89%	i
Lincoln National Convertible Securities Fund, Inc.	0.89%	i
TCW Convertible Securities Fund, Inc.	0.94%	i
Putnam High Income Convertible and Bond Fund	1.14%	a,b,g

CONVERTIBLE FUNDS (continued)

Fund	Expense Ratio	Footnote
Castle Convertible Fund, Inc.	1.14%	a,b,i
AIM Strategic Income Fund, Inc.	1.17%	o,i
Ellsworth Convertible Growth and Income Fund	1.20%	a,b,f
Bancroft Convertible Fund, Inc.	1.30%	k

DUAL PURPOSE FUNDS

Fund	Expense Ratio	Footnote
Quest For Value Dual Purpose Fund, Inc.	0.77%	o,i
Convertible Holdings, Inc.	0.83%	i
Hampton Utilities Trust	1.33%	i
Counsellors Tandem Securities Fund, Inc.	1.35%	o,i

BOND FUNDS

Fund	Expense Ratio	Footnote
InterCapital Income Securities, Inc.	0.66%	a,b,f
American Adjustable Rate Term Trust Inc. --1998	0.69%	a,d,g
Montgomery Street Income Securities, Inc.	0.69%	o,i
State Mutual Securities Trust	0.77%	i
The Blackrock 1998 Term Trust Inc.	0.78%	a,d,j
John Hancock Income Securities Trust	0.74%	i
John Hancock Investors Trust	0.74%	i
American Capital Bond Fund, Inc.	0.72%	o,a,i
Dean Witter Government Income Trust	0.72%	a,b,f
AMEV Securities. Inc.	0.82%	a,b,h
Mutual of Omaha Interest Shares, Inc.	0.82%	i
Pacific American Income Shares, Inc.	0.84%	o,i
Dreyfus Strategic Governments Income, Inc.	0.87%	a,b,j
First Boston Income Fund, Inc.	0.87%	i
Putnam Premier Income Trust	0.88%	a,b,h
Transamerica Income Shares, Inc.	0.68%	f
Current Income Shares, Inc.	0.90%	i
Independence Square Income Securities, Inc.	0.90%	i
Vestaur Securities, Inc.	0.90%	j
High Income Advantage Trust II	0.92%	a,b,h
The Blackrock Target Term Trust Inc.	0.92%	k
Fort Dearborn Income Securities, Inc.	0.92%	a,b,f
INA Investment Securities, Inc.	0.93%	i
Kemper Intermediate Government Trust	0.93%	j
Circle Income Shares, Inc.	0.94%	a,c,f

BOND FUNDS (continued)

FUND	EXPENSE RATIO	FOOTNOTE
The Blackrock Strategic Term Trust Inc.	0.96%	a,d,j
1838 Bond-Debenture Trading Fund	0.97%	o,f
Lincoln National Income Fund, Inc.	0.97%	o,i
Excelsior Income Shares, Inc.	0.98%	i
Putnam Master Intermediate Income Trust	0.98%	a,b,f
Hatteras Income Securities, Inc.	0.99%	i
The New America High Income Fund, Inc.	1.97%	o,i
ACM Government Securities Fund, Inc.	1.83%	i
American Adjustable Rate Term Trust Inc. --1997	1.89%	a,b,g
Colonial Intermediate High Income Fund	1.38%	k
MFS Special Value Trust	1.37%	k
USF&G Pacholder Fund, Inc.	1.37%	i
ACM Government Spectrum Fund, Inc.	1.35%	a,b,i
USLife Income Fund, Inc.	1.32%	o,i
ACM Government Income Fund, Inc.	1.30%	o,i
The Blackrock Advantage Term Trust Inc.	1.30%	o,i
The High Yield Plus Fund, Inc.	1.28%	o,f
MassMutual Participation Investors	1.28%	i
CIGNA High Income Shares	1.26%	o,i
ACM Government Opportunity Fund, Inc.	1.23%	a,b,h
The High Yield Income Fund, Inc.	1.21%	o,a,b,g
Oppenheimer Multi-Government Trust	1.21%	k
High Income Advantage Trust III	1.17%	h
RAC Income Fund, Inc.	1.17%	o,k
Oppenheimer Multi-Sector Income Trust	1.16%	k
Tyler Cabot Mortgage Securities	1.16%	o,k
American Government Term Trust Inc.	1.13%	o,j
MFS Multimarket Income Trust	1.11%	o,k
ACM Managed Income Fund, Inc.	1.11%	a,b,g
Hyperion Total Return Fund, Inc.	1.10%	o,j
Putnam Master Income Trust	1.10%	k
The Blackrock Income Trust Inc.	1.08%	o,k
Colonial InterMarket Income Trust I	1.07%	j
High Income Advantage Trust	1.07%	a,b,f
Bunker Hill Income Securities, Inc.	1.06%	a,b,f
CNA Income Shares, Inc.	1.05%	i
MFS Government Markets Income Trust	1.04%	j

BOND FUNDS (continued)

FUND	EXPENSE RATIO	FOOTNOTE
American Capital Income Trust	1.03%	i
Franklin Principal Maturity Trust	1.03%	o,j
American Government Income Fund Inc.	1.02%	o,k
MFS Charter Income Trust	1.02%	j
American Government Income Portfolio, Inc.	1.01%	o,k
Putnam Intermediate Government Income Trust	1.01%	j
First Boston Strategic Income Fund, Inc.	1.00%	i
Kemper Multi-Market Income Trust	1.00%	j
MFS Intermediate Income Trust	1.00%	k
American Adjustable Rate Term Trust Inc. --1996	2.04%	a,b,g
Zenix Income Fund, Inc.	2.15%	o,f
Kemper High Income Trust	2.22%	j
Prospect Street High Income Portfolio Inc.	2.23%	o,k
CIM High Yield Securities	2.46%	o,i
Van Kampen Merritt Intermediate Term High Income Trust	2.51%	i
American Adjustable Rate Term Trust Inc. --1995	2.67%	a,b,g
Van Kampen Merritt Limited Term High Income Trust	2.73%	i
MassMutual Corporate Investors	2.77%	i
American Opportunity Income Fund Inc.	2.97%	a,b,g
Franklin Universal Trust	3.45%	a,b,g

MUNICIPAL BOND FUNDS

FUND	EXPENSE RATIO	FOOTNOTE
MuniYield Fund, Inc.	0.51%	a,d,e
InterCapital Insured Municipal Trust	0.54%	a,d,e
Minnesota Municipal Term Trust Inc.	0.55%	a,d,i
Seligman Quality Municipal Fund, Inc.	0.55%	a,d,e
American Municipal Term Trust Inc.	0.56%	a,d,i
American Municipal Term Trust Inc. II	0.58%	a,d,i
MuniVest Fund, Inc.	0.65%	a,b,g
Nuveen Premium Income Municipal Fund, Inc.	0.65%	a,b,j
The Blackrock Municipal Target Term Inc.	0.66%	a,d,i
MuniEnhanced Fund, Inc.	0.70%	h
Allstate Municipal Income Trust	0.72%	a,b,g

MUNICIPAL BOND FUNDS (continued)

FUND	EXPENSE RATIO	FOOTNOTE
Kemper Municipal Income Trust	0.72%	j
Nuveen Municipal Income Fund, Inc.	0.72%	a,b,h
Nuveen California Municipal Income Fund, Inc.	0.73%	j
Nuveen New York Quality Income Municipal Fund, Inc.	0.73%	a,d,f
Nuveen Performance Plus Municipal Fund, Inc.	0.74%	a,b,j
Nuveen Quality Income Municipal Fund, Inc.	0.74%	a,d,k
Nuveen California Select Quality Municipal Fund, Inc.	0.75%	a,d,k
Nuveen Investment Quality Municipal Fund, Inc.	0.75%	k
Nuveen Municipal Market Opportunity Fund, Inc.	0.75%	k
Nuveen Florida Investment Quality Municipal Fund, Inc.	0.76%	a,d,k
Nuveen Municipal Advantage Fund, Inc.	0.76%	k
Nuveen New Jersey Investment Quality Municipal Fund, Inc.	0.76%	a,k
Kemper Strategic Municipal Income Trust	0.77%	j
Nuveen Insured Municipal Opportunity Fund, Inc.	0.77%	a,d,k
Nuveen Insured Quality Municipal Fund, Inc.	0.77%	a,d,k
Nuveen California Investment Quality Municipal Fund, Inc.	0.78%	a,d,k
Nuveen California Performance Plus Municipal Fund, Inc.	0.78%	k
Nuveen Florida Quality Income Municipal Fund, Inc.	0.79%	a,d,i
Nuveen Michigan Quality Income Municipal Fund, Inc.	0.79%	a,d,j
Nuveen New York Investment Quality Municipal Fund, Inc.	0.79%	a,b,f
Nuveen Select Quality Municipal Fund, Inc.	0.79%	a,d,k
InterCapital Quality Municipal Investment Trust	0.80%	a,b,e
Nuveen California Municipal Market Opportunity Fund, Inc.	0.80%	k

MUNICIPAL BOND FUNDS (continued)

FUND	EXPENSE RATIO	FOOTNOTE
Nuveen New York Municipal Income Fund, Inc.	0.80%	a,b,f
Nuveen New York Performance Plus Municipal Fund, Inc.	0.81%	a,f
Nuveen Pennsylvania Investment Quality Municipal Fund	0.81%	a,d,k
Nuveen New York Select Quality Municipal Fund, Inc.	0.82%	a,f
Apex Municipal Fund, Inc.	0.83%	a,b,i
Nuveen California Municipal Value Fund, Inc.	0.83%	a,b,h
Nuveen Municipal Value Fund, Inc.	0.83%	j
Nuveen New York Municipal Market Opportunity Fund, Inc.	0.83%	a,b,f
Nuveen New Jersey Quality Income Municipal Fund, Inc.	0.85%	a,d,i
Allstate Municipal Income Trust II	0.86%	i
Dreyfus Municipal Income, Inc.	0.86%	a,b,f
Nuveen Pennsylvania Quality Income Municipal Fund	0.86%	a,d,i
Taurus MuniNew York Holdings	0.86%	k
Colonial Investment Grade Municipal Trust	0.87%	i
Colonial Municipal Income Trust	0.87%	j
Nuveen Texas Quality Income Municipal Fund, Inc.	0.87%	a,d,j
Dreyfus Strategic Municipal Bond Fund, Inc.	0.88%	j
Dreyfus Strategic Municipals, Inc.	0.88%	a,b,f
MuniInsured Fund, Inc.	0.88%	a,b,f
Nuveen Ohio Quality Income Municipal Fund, Inc.	0.89%	a,d,j
Municipal High Income Fund, Inc.	0.90%	k
Seligman Select Municipal Fund, Inc.	0.90%	i
Taurus MuniCalifornia Holdings	0.91%	k
Nuveen New York Municipal Value Fund, Inc.	0.91%	a,b,h
Colonial High Income Municipal Trust	0.97%	i
InterCapital Insured Municipal Bond Trust	0.98%	a,b,e
Allstate Municipal Income Trust III	1.00%	a,b,g
The New York Tax-Exempt Income Fund, Inc.	1.03%	a,b,e
Allstate Municipal Income Opportunities Trust	1.06%	a,b,j

MUNICIPAL BOND FUNDS (continued)

FUND	EXPENSE RATIO	FOOTNOTE
Allstate Municipal Income Opportunities Trust II	1.06%	g
Dreyfus New York Municipal Income, Inc.	1.10%	a,b,f
Dreyfus California Municipal Income, Inc.	1.12%	a,b,f
Putnam High Yield Municipal Trust	1.13%	f
Allstate Municipal Income Opportunities Trust III	1.14%	f
Duff & Phelps Utilities Tax-Free Income, Inc.	1.19%	o,d,e
MFS Municipal Income Trust	1.27%	k
Putnam Managed Municipal Income Trust	1.33%	k
Allstate Municipal Premium Income Trust	1.44%	a,b,j
Van Kampen Merritt Municipal Income Trust	1.44%	a,b,i
Putnam Investment Grade Municipal Trust	1.46%	j
Van Kampen Merritt Municipal Trust	1.49%	a,d,g
Van Kampen Merritt Investment Grade Municipal Trust	1.53%	k
Van Kampen Merritt California Quality Municipal Trust	1.57%	a,d,g
Van Kampen Merritt Pennsylvania Quality Municipal Trust	1.61%	a,d,g
Van Kampen Merritt Florida Quality Municipal Trust	1.66%	a,d,g
Van Kampen Merritt New York Quality Municipal Trust	1.73%	a,d,g
Van Kampen Merritt Ohio Quality Municipal Trust	1.84%	a,d,g
Van Kampen Merritt California Municipal Income Trust	2.26%	a,b,i

FOREIGN BOND FUNDS

FUND	EXPENSE RATIO	FOOTNOTE
Templeton Global Income Fund, Inc.	0.81%	a,b,g
The Global Yield Fund, Inc.	0.99%	o,i
The Global Government Plus Fund, Inc.	1.07%	i
Templeton Global Governments Income Trust	1.09%	a,b,g
Global Income Plus Fund	1.13%	k
The First Australia Prime Income Fund, Inc.	1.59%	o,k
Kleinwort Benson Australian Income Fund, Inc.	1.62%	a,b,e
ACM Managed Multi-Market Trust, Inc.	3.37%	j

MISCELLANEOUS & OTHER

FUND	EXPENSE RATIO	FOOTNOTE
The Zweig Total Return Fund	1.11%	i
Pilgrim Prime Rate Trust	1.42%	g
America's All Season Fund, Inc.	2.36%	i
Franklin Multi-Income Trust	3.21%	f

FOOTNOTES:

a. annualized
b. six month period
c. nine month period
d. from commencement
e. period ended 4/30/92
f. period ended 3/31/92
g. period ended 2/29/92
h. period ended 1/31/92
i. period ended 12/31/91
j. period ended 11/30/91
k period ended 10/31/91
l. period ended 9/30/91
o. operating expense ratio

Income Ratio Survey
(net investment income to average net assets)

"Yield" continues to be one of the most confusing terms applied to closed-end fund analysis. Many investors and newspapers mistakenly include capital gains distributions and return of capital as part of this calculation. This can be as misleading as it would be for a depositor of $100 in a savings bank earning 5% interest who withdraws the $5 in interest, plus an additional $2 at the end of the year and mistakenly calculates his "yield" as 7%, ignoring the $2 reduction of his account balance to $98. The income ratio (net income per share divided by average net assets) is what we believe to be a better measure of "yield" for an investment company.

Please note that figures presented for the dual purpose funds show the ratio of net investment income to average net assets of both capital and income shares combined, even though, in most cases, the income shares receive all the income.

FUND	INCOME RATIO	FOOTNOTE
EQUITY FUNDS		
Source Capital Inc.	4.22%	i
The Charles Allmon Trust, Inc.	4.17%	i
The Salomon Brothers Fund, Inc.	3.01%	i
Tri-Continental Corporation	2.90%	i
Adams Express Company	2.74%	i
Baker, Fentress & Company	2.53%	i
Jundt Growth Fund, Inc.	2.45%	a,d,i
The Gabelli Equity Trust Inc.	2.34%	i
Niagara Share Corporation	2.12%	i
Central Securities Corporation	1.78%	i
Blue Chip Value Fund, Inc.	1.66%	i
Liberty All-Star Equity Fund	1.66%	i
The Inefficient-Market Fund, Inc.	1.26%	i
Bergstrom Capital Corporation	1.25%	i
Royce Value Trust	1.52%	i
General American Investors Company, Inc.	0.37%	i
Engex, Inc.	(0.03%)	l
FOREIGN EQUITY FUNDS		
The Brazil Fund, Inc.	8.13%	i
Templeton Global Utilities, Inc.	4.98%	a,b,g
The Mexico Equity and Income Fund, Inc.	4.61%	a,b,h
The Chile Fund, Inc.	3.97%	i
The United Kingdom Fund, Inc.	3.73%	f
The Growth Fund of Spain, Inc.	3.32%	j
The Turkish Investment Fund, Inc.	3.28%	k
The First Australia Fund, Inc.	3.11%	k

FUND	INCOME RATIO	FOOTNOTE
FOREIGN EQUITY FUNDS (continued)		
The First Iberian Fund, Inc.	2.96%	l
The Argentina Fund, Inc.	2.54%	a,d,k
The Thai Fund, Inc.	2.45%	i
The Latin American Equity Fund, Inc.	2.35%	a,d,i
Morgan Stanley Emerging Markets	2.32%	a,d,i
The Europe Fund, Inc.	2.30%	i
The Latin American Investment Fund, Inc.	2.30%	i
The Italy Fund, Inc.	2.17%	h
Scudder New Europe Fund, Inc.	1.74%	k
The Irish Investment Fund, Inc.	1.55%	k
The Global Health Sciences Fund	1.52%	a,d,e
The Singapore Fund, Inc.	1.47%	k
The France Growth Fund, Inc.	1.46%	i
The Thai Capital Fund, Inc.	1.36%	i
The Spain Fund, Inc.	1.33%	j
The Future Germany Fund, Inc.	1.22%	k
The Portugal Fund, Inc.	1.20%	i
The Germany Fund, Inc.	1.17%	i
The New Germany Fund, Inc.	1.02%	i
Alliance Global Environment Fund, Inc.	0.95%	k
The Malaysia Fund, Inc.	0.77%	i
The Emerging Germany Fund, Inc.	0.76%	i
The Asia Pacific Fund, Inc.	0.70%	f
The First Philippine Fund, Inc.	0.64%	a,b,i
Jakarta Growth Fund, Inc.	0.63%	f
Pacific-European Growth Fund Inc.	0.60%	g
Scudder New Asia Fund, Inc.	0.54%	i
Worldwide Value Fund, Inc.	0.50%	i

FOREIGN EQUITY FUNDS (continued)

FUND	INCOME RATIO	FOOTNOTE
The Indonesia Fund, Inc.	0.49%	i
The Emerging Mexico Fund, Inc.	0.39%	a,b,i
Templeton Emerging Markets Fund, Inc.	0.38%	a,b,g
GT Greater Europe Fund	0.21%	k
The Swiss Helvetia Fund, Inc.	0.07%	i
The R.O.C. Taiwan Fund	(0.15%)	i
The Mexico Fund, Inc.	(0.16%)	a,h
Japan OTC Equity Fund, Inc.	(0.58%)	g
The India Growth Fund, Inc.	(0.65%)	a,b,i
The Korea Fund, Inc.	(0.66%)	a,b,i
The Taiwan Fund, Inc.	(0.78%)	a,b,g
The European Warrant Fund	(0.79%)	f
Clemente Global Growth Fund, Inc.	(0.11%)	i
The Austria Fund, Inc.	(1.16%)	a,b,g

SPECIALIZED EQUITY FUNDS

FUND	INCOME RATIO	FOOTNOTE
Real Estate Securities Income Fund	9.26%	i
Preferred Income Fund Incorporated	9.18%	a,d,j
Patriot Premium Dividend Fund II	8.13%	k
Duff & Phelps Utilities Income, Inc.	7.75%	i
Patriot Select Dividend Trust	7.19%	a,b,i
Putnam Dividend Income Fund	7.16%	a,b,i
Patriot Premium Dividend Fund I	6.90%	a,b,f
ASA Limited	3.70%	j
Petroleum & Resources Corporation	3.06%	i
Pilgrim Regional BankShares	2.68%	i
The Zweig Fund, Inc.	2.37%	i
Capital Southwest Corporation	2.30%	f
Dover Regional Financial Shares	1.62%	i
The Southeastern Thrift and Bank Fund, Inc.	1.49%	a,b,i
First Financial Fund, Inc.	1.33%	f
Z-Seven Fund, Inc.	(0.15%)	i
H&Q Healthcare Investors	(0.30%)	a,b,f
Sterling Capital Corporation	(0.30%)	i
Morgan Grenfell SMALLCap Fund, Inc.	(0.85%)	i

CONVERTIBLE FUNDS

FUND	INCOME RATIO	FOOTNOTE
Putnam High Income Convertible and Bond Fund	11.56%	a,b,g
AIM Strategic Income Fund, Inc.	9.04%	i
Castle Convertible Fund, Inc.	7.37%	a,b,i

CONVERTIBLE FUNDS (continued)

FUND	INCOME RATIO	FOOTNOTE
Bancroft Convertible Fund, Inc.	6.70%	k
American Capital Convertible Securities, Inc.	6.41%	i
Ellsworth Convertible Growth and Income Fund	6.50%	a,b,f
Lincoln National Convertible Securities Fund, Inc.	5.96%	i
TCW Convertible Securities Fund, Inc.	5.68%	i

DUAL PURPOSE FUNDS

FUND	INCOME RATIO	FOOTNOTE
Convertible Holdings, Inc.	7.24%	i
Counsellors Tandem Securities Fund, Inc.	3.45%	i
Hampton Utilities Trust	4.96%	i
Quest For Value Dual Purpose Fund, Inc.	4.39%	i

BOND FUNDS

FUND	INCOME RATIO	FOOTNOTE
High Income Advantage Trust	16.02%	a,b,f
Van Kampen Merritt Intermediate Term High Income Trust	15.86%	i
CIGNA High Income Shares	15.49%	i
High Income Advantage Trust II	15.13%	a,b,h
Colonial Intermediate High Income Fund	14.40%	k
Zenix Income Fund, Inc.	14.16%	f
Kemper High Income Trust	13.78%	j
Van Kampen Merritt Limited Term High Income Trust	13.59%	i
High Income Advantage Trust III	13.53%	h
USF&G Pacholder Fund, Inc.	12.94%	i
American Opportunity Income Fund Inc.	12.83%	a,b,g
American Government Income Portfolio, Inc.	12.75%	k
American Government Income Fund Inc.	12.72%	k
The New America High Income Fund, Inc.	12.62%	i
Kemper Multi-Market Income Trust	12.60%	j
CIM High Yield Securities	12.59%	i
The High Yield Income Fund, Inc.	12.44%	a,b,g
First Boston Strategic Income Fund, Inc.	12.13%	i
American Capital Income Trust	12.11%	i
The Blackrock Income Trust Inc.	11.95%	k
The Blackrock Target Term Trust Inc.	11.82%	k
The Blackrock Advantage Term Trust Inc.	11.79%	i
RAC Income Fund, Inc.	11.79%	k
ACM Government Income Fund, Inc.	11.66%	i

BOND FUNDS (continued)

FUND	INCOME RATIO	FOOTNOTE
The High Yield Plus Fund, Inc.	11.69%	f
ACM Government Securities Fund, Inc.	11.59%	i
CNA Income Shares, Inc.	11.58%	i
American Government Term Trust Inc.	11.48%	j
Colonial InterMarket Income Trust I	11.23%	j
The Blackrock Strategic Term Trust Inc.	11.14%	a,d,j
Hyperion Total Return Fund, Inc.	11.14%	j
First Boston Income Fund, Inc.	11.12%	i
Oppenheimer Multi-Government Trust	11.06%	k
ACM Government Spectrum Fund, Inc.	11.05%	i
Oppenheimer Multi-Sector Income Trust	10.80%	k
InterCapital Income Securities, Inc.	10.44%	a,b,f
MFS Charter Income Trust	10.34%	j
USLife Income Fund, Inc.	10.26%	a,b,i
Bunker Hill Income Securities, Inc.	10.11%	a,b,f
AMEV Securities. Inc.	10.06%	a,b,h
Kemper Intermediate Government Trust	10.02%	j
Hatteras Income Securities, Inc.	9.93%	i
Putnam Master Income Trust	9.74%	k
Tyler Cabot Mortgage Securities	9.71%	k
MassMutual Corporate Investors	9.70%	i
Montgomery Street Income Securities, Inc.	9.60%	i
Pacific American Income Shares, Inc.	9.60%	i
Putnam Premier Income Trust	9.56%	a,b,h
MassMutual Participation Investors	9.50%	i
Franklin Principal Maturity Trust	9.41%	j
American Adjustable Rate Term Trust Inc. --1995	9.37%	a,b,g
John Hancock Investors Trust	9.33%	i
State Mutual Securities Trust	9.29%	i
John Hancock Income Securities Trust	9.28%	i
Dreyfus Strategic Governments Income, Inc.	9.24%	a,b,j
Prospect Street High Income Portfolio Inc.	9.24%	k
ACM Managed Income Fund, Inc.	9.22%	a,b,g
MFS Multimarket Income Trust	9.22%	k
Circle Income Shares, Inc.	9.13%	a,c,f
Transamerica Income Shares, Inc.	8.98%	f
Independence Square Income Securities, Inc.	8.97%	i
1838 Bond-Debenture Trading Fund	8.85%	f
Putnam Master Intermediate Income Trust	8.84%	a,b,f

BOND FUNDS (continued)

FUND	INCOME RATIO	FOOTNOTE
ACM Government Opportunity Fund, Inc.	8.71%	a,b,h
Mutual of Omaha Interest Shares, Inc.	8.63%	i
Current Income Shares, Inc.	8.60%	i
The Blackrock 1998 Term Trust Inc.	8.53%	a,d,j
American Capital Bond Fund, Inc.	8.52%	a,b,i
Vestaur Securities, Inc.	8.50%	j
INA Investment Securities, Inc.	8.49%	i
American Adjustable Rate Term Trust Inc. --1996	8.47%	a,b,g
MFS Government Markets Income Trust	8.38%	j
MFS Intermediate Income Trust	8.10%	k
Lincoln National Income Fund, Inc.	8.05%	i
Excelsior Income Shares, Inc.	8.01%	i
MFS Special Value Trust	7.97%	k
American Adjustable Rate Term Trust Inc. --1997	7.95%	a,b,g
Dean Witter Government Income Trust	7.92%	a,b,f
Fort Dearborn Income Securities, Inc.	7.82%	a,b,f
American Adjustable Rate Term Trust Inc. --1998	7.60%	a,d,g
Putnam Intermediate Government Income Trust	7.51%	j
Franklin Universal Trust	6.60%	a,b,g

MUNICIPAL BOND FUNDS

FUND	INCOME RATIO	FOOTNOTE
Putnam High Yield Municipal Trust	8.77%	f
Dreyfus Strategic Municipals, Inc.	8.52%	a,b,f
Apex Municipal Fund, Inc.	8.38%	a,b,i
Colonial High Income Municipal Trust	8.30%	i
Colonial Municipal Income Trust	8.29%	j
Van Kampen Merritt Municipal Income Trust	8.16%	a,b,i
Dreyfus Municipal Income, Inc.	8.15%	a,b,f
Van Kampen Merritt Investment Grade Municipal Trust	8.12%	k
Colonial Investment Grade Municipal Trust	8.11%	i
Allstate Municipal Income Opportunities Trust	7.99%	a,b,j
InterCapital Insured Municipal Bond Trust	7.92%	a,b,e
Municipal High Income Fund, Inc.	7.90%	k
Allstate Municipal Income Opportunities Trust II	7.87%	g

MUNICIPAL BOND FUNDS (continued)

FUND	INCOME RATIO	FOOTNOTE
InterCapital Quality Municipal Investment Trust	7.80%	a,b,e
MFS Municipal Income Trust	7.79%	k
Allstate Municipal Premium Income Trust	7.75%	a,b,j
Putnam Managed Municipal Income Trust	7.69%	k
Allstate Municipal Income Opportunities Trust III	7.61%	f
Duff & Phelps Utilities Tax-Free Income Inc.	7.54%	a,d,e
Dreyfus California Municipal Income, Inc.	7.36%	a,b,f
Kemper Strategic Municipal Income Trust	7.31%	j
Dreyfus Strategic Municipal Bond Fund, Inc.	7.27%	j
Putnam Investment Grade Municipal Trust	7.26%	j
Allstate Municipal Income Trust II	7.05%	i
Nuveen Municipal Income Fund, Inc.	7.03%	a,b,h
Nuveen Municipal Value Fund, Inc.	6.98%	j
Allstate Municipal Income Trust	6.95%	a,b,g
Van Kampen Merritt California Municipal Income Trust	6.91%	a,b,i
Nuveen New York Municipal Income Fund, Inc.	6.79%	a,b,f
Kemper Municipal Income Trust	6.76%	j
Nuveen Premium Income Municipal Fund, Inc.	6.76%	a,b,j
Nuveen California Municipal Income Fund, Inc.	6.75%	j
Nuveen Municipal Advantage Fund, Inc.	6.70%	k
Nuveen Municipal Market Opportunity Fund, Inc.	6.70%	k
Taurus MuniNew York Holdings	6.70%	k
Nuveen Investment Quality Municipal Fund, Inc.	6.67%	k
Taurus MuniCalifornia Holdings	6.60%	k
MuniVest Fund, Inc.	6.59%	a,b,g
Nuveen Performance Plus Municipal Fund, Inc.	6.46%	a,b,j
Nuveen New York Municipal Value Fund, Inc.	6.44%	a,b,h
Dreyfus New York Municipal Income, Inc.	6.43%	a,b,f
Nuveen California Municipal Value Fund, Inc.	6.43%	a,b,h
MuniEnhanced Fund, Inc.	6.41%	h
Nuveen New York Performance Plus Municipal Fund, Inc.	6.35%	a,k
Allstate Municipal Income Trust III	6.33%	a,b,g
Seligman Select Municipal Fund, Inc.	6.33%	i
Nuveen New York Municipal Market Opportunity Fund, Inc.	6.31%	a,b,f
MuniYield Fund, Inc.	6.29%	a,d,e
The New York Tax-Exempt Income Fund, Inc.	6.28%	a,b,e

MUNICIPAL BOND FUNDS (continued)

FUND	INCOME RATIO	FOOTNOTE
Nuveen California Performance Plus Municipal Fund, Inc.	6.28%	k
American Municipal Term Trust Inc.	6.27%	a,d,i
Nuveen California Municipal Market Opportunity Fund, Inc.	6.25%	k
American Municipal Term Trust Inc. II	6.24%	a,d,i
MuniInsured Fund, Inc.	6.18%	a,b,f
Van Kampen Merritt Municipal Trust	6.16%	a,d,g
Nuveen Insured Quality Municipal Fund, Inc.	6.14%	a,d,k
Nuveen New York Investment Quality Municipal Fund, Inc.	6.02%	a,b,f
Nuveen California Investment Quality Municipal Fund, Inc.	5.85%	a,d,k
Nuveen Select Quality Municipal Fund, Inc.	5.81%	a,d,k
Seligman Quality Municipal Fund, Inc.	5.77%	a,d,e
Nuveen New York Select Quality Municipal Fund, Inc.	5.75%	a,f
Van Kampen Merritt New York Quality Municipal Trust	5.58%	a,d,g
Nuveen Pennsylvania Investment Quality Municipal Fund	5.50%	a,d,k
Nuveen Florida Investment Quality Municipal Fund, Inc.	5.47%	a,d,k
Van Kampen Merritt Pennsylvania Quality Municipal Trust	5.40%	a,d,g
Van Kampen Merritt Florida Quality Municipal Trust	5.25%	a,d,g
Van Kampen Merritt California Quality Municipal Trust	5.20%	a,d,g
Nuveen California Select Quality Municipal Fund, Inc.	5.13%	a,d,k
Nuveen Quality Income Municipal Fund, Inc.	5.13%	a,d,k
Nuveen New Jersey Investment Quality Municipal Fund, Inc.	5.06%	a,k
InterCapital Insured Municipal Trust	4.97%	a,d,g
Nuveen New York Quality Income Municipal Fund, Inc.	4.51%	a,d,f
Van Kampen Merritt Ohio Quality Municipal Trust	4.45%	a,d,g
Nuveen Florida Quality Income Municipal Fund, Inc.	4.28%	a,d,i

MUNICIPAL BOND FUNDS (continued)

FUND	INCOME RATIO	FOOTNOTE
Nuveen New Jersey Quality Income Municipal Fund, Inc.	4.28%	a,d,i
Nuveen Pennsylvania Quality Income Municipal Fund	4.13%	a,d,i
Nuveen Insured Municipal Opportunity Fund, Inc.	4.00%	a,d,k
The Blackrock Municipal Target Term Inc.	3.89%	a,d,i
Nuveen Michigan Quality Income Municipal Fund, Inc.	3.59%	a,d,j
Nuveen Texas Quality Income Municipal Fund, Inc.	3.58%	a,d,j
Nuveen Ohio Quality Income Municipal Fund, Inc.	3.52%	a,d,j
Minnesota Municipal Term Trust Inc.	0.55%	a,d,i

FOREIGN BOND FUNDS

FUND	INCOME RATIO	FOOTNOTE
ACM Managed Multi-Market Trust, Inc.	11.62%	j
The First Australia Prime Income Fund, Inc.	11.11%	k
Templeton Global Income Fund, Inc.	9.75%	a,b,g
The Global Yield Fund, Inc.	9.69%	i
Global Income Plus Fund	9.50%	k
Templeton Global Governments Income Trust	9.37%	a,b,g
The Global Government Plus Fund, Inc.	8.30%	i
Kleinwort Benson Australian Income Fund, Inc.	8.12%	a,b,e

MISCELLANEOUS & OTHER

FUND	INCOME RATIO	FOOTNOTE
Franklin Multi-Income Trust	7.64%	f
Pilgrim Prime Rate Trust	7.62%	g
The Zweig Total Return Fund	4.74%	i
America's All Season Fund, Inc.	3.71%	i

FOOTNOTES:

a. annualized
b. six month period
c. nine month period
d. from commencement
e. period ended 4/30/92
f. period ended 3/31/92
g. period ended 2/29/92
h. period ended 1/31/92
i. period ended 12/31/91
j. period ended 11/30/91
k. period ended 10/31/91
l. period ended 9/30/91

RANK	FUND	% CHANGE NAV	RANK	FUND	% CHANGE PRICE
EQUITY FUNDS			**EQUITY FUNDS**		
1	Bergstrom Capital	72.41%	1	Bergstrom Capital	105.10%
2	General American Investors	60.66%	2	General American Investors	77.23%
3	Engex	53.68%	3	Liberty All-Star Equity Fund	51.87%
4	Royce Value Trust**	39.39%	4	Engex	50.54%
5	Liberty All-Star Equity Fund	38.22%	5	Blue Chip Value Fund	43.08%
6	Blue Chip Value Fund	35.75%	6	Salomon Brothers Fund	42.39%
7	Adams Express	31.13%	7	Tri-Continental Corp.	41.07%
8	Salomon Brothers Fund	29.80%	8	Adams Express	39.86%
9	Tri-Continental Corp.	28.10%	9	Royce Value Trust**	35.20%
10	Central Securities	24.97%	10	Niagara Share Corp.	34.39%
11	Baker, Fentress & Company	24.84%	11	Baker, Fentress & Company	33.45%
12	Source Capital	22.23%	12	Central Securities	30.49%
13	Niagara Share Corp.	19.63%	13	Source Capital	29.32%
14	Gabelli Equity Trust***	15.19%	14	Gabelli Equity Trust***	10.81%
15	Charles Allmon Trust	11.90%	15	Charles Allmon Trust	1.48%
	AVERAGE NAV TOTAL RETURN EQUITY FUNDS	33.86%		*AVERAGE PRICE TOTAL RETURN EQUITY FUNDS*	41.75%
FOREIGN EQUITY FUNDS			**FOREIGN EQUITY FUNDS**		
1	Brazil Fund	152.93%	1	Latin American Inv. Fund	178.78%
2	Latin American Inv. Fund	112.97%	2	Emerging Mexico Fund	130.26%
3	Chile Fund	92.46%	3	Brazil Fund	118.52%
4	Emerging Mexico Fund	88.88%	4	Templeton Emerging Markets	98.10%
5	Mexico Fund	75.91%	5	Mexico Fund	79.98%
6	Templeton Emerging Markets	72.92%	6	Chile Fund	74.40%
7	Mexico Equity & Income Fd.	43.84%	7	Asia Pacific Fund	52.20%
8	India Growth Fund	29.33%	8	ROC Taiwan Fund	41.94%
9	First Australia Fund	28.64%	9	Mexico Equity & Income Fd.	40.20%
10	First Philippine Fund	28.63%	10	Thai Capital Fund	38.89%
11	Taiwan Fund	26.47%	11	First Philippine Fund	38.27%
12	Templeton Global Utilities	24.49%	12	India Growth Fund	34.23%
13	Thai Fund	23.39%	13	First Australia Fund	30.14%
14	Asia Pacific Fund	23.09%	14	Japan OTC Equity Fund	28.06%
15	Japan OTC Equity Fund	16.13%	15	Scudder New Asia Fund	26.27%
16	Singapore Fund	16.02%	16	Singapore Fund	24.01%
17	Clemente Global Growth	15.53%	17	Spain Fund	22.94%
18	Spain Fund	15.09%	18	Irish Investment Fund	19.19%
19	Growth Fund of Spain	14.24%	19	Growth Fund of Spain	19.06%
20	Thai Capital Fund	13.05%	20	Europe Fund	17.94%
21	ROC Taiwan Fund	12.47%	21	Templeton Global Utilities	16.91%
22	Scudder New Asia Fund	12.38%	22	Turkish Investment Fund	16.52%
23	Irish Investment Fund	11.75%	23	Taiwan Fund	15.88%
24	Pacific European Growth Fund	10.83%	24	Pacific European Growth Fund	12.32%
25	Malaysia Fund	9.20%	25	France Growth Fund	12.19%
26	First Iberian Fund	8.80%	26	Future Germany Fund	12.13%

RANK	FUND	% CHANGE NAV	RANK	FUND	% CHANGE PRICE
FOREIGN EQUITY FUNDS (continued)			**FOREIGN EQUITY FUNDS** (continued)		
27	Worldwide Value Fund	6.63%	27	Swiss Helvetia Fund	11.83%
28	Alliance Global Environment	6.03%	28	Germany Fund	11.24%
29	France Growth Fund	5.33%	29	Clemente Global Growth	11.47%
30	Swiss Helvetia Fund	5.17%	30	United Kingdom Fund	10.61%
31	Europe Fund	4.81%	31	Thai Fund	10.11%
32	United Kingdom Fund	4.55%	32	Alliance Global Environment	9.81%
33	Future Germany Fund	3.76%	33	Malaysia Fund	7.45%
34	Korea Fund	2.07%	34	Portugal Fund	5.48%
35	Germany Fund	1.90%	35	Korea Fund	5.25%
36	GT Greater Europe Fund	0.89%	36	Worldwide Value Fund	4.82%
37	Italy Fund	0.44%	37	GT Greater Europe Fund	3.89%
38	New Germany Fund	-0.24%	38	Scudder New Europe Fund	3.58%
39	Portugal Fund	-0.57%	39	Emerging Germany Fund	1.64%
40	Scudder New Europe Fund	-2.09%	40	First Iberian Fund	0.32%
41	Emerging Germany Fund	-4.70%	41	Italy Fund	-4.35%
42	Turkish Investment Fund	-5.45%	42	New Germany Fund	-4.88%
43	European Warrant Fund	-18.43%	43	European Warrant Fund	-6.29%
44	Austria Fund	-20.34%	44	Austria Fund	-9.90%
45	Indonesia Fund	-25.09%	45	Jakarta Growth Fund	-12.15%
46	Jakarta Growth Fund	-28.05%	46	Indonesia Fund	-15.75%
	AVERAGE NAV TOTAL RETURN FOREIGN EQUITY FUNDS	19.91%		*AVERAGE PRICE TOTAL RETURN FOREIGN EQUITY FUNDS*	27.03%
	SPECIALIZED EQUITY			**SPECIALIZED EQUITY**	
1	H&Q Healthcare Investors	92.93%	1	H&Q Healthcare Investors	132.18%
2	First Financial Fund	89.92%	2	First Financial Fund	83.44%
3	Morgan Grenfell Small Cap.	56.61%	3	Z-Seven Fund*	67.35%
4	Real Estate Securities Income	52.76%	4	Real Estate Securities Income	64.32%
5	Pilgrim Regional BankShares	48.19%	5	Morgan Grenfell Small Cap.	58.23%
6	Z-Seven Fund*	46.85%	6	SE Savings Institutions*	57.38%
7	SE Savings Institutions*	44.60%	7	Pilgrim Regional BankShares	49.00%
8	Patriot Premium Dividend II	31.71%	8	Patriot Premium Dividend II	45.22%
9	Patriot Premium Dividend	29.70%	9	Patriot Select Dividend Trust	37.31%
10	Zweig Fund**	29.60%	10	Patriot Premium Dividend	34.32%
11	Patriot Select Dividend Trust	28.73%	11	Zweig Fund**	33.66%
12	Putnam Dividend Income	28.11%	12	Putnam Dividend Income	28.90%
13	Duff & Phelps Utilities Income	24.37%	13	Duff & Phelps Utilities Income	24.87%
14	Inefficient Market Fund	23.27%	14	ASA Ltd.	14.33%
15	Dover Regional Financial*	21.89%	15	Inefficient Market Fund	13.70%
16	Petroleum & Resources	6.81%	16	Dover Regional Financial*	13.48%
17	ASA Ltd.	-2.82%	17	Petroleum & Resources	11.49%
18	Central Fund of Canada	-8.17%	18	Central Fund of Canada	-4.37%
	AVERAGE NAV TOTAL RETURN SPECIALIZED EQUITY	35.84%		*AVERAGE PRICE TOTAL RETURN SPECIALIZED EQUITY*	42.49%
	DUAL PURPOSE			**DUAL PURPOSE**	
1	Convertible Holdings cap. shs.	44.49%	1	Convertible Holdings cap. shs.	66.67%
2	Gemini II Fund cap. shs.	43.42%	2	Quest for Value cap. shs.	48.54%
3	Quest for Value cap. shs.	34.47%	3	Gemini II Fund cap. shs.	43.68%

RANK	FUND	% CHANGE NAV	RANK	FUND	% CHANGE PRICE
	DUAL PURPOSE (continued)			**DUAL PURPOSE (continued)**	
4	Counsellors Tandem (common)	32.66%	4	Hampton Utilities cap. shs.	38.25%
5	Hampton Utilities cap. shs.	27.50%	5	Counsellors Tandem (common)	37.30%
6	Convertible Holdings inc. shs.	15.27%	6	Gemini II Fund inc. shs.	35.78%
7	Quest for Value inc. shs.	12.06%	7	Convertible Holdings inc. shs.	28.97%
8	Gemini II Fund inc. shs.	10.55%	8	Hampton Utilities inc. shs.	22.91%
9	Hampton Utilities inc. shs.	9.10%	9	Quest for Value inc. shs.	15.63%
	AVERAGE NAV TOTAL RETURN DUAL PURPOSE	25.50%		*AVERAGE PRICE TOTAL RETURN DUAL PURPOSE*	37.53%
	MISCELLANEOUS			**MISCELLANEOUS**	
1	Franklin Multi-Income	49.83%	1	Franklin Multi-Income	45.27%
2	Zweig Total Return Fund	19.49%	2	Zweig Total Return Fund	35.77%
3	America's All-Season Fund*	12.55%	3	America's All-Season Fund*	-5.48%
	AVERAGE NAV TOTAL RETURN MISCELLANEOUS	27.29%		*AVERAGE PRICE TOTAL RETURN MISCELLANEOUS*	25.18%
	CONVERTIBLE FUNDS			**CONVERTIBLE FUNDS**	
1	Putnam High Income Conv.	41.49%	1	Putnam High Income Conv.	73.84%
2	Lincoln National Convertible	39.01%	2	Lincoln National Convertible	40.04%
3	TCW Convertible Securities	31.91%	3	Castle Convertible Fund	38.15%
4	Castle Convertible Fund	31.06%	4	TCW Convertible Securities	34.60%
5	Ellsworth Conv. Growth&Income	24.36%	5	American Capital Convertible	27.08%
6	Bancroft Convertible Fund	23.49%	6	Ellsworth Conv. Growth&Income	26.48%
7	American Capital Convertible	22.37%	7	Bancroft Convertible Fund	26.03%
8	AIM Strategic Income	15.80%	8	AIM Strategic Income	16.81%
	AVERAGE NAV TOTAL RETURN CONVERTIBLE FUNDS	28.69%		*AVERAGE PRICE TOTAL RETURN CONVERTIBLE FUNDS*	35.38%
	BOND FUNDS			**BOND FUNDS**	
1	CIGNA High Income Shares	61.68%	1	CIGNA High Income Shares	115.53%
2	Kemper High Income Trust	51.79%	2	VKM Intermediate Term	92.88%
3	Franklin Universal Trust	51.39%	3	New America High Income	67.46%
4	Kemper Multi-Income Trust	50.16%	4	Colonial Intermediate High Inc.	66.38%
5	VKM Intermediate Term	47.83%	5	CIM High Yield Securities	65.56%
6	High Income Advantage Trust	47.17%	6	VKM Limited High Income	64.29%
7	High Income Advantage Trust II	46.29%	7	Franklin Universal Trust	62.40%
8	VKM Limited High Income	46.09%	8	Kemper High Income Trust	61.25%
9	Colonial Intermediate High Inc.	45.82%	9	USF&G Pacholder Fund	59.92%
10	High Income Advantage Trust III	43.25%	10	High Income Advantage Trust II	59.21%
11	High Yield Plus Fund	40.73%	11	High Income Advantage Trust	55.86%
12	CIM High Yield Securities	40.44%	12	MFS Special Value Trust	54.60%
13	Prospect Street High Income	40.07%	13	High Yield Income Fund	53.10%
14	High Yield Income Fund	39.01%	14	Prospect Street High Income	52.00%
15	MFS Special Value Trust	38.35%	15	First Boston Strategic Income	49.35%
16	Zenix Income Fund	38.35%	16	Kemper Multi-Income Trust	48.23%
17	USF&G Pacholder Fund	32.63%	17	American Capital Income Fund	47.64%
18	American Capital Income Fund	30.23%	18	Zenix Income Fund	46.79%
19	CNA Income Shares	28.34%	19	First Boston Income Fund	45.49%
20	New America High Income	28.11%	20	High Income Advantage Trust III	45.25%

RANK	FUND	% CHANGE NAV	RANK	FUND	% CHANGE PRICE
	BOND FUNDS (continued)			**BOND FUNDS** (continued)	
21	American Government Portfolio	27.57%	21	MassMutual Corporate Inv.	44.94%
22	First Boston Income Fund	27.49%	22	High Yield Plus Fund	43.45%
23	American Government Income	26.15%	23	CNA Income Shares	42.43%
24	First Boston Strategic Income	25.12%	24	MassMutual Participation Inv.	41.58%
25	ACM Managed Income	24.22%	25	AMEV Securities	34.51%
26	American Opportunity Income Fd.	23.94%	26	USLIFE Income Fund	33.93%
27	MFS Charter Income Fund	23.83%	27	John Hancock Investors Trust	32.97%
28	USLIFE Income Fund	23.05%	28	Bunker Hill Income Securities	32.80%
29	Putnam Master Income Trust	22.99%	29	Circle Income Shares	31.85%
30	Franklin Principal Maturity	22.72%	30	American Capital Bond Fund	31.34%
31	Blackstone Income Trust	22.55%	31	Intercapital Income Securities	31.09%
32	Putnam Master Intermediate	21.78%	32	MFS Charter Income Fund	30.69%
33	Putnam Diversified Premium	22.14%	33	Hatteras Income Securities	30.32%
34	MFS Multimarket Income	22.18%	34	ACM Managed Income	29.72%
35	AMEV Securities	22.13%	35	Putnam Master Income Trust	28.84%
36	Montgomery Street Income	21.54%	36	Blackstone Income Trust	28.83%
37	ACM Government Opportunities	21.24%	37	INA Investments	28.47%
38	Blackstone Advantage Term	20.90%	38	Oppenheimer Multi-Sector	28.04%
39	1838 Bond-Debenture Trading	20.17%	39	Putnam Master Intermediate	27.63%
40	Current Income Shares	20.03%	40	Pacific American Income	27.48%
41	Blackstone Target Term	19.94%	41	Colonial Intermarket Income I	26.11%
42	American Government Term	19.65%	42	Oppenheimer Multi-Govern.	26.01%
43	Lincoln National Income Fund	19.54%	43	Transamerica Income	25.85%
44	Intercapital Income Securities	19.41%	44	Putnam Diversified Premium	25.44%
45	State Mutual Securities	19.35%	45	American Opportunity Income Fd.	25.39%
46	Oppenheimer Multi-Sector	19.20%	46	Lincoln National Income Fund	25.30%
47	Pacific American Income	19.15%	47	MFS Multimarket Income	24.42%
48	Colonial Intermarket Income I	18.68%	48	John Hancock Income Securities	24.10%
49	Putnam Premier Income	18.46%	49	State Mutual Securities	23.68%
50	INA Investments	18.30%	50	Hyperion Total Return	23.65%
51	Hatteras Income Securities	18.26%	51	RAC Income Fund	23.35%
52	Fort Dearborn Income	18.06%	52	Franklin Principal Maturity	23.23%
53	MassMutual Corporate Inv.	17.99%	53	Tyler Cabot Mortgage Securities	22.64%
54	Blackstone Strategic	17.54%	54	ACM Government Opportunities	21.98%
55	Transamerica Income	17.51%	55	Blackstone Advantage Term	21.55%
56	Vestaur Securities	17.39%	56	Putnam Premier Income	21.47%
57	Independence Square Income	17.34%	57	Mutual Of Omaha Interest	20.94%
58	Bunker Hill Income Securities	17.19%	58	Current Income Shares	20.76%
59	John Hancock Investors Trust	17.17%	59	Montgomery Street Income	20.48%
60	RAC Income Fund	16.68%	60	Vestaur Securities	20.22%
61	Tyler Cabot Mortgage Securities	16.68%	61	American Government Portfolio	20.01%
62	Circle Income Shares	16.43%	62	Excelsior Income Shares	19.69%
63	John Hancock Income Securities	16.42%	63	Independence Square Income	19.17%
64	ACM Government Income Fund	16.25%	64	ACM Government Income Fund	19.00%
65	Hyperion Total Return	16.21%	65	Fort Dearborn Income	18.98%
66	ACM Government Securities	15.89%	66	ACM Government Securities	18.85%
67	Oppenheimer Multi-Govern.	15.66%	67	ACM Government Spectrum	17.81%
68	ACM Government Spectrum	15.40%	68	American Government Income	17.11%
69	American Capital Bond Fund	15.35%	69	Blackstone Target Term	16.79%

RANK	FUND	% CHANGE NAV	RANK	FUND	% CHANGE PRICE
	BOND FUNDS (continued)			**BOND FUNDS (continued)**	
70	Mutual Of Omaha Interest	15.14%	70	MFS Intermediate Income	16.52%
71	Excelsior Income Shares	15.07%	71	1838 Bond-Debenture Trading	15.86%
72	MassMutual Participation Inv.	14.66%	72	Blackstone Strategic	15.80%
73	Kemper Int. Government Trust	14.20%	73	Dean Witter Government Inc.	14.93%
74	Putnam Intermediate Govern.	14.13%	74	Dreyfus Strategic Government	14.85%
75	Dreyfus Strategic Government	13.03%	75	MFS Government Markets	14.62%
76	American Adjustable Rate 1995	12.89%	76	American Government Term	14.24%
77	MFS Government Markets	12.34%	77	Putnam Intermediate Govern.	14.14%
78	Dean Witter Government Inc.	12.10%	78	American Adjustable Rate 1995	12.28%
79	MFS Intermediate Income	11.64%	79	American Adjustable Rate 1996	11.44%
80	American Adjustable Rate 1996	11.18%	80	Kemper Int. Government Trust	9.80%
	AVERAGE NAV TOTAL RETURN BOND FUNDS	24.59%		*AVERAGE PRICE TOTAL RETURN BOND FUNDS*	33.28%
	FOREIGN BOND FUNDS			**FOREIGN BOND FUNDS**	
1	First Australia Prime Income	22.55%	1	Kleinwort Benson Australian	34.82%
2	Kleinwort Benson Australian	20.87%	2	First Australia Prime Income	32.82%
3	Templeton Global Income	14.14%	3	Global Income Plus	19.68%
4	Templeton Global Government	13.44%	4	ACM Managed Multi-Market	16.98%
5	Global Income Plus	12.16%	5	Templeton Global Income	16.18%
6	ACM Managed Multi-Market	10.92%	6	Global Government Plus	14.92%
7	Global Government Plus	9.06%	7	Templeton Global Government	13.37%
8	Global Yield Fund	7.27%	8	Global Yield Fund	7.63%
	AVERAGE NAV TOTAL RETURN FOREIGN BOND FUNDS	13.80%		*AVERAGE PRICE TOTAL RETURN FOREIGN BOND FUNDS*	19.55%
	MUNICIPAL BOND FUNDS			**MUNICIPAL BOND FUNDS**	
1	Nuveen NY Muni. Market Opp.	18.85%	1	Putnam High Yield Municipal	29.97%
2	Nuveen NY Perf. Plus Muni.	18.18%	2	MuniEnhanced Fund	28.66%
3	Taurus MuniNew York Holdings	16.20%	3	MuniVest Fund, Inc.	25.70%
4	Allstate Municipal Premium	16.16%	4	Allstate Municipal Inc. Opp. II	20.94%
5	Putnam Investment Grade Muni.	16.05%	5	Allstate Municipal Inc. Opp. III	20.78%
6	VKM Municipal Income Trust	15.81%	6	VKM Municipal Income Trust	20.60%
7	Nuveen Municipal Market Opp.	15.75%	7	Putnam Investment Grade Muni.	20.34%
8	Nuveen Performance Plus	15.74%	8	Nuveen Municipal Market Opp.	20.16%
9	Nuveen Investment Quality	15.71%	9	Nuveen Premium Income Muni.	19.90%
10	Kemper Municipal Income	15.69%	10	Putnam Managed Municipal	19.58%
11	Nuveen Municipal Advantage	15.40%	11	Kemper Municipal Income	18.84%
12	Nuveen NY Inv. Quality Muni.	15.08%	12	Taurus MuniCalifornia Holdings	18.31%
13	MuniEnhanced Fund	15.06%	13	Taurus MuniNew York Holdings	18.03%
14	Seligman Select Municipal	14.99%	14	Nuveen NY Muni. Market Opp.	18.22%
15	MuniVest Fund, Inc.	14.98%	15	Allstate Municipal Premium	18.12%
16	Nuveen Premium Income Muni.	14.90%	16	VKM Investment Grade Muni.	17.92%
17	Putnam Managed Municipal	14.85%	17	Seligman Select Municipal	17.66%
18	Nuveen Cal. Muni. Market Opp.	14.67%	18	Nuveen Performance Plus	17.51%
19	Nuveen Insured Quality Muni.	13.85%	19	Allstate Municipal Income Tr.	17.49%
20	VKM Investment Grade Muni.	13.83%	20	Nuveen Municipal Advantage	17.05%
21	Nuveen Cal. Pref. Plus Muni.	13.78%	21	MuniInsured Fund Inc.	16.96%
22	Dreyfus Municipal Income	13.40%	22	Dreyfus Strategic Municipals	16.76%

RANK	FUND	% CHANGE NAV	RANK	FUND	% CHANGE PRICE
MUNICIPAL BOND FUNDS (continued)			**MUNICIPAL BOND FUNDS** (continued)		
23	Nuveen NY Municipal Value	13.36%	23	Nuveen Investment Quality	15.83%
24	VKM California Municipal	13.23%	24	Nuveen Municipal Income	14.80%
25	Taurus MuniCalifornia Holdings	13.05%	25	Nuveen Municipal Value	14.80%
26	Allstate Municipal Income II	12.92%	26	MFS Municipal Income Trust	14.64%
27	Nuveen NY Municipal Income	12.78%	27	Allstate Municipal Income II	14.18%
28	Allstate Municipal Income III	12.68%	28	Nuveen Cal. Municipal Value	13.98%
29	MuniInsured Fund Inc.	12.66%	29	Nuveen NY Municipal Value	13.92%
30	Nuveen Cal. Inv. Qual. Muni.	12.55%	30	Dreyfus Municipal Income	13.47%
31	Dreyfus New York Municipal	12.45%	31	Allstate Municipal Income III	13.35%
32	Kemper Strategic Muni. Income	12.16%	32	New York Tax-Exempt Income	13.27%
33	Nuveen Municipal Income	11.77%	33	Nuveen NY Perf. Plus Muni.	12.97%
34	Nuveen Municipal Value	11.44%	34	Allstate Municipal Income Opp	12.91%
35	Dreyfus Strategic Municipals	11.41%	35	Nuveen Cal. Municipal Income	12.18%
36	Allstate Municipal Income Tr.	11.32%	36	Kemper Strategic Muni. Income	12.15%
37	New York Tax-Exempt Income	10.99%	37	Nuveen Insured Quality Muni.	11.73%
38	Dreyfus Strategic Municipal Bond	10.78%	38	Dreyfus Strategic Municipal Bond	11.62%
39	Colonial Investment Grade Mun.	10.55%	39	Colonial Investment Grade Mun.	11.16%
40	Allstate Municipal Inc. Opp. III	10.36%	40	Dreyfus New York Municipal	10.75%
41	Putnam High Yield Municipal	10.29%	41	Apex Municipal Fund	10.45%
42	Municipal High Income Fund	10.12%	42	Nuveen Cal. Pref. Plus Muni.	10.22%
43	Nuveen Cal. Municipal Value	10.05%	43	Municipal High Income Fund	9.61%
44	Allstate Municipal Inc. Opp. II	9.78%	44	Nuveen NY Inv. Quality Muni.	9.57%
45	Nuveen Cal. Municipal Income	9.35%	45	Nuveen Cal. Muni. Market Opp.	9.38%
46	Allstate Municipal Income Opp	8.98%	46	Nuveen NY Municipal Income	9.34%
47	MFS Municipal Income Trust	8.46%	47	VKM California Municipal	8.31%
48	Colonial High Income Municipal	7.53%	48	Nuveen Cal. Inv. Qual. Muni.	7.89%
49	Dreyfus Cal. Municipal Income	7.24%	49	Colonial High Income Municipal	7.23%
50	Colonial Municipal Income Tr.	5.36%	50	Colonial Municipal Income Tr.	4.20%
51	Apex Municipal Fund	4.24%	51	Dreyfus Cal. Municipal Income	-2.36%
	AVERAGE NAV TOTAL RETURN MUNICIPAL BOND FUNDS	*12.68%*		*AVERAGE PRICE TOTAL RETURN MUNICIPAL BOND FUNDS*	*14.92%*

*these funds traded OTC with spreads between the bid and ask usually as wide as 5%, therefore if the stock trades on the bid and then on the ask it would appear that it has gained 5%, when actually the bid and ask may have remained unchanged.

** not adjusted for rights offering

***adjusted for rights offering

#For NAV total return, 12/30/90 through 1/3/92; for price total return, 12/30/90 through 12/31/91

The following formula is used to calculate total return:
((ending value + dividends) - beginning value) / beginning value

Dividends are indicated by ex-dividend date.

THOMAS J. HERZFELD ADVISORS, INC.
PERFORMANCE RANKINGS FOR THE YEAR 1992
(adjusted for dividends and distributions)

RANK	FUND	% CHANGE NAV	RANK	FUND	% CHANGE PRICE
	EQUITY FUNDS			**EQUITY FUNDS**	
1	Central Securities	26.16%	1	Central Securities	34.97%
2	Royce Value Trust	19.63%	2	Royce Value Trust	26.75%
3	Gabelli Equity Trust***	13.70%	3	Source Capital	16.05%
4	Source Capital	12.33%	4	Gabelli Equity Trust***	15.21%
5	Inefficient Market Fund	9.70%	5	General American Investors	14.56%
6	Adams Express	8.55%	6	Adams Express	13.79%
7	Tri-Continental Corp.***	6.70%	7	Liberty All-Star Equity Fund**	13.44%
8	Liberty All-Star Equity Fund**	5.43%	8	Inefficient Market Fund	11.83%
9	Baker, Fentress & Company	4.96%	9	Blue Chip Value Fund	11.74%
10	Engex	4.36%	10	Bergstrom Capital	9.38%
11	Salomon Brothers Fund	3.32%	11	Baker, Fentress & Company	6.72%
12	Charles Allmon Trust	3.07%	12	Salomon Brothers Fund	6.31%
13	General American Investors	2.79%	13	Charles Allmon Trust	4.39%
14	Bergstrom Capital	0.37%	14	Engex	4.29%
15	Blue Chip Value Fund	-0.24%	15	Tri-Continental Corp.***	0.74%
16	Jundt Growth Fund	-0.51%	16	Jundt Growth Fund	-7.03%
	AVERAGE NAV TOTAL RETURN EQUITY FUNDS	7.52%		*AVERAGE PRICE TOTAL RETURN EQUITY FUNDS*	11.45%
	FOREIGN EQUITY FUNDS			**FOREIGN EQUITY FUNDS**	
1	Thai Fund	39.65%	1	Chile Fund	52.76%
2	Thai Capital Fund	31.94%	2	Malaysia Fund	38.30%
3	Mexico Fund***	20.98%	3	Asia Pacific Fund	31.25%
4	Malaysia Fund	20.88%	4	Mexico Fund***	29.71%
5	Mexico Equity & Income Fd.	19.06%	5	Mexico Equity & Income Fd.	29.36%
6	Emerging Mexico Fund	18.47%	6	First Philippine Fund	25.45%
7	First Philippine Fund	17.62%	7	Jakarta Growth Fund	25.30%
8	Asia Pacific Fund	14.94%	8	Morgan Stanley Emerging Mkts.	25.14%
9	Morgan Stanley Emerging Mkts.	13.24%	9	Emerging Mexico Fund	23.75%
10	Chile Fund	12.10%	10	European Warrant Fund	22.94%
11	Templeton Global Utilities	8.63%	11	Thai Capital Fund	21.92%
12	Templeton Emerging Markets	8.07%	12	Thai Fund	20.74%
13	European Warrant Fund	6.68%	13	Templeton Global Utilities	18.33%
14	Swiss Helvetia Fund	5.97%	14	Latin America Equity Fund	16.37%
15	Latin American Inv. Fund	5.69%	15	India Growth Fund	12.96%
16	Jakarta Growth Fund	3.75%	16	Korea Fund	11.76%
17	United Kingdom Fund	3.35%	17	United Kingdom Fund	8.77%
18	Latin America Equity Fund	2.94%	18	Indonesia Fund	7.46%
19	Scudder New Asia Fund	1.43%	19	Swiss Helvetia Fund	4.91%
20	Indonesia Fund	0.91%	20	France Growth Fund	4.70%
21	France Growth Fund	-0.55%	21	Latin American Inv. Fund	1.23%
22	Korea Fund	-0.60%	22	Singapore Fund	-0.49%
23	Brazil Fund	-2.09%	23	Brazil Fund	-0.64%
24	Clemente Global Growth	-3.33%	24	Scudder New Asia Fund	-1.62%

RANK	FUND	% CHANGE NAV	RANK	FUND	% CHANGE PRICE
	FOREIGN EQUITY FUNDS (continued)			**FOREIGN EQUITY FUNDS** (continued)	
25	Singapore Fund	-5.37%	25	Worldwide Value Fund	-4.68%
26	GT Greater Europe Fund	-6.04%	26	Clemente Global Growth	-4.93%
27	India Growth Fund	-6.45%	27	GT Greater Europe Fund	-5.26%
28	Germany Fund	-7.55%	28	Scudder New Europe Fund	-5.85%
29	Europe Fund	-8.11%	29	Europe Fund	-6.48%
30	Worldwide Value Fund	-8.19%	30	Future Germany Fund	-7.38%
31	Taiwan Fund	-8.29%	31	Templeton Emerging Markets	-8.85%
32	Future Germany Fund	-9.04%	32	New Germany Fund	-9.95%
33	Scudder New Europe Fund	-9.20%	33	Irish Investment Fund	-10.10%
34	ROC Taiwan Fund	-10.49%	34	First Australia Fund	-11.80%
35	New Germany Fund	-11.62%	35	Emerging Germany Fund	-13.35%
36	Argentina Fund	-12.01%	36	Germany Fund	-13.36%
37	Emerging Germany Fund	-13.47%	37	Argentina Fund	-13.93%
38	Alliance Global Environment	-13.54%	38	ROC Taiwan Fund	-14.44%
39	First Australia Fund	-15.27%	39	Italy Fund	-15.49%
40	Portugal Fund	-16.03%	40	Alliance Global Environment	-15.66%
41	Irish Investment Fund	-17.32%	41	Portugal Fund	-17.35%
42	First Iberian Fund	-19.11%	42	First Iberian Fund	-17.70%
43	Austria Fund	-19.47%	43	Growth Fund of Spain	-18.67%
44	Growth Fund of Spain	-21.95%	44	Austria Fund	-19.28%
45	Italy Fund	-28.71%	45	Taiwan Fund	-21.85%
46	Spain Fund	-28.91%	46	Japan OTC Equity Fund	-26.51%
47	Japan OTC Equity Fund	-32.02%	47	Turkish Investment Fund	-30.62%
48	Turkish Investment Fund	-38.62%	48	Spain Fund	-35.15%
	AVERAGE NAV TOTAL RETURN FOREIGN EQUITY FUNDS	-2.44%		*AVERAGE PRICE TOTAL RETURN FOREIGN EQUITY FUNDS*	1.70%
	SPECIALIZED EQUITY			**SPECIALIZED EQUITY**	
1	SE Thrift & Bank*	76.13%	1	SE Thrift & Bank*	86.53%
2	First Financial Fund	70.24%	2	First Financial Fund	82.34%
3	Dover Regional Financial*	36.34%	3	Dover Regional Financial*	68.90%
4	Pilgrim Regional BankShares	30.87%	4	Pilgrim Regional BankShares	30.89%
5	Preferred Income Fund	23.54%	5	Putnam Dividend Income	23.26%
6	Real Estate Securities Income	13.22%	6	Real Estate Securities Income	21.82%
7	Putnam Dividend Income	11.17%	7	Patriot Premium Dividend	18.49%
8	Patriot Premium Dividend	10.07%	8	Preferred Income Fund	18.42%
9	Duff & Phelps Utilities Income	9.54%	9	Patriot Select Dividend Trust	15.00%
10	Patriot Premium Dividend II	8.99%	10	Duff & Phelps Utilities Income	12.80%
11	Patriot Select Dividend Trust	7.02%	11	Patriot Premium Dividend II	8.82%
12	Petroleum & Resources	4.95%	12	Zweig Fund	5.45%
13	Zweig Fund	3.63%	13	Petroleum & Resources	4.81%
14	Morgan Grenfell Small Cap.	1.76%	14	Morgan Grenfell Small Cap.	1.36%
15	Central Fund of Canada	-6.10%	15	Central Fund of Canada	-6.19%
16	H&Q Healthcare Investors	-12.13%	16	Z-Seven Fund*	-17.07%
17	Z-Seven Fund*	-14.57%	17	H&Q Healthcare Investors	-25.49%
18	ASA Ltd.	-26.38%	18	ASA Ltd.	-28.27%
	AVERAGE NAV TOTAL RETURN SPECIALIZED EQUITY	13.79%		*AVERAGE PRICE TOTAL RETURN SPECIALIZED EQUITY*	17.88%

RANK	FUND	% CHANGE NAV	RANK	FUND	% CHANGE PRICE
	DUAL PURPOSE			**DUAL PURPOSE**	
1	Quest for Value cap. shs.	22.55%	1	Convertible Holdings cap. shs.	38.11%
2	Gemini II Fund inc. shs.	22.14%	2	Quest for Value cap. shs.	37.84%
3	Convertible Holdings cap. shs.	17.89%	3	Gemini II Fund cap. shs.	12.87%
4	Gemini II Fund cap. shs.	14.82%	4	Hampton Utilities cap. shs.	9.16%
5	Convertible Holdings inc. shs.	14.48%	5	Quest for Value inc. shs.	7.24%
6	Quest for Value inc. shs.	11.47%	6	Hampton Utilities inc. shs.	1.85%
7	Hampton Utilities inc. shs.	8.65%	7	Counsellors Tandem (common)	0.00%
8	Hampton Utilities cap. shs.	8.55%	8	Convertible Holdings inc. shs.	-0.12%
9	Counsellors Tandem (common)	-2.13%	9	Gemini II Fund inc. shs.	-1.50%
	AVERAGE NAV TOTAL RETURN DUAL PURPOSE	13.16%		*AVERAGE PRICE TOTAL RETURN DUAL PURPOSE*	11.72%
	MISCELLANEOUS			**MISCELLANEOUS**	
1	Franklin Multi-Income	15.41%	1	Franklin Multi-Income	14.33%
2	Zweig Total Return Fund	3.38%	2	Zweig Total Return Fund	2.70%
3	America's All-Season Fund*	-7.92%	3	America's All-Season Fund*	-1.67%
	AVERAGE NAV TOTAL RETURN MISCELLANEOUS	3.62%		*AVERAGE PRICE TOTAL RETURN MISCELLANEOUS*	5.12%
	CONVERTIBLE FUNDS			**CONVERTIBLE FUNDS**	
1	Putnam High Income Conv.	25.72%	1	Putnam High Income Conv.	27.25%
2	Castle Convertible Fund	15.44%	2	Castle Convertible Fund	23.23%
3	Ellsworth Conv Growth&Income	15.28%	3	Bancroft Convertible Fund	21.92%
4	Bancroft Convertible Fund	15.06%	4	Lincoln National Convertible	21.87%
5	TCW Convertible Securities	13.16%	5	Ellsworth Conv Growth&Income	20.28%
6	American Capital Convertible	11.35%	6	AIM Strategic Income	16.53%
7	Lincoln National Convertible	10.57%	7	TCW Convertible Securities	13.89%
8	AIM Strategic Income	9.83%	8	American Capital Convertible	11.97%
	AVERAGE NAV TOTAL RETURN CONVERTIBLE FUNDS	14.55%		*AVERAGE PRICE TOTAL RETURN CONVERTIBLE FUNDS*	19.62%
	BOND FUNDS			**BOND FUNDS**	
1	New America High Income	27.38%	1	Prospect Street High Income	44.46%
2	Prospect Street High Income	20.41%	2	VKM Limited High Income	38.00%
3	VKM Intermediate Term	19.76%	3	New America High Income	28.86%
4	CIGNA High Income Shares	19.54%	4	High Income Advantage Trust	28.74%
5	Franklin Universal Trust	18.95%	5	High Income Advantage Trust II	28.02%
6	Zenix Income Fund	18.22%	6	American Opportunity Income Fd.	27.00%
7	CIM High Yield Securities	18.00%	7	High Yield Plus Fund	26.29%
8	USF&G Pacholder Fund	17.99%	8	CIM High Yield Securities	25.43%
9	High Yield Plus Fund	17.21%	9	ACM Managed Income	25.26%
10	Kemper High Income Trust	17.17%	10	CIGNA High Income Shares	24.67%
11	Colonial Intermediate High Inc.	16.88%	11	USF&G Pacholder Fund	24.41%
12	MassMutual Corporate Inv.	16.77%	12	American Government Income	22.66%
13	High Yield Income Fund	16.43%	13	High Yield Income Fund	22.59%
14	Kemper Multi-Income Trust	16.02%	14	USLIFE Income Fund	22.41%
15	VKM Limited High Income	15.97%	15	Franklin Universal Trust	22.26%
16	ACM Managed Income	15.75%	16	High Income Advantage Trust III	21.37%

RANK	FUND	% CHANGE NAV	RANK	FUND	% CHANGE PRICE
	BOND FUNDS (continued)			**BOND FUNDS (continued)**	
17	High Income Advantage Trust II	15.73%	17	American Government Portfolio	20.48%
18	American Opportunity Income Fd.	15.72%	18	Kemper Multi-Income Trust	20.21%
19	American Government Portfolio	15.57%	19	Kemper High Income Trust	19.83%
20	American Strategic Income	15.57%	20	State Mutual Securities	19.72%
21	American Government Income	14.52%	21	Zenix Income Fund	19.61%
22	High Income Advantage Trust	14.27%	22	Colonial Intermediate High Inc.	19.40%
23	High Income Advantage Trust III	14.15%	23	VKM Intermediate Term	18.65%
24	American Capital Income Fund	13.11%	24	Putnam Master Income Trust	17.98%
25	First Boston Strategic Income	12.53%	25	Lincoln National Income Fund	15.78%
26	USLIFE Income Fund	12.43%	26	American Capital Income Fund	15.51%
27	MFS Special Value Trust	12.29%	27	CNA Income Shares	14.92%
28	Putnam Master Income Trust	11.68%	28	Montgomery Street Income	14.88%
29	Putnam Master Intermediate	11.56%	29	MFS Special Value Trust	14.43%
30	First Boston Income Fund	11.22%	30	Putnam Master Intermediate	14.06%
31	Bunker Hill Income Securities	11.21%	31	Putnam Premier Income	14.06%
32	Putnam Premier Income	11.15%	32	American Government Term	13.57%
33	State Mutual Securities	10.94%	33	Colonial Intermarket Income I	12.74%
34	Independence Square Income	10.80%	34	Independence Square Income	12.52%
35	Intercapital Income Securities	10.63%	35	Mutual Of Omaha Interest	11.58%
36	American Capital Bond Fund	10.06%	36	Hatteras Income Securities	11.43%
37	Hatteras Income Securities	9.94%	37	American Strategic Income	10.76%
38	ACM Government Securities	9.78%	38	Dreyfus Strategic Government	10.04%
39	Colonial Intermarket Income I	9.69%	39	First Boston Income Fund	9.85%
40	Montgomery Street Income	9.39%	40	ACM Government Securities	9.74%
41	ACM Government Income Fund	9.32%	41	ACM Government Opportunities	9.28%
42	John Hancock Income Securities	9.23%	42	American Capital Bond Fund	9.17%
43	Current Income Shares	9.04%	43	ACM Government Spectrum	8.86%
44	John Hancock Investors Trust	9.03%	44	MFS Multimarket Income	8.81%
45	MassMutual Participation Inv.	8.86%	45	Hyperion Total Return	8.48%
46	Fort Dearborn Income	8.79%	46	Kemper Int. Government Trust	7.75%
47	CNA Income Shares	8.61%	47	Pacific American Income	7.30%
48	Pacific American Income	8.55%	48	Oppenheimer Multi-Sector	7.05%
49	AMEV Securities	8.50%	49	AMEV Securities	6.86%
50	Mutual Of Omaha Interest	7.93%	50	John Hancock Income Securities	6.62%
51	Vestaur Securities	7.92%	51	ACM Government Income Fund	6.58%
52	INA Investments	7.69%	52	American Adjustable Rate 1997	6.15%
53	Franklin Principal Maturity	7.65%	53	RAC Income Fund	6.08%
54	Oppenheimer Multi-Sector	7.56%	54	MFS Charter Income Fund	6.05%
55	Transamerica Income	7.45%	55	Bunker Hill Income Securities	5.84%
56	BlackRock 1998 Term Trust	7.27%	56	1838 Bond-Debenture Trading	5.73%
57	Lincoln National Income Fund	7.18%	57	Putnam Intermediate Govern.	5.72%
58	Excelsior Income Shares	7.17%	58	John Hancock Investors Trust	5.69%
59	BlackRock Target Term	7.02%	59	INA Investments	5.49%
60	Putnam Intermediate Govern.	7.02%	60	Fort Dearborn Income	5.32%
61	ACM Government Spectrum	6.92%	61	Transamerica Income	4.99%
62	MFS Charter Income Fund	6.63%	62	American Adjustable Rate 1995	4.55%
63	1838 Bond-Debenture Trading	6.50%	63	Excelsior Income Shares	4.53%
64	BlackRock Strategic Term	6.03%	64	Vestaur Securities	4.44%

RANK	FUND	% CHANGE NAV	RANK	FUND	% CHANGE PRICE
	BOND FUNDS (continued)			**BOND FUNDS (continued)**	
65	Circle Income Shares	5.99%	65	American Adjustable Rate 1996	3.46%
66	American Adjustable Rate 1997	5.81%	66	MassMutual Corporate Inv.	3.30%
67	Dean Witter Government Inc.	5.75%	67	Dean Witter Government Inc.	3.12%
68	Kemper Int. Government Trust	5.63%	68	Current Income Shares	3.06%
69	ACM Government Opportunities	5.27%	69	Oppenheimer Multi-Govern.	2.95%
70	Hyperion Total Return	5.23%	70	First Boston Strategic Income	2.89%
71	MFS Multimarket Income	5.20%	71	BlackRock Advantage Term	2.41%
72	American Adjustable Rate 1996	4.95%	72	MFS Intermediate Income	2.16%
73	Dreyfus Strategic Government	4.94%	73	Franklin Principal Maturity	1.50%
74	American Adjustable Rate 1995	4.85%	74	BlackRock 1998 Term Trust	1.47%
75	American Government Term	4.63%	75	MFS Government Markets	1.36%
76	RAC Income Fund	4.62%	76	Intercapital Income Securities	0.31%
77	BlackRock Advantage Term	4.48%	77	BlackRock Strategic Term	0.19%
78	Oppenheimer Multi-Govern.	3.74%	78	BlackRock Target Term	-0.04%
79	MFS Intermediate Income	3.64%	79	Circle Income Shares	-3.23%
80	MFS Government Markets	3.24%	80	MassMutual Participation Inv.	-5.68%
81	BlackRock Income Trust	2.18%	81	BlackRock North American	-6.35%
82	BlackRock North American	-1.11%	82	BlackRock Income Trust	-11.52%
	AVERAGE NAV TOTAL RETURN BOND FUNDS	10.41%		*AVERAGE PRICE TOTAL RETURN BOND FUNDS*	11.62%
	FOREIGN BOND FUNDS			**FOREIGN BOND FUNDS**	
1	Global Income Plus	2.30%	1	Templeton Global Income	10.87%
2	Templeton Global Income	1.58%	2	Global Yield Fund	2.15%
3	Global Government Plus	0.12%	3	First Australia Prime Income	2.01%
4	Templeton Global Government	-0.49%	4	Global Government Plus	1.55%
5	Global Yield Fund	-0.78%	5	Templeton Global Government	0.53%
6	Kleinwort Benson Australian	-1.80%	6	Kleinwort Benson Australian	-3.45%
7	First Australia Prime Income	-2.47%	7	Global Income Plus	-6.19%
8	ACM Managed Multi-Market	-4.70%	8	ACM Managed Multi-Market	-22.83%
	AVERAGE NAV TOTAL RETURN FOREIGN BOND FUNDS	-0.78%		*AVERAGE PRICE TOTAL RETURN FOREIGN BOND FUNDS*	-1.92%
	MUNICIPAL BOND FUNDS			**MUNICIPAL BOND FUNDS**	
1	VKM PA Quality Muncipal Trust	14.29%	1	VKM Municipal Income Trust	20.71%
2	VKM New York Quality	13.63%	2	Taurus MuniNew York Holdings	19.00%
3	Putnam Investment Grade Muni	13.52%	3	New York Tax-Exempt Income	16.88%
4	VKM Municipal Income Trust	13.31%	4	Allstate Municipal Premium	15.27%
5	VKM Municipal Trust	12.71%	5	Putnam Managed Municipal	14.66%
6	Putnam Managed Municipal	12.69%	6	Taurus MuniCalifornia Holdings	14.62%
7	MuniYield Fund	12.16%	7	Intercapital Insured Muni Bond	14.47%
8	VKM FL Quality Municipal Trust	12.15%	8	Dreyfus New York Municipal	14.15%
9	American Municipal Term Trust	12.10%	9	VKM New York Quality	14.15%
10	VKM Ohio Quality	12.08%	10	Nuveen NY Muni. Market Opp	13.96%
11	Putnam High Yield Municipal	12.04%	11	Dreyfus Municipal Income	13.85%
12	Nuveen NY Perf. Plus Muni	11.98%	12	Putnam High Yield Municipal	13.44%
13	Nuveen NY Muni. Market Opp	11.94%	13	Putnam Investment Grade Muni	13.34%
14	American Municipal Term Tr II	11.84%	14	VKM CA Municipal Trust	13.02%

RANK	FUND	% CHANGE NAV	RANK	FUND	% CHANGE PRICE
MUNICIPAL BOND FUNDS (continued)			**MUNICIPAL BOND FUNDS** (continued)		
15	Nuveen NY Inv Quality Muni	11.79%	15	Nuveen CA Inv. Qual. Muni.	12.67%
16	Nuveen NY Select Quality	11.70%	16	American Municipal Term Trust	12.60%
17	MuniEnhanced Fund	11.66%	17	Dreyfus Strategic Municipal Bond	12.45%
18	Nuveen Insured Quality Muni.	11.57%	18	Nuveen NY Municipal Value	12.07%
19	Taurus MuniNew York Holdings	11.29%	19	Allstate Municipal Income II	12.02%
20	Seligman Select Municipal	11.16%	20	Nuveen NY Perf. Plus Muni	11.87%
21	Allstate Municipal Premium	11.08%	21	Nuveen Insured Quality Muni.	11.76%
22	Intercapital Insured Muni Bond	11.03%	22	Municipal High Income Fund	11.64%
23	Nuveen CA Perf Plus Muni	10.99%	23	VKM Municipal Trust	11.24%
24	Nuveen PA Inv. Quality Muni.	10.98%	24	VKM PA Quality Muncipal Trust	11.16%
25	VKM CA Municipal Trust	10.92%	25	Seligman Select Municipal	11.07%
26	Minnesota Municipal Term Trust	10.84%	26	Nuveen NJ Quality Income Muni	10.72%
27	Nuveen Quality Income Muni	10.84%	27	Nuveen Select Quality Municipal	10.66%
28	Nuveen CA Inv. Qual. Muni.	10.75%	28	Nuveen Investment Quality	10.59%
29	Nuveen FL Quality Income Municipal	10.62%	29	Nuveen Municipal Advantage	10.56%
30	Kemper Municipal Income	10.59%	30	Nuveen CA Select Quality	10.49%
31	VKM CA Quality Municipal Trust	10.59%	31	VKM FL Quality Municipal Trust	10.35%
32	Nuveen MI Quality Income Muni	10.56%	32	Nuveen FL Quality Income Municipal	10.02%
33	Nuveen Municipal Market Opp.	10.47%	33	Nuveen Municipal Value	9.91%
34	Nuveen PA Quality Income Muni	10.47%	34	VKM CA Quality Municipal Trust	9.90%
35	Nuveen Insured Municipal Opp	10.45%	35	MuniEnhanced Fund	9.85%
36	Nuveen Municipal Advantage	10.44%	36	Nuveen FL Inv. Quality Muni.	9.82%
37	Nuveen Investment Quality	10.34%	37	Nuveen NY Municipal Income	9.81%
38	Nuveen CA Select Quality	10.19%	38	Nuveen NY Inv Quality Muni	9.80%
39	MuniVest Fund, Inc.	10.07%	39	Nuveen Performance Plus	9.74%
40	Dreyfus New York Municipal	10.02%	40	Nuveen Municipal Market Opp.	9.71%
41	Nuveen FL Inv. Quality Muni.	10.02%	41	Nuveen CA Muni. Market Opp.	9.57%
42	Nuveen Performance Plus	9.96%	42	Duff & Phelps Utilities Tax Free	9.51%
43	Nuveen OH Quality Income Municipal	9.88%	43	Nuveen NJ Inv. Quality Muni.	9.50%
44	Nuveen NY Quality Income Muni	9.86%	44	Nuveen CA Perf Plus Muni	9.38%
45	Nuveen Select Quality Municipal	9.85%	45	Nuveen PA Quality Income Muni	9.03%
46	Intercapital Quality Municipal	9.79%	46	Kemper Municipal Income	8.98%
47	Seligman Quality Municipal	9.78%	47	American Municipal Term Tr II	8.81%
48	Nuveen Premier Insured Muni	9.77%	48	BlackRock Municipal Tgt Term	8.69%
49	Duff & Phelps Utilities Tax Free	9.69%	49	MuniVest Fund, Inc.	8.64%
50	Nuveen Premier Muni Income	9.67%	50	Nuveen MI Quality Income Muni	8.61%
51	Nuveen CA Muni. Market Opp.	9.56%	51	Kemper Strategic Muni. Income	8.53%
52	Nuveen TX Quality Income Municipal	9.55%	52	Colonial Municipal Income Tr.	8.48%
53	BlackRock Municipal Tgt Term	9.50%	53	Nuveen NY Select Quality	8.41%
54	Nuveen NJ Quality Income Muni	9.44%	54	Dreyfus Cal. Municipal Income	8.17%
55	Nuveen NJ Inv. Quality Muni.	9.39%	55	VKM Ohio Quality	7.61%
56	Nuveen Premium Income Muni	9.36%	56	VKM Investment Grade Muni	7.52%
57	Nuveen CA Quality Inc. Muni	8.86%	57	Nuveen Premier Income Muni	7.27%
58	Kemper Strategic Muni. Income	8.83%	58	Colonial Investment Grade Mun.	7.20%
59	Taurus MuniCalifornia Holdings	8.79%	59	Intercapital Quality Municipal	7.18%
60	Nuveen NY Municipal Value	8.78%	60	MuniYield Fund	7.16%
61	Nuveen Municipal Value	8.62%	61	Nuveen OH Quality Income Municipal	6.84%
62	Dreyfus Municipal Income	8.60%	62	Allstate Municipal Income Tr.	6.62%

RANK	FUND	% CHANGE NAV	RANK	FUND	% CHANGE PRICE
	MUNICIPAL BOND FUNDS (continued)			**MUNICIPAL BOND FUNDS** (continued)	
63	Municipal High Income Fund	8.40%	63	Nuveen Municipal Income	6.59%
64	Dreyfus Strategic Municipal Bond	8.28%	64	Nuveen Quality Income Muni	6.23%
65	MuniInsured Fund Inc.	8.25%	65	Nuveen TX Quality Income Municipal	6.17%
66	New York Tax-Exempt Income	8.12%	66	Nuveen CA Municipal Value	6.08%
67	Nuveen Municipal Income	7.99%	67	Nuveen CA Quality Inc. Muni	6.03%
68	Allstate Municipal Income Tr.	7.86%	68	MuniInsured Fund Inc.	5.70%
69	Allstate Municipal Income II	7.85%	69	Nuveen Insured Municipal Opp	4.95%
70	Dreyfus Strategic Municipals	7.73%	70	Nuveen PA Inv. Quality Muni.	4.84%
71	Nuveen CA Municipal Income	7.50%	71	Allstate Municipal Income III	4.22%
72	Nuveen CA Municipal Value	7.48%	72	Allstate Municipal Inc. Opp. III	3.97%
73	MFS Municipal Income Trust	7.28%	73	Nuveen NY Quality Income Muni	3.84%
74	Dreyfus Cal. Municipal Income	7.27%	74	Dreyfus Strategic Municipals	3.66%
75	Nuveen NY Municipal Income	6.87%	75	Colonial High Income Municipal	3.58%
76	Allstate Municipal Income III	6.73%	76	Nuveen CA Municipal Income	2.81%
77	Colonial Investment Grade Mun.	6.46%	77	Seligman Quality Municipal	2.55%
78	Colonial Municipal Income Tr.	6.28%	78	MFS Municipal Income Trust	2.40%
79	VKM Investment Grade Muni	6.28%	79	Minnesota Municipal Term Trust	2.22%
80	Colonial High Income Municipal	6.10%	80	Nuveen Premium Muni Income	-0.32%
81	Allstate Municipal Inc. Opp. III	5.53%	81	Nuveen Premier Insured Muni	-1.67%
82	Allstate Municipal Inc. Opp. II	2.87%	82	Allstate Municipal Income Opp	-5.78%
83	Apex Municipal Fund	2.31%	83	Allstate Municipal Inc. Opp. II	-8.31%
84	Allstate Municipal Income Opp	1.94%	84	Apex Municipal Fund	-8.75%
	AVERAGE NAV TOTAL RETURN MUNICIPAL BOND FUNDS	9.65%		*AVERAGE PRICE TOTAL RETURN MUNICIPAL BOND FUNDS*	8.65%

*these funds trade OTC with spreads between the bid and ask usually as wide as 5%, therefore if the stock trades on the bid and then on the ask it would appear that it has gained 5%, when actually the bid and ask may have remained unchanged.

** not adjusted for rights offering

***adjusted for rights offering

#AMV has changed its name to Fortis Securities, symbol FOR; TMF shares were converted into Capstead Mortgage Series B preferred shares

The following formula is used to calculate total return:
((ending value + dividends) - beginning value) / beginning value

Dividends are indicated by ex-dividend date.

THOMAS J. HERZFELD ADVISORS, INC.
PERFORMANCE SURVEY FOR THE YEAR 1992
(adjusted for dividends and distributions)

SYMBOL	FUND	NAV 1/3/92	Price 12/31/91	1st Qtr.	2nd Qtr.	3rd Qtr.	4th Qtr.	NAV 12/31/92	Price 12/31/92	% Change NAV	% Change Price
				--- Dividends and Distributions---						-Year-Ended 12/31/92-	
	EQUITY FUNDS										
ADX	Adams Express	20.36	19.00	0.12	0.12	0.12	1.26	20.48	20.00	8.55%	13.79%
BKF	Baker, Fentress & Company	21.57	17.63	0	0.2	0	1.61	20.83	17.00	4.96%	6.72%
BEM	Bergstrom Capital	104.24	122.63	0	0	0	2	102.63	132.13	0.37%	9.38%
BLU	Blue Chip Value Fund	8.42	7.63	0	0.2	0.19	0.38	7.63	7.75	-0.24%	11.74%
CET	Central Securities	11.66	9.25	0	0.1	0	0.76	13.85	11.63	26.16%	34.97%
GSO	Charles Allmon Trust	10.40	10.00	0.0071		0	0.4317	10.28	10.00	3.07%	4.39%
EGX	Engex	11.48	8.75	0	0	0	0	11.98	9.13	4.36%	4.29%
GAB	Gabelli Equity Trust***	10.55	10.13	0.25	0.25	0.605	0.31	10.58	10.25	13.70%	15.21%
GAM	General American Investors	30.78	28.88	1.08	0	0	2	28.56	30.00	2.79%	14.56%
IMF	Inefficient Market Fund	10.52	8.88	0	0.04	0	0.01	11.49	9.88	9.70%	11.83%
JF	Jundt Growth Fund	15.65	16.00	0	0	0	0	15.57	14.88	-0.51%	-7.03%
USA	Liberty All-Star Equity Fund**	11.24	10.75	0.27	0.27	0.26	0.27	10.78	11.13	5.43%	13.44%
NGS	Niagara Share Corp.	15.33	14.63					MERGED WITH OPEN-END FUND			
RVT	Royce Value Trust	11.21	10.38	0	0	0	0.9	12.51	12.25	19.63%	26.75%
SBF	Salomon Brothers Fund	15.64	13.88	0	0.15	0.15	0.7	15.16	13.75	3.32%	6.31%
SOR	Source Capital	41.37	44.25	0.9	0.9	0.9	0.9	42.87	47.75	12.33%	16.05%
TY	Tri-Continental Corp.***	28.57	27.75	0.18	0.18	0.19	0.93	28.03	25.50	6.70%	0.74%
	FOREIGN EQUITY FUNDS										
AEF	Alliance Global Environment	13.37	11.63	0	0	0	0.18	11.38	9.63	-13.54%	-15.66%
AF	Argentina Fund	11.16	14.25	0	0	0	0.14	9.68	12.13	-12.01%	-13.93%
APB	Asia Pacific Fund	12.35	12.75	0	0	1.21	0.525	12.46	15.00	14.94%	31.25%
OST	Austria Fund	9.48	8.88	0	0	0	0.164	7.47	7.00	-19.47%	-19.28%
BZF	Brazil Fund	15.10	14.75	0	0.275	0	0.38	14.13	14.00	-2.09%	-0.64%
BZL	Brazilian Equity Fund					0	0.0256	9.49	9.00	NEW FUND	
CH	Chile Fund	30.60	23.88	0	0	1.5385	1.6833	31.08	33.25	12.10%	52.76%
CHN	The China Fund					0	0.0434	14.19	13.00	NEW FUND	
CLM	Clemente Global Growth	10.81	9.13	0	0	0	1.05	9.40	7.63	-3.33%	-4.93%
FRG	Emerging Germany Fund	9.13	7.75	0.23	0	0	0.11	7.56	6.38	-13.47%	-13.35%
MEF	Emerging Mexico Fund	18.62	18.00	0	0	0	4.9	17.16	17.38	18.47%	23.75%
EWF	European Warrant Fund	7.11	6.13	0	0	0	0.155	7.43	7.38	6.68%	22.94%
EF	Europe Fund	12.58	11.50	0	0	0	0.88	10.68	9.88	-8.11%	-6.48%
IAF	First Australia Fund	10.56	9.13	0.11	0.09	0	0.098	8.65	7.75	-15.27%	-11.80%
ISL	First Israel Fund						0	14.32	12.75	NEW FUND	

FOREIGN EQUITY FUNDS (continued)

SYMBOL	FUND	NAV 1/3/92	Price 12/31/91	1st Qtr.	2nd Qtr.	3rd Qtr.	4th Qtr.	NAV 12/31/92	Price 12/31/92	% Change NAV	% Change Price
				--- Dividends and Distributions---						-Year-Ended 12/31/92-	
IBF	First Iberian Fund	9.00	7.63	0	0.06	0	0.34	6.88	5.88	-19.11%	-17.70%
FPF	First Philippine Fund	11.58	8.63	0	0	0	0.57	13.05	10.25	17.62%	25.45%
FRF	France Growth Fund	10.63	8.88	0	0	0	0.042	10.53	9.25	-0.55%	4.70%
FGF	Future Germany Fund	14.60	12.88	0	0	0	0.3	12.98	11.63	-9.04%	-7.38%
GER	Germany Fund	10.99	12.13	0	0	0	0.38	9.78	10.13	-7.55%	-13.36%
GHS	Global Health Sciences							13.12	11.25	NEW FUND	NEW FUND
GCH	Greater China Fund							13.41	12.38	NEW FUND	NEW FUND
GSP	Growth Fund of Spain	11.48	9.38	0	0	0	0	8.96	7.63	-21.95%	-18.67%
GTF	GT Greater Europe Fund	11.25	9.50	0	0	0	0	10.57	9.00	-6.04%	-5.26%
IGF	India Growth Fund	17.06	13.50	0	0	0	0	15.96	15.25	-6.45%	12.96%
IF	Indonesia Fund	7.71	8.38	0	0	0	0	7.78	9.00	0.91%	7.46%
IRL	Irish Investment Fund	9.76	7.63	0	0	0	0.23	7.84	6.63	-17.32%	-10.10%
ITA	Italy Fund	10.97	8.88	0	0	0	0	7.82	7.50	-28.71%	-15.49%
JGF	Jakarta Growth Fund	6.13	5.75	0	0	0	0.08	6.28	7.13	3.75%	25.30%
JEQ	Japan Equity Fund							9.93	8.75	NEW FUND	NEW FUND
JOF	Japan OTC Equity Fund	10.18	10.38	0	0	0	0	6.92	7.63	-32.02%	-26.51%
JFC	Jardine Fleming China Reg. Fund							15.13	13.88	NEW FUND	NEW FUND
KF	Korea Fund	10.92	12.63	0	0	0.235	0.07	10.62	13.88	-0.60%	11.76%
KIF	Korea Investment Fund						0.012	9.93	10.63	NEW FUND	NEW FUND
LDF	Latin American Discovery Fund							15.23	13.25	NEW FUND	NEW FUND
LAM	Latin American Inv. Fund	26.39	26.50	0	0	2.4511	0	25.44	24.38	5.69%	1.23%
LAQ	Latin America Equity Fund	15.65	13.50	0	0	0.0763	1.6341	14.40	14.00	2.94%	16.37%
MF	Malaysia Fund	13.46	11.75	0	0	0	0	16.27	16.25	20.88%	38.30%
MXE	Mexico Equity & Income Fd.	15.27	12.88	0	0.2548	0	1.53	16.65	15.13	19.06%	29.36%
MXF	Mexico Fund***	23.36	20.40	0	0	0	2.701	25.31	23.50	20.98%	29.71%
MSF	Morgan Stanley Emerging Mkts.	14.80	14.50	0	0	0.02	0	16.74	18.13	13.24%	25.14%
GF	New Germany Fund	12.65	10.75	0	0	0	0.18	11.00	9.50	-11.62%	-9.95%
										OPEN-ENDED	
PEF	Pacific European Growth Fund	10.26	8.63	0	0	0	0.058	8.91	8.00	-16.03%	-17.35%
PGF	Portugal Fund	10.68	9.75	0	0	0	0.02	8.51	8.75	-10.49%	-14.44%
ROC	ROC Taiwan Fund	9.53	10.25	0	0	0	0	—	—	1.43%	-1.62%
SAF	Scudder New Asia Fund	15.02	15.13	0.04	0	0	0.465	14.73	14.38	-9.20%	-5.85%
NEF	Scudder New Europe Fund	10.00	8.38	0	0	0	0.26	8.82	7.63	-5.37%	-0.49%
SGF	Singapore Fund	12.01	10.25	0	0	0	0.325	11.04	9.88	-28.91%	-35.15%
SNF	Spain Fund	11.76	13.00	0	0	0	0.18	8.18	8.25	5.97%	4.91%
SWZ	Swiss Helvetia Fund	13.81	13.25	0	0	0	0.025	14.61	13.88	-8.29%	-21.85%
TWN	Taiwan Fund	20.88	24.63	0	0	0	0.12	19.03	19.13	8.07%	-8.85%
EMF	Templeton Emerging Markets	16.97	22.38	0	0	0	6.02	12.32	14.38		

114

SYMBOL	FUND	NAV 1/3/92	Price 12/31/91	1st Qtr.	2nd Qtr.	3rd Qtr.	4th Qtr.	NAV 12/31/92	Price 12/31/92	% Change NAV	% Change Price
				\-\-\- Dividends and Distributions\-\-\-						-Year-Ended 12/31/92-	
	FOREIGN EQUITY FUNDS (continued)										
TGU	Templeton Global Utilities	12.86	12.25	0.15	0.15	0.15	0.42	13.10	13.63	8.63%	18.33%
TC	Thai Capital Fund	9.11	9.13	0	0	0	0	12.02	11.13	31.94%	21.92%
TTF	Thai Fund	15.46	16.25	0	0	0	0.87	20.72	18.75	39.65%	20.74%
TKF	Turkish Investment Fund	7.56	7.63	0	0	0	0.04	4.60	5.25	-38.62%	-30.62%
UKM	United Kingdom Fund	10.44	9.13	0	0.09	0	0.46	10.24	9.38	3.35%	8.77%
VLU	Worldwide Value Fund	15.39	12.50	0	0	0.04	0	14.09	11.88	-8.19%	-4.68%
	SPECIALIZED EQUITY										
ASA	ASA Ltd.	41.85	46.88	0.5	0.5	0.5	0.5	28.81	31.63	-26.38%	-28.27%
CEF	Central Fund of Canada	4.26	3.88	0	0	0	0.01	3.99	3.63	-6.10%	-6.19%
DVRFS	Dover Regional Financial*	5.49	3.88	0	0.045	0	0	7.44	6.50	36.34%	68.90%
DNP	Duff & Phelps Utilities Income	9.54	10.00	0.18	0.18	0.18	0.24	9.67	10.50	9.54%	12.80%
ETF	Emerging Markets Telecom.					0	0.25	13.28	13.13	NEW FUND	
FF	First Financial Fund	9.29	8.13	0.03	0	0	2.035	13.75	12.75	70.24%	82.34%
HQH	H&Q Healthcare Investors	23.42	25.50	0	0	0	0	20.58	19.00	-12.13%	-25.49%
HQL	H&Q Life Sciences Inv. Fund					0	0	15.28	14.63	NEW FUND	
MGC	Morgan Grenfell Small Cap.	12.53	12.88	0	0	0	0.8005	11.95	12.25	1.76%	1.36%
PDF	Patriot Premium Dividend	10.17	9.38	0.1334	0.2001	0.2001	0.2001	10.46	10.38	10.07%	18.49%
PDT	Patriot Premium Dividend II	12.35	11.63	0.225	0.225	0.225	0.225	12.56	11.75	8.99%	8.82%
DIV	Patriot Select Dividend Trust	16.57	16.75	0.275	0.4125	0.4125	0.4125	16.22	17.75	7.02%	15.00%
PEO	Petroleum & Resources	28.26	26.00	0.2	0.2	0.2	1.4	27.66	25.25	4.95%	4.81%
PBS	Pilgrim Regional BankShares	10.14	9.50	0.19	0.2	0.2	0.22	12.46	11.63	30.87%	30.89%
PFD	Preferred Income Fund	16.23	18.00	0.36	0.36	0.36	1.86	17.11	18.38	23.54%	18.42%
PFO	Preferred Income Opportunity Fd.				0.165	0.2475	0.725	12.24	13.00	NEW FUND	
PDI	Putnam Dividend Income	11.41	10.88	0.3	0.285	0.285	0.285	11.53	12.25	11.17%	23.26%
RIF	Real Estate Securities Income	7.34	7.13	0.17	0.17	0.17	0.17	7.63	8.00	13.22%	21.82%
STBF	SE Thrift & Bank*	8.84	7.13	0.02	0.02	0	0	15.53	13.25	76.13%	86.53%
ZSEV	Z-Seven Fund*	17.71	20.50	0	0	0	0	15.13	17.00	-14.57%	-17.07%
ZF	Zweig Fund	12.41	13.75	0.29	0.29	0.28	0.64	11.36	13.00	3.63%	5.45%
	DUAL PURPOSE										
CNV	Convertible Holdings cap. shs.	11.01	6.88	0	0	0	0.12	12.86	9.38	17.89%	38.11%
CNVpr	Convertible Holdings inc. shs.	9.32	12.63	0	0.36	0.37	0.63	9.31	11.25	14.48%	-0.12%
CTF	Counsellors Tandem (common)	16.90	14.13	0	0	0	0	16.54	14.13	-2.13%	0.00%
GMI	Gemini II Fund cap. shs.	16.46	13.25	0	0	0	0.08	18.82	14.88	14.82%	12.87%
GMIpr	Gemini II Fund inc. shs.	9.35	13.63	0.26	0.25	0	0.91	10.00	12.00	22.14%	-1.50%
HU	Hampton Utilities cap. shs.	14.85	13.38	0	0	0	0.35	15.77	14.25	8.55%	9.16%

115

SYMBOL	FUND	NAV 1/3/92	Price 12/31/91	1st Qtr.	2nd Qtr.	3rd Qtr.	4th Qtr.	NAV 12/31/92	Price 12/31/92	% Change NAV	% Change Price
				--- Dividends and Distributions---						-Year-Ended 12/31/92-	
	DUAL PURPOSE (continued)										
HUpr	Hampton Utilities inc. shs.	49.34	54.00	1	1	1	1	49.61	51.00	8.65%	1.85%
KFV	Quest for Value cap. shs.	22.51	17.63	0	0	0	1.295	26.29	23.00	22.55%	37.84%
KFVpr	Quest for Value inc. shs.	11.62	13.38	0.3	0.3	0.335	0.408	11.61	13.00	11.47%	7.24%
	MISCELLANEOUS										
FUND	America's All-Season Fund*	6.01	4.56	0	0.15	0.14	0.134	5.11	4.06	-7.92%	-1.67%
FMI	Franklin Multi-Income	10.10	9.50	0.2425	0.24	0.234	0.27	10.67	9.88	15.41%	14.33%
ZTR	Zweig Total Return Fund	9.77	10.75	0.24	0.24	0.24	0.32	9.06	10.00	3.38%	2.70%
	CONVERTIBLE FUNDS										
AST	AIM Strategic Income	9.16	8.50	0.1575	0.155	0.15	0.3175	9.28	9.13	9.83%	16.53%
ACS	American Capital Convertible	22.29	19.25	0.3	0.3	0.29	0.29	23.64	20.38	11.35%	11.97%
BCV	Bancroft Convertible Fund	21.31	18.50	0.34	0.34	0.34	1.16	22.34	20.38	15.06%	21.92%
CVF	Castle Convertible Fund	23.70	20.75	0.4	0.4	0.4	0.62	25.54	23.75	15.44%	23.23%
ECF	Ellsworth Conv Growth&Income	8.71	7.38	0.135	0.135	0.135	0.216	9.42	8.25	15.28%	20.28%
LNV	Lincoln National Convertible	18.07	15.50	0	0.24	0.24	1.66	17.84	16.75	10.57%	21.87%
PCF	Putnam High Income Conv.	7.59	7.75	0.213	0.213	0.213	0.223	8.68	9.00	25.72%	27.25%
CVT	TCW Convertible Securities	8.13	8.75	0.21	0.21	0.21	0.21	8.36	9.13	13.16%	13.89%
	BOND FUNDS										
ACG	ACM Government Income Fund	10.52	11.25	0.22	0.24	0.24	0.29	10.51	11.00	9.32%	6.58%
AOF	ACM Government Opportunities	9.73	9.63	0.1325	0.1988	0.1988	0.6128	9.10	9.38	5.27%	9.28%
GSF	ACM Government Securities	10.48	10.63	0.265	0.24	0.24	0.29	10.47	10.63	9.78%	9.74%
SI	ACM Government Spectrum	9.06	9.00	0.1508	0.1988	0.1988	0.2488	8.89	9.00	6.92%	8.86%
AMF	ACM Managed Income	8.81	9.00	0.197	0.237	0.259	0.455	9.05	10.13	15.75%	25.26%
ADJ	American Adjustable Rate 1995	9.94	10.38	0.129	0.1895	0.1775	0.226	9.70	10.13	4.85%	4.55%
BDJ	American Adjustable Rate 1996	9.68	10.25	0.129	0.1895	0.179	0.232	9.43	9.88	4.95%	3.46%
CDJ	American Adjustable Rate 1997	9.64	10.00	0.132	0.194	0.182	0.232	9.46	9.88	5.81%	6.15%
DDJ	American Adjustable Rate 1998			0.059	0.177	0.177	0.236	9.48	9.88	NEW FUND	
EDJ	American Adjustable Rate 1999				0	0	0.1635	9.43	10.00	NEW FUND	
ACB	American Capital Bond Fund	19.78	20.13	0.42	0.42	0.42	0.46	20.05	20.25	10.06%	9.17%
ACD	American Capital Income Trust	7.73	7.38	0.21	0.21	0.21	0.2638	7.85	7.63	13.11%	15.51%
AGF	American Government Income	8.00	8.13	0.128	0.202	0.207	0.5542	8.07	8.88	14.52%	22.66%
AAF	American Government Portfolio	10.38	10.63	0.16	0.255	0.26	1.0007	10.32	11.13	15.57%	20.48%
AGT	American Government Term	9.97	10.63	0.157	0.2355	0.2355	0.314	9.49	11.13	4.63%	13.57%
OIF	American Opportunity Income Fd	10.48	10.75	0.1666	0.2499	0.2699	1.3412	10.10	11.63	15.72%	27.00%
ASP	American Strategic Income	14.15	15.13	0.225	0.3375	0.3375	0.6025	14.85	15.25	15.57%	10.76%

BOND FUNDS (continued)

SYMBOL	FUND	NAV 1/3/92	Price 12/31/91	1st Qtr	2nd Qtr	3rd Qtr	4th Qtr	NAV 12/31/92	Price 12/31/92	% Change NAV	% Change Price
				--- Dividends and Distributions ---						Year-Ended 12/31/92	
BSP	American Strategic Income II					0.1125	0.45	13.83	15.13	NEW FUND	NEW FUND
AMV#	AMEV Securities	10.12	11.38	0.2625	0.2575	0.255	0.255	9.95	11.13	8.50%	6.86%
BAT	BlackRock Advantage Term	10.84	11.25	0.1584	0.2313	0.2313	0.275	10.43	10.63	4.48%	2.41%
BKT	BlackRock Income Trust	9.68	10.63	0.2134	0.2376	0.2376	0.2124	8.99	8.50	2.18%	-11.52%
BQT	BlackRock Investment Qual Term					0.2025	0.27	9.57	9.38	NEW FUND	NEW FUND
BBT	BlackRock 1998 Term Trust	10.31	10.50	0.1375	0.2001	0.2001	0.2416	10.28	9.88	7.27%	1.47%
BNN	BlackRock 1999 Term Trust					0	0.1812	9.40	9.00	NEW FUND	NEW FUND
BLK	BlackRock 2001 Term Trust									NEW FUND	NEW FUND
BNA	BlackRock North American	14.19	14.75	0.2188	0.3282	0.3282	0.4376	12.72	12.50	-1.11%	-6.35%
BGT	BlackRock Strategic Term	10.05	10.75	0.1583	0.2312	0.2312	0.275	9.76	9.88	6.03%	0.19%
BTT	BlackRock Target Term	10.42	10.88	0.1542	0.225	0.225	0.2668	10.28	10.00	7.02%	-0.04%
BHL	Bunker Hill Income Securities	15.43	15.75	0.38	0.36	0.34	0.34	15.74	15.25	11.21%	5.84%
HIS	CIGNA High Income Shares	6.69	7.13	0.225	0.225	0.225	0.3325	6.99	7.88	19.54%	24.67%
CIM	CIM High Yield Securities	7.11	6.63	0.195	0.195	0.195	0.225	7.58	7.50	18.00%	25.43%
CINS	Circle Income Shares	12.18	12.38	0.255	0.255	0.235	0.23	11.94	11.00	5.99%	-3.23%
CNN	CNA Income Shares	10.57	11.13	0.29	0.29	0.29	0.29	10.32	11.63	8.61%	14.92%
CMK	Colonial Intermarket Income I	11.35	10.75	0.3	0.28	0.27	0.27	11.33	11.00	9.69%	12.74%
CIF	Colonial Intermediate High Inc.	6.19	5.88	0.195	0.195	0.195	0.18	6.47	6.25	16.88%	19.40%
CUR	Current Income Shares	13.17	13.25	0.26	0.26	0.26	0.25	13.33	12.63	9.04%	3.06%
GVT	Dean Witter Government Inc.	9.78	9.38	0.195	0.195	0.1725	0.23	9.55	8.88	5.75%	3.12%
DSI	Dreyfus Strategic Government	11.33	11.50	0.265	0.255	0.255	0.255	10.86	11.63	4.94%	10.04%
BDF	1838 Bond-Debenture Trading	21.17	22.50	0	0.455	0.455	0.255	21.38	22.63	6.50%	5.73%
EIS	Excelsior Income Shares	18.56	18.00	0	0.34	0.31	0.79	18.45	17.38	7.17%	4.53%
FBF	First Boston Income Fund	8.33	8.38	0.225	0.225	0.225	0.15	8.44	8.38	11.22%	9.85%
FBI	First Boston Strategic Income	9.66	10.38	0.3	0.3	0.275	0.175	9.82	9.63	12.53%	2.89%
FTD	Fort Dearborn Income	16.15	16.25	0.31	0.31	0.31	0.31	16.33	15.88	8.79%	5.32%
FPT	Franklin Principal Maturity	8.24	8.00	0.18	0.14	0.15	0.15	8.25	7.50	7.65%	1.50%
FT	Franklin Universal Trust	8.06	7.38	0.2045	0.1875	0.1875	0.1875	8.82	8.25	18.95%	22.26%
HAT	Hatteras Income Securities	15.99	17.50	0.375	0.375	0.375	0.375	16.08	18.00	9.94%	11.43%
YLD	High Income Advantage Trust	5.34	5.00	0.1	0.15	0.15	0.412	5.29	5.63	14.27%	28.74%
YLT	High Income Advantage Trust II	5.76	5.25	0.105	0.1575	0.1575	0.426	5.82	5.88	15.73%	28.02%
YLH	High Income Advantage Trust III	6.46	6.13	0.12	0.18	0.18	0.454	6.44	6.50	14.15%	21.37%
HYI	High Yield Income Fund	7.06	6.75	0.225	0.225	0.225	0.225	7.32	7.38	16.43%	22.59%
HYP	High Yield Plus Fund	7.61	7.00	0.21	0.21	0.21	0.21	8.08	8.00	17.21%	26.29%
HTA	Hyperion 1997 Term Trust						0.0933	9.49	9.75	NEW FUND	NEW FUND
HTT	Hyperion 1999 Term Trust					0.1334	0.2001	8.80	9.88	NEW FUND	NEW FUND
HTB	Hyperion 2002 Term Trust						0.0967	9.42	9.75	NEW FUND	NEW FUND

SYMBOL	FUND	NAV 1/3/92	Price 12/31/91	1st Qtr.	2nd Qtr.	3rd Qtr.	4th Qtr.	NAV 12/31/92	Price 12/31/92	% Change NAV	% Change Price
				--- Dividends and Distributions---						-Year-Ended 12/31/92-	
	BOND FUNDS (continued)										
HTR	Hyperion Total Return	11.29	11.38	0.3	0.21	0.29	0.29	10.79	11.25	5.23%	8.48%
IIS	INA Investments	18.78	17.75	0.38	0.38	0.33	0.385	18.75	17.25	7.69%	5.49%
IOF	Income Opportunities 1999						0.1803	9.37	9.25	NEW FUND	NEW FUND
IFT	Income Opportunities 2000						0	9.64	10.00	NEW FUND	NEW FUND
ISIS	Independence Square Income	17.31	16.50	0.24	0.36	0.36	0.48	17.74	17.13	10.80%	12.52%
ICB	Intercapital Income Securities	18.21	21.13	0.465	0.465	0.465	0.42	18.33	19.38	10.63%	0.31%
JHS	John Hancock Income Securities	16.19	17.00	0.35	0.3475	0.3425	0.335	16.31	16.75	9.23%	6.62%
JHI	John Hancock Investors Trust	21.54	24.00	0.47	0.47	0.47	0.455	21.62	23.50	9.03%	5.69%
KHI	Kemper High Income Trust	8.27	8.63	0.24	0.24	0.24	0.24	8.73	9.38	17.17%	19.83%
KGT	Kemper Int. Government Trust	9.10	8.88	0.1875	0.1875	0.1875	0.25	8.80	8.75	5.63%	7.75%
KMM	Kemper Multi-Income Trust	10.36	9.50	0.27	0.27	0.27	0.36	10.85	10.25	16.02%	20.21%
LTT	Liberty Term Trust, Inc.--1999					0.23	0.236	9.09	10.25	NEW FUND	NEW FUND
LND	Lincoln National Income Fund	29.65	27.63	0	0.57	0.57	2.22	28.42	28.63	7.18%	15.78%
MCI	MassMutual Corporate Inv.	28.74	28.00	0	0.7	0.7	1.4	30.76	26.13	16.77%	3.30%
MPV	MassMutual Participation Inv.	8.58	8.63	0	0.22	0.18	0.36	8.58	7.38	8.86%	-5.68%
MIT	Merrill Lynch & Co. S&P 500									NEW FUND	
MCR	MFS Charter Income Fund	10.71	10.25	0.25	0.3	0.3	0.27	10.30	9.75	6.63%	6.05%
MGF	MFS Government Markets	8.24	7.88	0.2205	0.2205	0.2205	0.1955	7.65	7.13	3.24%	1.36%
MIN	MFS Intermediate Income	8.39	7.88	0.2025	0.2025	0.2025	0.1875	7.90	7.25	3.64%	2.16%
MMT	MFS Multimarket Income	8.07	7.38	0.231	0.231	0.231	0.207	7.59	7.13	5.20%	8.81%
MFV	MFS Special Value Trust	14.90	14.88	0.4125	0.4125	0.4125	1.0335	14.46	14.75	12.29%	14.43%
MTS	Montgomery Street Income	19.17	19.63	0	0.43	0.41	0.83	19.30	20.88	9.39%	14.88%
MUO	Mutual Of Omaha Interest	14.12	14.25	0.28	0.29	0.29	0.29	14.09	14.75	7.93%	11.58%
HYB	New America High Income	3.82	3.63	0.135	0.125	0.12	0.166	4.32	4.13	27.38%	28.86%
OGT	Oppenheimer Multi-Govern.	9.04	9.25	0.304	0.198	0.198	0.198	8.48	8.63	3.74%	2.95%
OMS	Oppenheimer Multi-Sector	10.72	11.00	0.291	0.291	0.291	0.277	10.38	10.63	7.56%	7.05%
PAI	Pacific American Income	15.90	15.75	0.35	0.35	0.35	0.35	15.86	15.50	8.55%	7.30%
PHY	Prospect Street High Income	3.87	3.25	0.09	0.1	0.12	0.26	4.09	4.13	20.41%	44.46%
PGT	Putnam Intermediate Govern.	9.46	9.25	0.21	0.19	0.18	0.574	8.97	8.63	7.02%	5.72%
PMT	Putnam Master Income Trust	9.02	8.25	0.2325	0.2325	0.2325	0.286	9.09	8.75	11.68%	17.98%
PIM	Putnam Master Intermediate	8.39	7.75	0.2025	0.2025	0.2025	0.2321	8.52	8.00	11.56%	14.06%
PPT	Putnam Premier Income	8.43	7.75	0.2175	0.2175	0.2175	0.1875	8.53	8.00	11.15%	14.06%
RMF	RAC Income Fund	11.68	12.00	0.315	0.315	0.315	0.285	10.99	11.50	4.62%	6.08%
SMS	State Mutual Securities	11.06	10.63	0.23	0.23	0.23	0.28	11.30	11.75	10.94%	19.72%
TRM	TCW/DW Term Trust 2002							9.54	10.13	NEW FUND	NEW FUND
TAI	Transamerica Income	24.41	26.00	0.54	0.5025	0.5025	0.5025	24.18	25.25	7.45%	4.99%
	Triple A & Government '95							991.97	995.00	NEW FUND	

SYMBOL	FUND	NAV 1/3/92	Price 12/31/91	1st Qtr.	2nd Qtr.	3rd Qtr.	4th Qtr.	NAV 12/31/92	Price 12/31/92	% Change NAV	% Change Price
				\-\-\- Dividends and Distributions\-\-\-						-Year-Ended 12/31/92-	
	BOND FUNDS (continued)										
TTR	Triple A & Government '97							984.07	990.00		
TMF#	2002 Target Term Trust							NEW FUND	NEW FUND		
	Tyler Cabot Mortgage Securities	11.54	12.13	0.21	0.315	0.315	0.245	BECAME Capstead Mortgage Pr. Series B			
PHF	USF&G Pacholder Fund	17.37	17.25	0	0.45	0.45	1.185	18.41	19.38	17.99%	24.41%
UIF	USLIFE Income Fund	9.49	9.13	0.23	0.23	0.23	0.23	9.75	10.25	12.43%	22.41%
VIT	VKM Intermediate Term	5.96	6.88	0.21	0.2125	0.2375	0.2475	6.23	7.25	19.76%	18.65%
VLT	VKM Limited High Income	7.67	7.50	0.235	0.225	0.245	0.27	7.92	9.38	15.97%	38.00%
VES	Vestaur Securities	14.89	14.88	0.29	0.29	0.29	0.29	14.91	14.38	7.92%	4.44%
ZIF	Zenix Income Fund	6.07	6.13	0.21	0.208	0.204	0.204	6.35	6.50	18.22%	19.61%
	FOREIGN BOND FUNDS										
MMF	ACM Managed Multi-Market	11.01	12.63	0.18	0.27	0.2475	0.295	9.50	8.75	-4.70%	-22.83%
AWG	Alliance World Dollar Gvt Fund						0.2498	14.17	14.75	NEW FUND	
BNA	Blackrock North America					0.3282	0.3282	12.72	12.50	NEW FUND	
EMD	Emerging Markets Income						0.24	13.89	14.25	NEW FUND	
FAX	First Australia Prime Income	10.87	11.13	0.27	0.27	0.27	0.351	9.44	10.19	-2.47%	2.01%
FCO	First Commonwealth Fund				0.315	0.315	0.3025	12.54	11.88	NEW FUND	
GOV	Global Government Plus	8.24	7.75	0.175	0.175	0.175	0.345	7.38	7.00	0.12%	1.55%
GLI	Global Income Plus	9.82	10.25	0	0.21	0.215	0.4406	9.18	8.75	2.30%	-6.19%
PGY	Global Yield Fund	8.97	8.13	0.2	0.2	0.2	0.2	8.10	7.50	-0.78%	2.15%
KBA	Kleinwort Benson Australian	11.42	10.88	0.16	0.21	0.21	0.795	9.84	9.13	-1.80%	-3.45%
LBF	Latin America Dollar Income					0	0.5	12.95	12.88	NEW FUND	
PGD	Patriot Global Dividend Fund					0	0.3093	13.74	13.63	NEW FUND	
SGL	Strategic Global Income				0.16	0.3275	0.49	13.47	12.13	NEW FUND	
TGG	Templeton Global Government	9.16	9.50	0.21	0.21	0.205	0.3	8.19	8.63	-0.49%	0.53%
GIM	Templeton Global Income	8.87	8.88	0.21	0.21	0.21	0.21	8.17	9.00	1.58%	10.87%
	MUNICIPAL BOND FUNDS										
AMO	Allstate Municipal Income Opp	9.38	9.13	0.18	0.18	0.18	0.1824	8.84	7.88	1.94%	-5.78%
AOT	Allstate Municipal Inc. Opp. II	9.43	9.50	0.195	0.18	0.18	0.1559	8.99	8.00	2.87%	-8.31%
AIO	Allstate Municipal Inc. Opp. III	9.63	9.50	0.18	0.18	0.1879	0.2045	9.41	9.13	5.53%	3.97%
ALM	Allstate Municipal Income Tr.	10.56	10.88	0.18	0.18	0.18	0.18	10.67	10.88	6.62%	6.62%
ALT	Allstate Municipal Income II	10.35	10.00	0.1725	0.1725	0.1725	0.1845	10.46	10.50	7.86%	12.02%
ALL	Allstate Municipal Income III	9.75	9.63	0.165	0.15	0.15	0.1913	9.75	9.38	7.85%	4.22%
ALI	Allstate Municipal Premium	10.00	9.88	0.18	0.1875	0.1875	0.203	10.35	10.63	6.73%	15.27%
AXT	American Municipal Term Trust	10.00	10.13	0.1084	0.1626	0.1626	0.2168	10.56	10.75	11.08%	12.60%
BXT	American Municipal Term Tr II	9.72	9.88	0.1034	0.1551	0.1551	0.2068	10.25	10.13	12.10%	11.84%

SYMBOL	FUND	NAV 1/3/92	Price 12/31/91	1st Qtr.	2nd Qtr.	3rd Qtr.	4th Qtr.	NAV 12/31/92	Price 12/31/92	-Year-Ended 12/31/92- % Change NAV	% Change Price
	MUNICIPAL BOND FUNDS		(continued)	--- Dividends and Distributions---							
CXT	American Municipal Term Tr III						0.0475	9.58	9.88	NEW FUND	
APX	Apex Municipal Fund	10.76	11.50	0.2277	0.222	0.2125	0.2069	10.14	9.63	2.31%	-8.75%
BFC	BlackRock Cal. Insured 2008						0.0713	14.18	13.88	NEW FUND	
BRF	BlackRock Fl. Insured 2008						0.0719	14.29	14.25	NEW FUND	
BMT	BlackRock Insured Municipal				0	0.1562	0.1562	9.92	9.88	NEW FUND	
BRM	BlackRock Insured Muni 2008						0.0738	14.31	13.75	NEW FUND	
BMN	BlackRock Municipal Tgt Term	9.59	9.63	0.1538	0	0.1538	0.1538	10.04	10.00	9.50%	8.69%
BLN	BlackRock NY Insured 2008						0.0713	14.33	13.75	NEW FUND	
CXE	Colonial High Income Municipal	8.92	8.63	0.171	0.171	0.171	0.171	8.78	8.25	6.10%	3.58%
CXH	Colonial Investment Grade Mun.	11.09	11.75	0.216	0.216	0.207	0.207	10.96	11.75	6.46%	7.20%
CMU	Colonial Municipal Income Tr.	8.06	7.50	0.159	0.159	0.159	0.159	7.93	7.50	6.28%	8.48%
DCM	Dreyfus Cal. Municipal Income	9.35	8.88	0.15	0.15	0.15	0.15	9.43	9.00	7.27%	8.17%
DMF	Dreyfus Municipal Income	9.88	10.00	0.18	0.18	0.18	0.22	9.97	10.63	8.60%	13.85%
DNM	Dreyfus New York Municipal	9.78	9.75	0.1575	0.1575	0.1575	0.1575	10.13	10.50	10.02%	14.15%
DSM	Dreyfus Strategic Municipal Bond	9.71	9.75	0.1785	0.1785	0.1785	0.1785	9.80	10.25	8.28%	12.45%
LEO	Dreyfus Strategic Municipals	10.06	10.75	0.195	0.195	0.195	0.183	10.07	10.38	7.73%	3.66%
DTF	Duff & Phelps Utilities Tax Free	14.30	14.88	0.195	0.24	0.24	0.24	14.77	15.38	9.69%	9.51%
IMB	Intercapital Insured Muni Bond	14.87	15.75	0.2625	0.2725	0.2775	0.4673	15.23	16.75	11.03%	14.47%
IMT	Intercapital Insured Muni Trust				0.1625	0.2438	0.4325	14.94	15.25	NEW FUND	
IQT	Intercapital Quality Municipal	14.40	14.63	0.255	0.265	0.27	0.51	14.51	14.38	9.79%	7.18%
KTF	Kemper Municipal Income	12.11	12.50	0.2175	0.2175	0.2175	0.2205	12.52	12.75	10.59%	8.98%
KSM	Kemper Strategic Muni. Income	11.78	12.25	0.225	0.225	0.225	0.245	11.90	12.38	8.83%	8.53%
MMU	Managed Municipal Portfolio					0.061	0.211	12.32	11.63	NEW FUND	
MTU	Managed Municipals Portfolio II						0.06	12.25	11.38	NEW FUND	
MFM	MFS Municipal Income Trust	8.97	8.88	0.18	0.18	0.178	0.175	8.91	8.38	7.28%	2.40%
MNA	Minnesota Municipal Term Trust	9.69	10.63	0.1018	0.1527	0.1527	0.2036	10.13	10.25	10.84%	2.22%
MNB	Minnesota Municipal Term Tr II				0	0.0492	0.0984	9.74	10.38	NEW FUND	
MHF	Municipal High Income Fund	9.49	9.13	0.1725	0.1725	0.1725	0.1695	9.60	9.50	8.40%	11.64%
MEN	MuniEnhanced Fund	12.08	12.88	0.2255	0.2277	0.2343	0.5808	12.22	12.88	11.66%	9.85%
MIF	MuniInsured Fund Inc.	10.08	10.38	0.1568	0.1544	0.1575	0.3724	10.07	10.13	8.25%	5.70%
MVF	MuniVest Fund, Inc.	9.98	10.88	0.1994	0.2033	0.2069	0.4551	9.92	10.75	10.07%	8.64%
MYC	MuniYield California Fund				0.2256	0.2482	0.3298	14.69	14.38	NEW FUND	
MIC	MuniYield California Insured					0.1047	0.2573	14.10	14.25	NEW FUND	
MCA	MuniYield California Insured II						0	14.66	14.75	NEW FUND	
MYF	MuniYield Florida Fund				0.2208	0.2461	0.2781	14.86	15.88	NEW FUND	
MFT	MuniYield Florida Insured Fund						0	14.74	14.88	NEW FUND	
MYD	MuniYield Fund	14.60	15.50	0.2535	0.2671	0.2779	0.437	15.14	15.38	12.16%	7.16%

MUNICIPAL BOND FUNDS (continued)

SYMBOL	FUND	NAV 1/3/92	Price 12/31/91	1st Qtr.	2nd Qtr.	3rd Qtr.	4th Qtr.	NAV 12/31/92	Price 12/31/92	% Change NAV	% Change Price
				--- Dividends and Distributions---						-Year-Ended 12/31/92-	
MYI	MuniYield Insured Fund				0.2146	0.2546	0.3479	14.89	14.63	NEW FUND	NEW FUND
MTI	MuniYield Insured Fund II						0	14.68	14.13	NEW FUND	NEW FUND
MYJ	MuniYield New Jersey Fund				0.159	0.2797	0.2486	14.56	15.00	NEW FUND	NEW FUND
MJI	MuniYield New Jersey Insured Fd						0	14.55	15.25	NEW FUND	NEW FUND
MYN	MuniYield New York Insured Fd				0.2146		0.25	15.09	15.25	NEW FUND	NEW FUND
MYT	MuniYield NY Insured Fund II					0.2528	0.2369	14.20	14.75	NEW FUND	NEW FUND
MYY	MuniYield NY Insured Fund III					0.1089		14.22	15.00	NEW FUND	NEW FUND
MYM	MuniYield Michigan Fund				0.2248	0.2557	0.3066	14.86	15.38	NEW FUND	NEW FUND
MIY	MuniYield Michigan Insured Fund						0	14.77	15.38	NEW FUND	NEW FUND
MPA	MuniYield Pennsylvania Fund						0	14.52	15.38	NEW FUND	NEW FUND
MQY	MuniYield Quality					0.1232	0.2472	14.17	13.63	NEW FUND	NEW FUND
MQT	MuniYield Quality II					0	0.2362	14.40	14.25	NEW FUND	NEW FUND
XTX	New York Tax-Exempt Income	10.33	10.13	0.159	0.159	0.159	0.232	10.46	11.13	8.12%	16.88%
NAZ	Nuveen AZ Premium Income Muni					0	0			NEW FUND	NEW FUND
NQC	Nuveen CA Inv. Qual. Muni.	14.90	15.13	0.252	0.252	0.264	0.2735	15.46	16.00	10.75%	12.67%
NCM	Nuveen CA Municipal Income	12.00	13.00	0.1995	0.1995	0.1995	0.1413	12.16	12.63	7.50%	2.81%
NCO	Nuveen CA Muni. Market Opp.	15.16	15.25	0.255	0.255	0.1665	0.283	15.65	15.75	9.56%	9.57%
NCA	Nuveen CA Municipal Value	10.41	11.00	0.1665	0.1665	0.1665	0.1693	10.52	11.00	7.48%	6.08%
NCP	Nuveen CA Perf Plus Muni	15.08	15.38	0.255	0.255	0.273	0.284	15.67	15.75	10.99%	9.38%
NUC	Nuveen CA Quality Inc. Muni	14.20	14.38	0.15	0.225	0.225	0.2675	14.59	14.38	8.86%	6.03%
NVC	Nuveen CA Select Quality	14.63	14.50	0.243	0.243	0.248	0.2873	15.10	15.00	10.19%	10.49%
NQF	Nuveen FL Inv. Quality Muni.	14.79	15.50	0.2475	0.2475	0.2525	0.2749	15.25	16.00	10.02%	9.82%
NUF	Nuveen FL Quality Income Munic	14.34	14.50	0.228	0.228	0.228	0.2689	14.91	15.00	10.62%	10.02%
NPC	Nuveen Insured CA Premium Fund						0	14.09	14.88	NEW FUND	NEW FUND
NXC	Nuveen Ins CA Select Tax-Free					0.0681	0.2043	14.05	15.00	NEW FUND	NEW FUND
NFL	Nuveen Insured FL Premium Fund						0	14.03	15.13	NEW FUND	NEW FUND
NIO	Nuveen Insured Municipal Opp	14.42	14.88	0.2355	0.2355	0.2455	0.2705	14.94	14.63	10.45%	4.95%
NNF	Nuveen Insured NY Premium Fund						0	13.98	15.00	NEW FUND	NEW FUND
NXN	Nuveen Ins NY Select Tax- Free					0.0668	0.2004	13.94	13.25	NEW FUND	NEW FUND
NPE	Nuveen Ins Premium Municipal Fd						0	14.05	15.13	NEW FUND	NEW FUND
NQI	Nuveen Insured Quality Muni.	15.10	15.88	0.261	0.261	0.284	0.3107	15.73	16.63	11.57%	11.76%
NQM	Nuveen Investment Quality	15.35	16.13	0.285	0.285	0.302	0.3355	15.73	16.63	10.34%	10.59%
NMP	Nuveen MI Premium Income Muni						0	13.97	15.00	NEW FUND	NEW FUND
NUM	Nuveen MI Quality Income Muni	14.28	15.13	0.2265	0.2265	0.2265	0.248	14.86	15.50	10.56%	8.61%
NMA	Nuveen Municipal Advantage	15.13	16.00	0.2775	0.2775	0.2965	0.338	15.52	16.50	10.44%	10.56%
NMI	Nuveen Municipal Income	12.12	12.88	0.213	0.213	0.213	0.209	12.24	12.88	7.99%	6.59%
NMO	Nuveen Municipal Market Opp.	15.36	16.00	0.282	0.282	0.292	0.3221	15.79	16.38	10.47%	9.71%

121

MUNICIPAL BOND FUNDS (continued)

SYMBOL	FUND	NAV 1/3/92	Price 12/31/91	1st Qtr.	2nd Qtr.	3rd Qtr.	4th Qtr.	NAV 12/31/92	Price 12/31/92	% Change NAV (Year-Ended 12/31/92)	% Change Price (Year-Ended 12/31/92)
NUV	Nuveen Municipal Value	10.50	11.00	0.1775	0.177	0.177	0.1838	10.69	11.38	8.62%	9.91%
NQJ	Nuveen NJ Inv. Quality Muni.	14.60	15.38	0.2325	0.2325	0.2325	0.2632	15.01	15.88	9.39%	9.50%
NNJ	Nuveen NJ Premium Income						0	14.02	15.13	NEW FUND	10.72%
NUJ	Nuveen NJ Quality Income Muni	14.29	14.50	0.222	0.222	0.234	0.251	14.71	15.13	9.44%	9.80%
NQN	Nuveen NY Inv Quality Muni	15.25	16.00	0.2595	0.2595	0.2745	0.2745	15.98	16.50	11.79%	9.81%
NNM	Nuveen NY Municipal Income	12.02	12.25	0.1965	0.1965	0.1965	0.2367	12.02	12.63	6.87%	13.96%
NNO	Nuveen NY Muni. Market Opp	15.41	15.63	0.27	0.27	0.293	0.3476	16.07	16.63	11.94%	12.07%
NNY	Nuveen NY Municipal Value	10.50	10.88	0.1689	0.1689	0.1689	0.3054	10.61	11.38	8.78%	11.87%
NNP	Nuveen NY Perf. Plus Muni	15.10	15.75	0.2655	0.2655	0.2875	0.301	15.79	16.50	11.98%	3.84%
NUN	Nuveen NY Quality Income Muni	14.22	14.63	0.1476	0.2214	0.2214	0.2214	14.81	14.38	9.86%	8.41%
NVN	Nuveen NY Select Quality	14.71	14.88	0.2385	0.2385	0.2455	0.2791	15.43	15.13	11.70%	6.84%
NOH	Nuveen OH Premium Income Fund						0	13.96	15.63	NEW FUND	4.84%
NUO	Nuveen OH Quality Income Munic	14.16	15.25	0.219	0.219	0.219	0.2613	14.64	15.38	9.88%	9.03%
NQP	Nuveen PA Inv. Quality Muni.	14.90	16.25	0.249	0.249	0.26	0.2785	15.50	16.00	10.98%	9.74%
NPA	Nuveen PA Premium Income Fund						0	14.00	15.13	NEW FUND	-1.67%
NUP	Nuveen PA Quality Income Muni	14.42	15.00	0.2295	0.2295	0.2425	0.2776	14.95	15.38	10.47%	-0.32%
NPP	Nuveen Performance Plus	14.94	15.13	0.261	0.261	0.278	0.2985	15.33	15.50	9.96%	7.27%
NF	Nuveen Premier Insured Muni	14.02	15.00	0.075	0.225	0.225	0.225	14.64	14.00	9.77%	6.23%
NPF	Nuveen Premier Muni Income	14.02	15.13	0.08	0.24	0.24	0.2661	14.55	14.25	9.67%	10.66%
NPI	Nuveen Premium Income Muni	15.78	16.88	0.285	0.285	0.324	0.333	16.03	16.88	9.36%	6.17%
NPM	Nuveen Premium Income Muni II					0	0	13.95	13.25	NEW FUND	13.44%
NPN	Nuveen Premium Income Muni III						0.2268	14.33	13.75	NEW FUND	13.34%
NQU	Nuveen Quality Income Muni	14.61	14.75	0.252	0.252	0.263	0.277	15.15	14.63	10.84%	
NIM	Nuveen Select Maturity Muni						0	11.43	10.88	NEW FUND	
NIR	Nuveen Select Maturity Muni II					0	0.0536	11.40	10.75	NEW FUND	
NQS	Nuveen Select Quality Municipal	14.91	15.00	0.255	0.255	0.285	0.304	15.28	15.50	9.85%	
NXP	Nuveen Select Tax-Free Income				0.079	0.237	0.237	14.63	14.63	NEW FUND	
NXQ	Nuveen Select Tax-Free Income 2				0	0.1512	0.2268	14.46	13.63	NEW FUND	
NXR	Nuveen Select Tax-Free Income 3					0	0.2118	13.88	13.13	NEW FUND	
NXS	Nuveen Select Tax-Free Income 4					0	0.1454	14.14	13.75	NEW FUND	
NTE	Nuveen TX Premium Income Fund					0	0	13.90	15.00	NEW FUND	
NTX	Nuveen TX Quality Income Munic	14.24	15.25	0.2265	0.2265	0.2265	0.2611	14.66	15.25	9.55%	
PPM	Painewebber Premium Tax-Free					0	0	15.35	15.13	NEW FUND	
PCA	Putnam CA Investment Grade					0	0	14.55	15.00	NEW FUND	
PYM	Putnam High Yield Municipal	9.05	9.75	0.2025	0.2025	0.2025	0.2025	9.33	10.25	12.04%	
PMG	Putnam Investment Grade Muni II				0	0		14.59	15.00	NEW FUND	
PGM	Putnam Investment Grade Muni	11.82	12.50	0.222	0.222	0.234	0.24	12.50	13.25	13.52%	

-Year-Ended 12/31/92-

SYMBOL	FUND	NAV 1/3/92	Price 12/31/91	1st Qtr.	2nd Qtr.	3rd Qtr.	4th Qtr.	NAV 12/31/92	Price 12/31/92	% Change NAV	% Change Price
		(continued)		--- Dividends and Distributions ---							
	MUNICIPAL BOND FUNDS										
PMM	Putnam Managed Municipal	9.62	10.00	0.1905	0.1905	0.1905	0.2695	10.00	10.63	12.69%	14.66%
PMN	Putnam NY Inv Grade Municipal						0	14.35	15.00	NEW FUND	NEW FUND
PMH	Putnam Tax Free Health Care Fd				0	0.1688	0.3216	14.26	14.00	NEW FUND	NEW FUND
SQF	Seligman Quality Municipal	14.18	14.75	0.1564	0.2346	0.2346	0.2506	14.69	14.25	9.78%	2.55%
SEL	Seligman Select Municipal	11.97	12.25	0.21	0.21	0.21	0.226	12.45	12.75	11.16%	11.07%
SBI	Smith Barney Intermediate Muni				0.98	0.147	0.196	10.36	10.13	NEW FUND	NEW FUND
SBT	Smith Barney Municipal Fund					0.02	0.259	14.81	14.25	NEW FUND	NEW FUND
MCF	Taurus MuniCalifornia Holdings	11.75	12.13	0.2217	0.2202	0.2222	0.359	11.76	12.88	8.79%	14.62%
MNY	Taurus MuniNew York Holdings	11.83	12.00	0.2231	0.2276	0.2291	0.2256	12.26	13.38	11.29%	19.00%
VKA	VKM Advantage Muni Income						0.0785	15.40	14.25	NEW FUND	NEW FUND
VAP	VKM Advantage PA Municipal						0.073	15.25	14.38	NEW FUND	NEW FUND
VKC	VKM CA Municipal Trust	9.98	9.75	0.165	0.165	0.165	0.2749	10.30	10.25	10.92%	13.02%
VQC	VKM CA Quality Municipal Trust	15.09	14.38	0.2346	0.2346	0.2346	0.3442	15.64	14.75	10.59%	9.90%
VFM	VKM FL Quality Municipal Trust	15.27	15.13	0.2496	0.2496	0.2496	0.3171	16.06	15.63	12.15%	10.35%
VIG	VKM Investment Grade Muni	11.63	12.38	0.2325	0.2325	0.2325	0.2325	11.43	12.38	6.28%	7.52%
VMT	VKM Municipal Income Trust	10.26	10.75	0.201	0.201	0.205	0.3691	10.65	12.00	13.31%	20.71%
VMO	VKM Municipal Opportunity Tr				0	0.255	0.3122	15.65	15.00	NEW FUND	NEW FUND
VKQ	VKM Municipal Trust	15.26	15.13	0.2721	0.2721	0.2721	0.383	16.00	15.63	12.71%	11.24%
VNM	VKM New York Quality	15.26	14.63	0.2496	0.2496	0.2496	0.3206	16.27	15.63	13.63%	14.15%
VOQ	VKM Ohio Quality	15.19	15.50	0.2457	0.2457	0.2457	0.3177	15.97	15.63	12.08%	7.61%
VPQ	VKM PA Quality Muncipal Trust	15.28	15.00	0.2532	0.2532	0.2532	0.4143	16.29	15.50	14.29%	11.16%
VIM	VKM Trust for Insured Muni.						0.3114	15.95	14.88	NEW FUND	NEW FUND
VIC	VKM Trust For Inv Grade CA Muni				0.225	0.225	0.3674	15.42	14.50	NEW FUND	NEW FUND
VTF	VKM Tr For Inv Grade FL Muni				0.077	0.231	0.2363	15.82	15.13	NEW FUND	NEW FUND
VGM	VKM Trust for Investment Grade				0.078	0.234	0.3376	16.05	15.38	NEW FUND	NEW FUND
VTJ	VKM Tr For Inv Grade NJ Muni				0.255	0.255	0.323	15.67	15.13	NEW FUND	NEW FUND
VTN	VKM Tr For Inv Grade NY Muni				0.077	0.231	0.255	15.50	15.13	NEW FUND	NEW FUND
VTP	VKM Tr For Inv Grade PA Muni				0.085	0.255	0.2592	15.66	15.13	NEW FUND	NEW FUND
VMN	Voyageur Minnesota Municipal			0	0.083	0.249	0.2325	14.07	15.50	NEW FUND	NEW FUND

New Issues
(not listed in Chapter 12)

Alliance World Dollar Government Fund, Inc.
Listed: AWG, NYSE
1345 Avenue of the Americas, New York, NY 10105
Phone: 800-247-4154; 800-426-5523

**American Adjustable Rate Term Trust, Inc.-
1999**
Listed: EDJ, NYSE
American Strategic Income Portfolio, Inc. II
Listed: BSP, NYSE
PO Box 419432, Kansas City, MO 64141
Phone: 800-543-1627; 800-333-6000

American Municipal Term Trust III
Listed: CXT, NYSE
222 S. 9th St., Minneapolis, MN 55402
Phone: 800-866-7778

**The BlackRock California Insured 2008
Municipal Term Trust**
Listed: BFC, NYSE
**The BlackRock Florida Insured 2008
Municipal Term Trust**
Listed: BRF, NYSE
**The BlackRock Insured Municipal 2008
Term Trust**
Listed: BRM, NYSE
**The BlackRock New York Insured 2008
Municipal Term Trust**
Listed: BLN, NYSE
800 Scudders Mill Road, Plainsboro, NJ 08536
Phone: 212-214-1215; 800-227-7236; 800-451-6788

The BlackRock 2001 Term Trust
Listed: BLK, NYSE
1285 Avenue of the Americas, New York, NY 10019
Phone: 212-713-2848

The China Fund, Inc.
Listed: CHN, NYSE
405 Lexington Ave, New York, NY 10174
Phone: 212-808-0500

The Emerging Markets Income Fund
Listed: EMD, NYSE
153 East 53rd St., 50th Fl., New York, NY 10022
Phone: 1-800-726-6666

The First Israel Fund, Inc.
Listed: ISL, NYSE
One Citicorp Center, 58th Fl., 153 East 53rd St.,
New York, NY 10022
Phone: 212-832-2626

The Greater China Fund
Listed: GCH, NYSE
1285 Avenue of the Americas
New York, NY 10019
Phone: 212-713-2000

Hyperion 1997 Term Trust, Inc.
Listed: HTA, NYSE
Hyperion 2002 Term Trust, Inc.
Listed: HTB, NYSE
Hyperion Capital, 520 Madison Ave., 10th Fl.,
New York, NY 10022
Phone: 212-980-8400

Income Opportunities Fund 1999 Inc.
Listed: IOF, NYSE
Income Opportunities Fund 2000 Inc.
Listed: IFT, NYSE
PO Box 9011, Princeton, NJ 08543-9011
Phone: 609-282-2800

InterCapital Quality Municipal Income Trust
Listed: IQI, NYSE
Two World Trade Center, New York, NY 10048
Phone: 212-392-1600; 212-392-2500

Japan Equity Fund
Listed: JEQ, NYSE
c/o Daiwa Securities Trust Co.,
One Evertrust Plaza, Jersey City, NJ 07302
Phone: 800-933-3440

Jardine Fleming China Region Fund, Inc.
Listed: JFC, NYSE
100 East Pratt Street, Baltimore, MD 21202
Phone: 800-638-8540

Latin America Dollar Income Fund
Listed: LBF, NYSE
345 Park Avenue, New York, NY 10154
Phone: 617-330-5602; 800-225-5163 ext. 5602

(continued)
Managed Municipal Portfolio
Listed: MMU, NYSE
Managed Municipal Portfolio II
Listed: MTO, NYSE
Two World Trade Center, New York, NY 10048
Phone: 212-464-8068

Merrill Lynch & Co. S&P 500
Listed: MIT, NYSE
PO Box 9011, Princeton, NJ 08543-9011
Phone: 609-282-8837

MuniYield California Insured Fund, Inc.
Listed: MIC, NYSE
MuniYield California Insured Fund II, Inc.
Listed: MCA, NYSE
MuniYield Florida Insured Fund, Inc.
Listed: MFT, NYSE
MuniYield Insured Fund II
Listed: MTI, NYSE
MuniYield Michigan Insured Fund, Inc.
Listed: MIY, NYSE
MuniYield New Jersey Insured Fund, Inc.
Listed: MJI, NYSE
MuniYield New York Insured Fund II, Inc.
Listed: MYT, NYSE
MuniYield New York Insured Fund III, Inc.
Listed: MYY, NYSE
MuniYield Pennsylvania Fund, Inc.
Listed: MPA, NYSE
MuniYield Quality Fund, Inc.
Listed: MQY, NYSE
MuniYield Quality Fund II, Inc.
Listed: MQT, NYSE
800 Scudders Mill Road, Plainsboro, NJ 08536
Phone: 609-282-2800

Nuveen Arizona Premium Income Municipal Fund
Listed: NAZ, NYSE
Nuveen Insured California Premium Inc. Municipal Fund
Listed: NPC, NYSE
Nuveen Insured Florida Premium Fund
Listed: NFL, NYSE
Nuveen Insured New York Premium Fund
Listed: NNF, NYSE
Listed: NMP, NYSE

(continued)
Nuveen Insured Premium Municipal Fund
Listed: NPE, NYSE
Nuveen Michigan Premium Income Municipal Fund
Nuveen New Jersey Premium Income Fund
Listed: NNJ, NYSE
Nuveen Ohio Premium Income Fund
Listed: NOH, NYSE
Nuveen Pennsylvania Premium Income Fund
Listed: NPA, NYSE
Nuveen Premium Income Municipal Fund II
Listed: NPM, NYSE
Nuveen Premium Income Municipal Fund III
Listed: NPN, NYSE
Nuveen Select Maturities Municipal Fund
Listed: NIM, NYSE
Nuveen Select Maturities Municipal Fund II
Listed: NIR, NYSE
Nuveen Select Tax-Free Income Portfolio 3
Listed: NXR, NYSE
Nuveen Select Tax-Free Income Portfolio 4
Listed: NXS, NYSE
Nuveen Texas Premium Income Fund
Listed: NTE, NYSE
333 West Wacker Drive, Chicago, IL 60606
Phone: 800-351-4100; 800-526-0934

PaineWebber Premium Tax-Free Income Fund
Listed: PPM, NYSE
1285 Avenue of the Americas, New York, NY 10019
Phone: 212-713-2000 ext. 3678

Patriot Global Dividend Fund
Listed: PGD, NYSE
101 Huntington Avenue, Boston, MA 02199-7603
Phone:617-375-1808; 800-843-0090

Putnam California Investment Grade Municipal Trust
Listed: PCA, ASE
Putnam Investment Grade Municipal Trust II
Listed: PMG, NYSE
Putnam New York Investment Grade Municipal Trust
Listed: PMN, ASE
1 Putnam Pl., 859 Willard St., Quincy, MA 02269
Phone: 800-634-1587; 800-354-4000

(continued)
Smith Barney Municipal Fund
Listed: SBT, NYSE
1345 Avenue of the Americas, New York, NY 10155
Phone: 212-698-5349; 800-544-7835

TCW/DW Term Trust 2002
Listed: TRM, NYSE
2 World Trade Center, New York, NY 10048
Phone: 212-392-1600

Van Kampen Merritt Advantage Municipal Income Trust
Listed: VKA, NYSE
Van Kampen Merritt Advantage Pennsylvania Municipal Income Trust
Listed: VAP, NYSE
One Parkview Plaza, Oakbrook Terrace, IL 60181
Phone: 800-225-2222; 800-341-2929

Reorganizations and Other Updates
(these funds are still listed in Chapter 12 but some are no longer closed-end funds)

Niagara Share Corporation
has been acquired by Scudder Growth and Income Fund (an open-end fund) in a tax-free transaction.

Pacific-European Growth Fund, Inc.
converted from a closed-end fund to an open-end series fund of Piper Global Funds on August 31, 1992.

Tyler Cabot Mortgage Securities
has merged with Capstead Mortgage Corp. (CMO, NYSE). Tyler Cabot Mortgage Securities shareholders were issued $1.26 cumulative convertible preferred stock series B with a liquidation preference of $11.38 per share.

AMEV Securities, Inc.
Name has been changed to Fortis Securities, symbol: FOR, NYSE, Cusip #: 34955T100

Allstate Municipal Income Opportunities Trust
Name has been changed to Municipal Income Opportunities Trust, symbol: OIA, NYSE,Cusip #: 62621Q101

Allstate Municipal Income Opportunities Trust II
Name has been changed to Municipal Income Opportunities Trust II, symbol: OIB, NYSE, Cusip#: 62621R109

Allstate Municipal Income Opportunities Trust III
Name has been changed to Municipal Income Opportunities Trust III, symbol: OIC, NYSE, Cusip #: 62621T105

Allstate Municipal Income Trust
Name has been changed to Municipal Income Trust, symbol: TFA, NYSE, Cusip #: 626216105

Allstate Municipal Income Trust II
Name has been changed to Municipal Income Trust II, symbol: TFB, NYSE, Cusip #: 626217103

Allstate Municipal Income Trust III
Name has been changed to Municipal Income Trust III, symbol: TFC, NYSE, Cusip #: 62621P103

Allstate Municipal Premium Income Trust
Name has been changed to Municipal Premium Income Trust, symbol: PIA, NYSE, Cusip #: 625923107

12
Individual
Closed-End
Fund Coverage

Each closed-end fund covered in this section contains information organized in the format that follows and using the guidelines described.

Fund's name, address, phone number
stock exchange symbol, principal exchanges,
and commencement of fund operations

Category that best describes
the fund's portfolio or objectives

Fund's net asset value and share price
total return for 1990 and 1991
(see Chapter 11 for formulas and
total return for 1992)

Premium and Discount range
for period 1/1/91 to 6/30/92

FUND NAME

Address   **Category:**

Phone: **1991/mid-1992 Range of Premium/Disc:**
Listed: **1991/mid-1992 Range of Price:**
Commenced Operations: **NAV Total Return 1990:**   **1991:**
Cusip: **Share Price Total Return 1990:**   **1991:**
                      Herzfeld Ranking 1991:

Investment Objective:

      Officers:

Investment Advisor:
Advisory Fee:
Administrator:
Administration Fee:

Capital Structure: *Common stock:*
                     Debt:

Portfolio Highlights (as of   ):

Historical Financial Statistics (fiscal year-end:)

	1991	1990	1989	1988	1987	1986
Value of net assets (000)						
NAV						
Net investment income						
Dividends from net investment income						
Dividends from net realized gains						
Expense ratio						
Income ratio						
Portfolio turnover						

Special considerations:
Shareholders over 5%:

Share price range for
period 1/1/91 to 6/30/92

How the fund ranked for
the period 12/30/90 to
12/28/91 by category

Graph of share price and
NAV from 12/31/88
to 6/30/92

Financial data as of fiscal
year-end unless otherwise
indicated

Ratio of expenses to
average net assets; see
Chapter 11 for
complete description

Ratio of net investment income
to average net assets; see
Chapter 11 for complete
description

Any special conditions of the fund, automatic open-ending proposals,
anti-takeover provisions, important announcements by the fund, and
large shareholder positions (if applicable)

ACM Government Income Fund, Inc.

1345 Avenue of the Americas, New York, NY 10105   **Category**: Bond Fund

Phone: 212-969-1000; 800-247-4154	**1991/mid-1992 Range of Premium/Disc**: +14% to 0%
Listed: ACG, NYSE	**1991/mid-1992 Range of Price**: $11 3/4 to $10 1/8
Commenced Operations: August, 1987	**NAV Total Return 1990**: +7.32%; **1991**: +16.25%
Cusip: 000912105	**Share Price Total Return 1990**: +8.69%; **1991**: +19.00%
	Herzfeld Ranking 1991: 64th of 80 bond funds

Investment Objective: High current income consistent with preservation of capital principally through investment in U.S. government securities.

Officers:

D.H. Dievler   Chairman
W.D. Lyski   President

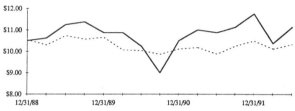

Investment Advisor: Alliance Capital Management L.P.

Advisory Fee: Monthly fee at annualized rate of 0.30% of the average weekly net assets up to $250 mil. and 0.25% of average weekly net assets in excess of $250 mil. plus 5.25% of the daily gross income accrued by the fund during the month. The fee shall not exceed in the aggregate 1/12th of 1% of the fund's average weekly net assets during the months. Annual fee approximately 1%. Fee for year-ended 12/31/91 was $4,654,851.

Administrator: Mitchell Hutchins Asset Management Inc.

Administration Fee: Annualized rate of 0.20% of the fund's average weekly net assets up to $100 mil., 0.18% of the fund's average weekly net assets on the next $200 mil., and 0.16% of the fund's average weekly net assets over $300 mil. Fee for year-ended 12/31/91 was $855,509.

Capital Structure: *Common stock*: 300 mil. shares authorized; 48,084,000 shares outstanding at 12/31/91
     Debt: Revolving credit agreement with Morgan Guaranty Trust Company of New York, $45 mil. outstanding 12/31/91; interest based on London Interbank Offered Rate.

Portfolio Highlights (as of 12/31/91): U.S. government and agency obligations 91.6%, debt obligations 16.9%, foreign securities 11.6%, preferred stocks 2.9%, call options purchased 0.5%, warrant 0.2%, repurchase agreement 1.1%, other assets less liabilities (24.8%). Largest sector concentrations: U.S. treasury securities 47.8%, federal agency securities 43.1%, mortgage-related securities 10.7%. **Largest issuers**: U.S. treasury bonds and notes; Student Loan Marketing Association; FNMA; Resolution Funding Corporation; French Government OATS.

Historical Financial Statistics (fiscal year-end: 12/31/91):

	1991	1990	1989	1988	8/28/87 to 12/31/87
Value of net assets (000)	509,206	483,006	504,070	493,456	517,536
NAV	10.59	10.15	10.66	10.55	11.23
Net investment income	1.18	1.23	1.21	1.25	0.40
Dividends from net investment income	1.25	1.32	1.24	1.23	0.39
Distributions from net realized gains and currency transactions	--	--	--	0.22	0.05
Expense ratio	1.93%	2.21%	1.79%	1.99%	1.63% ann.
Operating expense ratio	1.30%	1.37%	1.40%	1.32%	1.24% ann.
Income ratio	11.66%	12.16%	11.48%	11.40%	10.57% ann.
Portfolio turnover	516%	348%	310%	288%	103%

Special considerations: The board considers making a tender offer every quarter to reduce or eliminate discounts from net asset value; after January, 1992, if certain conditions are met, the fund may convert to an open-end fund with a 2/3 vote of outstanding shares. The fund has a staggered board of directors and its Articles of Incorporation contain various anti-takeover provisions. As of 12/31/91 the fund had a capital loss carryforward of approximately $23.5 mil. available through 1998.

ACM Government Opportunity Fund, Inc.

1345 Avenue of the Americas, New York, NY 10105

Category: Bond Fund

Phone: 212-969-1000; 800-247-4154
Listed: AOF, NYSE
Commenced Operations: August, 1988
Cusip: 000918102

1991/mid-1992 Range of Premium/Disc: +7% to -4%
1991/mid-1992 Range of Price: $10 3/8 to $8 3/4
NAV Total Return 1990: +7.08%; **1991**: +21.24%
Share Price Total Return 1990: +6.03%; **1991**: +21.98%
Herzfeld Ranking 1991: 37th of 80 bond funds

Investment Objective: High current income consistent with prudent investment risk, with a secondary objective of capital growth. The fund invests primarily in obligations issued or guaranteed by the U.S. government, its agencies or instrumentalities.

Officers:

D.H. Dievler   Chairman & President

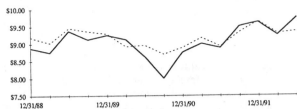

Investment Advisor: Alliance Capital Management L.P.
Advisory Fee: Monthly fee of 0.0625% of the average weekly net assets (about 0.75% annually). Fee for six months ended 1/31/92 was $415,126.
Administrator: The Boston Company Advisors, Inc.
Administration Fee: Monthly fee at annual rate of 0.25% of the average weekly net assets. Fee for six months ended 1/31/92 was $99,631.

Capital Structure: *Common stock*: 300 mil. shares authorized; 11,902,876 shares outstanding on 1/31/92

Portfolio Highlights (as of 1/31/92): U.S. government and agency obligations 92.6%, foreign securities 5.8%, common stocks 13.4%, convertible bonds 5.5%, preferred stocks 4.5%, convertible preferred stock 0.3%, commercial paper 4.9%, call options purchased 0.5%, other assets less liabilities (27.5%). **Largest issuers**: U.S. treasury bonds and notes; Resolution Funding Corporation zero coupon; Federal National Mortgage Association Stripped Mortgage-Backed Securities; Student Loan Marketing Association 16-94; Government of Spain 11.30-02.

Historical Financial Statistics (fiscal year-end: 7/31/91):

	six months 1/31/92	1991	1990	8/26/88 to 7/31/89
Value of net assets (000)	113,386	105,936	104,121	110,406
NAV	9.53	9.02	9.01	9.59
Net investment income	0.41	0.90	0.92	0.95
Dividends from net investment income	0.50	1.06	1.01	0.84
Distributions from net realized gains	0.04	--	0.03	0.11
Expense ratio	1.23% ann.	1.22%	1.24%	1.23% ann.
Income ratio	8.71% ann.	9.97%	10.08%	11.04% ann.
Portfolio turnover	326%	365%	287%	123%

Special considerations: The fund is permitted to use leverage. The board considers making a tender offer every quarter; after January, 1994, if certain conditions are met, the fund may convert to an open-end fund with a 2/3 vote of shareholders. The fund has a staggered board of directors and its Articles of Incorporation contain various anti-takeover provisions. The fund announced a dividend reduction to a monthly rate of $0.06625 beginning with the February, 1992, dividend.

ACM Government Securities Fund, Inc.

1345 Avenue of the Americas, New York, NY 10105

Category: Bond Fund

Phone: 212-969-1000; 800-247-4154
Listed: GSF, NYSE
Commenced Operations: January, 1988
Cusip: 000914101

1991/mid-1992 Range of Premium/Disc: +9% to -3%
1991/mid-1992 Range of Price: $11 5/8 to $9 3/8
NAV Total Return 1990: +5.61%; **1991:** +15.89%
Share Price Total Return 1990: +2.93%; **1991:** +18.85%
Herzfeld Ranking 1991: 66th of 80 bond funds

Investment Objective: High current income consistent with preservation of capital principally through investment in U.SA. government. The fund may invest up to 35% of assets in other fixed-income securities, including those issued by stable foreign governments and may utilize other investment techniques including options and futures.

Officers:

D.H. Dievler — Chairman
W.D. Lyski — President

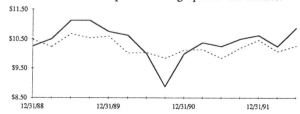

Investment Advisor: Alliance Capital Management L.P.

Advisory Fee: Monthly fee at annualized rate of 0.30% of the average weekly net assets up to $250 mil. and 0.25% of average weekly net assets in excess of $250 mil. plus 5.25% of the daily gross income accrued by the fund during the month. The fee shall not exceed in the aggregate 1/12th of 1% of the fund's average weekly net assets during the month. Annual fee is approximately 1%. Advisory fee of 1991 was $6,387,781.

Administrator: Mitchell Hutchins Asset Management, Inc.

Administration Fee: Annualized rate of 0.20% of the fund's average weekly net assets up to $100 mil., 0.18% of the fund's average weekly net assets on the next $200 mil., and 0.16% of the fund's average weekly net assets over $300 mil. Administrative fee for 1991 was $1,160,289.

Capital Structure: *Common stock*: 300 mil. shares authorized; 67,037,388 shares outstanding at 12/31/91. *Debt:* Revolving credit agreement with Morgan Guaranty Trust Company of New York, $55 mil. outstanding 12/31/91 of which $30 mil. will mature 2/18/92, and $25 mil. on 3/18/92. Interest based on London Interbank Offered Rate.

Portfolio Highlights (as of 12/31/91): U.S. government and agency obligations 89.5%, debt obligations 16.2%, foreign securities 12.9%, preferred stock 3.0%, warrants 0.3%, call option purchased 0.5%, repurchase agreement 1.5%, other assets less liabilities (23.9%). Foreign sector breakdown: France 8.7%, Australia 3.7%, Germany 0.1%, Canada 0.1%, Ireland 0.1%, Japan 0.1%, United Kingdom 0.1%. **Largest issuers:** U.S. treasury bonds and notes; Student Loan Marketing Association; Resolution Funding Corporation zero coupon; Mortgage Backed Securities Trust; Federal National Mortgage Association 17-92.

Historical Financial Statistics (fiscal year-end: 12/31/91):

	1991	1990	1989	1/28/88 to 12/31/88
Value of net assets (000)	707,043	673,218	698,563	681,895
NAV	10.55	10.16	10.60	10.48
Net investment income	1.17	1.22	1.20	1.12
Dividends from net investment income	1.26	1.28	1.26	1.10
Distributions from net realized gains and currency transactions	--	--	--	0.06
Expense ratio	1.83%	2.05%	1.65%	1.77% ann.
Operating expense ratio	1.28%	1.32%	1.27%	1.30% ann.
Income ratio	11.59%	12.09%	11.33%	11.24% ann.
Portfolio turnover	480%	360%	303%	267%

Special considerations: The fund is permitted to use leverage. The board considers making a tender offer every quarter to attempt to reduce or eliminate a market value discount from net asset value; after January, 1993, if certain conditions are met, the fund may convert to an open-end fund with a 2/3 vote of shareholders. The fund has a staggered board of directors and its Articles of Incorporation contain various anti-takeover provisions. As of 12/31/91 the fund had a capital loss carryforward of approximately $27.1 mil. available through 1998.

ACM Government Spectrum Fund, Inc.

1345 Avenue of the Americas, New York, NY 10105

Category: Bond Fund

Phone: 212-969-1000; 800-247-4154
Listed: SI, NYSE
Commenced Operations: May, 1988
Cusip: 000917104

1991/mid-1992 Range of Premium/Disc: +8% to -7%
1991/mid-1992 Range of Price: $9 1/2 to $8 1/4
NAV Total Return 1990: +7.77%; **1991:** +15.40%
Share Price Total Return 1990: +5.19%; **1991:** +17.81%
Herzfeld Ranking 1991: 68th of 80 bond funds

Investment Objective: High current income consistent with preservation of capital primarily through investment in obligations issued or guaranteed by the U.S. government, its agencies or instrumentalities (up to 35% may be invested in foreign government securities).

Officers:

D.H. Dievler	Chairman
W.D. Lyski	President

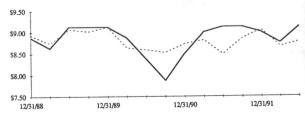

Investment Advisor: Alliance Capital Management L.P.
Advisory Fee: Monthly fee at annualized rate of 0.30% of the average weekly net assets up to $250 mil. and 0.25% of average weekly net assets in excess of $250 mil. plus 5.25% of the daily gross income accrued by the fund during the month. The fee shall not exceed in the aggregate 1/12th of 1% of the fund's average weekly net assets during the month. Annual fee approximately 1%. Fee for year-ended 12/31/91 was $2,607,017.
Administrator: Mitchell Hutchins Asset Management Inc.
Administration Fee: Annualized rate of 0.20% of the fund's average weekly net assets up to $100 mil., 0.18% of the fund's average weekly net assets on the next $200 mil., and 0.16% of the fund's average weekly net assets over $300 mil. Fee for year-ended 12/31/91 was $514,499.

Capital Structure: *Common stock:* 300 mil. shares authorized; 31,530,920 shares outstanding at 12/31/91

Portfolio Highlights (as of 12/31/91): U.S. government and agency obligations 107.4%, foreign securities 9.5%, call options purchased 0.5%, repurchase agreement 2.1%, other assets less liabilities (19.5%). **Largest issuers:** U.S. treasury notes and bonds; Federal National Mortgage Association 17-93; Resolution Funding Corporation zero coupons; French Government OATS; Student Loan Marketing Association 16-94; Commonwealth of Australia 10-02.

Historical Financial Statistics (fiscal year-end: 12/31/91):

	1991	1990	1989	5/27/88 to 12/31/88
Value of net assets (000)	**288,664**	274,333	285,378	277,758
NAV	**9.15**	8.76	9.13	8.93
Net investment income	**0.96**	1.04	0.97	0.56
Dividends from net investment income	**1.01**	1.10	0.97	0.55
Distributions from net realized gains	--	--	--	0.09
Expense ratio	**1.35%**	1.42%	1.34%	1.32% ann.
Income ratio	**11.05%**	12.01%	10.78%	10.29% ann.
Portfolio turnover	**442%**	419%	353%	171%

Special considerations: The fund is permitted to borrow funds or issue senior securities. The board considers repurchasing shares every quarter to attempt to reduce or eliminate a market value discount from net asset value; after January, 1993, if certain conditions are met, the fund may convert to an open-end fund with a 2/3 vote of outstanding shares. The fund has a staggered board of directors and its Articles of Incorporation contain various anti-takeover provisions.

ACM Managed Income Fund, Inc.

1345 Avenue of the Americas, New York, NY 10105

Category: Bond Fund

Phone: 212-969-1000; 800-247-4154
Listed: AMF, NYSE
Commenced Operations: October, 1988
Cusip: 000919100

1991/mid-1992 Range of Premium/Disc: +9% to -7%
1991/mid-1992 Range of Price: $9 5/8 to $7 1/2
NAV Total Return 1990: +0.20%; **1991:** +24.22%
Share Price Total Return 1990: +0.09%; **1991:** +29.72%
Herzfeld Ranking 1991: 25th of 80 bond funds

Investment Objective: High total return including current income and capital appreciation through active management of a portfolio of fixed-income securities, primarily U.S. government, its agencies or instrumentalities and corporate fixed-income securities, including high-yielding lower-rated or non-rated fixed-income securities.

Officers:
D.H. Dievler   Chairman & President

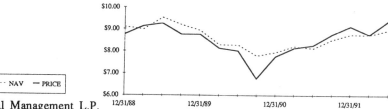

Investment Advisor: Alliance Capital Management L.P.
Advisory Fee: Monthly fee of 0.05416% of average weekly adjusted assets (approximately 0.65% annually). Fee for six months ended 2/29/92 was $840,709.
Administrator: Princeton Administrators, Inc.
Administration Fee: Monthly fee at annual rate of 0.20% of the fund's average weekly adjusted total assets. Fee for six months ended 2/29/92 was $258,680.

Capital Structure: *Common stock:* 299,998,100 shares authorized; 18,219,633 shares outstanding at 2/29/92
Remarketed Preferred Stock: 1,900 shares authorized, 950 shares outstanding 2/29/92; liquidation value $100,000. Dividend rate is set every 28 days by the remarketing agent.

Portfolio Highlights (as of 2/29/92): U.S. government and agency obligations 59.1%, corporate obligations 36.7%, Yankees 1.8%, preferred stocks 5.4%, warrants 0.4%, common stock 0.4%, repurchase agreement 4.9%, other (8.7%). Largest industry concentrations (corporate obligations): media 6.9%, container 6.1%, banking & finance 5.4%.
Largest Issuers: U.S. treasury bonds & notes; FNMA Stripped Mortgage Backed Securities; FNMA collateralized mortgage obligations; Owens-Illinois, Inc. 7.625-01; Tele-Communications Inc. 9.8-12.

Historical Financial Statistics (fiscal year-end: 8/31/91):

	six months 2/29/92	1991	1990	11/3/88 to 8/31/89
Value of net assets (000)	254,865	257,905	248,597	182,145
NAV	8.77	8.39	7.93	9.40
Net investment income	0.63	1.45	1.29	0.77
Dividends from net investment income	0.50	1.01	1.01	0.76
Common stock equivalent of dividends to remarketed preferred shares	0.13	0.36	0.30	--
Expense ratio	1.10% ann.	1.11%	1.09%	1.06% ann.
Income ratio	9.22% ann.	11.20%	10.68%	10.19% ann.
Portfolio turnover	346%	293%	310%	129%

Special considerations: The prospectus stated that during the fourth quarter of 1991, under certain circumstances, the fund will make a tender offer for all shares of the fund at net asset value. If the fund's Board of Directors does not repurchase shares pursuant to the tender offer, the fund will make additional tender offers. If shares are still outstanding on 7/31/92, the board must submit a proposal to open-end the fund. The fund did make such a tender offer in 1991, and ,472,417 shares were redeemed. Any time after 10/1/91, the fund may open-end with a majority vote of shareholders. The fund's Articles of Incorporation contain various anti-takeover provisions, including a staggered board of directors and ability of the board to reclassify any unissued shares.

ACM Managed Multi-Market Trust, Inc.

1345 Avenue of the Americas, New York, NY 10105

Category: Foreign Bond Fund

Phone: 212-969-1000; 800-247-4154
Commenced Operations: January, 1990
Listed: MMF, NYSE
Cusip: 000928101

1991/mid-1992 Range of Premium/Disc: +19% to -3%
1991/mid-1992 Range of Price: $12 7/8 to $10 5/8
NAV Total Return 1991: +10.92%
Share Price Total Return 1991: +16.98%
Herzfeld Ranking 1991: 6th of 8 foreign bond funds

Investment Objective: The highest level of current income, consistent with what the fund's investment advisor considers to be prudent investment risk, that is available from a portfolio of high-quality debt securities having remaining maturities of not more than 5 years.

Officers:

D.H. Dievler   Chairman & President

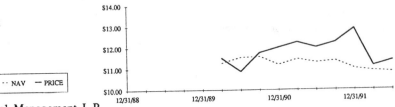

Investment Advisor: Alliance Capital Management L.P.
Advisory Fee: Monthly management fee at an annual rate of 0.65 of 1% of average weekly adjusted total assets. Fee for year-ended 11/30/91 was $916,037.
Administrator: Prudential Mutual Fund Management, Inc.
Administration Fee: Monthly fee at an annual rate of 0.20 of 1% of average weekly adjusted total assets up to $100 million, 0.18 of 1% of next $150 million, and 0.16 of 1% of average weekly adjusted total net assets over $250 million. Fee for year-ended 11/30/91 was $273,676.

Capital Structure: *Common stock*: 300 million shares authorized; 9,903,388 shares outstanding 12/31/91. *Debt*: Multi-currency credit agreement with Morgan Guaranty Trust Company of New York for a maximum credit availability of $30 mil. Loan outstanding 11/30/91, $28,750,000. Interest payment is based on the London Interbank Offered Rate.the revolving credit.

Portfolio Highlights (as of 11/30/91): Government/agency 47.5%, debt obligations 55.7%, certificate of deposit 5.3%, commercial paper 13.7%, treasury bills 0.7%, put option purchased 0.2%, outstanding call options written (0.1%). Quality ratings: AAA 43.4%, AA 44.4%, A1/P1 12.2%. Largest geographic concentrations: Canada 30.2%, United Kingdom 17.2%, Spain 12.8%, European Currency Units 11.1%, Denmark 10.0%, Australia 9.9%, Italy 9.3%, Sweden 8.2%. **Largest issuers:** Government of Spain 13.45-96; Halifax Building Society FRN zero coupon; Government of Canada; Swedish Export Credit 16.35-92; Kingdom of Denmark 9.6-94.

Historical Financial Statistics (fiscal year-end: 11/30/91):

	1991	1/26/90 to 11/30/90
Value of net assets (000)	111,133	113,252
NAV	11.22	11.53
Net investment income	1.33	1.24
Dividends from net investment income	1.34	1.18
Distributions from net realized gains	0.17	--
Expense ratio	3.37%	2.90% ann.
Operating expense ratio	1.51%	1.39% ann.
Income ratio	11.62%	12.90% ann.
Portfolio turnover	95%	101%

Special considerations: The fund may use hedging strategies including forward currency exchange contracts, options, futures contracts, options on futures contracts and options on foreign currencies. The Board of Directors will submit an open-ending proposal no later than 12/31/95. If an open-ending is not approved by shareholders, the fund will dissolve and net assets will be distributed to shareholders. The fund may repurchase shares or make tender offer, such actions will be considered on a quarterly basis by the board.

Adams Express Company

7 St. Paul Street, Suite 1140, Baltimore, MD 21202

Category: Equity Fund

Phone: 410-752-5900
Listed: ADX, NYSE, Pacific Stock Exchange
Commenced Operations: 1854
    (became a closed-end fund in 1929)
Cusip: 006212104

1991/mid-1992 Range of Premium/Disc: 0% to 15%
1991/mid-1992 Range of Price: $20 1/4 to $14 1/4
NAV Total Return 1990: +0.76%; **1991:** +31.13%
Share Price Total Return 1990: +5.41%; **1991:** +39.86%
Herzfeld Ranking 1991: 7th of 15 equity funds

Investment Objective: Preservation of capital, attainment of reasonable income and opportunity for capital appreciation.

Officers:

D.G. Ober   Chairman, Chief Executive Officer
J.M. Truta   President

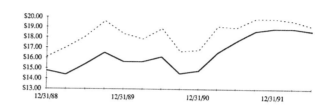

Investment Advisor: internally managed
Advisory Fee: Officers and directors' fees in 1991, $1,150,693.
Administrator: internally administered
Administration Fee: Administration and operations expense in 1991, $691,655.

Capital Structure: *Common stock:* 50 mil. shares authorized; 32,747,497 shares outstanding 12/31/91

Portfolio Highlights (as of 3/31/92): Stocks and convertible securities 96.0%, short-term investments 3.7%. Largest industries: consumer 35.9%, utilities 15.2%, producer goods 12.3%, financial 11.0%, energy 10.3%, basic industries 8.9%. **Largest positions:** Petroleum & Resources Corporation, Wal-Mart Stores Inc., International Flavors & Fragrances Inc., General Electric Co., American International Group Inc., Home Depot Inc. conv. sub. notes 6.0-97, Medco Containment Services Inc., Texaco Inc., Abbott Laboratories, Pall Corp.

Historical Financial Statistics (fiscal year-end: 12/31/91):

	1991	1990	1989	1988	1987	1986
Value of net assets (000)	661,896	529,483	550,091	455,825	427,225	468,344
NAV	20.21	16.82	18.35	16.11	15.92	19.51
Net investment income	0.53	0.63	0.70	0.54	0.57	0.61
Dividends from net investment income	0.54	0.66	0.70	0.50	0.78	0.71
Distributions from net realized gains	1.09	1.06	1.36	1.32	2.66	3.74
Expense ratio	0.58%	0.50%	0.51%	0.55%	0.48%	0.53%
Income ratio	2.74%	3.57%	3.87%	3.20%	2.68%	2.81%
Portfolio turnover	17.64%	24.71%	26.04%	18.00%	27.58%	34.52%

Special considerations: Another closed-end fund, Petroleum & Resources Corporation, is a non-controlled affiliate of Adams Express. Adams Express added 63,807 shares of Petroleum & Resources Corporation to its holding through the dividend reinvestment plan and holds 1,085,249 shares. The fund may purchase shares of its common stock from time to time at such prices and amounts as the Board of Directors may deem advisable. No purchases were made during the year-ended 12/31/91.

AIM Strategic Income Fund, Inc.

11 Greenway Plaza, Suite 1919, Houston, TX 77046

Category: Convertible Fund

Phone: 713-626-1919; 800-347-1919
Listed: AST, ASE
Commenced Operations: March, 1989
Cusip: 00142G103

1991/mid-1992 Range of Premium/Disc: 0% to -12%
1991/mid-1992 Range of Price: $9 1/4 to $7 1/2
NAV Total Return 1990: +5.92%; **1991:** +15.80%
Share Price Total Return 1990: -7.49%; **1991:** +16.81%
Herzfeld Ranking 1991: 8th of 8 convertible funds

Investment Objective: High current income consistent with stability of principal primarily by pursuing a strategy of investing in convertible securities and by employing short selling to enhance income and hedge against market risk.

Officers:

C.T. Bauer   President

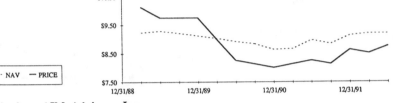

Investment Advisor and Administrator: AIM Advisors, Inc.
Advisory and Administration Fee: Monthly fee in an amount equal to an annualized rate of 0.80% of the fund's average weekly net assets. $52,476 of the fee was waived for the year-ended 12/31/90. Fee for 1991 was $484,295.

Capital Structure: *Common stock*: 200 million shares authorized; 6,895,842 shares outstanding 12/31/91.

Portfolio Highlights (as of 12/31/91): Convertible bonds and notes 81.69%, convertible preferred stocks 15.55%, short-term investments 4.61%, other assets less liabilities (1.87%), short sales (46.2%). Largest sector concentrations: retail 15.47%, capital goods 16.38%, consumer durables 8.40%, consumer services 8.03%. Largest holdings: Home Depot Inc., Alza Corp., Chiron Corp., Genzyme Corp., Petrie Stores Corp.

Historical Financial Statistics (fiscal year-end: 12/31/91):

	1991	1990	3/23/89 to 12/31/89
Value of net assets (000)	63,068	59,585	62,141
NAV	9.15	8.64	9.12
Net investment income	0.80	0.98	0.77
Dividends from net investment income	0.80	0.98	0.77
Distributions from net realized gains on investments	0.05	0.04	--
Operating expense ratio	1.17%	1.16%*	0.97%*
Income ratio	9.04%	10.96%*	10.86% ann.*
Portfolio turnover	89.40%	91.73%	161.82%

*after partial waiver of advisory and administrative fees.

Special considerations: In efforts to reduce discounts which may develop, the fund may repurchase shares in the open-market or make tender offers. Such actions will be considered by the board on a quarterly basis. Beginning 1/1/94 and in each fiscal year thereafter, if the shares have traded at an average discount from net asset value of greater than 10% and if the fund receives written requests from shareholders of 10% or more of the fund's common shares requesting it, the fund will submit a proposal to convert to an open-end fund unless the board determines such conversion would impair the ability of the fund to seek its investment objective. The fund's Articles of Incorporation and Bylaws contain various anti-takeover provisions including a 66 2/3% vote of shareholders for, among other things, merger with another corporation, issuance of any securities of the fund to any person or entity for cash, or sale of a substantial part of the assets of the fund. The monthly dividend was reduced to $0.05 per share beginning with the June, 1992, dividend.

Alliance Global Environment Fund, Inc.

1345 Avenue of the Americas, New York, NY 10105

Category: Foreign Equity Fund

Phone: 212-969-1000; 800-247-4154
Listed: AEF, NYSE
Commenced Operations: June, 1990
Cusip: 01859L103

1991/mid-1992 Range of Premium/Disc: -5% to -20%
1991/mid-1992 Range of Price: $13 3/8 to $9 7/8
NAV Total Return 1991: +6.03%
Share Price Total Return 1991: +9.81%
Herzfeld Ranking 1991: 28th of 46 specialized equity funds

Investment Objective: Long-term capital appreciation through investment primarily in equity securities of companies expected to benefit from advances or improvements in products, processes or services intended to foster the protection of the environment.

Officers:

D.H. Dievler   Chairman
G. Wellman   President

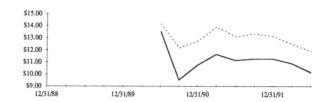

Investment Advisor: Alliance Capital Management L.P.
Advisory Fee: Monthly fee at annual rate of 1.10% of average weekly net assets up to $100 mil., 0.95% of next $100 mil., and 0.80% of any excess. Fee for year-ended 10/31/91 was $1,016,459.

Capital Structure: *Common stock:* 100 mil. shares authorized, 6,907,169 shares outstanding 10/31/91

Portfolio Highlights: (as of 10/31/91): Common stocks and other investments 82.6%, preferred stocks 1.7%, convertible bonds 0.3%, commercial paper 17.2%, currency call account 0.2%, other assets less liabilities (2.0%). Largest geographic concentrations: U.S. 52.0%, UK 19.5%, Germany 6.0%, France 5.6%, Japan 5.2%, Netherlands 4.6%. **Largest positions:** Wheelabrator Technologies Inc., Waste Management Inc., Betz Laboratories Inc., Ocean Group plc, Emcon Associates.

Historical Financial Statistics (fiscal year-end: 10/31/91):

	1991	6/1/90 to 10/31/90
Value of net assets (000)	90,612	86,041
NAV	13.12	12.46
Net investment income	0.13	0.20
Dividends from net investment income	0.25	--
Distributions from net realized gains	0.09	--
Expense ratio	1.49%	1.72% ann.
Income ratio	0.95%	3.59% ann.
Portfolio turnover	32%	4%

Special considerations: The fund may invest up to 25% of its total assets in securities which are not readily marketable. The fund may, under certain circumstances, repurchase its shares in the open market or private transactions. On a quarterly basis the fund will consider making tender offers for shares. The fund's Articles of Incorporation and By-Laws contain various anti-takeover provisions. At 10/31/91, the fund had a loss carryforward of $1,676,187 expiring through 1999.

Allied Capital Corporation

1666 K Street NW, Suite 901, Washington, DC 20006

Category: Miscellaneous

Phone: 202-331-1112
Listed: ALLC, OTC
Commenced Operations: 1958
Cusip: 019033109

1991/mid-1992 Range of Premium/Disc: N/A
1991/mid-1992 Range of Price: $20 to $13 3/4
NAV Total Return 1990: N/A; **1991:** N/A
Share Price Total Return 1990: N/A; **1991:** N/A
Herzfeld Ranking 1991: N/A

Investment Objective: The fund uses its own funds and money borrowed from the private sector for direct venture capital financing in exchange for equity positions. The fund also uses government-backed Small Business Investment Company (SBIC) funds to lend money to small companies with an option to buy stock.

Officers:

D. Gladstone   Chairman
G.C. Williams, III   President

Investment Advisor: Allied Capital Advisers, Inc.
Advisory Fee: 2 1/2% of assets. Fee for year-ended 12/31/91 was $2,717,000.
Administrator: Allied Capital Advisers, Inc.

Capital Structure: *Common stock:* 10 mil. shares authorized; 6,050,588 shares outstanding 3/20/92
Debt: $49,800,000 of subordinated debentures payable to the Small Business Administration at various interest rates. $2,761,000 reverse repurchase agreements.

Portfolio Highlights (as of 12/31/91): Diversification of loans and investments: radio stations 13%, pizza shops 9%, fast food restaurants 7%. **Largest holdings:** Environmental Air Control Inc. (MD); Broadcast Holdings, Inc. (DC); Visu-Com, Inc. (MD); Centennial Media Corp (CO); Montgomery Tank Lines (FL).

Historical Financial Statistics (fiscal year-end: 12/31/91):

	1991	1990	1989	1988	1987	1986
Value of net assets (000)	39,929	42,847	47,643	48,171	33,177	34,822
NAV	6.63	7.11	8.01	8.21	6.62	7.13
Net investment income	0.68	1.021	0.89	0.67	0.52	0.29
Dividends from ordinary income	0.66	1.02	0.95	0.63	0.50	0.34
Distributions from net realized gains	0.39	0.25	0.20	0.39	0.42	0.43
Distribution of stock of subsidiary	--	2.75	--	--	--	--

Special considerations: Most portfolio holdings are restricted securities. The fund retained a portion of the taxable net long-term capital gains in the amount of $0.135321 per share for the year-ended 12/31/90. Investors were able to take a credit on their 1990 tax returns equivalent to $0.046009 per share and increase their tax basis by $0.089312 per share.

Allied Capital Corporation II

1666 K Street NW, Suite 901, Washington, DC 20006

Category: Miscellaneous

Phone: 202-331-1112
Listed: ALII, OTC
Commenced Operations: 1989
Cusip: 019037100

1991/mid-1992 Range of Premium/Disc: N/A
1991/mid-1992 Range of Price: $24 1/2 to $14 1/2
NAV Total Return 1990: N/A; **1991:** N/A
Share Price Total Return 1990: N/A; **1991:** N/A
Herzfeld Ranking 1991: N/A

Investment Objective: The fund uses its own funds and money borrowed from the private sector for direct venture capital financing in exchange for equity positions. The fund also uses government-backed Small Business Investment Company (SBIC) funds to lend money to small companies with an option to buy stock.

Officers:

D. Gladstone   Chairman
W.F. Dunbar   President

Investment Advisor: Allied Capital Advisers, Inc.
Advisory Fee: The sum of 0.625% per quarter of each quarter-end value of consolidated invested assets and 0.125% per quarter of each quarter-end value of consolidated interim investments and cash. On an annual basis fee is equivalent to 2.5% on invested assets and 0.5% on interim investments and cash. Fee for year-ended 12/31/91 was $1,165,000.
Administrator: Allied Capital Advisers, Inc.

Capital Structure: *Common stock:* 10 mil. shares authorized; 6,791,708 shares outstanding 3/27/92
     Debt: $12,699,000 reverse repurchase agreements outstanding 12/31/91

Portfolio Highlights (as of 12/31/91): Largest positions: Williams Brothers Lumber Co. (GA); Montgomery Tank Lines (FL); Gateway Healthcare Corp. (VA); Arnold Moving Co (KY); Sunstates Refrigerated Services (GA).

Historical Financial Statistics (fiscal year-end: 12/31/91):

	1991	1990	10/11/89 to 12/31/89
Value of net assets (000)	90,387	92,443	91,376
NAV	13.45	13.76	13.91
Net investment income	0.98	1.10	0.173

Allstate Municipal Income Opportunities Trust

Two World Trade Ctr., 72nd Fl, New York, NY 10048 **Category: Municipal Bond Fund**

Phone: 212-392-2550
Listed: AMO, NYSE
Commenced Operations: September, 1988
Cusip: 019907104

1991/mid-1992 Range of Premium/Disc: +7% to -7%
NAV Total Return 1990: +7.01%; **1991**: +8.98%
1991/mid-1992 Range of Price: $10 to $8 5/8
Share Price Total Return 1990: -11.44%; **1991**: +12.91%
Herzfeld Ranking 1991: 46th of 51 municipal bond funds

Investment Objective: Optimum current income exempt from federal income tax primarily through investment in non-rated municipal obligations of medium quality.

Officers:

A.J. Melton, Jr.   Chairman
C.A. Fiumefreddo President & CEO

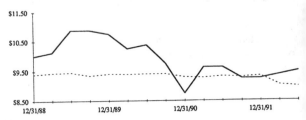

Investment Advisor: Allstate Investment Management Company
Advisory Fee: Monthly fee at annual rate of 0.60% of average weekly net assets. Fee for six months ended 11/30/91 was $605,038.
Administrator: Dean Witter Reynolds, Inc.
Administration Fee: Monthly fee at annual rate of 0.30% of average weekly net assets. Fee for six months ended 11/30/91 was $302,519.

Capital Structure: *Shares of Beneficial Interest* : unlimited number of shares authorized; 21,729,572 shares outstanding 11/30/91

Portfolio Highlights (as of 11/30/91): Municipal bonds 96.8%, short-term municipal obligations 0.5%. Largest industry concentrations: hospital revenue 32.1%, industrial development/pollution control revenue 20.7%, mortgage revenue/multifamily 15.7%, mortgage revenue/single family 13.7%. **Largest issuers**: Escambia County, Florida, Intermediate Care Facility/Mentally Retarded Revenue Bonds; Colorado Housing Finance Authority Single Family Mortgage Revenue Bonds Series B; Flagler County, Florida, Industrial Development Authority First Mortgage Revenue Bonds (RHA/South Florida Properties, Inc. Project) Series 1988 A 10.50-18; Broward County, Florida Industrial Development Revenue Refunding Bonds (Graphic Dynamics Inc. Project) Series 1989 A and B; Lexington County, South Carolina, Industrial Development Revenue Refunding Bonds (Ellett Brothers) 10.625-08.

Historical Financial Statistics (fiscal year-end: 5/31/91):				
	six months 11/30/91	1991	1990	9/19/88 to 5/31/89
Value of net assets (000)	201,748	202,418	199,173	194,698
NAV	9.28	9.39	9.44	9.56
Net investment income				
Dividends to shareholders	0.37	0.82	0.84	0.37
Expense ratio	1.06% ann.	1.10%	1.10%	1.11% ann.
Income ratio	7.99% ann.	8.37%	8.61%	7.03% ann.
Portfolio turnover	4%	7%	8%	9%

Special considerations: The trust may repurchase shares to attempt to reduce or eliminate discounts from net asset value, and trustees intend to consider making a tender offer for shares annually. The fund's Declaration of Trust contains various anti-takeover provisions.

Allstate Municipal Income Opportunities Trust II

Two World Trade Ctr., 72nd Fl, New York, NY 10048   **Category: Municipal Bond Fund**

Phone: 212-392-2550
Listed: AOT, NYSE
Commenced Operations: June, 1989
Cusip: 019911106

1991/mid-1992 Range of Premium/Disc: +9% to -8%
1991/mid-1992 Range of Price: $10 to $8 1/2
NAV Total Return 1990: +7.18%; **1991:** +9.78%
Share Price Total Return 1990: +0.47%; **1991:** +20.94%
Herzfeld Ranking 1991: 44th of 51 municipal bond funds

Investment Objective: High level of current income exempt from federal income tax, primarily through investment in a diversified portfolio of non-rated municipal obligations of medium quality which generally provide a higher current yield than municipal obligations of higher quality.

Officers:
A.J. Melton, Jr.   Chairman
C.A. Fiumefreddo   President & CEO

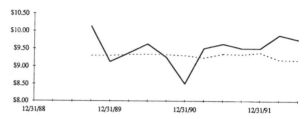

Investment Advisor: Allstate Investment Management Company
Advisory Fee: Monthly fee at annual rate of 0.60% of average weekly net assets. Fee for year-ended 2/29/92 was $1,168,241.
Administrator: Dean Witter Reynolds, Inc.
Administration Fee: Monthly fee at annual rate of 0.30% of average weekly net assets. Fee for year-ended 2/29/92 was $584,121.

Capital Structure: *Shares of Beneficial Interest:* unlimited number of shares authorized; 21,039,707 shares outstanding 2/29/92

Portfolio Highlights (as of 2/29/92): Municipal bonds 96.8%, short-term municipal obligations 1.1%, cash and other assets in excess of liabilities (2.1%). Largest industry concentrations: hospital revenue 28.5%, mortgage revenue/multi-family 18.4%, industrial development/pollution control revenue 15.3%, tax allocation 10.7%, transportation revenue 8.2%. **Largest issuers:** various Massachusetts Industrial Finance Agency; Michigan Strategic Fund Limited Obligation Revenue Bonds (Kasle Steel Corporation Project) Series 1989 (AMT); Village of Carol Stream, DuPage County, Illinois, Tax Increment Revenue Bonds (Carol Pointe Project), Series 1990A 9.5-10; various City of Eden Prairie, Minnesota, Multifamily Housing Revenue Refunding Bonds (Fountain Place Apartments Phase II) Series A 9.75-19; various Tarrant County, Texas, Health Facilities Development Corporation, Health Facilities Development Revenue Bonds (3927 Foundation Inc. Project) Series 1989; various Memphis, Tennessee, Center City Revenue Finance Corporation Multifamily Housing Revenue Refunding Bonds (Riverset Apartments Project Phase II)

Historical Financial Statistics (fiscal year-end: 2/29/92):

	1992	1991	6/30/89 to 2/28/90
Value of net assets (000)	194,251	190,386	189,980
NAV	9.23	9.28	9.34
Net investment income	0.73	0.75	0.39
Dividends to shareholders	0.78	0.74	0.34
Distributions to shareholders	--	0.01	--
Expense ratio	1.06%	1.06%	1.07% ann.
Income ratio	7.87%	7.99%	6.26% ann.
Portfolio turnover	5%	34%	0%

Special considerations: The trust may repurchase shares to attempt to reduce or eliminate discounts from net asset value, and trustees intend to consider making a tender offer for shares annually. The fund's Declaration of Trust contains various anti-takeover provisions. Dividend rate reduced to $0.06 per month in April, 1992.

Allstate Municipal Income Opportunities Trust II

Two World Trade Ctr., 72nd Fl, New York, NY 10048 **Category: Municipal Bond Fund**

Phone: 212-392-2550
Listed: AIO, NYSE
Commenced Operations: April, 1990
Cusip: 019915107

1991/mid-1992 Range of Premium/Disc: +4% to -10%
1991/mid-1992 Range of Price: $10 to $8 1/4
NAV Total Return 1991: +10.36%
Share Price Total Return 1991: +20.78%
Herzfeld Ranking 1991: 40th of 51 municipal bond funds

Investment Objective: High level of current income exempt from federal income tax, primarily through investment in a diversified portfolio of non-rated municipal obligations of medium quality which generally provide a higher current yield than municipal obligations of higher quality.

Officers:
A.J. Melton, Jr.   Chairman
C.A. Fiumefreddo   President & CEO

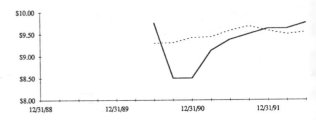

Investment Advisor: Allstate Investment Management Company
Advisory Fee: Monthly fee at annual rate of 0.60% of average weekly net assets. Fee for year-ended 3/31/92 was $661,230.
Administrator: Dean Witter Reynolds, Inc.
Administration Fee: Monthly fee at annual rate of 0.30% of average weekly net assets. Fee for year-ended 3/31/92 was $330,615.

Capital Structure: *Shares of Beneficial Interest* : unlimited number of shares authorized; 11,495,006 shares outstanding 3/31/92

Portfolio Highlights (as of 3/31/92): Municipal bonds 95.0%, short-term municipal obligations 2.5%, cash and other assets in excess of liabilities 2.5%. Largest industry concentrations: hospital revenue 32.7%, tax allocation 15.1%, mortgage revenue/multi-family 12.4%, mortgage revenue/single-family 11.2%, transportation facilities revenue 11.1%. **Largest issuers:** City and County of Denver, CO, Airport Systems Revenue Bonds; Massachusetts State Industrial Finance Agency Revenue; Main State Housing Authority, Mortgage Purchase Bonds 1990 Series A2 (AMT) 8.10-22; Washington State Housing Finance Commission, Multifamily Mortgage Revenue Refunding Bonds (FNMA Collateralized) Series 1990 A 7.5-23; Lely Community Development District, Florida, Special Assessment Bonds Series 1991 9.0-11.

Historical Financial Statistics (fiscal year-end: 3/31/92):

	1992	4/30/90 to 3/31/91
Value of net assets (000)	**109,326**	107,798
NAV	**9.51**	9.44
Net investment income	**0.73**	0.57
Dividends to shareholders	**0.72**	0.50
Distributions to shareholders	**0.06**	--
Expense ratio	**1.14%**	1.12% ann.
Income ratio	**7.61%**	6.72% ann.
Portfolio turnover	**11%**	10%

Special considerations: The trust may repurchase shares to attempt to reduce or eliminate discounts from net asset value, and trustees intend to consider making a tender offer for shares annually. The fund's Declaration of Trust contains various anti-takeover provisions.

Allstate Municipal Income Trust

Two World Trade Ctr., 72nd Fl, New York, NY 10048

Category: Municipal Bond Fund

Phone: 212-392-2550
Listed: ALM, NYSE
Commenced Operations: September, 1987
Cusip: 019904101

1991/mid-1992 Range of Premium/Disc: +4% to -4%
1991/mid-1992 Range of Price: $10 7/8 to $9 5/8
NAV Total Return 1990: +5.40%; **1991**: +11.32%
Share Price Total Return 1990: +0.87%; **1991**: +17.49%
Herzfeld Ranking 1991: 36th of 51 municipal bond funds

Investment Objective: Current income exempt from federal income tax principally through investment in a diversified portfolio of investment grade municipal obligations.

Officers:
C.A. Fiumefreddo   Chairman & CEO

Investment Advisor: Allstate Investment Management Company

Advisory Fee: Monthly fee at annual rate of 0.45% of average weekly net assets up to $250 mil., 0.35% on next $250 mil., 0.28% on next $250 mil., 0.22% on next $250 mil., 0.20% on excess. Fee for six months ended 2/29/92 was $727,343.

Administrator: Dean Witter Reynolds, Inc.

Administration Fee: Monthly fee at an annual rate of 0.20% of average weekly net assets up to $250 mil., 0.15% on next $250 mil., 0.12% on next $250 mil., 0.10% on excess. Fee for six months ended 2/29/92 was $320,599.

Capital Structure: *Shares of Beneficial Interest*: unlimited number of shares authorized; 33,153,050 shares outstanding 2/29/92

Portfolio Highlights (as of 2/29/92): Municipal bonds 97.9%, short-term municipal obligations 0.1%, cash and other assets in excess of liabilities 2.0%. Largest industry concentrations: hospital revenue 19.8%, industrial development/pollution control revenue 17.3%, electric revenue 10.8%, transportation facilities revenue 9.4%, educational facilities revenue 7.6%, mortgage revenue/single family 7.4%, water & sewer revenue 7.0%, general obligation 6.7%. **Largest issuers**: North Carolina Municipal Power Agency; City and County of Denver, Colorado, Airport System Revenue Bonds; Indiana Health Facilities Finance Authority (St. Anthony Hospital) 9.25-17; New York Energy Research & Development Authority Series 1987B Electric Facility Revenue (Consolidated Edison of New York) AMT 9.25-22; New York City, New York Series 1988 Group A. The fund maintained an average quality rating of "A", with an average maturity of approximately 25 years.

Historical Financial Statistics (fiscal year-end: 8/31/91):

	six month 2/29/92	1991	1990	1989	9/29/87 to 8/31/88
Value of net assets (000)	346,869	343,724	329,674	328,429	309,610
NAV	10.46	10.37	10.01	10.36	10.20
Net investment income	0.36	0.74	0.76	0.76	0.68
Dividends to shareholders	0.36	0.68	0.85	0.78	0.61
Distributions to shareholders	0.01	--	0.06	0.23	0.02
Expense ratio	0.72% ann.	0.75%	0.79%	0.76%	0.78% ann.
Income ratio	6.95% ann.	7.31%	7.38%	7.29%	7.42% ann.
Portfolio turnover	8%	5%	10%	18%	149%

Special considerations: Up to 35% of total assets may be invested in non-investment grade securities. The trust may repurchase shares to reduce or eliminate discounts which may develop. The trustees intend to annually consider making a tender offer for the fund's shares. The Declaration of Trust contains various anti-takeover provisions. As of 2/29/92 the fund had a capital loss carryforward of approximately $115,000 available through 1999. Dividend rate reduced to 0.06 per month.

Allstate Municipal Income Trust II

Two World Trade Ctr., 72nd Fl, New York, NY 10048

Category: Municipal Bond Fund

Phone: 212-392-2550
Listed: ALT, NYSE
Commenced Operations: June, 1988
Cusip: 019906106

1991/mid-1992 Range of Premium/Disc: +2% to -7%
1991/mid-1992 Range of Price: $10 5/8 to $9 1/8
NAV Total Return 1990: +5.91%; **1991:** +12.92%
Share Price Total Return 1990: +0.70%; **1991:** +14.18%
Herzfeld Ranking 1991: 26th of 51 municipal bond funds

Investment Objective: Current income exempt from federal income tax principally through investment in a diversified portfolio of investment grade municipal obligations.

Officers:

A.J. Melton, Jr.   Chairman
C.A. Fiumefreddo   President & CEO

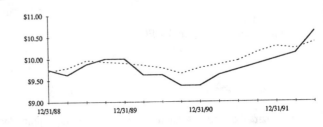

Investment Advisor: Allstate Investment Management Company
Advisory Fee: Monthly fee at annual rate of 0.50% of average weekly net assets up to $250 mil., 0.40% on next $250 mil., 0.333% on next $250 mil., 0.267% on excess. Fee for year-ended 12/31/91 was $1,401,832.
Administrator: Dean Witter Reynolds, Inc.
Administration Fee: Monthly fee at annual rate of 0.25% of average weekly net assets up to $250 mil., 0.20% on next $250 mil., 0.167% on next $250 mil., 0.133% on excess. Fee for year-ended 12/31/91 was $700,914.

Capital Structure: *Shares of Beneficial Interest:* unlimited number of shares authorized; 28,685,916 shares outstanding 12/31/91

Portfolio Highlights (as of 12/31/91): Municipal bonds 97.1%, short-term municipal obligations 2.7%, cash and other assets in excess of liabilities 0.2%. Largest sector concentrations: hospital revenue 20.3%, mortgage revenue/single family 11.4%, transportation facilities revenue 10.1%, resource recovery revenue 10.0%. As of 12/31/91 the fund maintained an average quality rating of "A" and an average maturity of approximately 25 years. **Largest issuers:** City of Tampa, FL, Capital Improvement Program Revenue Bonds; Boulder County, CO, Revenue Bonds Series 1988 (National Center for Atmospheric Research) 8.25-13; Lancaster County, PA, Solid Waste Management Authority Resource Recovery Systems (AMT) 8.5-10; County of Allegheny, PA, Airport revenue bonds; Indianapolis, IN, Local Public Improvement Bonds.

Historical Financial Statistics (fiscal year-end: 12/31/91):

	1991	1990	1989	6/1/88 to 12/31/88
Value of net assets (000)	296,554	280,344	285,124	274,062
NAV	10.34	9.79	9.90	9.71
Net investment income	0.71	0.77	0.71	0.36
Dividends to shareholders	0.67	0.73	0.73	0.37
Distributions to shareholders	0.03	0.02	0.07	0.01
Expense ratio	0.86%	0.88%	0.87%	0.86% ann.
Income ratio	7.05%	7.24%	7.20%	6.60% ann.
Portfolio turnover	15%	24%	35%	27%

Special considerations: Up to 35% of total assets may be invested in non-investment grade securities. The trust may repurchase shares to reduce or eliminate discounts which may develop. The trustees intend to annually consider making a tender offer for the fund's shares. The Declaration of Trust contains various anti-takeover provisions. Dividend rate reduced to $0.055 per month.

Allstate Municipal Income Trust III

Two World Trade Ctr., 72nd Fl, New York, NY 10048

Category: Municipal Bond Fund

Phone: 212-392-2550
Listed: ALL, NYSE
Commenced Operations: October, 1989
Cusip: 019912104

1991/mid-1992 Range of Premium/Disc: +4% to -6%
1991/mid-1992 Range of Price: $10 to $8 5/8
NAV Total Return 1990: +6.40%; **1991:** +12.68%
Share Price Total Return 1990: +4.58%; **1991:** +13.35%
Herzfeld Ranking 1991: 28th of 51 municipal bond funds

Investment Objective: Current income exempt from federal income tax principally through investment in a diversified portfolio of investment grade municipal obligations.

Officers:

A.J. Melton, Jr.   Chairman
C.A. Fiumefreddo   President & CEO

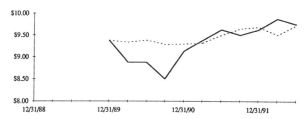

Investment Advisor: Allstate Investment Management Company

Advisory Fee: Monthly fee at annual rate of 0.50% of average weekly net assets up to $250 mil., 0.40% on next $250 mil., 0.333% on next $250 mil., 0.267% on excess. Fee for six months ended 2/29/92 was $158,260.

Administrator: Dean Witter Reynolds, Inc.

Administration Fee: Monthly fee at annual rate of 0.25% of average weekly net assets up to $250 mil., 0.20% on next $250 mil., 0.167% on next $250 mil., 0.133% on excess. Fee for six months ended 2/29/92 was $79,130.

Capital Structure: *Shares of Beneficial Interest*: unlimited number of shares authorized; 6,632,086 shares outstanding 2/29/92

Portfolio Highlights (as of 2/29/92): Municipal bonds 93.2%, short-term municipal obligations 5.2%, cash and other assets in excess of liabilities 1.6%. Largest industry concentrations: hospital revenue 25.5%, mortgage revenue/single family 22.3%, transportation revenue 18.1%, electric revenue 7.0%. **Largest issuers:** Saint Tammany, Louisiana, Public Trust Financing Authority Residual Revenue Convertible Capital Appreciation Refunding Bonds Series 1990B 7.25-11; Washington Public Power Supply System Nuclear Project #2 Revenue Refunding Series C 7.625-10; Alliance Airport Authority Inc., Texas Special Facilities Revenue Bonds Series 1990 (American Airlines Inc. Project (AMT) 7.5-29; Florence County, South Carolina, Law Enforcement and Civic Center Certificates of Participation 7.60-14; Idaho Housing Agency Single Family Mortgage Revenue Bonds Series D2 (AMT) 8.25-20.

Historical Financial Statistics (fiscal year-end: 8/31/91):

	six months 2/29/92	1991	10/5/89 to 8/31/90
Value of net assets (000)	63,086	63,565	62,147
NAV	9.51	9.60	9.32
Net investment income	0.31	0.68	0.57
Dividends to shareholders	0.33	0.66	0.55
Distributions to shareholders	0.06	0.04	--
Expense ratio	1.00% ann.	1.02%	1.10% ann.
Income ratio	6.33% ann.	7.20%	6.76% ann.
Portfolio turnover	5%	40%	150%

Special considerations: The trust may repurchase shares to reduce or eliminate discounts which may develop. The trustees intend to consider making a tender offer for the fund's shares annually. The Declaration of Trust contains various anti-takeover provisions. Dividend rate reduced to $0.05 per month in April, 1992.

Allstate Municipal Premium Income Trust

Two World Trade Ctr., 72nd Fl, New York, NY 10048   **Category: Municipal Bond Fund**

Phone: 212-392-2550	**1991/mid-1992 Range of Premium/Disc**: +4% to -4%
Listed: ALI, NYSE	**1991/mid-1992 Range of Price**: $10 5/8 to $8 3/4
Commenced Operations: February, 1989	**NAV Total Return 1990**: +5.38%; **1991**: +16.16%
Cusip: 019909100	**Share Price Total Return 1990**: +3.45%; **1991**: +18.12%
	Herzfeld Ranking 1991: 4th of 51 municipal bond funds

Investment Objective: Maximum current income exempt from federal income tax through investment in a diversified portfolio of investment-grade municipal obligations.

Officers:

A.J. Melton, Jr.   Chairman
C.A. Fiumefreddo   President & CEO

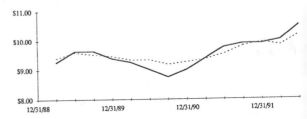

Investment Advisor: Allstate Investment Management Company

Advisory Fee: Monthly fee at annual rate of 0.50% of average weekly net assets. Fee for six months ended 11/30/91 was $941,920.

Administrator: Dean Witter Reynolds, Inc.

Administration Fee: Monthly fee at annual rate of 0.25% of average weekly net assets. Fee for six months ended 11/30/91 was $470,960.

Capital Structure: *Shares of Beneficial Interest*: unlimited number of shares authorized; 26,149,919 shares outstanding 2/29/92

Auction Rate preferred stock: 1 mil. shares authorized; 1,250 shares outstanding 2/29/92 in five series for total proceed of $125 mil., liquidation value $100,000 plus accumulated but unpaid dividends. Dividend rate is set every 28 days through auction. Rate ranged from 3.65% to 4.95% for six months ended 11/30/91

Portfolio Highlights (as of 11/30/91): Municipal bonds 96.0%, short-term municipal obligations 1.4%, cash and other assets in excess of liabilities 2.6%. Largest industry concentrations: hospital revenue 23.9%, mortgage revenue/single family 18.0%, industrial development/pollution control revenue 11.1%, general obligation 8.8%, mortgage revenue/multi-family 8.1%, electric revenue 6.5%. **Largest issuers**: City and County of Denver Colorado, Airport System Revenue Bonds; City of Minneapolis, Minnesota, Health Care Series; Industrial Development Authority of Pima County, Arizona Series 1988A (Tucson Electric & Power) 7.25-10; New York City general obligations; Alliance Airport Authority of Texas, Special Facilities Revenue Bonds Series 1990 (American Airlines Project) AMT 7.5-29.

Historical Financial Statistics (fiscal year-end: 5/31/91):

	six months 11/30/91	1991	1990	2/1/89 to 5/31/89
Value of net assets (000)	380,657	373,207	368,065	249,581
NAV	9.78	9.61	9.35	9.59
Net investment income	0.48	0.96	0.71	0.21
Dividends to shareholders	0.36	0.70	0.69	0.15
Distributions to common shareholders	--	0.07	0.11	--
Expense ratio	1.44% ann.	1.59%	1.02%	0.96% ann.
Income ratio (avail. to common shareholders)	7.75% ann.	7.32%	6.93%	7.18% ann.
Portfolio turnover	12%	56%	150%	106%

Special considerations: The trust may repurchase shares to reduce or eliminate discounts which may develop. The trustees intend to annually consider making a tender offer for the fund's shares. The Declaration of Trust contains various anti-takeover provisions. Dividend rate reduced to $0.0625 per month in April, 1992.

American Adjustable Rate Term Trust Inc.--1995

222 South Ninth St., Minneapolis, MN 55402

Category: Bond Fund

Phone: 612-342-6387; 800-333-6000 ext. 6384
Listed: ADJ, NYSE
Commenced Operations: March, 1990
Cusip: 02368L105

1991/mid-1992 Range of Premium/Disc: +10% to +1%
1991/mid-1992 Range of Price: $10 7/8 to $10
NAV Total Return 1991: +12.89%
Share Price Total Return 1991: +12.28%
Herzfeld Ranking 1991: 76th of 80 bond funds

Investment Objective: High level of current income and return of $10 per share to investors on 4/15/95. The trust will invest primarily in mortgage-backed securities having adjustable interest rates which reset at periodic intervals (ARMS).

Officers

E.J. Kohler   Chairman
B.S. Rinkey   President

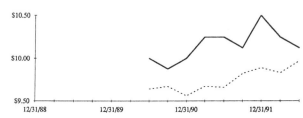

Investment Advisor: Piper Capital Management Incorporated
Advisory Fee: Monthly fee at the annual rate of 0.35% of average weekly net assets. Fee for six months ended 2/29/92 was $190,950.
Administrator: Piper Capital Management Incorporated
Administration Fee: Monthly fee at the annual rate of 0.15% of average weekly net assets. Fee for six months ended 2/29/92 was $81,836.

Capital Structure: *Shares of beneficial interest:* 1 bil. shares authorized; 11,110,000 shares outstanding 2/29/92
    Debt: Reverse repurchase agreements payable as of 2/29/92, $33.9 mil.

Portfolio Highlights (as of 2/29/92): U.S. government agency/adjustable rate mortgage-backed 36.6%, other AA-rated adjustable rate mortgage-backed 30.9%, U.S. government/agency 16.4%, tax-exempt zero-coupon bonds 8%, U.S. government agency collateralized mortgage-backed 3.8%, Canadian 1.4%, other 0.3%, short-term 2.6%. **Largest issuers:** FNMA; FHLMC; Resolution Trust Corporation ARM; Dime Savings ARM 8.74-18; Prudential Home Mortgage ARM 8.28-21.

Historical Financial Statistics (fiscal year-end: 8/31/91):

	six months 2/29/92	1991	3/29/90 to 8/31/90
Value of net assets (000)	109,855	108,438	107,414
NAV	9.89	9.76	9.67
Net investment income	0.46	0.90	0.36
Distributions from net investment income	0.39	0.88	0.31
Distributions from net realized gains	0.02	0.01	--
Expense ratio	2.67% ann.	3.29%	1.96% ann.
Operating expense ratio	0.66% ann.	0.73%	0.61% ann.
Income ratio	9.37% ann.	9.45%	9.00% ann.
Portfolio turnover	22%	66%	33%

Special considerations: S&P Rating: AA$_f$. The fund purchased 880 four-year U.S. treasury note put option contracts in the fiscal year 1990 for $480,200. The trust will be entitled to a cash payment during this exercise period of 3/15/95 to 4/15/95, if at such time yields on four-year U.S. treasury notes are in excess of the 11.25% yield specified in the option contracts. The fund pays monthly distributions from net investment income and annual distributions of realized capital gains. The fund's Articles of Incorporation contain various anti-takeover provisions. Dividend rate reduced to $0.0605 per month in May, 1992. **Shareholders over 5%:** Bongards Creameries, 6.08%

American Adjustable Rate Term Trust Inc.--1996

222 South Ninth St., Minneapolis, MN 55402

Category: Bond Fund

Phone: 612-342-6387; 800-333-6000 ext. 6384
Listed: BDJ, NYSE
Commenced Operations: September, 1990
Cusip: 02368M103

1991/mid-1992 Range of Premium/Disc: +9%to +1%
1991/mid-1992 Range of Price: $10 5/8 to $9 7/8
NAV Total Return 1991: +11.18%
Share Price Total Return 1991: +11.44%
Herzfeld Ranking 1991: 80th of 80 bond funds

Investment Objective: High level of current income and return of $10 per share to investors on 3/31/96. The trust will invest primarily in mortgage-backed securities having adjustable interest rates which reset at periodic intervals (ARMS).

Officers:
E.J. Kohler   Chairman
B.S. Rinkey   President

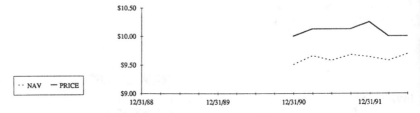

Investment Advisor: Piper Capital Management Incorporated
Advisory Fee: Monthly fee at the annual rate of 0.35% of average weekly net assets. Fee for six months ended 2/29/92 was $453,148.
Administrator: Piper Capital Management Incorporated
Administration Fee: Monthly fee at the annual rate of 0.15% of average weekly net assets. Fee for six months ended 2/29/92 was $194,206.

Capital Structure: *Shares of beneficial interest*: 1 bil. shares authorized; 26,930,000 shares outstanding 2/29/92
    Debt: Reverse repurchase agreements payable as of 2/29/92, $75.8 mil.

Portfolio Highlights (as of 2/29/92): U.S. government agency/adjustable rate mortgage-backed 43.2%, other AA-rated adjustable rate mortgage-backed 28.8%, U.S. government/agency 13.0%, tax-exempt zero-coupon bonds 8.5%, U.S. government agency collateralized mortgage-backed 4.2%, Canadian 1.1%, other 0.2%, short-term 1.0%. **Largest issuers:** FNMA; FHLMC; GNMA; Resolution Trust Corporation ARM; Ryland-First Nationwide ARM 8.03-18.

Historical Financial Statistics (fiscal year-end: 8/31/91):

	six months 2/29/92	9/27/90 to 8/31/91
Value of net assets (000)	259,317	259,506
NAV	9.63	9.64
Net investment income	0.41	0.83
Dividends from net investment income	0.41	0.77
Expense ratio	2.04% ann.	2.47% ann.
Operating expense ratio	0.62% ann.	0.64% ann.
Income ratio	8.47% ann.	9.09% ann.
Portfolio turnover	15%	60%

Special considerations: S&P Rating: AA$_f$. The fund purchased 870 four-year U.S. treasury note put option contracts for $748,800. The trust will be entitled to a cash payment during this exercise period of 3/1/96 to 3/31/96, if at such time yields on four-year U.S. treasury notes are in excess of the 11.25% yield specified in the option contracts. The fund pays monthly distributions from net investment income and annual distributions of realized capital gains. The fund's Articles of Incorporation contain various anti-takeover provisions. Dividend rate reduced to $0.0605 in May, 1992.

American Adjustable Rate Term Trust Inc.--1997

222 South Ninth St., Minneapolis, MN 55402

Category: Bond Fund

Phone: 612-342-6387; 800-333-6000 ext. 6384
Listed: CDJ, NYSE
Commenced Operations: July, 1991
Cusip: 02368N101

1991/mid-1992 Range of Premium/Disc: +7% to +2%
1991/mid-1992 Range of Price: $10 1/2 to $9 3/4
NAV Total Return 1991: N/A
Share Price Total Return 1991: N/A
Herzfeld Ranking 1991: N/A

Investment Objective: High level of current income and return of $10 per share to investors on 3/31/97. The trust will invest primarily in mortgage-backed securities having adjustable interest rates which reset at periodic intervals (ARMS).

Officers

E.J. Kohler — Chairman
J.B. Griffin — President

Investment Advisor: Piper Capital Management Incorporated
Advisory Fee: Monthly fee at the annual rate of 0.35% of average weekly net assets. Fee for six months ended 2/29/92 was $702,631.
Administrator: Piper Capital Management Incorporated
Administration Fee: Monthly fee at the annual rate of 0.15% of average weekly net assets. Fee for six months ended 2/29/92 was $301,128.

Capital Structure: *Shares of beneficial interest:* 1 bil. shares authorized; 50,540,612 shares outstanding 2/29/92
Debt: Reverse repurchase agreements payable as of 2/29/92, $144.9 mil.

Portfolio Highlights (as of 2/29/92): U.S. government agency/adjustable rate mortgage-backed 36.5%, other AA-rated adjustable rate mortgage-backed 32.1%, U.S. government/agency 17.2%, tax-exempt zero-coupon bonds 8.4%, U.S. government agency collateralized mortgage-backed 2.5%, Canadian 1.8%, short-term 1.5%. **Largest issuers:** FNMA; FHLMC; Resolution Trust Corporation ARM; Glendale Federal Savings ARM 7.36-29; GNMA.

Historical Financial Statistics (fiscal year-end: 8/31/91):

	six months 2/29/92	7/24/91 to 8/31/91
Value of net assets (000)	485,325	211,731
NAV	9.60	9.68
Net investment income	0.39	0.07
Dividends from net investment income	0.42	--
Distributions from net realized gains	0.03	--
Expense ratio	1.89% ann.	0.83% ann.
Operating expense ratio	0.59% ann.	0.60% ann.
Income ratio	7.95% ann.	7.88% ann.
Portfolio turnover	25%	10%

Special considerations: S&P Rating: AAf. The Board of Directors will at least annually consider making a tender offer at net asset value if shares are trading at a discount. They will also consider repurchases of shares in the open market. Hedging transactions may be used to protect against possible declines in market value resulting from downward trends in the debt securities markets. The fund pays monthly distributions from net investment income and annual distributions of realized capital gains. The fund's Articles of Incorporation contain various anti-takeover provisions. Dividend rate reduced to $0.062 per month in May, 1992.

American Adjustable Rate Term Trust Inc.--1998

222 South Ninth St., Minneapolis, MN 55402

Category: Bond Fund

Phone: 612-342-6387; 800-333-6000 ext. 6384	**1991/mid-1992 Range of Premium/Disc:**+8% to +2%
Listed: DDJ, NYSE	**1991/mid-1992 Range of Price:** $10 3/8 to $9 3/4
Commenced Operations: January, 1992	**NAV Total Return 1991:** N/A
Cusip: 02368P106	**Share Price Total Return 1991:** N/A
	Herzfeld Ranking 1991: N/A

Investment Objective: High level of current income and return of $10 per share to investors on 3/31/98. The trust will invest primarily in mortgage-backed securities having adjustable interest rates which reset at periodic intervals (ARMS).

Officers:

E.J. Kohler	Chairman
B.S. Rinkey	President

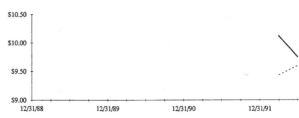

Investment Advisor: Piper Capital Management Incorporated

Advisory Fee: Monthly fee at the annual rate of 0.35% of average weekly net assets. Fee for period 1/30/92 to 2/29/92 was $98,323.

Administrator: Piper Capital Management Incorporated

Administration Fee: Monthly fee at the annual rate of 0.15% of average weekly net assets. Fee for period 1/30/92 to 2/29/92 was $41,139.

Capital Structure: *Shares of beneficial interest*: 1 bil. shares authorized; 38,910,000 shares outstanding 2/29/92
Debt: Reverse repurchase agreements payable as of 2/29/92, $100 mil.

Portfolio Highlights (as of 2/29/92): U.S. government agency/adjustable rate mortgage-backed 35.4%, other AA-rated adjustable rate mortgage-backed 31.3%, U.S. government/agency 12.7%, tax-exempt zero-coupon bonds 6.3%, U.S. government agency collateralized mortgage-backed 2.2%, Canadian 0.7%, short-term 1.4%. **Largest issuers:** FNMA; FHLMC; U.S. treasury notes; Ryland ARM; GNMA.

Historical Financial Statistics (fiscal year-end: 8/31/91):

	1/30/92 to 2/29/92
Value of net assets (000)	372,086
NAV	9.56
Net investment income	0.05
Dividends from net investment income	--
Distributions from net realized gains	--
Expense ratio	0.69% ann.
Operating expense ratio	0.57% ann.
Income ratio	7.60% ann.
Portfolio turnover	22%

Special considerations: S&P Rating: AA$_f$. The Board of Directors will at least annually consider making a tender offer at net asset value if shares are trading at a discount. They will also consider repurchases of shares in the open market. Hedging transactions may be used to protect against possible declines in market value resulting from downward trends in the debt securities markets. The fund pays monthly distributions from net investment income and annual distributions of realized capital gains. The fund's Articles of Incorporation contain various anti-takeover provisions.

American Capital Bond Fund, Inc.

2800 Post Oak Blvd., Houston, TX 77056

Category: Bond Fund

Phone: 713-993-0500
Listed: ACB, NYSE
Commenced Operations: 1970
Cusip: 024902108

1991/mid-1992 Range of Premium/Disc: +2% to -11%
1991/mid-1992 Range of Price: $20 1/8 to $16 5/8
NAV Total Return 1990: +6.13%; **1991:** +15.35%
Share Price Total Return 1990: +5.29%; **1991:** +31.34%
Herzfeld Ranking 1991: 69th of 80 bond funds

Investment Objective: Primary objective of income, with secondary objective of stability of principal, primarily through investment in investment grade corporate bonds.

Officers:
D.G. Powell   Chairman & President

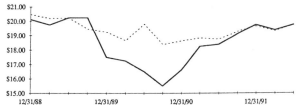

Investment Advisor: American Capital Asset Management, Inc.
Advisory Fee: Monthly fee at annual rate of 0.50% of average weekly net assets on first $150 mil., 0.45% on next $100 mil., 0.40% on next $100 mil., and 0.35% on amounts over $350 mil. Fee for six months ended 12/31/91 was $512,431.
Shareholder Service Agent: Boston Financial Data Services, Inc.
Shareholder Service Fee: Fee for 1991, $159,788

Capital Structure: *Common stock:* 15 mil. shares authorized; 10,970,124 shares outstanding 12/31/91
Convertible Extendible Notes: $26.2 mil. of 8.5% Five Year Convertible Extendible notes due 1/1/95, convertible at $19.20 per share.

Portfolio Highlights (as of 12/31/91): Corporate bonds and notes 99.32%, government agencies and obligations 8.19%, preferred stock 2.02%, repurchase agreement 1.14%, other assets and liabilities 1.33%. Largest industry concentrations: utilities 42.0%, energy 17.5%, producer/manufacturing 13.2%, financial 11.4%, government agencies & obligations 7.4%, consumer products & services 4.3%, misc./short-term 4.2%. Quality ratings: government/repurchase agreement 6.68%, AAA 5.02%, A 21.02%, A 63.73%, B and lower 1.73%, preferred stock 1.82%. **Largest issuers:** Cincinnati Gas & Electric Co. 1st mtg.; Phillips Petroleum Co. deb 11 1/4-13; Occidental Petroleum Corp.; Government National Mortgage Association; John Deere Credit Corp. sub. notes 9 5/8-98.

Historical Financial Statistics (fiscal year-end: 6/30/91):						
	six months 12/31/91	1991	1990	1989	1988	1987
Value of net assets (000)	218,187	204,408	204,862	220,80	232,040	231,300
NAV	19.89	18.68	18.72	20.34	21.49	21.87
Net investment income	0.82	1.76	2.07	1.90	1.95	1.94
Dividends from net investment income	0.84	1.77	2.075	2.20	2.20	2.20
Operating expense ratio	0.36%	0.72%	0.71%	0.71%	0.70%	0.71%
Convertible note expense ratio	0.53%	1.09%	1.55%	1.90%	1.95%	2.11%
Income ratio	4.26%	9.42%	10.65%	9.03%	9.22%	8.63%
Portfolio turnover	22%	18%	14%	13%	41%	41%

Special considerations: As of 6/30/91 the fund had an accumulated capital loss carryforward of approximately $42.4 mil. available through 1999.

American Capital Convertible Securities, Inc.

2800 Post Oak Blvd., Houston, TX 77056   **Category:ConvertibleFund**

Phone: 713-993-0500
Listed: ACS, NYSE
Commenced Operations: 1972
Cusip: 024905101

1991/mid-1992 Range of Premium/Disc:-6% to -15%
1991/mid-1992 Range of Price: $20 1/4 to$16 1/4
NAV Total Return 1990: -8.08%; **1991:** +22.37%
Share Price Total Return 1990: -11.59%; **1991:** +27.08%
Herzfeld Ranking 1991: 7th of 8 convertible funds

Investment Objective: Growth and income primarily through investment in convertible bonds, convertible preferred stocks and common stocks.

Officers:

D.G. Powell   Chairman & President

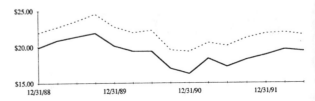

Investment Advisor: American Capital Asset Management, Inc.
Advisory Fee: Monthly fee at annual rate of 0.50% of average weekly net assets on first $150 mil., 0.45% on next $100 mil., 0.40% on next $100 mil., and 0.35% on amounts over $350 mil. Fee for 1991 was $333,652.
Shareholder Service Agent: Boston Financial Data Services, Inc.
Shareholder Service Fee: Fee for 1991, $54,122.

Capital Structure: *Common stock*: 12.5 mil. shares authorized; 3,242,000 shares outstanding 12/31/91

Portfolio Highlights (as of 12/31/91): Convertible corporate bonds 50.6%, non-convertible corporate bonds 15.0%, common stock 13.9%, convertible preferred stock 12.2%, U.S. treasury notes 2.3%, short-term investments & other assets & liabilities 6.0%. Largest industry concentrations: drugs 8.88%, foods 6.83%, tobacco 4.72%, utilities/telephone and telegraph 4.68%, banks 4.61%, office and business equipment 4.07%. **Largest issuers:** Texas Utilities Electric Co. 9 3/4-21; A.L. Laboratories Inc. sub. deb. 7 3/4-14; ConAgra Inc. sub. deb. 9 3/4-21; U.S. treasury notes 8-97; Caterpillar Inc. deb. 9 3/8-21.

Historical Financial Statistics (fiscal year-end: 12/31/91):

	1991	1990	1989	1988	1987	1986
Value of net assets (000)	**72,079**	62,938	73,696	70,332	65,593	81,990
NAV	**22.23**	19.41	22.73	21.94	21.46	27.34
Net investment income	**1.32**	1.47	1.51	1.44	1.35	1.60
Dividends from net investment income	**1.40**	1.40	1.57	1.47	2.13	1.80
Distributions from net realized gains	**--**	0.1425	0.745	1.3325	3.81	4.02
Expense ratio	**0.89%**	0.86%	0.84%	0.82%	0.76%	0.77%
Income ratio	**6.41%**	7.01%	6.47%	6.30%	4.72%	5.38%
Portfolio turnover	**168%**	95%	90%	69%	77%	84%

Special considerations: In April, 1973, the Board authorized the repurchase of up to 200,000 shares as it may be deemed advisable from time to time by the fund's officers. The fund did not repurchase any shares during 1991. As of 12/31/91 the fund had a capital loss carryforward of approximately $6.8 mil. available through 1999.

American Capital Income Trust

2800 Post Oak Blvd., Houston, TX 77056

Category: Bond Fund

Phone: 713-993-0500	**1991/mid-1992 Range of Premium/Disc:** +4% to -17%
Listed: ACD, NYSE	**1991/mid-1992 Range of Price:** $8 3/8 to $5 1/2
Commenced Operations: April, 1988	**NAV Total Return 1990:** -3.64%; **1991:** +30.23%
Cusip: 024915100	**Share Price Total Return 1990:** -12.04%; **1991:** +47.64%
	Herzfeld Ranking 1991: 18th of 80 bond funds

Investment Objective: High current income consistent with preservation of capital, primarily through investment in U.S. government securities and corporate fixed income securities, including high-yielding, lower-rated or nonrated securities.

Officers:

D.G. Powell   Chairman & President

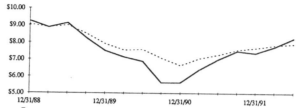

Investment Advisor: American Capital Asset Management Inc.

Advisory Fee: Monthly fee at annual rate of 0.65% of average weekly net assets. Fee for year-ended 12/31/91 was $714,587.

Administrator: American Capital Marketing, Inc.

Administration Fee: Monthly fee at annual rate of 0.10% of average weekly net assets on first $250 mil. , and 0.05% of average weekly net assets in excess of $250 mil. Fee for year-ended 12/31/91 was $109,937.

Shareholder Service Agent: Boston Financial Data Services, Inc.

Shareholder Service Fee: Fee for 1991, $37,441.

Capital Structure: *Shares of beneficial interest*: unlimited number of shares authorized; 15,113,000 shares outstanding 12/31/91

Portfolio Highlights (as of 12/31/91): U.S. agencies and government obligations 46.6%, corporate bonds 34.9%, preferred stocks 14.5%, misc. investments and other assets and liabilities 4.0%. **Largest issuers:** Federal Home Loan Banks; Government National Mortgage Association; U.S. treasury notes; Federal Farm Credit Banks; Bell and Howell $4.25 cum. payment-in-kind exchangeable.

Historical Financial Statistics (fiscal year-end: 12/31/91):

	1991	1990	1989	4/21/88 to 12/31/88
Value of net assets (000)	116,298	100,626	119,373	134,311
NAV	7.70	6.66	7.90	9.06
Net investment income	0.88	0.974	1.06	0.68
Dividends from net investment income	0.89	0.972	1.078	0.6695
Distributions from net realized gains	--	--	0.026	--
Expense ratio	1.03%	1.00%	0.97%	0.93% ann.
Income ratio	12.11%	13.25%	12.18%	11.26% ann.
Portfolio turnover	50%	29%	20%	46%

Special considerations: The fund may repurchase shares when the fund trades below net asset value. The fund's Declaration of Trust contains various anti-takeover provisions. As of 12/31/91 the fund had a net realized capital loss carryforward of approximately $24.4 mil. expiring through 1992.

American Government Income Fund Inc.

222 S. Ninth St., Minneapolis, MN 55402

Category: Bond Fund

Phone: 612-342-6387; 800-333-6000 ext. 6384
Listed: AGF, NYSE
Commenced Operations: April, 1988
Cusip: 025917105

1991/mid-1992 Range of Premium/Disc: +15% to 0%
1991/mid-1992 Range of Price: $9 to $7
NAV Total Return 1990: +10.13%; **1991:** +26.15%
Share Price Total Return 1990: +11.15%; **1991:** +17.11%
Herzfeld Ranking 1991: 23rd of 80 bond funds

Investment Objective: High current income with preservation of capital, principally through investment in obligations issued or guaranteed by the U.S. government, its agencies or instrumentalities.

Officers:

E.J. Kohler   Chairman
W. Bruntjen   President

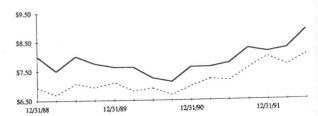

Investment Advisor: Piper Capital Management Incorporated
Advisory Fee: Monthly fee of 0.025% of average weekly net assets, about 0.30% annually, plus 5.25% of daily gross income (not to exceed 1/12 of 0.60% per month). Fee for year-ended 10/31/91 was $894,876.
Administrator: Piper Capital Management Incorporated
Administration Fee: Monthly fee of 0.20% of the fund's average weekly net assets. Fee for year-ended 10/31/91 was $298,292.

Capital Structure: *Common stock:* 1 bil. shares authorized; 20,718,748 shares outstanding 10/31/91
         Debt: Reverse repurchase agreements with certain broker-dealers of $35.8 mil. on 10/31/91

Portfolio Highlights (as of 10/31/91): U.S. government/agency 38.5%, Federal National Mortgage Association 21.1%, collateralized mortgage obligations and other mortgage-backeds 20.9%, Government National Mortgage Association 11.8%, Federal Home Loan Mortgage Corporation 3.5%.

Historical Financial Statistics (fiscal year-end: 10/31/91):

	1991	1990	1989	4/28/88 to 10/31/88
Value of net assets (000)	159,116	139,246	141,128	140,684
NAV	7.68	6.76	7.09	7.33
Net investment income	0.92	0.87	0.81	0.43
Distributions from net investment income	0.80	0.78	0.85	0.45
Distributions from net realized gains	--	--	0.03	--
Expense ratio*	2.56%	3.13%	2.63%	2.04% ann.
Operating expense ratio	1.02%	1.04%	1.42%	1.33% ann.
Income ratio	12.72%	12.68%	11.58%	11.72% ann.
Portfolio turnover	111%	61%	46.00%	55.00%

*includes interest expense

Special considerations: S&P Rating: AAf. The fund will consider making a tender offer for shares every quarter. The fund may convert to an open-end fund after 11/1/92, under certain circumstances, with a 2/3 vote. The fund's Articles of Incorporation contain various anti-takeover provisions as well as limits on director liability. Monthly dividend rate reduced from $0.07 to $0.064 per share. Investment guidelines have been amended to allow for various hedging transactions. As of 10/31/91 the fund had a capital loss carryforward of approximately $2.1 mil. available through 1999.

American Government Income Portfolio Inc.

222 S. Ninth Street, Minneapolis, MN 55402-3804   **Category: Bond Fund**

Phone: 800-866-7778 ext. 6384
Listed: AAF, NYSE
Commenced Operations: September, 1988
Cusip: 025919101

1991/mid-1992 Range of Premium/Disc: +9% to -1%
1991/mid-1992 Range of Price: $11 1/8 to $9
NAV Total Return 1990: +9.98%; **1991:** +27.57%
Share Price Total Return 1990: +12.44%; **1991:** +20.01%
Herzfeld Ranking 1991: 21st of 80 bond funds

Investment Objective: High current income with preservation of capital, principally through investment in obligations issued or guaranteed by the U.S. government, its agencies or instrumentalities.

Officers:

E.J. Kohler	Chairman
W. Bruntjen	President

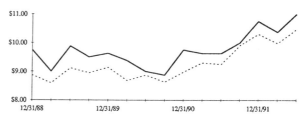

Investment Advisor: Piper Capital Management Incorporated
Advisory Fee: Monthly fee of 0.025% of weekly net assets plus 5.25% of daily gross income (not to exceed 1/12 of 0.60% per month), approximately 0.60% annually. Fee for year-ended 10/31/91 was $1,307,014.
Administrator: Piper Capital Management Incorporated
Administration Fee: Monthly fee of 0.20% of average weekly net assets. Fee for year-ended 10/31/91 was $435,671.

Capital Structure: *Common stock:* 1 bil. shares authorized; 23,412,054 shares outstanding 10/31/91
                                   Debt: Reverse repurchase agreements with certain broker-dealers of $61 mil. on 10/31/91

Portfolio Highlights (as of 10/31/91): U.S. government and agency 27.3%, collateralized mortgage obligations and other mortgage-backeds 26.1%, Federal National Mortgage Association 18.5%, Federal Home Loan Mortgage Corporation 14.2%, Government National Mortgage Association 8.6%, other 5.3%.

Historical Financial Statistics (fiscal year-end: 10/31/91):

	1991	1990	1989	9/29/88 to 10/31/88
Value of net assets (000)	234,479	203,736	205,563	202,088
NAV	10.02	8.73	9.16	9.37
Net investment income	1.19	1.04	1.03	0.08
Distributions from net investment income	1.00	0.97	1.10	0.09
Distributions from net realized gains	--	0.03	0.03	--
Expense ratio	2.76%	3.19%	2.59%*	1.83% ann.
Operating expense ratio	1.01%	1.03%	1.12%*	1.13% ann.
Income ratio	12.75%	11.72%	11.45%*	10.59% ann.
Portfolio turnover	94%	49%	65.54%	0.02%

*Management fees were waived for the year-ended 10/31/89; total expense ratio would have been 2.83%, and income ratio would have been 11.21% had they not been waived.

Special considerations: S&P Rating: AAf. Average life of portfolio holdings is 5 to 7 years and debt securities are rated AA or better (excluding certain short-term investments). The board will consider making tender offers for shares on a quarterly basis, and the fund may convert to an open-end fund after 11/1/92 if certain conditions are met and the proposal is approved by a 2/3 vote. The Articles of Incorporation contain various anti-takeover provisions. Monthly dividend rate reduced from $0.0885 to $0.08 per share. Investment guidelines have been amended to allow for various hedging transactions.

American Government Term Trust Inc.

222 South Ninth Street, Minneapolis, MN 55402

Category: Bond Fund

Phone: 612-342-6387; 800-333-6000 ext. 6384	**1991/mid-1992 Range of Premium/Disc**:+13% to +2%
Listed: AGT, NYSE	**1991/mid-1992 Range of Price**: $11 to $9 7/8
Commenced Operations: January, 1989	**NAV Total Return 1990**: +9.14%; **1991**: +19.65%
Cusip: 025920109	**Share Price Total Return 1990**: +11.00%;**1991**:+14.24%
	Herzfeld Ranking 1991: 42nd of 80 bond funds

Investment Objective: High current income and return of $10 per share to investors on or shortly before 8/31/2001, primarily through investment in mortgage-backed securities and zero coupon securities.

Officers:

E.J. Kohler	Chairman
B.S. Rinkey	President

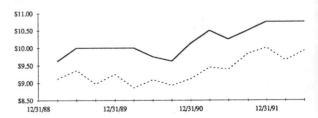

-- NAV — PRICE

Investment Advisor: Piper Capital Management Incorporated

Advisory Fee: Monthly fee at annual rate of 0.60% of average weekly net assets through 1/31/93; 0.45% annually 2/1/93 to 1/31/97; 0.30% annually 2/1/97 until termination of the fund. Fee for year-ended 11/30/91 was $459,429.

Administrator: Piper Capital Management Incorporated

Administration Fee: Monthly fee at annual rate of 0.15% of average weekly net assets through 1/31/93; 0.125% annually 2/1/93 to 1/31/97; 0.10% annually 2/1/97 until termination of the fund. Fee for year-ended 11/30/91 was $114,857.

Capital Structure: *Shares of beneficial interest*: 1 bil. shares authorized; 8,060,000 shares outstanding 11/30/91
Debt: Reverse repurchase agreements of $19,940,000 outstanding on 11/30/91

Portfolio Highlights (as of 10/31/91): U.S. government/agency 38.5%, Federal National Mortgage Association 21.1%, collateralized mortgage obligations and other mortgage-backeds 20.9%, Government National Mortgage Association 11.8%, Federal Home Loan Mortgage Corporation 3.5%.

Historical Financial Statistics (fiscal year-end: 11/30/91):

	1991	1990	1/26/89 to 11/30/89
Value of net assets (000)	80,370	73,590	75,279
NAV	9.97	9.13	9.34
Net investment income	1.09	0.95	0.74
Distributions from net investment income	0.95	0.90	0.81
Distributions from net realized gains	--	--	0.04
Expense ratio	3.05%	2.66%	1.26% ann.
Operating expense ratio	1.11%	1.05%	0.99% ann.
Income ratio	11.48%	10.59%	9.62% ann.
Portfolio turnover	53%	44%	94.21%

Special considerations: S&P Rating: AAAf. The fund's Articles of Incorporation contain various anti-takeover provisions. The fund's board will consider making tender offers for the fund's shares or authorizing repurchase of shares on a quarterly basis. The fund may borrow up to 33 1/3 of the fund's total assets, but it is expected that borrowing will not exceed 25% of total assets. Monthly dividend rate reduced from $0.08 to $0.0785 per share.

American Municipal Term Trust Inc.

222 South Ninth Street, Minneapolis, MN 55402   **Category:** Municipal Bond Fund

Phone: 612-342-6387; 800-333-6000 ext. 6384	**1991/mid-1992 Range of Premium/Disc**: +9% to -1%
Listed: AXT, NYSE	**1991/mid-1992 Range of Price**: $10 5/8 to $9 5/8
Commenced Operations: March, 1991	**NAV Total Return 1991**: N/A
Cusip: 027652106	**Share Price Total Return 1991**: N/A
	Herzfeld Ranking 1991: N/A

Investment Objective: High current income exempt from regular federal income tax and return to investors of $10.00 per share of common stock upon termination of the trust expected to occur on or shortly before April 15, 2001 (may be extended to April 15, 2006). The fund invests in a diversified portfolio of high-quality municipal obligations including municipal zero coupon securities.

Officers:

E.J. Kohler	Chairman
R.R. Reuss	President

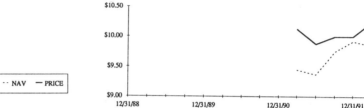

Investment Advisor: Piper Capital Management Incorporated

Advisory Fee: Monthly fee at annual rate of 0.25% of average weekly net assets. Fee for period 3/27/91 to 12/31/91 was $217,938.

Administrator: Piper Capital Management Incorporated

Administration Fee: Monthly fee at annual rate of 0.15% of average weekly net assets. Fee for period 3/27/91 to 12/31/91 was $130,763.

Capital Structure:

Common stock: 200 mil. shares authorized; 8,455,000 as of 12/31/91
Remarketed Preferred stock 1 mil. shares authorized, 850 shares outstanding with liquidation preference of $50,000 per share. Dividend adjusted every 7 days.

Portfolio Highlights (as of 3/31/92): Fixed-rate municipal securities 93.3%, insured bonds 66.7%, municipal zero coupon bonds 6.7%. Quality ratings: AAA 69.3%, AA 18.7%, A 9.3%, BBB 2.7%. Largest geographic concentrations (as of 12/31/91): Washington 18.8%, Texas 17.7%, Illinois 15.1%, Indiana 9.2%, Nevada 5.9%.

Largest issuers: (WA) Public Power Supply System; (IL) State Sales Tax Revenue; (TX) Houston Hotel Occupancy Tax Rev. 7-15; (WA) Port Longview Industrial Development Rev. 7.45-13; District of Columbia general obligation 6.75-08.

Historical Financial Statistics (fiscal year-end: 12/31/91):

	3/27/91 to 12/31/91
Value of net assets (000)	126,987
NAV	9.99
Net investment income	0.65
Distributions from net investment income paid to common shareholders	0.49
Distributions from net investment income paid to preferred shareholders	0.13
Expense ratio	0.56% ann.
Income ratio	6.27% ann.
Portfolio turnover	24%

Special considerations: S&P rating: AAf. The fund pays monthly dividends of net investment income after payment of dividends on preferred stock; net realized capital gains will generally be distributed at least annually. The initial dollar weighted average maturity of the trust's assets is expected to be from 18 to 25 years and will shorten during the term of the trust. Termination date will be extended if the trust is unable to distribute at least $10 per share to common shareholders.

American Municipal Term Trust Inc. II

222 South Ninth Street, Minneapolis, MN 55402

Category: Municipal Bond Fund

Phone: 612-342-6387; 800-333-6000 ext. 6384
Listed: BXT, NYSE
Commenced Operations: September, 1991
Cusip: 027653104

1991/mid-1992 Range of Premium/Disc: +8% to 0%
1991/mid-1992 Range of Price: $10 3/8 to $9 1/2
NAV Total Return 1991: N/A
Share Price Total Return 1991: N/A
Herzfeld Ranking 1991: N/A

Investment Objective: High current income exempt from regular federal income tax and return to investors of $10.00 per share of common stock upon termination of the trust expected to occur on or shortly before April 15, 2002 (may be extended to April 15, 2006). The fund invests in a diversified portfolio of high-quality municipal obligations including municipal zero coupon securities.

Officers:

E.J. Kohler   Chairman
R.R. Reuss   President

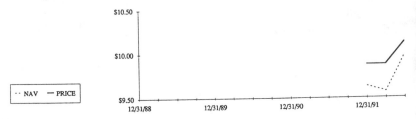

Investment Advisor: Piper Capital Management Incorporated
Advisory Fee: Monthly fee at annual rate of 0.25% of average weekly net assets. Fee for period 9/26/91 to 12/31/91 was $56,777.
Administrator: Piper Capital Management Incorporated
Administration Fee: Monthly fee at annual rate of 0.15% of average weekly net assets. Fee for period 9/26/91 to 12/31/91 was $34,066.

Capital Structure: *Common stock:* 200 mil. shares authorized; 7,355,820 shares outstanding 12/31/91
Remarketed Preferred stock: 1 mil. shares authorized, 740 shares outstanding with liquidation preference of $50,000 per share. Dividend adjusted every 7 days.

Portfolio Highlights (as of 3/31/92): Fixed rate municipal securities 92.8%, insured bonds 65.0%, municipal zero coupon securities 7.2%. Quality ratings: AAA 69.0%, AA 13.3%, A 10.4%, BBB 7.3%. Largest geographic concentrations (12/31/91): Illinois 21.4%, Washington 16.3%, Texas 13.0%, Indiana 11.0%, Florida 6.5%. **Largest issuers:** (WA) State Public Power Supply; (TX) Houston Hotel Occupancy 7-15; (IL) Cook County general obligation 6.75-11; (ND) Bismark Hospital Revenue-St. Alexius 6.9-06; (IL) Lake County Water and Sewer 6.75.

Historical Financial Statistics (fiscal year-end: 12/31/91):

	9/26/91 to 12/31/91
Value of net assets (000)	108,392
NAV	9.71
Net investment income	0.19
Distributions from net investment income paid to common shareholders	0.16
Distributions from net investment income paid to preferred shareholders	0.02
Expense ratio	0.58% ann.
Income ratio	6.24% ann.
Portfolio turnover	18%

Special considerations: S&P ratings: AA$_f$. The fund will pays monthly dividends of net investment income after payment of dividends on preferred stock; net realized capital gains will generally be distributed at least annually. The initial dollar weighted average maturity of the trust's assets is expected to be from 18 to 25 years and will shorten during the term of the trust. Termination date will be extended if the trust is unable to distribute at least $10 per share to common shareholders.

158

American Opportunity Income Fund Inc.

222 S. Ninth Street, Minneapolis, MN 55402-3804   **Category:** Bond Fund

Phone: 800-866-7778 ext. 6384	**1991/mid-1992 Range of Premium/Disc:** +11% to -4%
Listed: OIF, NYSE	**1991/mid-1992 Range of Price:** $11 3/4 to $9 3/8
Commenced Operations: September, 1989	**NAV Total Return 1990:** +12.18%; **1991:** +23.94%
Cusip: 028727105	**Share Price Total Return 1990:** +10.15%; **1991:** +25.39%
	Herzfeld Ranking 1991: 26th of 80 bond funds

Investment Objective: High level of current income with a secondary objective of capital appreciation, primarily through active management of a portfolio of securities of which at least 65% are mortgage-backed securities issued or guaranteed by the U.S. government or one of its agencies or instrumentalities; or issued by private issuers and rated, at the time of investment, either AAA or AA by S&P Corp.

Officers:

E.J. Kohler	Chairman
W. Bruntjen	President

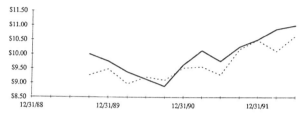

Investment Advisor: Piper Capital Management Incorporated

Advisory Fee: Monthly fee in the amount equal to the sum of 0.01667% of average weekly net assets during the month (approximately 0.20% on an annual basis) and 4.5% of daily gross income. The fee shall not exceed in the aggregate 1/12 of 0.725% of the fund's average weekly net assets during the month. Fee for six months ended 2/29/92 was $760,224.

Administrator: Piper Capital Management Incorporated

Administration Fee: Monthly fee at the annual rate of 0.20% of average weekly net assets. Fee for six months ended 2/29/92 was $214,847.

Capital Structure: *Shares of beneficial interest:* 250 mil. shares authorized; 21,048,671 outstanding 2/29/92
                                 Debt: Reverse repurchase agreements payable as of 2/29/92, $73.5 mil.

Portfolio Highlights (as of 2/29/92): Agency Collateralized Mortgage obligations 33%, Federal National Mortgage Association 21%, U.S. government 17%, Federal Home Loan Mortgage Corporation 11%, foreign 9%, Government National Mortgage Association 8%, short-term 1%. Of the securities, 90.1% were either U.S. government obligations or rated AAA, and 9.9% were rated AA. The fund has never held securities rated less than AA. **Largest issuers:** FNMA; U.S. treasury notes and bonds; FNMA; FHLMC; Resolution Trust Corp.; GNMA.

Historical Financial Statistics: (fiscal year-end: 8/31/91):

	six months 2/29/92	1991	1990
Value of net assets (000)	**216,197**	206,491	191,076
NAV	**10.27**	9.81	9.13
Net investment income	**0.65**	1.05	0.80
Distributions from net investment income	**0.54**	1.05	0.80
Distributions from net realized gains	**0.24**	0.08	0.07
Expense ratio	**2.97%** ann.	3.47%	2.72% ann.
Operating expense ratio	**1.22%** ann.	1.15%	1.05% ann.
Income ratio	**12.83%** ann.	11.06%	9.52% ann.
Portfolio turnover	**40%**	115%	124%

Special considerations: S&P Rating: AAf. Options and CMO's with inverse floating rates are utilized by the fund. At the July, 1992 annual meeting shareholders will vote on a proposal to remove the 5% restriction on investment in mortgage-backed securities, derivative mortgage-backed securities and similar instruments.

American Strategic Income Portfolio Inc.

222 South Ninth Street, Minneapolis, MN 55402

Category: Bond Fund

Phone: 612-342-6387; 800-333-6000 x 6387	**1991/mid-1992 Range of Premium/Disc:** +15% to +7%
Listed: ASP, NYSE	**1991/mid-1992 Range of Price:** $15 7/8 to $14 1/2
Commenced Operations: December, 1991	**NAV Total Return 1991:** N/A
Cusip: 030098107	**Share Price Total Return 1991:** N/A
	Herzfeld Ranking 1991: N/A

Investment Objective: High level of current income with a secondary objective of capital appreciation. The fund invests actively in a portfolio of securities which will initially emphasize investments in mortgage-related assets but may also invest in asset-backed securities, U.S. government securities, corporate debt securities, municipal obligations, unregistered securities, derivative mortgage-backed securities and mortgage servicing rights.

Officers:

E.J. Kohler	Chairman
W. Bruntjen	President

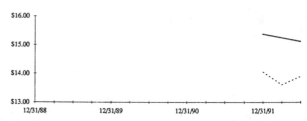

Investment Advisor: Piper Capital Management Incorporated

Advisory Fee: Monthly fee equal to the sum of 0.01667% of the average weekly net assets of the fund during the month and 4.5% of the daily gross income during the month; the fee shall not exceed in the aggregate 1/12 of 0.725% of average weekly net assets during the month (approximately 0.725% on an annual basis).

Administrator: Piper Capital Management Incorporated

Administration Fee: Monthly fee equal to the annualized rate of 0.20% of average weekly net assets.

Capital Structure: *Common stock:* 1 bil. shares authorized, 4.5 mil. shares outstanding 12/19/91

Portfolio Highlights (as of 3/31/92): Adjustable-rate mortgages 28%, treasuries 28%, fixed mortgages 24%, mortgages/CMOs 16%, derivative 4%. Average life, 9.2 years, implied duration 5.5 years.

Historical Financial Statistics:

	3/31/92
Value of net assets (000)	**70,811**
NAV	**13.61**

Special considerations: S&P ratings A_f. The fund may borrow up to 33 1/3% of total assets. The fund makes monthly distributions of net investment income and annual distributions of net realized capital gains. The board of directors will annually consider making tender offers at net asset value and will review the option to repurchase shares quarterly. The fund may use option and hedging strategies for hedging purposes.

America's All Season Fund, Inc.

201 West Canton Ave., Suite 100, Winter Park, FL 32789 **Category:** Miscellaneous

Phone: 407-629-1400	**1991/mid-1992 Range of Premium/Disc:** 6% to -26%
Listed: FUND, OTC	**1991/mid-1992 Range of Price:** $5 1/2 to $3 7/8
Commenced Operations: March, 1988	**NAV Total Return 1990:** +0.43%; **1991:** +12.55%
Cusip: 030603104	**Share Price Total Return 1990:** +6.60%; **1991:** -5.48%

Investment Objective: Long-term capital appreciation without undue risk to preservation of capital.

Officers:

D.J. Veitia   Chairman & CEO

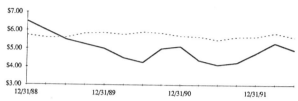

Investment Advisor and Administrator: Veitia & Assoc., Inc.

Advisory Fee: Monthly fee at annual rate of 1.0% of average daily net assets. If certain fund expenses exceed specified limits, the manager will adjust its fees downward to cause the fund's expenses to comply with those limits. Fee for year-ended 12/31/91 was $498,336.

Capital Structure: *Common stock:* 100 mil. shares authorized; 8,742,557 shares outstanding 12/31/91

Portfolio Highlights (as of 12/31/91): Common stocks 76.68%, foreign bank obligations 25.39%, index notes 1.67%, corporate bonds 0.22%. Largest sector concentrations: health and personal care 11.99%, merchandising 7.26%, telecommunications 5.06%, wholesale and international trade 4.98%, banking 4.32%. Largest geographic concentrations: United States 17.99%, Netherlands 9.83%, France 7.60%, Switzerland 7.34%, Sweden 6.91%. **Largest positions:** Astra BF, Roche Holding AG, Otra, Schering Plough, Archer Daniels Midland.

Historical Financial Statistics (fiscal year-end: 12/31/91):

	1991	1990	1989	3/2/88 to 12/31/88
Value of net assets (000)	**52,540**	48,830	51,711	45,510
NAV	**6.01**	5.59	5.91	5.52
Net investment income	**0.21**	0.25	0.24	0.28
Dividends from net investment income	**0.17**	0.24	0.23	0.25
Distributions from net realized gains	**0.11**	0.05	0.03	--
Distributions from other sources	**--**	--	--	0.05
Expense ratio	**2.36%**	2.48%	1.99%	2.17% ann.
Income ratio	**3.71%**	4.33%	4.34%	6.76% ann.
Portfolio turnover	**269%**	312%	244%	30%

Special considerations: The fund initially offered shares to the public in the period March, 1988, to September, 1988, through International Assets Advisory Corporation. The fund is permitted to use leverage and may invest up to 25% of assets in gold or silver bullion or other forms of gold. A proposal at the November, 1991, annual meeting to convert the fund to an open-end fund in approximately two years did not pass. The fund has adopted a 2 1/2% of net asset value quarterly payout policy.

AMEV Securities, Inc.

PO Box 64284, St. Paul, MN 55164

Category: Bond Fund

Phone: 612-738-4000, 800-800-2638 x4274
Listed: AMV, NYSE
Commenced Operations: 1972
Cusip: 001910108

1991/mid-1992 Range of Premium/Disc: +16% to -1%
1991/mid-1992 Range of Price: $11 3/4 to $9 1/8
NAV Total Return 1990: +3.89%; **1991**: +22.13%
Share Price Total Return 1990: -4.07%; **1991**: +34.51%
Herzfeld Ranking 1991: 34th of 80 bond funds

Investment Objective: High current income through investment in a diversified portfolio of marketable debt securities with a secondary objective of capital appreciation.

Officers:

A.R. Freedman   Chairman
E.M. Mahoney   President

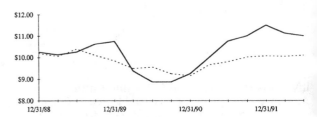

Investment Advisor: Fortis Advisers, Inc.
Advisory Fee: Annual rate of 0.45% of the first $100 mil. of average monthly net assets, 0.40% of average monthly net assets over $100 mil., plus 2% of net amount of dividend and interest income. Fee for six months ended 1/31/92 was $387,148.

Capital Structure: *Common stock*: 15 mil. shares authorized; 11,597,832 shares outstanding 1/31/92
                Debt: A $1 mil. line of credit is available; there were no borrowings during the six months ended 1/31/92.

Portfolio Highlights (as of 1/31/92): Equity securities 0.23%, long-term debt securities 97.87%, short-term investments 0.68%. Investment grade corporate, municipal and foreign debt securities 15.61%, non-investment grade corporate debt securities 25.28%, U.S. government & agencies 56.98%. **Largest issuers**: Federal National Mortgage Association; Federal Home Loan Mortgage Corp.; Federal Farm Credit Bank; U.S. treasury note 12.625-94; City of New York municipal obligations.

Historical Financial Statistics (fiscal year-end: 7/31/91):

	six months 1/31/92	1991	1990	1989	1988	1987
Value of net assets (000)	116,952	113,364	107,181	113,009	109,328	110,754
NAV	10.08	9.91	9.62	10.42	10.36	10.76
Net investment income	0.51	1.06	1.07	1.09	1.07	1.07
Distributions from net investment income	0.54	1.07	1.10	1.09	1.08	1.08
Expense ratio	0.82% ann.	0.88%	0.86%	0.86%	0.83%	0.83%
Income ratio	10.06% ann.	11.12%	10.95%	10.62%	10.25%	9.65%
Portfolio turnover	23%	67%	117%	100%	121%	165%

Special considerations: On 5/11/92 the fund's Board of Directors reduced the dividend rate from $0.0875 to $0.085 citing the steady decline in interest rates which has reduced the earnings of the fund.

Apex Municipal Fund, Inc.

Box 9011, Princeton, NJ 08543

Category: Municipal Bond Fund

Phone: 609-282-2800
Listed: APX, NYSE
Commenced Operations: July, 1989
Cusip: 037580107

1991/mid-1992 Range of Premium/Disc: +12% to 0%
1991/mid-1992 Range of Price: $12 to $10 3/4
NAV Total Return 1990: +8.46%; **1991**: +4.24%
Share Price Total Return 1990: +11.97%; **1991**: +10.45%
Herzfeld Ranking 1991: 51st of 51 municipal bond funds

Investment Objective: High current income exempt from federal income taxes through investment in a portfolio of medium to lower grade or unrated municipal obligations. The fund may hedge the portfolio through the use of options and futures transactions.

Officers:
A. Zeikel   President

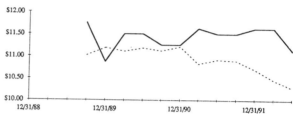

Investment Advisor: Fund Asset Management, Inc.
Advisory Fee: Monthly fee at the annual rate of 0.65% of average weekly net assets. Fee for six months ended 12/31/91 was $682,379.

Capital Structure: *Common stock*: 150 mil. shares authorized; 19,070,878 shares outstanding 12/31/91

Portfolio Highlights (as of 12/31/91): Municipal investments 97.0%, other assets less liabilities 3.0%. Largest geographic concentrations: Florida 11.6%, Pennsylvania 11.6%, Illinois 8.4%, Massachusetts 8.4%, Minnesota 7.9%, Texas 7.1%, New York 6.5%. **Largest issuers**: Saint Paul, Minnesota, Housing and Redevelopment Authority, Hospital Revenue Bonds (Healtheast Project); New York City, New York general obligation; Iowa Finance Authority, Health Care Facilities Revenue Bonds (Mercy Health Initiatives Project) 9.95-19; Florida Housing Finance Agency, M/F Housing Agency Revenue Bonds (Palm Aire) AMT 10-20; Washington Health Care Facilities Authority Revenue Bonds (Kadlec Medical Center--Richland) 9-11.

Historical Financial Statistics (fiscal year-end: 6/30/91):

	six months 12/31/91	1991	7/25/89 to 6/30/90
Value of net assets (000)	204,904	206,736	208,934
NAV	10.74	10.92	11.18
Net investment income	0.47	0.94	0.82
Dividends from net investment income	0.46	0.94	0.75
Expense ratio	0.83% ann.	0.84%	0.51% ann.*
Income ratio	8.38% ann.	8.49%	8.10% ann.
Portfolio turnover	1%	31%	122%

*after reimbursement of a portion of advisory fee; fee before reimbursement was 0.78% ann.

Special considerations: The fund's Articles of Incorporation contain various anti-takeover provisions, including a 75% vote to, among other things, merge with another corporation or liquidate the fund. As of 6/30/91 the fund had a capital loss carryforward of approximately $1.8 mil. expiring through 1999.

The Argentina Fund, Inc.

345 Park Avenue, New York, NY 10154

Category: Foreign Equity Fund

Phone: 212-326-6200, 617-330-5602
Listed: AF, NYSE
Commenced Operations: October, 1991
Cusip: 040112104

1991/mid-1992 Range of Premium/Disc: +45% to -5%
1991/mid-1992 Range of Price: $16 1/4 to $12
NAV Total Return 1991: N/A
Share Price Total Return 1991: N/A
Herzfeld Ranking 1991: N/A

Investment Objective: Long-term capital appreciation primarily through investment in equity securities of Argentine issuers. The fund may also invest in debt securities issued or guaranteed by the Argentine government and Argentine companies, and in certain related repurchase agreements.

Officers

E.D. Villani   Chairman
N. Bratt   President

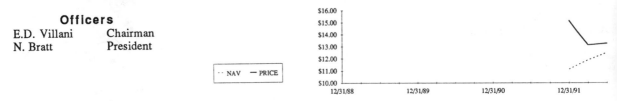

Investment Manager and Administrator: Scudder, Stevens & Clark Inc.
Management and Administrative Fee: Monthly fee at an annualized rate of 1.30% of the fund's average weekly net assets.
Argentine Sub-Advisor: Sociedad General de Negocious y Valores S.A.
Sub-Advisory Fee: (paid by Scudder, Stevens & Clark, Inc.) Monthly fee at the annualized rate of 0.36% of the fund's average weekly net assets.

Capital Structure: *Common stock*: 100 mil. shares authorized, 5,770,202 shares outstanding 6/3/92

Portfolio Highlights (as of 1/31/92): Equity securities 33.7%, debt securities 17.1%, repurchase agreements 4.2%, commercial paper 45.0%. Largest industry concentrations (equity securities): food and beverage 7.6%, conglomerates 6.7%, petroleum 4.1%. **Largest positions:** Argentina BONEX 89 floating rate note LIBOR 12/28/99; Pérez Companc, Astra Corporación, Argentina GRA (Guaranteed Refinancing Agreement) floating rate loan LIBOR plus 0.8125-06; Molinos Río De La Plata.

Historical Financial Statistics:
10/22/91 to 10/31/91

Value of net assets (000)	63,290
NAV	10.99
Net investment income	0.01
Expense ratio	2.55% ann.
Income ratio	2.54% ann.
Portfolio turnover	--

Special considerations: The fund may invest up to 25% of total assets in unlisted securities of Argentine companies. In order to hedge against currency exchange rate risks, the fund may enter into forward currency exchange contracts. The fund may also write covered call options. The fund will make annual distributions of its investment company taxable income and any net long-term capital gains in excess of net short-term capital losses. The fund's Articles of Incorporation and By-Laws contain various anti-takeover provisions including a 75% vote to merge with another fund or liquidate the fund.

ASA Limited

PO Box 269, Florham Park, NJ 07932

Phone: 201-377-3535
Listed: ASA, NYSE
Commenced Operations: 1958
Cusip: 002050102

Category: Specialized Equity Fund

1991/mid-1992 Range of Premium/Disc: +16% to -9%
1991/mid-1992 Range of Price: $56 to $38 1/8
NAV Total Return 1990: -31.81%; **1991:** -2.82%
Share Price Total Return 1990: -13.53%; **1991:** +14.33%
Herzfeld Ranking 1991: 17th of 18 specialized equity funds

Investment Objective: The fund invests over 50% of its assets in common shares of gold mining companies in South Africa. The remainder of assets may be invested in other South African companies subject to various restrictions. Limited investment outside of South Africa is permitted.

Officers:
W.A. Stanger, Jr. Chairman & Treasurer

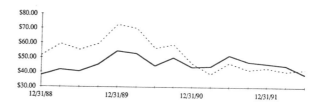

Investment Advisor: internally managed
Advisory Fee: Expenses for salaries and directors' fees for 1991 were $625,010.
Administrator: Lyons Associates
Administration Fee: Administrative expenses for 1991 (excluding salaries) were $291,315.

Capital Structure: *Common stock:* 24 mil. shares authorized; 9.6 mil. shares outstanding 2/29/92

Portfolio Highlights (as of 2/29/92): Ordinary shares of gold mining companies 67.0%, ordinary shares of other companies 30.8%, cash and other assets less payables 2.2%. Largest geographic concentrations: Far West Rand area 36.6%, Klerksdorp area 24.2%, Evander area 4.4%, Canadian gold mines 1.4%, Orange Free State area 0.4%.
Largest positions: Driefontein Consolidated Ltd., Kloof Gold Mining Company Ltd., Vaal Reefs Exploration and Mining Co. Ltd., De Beers Consolidated Mines Ltd./Centenary AG; Southvaal Holdings Ltd.

Historical Financial Statistics (fiscal year-end: 11/30/91):

	1991	1990	1989	1988	1987	1986
Value of net assets (000)	429,168	465,990	672,085	522,648	795,227	702,450
NAV	44.71	48.54	70.01	54.44	82.84	73.11
Net investment income	1.51	2.08	2.39	2.72	3.67	3.31
Dividends paid	3.00	3.50	3.50	3.50	4.50	3.00
Expense ratio	0.66%	0.43%	0.51%	0.52%	0.24%	0.31%
Income ratio	3.70%	3.12%	4.74%	5.24%	3.91%	5.55%
Portfolio turnover	0.36%	4.97%	3.21%	0.08%	2.37%	1.82%

Special considerations: Dividends to shareholders are subject to South African withholding tax. At the 1991 annual meeting various amendments to the Articles of Association were voted on including: having the Board of Directors fix the number of directors from time to time (between 5 and 15), decrease from 60% to 50% the number of directors which must be U.S. citizens and residents, make short-term rand denominated investments of up to 5% of total assets. Since December 1, 1987, the fund has been a "passive foreign investment company" under rules enacted by the Tax Reform Act of 1986. U.S. shareholders may treat the fund as a "qualified electing fund" to avoid realized gains being treated as ordinary income, but must elect such treatment. IRA Notice 88-125 describes how such an election must be made. The 1990 annual report contains additional information on tax issues. South Africa has a dual-rand system, a "financial rand" and a "commercial rand": the commercial rand is the official exchange rate while the financial rand "is the unit of currency used only by non-residents of South Africa for investment in South Africa." On 2/29/92 the fund's net asset value was R124.53, which translated to $43.85 using the commercial rand rate and to $32.51 using the financial rand rate. Dividend rate reduced to $0.50 per quarter in February, 1992.

The Asia Pacific Fund, Inc.
One Seaport Plaza, New York, NY 10292

Category: Foreign Equity Fund

Phone: 212-214-3334
Listed: APB, NYSE
Commenced Operations: April, 1987
Cusip: 044901106

1991/mid-1992 Range of Premium/Disc: +19% to -14%
1991/mid-1992 Range of Price: $17 to $10
NAV Total Return 1990: -15.62%; **1991**: +23.09%
Share Price Total Return 1990: -36.48%; **1991**: +52.20%
Herzfeld Ranking 1991: 14th of 46 foreign equity funds

Investment Objective: Long-term capital appreciation through investment primarily in equity securities of companies in Hong Kong, Korea, Malaysia, the Philippines, Singapore, Taiwan and Thailand.

Officers:
J.A. Morrell   Chairman
M.J. Downey   President

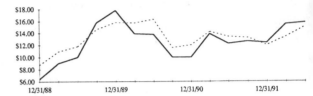

Investment Advisor: Baring International Investment (Far East) Limited

Advisory Fee: Monthly fee at annual rate of 1.10% of the fund's average weekly net assets up to $50 mil., 0.90% of assets between $50 mil. and $100 mil., and 0.70% of assets above $100 mil. Fee for year-ended 3/31/92 was $1,142,985.

Administrator: Prudential Mutual Fund Management, Inc.

Administration Fee: Monthly fee at annual rate of 0.25% of the fund's average weekly net assets.

Capital Structure: *Common stock*: 20 mil. authorized; 8,833,915 shares outstanding 3/31/92
Debt: Loan agreement with Baring Brothers & Co., $1.8 mil. at interest rate of 9.39%; uncommitted credit line with Baring Brothers & Co., loan outstanding 3/31/92, $2.5 mil. at interest rate of 4.8125%, maturity 4/30/92 (subsequent to 3/31/92 loan was extended and additional $7 mil. borrowed); PRICOA International Bank S.A., loan outstanding 3/31/92, $2.5 mil. at interest rate of 4.8125%, maturity 4/30/92 (subsequent to 3/31/92 loan was extended and additional $2 mil. borrowed).

Portfolio Highlights (as of 3/31/92): Equities and equity equivalents 104.4%, convertible bonds 0.2%, short-term investments 1.3%, liabilities in excess of other assets (5.9%). Largest geographic concentrations: Hong Kong 48.1%, Malaysia 17.0%, Thailand 16.8%, Singapore 14.5%, Korea 5.1%. **Largest positions**: Siam Cement Co. Ltd., Sun Hung Kai Properties Ltd., Swire-Pacific Ltd. "A", Henderson Land Development Co. Ltd., HSBC Holdings plc.

Historical Financial Statistics (fiscal year-end: 3/31/92):

	1992	1991	1990	1989	5/4/87 to 3/31/88
Value of net assets (000)	116,831	124,878	136,072	94,675	67,460
NAV	13.23	14.20	15.71	10.93	7.79
Net investment income (loss)	0.10	0.08	(0.02)	0.06	(0.02)
Dividends to shareholders	0.13	0.04	0.01	0.06	--
Distributions from foreign currency and other	2.34	1.24	0.14	0.01	--
Distributions from paid-in capital	--	--	0.03	--	--
Total expense ratio	2.19%	2.13%	2.41%	2.91%	2.96% ann.
Operating expense ratio	1.92%	1.85%	1.72%	2.02%	1.99% ann.
Income ratio (loss)	0.70%	0.56%	(0.12%)	0.67%	(0.28%) ann.
Portfolio turnover	63%	37%	46%	39%	45%

Special considerations: Dividend and interest income on foreign portfolio holdings is subject to withholding taxes as well as capital gains taxes in certain countries. The fund's Articles of Incorporation contain various anti-takeover provisions. At the 1990 annual meeting shareholders voted on a proposal to increase the borrowing capabilities of the fund to enable the fund to employ leverage and to permit investment in India, Pakistan, Sri Lanka and Indonesia. **Shareholders over 5%**: Harris Associates L.P., 6.4%

The Austria Fund, Inc.

1345 Avenue of the Americas, New York, NY 10105   **Category**: Foreign Equity Fund

Phone: 212-969-1000; 800-247-4154	**1991/mid-1992 Range of Premium/Disc**: +1% to -22%
Listed: OST, NYSE	**1991/mid-1992 Range of Price**: $12 3/4 to $7 7/8
Commenced Operations: September, 1989	**NAV Total Return 1990**: +2.29%; **1991**: -20.34%
Cusip: 052587102	**Share Price Total Return 1990**: -48.56%; **1991**: -9.90%
	Herzfeld Ranking 1991: 44th of 46 foreign equity funds

Investment Objective: Long-term capital appreciation primarily through investment in equity securities of Austrian companies.

Officers:
D.H. Williams   Chairman
D.H. Dievler   President

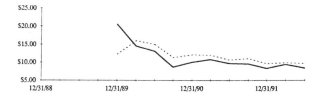

Investment Advisor: Alliance Capital Management L.P.

Administrator: Alliance Capital Management L.P.

Advisory and Administration Fee: Monthly fee at annual rate of 1.0% of average weekly net assets up to $50 mil., and 0.90% on excess. Fee for six months ended 2/29/92 was $397,754.

Sub-Advisor: Girozentrale Capital Management Beratungsgesellschaft m.b.H.

Sub-Advisory Fee: Monthly fee at the annual rate of 0.20% of average weekly net assets. Fee for six months ended 2/29/92 was $82,889.

Capital Structure: *Common stock*: 100 mil. shares authorized; 8,259,015 shares outstanding 2/29/92

Portfolio Highlights (as of 2/29/92): Common and preferred stocks and other investments 95.7%, currency call account 4.3%, convertible bond 0.5%, time deposit 0.3%, other assets less liabilities (0.8%). Largest sector concentrations: financial services 23.3%, capital goods 21.0%, basic industries 19.4%, consumer products & services 16.1%, utilities 11.7%, multi-industry companies 1.8%. **Largest positions**: Erste Allegemeine Generali AG 9.8%, OEMV AG 9.3%, Oesterreichische Elektrizitaetswirtschafts Cl. A 9.2%, Creditanstalt-Bankverein 5.6%, Oesterr Laenderbank AG 4.8%.

Historical Financial Statistics: (fiscal year-end: 8/31/91):

	six months 2/29/92	1991	2/28/89 to 8/31/90
Value of net assets (000)	85,899	89,927	120,088
NAV	10.40	10.89	14.54
Net investment income (loss)	(0.06)	(0.04)	0.12
Dividends from net investment income	--	0.06	0.06
Distributions from net realized gains	0.14	0.36	0.01
Expense ratio	1.83% ann.	1.78%	1.82% ann.
Income ratio (loss)	(1.16%) ann.	(0.35%)	0.89% ann.
Portfolio turnover	25%	34%	24%

Special considerations: In February, 1990, there was a secondary offering of 2.5 million shares at $17 per share. Up to 25% of total assets may be invested in securities which are not readily marketable. The fund may repurchase its shares in the open market, make tender offers, and after January, 1995, if certain conditions exist, convert to an open-end fund. On a quarterly basis, the fund will consider making tender offers for shares. The fund's Articles of Incorporation and By-Laws contain various anti-takeover provisions. At the 1990 annual meeting shareholders voted on amending the fund's investment restrictions to increase the amount of the fund's assets that may be invested in warrants and increased the maximum size of the Board of Directors. As of 2/29/92 the fund held 5.1% of assets in restricted securities.

Shareholders over 5%: Nomura International Trust Company, 24.91%; Brown Brothers Harriman & Co., 9.23%, Daiwa Securities Trust Company, 6.0%.

Baker, Fentress & Company

200 W. Madison Street, Ste. 3510, Chicago, IL 60606

Category: Equity Fund

Phone: 312-236-9190
Listed: BKF, NYSE
Commenced Operations: 1891
Cusip: 057213100

1991/mid-1992 Range of Premium/Disc: -11% to -22%
1991/mid-1992 Range of Price: $19 to $14 3/8
NAV Total Return 1990: -19.66%; **1991:** +24.84%
Share Price Total Return 1990: -24.09%; **1991:** +33.45%
Herzfeld Ranking 1991: 11th of 15 equity funds

Investment Objective: Capital appreciation and income consistent with capital appreciation principally through investment in common stocks and in other equity securities, including debt securities convertible into, or accompanied by, options to purchase, equity securities, and debt securities.

Officers:

J.P. Gorter   Chairman
D.D. Peterson   President & CEO

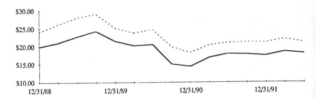

Investment Advisor: internally managed
Advisory Fee: Administration, operations and rent 1991, $1,064,060; directors' fees and expenses $177,056.
Administrator: internally administered

Capital Structure: *Common stock:* 40 mil. shares authorized; 19,422,829 outstanding 12/31/91

Portfolio Highlights (as of 3/31/92): Investments in unaffiliated issuers 71.75%, investments in non-controlled affiliates 3.05%, investments in controlled affiliates 18.53%, money market and fixed-income securities 6.68%, other assets less liabilities 0.01%. Largest industry concentrations: private placement portfolio 8.24%, health care 10.90%, finance 9.67%, technology 9.21%, basic industries 7.29%, merchandising & distribution 6.34%.
Largest holdings: Consolidated-Tomoka Land Co., MCI Communications Corporation, Sysco Corporation, Abbott Laboratories, Newell Co.

Historical Financial Statistics (fiscal year-end: 12/31/91):

	1991	1990	1989	1988	1987	1986
Value of net assets (000)	417,355	350,200	456,191	406,253	378,333	396,717
NAV	21.49	18.66	25.18	24.08	23.28	25.19
Net investment income	0.58	0.70	0.68	0.69	0.67	0.64
Dividends from net investment income	0.58	0.70	0.72	0.67	0.70	0.65
Distributions from net realized gains	1.15	1.25	2.72	1.59	1.63	1.90
Expense ratio	0.84%	0.68%	0.64%	0.64%	0.49%	0.53%
Income ratio	2.53%	3.03%	2.49%	2.78%	2.37%	2.33%
Portfolio turnover	50.70%	26.19%	35.47%	53.23%	28.58%	15.13%

Special considerations: The fund owns 79.9% of its controlled affiliate Consolidated-Tomoka Land Co., which generates income through land utilization and conversion, i.e., citrus operations, real estate developing, property leasing, etc., in the state of Florida. The fund has a staggered board of directors. Beginning in 1987 the fund initiated a policy of annually paying shareholders dividends and capital gain distributions which, when added together, equal at least 8% of the company's average net asset value for the 12 month period ended 10/31 of that year. In 1991 the fund celebrated its 100th anniversary. Beginning in 1992, the fund pays dividends twice a year, in June and December, rather than quarterly. During the quarter ended 3/31/92 the fund repurchased 91,600 shares at a discount of 20.7%.

Bancroft Convertible Fund, Inc.

56 Pine Street, New York, NY 10005

Category: Convertible Fund

Phone: 212-269-9236
Listed: BCV, ASE
Commenced Operations: 1971
Cusip: 059695106

1991/mid-1992 Range of Premium/Disc: -9% to -15%
1991/mid-1992 Range of Price: $19 7/8 to $15 3/8
NAV Total Return 1990: -4.35%; **1991:** +23.49%
Share Price Total Return 1990: -5.05%; **1991:** +26.03%
Herzfeld Ranking 1991: 6th of 8 convertible funds

Investment Objective: Current income and the potential for capital appreciation by investing principally in convertible securities.

Officers:
R.E. Dinsmore — Chairman
T.H. Dinsmore — President

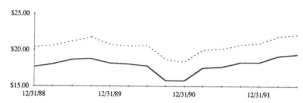

Investment Advisor: Davis/Dinsmore Management Company
Advisory Fee: Monthly fee at annual rate of 0.75% of first $100 mil. of net assets and 0.50% of excess over $100 mil. in net assets. The annual fee is subject to reduction to the extent that the ordinary expenses of the fund (excluding taxes and interest) exceed 1.5% of the first $100 mil. and 1% of the excess over $100 mil. of average monthly net assets. Fee for year-ended 10/31/91 was $391,165.

Capital Structure: *Common stock:* 9 mil. shares authorized; 2,612,954 shares outstanding 10/31/91

Portfolio Highlights (as of 1/31/92): Bonds and notes 82.2%, preferred stocks 15.0%, common stocks 1.0%, other assets and liabilities 1.8%. Largest sector concentrations: banking 14.8%, energy 11.7%, financial & insurance 10.8%, U.S. treasury notes 5.4%, electronics & instruments 5.2%, transportation 4.9%, building & real estate 4.6%.
Largest positions: U.S. treasury notes; various Time Warner Inc.; Old Republic International cv. sub. deb. 8-15; Pulte Home Credit Corp. cv. sub. deb. (cv. into PHM Corp. common stock) 8 1/2-08; Comsat International n.V. Euro cv. sub. deb. 7 3/4-98; IBM Corp. cv. sub. deb. 7 7/8-04.

Historical Financial Statistics (fiscal year-end: 10/31/91, was 3/31 before 3/88):

	10/31/91	10/31/90	10/31/89	10/31/88#	3/31/88	3/31/87
Value of net assets (000)	54,915	46,666	54,705	40,103	37,988	62,796
NAV	21.02	17.86	21.40	22.60	23.54	27.79
Net investment income	1.34	1.44	1.21	0.79	1.42	1.32
Dividends from net investment income	1.46	1.40	1.36	0.40	1.49	1.58
Distributions from net realized gains	--	0.20	0.25	0.91	2.81	5.10
Distributions of tax basis realized gains in excess of book basis realized gains	--	0.19	--	--	--	--
Expense ratio	1.3%***	1.4%***	1.5%***	1.7% ann.	2.4%*	1.8%**
Income ratio	6.7%	7.2%	6.8%	6.2% ann.	4.8%*	4.9%**
Portfolio turnover	38.8%	18.0%	51.4%	29.1% ann.	35.7%	38.7%

\# seven months ended 10/31/88
* includes $0.29/share expense from tender offer & related litigation
** includes $0.14/share expense from tender offer & related litigation
***includes $0.02/share legal expenses for litigation and shareholder proposals for 1989, $0.03 for 1990, and $0.01 for 1991

Special considerations: Fund changed its fiscal year-end to 10/31 from 3/31. The fund had a rights offering in 1988 at $17.32 per share. Dividend rate reduced to $0.34 per quarter in the first quarter of 1992.

Bando McGlocklin Capital Corporation

13555 Bishops Ct., Ste. 205, Brookfield, WI 53005

Category: Miscellaneous

Phone: 414-784-9010
Listed: BMCC, OTC
Commenced Operations: September, 1980
Cusip: 060003100

1991/mid-1992 Range of Premium/Disc: N/A
1991/mid-1992 Range of Price: $14 to $8 1/4
NAV Total Return 1990: N/A; **1991:** N/A
Share Price Total Return 1990: N/A; **1991:** N/A
Herzfeld Ranking 1991: N/A

Investment Objective: Small business investment company, engaging in financing small business concerns through secured loans.

Officers:

G.R. Schonath   Chairman
J. McGlocklin   President & Secretary

Investment Advisor: internally managed
Advisory Fee: salaries & employee benefits year-ended 6/30/90 $641,723.

Capital Structure: *Common stock:* 5 mil. shares authorized; 2,727,405 average shares outstanding period ending 12/31/91
Debt: $79 mil. which include: Small Business Administration debentures, reverse repurchase agreements, short-term borrowings, State of Wisconsin Investment Board note payable, and notes payable to banks.

Portfolio Highlights (as of 12/31/91): (As percentages of total assets) U.S. treasury notes 10%, [Small Business Loans in the following industries] wholesale goods 12.3%, metalworking machinery 12.1%, industrial machinery 10.2%, services 9.4%, commercial printing 7.6%.

Historical Financial Statistics (fiscal year-end: 6/30/91):

	1991	1990	1989	1988	1987
Shareholders' equity	11,554	7,297	8,424	8,882	9,326
NAV	4.29	3.57	4.12	4.34	4.56

Special considerations: Shareholders' equity as of 12/31/91, $11,908,463. The fund makes loans to manufacturing, wholesale, service, retail and other types of small businesses. There was a 3-for-1 stock split in 1987.
Shareholders over 5%: George R. Schonath, 10.3%; Salvatore L. Bando, 9.6%; Jon McGlockin, 11.9%; David A. Geraldson, 1.6%

Bergstrom Capital Corporation

(formerly Claremont Capital Corp.)
505 Madison Street, Suite 220, Seattle, WA 98104

Category: Equity Fund

Phone: 206-623-7302
Listed: BEM, ASE
Commenced Operations: 1968
Cusip: 084093103

1991/mid-1992 Range of Premium/Disc: +27% to -4%
1991/mid-1992 Range of Price: $127 to $59 1/2
NAV Total Return 1990: +10.68%; **1991**: +72.41%
Share Price Total Return 1990: -1.34%; **1991**: +105.10%
Herzfeld Ranking 1991: 1st of 15 equity funds

Investment Objective: Growth and income, primarily through investment in marketable equity securities.

Officers:
W.L. McQueen   President & Treasurer

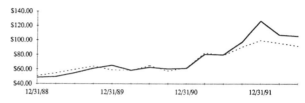

Investment Advisor: Bergstrom Advisers, Inc. (sub-advisory agreement with RCM Capital Management, approx. 28.0% of portfolio, and Frank A. Branson, Inc., approx. 28.0% of portfolio)

Advisory Fee: Annual fee of 0.75% of average net assets on first $50 mil., 0.50% of average net assets in excess of $50 mil. If in any fiscal year, the operating expenses exceed 1.5% of first $50 mil. of average net assets, plus 1% of average net assets in excess of $50 mil., the advisor will reimburse the fund for such excess up to the amount of the fee received by the advisor. Fee for year-ended 12/31/91 was $601,694.

Capital Structure: *Common stock*: 1,505,462 shares authorized; 1,237,500 outstanding 3/31/92

Portfolio Highlights (as of 3/31/92): Common stocks and convertible securities 86.2%, short-term notes 13.8%. Largest industry concentrations: biotechnology 34.9%, regulated investment companies 7.1%, telephone systems 6.8%, industrial and commercial services 6.1%. **Largest positions**: Amgen Inc., RCM Growth Equity Fund Inc., Southwestern Bell Corp., Baxter International Inc., Boole & Babbage Inc.

Historical Financial Statistics (fiscal year-end: 12/31/91):

	1991	1990	1989	1988	1987	1986
Value of net assets (000)	118,001	70,856	66,314	57,443	53,407	56,367
NAV	104.89	62.98	58.95	50.74	46.36	47.62
Net investment income	1.05	1.48	1.46	1.15	1.11	1.52
Dividends from net investment income	1.07	1.46	1.47	1.14	2.60	1.43
Distributions from net realized gains	1.93	1.54	4.93	2.16	2.10	0.71
Expense ratio	0.88%	0.99%	0.97%	1.06%	1.01%	0.98%
Income ratio	1.25%	2.47%	2.46%	2.24%	2.03%	3.14
Portfolio turnover	16.82%	9.84%	35.58%	16.12%	25.14%	44.15%

Special considerations: At 3/31/92 the fund had an aggregate of approximately $2 million invested in the closed-end fund shares of Convertible Holdings, Inc. capital shares and General American Investors. The fund had a rights offering in January, 1992, whereby shareholders received one right for every share held and could subscribe for one additional share for every ten rights at a subscription price of $106.00. 112,500 shares were issued. The fund had $6.6325 of retained long-term capital gains for the year 1991; shareholders were able to take a credit on their 1991 tax returns equivalent to $2.255 per share. **Shareholders over 5%**: Erik E. Bergstrom, 21.11%.

The BlackRock Advantage Term Trust Inc.

(formerly The Blackstone Advantage Term Trust, Inc.)
One Seaport Plaza, New York, NY 10292

Category: Bond Fund

Phone: 212-214-3332; 800-227-7236
Listed: BAT, NYSE
Commenced Operations: April, 1990
Cusip: 09247A101

1991/mid-1992 Range of Premium/Disc: +8% to 0%
1991/mid-1992 Range of Price: $11 3/8 to $10
NAV Total Return 1991: +20.90%
Share Price Total Return 1991: +21.55%
Herzfeld Ranking 1991: 38th of 80 bond funds

Investment Objective: To manage a portfolio of high quality securities that will return $10 per share (the initial offering price) to investors on or shortly before 12/31/05, while providing high monthly income.

Officers:

L.D. Fink   Chairman
R.L. Schlosstein President

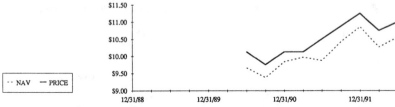

Investment Advisor: BlackRock Financial Management L.P. (formerly Blackstone Financial Management L.P.)
Advisory Fee: Monthly fee at annual rate of 0.60% of average weekly net assets through 12/31/95; 0.50% from that date to 12/31/00; and 0.40% from that date until the termination of the trust. Fee for year-ended 12/31/91 was $575,728.
Administrator: Prudential Mutual Fund Management Inc.
Administration Fee: Monthly fee at annual rate of 0.12% of average weekly net assets through 12/31/95; 0.10% from that date to 12/31/00; and 0.08% from that date until the termination of the trust. Fee for year-ended 12/31/91 was $115,146.

Capital Structure: *Common stock*: 200 mil. shares authorized; 9,510,667 shares outstanding 12/31/91
Debt: Reverse repurchase agreements with third party broker dealers; average daily balance of such reverse repurchase agreements outstanding during the year ended 12/31/91 was $22,919,743 at a weighted average interest rate of approximately 5.38%.

Portfolio Highlights (as of 12/31/91): Long-term investments 145.0%, short-term investments 3.0%, liabilities in excess of other assets (48.0%). Zero coupon securities 28%, U.S. treasury securities 25%, multiple-class mortgage pass-throughs 17%, CMO residuals 14%, mortgage pass-throughs 8%, stripped mortgage-backed securities 7%, asset-backed securities 1%. **Largest issuers**: U.S. treasury notes; U.S treasury strips 8/15/05; Federal National Mortgage Association Guaranteed REMIC Pass-Through Certificates; Government National Mortgage Association; Federal National Mortgage Association Stripped Mortgage-Backed Securities.

Historical Financial Statistics: (fiscal year-end: 12/31/91):

	1991	4/27/90 to 12/31/90
Value of net assets (000)	104,210	94,043
NAV	10.96	9.89
Net investment income	1.19	0.51
Dividends from net investment income	1.06	0.51
Distributions from short-term capital gains	--	0.06
Operating expense ratio	1.30%	1.17% ann.
Income ratio	11.79%	7.84% ann.
Portfolio turnover	254%	180%

Special considerations: The trust may repurchase shares from time to time. A tender offer at net asset value will be voted on by the board in 1995 and annually thereafter if the shares are trading at a discount from net asset value. The trust makes monthly distributions from net investment income and net short-term capital gains and retains, until final liquidation, income in an amount approximately equal to the tax exempt income attributable to its municipal zero coupon securities; but in no event greater than 1/10 of the trust's income per year. All or a portion of long-term capital gains is distributed at least annually. At the 1992 annual meeting shareholders approved a name change resulting from a reorganization of the advisor, "Blackstone" in the name was replaced by "BlackRock."

The BlackRock Income Trust Inc.

(formerly The Blackstone Income Trust, Inc.)

One Seaport Plaza, New York, NY 10292

Category: Bond Fund

Phone: 212-214-3332; 800-227-7236
Listed: BKT, NYSE
Commenced Operations: July, 1988
Cusip: 09247F100

1991/mid-1992 Range of Premium/Disc: +14% to 0%
1991/mid-1992 Range of Price: $11 to $8 1/8
NAV Total Return 1990: +15.82%; **1991:** +22.55%
Share Price Total Return 1990: +16.80%; **1991:** +28.83%
Herzfeld Ranking 1991: 31st of 80 bond funds

Investment Objective: Higher monthly income than investments in U.S. treasury securities consistent with preservation of capital through investment in high quality securities including mortgage-backed securities and asset-backed securities.

Officers:

L.D. Fink — Chairman
R.L. Schlosstein — President

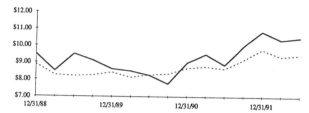

Investment Advisor: BlackRock Financial Management L.P. (formerly Blackstone Financial Management L.P.)
Advisory Fee: Monthly fee at annual rate of 0.65% of average weekly net assets. Fee for year-ended 10/31/91 was $3,517,740.
Administrator: Prudential Mutual Fund Management, Inc.
Administration Fee: Monthly fee at annual rate of 0.20% on first $500 mil. of weekly average net assets, 0.15% annual rate on excess. Fee for year-ended 10/31/91 was $1,065,908.

Capital Structure: *Common stock*: 200 mil. shares authorized; 61,818,895 shares outstanding 10/31/91
Debt: Reverse repurchase agreements with third party broker dealers; average daily balance outstanding during year ended 10/31/91 was $78,631,000 at a weighted average interest rate of 5.61%. Repurchase agreement outstanding 10/31/91 was $83,025,000.

Portfolio Highlights (as of 10/31/91): Long-term investments 132.8%, investments sold short (6.4%), other liabilities in excess of other assets (26.4%). Largest sector concentrations: mortgage pass-throughs 23%, U.S. government securities 23%, CMO residuals 21%, multiple class mortgage pass throughs 16%, stripped mortgage-backed securities 12%, asset backed securities 5%. Largest issues: U.S. treasury bonds and notes, Federal National Mortgage Association, Federal National Mortgage Association Stripped Mortgage-Backed Securities, Federal National Mortgage Association Guaranteed REMIC Pass-Through Certificates.

Historical Financial Statistics (fiscal year-end: 10/31/91):

	1991	1990	1989	7/88 to 10/88
Value of net assets (000)	582,845	519,429	511,110	567,413
NAV	9.43	8.49	8.42	9.44
Net investment income	1.05	1.13	1.00	0.21
Dividends from net investment income	1.03	1.06	1.03	0.18
Distributions from other sources	--	--	0.07	--
Operating expense ratio	1.07%	1.10%	1.12%	1.18% ann.
Income ratio	11.95%	13.58%	11.78%	9.00% ann.
Portfolio turnover	261%	77%	69%	74%

Special considerations: The fund maintains at least 80% of assets in investments rated AAA or Aaa, or issued or guaranteed by the U.S. government, its agencies or instrumentalities, with remaining assets also of high credit quality. The fund is permitted to repurchase shares when advantageous. Various anti-takeover provisions are contained in the fund's Articles of Incorporation. The fund reduced its monthly dividend rate to $0.0792 per share based on projected income levels for the fund. At the 1992 annual meeting shareholders approved a name change resulting from a reorganization of the advisor, "Blackstone" in the name was replaced by "BlackRock."

The BlackRock Insured Municipal Term Trust, Inc.

(formerly Blackstone Insured Municipal Term Trust)
One Seaport Plaza, New York, NY 10292

Category: Municipal Bond Fund

Phone: 212-713-2848; 800-227-7236	**1991/mid-1992 Range of Premium/Disc:** +8% to 0%
Listed: BMT, NYSE	**1991/mid-1992 Range of Price:** $10 1/8 to $9 1/4
Commenced Operations: February, 1992	**NAV Total Return 1991:** N/A
Cusip: 092474105	**Share Price Total Return 1991:** N/A
	Herzfeld Ranking 1991: N/A

Investment Objective: Current income exempt from regular federal income tax and return of $10.00 per share to investors on or about 12/31/10. At least 80% of total assets will be invested in a diversified portfolio of municipal obligations insured as to the timely payment of both principal and interest by issuers with claims-paying abilities which are rated AAA at the time of investment or which are of comparable claims-paying abilities.

Officers:

L.D. Fink   Chairman
R.L. Schlosstein   President

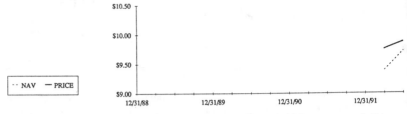

Investment Advisor: BlackRock Financial Management L.P. (formerly Blackstone Financial Management L.P.)
Advisory Fee: Monthly fee at annual rate of 0.35% of average weekly net assets.
Administrator: Mitchell Hutchins Asset Management, Inc.
Administration Fee: Monthly fee at annual rate of 0.10% of average weekly net assets.

Capital Structure: *Common stock*: 200 mil. shares authorized, 25,886,000 outstanding 6/26/92
                             Preferred stock: $125 mil. of preferred shares outstanding, dividend rate reset every 7 days
                             and every 28 days by series.

Portfolio Highlights: not yet published

Historical Financial Statistics:

	6/26/92
Value of net assets (000)	375,000
NAV	9.72

Special considerations: S&P rating AAAf. Monthly distributions are made from net investment income. The fund intends to retain until the final liquidating distribution, a small portion (not to exceed 10% in any year) of its net investment income to enhance the fund's ability to return to investors $10 per share upon termination of the fund. The Board of Directors will consider open market share repurchases at least annually to reduce discounts from net asset value which may occur. The fund's Articles of Incorporation contain various anti-takeover provisions, including a 75% voting requirement to convert to an open-end fund. At the 1992 annual meeting shareholders approved a name change resulting from a reorganization of the advisor. "Blackstone" in the name was replaced by "BlackRock." Initial dividend $0.05208 in May, 1992.

The BlackRock Investment Quality Term Trust Inc.

(formerly The Blackstone Investment Quality Term Trust, Inc.)

One Seaport Plaza, New York, NY 10292 **Category: Bond Fund**

Phone: 212-214-3332, 212-935-2626	**1991/mid-1992 Range of Premium/Disc**: +8% to 0%
Listed: BQT, NYSE	**1991/mid-1992 Range of Price**: $10 1/4 to $9 5/8
Commenced Operations: April, 1992	**NAV Total Return 1991**: N/A
Cusip: 09247J102	**Share Price Total Return 1991**: N/A
	Herzfeld Ranking 1991: N/A

Investment Objective: To manage a portfolio of fixed income securities that will return $10 per share to investors on or about 12/31/04 while providing high monthly income. The fund invests primarily in mortgage-backed securities and other securities issued or guaranteed by the U.S. government or its agencies and/or instrumentalities, mortgage-backed and asset-backed securities rated AAA or of equivalent quality, and corporate debt securities rated investment grade.

Officers:

L.D. Fink   Chairman

R.L. Schlosstein   President

Investment Advisor: BlackRock Financial Management L.P. (formerly Blackstone Financial Management L.P.)

Advisory Fee: Monthly fee at annual rate of 0.60% of average weekly net assets through 12/31/98, 0.50% from that date until 12/31/02, and 0.40% from that date until termination of the trust.

Administrator: Prudential Mutual Fund Management, Inc.

Administration Fee: Monthly fee at annual rate of 0.12% of average weekly net assets through 12/31/98, 0.10% from that date until 12/31/02, and 0.08% from that date until termination of the trust.

Capital Structure: *Common stock*: 200 mil. shares authorized, 32 mil. shares outstanding 4/23/92

Debt: An offering of preferred shares is planned for 3 to 6 months following the common stock offering.

Portfolio Highlights: not yet published

Historical Financial Statistics:

	4/23/92
Value of net assets (000)	300,800
NAV	9.40

Special considerations: Monthly distributions are made from net investment income. The fund intends to retain until the final liquidating distribution, income in an amount equal to the tax exempt income accrued on the Zero Coupon Securities, but in no event greater than 10% of the trust's net investment income per year. The Board of Directors will consider open market share repurchases at least annually to reduce discounts from net asset value which may occur. The fund's Articles of Incorporation contain various anti-takeover provisions, including a 75% voting requirement to convert to an open-end fund. At the 1992 annual meeting shareholders approved a name change resulting from a reorganization of the advisor, "Blackstone" in the name was replaced by "BlackRock."

The BlackRock Municipal Target Term Inc.

(formerly The Blackstone Municipal Target Term Inc.)
One Seaport Plaza, New York, NY 10292

Category: Municipal Bond Fund

Phone: 212-214-3332; 800-227-7236
Listed: BMN, NYSE
Commenced Operations: September, 1991
Cusip: 09247M105

1991/mid-1992 Range of Premium/Disc: +8% to -1%
1991/mid-1992 Range of Price: $10 1/8 to $9 3/8
NAV Total Return 1991: N/A
Share Price Total Return 1991: N/A
Herzfeld Ranking 1991: N/A

Investment Objective: To generate income that is exempt from federal income tax and to return $10.00 per share to investors on or about 12/31/06 by investing in a portfolio of high credit quality municipal securities.

Officers:

L.D. Fink   Chairman
R.L. Schlosstein President

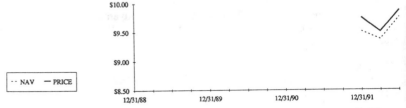

Investment Advisor: BlackRock Financial Management L.P. (formerly Blackstone Financial Management L.P.)
Advisory Fee: Monthly fee at annual rate of 0.35% of average weekly net assets. Fee for period 9/19/91 to 12/31/91 was $394,085.
Administrator: Prudential Mutual Fund Management, Inc.
Administration Fee: Monthly fee at annual rate of 0.07% of weekly average net assets. Fee for period 9/19/91 to 12/31/91 was $78,817.

Capital Structure: *Common stock*: 200 mil. shares authorized, 45,410,639 shares outstanding 12/31/91
Preferred stock: 4,500 reclassified shares in three series W7, F7 and W28, with a liquidation value of $50,000. Series W7 and F7 are cumulative at a rate reset every 7 days based on the results of an auction. Series W28 is cumulative and reset every 28 days based on the results of an auction. Dividend rates ranged from 3.75%-4.90% during fiscal 1991.

Portfolio Highlights (as of 12/31/91): Long-term 128.0%, short-term 29.7%, liabilities in excess of other assets (5.9%), liquidation value of preferred (51.8%). Largest industry concentrations: general obligations 23.41%, hospital 16.95%, transportation 9.71%, lease revenues 9.63%, water & sewer 9.0%, sales tax 8.54%, utility 6.36%. Largest geographic concentrations (long-term): IL 17.7%, NJ 16.6%, FL 9.5%, TX 9.1%, MI 9.0%, PA 8.0%, NY 7.9%, NV 7.8%, MA 7.6%. **Largest issuers:** New Jersey St. Tpk. Auth. Ser. C. 6.40%-07 American Municipal Bond Assurance Corporation; Jefferson (LA) Sales Tax Dist. Financial Guaranty Insurance Company; Massachusetts Bay Trans. Auth. General Trans. Sys. Ser. A Municipal Bond Insurance Association; (NY) Municipal Assistance Corp. American Municipal Bond Assurance Corporation; Illinois Health Facs. Auth. Elmhurst Mem. Hosp.

Historical Financial Statistics (fiscal year-end: 12/31/91):

	9/30/91 to 12/31/91
Value of net assets (000)	659,166
NAV	9.56
Net investment income avail. to common shares	0.11
Dividends from net investment income to common	0.05
Dividends from net investment income to preferred	0.02
Operating expense ratio	0.66% ann.
Income ratio avail. to common	3.89% ann.
Portfolio turnover	1%

Special considerations: Trust is rated AAAf by Standard & Poor's. At the 1992 annual meeting shareholders approved a name change resulting from a reorganization of the advisor, "Blackstone" in the name was replaced by "BlackRock."

The BlackRock 1998 Term Trust Inc.

(formerly The Blackstone 1998 Term Trust, Inc.)

One Seaport Plaza, New York, NY 10292

Category: Bond Fund

Phone: 212-214-3332; 800-227-7236	**1991/mid-1992 Range of Premium/Disc:** +7% to 0%
Listed: BBT, NYSE	**1991/mid-1992 Range of Price:** $10 3/4 to $9 7/8
Commenced Operations: April, 1991	**NAV Total Return 1991:** N/A
Cusip: 09247N103	**Share Price Total Return 1991:** N/A
	Herzfeld Ranking 1991: N/A

Investment Objective: To manage a portfolio of high quality securities that will return at least $10.00 per share to investors on or shortly before 12/31/98 while providing high monthly income. The trust invests primarily in mortgage-backed securities and zero coupon securities including zero coupon securities of municipal issuers.

Officers:

L.D. Fink   Chairman
R.L. Schlosstein   President

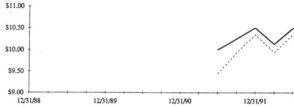

Investment Advisor: BlackRock Financial Management L.P. (formerly Blackstone Financial Management L.P.)

Advisory Fee: Monthly fee at annual rate of 0.50% of average weekly net assets through 12/31/94, 0.40% from then until 12/31/96, and 0.30% from then until termination of the trust. Fee from 4/19/91 to 11/30/91 was $1,581,223.

Administrator: Prudential Mutual Fund Management Inc.

Administration Fee: Monthly fee at annual rate of 0.12% of average weekly net assets through 12/31/94, 0.10% from then until 12/31/96, and 0.08% from then until termination of the trust. Fee from 4/19/91 to 11/30/91 was $379,494.

Capital Structure: *Common stock*: 200 mil. shares authorized; 58,660,527 shares outstanding 11/30/91
Debt: Reverse repurchase agreements with third party broker dealers; average daily balance of such reverse repurchase agreements outstanding during the year ended 11/30/91 was $104,970,000 at a weighted average interest rate of approximately 5.42%. Repurchase agreement outstanding 11/30/91 was $270,208,110.

Portfolio Highlights (as of 11/30/91): Long-term investments 148.0%, liabilities in excess of other assets (48.0%). Largest sector concentrations: mortgage pass-throughs 26%, multiple class mortgage pass-throughs 26%, U.S. government securities 12%, asset-backed securities 12%, CMO residuals 10%, taxable zero coupon bonds 9%, stripped mortgage-backed securities 4%, municipal zero coupon bonds 1%. **Largest Issuers:** FNMA mortgage pass-throughs; FHLMC multiclass mortgage participation certificates (guaranteed); U.S. treasury strips 2/15/99; Federal National Mortgage Association Guaranteed REMIC pass-through certificates.

Historical Financial Statistics:
4/30/91 to 11/30/91

Value of net assets (000)	595,698
NAV	10.16
Net investment income	0.48
Dividends from net investment income	0.42
Operating expense ratio	0.78% ann.
Income ratio	8.53% ann.
Portfolio turnover	154%

Special considerations: A tender offer at net asset value for any and all outstanding shares will be voted upon by the board of directors in 1996 if the shares are trading at a discount from net asset value. Open market share repurchases will be considered by the board at least annually. Zero coupon securities are expected to represent approximately 25% of the trust's initial assets. All trust assets will be rated AAA or Aaa or issued or guaranteed by the U.S. government or its agencies or instrumentalities. At the 1992 annual meeting shareholders approved a name change resulting from a reorganization of the advisor, "Blackstone" in the name was replaced by "BlackRock."

The BlackRock North American Government Income Trust Inc.

(formerly The Blackstone North American Government Income Trust, Inc.)

One Seaport Plaza, New York, NY 10292   **Category: Foreign Bond Fund**

Phone: 212-214-3332, 212-392-2550	**1991/mid-1992 Range of Premium/Disc:** +13% to +4%
Listed: BNA, NYSE	**1991/mid-1992 Range of Price:** $15 3/8 to $14 3/8
Commenced Operations: December, 1991	**NAV Total Return 1991:** N/A
Cusip: 092475102	**Share Price Total Return 1991:** N/A
	Herzfeld Ranking 1991: N/A

Investment Objective: To manage a portfolio of high grade securities to achieve high monthly income consistent with the preservation of capital. The fund will invest in Canadian and U.S. dollar-denominated securities, primarily securities issued or guaranteed by the federal governments of Canada and the U.S., their political subdivisions and agencies and instrumentalities. All assets will be government securities, securities rated AAA or of comparable credit quality.

Officers:

L.D. Fink   Chairman
R.L. Schlosstein   President

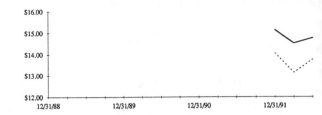

Investment Advisor: BlackRock Financial Management L.P. (formerly Blackstone Financial Management L.P.)
Advisory Fee: Monthly fee at annual rate of 0.60% of average weekly net assets.
Administrator: Prudential Mutual Fund Management Inc.
Administration Fee: Monthly fee at annual rate of 0.10% of average weekly net assets.

Capital Structure: *Shares of Beneficial Interest:* 200 mil. shares authorized, 32 mil. outstanding 12/20/91.

Portfolio Highlights: not yet published

Historical Financial Statistics:

	12/20/91
Value of net assets (000)	451,200
NAV	14.10

Special considerations: At least 65% of assets will be invested in government securities. The fund will distribute monthly dividends from net investment income, including all or a portion of net short-term capital gains. The Board of Directors will consider engaging in open market share repurchases at least annually in an effort to reduce any discounts from net asset value. The fund's Charter and By-Laws contain various anti-takeover provisions including a 75% voting requirement for conversion to an open-end fund and removal of a director. At the 1992 annual meeting shareholders approved a name change resulting from a reorganization of the advisor, "Blackstone" in the name was replaced by "BlackRock."

The BlackRock Strategic Term Trust Inc.

(formerly The Blackstone Strategic Term Trust, Inc.)

Two World Trade Center, New York, NY 10048

Category: Bond Fund

Phone: 212-392-2550; 800-869-3863	**1991/mid-1992 Range of Premium/Disc**: +12% to +4%
Listed: BGT, NYSE	**1991/mid-1992 Range of Price**: $11 to $9 7/8
Commenced Operations: January, 1991	**NAV Total Return 1991**: +17.54%
Cusip: 09247P108	**Share Price Total Return 1991**: +15.80%
	Herzfeld Ranking 1991: 54th of 80 bond funds

Investment Objective: High monthly income and to return at least $10 per share to investors on or shortly before 12/31/02 through investment in a high quality securities portfolio primarily in mortgage-backed securities and to a lesser extent in municipal securities.

Officers:

L.D. Fink — Chairman
R.L. Schlosstein — President

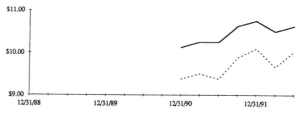

Investment Advisor: BlackRock Financial Management L.P. (formerly Blackstone Financial Management L.P.)

Advisory Fee: Monthly fee at annual rate of 0.60% of average weekly net assets through 12/31/94, 0.45% through 12/31/98 and 0.30% until termination. Fee for 12/12/90 to 11/30/91 was $2,968,068.

Administrator: Dean Witter Reynolds

Administration Fee: Monthly fee at annual rate of 0.15% of average weekly net assets through 12/31/94, 0.125% through 12/31/98 and 0.10% until termination. Fee for 12/12/90 to 11/30/91 was $742,017.

Capital Structure: *Shares of Beneficial Interest*: 200 mil. shares authorized, 57,510,639 shares outstanding 11/30/91

Debt: Reverse repurchase agreements with third party broker dealers; average daily balance of such reverse repurchase agreements outstanding during the year ended 11/30/91 was $74,981,472 at a weighted average interest rate of approximately 5.48%.

Portfolio Highlights (as of 11/30/91): Long-term investments 147.7%, short-term investments 0.7%, liabilities in excess of other assets (48.4%). Largest sector concentrations: multiple class mortgage pass-throughs 34%, mortgage pass-throughs 25%, CMO residuals 15%, taxable zero coupon bonds 13%, asset-backed securities 5%, municipal zero coupon bonds 4%, stripped mortgage-backed securities 4%. **Largest issuers**: FHLMC multiclass mortgage participation certificates; U.S. treasury strips; FNMA mortgage pass-throughs; FHLMC mortgage pass-throughs; FNMA guaranteed REMIC pass-through certificates.

Historical Financial Statistics:

	12/12/90 to 11/30/91
Value of net assets (000)	517,615
NAV	9.94
Net investment income	0.98
Dividends from net investment income	0.81
Operating expense ratio	0.96% ann.
Income ratio	11.14% ann.
Portfolio turnover	199%

Special considerations: The trust is rated AAAf by Standard & Poor's Corporation. The trust may invest in Eurodollar instruments and may invest up to 10% of its assets in securities issued by non-U.S. issuers. Various hedging transactions may be used to attempt to protect against possible declines in market value. A tender offer at net asset value for any and all of the outstanding shares will be voted upon by the board in 1994 and 1998 if the shares are trading at a discount. Various anti-takeover provisions are contained in the fund's Articles of Incorporation. At the 1992 annual meeting shareholders approved a name change resulting from a reorganization of the advisor, "Blackstone" in the name was replaced by "BlackRock."

The BlackRock Target Term Trust Inc.

(formerly The Blackstone Target Term Trust, Inc.)

One Seaport Plaza, New York, NY 10292   **Category: Bond Fund**

Phone: 212-214-3332, 800-227-7236	**1991/mid-1992 Range of Premium/Disc**: +12% to +2%
Listed: BTT, NYSE	**1991/mid-1992 Range of Price**: $11 1/8 to $9 7/8
Commenced Operations: November, 1988	**NAV Total Return 1990**: +11.45%; **1991**: +19.94%
Cusip: 092476100	**Share Price Total Return 1990**: +10.17%; **1991**: +16.79%
	Herzfeld Ranking 1991: 41st of 80 bond funds

Investment Objective: High monthly income, and the return of the $10.00 offering price to investors on or shortly before 12/31/2000. The fund invests primarily in mortgage-backed securities and zero coupon securities; all investments must be rated AAA or Aaa, or be issued or guaranteed by the U.S. government, its agencies or instrumentalities.

Officers:

L.D. Fink — Chairman
R.L. Schlosstein — President

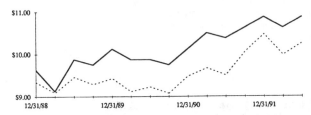

Investment Advisor: BlackRock Financial Management L.P. (formerly Blackstone Financial Management L.P.)
Advisory Fee: Monthly fee at annual rate of 0.60% of the fund's average weekly net assets until 12/31/92, 0.45% annually through 12/31/96 and 0.30% until termination of the fund. Fee for year-ended 10/31/91 was $5,540,958.
Administrator: Prudential Mutual Fund Management Inc.
Administration Fee: Monthly fee at annual rate of 0.15% of average weekly net assets on first $500 mil. plus 0.12% on excess until 12/31/92; 0.125% on first $500 mil. plus 0.10% on excess until 12/31/96 and 0.10% on first $500 mil. plus 0.08% on excess until termination of the fund. Fee for year-ended 10/31/91 was $1,260,663.

Capital Structure: *Common stock*: 200 mil. shares authorized; 95,460,639 shares outstanding 10/31/91
Debt: Reverse repurchase agreements with third party broker dealers; average daily balance of such reverse repurchase agreements outstanding during the year ended 10/31/91 was $46,611,000 at a weighted average interest rate of approximately 5.58%. Repurchase agreements outstanding 10/31/91 were $424,764,898.

Portfolio Highlights (as of 10/31/91): Long-term investments 152.8%, short-term investments 0.1%, liabilities in excess of other assets (52.9%). Sector concentrations: zero coupon securities 37%, CMO residuals 18%, U.S. government securities 14%, mortgage pass-throughs 13%, asset-backed securities 6%, multiple class mortgage pass-throughs 6%, pre-refunded municipal notes & bonds 4%, stripped mortgage-backed securities 2%. **Largest issuers**: U.S. treasury strips; FNMA, guaranteed REMIC pass-through certificates; FNMA pass-throughs; Government National Mortgage Association Series I 10.00% pass-through; Government Trust Certificates zero coupon bonds.

Historical Financial Statistics (fiscal year-end: 10/31/91):

	1991	1990	11/15/88 to 10/31/89
Value of net assets (000)	967,739	882,392	902,119
NAV	10.14	9.24	9.45
Net investment income	1.14	1.11	0.83
Dividends from net investment income	0.95	0.96	0.83
Operating expense ratio	0.92%	0.92%	0.92% ann.
Income ratio	11.82%	12.03%	9.66% ann.
Portfolio turnover	279%	114%	177%

Special considerations: The fund may repurchase shares when advantageous. The fund's Articles of Incorporation contain various anti-takeover provisions. The fund may invest up to 40% of total assets in securities which are not readily marketable, including those which are restricted as to disposition under securities law. At the 1992 annual meeting shareholders approved a name change resulting from a reorganization of the advisor, "Blackstone" in the name was replaced by "BlackRock."

Blue Chip Value Fund

633 17th Street, Suite 1800, Denver, CO 80270

Category: Equity Fund

Phone: 303-293-5999; **Hotline:** 303-293-5699
Listed: BLU, NYSE
Commenced Operations: April, 1987
Cusip: 095333100

1991/mid-1992 Range of Premium/Disc: +7% to -16%
1991/mid-1992 Range of Price: $8 1/4 to $5 1/2
NAV Total Return 1990: -2.17%; **1991:** +35.75%
Share Price Total Return 1990: -3.57%; **1991:** +43.08%
Herzfeld Ranking 1991: 6th of 15 equity funds

Investment Objective: High total return through capital appreciation and current income primarily through investment in a diversified portfolio of common stocks.

Officers:

K.V. Penland   Chairman
C.H. Anderson   President

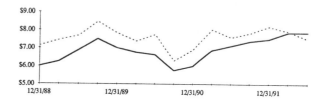

Investment Advisor: Denver Investment Advisors, Inc.
Advisory Fee: Monthly fee equal to 0.65% annually of average weekly net assets up to $100 mil., and 0.50% annually of excess. Fee for year-ended 12/31/91 was $469,671.
Administrator: American Data Services, Inc.
Administration Fee: Monthly fee equal to 0.10% annually of average weekly net assets up to $75 mil., 0.05% annually of average weekly net assets between $75 mil. and $125 mil. and 0.03% of excess; minimum $86,112 annually. Fee for year-ended 12/31/91 was $82,800.

Capital Structure:
        Common stock: 100 mil. shares authorized; 9,361,701 shares outstanding 12/31/91
        8 1/2% Senior Installment Notes: from the Aid Association for Lutherans for $7,375,500. Notes require monthly payment of principal and interest totaling $131,390.

Portfolio Highlights (as of 12/31/91): Common stocks 104.9%, money market fund 0.6%, other assets less liabilities 4.9%. Largest sector concentrations: consumer staples 36.5%, credit sensitive 27.3%, intermediate goods & services 15.9%, consumer cyclical 11.8%, capital goods 8.5%. Largest industry concentrations: diversified health care 9.2%, electric companies 8.0%, tobacco 6.9%, foods 6.9%, drugs 6.5%. **Largest positions:** Coca-Cola Co., Merck & Co. Inc., General Motor Corp. Class E, Abbott Laboratories, Kellogg Co.

Historical Financial Statistics (fiscal year-end: 12/31/91):

	1991	1990	1989	1988	2/4/87 to 12/31/87
Value of net assets (000)	78,221	65,300	73,317	66,787	62,516
NAV	8.36	6.97	7.83	7.13	6.68
Net investment income	0.13	0.14	0.25	0.20	0.15
Dividends from net investment income	0.13	0.14	0.30	0.19	0.11
Return of capital	0.83	0.61	0.48	--	--
Operating expense ratio (excl. interest)	1.31%	1.45%	1.38%	1.43%	1.37% ann.
Operating expense ratio (incl. interest)	1.63%	1.96%	1.98%	2.22%	2.12% ann.
Income ratio	1.66%	1.96%	3.25%	2.82%	2.46% ann.
Portfolio turnover	118.9%	103.88%	164.83%	135.06%	96.99%

Special considerations: The advisor uses its "Modern Value Investing" approach, in which it is generally fully invested in 50 common stocks that the advisor believes to be the best values of the 300 largest dividend-paying companies headquartered in the U.S. Under certain conditions, the fund will submit a proposal to redeem all outstanding shares at NAV on 6/30/93 but may repurchase shares whenever advantageous. The fund's Articles of Incorporation contain various anti-takeover provisions, including a staggered board of directors. As of 12/31/91 the fund had a capital loss carryforward of $8,505,071 expiring through 1998.

The Brazil Fund, Inc.
345 Park Avenue, New York, NY 10154

Category: Foreign Equity Fund

Phone: 617-330-5602
Listed: BZF, NYSE
Commenced Operations: April, 1988
Cusip: 105759104

1991/mid-1992 Range of Premium/Disc: +33% to -13%
1991/mid-1992 Range of Price: $23 5/8 to $6 3/8
NAV Total Return 1990: -51.41%; **1991**: +152.93%
Share Price Total Return 1990: -22.80%; **1991**: +118.52%
Herzfeld Ranking 1991: 1st of 46 foreign equity funds

Investment Objective: Long-term capital appreciation primarily through investment in equity securities of Brazilian issuers.

Officers:
J. Padegs   Chairman
N. Bratt   President

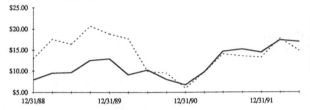

Investment Advisor: Scudder, Stevens & Clark Inc. (U.S. Advisor); Banco Icatu S/A (Brazilian advisor)
Advisory Fee: Monthly fee of 1.25% annually of average weekly net assets (Brazilian advisor paid by U.S. advisor from this fee). Fee for year-ended 12/31/91 was $1,751,651.
Administrator: Sodril S.A. Corretora de Titulos e Valores
Administration Fee: Annual fee payable quarterly in cruzeiros equal to $15,000 per year. Fee for year-ended 12/31/91 was $14,675.

Capital Structure: *Common stock*: 50 mil. shares authorized; 12,078,395 shares outstanding 12/31/91

Portfolio Highlights (as of 3/31/92): Equity securities 94.8%, short-term investment 1.0%, commercial paper 2.6%. Largest industry concentrations: telecommunications 17.4%, food and beverage 12.2%, mining 11.5%, forest products 11.4%, tobacco 6.7%, chemicals 6.2%, banking 5.1%. **Largest positions**: Telecomunicações Brasileiras S.A.; Companhia Vale do Rio Doce; Aracruz Celulose S.A. "B"; Sadia Concórdia S/A.

Historical Financial Statistics (fiscal year-end: 12/31/91):

	1991	1990	1989	4/8/88 to 12/31/88
Value of net assets (000)	166,719	72,142	226,986	154,895
NAV	13.80	5.97	18.85	12.90
Net investment income	0.95	1.32	0.88	0.42
Dividends from net investment income	--	0.12	0.89	0.41
Distributions from net realized gains on investments and foreign currency transactions	--	--	1.36	0.28
Distributions from paid-in capital	--	--	0.93	--
Operating expense ratio	2.15%	2.25%	2.01%	1.90% ann.
Income ratio	8.13%	11.27%	4.76%	4.70% ann.
Portfolio turnover	12.69%	4.31%	14.02%	0.74% ann.

Special considerations: Currency, political, and economic risks, including an extremely high inflation rate in Brazil, are present in addition to the usual risks of closed-end fund investing. The fund is subject to Brazilian withholding taxes on dividends and interest (U.S. shareholders may claim a tax credit). The fund's Articles of Incorporation contain various anti-takeover provisions, including a staggered board of directors. During March, 1990, major economic programs were initiated by the new Brazilian government. On 3/16/90 the Brazilian government changed the currency from the cruzado novo to the cruzeiro, froze 80% of the cruzados novos and virtually all accounts, including the maturity amount of the fund's holdings of short-term government instruments (LFT's) and interest-bearing cruzado novo account and imposed an 8% tax on LFT's. **Shareholders over 5%**: Bankers Trust Corp. 10.96%; Government of Kuwait, 7.4%

The Brazilian Equity Fund, Inc.

One Citicorp Center, 58th Floor, 153 East 53rd Street
New York, NY 10022

Category: Foreign Equity Fund

Phone: 212-832-2626	**1991/mid-1992 Range of Premium/Disc:** est. +28% to +6%
Listed: BZL, NYSE	**1991/mid-1992 Range of Price:** $17 3/4 to $12 1/8
Commenced Operations: April, 1992	**NAV Total Return 1991:** N/A
Cusip: 105884100	**Share Price Total Return 1991:** N/A
	Herzfeld Ranking 1991: N/A

Investment Objective: Long-term capital appreciation by investing primarily in Brazilian equity securities. The fund may also invest up to 25% of its assets in corporate and governmental debt securities of Brazilian issuers for the purpose of seeking long-term capital appreciation.

Officers:

E. Bassini   Chairman, Chief Executive Officer

Investment Advisor: BEA Associates

Advisory Fee: Quarterly fee at an annual rate of 1.35% of the first $100 mil. of average weekly net assets and 1.05% of amounts above $100 mil.

Co-Advisor: Garantia Administracao de Recursos S.A.

Co-Advisory Fee: Fee paid by BEA Associates at the annual rate of 0.25% of the first $100 mil. of average weekly net assets and 0.10% of amounts above $100 mil. (BEA Associates may pay the co-advisor in cruzeiros, this will reduce the amount payable to BEA Associates by the fund.)

Administrator: Mitchell Hutchins Asset Management Inc.

Administration Fee: Fee equal to the annual rate of 0.15% of the average weekly net assets of the fund.

Brazilian Administrator: Banco de Investimentos Garantia S.A.

Brazilian Administration Fee: Fee equal to the annual rate of 0.05% of the average weekly net assets of the fund invested in Brazil.

Capital Structure: *Common stock*: 100 mil. shares authorized, 4 mil. shares outstanding 4/3/92

Portfolio Highlights: not yet published

Historical Financial Statistics:

	4/3/92
Value of net assets (000)	55,800
NAV	13.95

Special considerations: The fund makes annual distributions of substantially all net investment income and net realized long-term capital gains in excess of net realized short-term capital losses. The fund's Articles of Incorporation and Bylaws contain various anti-takeover provisions including a 75% vote to merge with another fund or to liquidate the fund. Open-ending of the fund would require at least a 75% affirmative vote of the directors and a 75% vote of shareholders unless approved by 75% of the continuing directors. **Shareholders over 5%:** Teton Partners, L.P. & Noble Partners L.P., 5.5%.

Bunker Hill Income Securities, Inc.

156 West 56th Street, New York, NY 10019

Category: Bond Fund

Phone: 213-229-1172; 800-332-3863
Listed: BHL, NYSE
Commenced Operations: June, 1973
Cusip: 120609102

1991/mid-1992 Range of Premium/Disc: +5% to -11%
1991/mid-1992 Range of Price: $16 5/8 to $13
NAV Total Return 1990: +0.16%; **1991:** +17.19%
Share Price Total Return 1990: -13.48%; **1991:** +32.80%
Herzfeld Ranking 1991: 58th of 80 bond funds

Investment Objective: High current income consistent with prudent investment risk, primarily through investment in a diversified portfolio of high-quality marketable debt securities.

Officers:

G.F. Sanford   Chairman

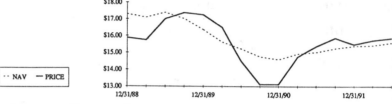

Investment Advisor: Security Pacific Investment Managers, Inc.

Advisory Fee: Quarterly fee of 0.5% annually on first $100 mil. net assets, and 0.35% of net assets on excess. The advisor will reimburse the fund for all expenses (excluding interest, taxes, brokerage commissions and certain other expenses, if any) borne by the fund in any fiscal year in excess of 1.5% of average net assets up to $30 mil., and 1% of average net assets in excess of $30 mil.

Capital Structure: *Common stock:* 6 mil. shares authorized; 2,758,792 shares outstanding 3/31/92
                          Preferred stock: 3 mil. shares authorized; none outstanding 3/31/92

Portfolio Highlights (as of 3/31/92): Bonds 92.5%, U.S. government agency note 2.1%, U.S. government obligation 1.4%, short-term investment 4.1%, liabilities in excess of other assets (0.1%). Quality ratings: U.S. government & agency 3.47%, AAA 0.36%, AA 13.97%, A 11.31%, BBB 52.69%, BB 7.36%, B 6.70%, not rated 4.14%. Largest industry concentrations: utilities/domestic 17.1%, finance 14.6%, oil & gas 11.5%, municipal bonds/Canadian 9.6%, air transportation 9.9%, utilities/Canadian 8.5%, retail trade 7.2%. **Largest Issuers:** Province of Ontario deb. 15 1/8-11; British Columbia Hydro Power bonds 15 1/2-11; Systems Energy Resources 1st mtg. 14-94; Continental Bank N.A. sub. notes 12 1/2-01; Coastal Corp. sr. deb. 11 3/4-06.

Historical Financial Statistics (fiscal year-end: 9/30/91):

	six months 3/31/92	1991	1990	1989	1988	1987
Value of net assets (000)	42,690	41,807	40,528	46,426	47,881	47,547
NAV	15.47	15.22	14.79	17.02	17.56	17.56
Net investment income	0.78	1.68	1.85	1.98	1.88	2.17
Dividends from net investment income	0.83	1.77	1.93	1.87	2.01	2.16
Expense ratio	1.06% ann.	1.09%	1.06%	1.05%	1.02%	1.12%
Income ratio	10.11% ann.	11.16%	11.65%	11.35%	10.63%	12.04%
Portfolio turnover	53.01%	54.79%	83.92%	88.48%	133%	79%

Special considerations: The fund may borrow up to 33 1/3% of total assets less liabilities (other than liabilities represented by borrowings which are not temporary).

Capital Southwest Corporation

12900 Preston Rd., Suite 700, Dallas, TX 75230   **Category:** Specialized Equity Fund

Phone: 214-233-8242
Listed: CSWC, OTC
Commenced Operations: 1961
Cusip: 140501107

1991/mid-1992 Range of Premium/Disc: N/A
1991/mid-1992 Range of Price: $28 1/4 to $17 3/4
NAV Total Return 1990: N/A; **1991:** N/A
Share Price Total Return 1990: N/A; **1991:** N/A

Investment Objective: Capital appreciation primarily through investment in businesses believed to have favorable growth potential. The fund is a venture capital investment company.

Officers:

W.R. Thomas   Chairman & President

Investment Advisor: internally managed
Advisory Fee: Operating expense ratio for year-ended 3/31/92, 1.1%.

Capital Structure: *Common stock:* 5 mil. shares authorized; 3,643,751 shares outstanding 3/31/92
Debt: $11 mil. subordinated debentures of Capital Southwest Venture Corporation (wholly-owned subsidiary of Capital Southwest Corporation)

Portfolio Highlights (as of 3/31/92): Largest Issuers: Skylawn Corporation ($43.0 mil.); Alamo Group Inc. ($29.5 mil.); The RectorSeal Corporation ($16.5 mil.); The Whitmore Manufacturing Company ($11.1 mil.); Denver Technologies, Inc. ($6.2 mil.); Encore Wire Corporation ($4.8 mil.); Palm Harbor Homes, Inc. ($3.9 mil.); Intelligent Electronics, Inc. ($3.0 mil.).

Historical Financial Statistics (fiscal year-end: 3/31/92):

	1992	1991	1990	1989	1988	1987
Value of net assets (000)	107,522	97,139	94,610	83,124	78,375	69,285
NAV	29.51	26.86	26.16	23.33	22.00	18.35
Net investment income	0.65	0.58	0.48	0.20	0.01	0.01
Distributions from net investment income	0.60	0.50	0.40	0.30	0.10	0.11
Distributions from net realized gain on investments	--	--	1.04	--	--	--
Operating expense ratio	1.1%	1.1%	1.0%	1.2%	1.0%	1.5%
Income ratio	2.3%	2.2%	1.9%	0.9%	--0.1%	
Portfolio turnover	6.5%	0.1%	6.9%	--	2.5%	2.5%

figures adjusted for 2-for-1 stock split in 1987)

Special considerations: The fund had $5.9375 of retained long-term capital gains for the year 1991; shareholders were able to take a credit on their 1991 tax returns equivalent to $2.0187 per share. **Shareholders over 5%:** William R. Thomas, 33.1%; J. Bruce Duty, 18.8%; Gary L. Martin, 6.3%; Randolph C. Storer, 5.7%; David M. Smith, 5.6%.

Castle Convertible Fund, Inc.

75 Maiden Lane, New York, NY 10038

Category: Convertible Fund

Phone: 212-806-8800; 800-992-3863
Listed: CVF, ASE
Commenced Operations: 1971
Cusip: 148443104

1991/mid-1992 Range of Premium/Disc: -8% to -18%
1991/mid-1992 Range of Price: $22 1/8 to $16 1/4
NAV Total Return 1990: -3.66%; **1991:** +31.06%
Share Price Total Return 1990: -4.48%; **1991:** +38.15%
Herzfeld Ranking 1991: 4th of 8 convertible funds

Investment Objective: Current income and possible long-term capital appreciation by investing principally in convertible debt and convertible preferred securities.

Officers:

F.M. Alger   Chairman & President

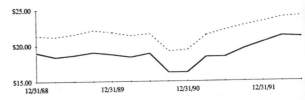

Investment Advisor: Fred Alger Management, Inc.

Advisory Fee: Monthly fee at annual rate of 0.75% of average weekly net assets; however, if aggregate expenses of the fund exceed 1.5% of the first $30 mil. average net assets and 1.0% of average net assets in excess of $30 mil., the investment advisor will reimburse the fund for the excess expenses. Fee for six months ended 12/31/91 was $190,631.

Capital Structure: *Common stock:* 10 mil. shares authorized; 2,211,863 shares outstanding 12/31/91

Portfolio Highlights (as of 3/31/92): Convertible corporate bonds 61.6%, convertible preferred stocks 22.6%, common stocks 12.0%, short-term corporate notes 4.3%, liabilities in excess of other assets (0.5%). Largest industry concentrations: energy 9.2%, insurance 8.3%, drugs & healthcare 7.9%, paper, packaging & forest products 7.6%, building & construction 7.2%. **Largest positions:** Enron Corporation sr. notes 10.75-98; Beverly Enterprises, cv. sub. deb. 7.625-03; James River Corp. dep. shrs. exch. pfd. Series L; Kroger Co. cv. sub. deb. 8.25-11; International Business Machines Corporation cv. sub. deb. 7.875-04.

Historical Financial Statistics (fiscal year-end: 6/30/91):

	six months 12/31/91	1991	1990	1989	1988	1987
Value of net assets (000)	52,138	49,058	47,883	47,760	49,703	60,250
NAV	23.57	22.18	21.65	21.59	22.53	27.90
Net investment income	0.83	1.61	1.70	1.96	1.96	2.23
Dividends from net investment income	0.90	1.66	1.67	1.88	2.98	2.20
Distributions from net realized gains	--	--	--	--	1.17	1.00
Expense ratio	1.14% ann.	1.15%	1.16%	1.26%	1.20%	1.13%
Income ratio	7.37% ann.	7.79%	7.84%	9.00%	8.09%	8.02%
Portfolio turnover	32.70%	48.37%	64.93%	71.29%	68.29%	46.29%

Special considerations: Shareholders over 5%: Alger Associates, 13.84%

Central Securities Corporation

375 Park Avenue, New York, NY 10152

Category: Equity Fund

Phone: 212-688-3011
Listed: CET, ASE
Commenced Operations: October, 1929
Cusip: 155123102

1991/mid-1992 Range of Premium/Disc: -15% to -23%
1991/mid-1992 Range of Price: $10 1/4 to $7 1/2
NAV Total Return 1990: -11.45%; **1991:** +24.97%
Share Price Total Return 1990: -13.51%; **1991:** +30.49%
Herzfeld Ranking 1991: 10th of 15 equity funds

Investment Objective: Growth of capital with a secondary objective of income.

Officers:
W.H. Kidd   President

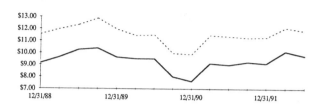

Investment Advisor: internally managed
Advisory Fee: Compensation to executive officers for 1991 (including contributions to profit sharing plan) totaled $361,183; expenses for administration and operations for 1991 totaled $246,989.
Administrator: internally administered

Capital Structure:
Common stock: 14 mil. shares authorized; 10,244,378 shares outstanding 12/31/91
Preferred Stock: $2.00 Series D Convertible Preference Stock, liquidation preference $25.00 per share(redeemable at corporation's option at $27.50 per share and convertible into 2.735 shares of common;750,000 shares authorized, 400,884 shares outstanding 12/31/91)

Portfolio Highlights (as of 12/31/91): Notes and debentures 3.9%, stocks 84.8%, short-term debt investments 12.0%. Largest sector concentrations: insurance 18.9%, electronics 11.8%, business services 10.8%, energy 8.6%, industrial equipment 8.4%, communications 7.4%. **Largest positions:** The Reynolds & Reynolds Company 10.0%, The Plymouth Rock Company Inc. 9.3%, Analog Devices Inc. 7.2%, The Chubb Corporation 5.9%, W.H. Brady Co. 4.8%, Murphy Oil Corporation 4.4%, Intel Corporation 3.7%, Rohm and Haas Company 3.3%, General Re Corporation 3.1%, GTE Corporation 2.6%.

Historical Financial Statistics (fiscal year-end: 12/31/91):

	1991	1990	1989	1988	1987	1986
Value of net assets (000)	131,640	111,152	129,377	118,930	110,629	116,731
NAV	11.87	10.00	12.24	11.77	11.36	13.26
Net investment income	0.14	0.17	0.17	0.16	0.17	0.18
Dividends from net investment income	0.14	0.20	0.35	0.16	0.22	0.23
Distributions from net realized gains	0.42	0.03	0.09	0.92	1.55	3.47
Distribution from capital surplus	0.14	0.47	0.56	--	--	--
Expense ratio	0.96%	0.98%	0.92%	0.89%	0.87%	0.84%
Income ratio	1.78%	2.11%	1.83%	1.88%	1.74%	1.61%
Portfolio turnover	17%	7%	14%	9%	33%	35%

Special considerations: The fund has been declaring an optional stock distribution each year. In 1991 the fund declared a distribution of 1 share for every 14 1/2 shares held or $0.70 in cash; in 1990 the fund declared a distribution of 1 share for every 12 shares held or $0.60 in cash; in 1989 the fund declared a distribution of 1 share for every 10 shares held or $0.90 in cash; in 1988 it declared 1 common share for every 12 shares held or $0.75 in cash. The fund repurchased 250,940 common shares in 1990 at an average discount of 18.5% and repurchased 390,994 shares in 1991 at an average discount of 18.4%. **Shareholders over 5%:** Christian A. Johnson Endeavor Foundation, preferred Stock 62.2%, common stock 37.6%; Mrs. Cristian A. Johnson, preferred stock 12.1%, common stock 9.6%; Wilmot H. Kidd, preferred stock 5.7%, common stock 7.2%.

The Charles Allmon Trust, Inc.

(formerly Growth Stock Outlook Trust, Inc)
4405 East-West Highway, Bethesda, MD 20814

Category: Equity Fund

Phone: 301-986-5866
Listed: GSO, NYSE
Commenced Operations: March, 1986
Cusip: 019756105

1991/mid-1992 Range of Premium/Disc: +6% to -9%
1991/mid-1992 Range of Price: $10 5/8 to $9 1/2
NAV Total Return 1990: +4.00%; **1991**: +11.90%
Share Price Total Return 1990: +11.24%; **1991**: +1.48%
Herzfeld Ranking 1991: 15th of 15 equity funds

Investment Objective: Long-term capital appreciation primarily through investment in a diversified portfolio of equity securities, with a secondary objective of income, in each case with emphasis on preservation of capital. The company invests in small, lesser known companies.

Officers:

C. Allmon   Chairman & President

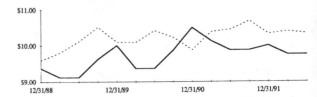

Investment Advisor: Growth Stock Outlook, Inc.
Advisory Fee: Quarterly fee of 0.25% of average weekly net assets (1% annually). Fee for year-ended 12/31/91 was $1,254,743.

Capital Structure: *Shares of beneficial interest*: 20 mil. shares authorized; 12,052,596 shares outstanding 3/31/92

Portfolio Highlights (as of 3/31/92): Common stocks 26.0%, convertible securities 0.1%, U.S. government obligations 69.2%, cash and other assets 4.7%. **Largest positions**: U.S. treasury bills and notes (69.2%), St. Jude Medical Inc., Crawford & Company Class 'A' and 'B', Lindsay Manufacturing, Harleysville Group Inc., Block Drug Company.

Historical Financial Statistics (fiscal year-end: 12/31/91):

	1991	1990	1989	1988	1987	3/14/86 to 12/31/86
Value of net assets (000)	125,330	120,906	124,278	127,843	127,426	136,905
NAV	10.40	9.90	10.10	9.59	9.18	9.52
Net investment income	0.44	0.54	0.57	0.41	0.36	0.29
Dividends from net investment income	0.44	0.54	0.57	0.41	0.64	--
Distributions from net realized gains	0.21	0.08	0.07	--	0.11	--
Expense ratio	1.31%	1.48%	1.43%	1.46%	1.51%	1.14%
Income ratio	4.17%	5.30%	5.58%	4.24%	3.59%	3.14%
Portfolio turnover	25%	41%	25%	24%	81%	45%

Special considerations: The fund may repurchase shares when trading at a discount from net asset value, and the board of directors announced it had authorized the repurchase of up to 500,000 shares in the open market or in privately negotiated transactions during the 12 months ending 4/30/93 when the shares are trading below net asset value. The fund repurchased 90,200 shares during the year-ended 12/31/90 at a weighted average discount of 9.2% and 156,600 shares during the year-ended 12/31/91 at a weighted average discount of 5.8%. The fund's Articles of Incorporation contain various anti-takeover provisions.

The Chile Fund, Inc.

One Citicorp Center, 58th Floor, 153 East 53rd St.
New York, NY 10022

Category: Foreign Equity Fund

Phone: 212-832-2626
Listed: CH, NYSE
Commenced Operations: September, 1989
Cusip: 168834109

1991/mid-1992 Range of Premium/Disc: 0% to -27%
1991/mid-1992 Range of Price: $41 1/4 to $15
NAV Total Return 1990: +27.30%; **1991:** +92.46%
Share Price Total Return 1990: +7.20%; **1991:** +74.40%
Herzfeld Ranking 1991: 3rd of 46 foreign equity funds

Investment Objective: Total return, consisting of capital appreciation and income through investment primarily in Chilean equity and debt securities.

Officers:
E. Bassini — President, Chief Investment Officer, & Chief Financial Officer

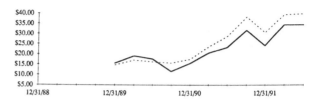

Investment Advisor: BEA Associates **Chilean Sub-Advisor:** Celsius Agente de Valores Limitada
Advisory Fee: Fee at the annual rate of 1.20% of the first U.S. $50 mil. of average monthly net assets, 1.15% on the next $50 mil., and 1.10% and any excess. Advisory fees for year-ended 12/31/91 were $1,791,320. **Sub-Advisory Fee** (paid by investment advisor): Annual fee at the rate of 0.15% of the first U.S. $50 mil. of average monthly net assets, 0.10% of the next $50 mil., and 0.05% on any excess.
Administrator: Provident Financial Processing Corporation **Chilean Administrator:** BEA Administration, Administradora de Fondos de Inversion de Capital Extranjero S.A.
Administration Fee: Fee at the annual rate of 0.1% of average monthly net assets, with a minimum annual fee. Fee for year-ended 12/31/91 was $199,143. **Chilean Administration Fee** (paid by Investment Advisor): Fee at 0.05% of average monthly net assets.

Capital Structure: *Common stock:* 100 mil. shares authorized, 5,402,554 shares outstanding 12/31/91

Portfolio Highlights (as of 12/31/91): Common stock 86.69%, time deposits 5.13%, Chilean government securities 1.79%, U.S. government securities 0.44%, participation contract for metal/mining extraction/Chile 0.28%, money market instruments/Chile 5.67%. Of the common stocks: Chile 84.95%, UK 1.72%, Canada 0.02%. **Largest positions:** Enersis, Endesa de Chile, Telefonos de Chile, Chilectra, Cartones.

Historical Financial Statistics (fiscal year-end: 12/31/91):

	1991	1990	9/27/89 to 12/31/89
Value of net assets (000)	160,360	93,744	79,494
NAV	29.68	17.44	14.79
Net investment income	0.97	1.55	0.04
Dividends from net investment income	0.98	1.25	0.05
Dividends from net short-term capital gains	2.18	--	--
Distributions in excess of net investment income	--	--	0.29
Expense ratio	1.75%*	2.04%	1.98% ann.
Income ratio	3.97%*	9.56%	1.44% ann.
Portfolio turnover	19.32%	12.63%	9.52% ann.

*ratios after taking into effect repatriation tax would have been: expense ratio 2.13%, income ratio 3.41%.

Special considerations: The fund may not repatriate capital for five years after investment in Chile except under limited circumstances to pay expenses. Certain provisions in the fund's Articles of Incorporation may have the effect of depriving shareholders of the opportunity to sell their shares at a premium over prevailing market prices, inhibiting the fund's possible conversion to an open-end fund. Shareholders approved future rights offerings at prices below market price at the 1992, annual meeting. **Shareholders over 5%:** G.T. Capital Management, 12.3%; Barings plc, 6.1%

CIGNA High Income Shares

One Financial Plaza, Springfield, MA 01103

Category: Bond Fund

Phone: 413-784-0100, 800-523-2097
Listed: HIS, NYSE
Commenced Operations: August, 1988
Cusip: 12551D109

1991/mid-1992 Range of Premium/Disc: +12% to -16%
1991/mid-1992 Range of Price: $8 to $3 3/4
NAV Total Return 1990: -21.86%; **1991**: +61.68%
Share Price Total Return 1990: -37.94%; **1991**: +115.53%
Herzfeld Ranking 1991: 1st of 80 bond funds

Investment Objective: High current income while preserving shareholders' capital through investment in a professionally managed, diversified portfolio of of high yield fixed-income securities; secondary objective is capital appreciation when consistent with first objective.

Officers:

G.R. Trumbull   Chairman
R.B. Albro   President

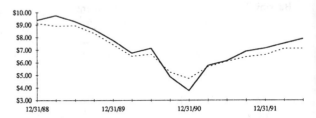

Investment Advisor: CIGNA Investments, Inc.
Advisory Fee: Monthly fee at annual rate of 0.75% of average weekly net assets under $200 mil., and 0.50% annual rate on average weekly net assets in excess of $200 mil. Fee for 1991 was $1,571,000.

Capital Structure:

Common stock: unlimited shares of beneficial interest authorized; 24,656,876 outstanding 12/31/91

Debt: Revolving credit agreement to borrow the lesser of $76,300,000 or 1/3 of the fund's eligible assets. Average borrowings outstanding during the year ended 12/31/91 were $59,013,000 at an average interest rate of 7.35%.

Portfolio Highlights (as of 12/31/91): Bonds and notes 133.4%, unites 0.6%, convertible preferred stock 0.1%, common stock 0.1%, warrants 0.1%, liabilities, less cash and other assets (34.3%). Quality ratings: Ba/BB 10.6%, B/B 77.2%, below B 4.2%, not rated 8.0%. Largest sector concentrations: food and beverages 21.9%, communications 18.3%, transportation 15.7%, containers and paper 14.8%, auto and truck 14.5%, chemicals 10.3%, financial 8.8%, industrial and misc. 7.6%, retail 7.4%. Average maturity 7.3 years, average credit quality B.   **Largest positions:** various I.C.H. Corp.; SCI Holdings Inc. 15-97; Container Corp. of America 14-01; Quantum Chemical Corp. 13-04; McCaw Cellular Communications Inc. 14-98.

Historical Financial Statistics (fiscal year-end: 12/31/91):

	1991	1990	1989	8/88 to 12/88
Value of net assets (000)	163,173	127,414	194,168	228,473
NAV	6.62	4.73	7.41	9.11
Net investment income	0.94	1.04	1.21	0.46
Distributions from net investment income	0.96	1.04	1.22	0.45
Distributions from paid-in capital	--	0.02	--	--
Operating expense ratio	1.26%	1.34%	1.08%	1.01% ann.
Interest expense ratio	2.79%	4.00%	3.43%	2.08% ann.
Income ratio	15.49%	16.98%	14.06%	12.86% ann.
Portfolio turnover	35%	14%	32%	9%

Special considerations: Before 1993 an open-ending proposal would require a 2/3 vote of shareholders to pass; after 12/31/93 a majority vote is required. The fund may repurchase shares or make tender offers if the Board deems it advantageous. The fund made a tender offer on 7/5/91, approximately 2.8 mil. shares were tendered at $6.30 per share. As of 12/31/91 the fund had a capital loss carryover for federal income tax purposes of $72,735,610, of which $162,500 expires in 1996, $10,011,421 expires in 1997, $32,490,863 expires in 1998, and $30,070,826 expires in 1999.

CIM High Yield Securities

153 E. 53rd Street, 24th Floor, New York, NY 10022   **Category: Bond Fund**

Phone: 212-891-6500; 617-573-1386 ext.6653   **1991/mid-1992 Range of Premium/Disc:** +5% to -21%
Listed: CIM, ASE   **1991/mid-1992 Range of Price:** $8 to $4 1/2
Commenced Operations: November, 1987   **NAV Total Return 1990:** -13.64%; **1991:** +40.44%
Cusip: 125527101   **Share Price Total Return 1990:** -23.29%; **1991:** +65.56%
   Herzfeld Ranking 1991: 12th of 80 bond funds

Investment Objective: High current income and preservation of capital primarily through investment in fixed income securities of domestic corporate issuers, mostly in the lower rating categories or non-rated.

Officers:
R.G. Wade, Jr.   Chairman
               & President

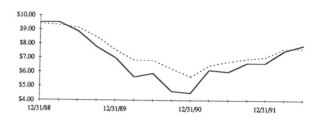

Investment Advisor: Chancellor Trust Company
Advisory Fee: Monthly fee at annual rate of 0.50% of average weekly net assets. Fee for 1991 was $130,505.
Administrator: The Boston Company Advisors, Inc.
Administration Fee: Monthly fee at annual rate of 0.09% of average weekly net assets, with a minimum fee of $40,000 per year. Fee for 1991 was $11,708.

Capital Structure: *Common stock:* unlimited number of shares of beneficial interest authorized; 3,947,265 outstanding 12/31/91
     Debt: Bank note payable equal to underwriting discount and organizational and offering expenses, $575,336 as of 12/31/91 at fixed annual rate of 10.54% to be repaid in 20 equal quarterly installments of $141,955.

Portfolio Highlights (as of 12/31/91): Corporate bonds and notes 99.2%, common stock 0.8%, warrants 0.2%, U.S. government securities 2.1%, other assets and liabilities (2.3%). Largest industry concentrations: retail 12.1%, communications 10.3%, food 9.6%, health care 8.3%, industrial 7.5%, leisure time 7.3%, broadcasting 5.7%, transportation 5.0%. **Largest positions:** Hospital Corporation of America jr. sub. deb. 17.5-05; McCaw Cellular Communications sr. sub. deb. 14-98; Wickes Companies, Inc. sub. notes 15-95; Owens-Illinois, Inc. jr. sub. deb. pay-in-kind 14.5-03.

Historical Financial Statistics (fiscal year-end: 12/31/91):

	1991	1990	1989	1988	11/18/87 to 12/31/87
Value of net assets (000)	28,015	22,283	29,122	36,394	34,220
NAV	7.10	5.65	7.38	9.41	9.35
Net investment income	0.84	0.86	1.13	1.16	0.08
Dividends from net investment income	0.83	0.87	1.15	1.13	0.09
Distributions from net realized gains	--	--	0.05	0.09	--
Operating expense ratio	2.46%	2.35%	2.28%	2.36%	2.18% ann.*
Income ratio	12.59%	13.00%	12.78%	12.07%	6.41% ann.*
Portfolio turnover	51.2%	34.9%	77.4%	209.6%	6.0%

*Advisory fee of $10,026 waived for period ended 12/31/87.

Special considerations: Under certain conditions, beginning in 1993, the fund will annually submit an open-ending proposal. Trustees will also consider, at least annually, repurchasing or making a tender offer for the fund's shares. The fund may borrow up to 15% of total assets. The Declaration of Trust contains various anti-takeover provisions. At 12/31/91 the fund had available for federal tax purposes an unused capital loss carryforward of $532,345 expiring in 1997, $1,428,262 expiring in 1998, and $3,316,747 expiring in 1999.

Circle Income Shares, Inc.

PO Box 44027, Indianapolis, IN 46244

Category: Bond Fund

Phone: 317-321-8180
Listed: CINS, OTC
Commenced Operations: July, 1973
Cusip: 172572109

1991/mid-1992 Range of Premium/Disc: +10% to -9%
1991/mid-1992 Range of Price: $13 1/4 to $10 1/4
NAV Total Return 1990: +3.54%; **1991:** +16.43%
Share Price Total Return 1990: +1.24%; **1991:** +31.85%
Herzfeld Ranking 1991: 62nd of 80 bond funds

Investment Objective: High income, primarily through investment in fixed-income securities.

Officers:

L.E. Nulsen   President & CEO

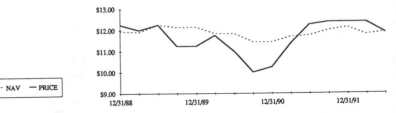

Investment Advisor: Bank One, Indianapolis, NA
Advisory Fee: Monthly fee at annual rate of 0.50% on first $50 mil. of average weekly net assets plus 0.40% of average weekly net assets on the excess. (The advisory fee may be reduced if certain annual expenses exceed 1 1/2% of the first $30 mil. of average weekly net assets and 1% of the remaining average net assets). Fee for nine months ended 3/31/92 was $123,334.

Capital Structure: *Common stock:* 10 mil. shares authorized; 2,776,884 shares outstanding 3/31/92

Portfolio Highlights (as of 3/31/92): U.S. government instrumentality obligations 27.9%, corporate obligations 69.2%, short-term obligations 1.3%. **Largest issues:** Federal Home Loan Mortgage Corporation; Federal National Mortgage Association; Government National Mortgage Association; Arizona Public Service First Mortgage Bonds 10 3/4-19; Beneficial Corp. notes 12 3/4-94.

Historical Financial Statistics (fiscal year-end: 6/30/91):	nine months 3/31/92	1991	1990	1989	1988	1987
Value of net assets (000)	32,867	32,130	32,323	33,363	32,821	32,549
NAV	11.84	11.75	11.84	12.25	12.32	12.48
Net investment income	0.80	1.18	1.19	1.19	1.21	1.28
Dividends from net investment income	0.82	1.20	1.17	1.32	1.32	1.32
Expense ratio*	0.94% ann.	0.98%	0.98%	0.99%	0.94%	0.89%
State and federal taxes to average net assets	--	(0.07%)	0.13%	0.13%	0.19%	0.06%
Income ratio	9.13% ann.	10.19%	9.88%	9.87%	9.84%	9.98%
Portfolio turnover	31.09%	15.30%	12.01%	44.51%	42.43%	29.80%

*excludes state and federal taxes

Special considerations: The fund had a total capital loss carryforward at 6/30/91 of $2,316,021 expiring through 1999. Dividend rate reduced to $0.085 in January, 1992.

Clemente Global Growth Fund, Inc.

152 West 57th Street, 25th Fl., New York, NY 10019

Category: Foreign Equity Fund

Phone: 212-765-0700
Listed: CLM, NYSE
Commenced Operations: June, 1987
Cusip: 185569100

1991/mid-1992 Range of Premium/Disc: -8% to -19%
1991/mid-1992 Range of Price: $9 7/8 to $7 7/8
NAV Total Return 1990: -15.03%; **1991:** +15.53%
Share Price Total Return 1990: -13.40%; **1991:** +11.47%
Herzfeld Ranking 1991: 17th of 46 foreign equity funds

Investment Objective: Long-term capital appreciation through investment in equity securities of small and medium sized companies located throughout the world, concentrating on securities markets in the U.S., Japan, Europe, the Asia/Pacific countries, Canada, Australia and emerging securities markets in certain developing countries.

Officers:

L.C. Clemente   Chairman
L.M. Clemente, Jr.   President

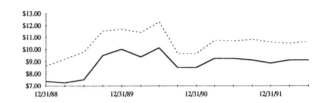

Investment Advisor: Clemente Capital Inc.

Advisory Fee: Monthly fee at annual rate of 1% of average monthly net assets to be increased to 1.50% annually or reduced to 0.50% annually as determined by relative performance to the FT-Actuaries World Index. Fee for year-ended 12/31/91 was $933,803 (which includes a $298,983 performance adjustment).

Administrator: Furman Selz Mager Dietz & Birney Incorporated

Administration Fee: Quarterly fee at annual rate of 0.20% of the fund's average weekly net assets. Fee for year-ended 12/31/91 was $126,940.

Capital Structure: *Common stock*: 25 mil. shares authorized; 5,892,400 shares outstanding 12/31/91

Portfolio Highlights (as of 3/31/92): Common stock 94.82%, corporate bonds 2.03%, preferred stock 1.28%, short-term investments 1.06%. Largest geographic concentrations: Far East 39.8%, Europe 28.0%, Latin America 12.8%, North America 17.5%. **Largest positions:** Astra AB A Free, Tolmex S.A. de C.V. Class B2, Tian An China, Shun Tak Enterprises Corp. Ltd., Raito Kogyo Co. Ltd.

Historical Financial Statistics (fiscal year-end: 12/31/91):

	1991	1990	1989	1988	6/30/87 to 12/31/87
Value of net assets (000)	63,783	57,671	69,013	51,380	46,047
NAV	10.82	9.79	11.71	8.72	7.66
Net investment income (loss)	(0.01)	(0.05)	(0.05)	0.01	0.03
Dividends from net investment income	--	--	--	0.02	--
Distributions from net realized gains	0.35	0.16	0.16	0.04	--
Expense ratio	2.74%	3.08%	3.05%	2.59%	2.94% ann.
Income ratio (loss)	(0.11%)	(0.42% loss)	(0.47% loss)	0.11%	0.74% ann.
Portfolio turnover	66.11%	28.69%	67.35%	97.64%	45.38%

Special considerations: At the April 29, 1992, annual meeting, shareholders voted against a proposal to open-end the fund in line with management's recommendations. Management also announced a 10% distribution policy. The fund may repurchase shares whenever shares trade at discounts of 10% of more. The fund's Articles of Incorporation contain various anti-takeover provisions.

CNA Income Shares, Inc.

CNA Plaza, Chicago, IL 60685

Category: Bond Fund

Phone: 312-822-4181
Listed: CNN, NYSE
Commenced Operations: 1973
Cusip: 126119106

1991/mid-1992 Range of Premium/Disc: +17% to -7%
1991/mid-1992 Range of Price: $12 3/4 to $8 1/2
NAV Total Return 1990: +0.39%; **1991:** +28.34%
Share Price Total Return 1990: -16.38%; **1991:** +42.43%
Herzfeld Ranking 1991: 19th of 80 bond funds

Investment Objective: High current income with secondary objective of capital appreciation, primarily through investment in debt securities rated in the four highest rating categories.

Officers:

D.C. Rycroft   Chairman & President

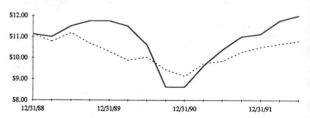

Investment Advisor: Continental Assurance Company
Advisory Fee: Monthly fee at annual rate of 0.5% of average weekly net assets. The fund also pays certain other expenses of operating the fund to a prescribed amount; expenses above that amount are reimbursed to the fund. Fee for year-ended 12/31/91 was $381,816.

Capital Structure: *Common stock*: 15 mil. shares authorized; 7,682,608 shares outstanding 12/31/91
Debt: $28,800,000 Five Year Convertible Extendible Notes repayable 5/31/92 at the option of the holder. Reset rate on the 9.125% Five Year Extendible Notes will be 1.25 percentage points over the 5-year Treasury note on 5/1/92 and will take effect on 6/1/92. Conversion price $11.73.

Portfolio Highlights (as of 12/31/91): Debt securities 133.9%, warrants 0.2%, short-term notes 1.1%. Largest industry concentrations: utilities 26.5%, government debt 23.6%, mortgage-backed 14.7%, transportation 9.5%, consumer products 8.5%, energy 7.5%, aerospace technology 6.3%, automotive 6.0%. **Largest issuers:** Federal Home Loan Mortgage Corporation multi-class PCs; Student Loan Marketing Association; Federal National Mortgage Association; International Bank for Reconstruction and Development; Occidental Petroleum Corporation sr. deb. 11.75-11.

Historical Financial Statistics (fiscal year-end: 12/31/91):

	1991	1990	1989	1988	1987	1986
Value of net assets (000)	81,151	69,626	77,001	80,417	78,384	75,509
NAV	10.56	9.16	10.29	11.12	11.03	11.96
Net investment income	1.15	1.21	1.26	1.25	1.25	1.25
Dividends from net investment income	1.16	1.20	1.24	1.29	1.35	1.20
Expense ratio	1.05%	0.97%	0.88%	0.88%	0.90%	0.88%
Income ratio	11.58%	12.35%	11.60%	11.03%	10.90%	10.67%
Portfolio turnover	39.77%	35.16%	39.12%	33.95%	29.67%	66.53%

Colonial High Income Municipal Trust

One Financial Center, Boston, MA 02111

Category: Municipal Bond Fund

Phone: 617-426-3750
Listed: CXE, NYSE
Commenced Operations: February, 1989
Cusip: 195743109

1991/mid-1992 Range of Premium/Disc: +5% to -6%
1991/mid-1992 Range of Price: $9 1/2 to $8 1/4
NAV Total Return 1990: +5.43%; **1991:** +7.53%
Share Price Total Return 1990: +2.49%; **1991:** +7.23%
Herzfeld Ranking 1991: 48th of 51 municipal bond funds

Investment Objective: High current income, generally exempt from federal income taxes primarily through investment in medium and lower quality bonds and notes issued by or on behalf of state and local governmental units whose interest is exempt from federal income tax.

Officers:
T. Bleasdale   Chairman
J.A. McNeice, Jr. President

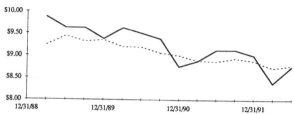

Investment Advisor: Colonial Management Associates, Inc.
Advisory Fee: Monthly fee at annual rate of 0.80% of average weekly net assets. Fee for 1991 was $2,181,000.
Administrator: Colonial Management Associates, Inc. (various bookkeeping and pricing services)
Administration Fee: $18,000 annually plus the following: no charge for first $50 mil., 0.0233% on next $950 mil., 0.0167% on next $1 bil., 0.01% on next $1 bil., 0.0007% on excess.

Capital Structure: *Shares of beneficial interest:* unlimited number of shares authorized; 30,658,000 outstanding 12/31/91

Portfolio Highlights (as of 12/31/91): Municipal bonds 97.2%, short-term obligations 0.9%, other assets & liabilities 1.9%. Largest sector concentrations: nursing homes 25.0%, hospitals & health care 18.5%, housing 14.7%, pollution control revenue 13.3%, electric 7.1%. **Largest issuers:** NJ Salem County Public Service Electric & Gas Co. 10.5-14; TX Harris County Memorial Hospital 10.875-14; IN Indianapolis Power & Light Co. 10.625-14; TX Bexar Housing Finance 8.2-22; TX Houston Airport 10.875-13.

Historical Financial Statistics (fiscal year-end: 12/31/91):

	1991	1990	2/16/89 to 12/31/89
Value of net assets (000)	273,207	273,864	282,016
NAV	8.91	9.00	9.35
Net investment income	0.742	0.784	0.624
Dividends from net investment income	0.758	0.827	0.565
Expense ratio	0.97%	0.96%	0.90% ann.
Income ratio	8.30%	8.56%	7.71% ann.
Portfolio turnover	17%	23%	58%

Special considerations: The fund may repurchase shares when trading at a discount of 10% or more from net asset value. The fund has a staggered board of trustees, and its Declaration of Trust contains various anti-takeover provisions. On 12/31/91 the fund had capital loss carryforwards of $3,066,000 expiring in 1998 and $3,140,000 expiring in 1999.

Colonial InterMarket Income Trust I

One Financial Center, Boston, MA 02111

Category: Bond Fund

Phone: 617-426-3750
Listed: CMK, NYSE
Commenced Operations: September, 1989
Cusip: 195762109

1991/mid-1992 Range of Premium/Disc: 0% to -10%
1991/mid-1992 Range of Price: $11 1/2 to $9 1/2
NAV Total Return 1990: +5.62%; **1991**: +18.68%
Share Price Total Return 1990: +0.79%; **1991**: +26.11%
Herzfeld Ranking 1991: 48th of 80 bond funds

Investment Objective: Maximum current income through investment in the following sectors: securities issued or guaranteed as to principal and interest by the U.S. government, its agencies, authorities or instrumentalities; debt securities issued by foreign governments and their political subdivisions; and high yield securities.

Officers:
J.A. McNeice, Jr. Chairman & President

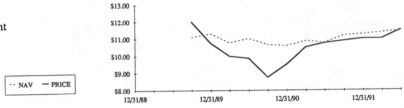

Investment Advisor: Colonial Management Associates, Inc.
Advisory Fee: Monthly fee at annual rate of 0.65% of average weekly net assets. Fee for year-ended 11/30/91 was $904,000.
Administrator: Colonial Management Associates, Inc. (various bookkeeping and pricing services)
Administration Fee: $18,000 annually plus the following: no charge for first $50 mil., 0.0233% on next $950 mil., 0.0167% on next $1 bil., 0.01% on next $1 bil., 0.0007% on excess.

Capital Structure: *Shares of beneficial interest*: unlimited number of shares authorized, 11,009,000 shares outstanding 11/30/91

Portfolio Highlights (as of 11/30/91): Corporate bonds & notes 46.6%, government & agency obligations 50.3%, preferred stocks 0.9%, common stocks 0.1%, short-term obligations 3.0%, liability for written call options (0.1%), other assets & liabilities (0.8%). Largest sector concentrations: government & agency obligations 50.3%, consumer non-durables 25.6%, government agencies 13.1%, manufacturing 9.4%, energy 4.1%. **Largest issuers**: Government National Mortgage Association; Government of Spain 13.45-96; U.S. treasury note 13.75-92; Victoria Finance Corp. 13.5-03; Quebec Province 10.25-01.

Historical Financial Statistics (fiscal year-end: 11/30/91):

	1991	1990	9/22/89 to 11/30/89
Value of net assets (000)	124,778	117,083	123,936
NAV	11.33	10.64	11.26
Net investment income	1.229	1.285	0.181
Dividends from net investment income	1.229	1.346	0.12
Dividends from net realized gains	0.006	0.004	--
Expense ratio	1.07%	1.11%	0.90% ann.
Income ratio	11.23%	11.88%	9.95% ann.
Portfolio turnover	109%	153%	--

Special considerations: The trust may repurchase shares in the open market at the discretion of the trustees and will do so in order to eliminate discounts which may develop. Beginning 12/1/94, under certain circumstances, including written requests from holders of 10% or more of the trust's outstanding shares, an open-ending proposal will be submitted to shareholders. The fund has a staggered board of trustees. The fund reduced its monthly dividend rate to $0.09 per share beginning with the 6/1/92 dividend.

Colonial Intermediate High Income Fund

One Financial Center, Boston, MA 02111

Category: Bond Fund

Phone: 617-426-3750
Listed: CIF, NYSE
Commenced Operations: July, 1988
Cusip: 195763107

1991/mid-1992 Range of Premium/Disc: +5% to -24%
1991/mid-1992 Range of Price: $6 7/8 to $3 5/8
NAV Total Return 1990: -25.51%; **1991:** +45.82%
Share Price Total Return 1990: -30.41%; **1991:** +66.38%
Herzfeld Ranking 1991: 9th of 80 bond funds

Investment Objective: High current income through investment in high yield fixed income securities. The dollar-weighted average maturity of the fund's debt securities will be between 3 and 10 years, with at least 80% of total assets invested in the lower rating categories.

Officers:

J.A McNeice, Jr. Chairman & President

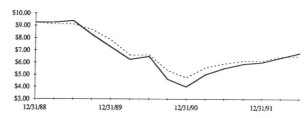

Investment Advisor: Colonial Management Associates, Inc.
Advisory Fee: Monthly fee at annual rate of 0.80% of average weekly net assets; fee for bookkeeping and pricing services at a base fee of $18,000 annually plus the following: no charge for first $50 mil., 0.0233% on next $950 mil., 0.0167% on next $1 bil., 0.01% on next $1 bil., 0.0007% on excess. Fee for year-ended 10/31/91 was $480,000.
Administrator: The Boston Company Advisors, Inc.
Administration Fee: Monthly fee at annual rate of 0.25% of gross assets less liabilities other than indebtedness for borrowings including notes. (This fee is for services of the administrator, custodial, transfer and dividend paying agent and registrar.) Fee for year-ended 10/31/91 was $202,000.

Capital Structure: *Common stock*: unlimited number of shares authorized; 13,284,000 outstanding 10/31/91
Debt: $27,400,000 Senior Extendible Notes to mature in 1993, unless extended, at an interest rate of 9.93% per annum through 7/14/93.

Portfolio Highlights (as of 10/31/91): Corporate bonds & notes 99.7%, common stock 0.3%, other assets & liabilities (23.8%). Largest sector concentrations: manufacturing 34.1%, consumer non-durables 20.9%, retail 13.9%, transportation 11.7%, banking & financial services 8.1%, energy 7.7%, technology 2.5%. **Largest issuers:** Owens-Illinois Inc. 12.75-99; Clajon Capital Inc. 13-99; Jones Intercable Inc. 13-00; Mark IV Industries Inc. 12.75-01; Flexi Van Leasing Inc. 13.5-98.

Historical Financial Statistics (fiscal year-end: 10/31/91):

	1991	1990	1989	7/29/88 to 10/31/88
Value of net assets (000)	83,613	64,872	107,769	116,613
NAV	6.29	4.88	8.26	9.22
Net investment income	0.80	1.072	1.223	0.257
Dividends from net investment income	0.775	1.106	1.20	0.245
Distributions from paid-in capital	--	0.014	--	--
Operating expense ratio	1.38%	1.31%	1.24%	1.04% ann.
Interest expense ratio	3.80%	4.23%	3.26%	3.26% ann.
Income ratio	14.40%	15.86%	13.48%	11.06% ann.
Portfolio turnover	30%	12%	23%	34% ann.

Special considerations: The fund may repurchase shares or make tender offers when advantageous; and after 11/1/93, if certain conditions are met, may convert to an open-end fund with a 2/3 vote of outstanding shares.

Colonial Investment Grade Municipal Trust

One Financial Center, Boston, MA 02111

Category: Municipal Bond Fund

Phone: 617-426-3750
Listed: CXH, NYSE
Commenced Operations: May, 1989
Cusip: 195768106

1991/mid-1992 Range of Premium/Disc: +10% to +3%
1991/mid-1992 Range of Price: $12 1/4 to $11 1/4
NAV Total Return 1990: +6.94%; **1991:** +10.55%
Share Price Total Return 1990: +3.75%; **1991:** +11.16%
Herzfeld Ranking 1991: 39th of 51 municipal bond funds

Investment Objective: Current income, generally exempt from federal income taxes through investment primarily in investment grade bonds and notes issued by or on behalf of state and local governmental units whose interest is exempt from federal income tax.

Officers:
J.A McNeice, Jr. Chairman & President

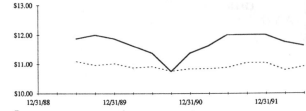

Investment Advisor: Colonial Management Associates, Inc.
Advisory Fee: Monthly fee equal to 0.65% annually of the fund's average weekly net assets. Fee for 1991 was $818,000.
Administrator: Colonial Management Associates, Inc. (various bookkeeping and pricing services)
Administration Fee: $18,000 annually plus 0.0233% of the fund's average weekly net assets over $50 million.

Capital Structure: *Shares of beneficial interest:* unlimited number of shares authorized; 11,509,000 outstanding 12/31/91
Debt: Loan outstanding at 12/31/91, $4,208 at a weighted average interest rate of 8.00%

Portfolio Highlights (as of 12/31/91): Municipal bonds 97.2%, short-term obligations 1.3%, other assets & liabilities 1.5%. Largest industry concentrations: housing 20.9%, hospitals & health care 17.7%, nursing homes 11.5%, public facility & improvement 9.6%, pollution control 8.2%, electric 7.9%, transportation 5.6%. **Largest issuers:** GA Burke County Pollution Control; PA Erie County Hospital 11.75-06; FL St. Lucie County Power & Light 11-19; NE Investment Finance RIB 10.223% variable rate 3/31/31; LA South Louisiana Port Commission 14.5-11.

Historical Financial Statistics (fiscal year-end: 12/31/91):

	1991	1990	5/26/89 to 12/31/89
Value of net assets (000)	127,589	124,871	126,856
NAV	11.09	10.85	11.02
Net investment income	0.886	0.942*	0.535*
Dividends from net investment income	0.894	0.945	0.524
Expense ratio*	0.87%	0.45%*	0%*
Income ratio	8.11%	8.66%*	8.30% ann.*
Fees and expenses waived or borne by advisor	--	0.43%	0.81% ann.
Portfolio turnover	15%	22%	32% ann.

*net of fees waived or borne by the advisor

Special considerations: The fund may use hedging techniques. The fund may repurchase shares from time to time to prevent discounts which may develop. Beginning in January, 1995, and each year thereafter, if certain conditions exist, a proposal to open-end the fund will be submitted to shareholders. The Declaration of Trust contains various anti-takeover provisions, including a staggered board of trustees.

Colonial Municipal Income Trust

One Financial Center, Boston, MA 02111   **Category:** Municipal Bond Fund

Phone: 617-426-3750
Listed: CMU, NYSE
Commenced Operations: March, 1987
Cusip: 195799101

1991/mid-1992 Range of Premium/Disc: +9% to -7%
1991/mid-1992 Range of Price: $8 7/8 to $7
NAV Total Return 1990: +5.73%; **1991:** +5.36%
Share Price Total Return 1990: -8.32%; **1991:** +4.20%
Herzfeld Ranking 1991: 50th of 51 municipal bond funds

Investment Objective: High current income exempt from federal income taxes with a secondary objective of capital preservation, primarily through investment in medium and lower quality bonds and notes issued by or on behalf of state and local governmental units.

Officers:
J.A. McNeice, Jr. Chairman & President

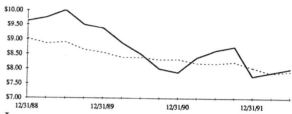

Investment Advisor: Colonial Management Associates, Inc.
Advisory Fee: Monthly fee at annual rate of 0.80% of average weekly net assets. Fee for year-ended 11/30/91 was $1,431,000.
Administrator: Colonial Management Associates, Inc. (various bookkeeping and pricing services)
Administration Fee: $18,000 annually plus the following: no charge for first $50 mil., 0.0233% on next $950 mil., 0.0167% on next $1 bil., 0.01% on next $1 bil., 0.0007% on excess.

Capital Structure: *Shares of beneficial interest:* unlimited number of shares authorized; 26,850,000 shares outstanding 11/30/91

Portfolio Highlights (as of 11/30/91): Municipal bonds 98.9%, short-term obligations 2.5%, other assets & liabilities (1.4%). Largest sector concentrations: hospitals & health care 24.7%, nursing homes 21.3%, housing 18.8%, public facility & improvement 10.9%, pollution control 10.4%. **Largest positions:** various TX Brazos River; PA Washington County Hospital 9.5-17; VA Dickenson County Volunteer Healthcare Systems Inc. 10.75-18; various PA Philadelphia Housing Redevelopment stepped-coupon; various AL Marshall County.

Historical Financial Statistics (fiscal year-end: 11/30/91):

	1991	1990	1989	1988	3/19/87 to 11/30/87
Value of net assets (000)	216,394	223,091	229,209	235,863	232,503
NAV	8.06	8.37	8.65	8.98	8.93
Net investment income	0.682	0.751	0.768	0.778	0.46
Dividends from net investment income	0.713	0.72	0.777	0.78	0.448
Expense ratio	0.87%	0.86%	0.87%	0.87%	0.80% ann.
Income ratio	8.29%	8.92%	8.66%	8.70%	7.19% ann.
Portfolio turnover	12%	20%	18%	52%	114% ann.

Special considerations: The fund may repurchase shares when they trade at discounts of 10% or more. The fund's Declaration of Trust contains various anti-takeover provisions including staggered terms for trustees.

Convertible Holdings, Inc.

PO Box 9011, Princeton, NJ 08543-9011

Category: Dual Purpose Fund

Phone: 609-282-2800
Listed: CNV (capital shares), NYSE
    CNVpr (income shares), NYSE
Commenced Operations: August, 1985
Cusip (capital shares): 212551204
Cusip (income shares): 212558100

1991/mid-1992 Range of Premium/Disc:
capital shares: -33% to -48%; income shares: +35% to +15%
1991/mid-1992 Range of Price:
capital shares: $7 3/4 to $4; income shares: $13 to $10 5/8
NAV Total Return CNV **1990:** -24.70%; **1991:** +44.49%
NAV Total Return CNVpr **1990:** +14.84%; **1991:** +15.27%
Share Price Total Return CNV **1990:** -25.00%; **1991:** +66.67%
Share Price Total Return CNVpr **1990:** +6.57%; **1991:** +28.97%

Investment Objective: Long-term appreciation and current and long-term growth of income. The fund invests primarily in convertible debt securities and convertible preferred stocks.

Officers:

A. Zeikel   President

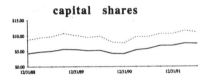
capital shares

income shares

Investment Advisor: Merrill Lynch Asset Management, Inc.
Advisory Fee: Quarterly fee at annual rate of 0.60% of average weekly net assets. The fee is reduced by 25% in any quarter that the fund does not achieve a minimum annualized rate of income return equal to 85% of the yield of the Value Line Convertible Index. Fee for year-ended 12/31/91 was $1,582,777.

Capital Structure: *Common stock*: 15 mil. shares authorized; 13,605,400 shares outstanding 12/31/92
    Preferred stock: 15 mil. shares authorized; 13,605,400 shares outstanding 12/31/92

Portfolio Highlights (as of 3/31/92): Convertible debentures 64.8%, corporate bonds 0.7%, convertible preferred stocks 14.6%, common stocks 12.9%, short-term 6.5%, short sales (1.9%), other assets 2.4%. Largest industry concentrations: banking & finance 13.2%, drugs 7.3%, computers 5.3%. **Largest Issuers:** Bristol-Myers Squibb Co., West One Bancorp, ITT Corp., Oakwood Homes Corp., Old National Bancorp., Advanced Micro Devices Inc.

Historical Financial Statistics (fiscal year-end: 12/31/91):

	1991	1990	1989	1988	1987*	6/30/87
Value of net assets (000)	275,045	230,851	264,339	245,077	243,073	292,704
NAV capital shares	10.91	7.67	10.12	8.69	8.49	11.88
NAV income shares	9.31	9.30	9.30	9.32	9.38	9.64
Net investment income	1.41	1.38	1.39	1.41	0.65	1.31
Dividends from net investment income (income shares)	1.40	1.38	1.41	1.47	0.91	1.30
Expense ratio	0.83%	0.86%	0.80%	0.79%	0.83% ann.	0.75%
Income ratio	7.24%	7.39%	7.15%	7.55%	6.37% ann.	6.08%
Portfolio turnover	54.90%	40.28%	50.47%	48.72%	23.09%	62.35%

*six months ended 12/31/87; fund's year-end has changed to 12/31 from 6/30

Special considerations: The fund terminates on 7/31/97; income shares will be redeemed at $9.30 per share plus accumulated and unpaid dividends. The Board will then recommend either to liquidate the remaining capital shares or to convert to an open-end fund. The fund's Articles of Incorporation contain various anti-takeover provisions including the requirement of a 2/3 vote of each class of shareholders, voting as a class, to terminate the fund or merge with an open-end fund. Capital shares are entitled to all portfolio appreciation, receive no distributions from net income as long as income shares are outstanding, bear none of the company's expenses, and have the potential for capital appreciation. Income shares are entitled to all the portfolio's net income (minimum cumulative dividend $1.00 ann.); pay all the company's expenses and have the potential for portfolio growth. A shareholder proposal in 1990 to liquidate the fund and another to replace the investment advisor, did not pass. The SEC granted the fund an exemptive order permitting it to buy back equal numbers of income and capital shares. As of 4/11/92, 94,300 shares of each class had been repurchased.
Shareholders over 5% (capital shares): NorthWest Quadrant, Inc., 14.7%; Stanislaw H. Bednarski, 5.5%

Counsellors Tandem Securities Fund, Inc.

466 Lexington Avenue, New York, NY 10017

Category: Dual Purpose Fund

Phone: 212-878-9204; 800-888-6878
Listed: CTF, NYSE
      CTFpr, NYSE
Commenced Operations: October, 1986
Cusip (common shares): 222269102
Cusip (preferred shares): 222269201

1991/mid-1992 Range of Premium/Disc:
common shares: -9% to -15%; preferred shares: N/A
1991/mid-1992 Range of Price:
common shares: $14 3/4 to $10 1/8; preferred shares: $50 5/8 to $45 1/4
NAV Total Return CTF **1990:** -2.56%; **1991:** +32.66%
Share Price Total Return CTF **1990:** -8.74%; **1991:** +37.30%

Investment Objective: Long-term capital appreciation consistent with preservation of capital and stability and dependability of income through investment in common and preferred stocks of utility companies. The fund may invest up to 45% of assets in nonutilities and up to 55% in utilities and cash holdings.

Officers:

| L.I. Pincus | Chairman |
| A.G. Orphanos | President |

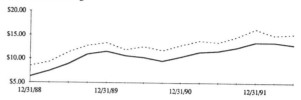

Investment Advisor: Warburg, Pincus Counsellors, Inc.
Advisory Fee: Quarterly fee at annual rate of 0.75% of average weekly net assets. Fee for 1991 was $517,781.
Administrator: Provident Institutional Management Corp.
Administration Fee: Annual fee of 0.10% on first $200 mil. average weekly net assets, 0.0075% on next $200 mil. average net assets, 0.005% on next $100 mil. average weekly net assets, and 0.003% on remaining average weekly net assets. Fee for 1991 was $100,000.

Capital Structure: *Common stock:* 30 mil. shares authorized; 2,845,562 shares outstanding 12/31/91
    Preferred stock: 6 mil. shares authorized; 576,958 shares outstanding 12/31/91. Quarterly dividends at the rate of 7 1/4% of the initial public offering price of $50.00 plus additional dividends. Preferred shares are redeemable at the option of the fund on or after 10/30/89.

Portfolio Highlights (as of 12/31/91): Common stock 95.5%, U.S. treasuries 0.3%, short-term 4.2%. Largest industry concentrations: other (non-utility) 46.5%: Utilities: electric 35.8%, telecommunications 8.6%, gas 4.6%.
Largest positions: Houston Industries, Merck & Co., Syntex Corp., Central & South West Corporation, Tambrands.

Historical Financial Statistics (fiscal year-end: 12/31/91):

	1991	1990	1989	1988	1987	10/30/86 to 12/31/86
Value of net assets (000)	76,879	64,974	108,457	84,891	73,685	85,760
NAV common shares	16.88	12.67	13.29	8.43	6.12	8.50
NAV preferred shares	50.00	50.00	50.00	50.00	50.00	50.63
Net investment income common shares	0.10	0.03	0.10	0.13	0.18	0.08
Net investment income preferred shares	3.63	3.63	3.63	3.63	3.63	0.63
Dividends from net investment income (common)	0.12	0.12	0.20	--	0.14	--
Dividends from net investment income (preferred)	3.63	3.63	3.63	3.63	4.57	--
Operating expense ratio	1.35%	2.33%	1.08%	1.34%	1.35%	1.18% ann.
Income ratio	3.45%	3.10%	3.75%	4.69%	5.18%	6.26% ann.
Portfolio turnover	26%	41%	67%	51%	87%	0%

Special considerations: Under certain circumstances, if the common shares have been trading at a 20% or greater discount, a vote of 75% of common share holders will cause redemption of the preferred shares. In early 1990, the fund accepted 2 mil. common shares at $10.85 each in a self-tender and 303,030 preferred shares at $49.50 each. The fund may repurchase shares in the open market at more than a 10% discount; during 1991, 6,111 shares were repurchased at a 15% discount. The fund had $0.1288 of retained long-term capital gains for the year 1991. **Shareholders over 5%:** CTF: Warburg Pincus Counsellors Inc., 12,.71% CTFpr: American Express Company, 5.86%.

Current Income Shares, Inc.

PO Box 30151, Terminal Annex , Los Angeles, CA 90030

Category: Bond Fund

Phone: 213-236-7940
Listed: CUR, NYSE
Commenced Operations: November, 1972
Cusip: 231298100

1991/mid-1992 Range of Premium/Disc: +5% to -4%
1991/mid-1992 Range of Price: $13 5/8 to $11 5/8
NAV Total Return 1990: +5.53%; **1991:** +20.03%
Share Price Total Return 1990: +5.92%; **1991:** +20.76%
Herzfeld Ranking 1991: 40th of 80 bond funds

Investment Objective: High current income through investment in a diversified portfolio of high quality marketable debt securities.

Officers:

M.A. Densmore   Chairman
R.E. Grayson   President

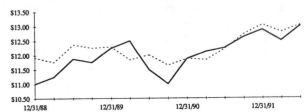

Investment Advisor: Union Bank

Advisory Fee: Fee calculated at annual rate of 0.5% of average net assets; advisor must reimburse the fund for certain expenses if they exceed 1 1/2% of first $30 mil. of average net assets, and 1% of average net assets in excess of $30 mil. Fee for year-ended 12/31/91 was $227,820.

Capital Structure: *Common stock:* 25 mil. shares authorized; 3,673,334 shares outstanding 12/31/91

Portfolio Highlights (as of 12/31/91): Bonds 97.76%, other assets and liabilities 2.24%. Largest sector concentrations: utilities 43.17%, industrial 31.12%, Canadians (payable in U.S. dollars) 11.07%, transportation 4.38%, U.S. government 4.24%, finance 3.78%. Quality ratings: AAA 11.75%, AA 11.21%, A 46.40%, BBB 21.92%, BB 8.72%. **Largest Issuers:** GTE Corporation 10 3/4-17; RJR Nabisco Inc. cap. corp. 10 1/2-98; Houston Industries 9 3/8-01; GTE North Tel. Facility 9.19-22; ITT Corp. 9 3/4-21.

Historical Financial Statistics (fiscal year-end: 12/31/91):

	1991	1990	1989	1988	1987	1986
Value of net assets (000)	48,359	43,363	45,178	43,796	43,665	48,425
NAV	13.16	11.80	12.30	11.92	11.89	13.18
Net investment income	1.07	1.10	1.12	1.11	1.13	1.13
Dividends from net investment income	1.09	1.10	1.12	1.12	1.38	1.12
Expense ratio	0.9%	0.9%	0.9%	0.9%	1.0%	0.8%
Income ratio	8.6%	9.3%	9.2%	9.3%	9.0%	8.8%
Portfolio turnover	82.38%	106.2%	84.5%	129.0%	114.1%	171.0%

Special considerations: The fund had a loss carryforward on 12/31/91 of $1,672,616 available through 1998. The quarterly dividend rate was reduced to $0.26 in February, 1992.

Dean Witter Government Income Trust

Two World Trade Ctr., 72nd Floor, New York, NY 10048

Category: Bond Fund

Phone: 212-392-2550
Listed: GVT, NYSE
Commenced Operations: February, 1988
Cusip: 241914100

1991/mid-1992 Range of Premium/Disc: +1% to -6%
1991/mid-1992 Range of Price: $9 3/4 to $8 7/8
NAV Total Return 1990: +9.99%; **1991:** +12.10%
Share Price Total Return 1990: +10.50%; **1991:** +14.93%
Herzfeld Ranking 1991: 78th of 80 bond funds

Investment Objective: High level of current income consistent with safety of principal primarily through investment in debt securities issued by the U.S. government, its agencies or instrumentalities.

Officers:
C.A. Fiumefreddo Chairman & CEO

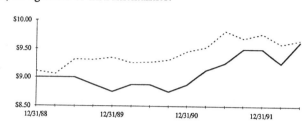

Investment Advisor: Dean Witter Reynolds, Inc.
Advisory Fee: Monthly fee at annual rate of 0.60% of average weekly net assets. Fee for six months ended 3/31/92 was $1,692,438.
Administrator: InterCapital Division of Dean Witter Reynolds, Inc.
Administration Fee: included in advisory fee, no separate fee.

Capital Structure: *Shares of beneficial interest:* unlimited number of shares authorized; 57,838,800 shares outstanding 3/31/92

Portfolio Highlights (as of 3/31/92): U.S. government agency mortgage pass-through certificates (91.4%), U.S. government agency 1.2%, commercial paper 3.5%, cash and other assets in excess of liabilities 3.9%. **Largest issuers:** Federal Home Loan Mortgage Corp. 59.8%; Federal National Mortgage Assoc. 17.6%; Government National Mortgage Assoc. 14.0%.

Historical Financial Statistics (fiscal year-end: 9/30/91):

	six months 3/31/92	1991	1990	1989	2/29/88 to 9/30/88
Value of net assets (000)	555,243	561,317	538,889	538,798	603,720
NAV	9.60	9.70	9.32	9.31	9.43
Net investment income	0.39	0.83	0.84	0.85	0.57
Dividends to shareholders	0.39	0.84	0.87	0.98	0.40
Expense ratio	0.72% ann.	0.72%	0.75%	0.74%	0.73% ann.
Income ratio	7.92% ann.	8.81%	9.01%	9.12%	10.31% ann.
Portfolio turnover	14%	10%	20%	64%	252%

Special considerations: The trust may repurchase shares to attempt to reduce or eliminate discounts from net asset value. The trust may invest up to 35% of total assets in foreign government securities. The Declaration of Trust contains various anti-takeover provisions. At 9/30/91 the trust had a net capital loss carryforward of $19,501,000 expiring through 1999.

Dover Regional Financial Shares

1521 Locust St., Ste. 500, Philadelphia, PA 19102

Category: Specialized Equity Fund

Phone: 215-735-5001
Listed: DVRFS, OTC
Commenced Operations: September, 1986
Cusip: 260409107

1991/mid-1992 Range of Premium/Disc: -15% to -32%
1991/mid-1992 Range of Price: $4 5/8 to $3 1/2
NAV Total Return 1991: +21.89%
Share Price Total Return 1991: +13.48%
Herzfeld Ranking 1991: 15th of 18 specialized equity funds

Investment Objective: Long-term capital appreciation, with secondary objective of current income, primarily through investment in equity securities of regional banks, stock savings institutions and their holding companies.

Officers:

B.Z. Cohen   Chairman

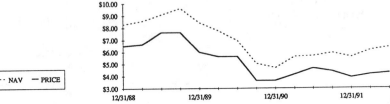

Investment Advisor: Dover Financial Management Corporation
Advisory Fee: Monthly fee at annual rate of 1% of average weekly net assets. The fee for 1991 was $42,736.

Capital Structure: *Shares of beneficial interest:* 3 mil. shares authorized; 747,000 shares outstanding 12/31/91

Portfolio Highlights (as of 12/31/91): Common stocks 51.8%, preferred stock 0.7%, thrifts 2.0%, short-term investments 47.5%. Largest sector concentrations: commercial banks 49.8%, thrifts 2.0%. **Largest positions:** Provident Bankshares Corporation (MD), First Fidelity Bancorporation (NJ), Commerce Bancorp Inc. (NJ), UJB Financial Corp (NJ), Franklin Financial Services Corp. (PA).

Historical Financial Statistics (fiscal year-end: 12/31/91):

	1991	1990	1989	1988	1987	9/29/86 to 12/31/86
Value of net assets (000)	4,136	3,486	6,287	6,195	6,225	6,845
NAV	5.54	4.67	8.42	8.29	8.33	9.16
Net investment income	0.09	0.30	0.14	0.15	0.21	0.07
Dividends from net investment income	0.10	0.29	0.14	0.19	0.22	--
Distributions from net realized gains	--	--	--	0.06	--	--
Return of capital	0.14	--	--	--	--	--
Expense ratio	2.50%	2.02%	1.96%	1.99%	1.80%	2.00% ann.
Income ratio	1.62%	4.59%	1.63%	1.73%	2.29%	2.79% ann.
Portfolio turnover	0%	0%	3.37%	6.80%	0%	0%

Special considerations: Beginning in 1992, the fund will make semi-annual distributions rather than quarterly distributions. The fund may invest up to 20% of its assets in restricted securities. Three positions were written off as worthless during 1991, Ball Savings Bank (PA), Metropolitan Savings & Loan Association (TN) and Southeastern Savings & Loan Association (NC). On 12/31/91 the fund had a capital loss carryforward of $761,174. **Shareholders over 5%:** Spector Gadon & Rosen P.C. Profits Sharing Plan, 4.4%

Dreyfus California Municipal Income, Inc.

144 Glenn Curtiss Blvd., Uniondale, NY 11556

Category: Municipal Bond Fund

Phone: 412-236-8000; 800-526,0801
Listed: DCM, ASE
Commenced Operations: October, 1988
Cusip: 261881106

1991/mid-1992 Range of Premium/Disc: +9% to -6%
1991/mid-1992 Range of Price: $10 1/4 to $8 3/4
NAV Total Return 1990: +5.25%; **1991:** +7.24%
Share Price Total Return 1990: +6.21%; **1991:** -2.36%
Herzfeld Ranking 1991: 49th of 51 municipal bond funds

Investment Objective: Maximum current income exempt from federal and California personal income taxes, consistent with preservation of capital; primarily through investment in investment grade California municipal obligations.

Officers:

R.J. Moynihan   President & Chief
                Investment Officer

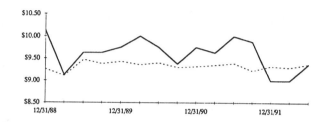

Investment Advisor: The Dreyfus Corporation
Advisory Fee: Monthly fee at annual rate of 0.70% of average weekly net assets. Fee for six months ended 3/31/92 was $143,585.

Capital Structure: *Common stock:* 110 mil. shares authorized; 4,420,896 shares outstanding 3/31/92

Portfolio Highlights (as of 3/31/92): Municipal bonds 100%. Quality ratings: AAA 11.8%, AA 7.7%, A 29.2%, BBB 16.0%, not rated 35.3%. **Largest issuers:** City of Vallejo, Multi-Family Hsg. Rev. (Sea Breeze Apt.) 9.50% 27; Orange County Community Facs. Dist. Sp. Tax; Fountain Vy. Agy. for Community Dev. Tax Allocation (City Ctr. Area Redev. Proj.) 9.10-15; Capistrano Uni. Sch. Dist. Community Facs. Dist. Spl. Tax (Aliso Viejo Proj.) 8.375-20; Northern California Power Agency Pub. Power. Rev. Ref.

Historical Financial Statistics (fiscal year-end: 9/30/91):

	six months 3/31/92	1991	1990	10/21/88 to 9/30/89
Value of net assets (000)	41,141	40,661	40,509	40,344
NAV	9.31	9.22	9.30	9.38
Net investment income	0.29	0.65	0.65	0.58
Dividends from net investment income	0.30	0.63	0.64	0.48
Dividends from net realized gain on investments	--	0.03	0.02	--
Expense ratio	1.12% ann.	1.04%	1.00%	1.07% ann.
Income ratio	7.36% ann.	8.00%	7.97%	7.86% ann.
Portfolio turnover	11.62% not ann.	15.43%	29.53%	14.33% not ann.

Special considerations: The fund may be open-ended at any time with a 75% vote of outstanding shares of both classes of stock, unless approved by 2/3 of the Directors. The fund may repurchase shares when the directors deem it advantageous. The fund's Articles of Incorporation contain various anti-takeover provisions, including a staggered board of directors.

Dreyfus Municipal Income, Inc.

144 Glenn Curtiss Blvd., Uniondale, NY 11556

Category: Municipal Bond Fund

Phone: 412-236-8000; 800-526-0801
Listed: DMF, ASE
Commenced Operations: October, 1988
Cusip: 26201R102

1991/mid-1992 Range of Premium/Disc: +6% to 0%
1991/mid-1992 Range of Price: $10 1/2 to $9 1/8
NAV Total Return 1990: +6.53%; **1991:** +13.40%
Share Price Total Return 1990: +2.20%; **1991:** +13.47%
Herzfeld Ranking 1991: 22nd of 80 municipal bond funds

Investment Objective: Maximum current income exempt from federal income tax, consistent with preservation of capital; primarily through investment in investment grade municipal obligations.

Officers:

R.J. Moynihan   President & Chief
                 Investment Officer

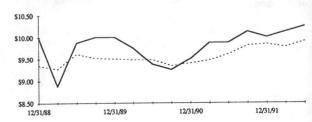

Investment Advisor: The Dreyfus Corporation
Advisory Fee: Monthly fee at annual rate of 0.70% of average weekly net assets. Fee for six months ended 3/31/92 was $660,128.

Capital Structure: *Common stock*: 110 mil. shares authorized; 19,345,010 shares outstanding 3/31/92
Preferred stock: An offering of preferred stock has been postponed until more favorable market conditions exist

Portfolio Highlights (as of 3/31/92): Municipal bonds 100%. Quality ratings: AA 14.7%, A 23.0%, BBB 29.7%, BB 2.7%, not rated 29.9%. Largest geographic concentrations: Texas 19.6%, Illinois 15.6%, Colorado 8.9%, New York 8.6%, Florida 8.4%, Massachusetts 5.7%, Pennsylvania 5.4%. **Largest issuers:** Chicago O'Hare International Airport Spl. Fac. Rev.; New York City general obligations; City and County of Denver Airport Rev.; Texas Housing Agency Single Family Mortgage Revenue; Illinois Dev. Fin. Auth. Revenue (Community Rehabilitation Providers Fac. Acquisition).

Historical Financial Statistics (fiscal year-end: 9/30/91):

	six months 3/31/92	1991	1990	10/24/88 to 9/30/89
Value of net assets (000)	189,453	188,441	176,356	176,757
NAV	9.79	9.83	9.34	9.52
Net investment income	0.36	0.72	0.73	0.64
Dividends from net investment income	0.34	0.68	0.70	0.52
Dividends from net realized gain on investments	0.08	0.04	0.02	--
Expense ratio	0.86% ann.	0.88%	0.85%	0.88% ann.
Income ratio	8.15% ann.	8.49%	8.58%	8.25% ann.
Portfolio turnover	10.25% not ann.	36.40%	27.11%	95.24% not ann.

Special considerations: The fund may be open-ended at any time with a 75% vote of outstanding shares of both classes of stock, unless approved by 2/3 of the Directors. The fund may repurchase shares when the Directors deem it advantageous. The fund's Articles of Incorporation contain various anti-takeover provisions, including a staggered board of directors.

Dreyfus New York Municipal Income, Inc.

Category: Municipal Bond Fund

144 Glenn Curtiss Blvd., Uniondale, NY 11556

Phone: 412-236-8000; 800-526-0801
Listed: DNM, ASE
Commenced Operations: October, 1988
Cusip: 26201T108

1991/mid-1992 Range of Premium/Disc: +5% to -4%
1991/mid-1992 Range of Price: $10 1/8 to $9
NAV Total Return 1990: +4.39%; **1991:** +12.45%
Share Price Total Return 1990: +5.05%; **1991:** +10.75%
Herzfeld Ranking 1991: 31st of 51 municipal bond funds

Investment Objective: Maximum current income exempt from federal, New York State, and New York City income tax, consistent with preservation of capital, primarily through investment in investment grade New York municipal obligations.

Officers:
R.J. Moynihan — President & Chief Investment Officer

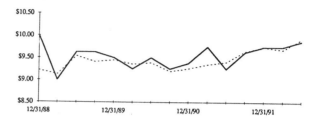

Investment Advisor: The Dreyfus Corporation

Advisory Fee: Monthly fee at annual rate of 0.70% of average weekly net assets. Fee for six months ended 3/31/92 was $122,482.

Capital Structure:

Common stock: 110 mil. shares authorized; 3,616,400 shares outstanding 3/31/92
Preferred stock: An offering of preferred stock has been postponed until more favorable market conditions exist.

Portfolio Highlights (as of 3/31/92): Municipal bonds 99.7%, short-term tax exempt investments 0.3%. Quality ratings: AA 10.4%, A 29.3%, BBB 49.0%, F-1 0.3%, not rated 11.0%. **Largest issuers:** Puerto Rico Commonwealth Hwy. Auth. Hwy. Rev.; New York State Energy, Resh. and Dev. Auth. Pollution Control Rev.; New York State Dorm. Auth. Rev.; New York City Indl. Dev. Agy. Civic Fac. Rev.; New York State Mortgage Agy.

Historical Financial Statistics (fiscal year-end: 9/30/91):

	six months 3/31/92	1991	1990	10/21/88 to 9/30/89
Value of net assets (000)	35,104	34,860	32,844	33,007
NAV	9.71	9.67	9.20	9.41
Net investment income	0.31	0.63	0.63	0.57
Dividends from net investment income	0.29	0.63	0.66	0.48
Dividends from net realized gains	0.02	0.01	--	--
Expense ratio	1.10% ann.	1.10%	1.07%	1.15% ann.
Income ratio	6.43% ann.	6.70%	6.68%	7.80% ann.
Portfolio turnover	6.19% not ann.	15.53%	11.76%	38.28% not ann.

Special considerations: The fund may be open-ended at any time with a 75% vote of outstanding shares of both classes of stock, unless approved by 2/3 of the Directors. The fund may repurchase shares when the directors deem it advantageous. The fund's Articles of Incorporation contain various anti-takeover provisions, including a staggered board of directors.

Dreyfus Strategic Governments Income, Inc.

Category: Bond Fund

144 Glenn Curtiss Blvd., Uniondale, NY 11556

Phone: 412-236-8000; 800-526-0801	**1991/mid-1992 Range of Premium/Disc:** +7% to -3%
Listed: DSI, NYSE	**1991/mid-1992 Range of Price:** $12 to $10 5/8
Commenced Operations: June, 1988	**NAV Total Return 1990:** +9.21%; **1991:** +13.03%
Cusip: 261938104	**Share Price Total Return 1990:** +15.23%; **1991:** +14.85%
	Herzfeld Ranking 1991: 75th of 80 bond funds

Investment Objective: Maximize current income, consistent with capital preservation, primarily through investment in obligations issued or guaranteed by the U.S. government, its agencies or instrumentalities, and in obligations issued or guaranteed by one or more foreign governments or any of their political subdivisions, agencies or instrumentalities. (Up to 50% of assets may be invested in foreign government securities.)

Officers:

J.S. DiMartino   President

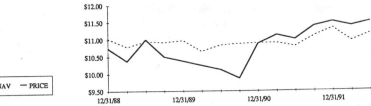

Investment Advisor: The Dreyfus Corporation

Advisory Fee: Monthly fee at annual rate of 0.70% of average weekly net assets. Fee for six months ended 11/30/91 was $562,117.

Capital Structure: *Common stock:* 100 mil. shares authorized; 14,702,688 outstanding 11/30/91

Portfolio Highlights (as of 11/30/91): Bonds and notes 93.8%, short-term investments 5.6%, cash and receivables net 0.6%. Largest industry concentrations: U.S. government and agencies 61.4%, foreign/governmental 15.4%, banking and finance 7.3%. **Largest Issuers:** U.S. treasury bonds and notes; International Bank for Reconstruction and Development; General Electric Capital notes; New Zealand government bonds 10-02; Hydro-Quebec deb.

Historical Financial Statistics (fiscal year-end: 5/31/91):				
	six months 11/30/91	1991	1990	6/24/88 to 5/31/89
Value of net assets (000)	164,707	159,751	156,198	156,985
NAV	11.20	10.92	10.70	10.76
Net investment income	0.51	1.06	1.10	1.00
Dividends from net investment income	0.54	1.08	1.08	0.94
Distributions from net realized gains	--	--	--	0.03
Expense ratio	0.87% ann.	0.87%	0.89%	0.89% ann.
Income ratio	9.24% ann.	9.67%	10.11%	10.89% ann.
Portfolio turnover	15.08% not ann.	11.92%	16.34%	83.78%

Special considerations: Under certain conditions, in the second quarter of 1991 the fund will commence an offer to repurchase all outstanding shares at net asset value. If not all shares are tendered, an open-ending proposal will be submitted by the Board of Directors. Also, in each year after 1/1/93, under certain conditions, the board will submit an open-ending proposal at the next succeeding annual meeting of shareholders. The fund may also repurchase shares under certain circumstances. The fund's Articles of Incorporation contain various anti-takeover provisions, including a staggered board of directors. As of 11/30/91 the fund had a capital loss carryover of approximately $392,000 available through 1998. Dividend rate reduced to $0.085 per month in March, 1992.

Dreyfus Strategic Municipal Bond Fund, Inc.

144 Glenn Curtiss Blvd., Uniondale, NY 11556

Category: Municipal Bond Fund

Phone: 800-331-1710; 800-334-6899; 800-331-1710; 617-720-5576	**1991/mid-1992 Range of Premium/Disc:** +4% to -$
	1991/mid-1992 Range of Price: $10 1/4 to $8 3/4
Listed: DSM, NYSE	**NAV Total Return 1990:** +7.10%; **1991:** +10.78%
Commenced Operations: November, 1989	**Share Price Total Return 1990:** +0.22%; **1991:** +11.62%
Cusip: 26202F107	**Herzfeld Ranking 1991:** 38th of 51 municipal bond funds

Investment Objective: Maximum current income exempt from federal income tax primarily through investment in a diversified portfolio of municipal obligations.

Officers:

R.J. Moynihan   President & Chief Investment Officer

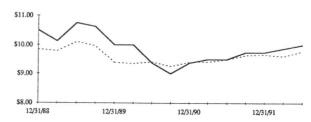

Investment Advisor: The Dreyfus Corporation

Advisory Fee: Monthly fee at annual rate of 0.50% of average weekly net assets. Fee for year-ended 11/30/91 was $1,987,711.

Administrator: The Boston Company Advisors, Inc.

Administration Fee: Monthly fee at annual rate of 0.25% of average weekly net assets. Fee for year-ended 11/30/91 was $993,856.

Capital Structure: *Common stock:* 110 mil. shares authorized; 41,485,390 shares outstanding 11/30/91

Preferred stock: An offering of preferred stock has been postponed until more favorable market conditions exist.

Portfolio Highlights (as of 11/30/91): Municipal bonds 98.8%, short-term tax exempt investments 1.2%. Quality ratings: AAA 2.6%, AA 9.4%, A 17.7%, BBB 24.8%, F-1+ 1.2%, not rated 44.3%. Largest geographic concentrations: Pennsylvania 12.7%, New York 11.6%, Massachusetts 11.1%, Texas 10.7%, Illinois 9.0%, Utah 6.2%, Colorado 5.3%. **Largest issuers:** New York City General Obligation; Erie Cnty. Gen. Dev. Auth. Rev. (First Mtg.-Sr. Living Services Inc. Proj.) 8.625-19; Massachusetts Hsg. Fin. Agy. Res. Hsg. Rev.; Chicago O'Hare Intl. Arpt. Spl. Fac. Rev. (Utd. Airlines Inc. Proj.); Denver City and Cnty. Arpt. Rev.

Historical Financial Statistics (fiscal year-end: 11/30/91):

	1991	1990	11/22/89 to 11/30/89
Value of net assets (000)	408,314	389,342	326,391
NAV	9.61	9.44	9.32
Net investment income	0.69	0.69	--
Dividends from net investment income	0.71	0.59	--
Expense ratio	0.88%	0.56%	--
Income ratio	7.27%	7.49%	--
Portfolio turnover	22.41%	16.51%	--

Special considerations: Prior to 1994, conversion to an open-end fund will require a 2/3 shareholder vote of each class of shares, if applicable; after 1994 a majority will be required. After 1994, if certain conditions exist, the fund will submit an open-ending proposal at the next annual meeting. The fund may repurchase shares or make tender offers, and the board will consider such actions at least once a year. The fund's Articles of Incorporation contain various anti-takeover provisions, including a 2/3 vote for liquidation of the fund or merger with another corporation. As of 11/30/91 the fund had a capital loss carryover of approximately $27,000 available through 1998.

Dreyfus Strategic Municipals, Inc.

144 Glenn Curtiss Blvd., Uniondale, NY 11556   **Category: Municipal Bond Fund**

Phone: 800-524-4458; 800-334-6899
Listed: LEO, NYSE
Commenced Operations: September, 1987
Cusip: 261932107

1991/mid-1992 Range of Premium/Disc: +12% to +2%
1991/mid-1992 Range of Price: $11 1/8 to $9 7/8
NAV Total Return 1990: +6.48%; **1991:** +11.41%
Share Price Total Return 1990: -0.49%; **1991:** +16.76%
Herzfeld Ranking 1991: 35th of 51 municipal bond funds

Investment Objective: Maximize current income exempt from federal income tax to the extent consistent with preservation of capital, primarily through investment in a diversified portfolio of municipal obligations.

Officers:

R.J. Moynihan   President & Chief Investment Officer

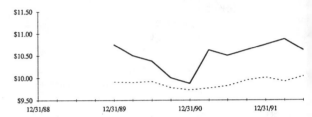

Investment Advisor: The Dreyfus Corporation

Advisory Fee: Monthly fee at annual rate of 0.75% of average weekly net assets. The advisor must reimburse the fund if various expenses exceed the lesser of 2% of the first $10 mil., 1 1/2% of next $20 mil., and 1% of excess net assets; or the expense limitation of any state having jurisdiction over the fund. Fee for six months ended 3/31/92 was $1,926,155.

Capital Structure: *Common stock:* 500 mil. shares authorized; 52,018,371 shares outstanding 3/31/92

Portfolio Highlights (as of 3/31/92): Municipal bonds 99.3%, short-term tax exempt investments 0.7%. Quality ratings: AAA 4.7%, AA 4.6%, A 14.2%, BBB 40.9%, F-1 0.7%, not rated 34.9%. Largest geographic concentrations: Pennsylvania 9.2%, New York 9.0%, Colorado 8.7%, Florida 8.2%, Texas 8.2%, Michigan 6.5%, Illinois 5.0%. **Largest issuers:** Greater Detroit (MI) Res. Recovery Auth. Rev.; City and County of Denver (CO) Airport Rev.; Burke County Dev. Auth Pollution Control Rev. (Georgia Power Co. Plt. Vogtle Proj.); Jacksonville (FL) Health Facs. Auth. Hosp. Rev. Ref. (Methodist Hosp. Proj.); Tulsa Municipal Airport Trust Rev. (American Airlines) 9.5-20.

	Historical Financial Statistics (fiscal year-end: 9/30/91):					
	six months 3/31/92	1991	1990	1989	1988	9/23/87 to 9/30/87
Value of net assets (000)	516,412	510,120	482,515	474,556	452,528	415,795
NAV	9.93	9.96	9.79	9.97	9.91	9.24
Net investment income	0.38	0.78	0.78	0.78	0.77	--
Dividends from net investment income	0.37	0.76	0.76	0.78	.70	--
Distributions from net realized gains	0.03	0.17	0.05	0.15	--	--
Expense ratio	0.88% ann.	0.88%	0.89%	0.91%	0.69%	--
Income ratio	8.52% ann.	8.87%	8.83%	8.79%	8.60%	--
Portfolio turnover	8.96% not ann.	6.43%	10.51%	11.43%	55.55%	--

Special considerations: At least 50% of assets must be invested in investment grade municipal obligations. The fund may repurchase shares under certain circumstances. The fund's Articles of Incorporation contain various anti-takeover provisions.

Duff & Phelps Utilities Income Inc.

55 East Monroe Street, Chicago, IL 60603

Category: Specialized Equity Fund

Phone: 312-368-5510; 800-426-5523
Listed: DNP, NYSE, MSE
Commenced Operations: January, 1987
Cusip: 264324104

1991/mid-1992 Range of Premium/Disc: +12% to +2%
1991/mid-1992 Range of Price: $10 3/8 to $8 1/8
NAV Total Return 1990: +2.14%; **1991:** +24.37%
Share Price Total Return 1990: +8.81%; **1991:** +24.87%
Herzfeld Ranking 1991: 13th of 18 specialized equity funds

Investment Objective: Current income and long-term growth of income, with capital appreciation as the secondary objective. The fund invests primarily in a diversified portfolio of equity and fixed income securities of companies in the public utilities industry.

Officers:

C.V. Hansen, CFA   Chairman
R.D. Milne, CFA   President & CEO

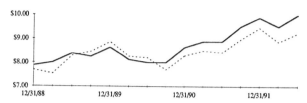

Investment Advisor: Duff & Phelps Investment Management Co.
Advisory Fee: Quarterly fee at annual rate of 0.60% of average weekly net assets and 0.50% of average weekly net assets in excess thereof. Fee for year-ended 12/31/91 was $10,297,466.
Administrator: J.J.B. Hilliard, W.L. Lyons, Inc.
Administration Fee: Quarterly fee at annual rate of 0.25% of average weekly net assets up to $100 mil, 0.20% from $100 mil. to $1 bil., and 0.10% of excess. Fee for year-ended 12/31/91 was $2,752,227.

Capital Structure: *Common stock*: 250 mil. shares authorized; 142,839,558 shares outstanding 12/31/91
Remarketed Preferred stock: 100 mil. shares authorized; 5000 shares outstanding 12/31/91, liquidation preference $100,000 per share. The dividend rate is set every 49 days and ranged between 4.05% and 6.40% during the year-ended 12/31/91. The remarketed preferred stock is redeemable at the fund's option at the issue price ($100,000) plus accumulated and unpaid dividends and is subject to mandatory redemption beginning in 2012, ending in 2024 by series.
Debt: Senior note payable of $33,596,217 at fixed rate of 8.75% annually.

Portfolio Highlights (as of 3/31/92): Common stocks 51.6%, bonds 48.4%. Largest industry concentrations: electric 76.4%, telecommunications 16.6%, gas 7.0%. **Largest positions/issuers:** various GTE Corp.; Texas Utilities Co.; FPL Group Inc.; American Electric Power Co. Inc.; American Electric Power Co. Inc.; NYNEX Corp.

Historical Financial Statistics (fiscal year-end: 12/31/91):

	1991	1990	1989	1988	1/21/87 to 12/31/87
Value of net assets (000)	1,863,427	1,663,348	1,728,352	1,548,727	1,004,137
NAV	9.55	8.29	8.86	7.69	7.57
Net investment income	0.95	0.99	1.02	0.75	0.60
Dividends to common stock from net investment income	0.77	0.76	0.76	0.75	0.56
Dividends on preferred stock from net investment income	0.17	0.25	0.27	0.02	--
Dividends to common stock from net realized gains	--	--	--	--	0.05
Expense ratio	1.17%	1.27%	1.33%	1.59%	1.61% ann.
Income ratio	7.75%	8.37%	8.71%	9.13%	7.67% ann.
Portfolio turnover	41.09%	58.99%	92.25%	65.68%	29.50%

Special considerations: Beginning 1/1/92 the Board may recommend open-ending of the fund if it believes it advisable; a majority vote of shareholders would be required. The fund may repurchase shares when the Board thinks it is advantageous. The fund's Articles of Incorporation contain various anti-takeover provisions.

Duff & Phelps Utilities Tax-Free Income Inc.

55 East Monroe Street, Chicago, IL 60603   **Category: Municipal Bond Fund**

Phone: 312-368-5510; 800-426-5523
Listed: DTF, NYSE
Commenced Operations: November, 1991
Cusip: 264325101

1991/mid-1992 Range of Premium/Disc: +12% to +2%
1991/mid-1992 Range of Price: $15 3/4 to $14 5/8
NAV Total Return 1991: N/A
Share Price Total Return 1991: N/A
Herzfeld Ranking 1991: N/A

Investment Objective: Current income exempt from regular federal income tax consistent with the preservation of capital. The fund invests primarily in a diversified portfolio of investment grade tax-exempt utility obligations.

Officers:

F.E. Jeffries	Chairman
R.D. Milne	President & CEO

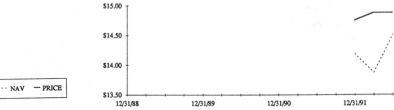

Investment Advisor: Duff & Phelps Investment Management Co.
Advisory Fee: Monthly fee at annual rate of 0.50% of average weekly managed assets. Fee for period 11/20/91 to 4/30/92 was $295,020.
Administrator: Prudential Mutual Fund Management, Inc.
Administration Fee: Monthly fee at annual rate of 0.15% of average weekly managed assets. Fee for period 11/20/91 to 4/30/92 was $88,506.

Capital Structure: *Common stock*: 600 mil. shares authorized, 8,262,445 shares outstanding 4/30/92
Preferred stock: 1,300 shares outstanding, dividend rate reset every 7 days. Dividend rate ranged from $3.00% to 3.80% for period from inception to 4/30/92

Portfolio Highlights (as of 4/30/92): Long-term investments 97.7%, short-term investments 0.2%. Largest geographic concentrations: New York 12.3%, Texas 12.0%, Illinois 11.0%, Washington 10.2%, Colorado 4.1%.
Largest issuers: San Antonio Elec. & Gas. Rev.; New York City Municipal Water Fin. Auth. Water & Sewer System Revenue 7.10-12; San Francisco City & County Pub. Utilities Comm. Water Revenue 6.5-17; New York State Power Auth. Revenue; South Carolina State Public Service Auth. Rev.

Historical Financial Statistics:

	11/20/91 to 4/30/92
Value of net assets (000)	180,538
NAV	13.98
Net investment income avail. to common shares	0.38
Dividends from net investment income to common shares	0.24
Operating expense ratio	1.19% ann.
Income ratio	6.45% ann.
Portfolio turnover	42%

Special considerations: The fund makes monthly distributions from net investment income; net capital gains are distributed annually. The Board of Directors will consider from time to time open market repurchases of and/or tender offers for the shares of common stock to seek to reduce any market discount from net asset value that may develop. In connection with the management of the fund's portfolio, the fund may enter into related hedging and risk management transactions. The fund's Charter contains various anti-takeover provisions, including a 75% voting requirement for open-ending the fund. Dividend rate for the first half of 1992, $0.08 per month.

1838 Bond-Debenture Trading Fund

Five Radnor Corporate Ctr., Suite 320, 100 Matsonford Road, Radnor, PA 19087   **Category**: Bond Fund

Phone: 215-293-4300
Listed: BDF, NYSE
Commenced Operations: 1971
Cusip: 282520105

1991/mid-1992 Range of Premium/Disc: +11% to 0%
1991/mid-1992 Range of Price: $24 1/4 to $20
NAV Total Return 1990: +2.56%; **1991**: +20.17%
Share Price Total Return 1990: +4.53%; **1991**: +15.86%
Herzfeld Ranking 1991: 39th of 80 bond funds

Investment Objective: Seek a high rate of return from interest income and trading activity from a portfolio consisting principally of debt securities.

Officers:

J.H. Donaldson   President

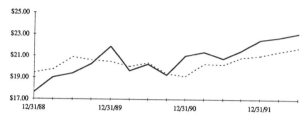

Investment Advisor: 1838 Investment Advisors, L.P.
Advisory Fee: Monthly fee at annual rate of 0.625% on first $40 mil., and 0.5% on excess average net assets.

Capital Structure: *Common stock*: 10 mil. shares authorized; 2,626,239 shares outstanding 3/31/92
                    Debt: Bank loan $1,678,975 as of 3/31/92

Portfolio Highlights (as of 3/31/92): Long-term debt securities 99.56%, preferred stocks 0.5%, common stocks 0.03%, investment companies 0.7%. Largest industry concentrations: industrial & misc. 32.03%, U.S. government & agencies 27.56%, electric utilities 22.63%, collateralized mortgage obligations 15.45%. Quality ratings: U.S. treasuries & agencies and AAA rated 42.7%, AA 6.1%, A 14.1%, BBB 27.9%, BB 3.0%, B 5.1%, not rated 1.1%. **Largest issuers**: U.S. treasury bonds and notes; Investments GNMA Mortgage-backed securities Series 1983-1 11 3/8-13; Shearson Lehman Collateral Mortgage Obligation Series R-2 8 1/2-03; Long Island Lighting Co. deb. Series AA 11 3/8-19; Gulf States Utilities 1st Mortgage 12 1/8-16.

Historical Financial Statistics (fiscal year-end: 3/31/92):

	1992	1991	1990	1989	1988	1987
Value of net assets (000)	56,163	52,793	51,852	50,916	51,901	54,161
NAV	21.39	20.27	20.04	19.75	20.18	21.25
Net investment income	1.83	1.85	1.82	1.81	1.86	1.93
Dividends from net investment income	1.83	1.87	1.82	1.86	1.86	2.00
Operating expense ratio	0.97%	1.05%	0.95%	1.11%	0.99%	1.03%
Income ratio	8.85%	9.39%	8.95%	9.20%	9.37%	9.30%
Portfolio turnover	73.11%	88.26%	135.34%	76.67%	95.71%	63.23%

Special considerations: Fund was named Drexel Bond-Debenture Trading Fund prior to 10/5/88. At 3/31/92 the fund had a loss carry-forward of approximately $2494,015 expiring through 1999. At the 1991 annual meeting shareholders voted on amending the fund's fundamental investment policy on purchasing restricted securities to permit acquisition of 144A securities (securities which may be resold to qualified institutional buyers without registration under the Securities Act of 1933).

Ellsworth Convertible Growth and Income Fund

56 Pine Street, New York, NY 10005

Category: Convertible Fund

Phone: 212-269-9236
Listed: ECF, ASE
Commenced Operations: June, 1986
Cusip: 289074106

1991/mid-1992 Range of Premium/Disc: -7% to -17%
1991/mid-1992 Range of Price: $8 to $6 1/4
NAV Total Return 1990: -5.42%; **1991:** +24.36%
Share Price Total Return 1990: -8.67%; **1991:** +26.48%
Herzfeld Ranking 1991: 5th of 8 convertible bond funds

Investment Objective: High level of total return including current income and capital appreciation, primarily through investment in convertible securities and by using investment techniques to enhance income and to hedge against market risks.

Officers:
R.E. Dinsmore   Chairman
T.H. Dinsmore   President

Investment Advisor: Davis/Dinsmore Management Company
Advisory Fee: Monthly fee at annual rate of 0.75% on first $100 mil., 0.5% on excess average net assets. The fee is reduced if ordinary expenses exceed 1.5% of the first $100 mil. or 1% of excess average monthly net assets. Fee for six months ended 3/31/92 was $196,294.

Capital Structure: *Common stock:* 20 mil. shares authorized; 6,118,443 outstanding 3/31/92

Portfolio Highlights (as of 3/31/92): Bonds and notes 73.8%, preferred stocks 17.3%, common stocks 5.0%, other assets and liabilities 3.9%. Largest sector concentrations: banking 17.5%, financial & insurance 11.5%, energy 9.8%, broadcasting & cable 5.6%, textiles 5.5%, transportation 4.8%, electronics & instruments 4.5%, building & real estate 4.5%, office equipment 4.4%. **Largest positions:** Old Republic International cv. sub. deb. 8-15; various Time Warner Inc. cv. exch. pfd.; various Barnett Banks Inc. cum cv. pfd.; PHM Corp. common stock; Park Communications Inc. cv. sub. deb. 6 7/8-11.

Historical Financial Statistics (fiscal year-end: 9/30/91):						
	six months 3/31/92	1991	1990	1989	1988	1987
Value of net assets (000)	54,680	51,687	45,872	53,846	51,777	57,025
NAV	8.94	8.45	7.50	9.00	8.66	9.93
Net investment income	0.28	0.53	0.58	0.66	0.56	0.55
Dividends from net investment income	0.24	0.58	0.65	0.56	0.55	0.57
Distributions from net realized gains	--	--	0.16	0.20	0.45	--
Expense ratio	1.2% ann.	1.4%	1.3%	1.4%	1.4%	1.4%
Income ratio	6.5% ann.	6.7%	7.0%	7.6%	6.7%	5.6%
Portfolio turnover	25%	37%	23%	34%	32%	35%

Special considerations: Beginning at the end of 1991, if the market price of the stock is less than 95% of net asset value for a 12 week period, the fund will have shareholders vote on a plan which, if passed with a two-third majority, will put into place a program which would allow shareholders to put their stock back to the company at NAV. At the January, 1992, annual meeting, shareholders voted against a proposal to amend and restate the Articles of Incorporation requiring the Board of Directors to consider giving the shareholders the right to tender their shares during the current fiscal year.

The Emerging Germany Fund, Inc.

One Battery Park Plaza, New York, NY 10004

Category: Foreign Equity Fund

Phone: 212-363-5100	**1991/mid-1992 Range of Premium/Disc**: -3% to -23%
Listed: FRG, NYSE	**1991/mid-1992 Range of Price**: $9 1/4 to $6 3/8
Commenced Operations: April, 1990	**NAV Total Return 1991**: -4.70%
Cusip: 290913102	**Share Price Total Return 1991**: +1.64%
	Herzfeld Ranking 1991: 41st of 46 foreign equity funds

Investment Objective: Long-term capital appreciation through investment in equity and equity-linked securities of medium and smaller-sized West German companies likely to benefit from political, legal and economic developments in East Germany.

Officers:

H. Hofmann   Chairman
T. Schmidt-Scheuber   President

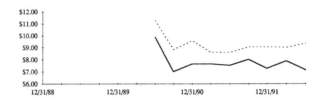

Investment Advisor: Asset Management Advisors of Dresdner Bank-Gesellschaft Für Vermögensanlageberatung mbH

Advisory Fee: Fee at the annual rate of 0.70% of average weekly net assets up to $100 mil. and 0.60% of any excess. Fee for 1991 was $859,054.

Investment Manager: ABD Securities Corporation

Management Fee: Fee at annual rate of 0.30% of average weekly net assets up to $100 mil. and 0.20% of any excess. Fee for 1991 was $353,017.

Capital Structure: *Common stock*: 100 mil. shares authorized; 14,008,334 outstanding 12/31/91

Portfolio Highlights (as of 3/31/92): Investments in German securities 96.62%, investments in short-term securities 0.20%. Common stocks 92.42%, preferred stocks 4.20%, assets in excess of liabilities 3.18%. Largest industry concentrations: banking 15.80%, machinery & engineering 10.73%, automobiles 9.86%, insurance 8.40%, multi-industry 6.58%, electric & gas 6.56%, electrical & electronics 6.42%. **Largest positions**: Siemens AG, Deutsche Bank AG, Mercedes Automobil Holding AG, Bayerische Vereinsbank AG, Commerzbank AG, Veba AG.

Historical Financial Statistics (fiscal year-end: 12/31/91):

	1991	4/5/90 to 12/31/90
Value of net assets (000)	124,069	131,747
NAV	8.86	9.40
Net investment income	0.07	0.16
Dividends from net investment income	0.07	0.16
Distributions from net realized gains	0.16	0.04
Expense ratio	1.70%	1.51% ann.
Income ratio	0.76%	3.62% ann.
Portfolio turnover	52%	13%

Special considerations: The fund may repurchase shares or make tender offers from time to time. At least annually the fund will distribute all net investment income and net realized capital gains. The fund's Articles of Incorporation and Bylaws contain various anti-takeover provisions including a 75% shareholder vote for merger with another fund, liquidation of the fund, and amending the Articles of Incorporation to convert to an open-end fund.

The Emerging Markets Telecommunications Fund, Inc.

One Citicorp Center, 58th Floor, 153 East 53rd Street
New York, NY 10022

Category: Specialized Equity Fund

Phone: 212-832-2626	**1991/mid-1992 Range of Premium/Disc**: +9% to +8%
Listed: ETF, NYSE	**1991/mid-1992 Range of Price**: $15 1/8 to $15
Commenced Operations: June, 1992	**NAV Total Return 1991**: N/A
Cusip: 290887108	**Share Price Total Return 1991**: N/A
	Herzfeld Ranking 1991: N/A

Investment Objective: Long-term capital appreciation primarily through investments in equity securities of telecommunications companies in emerging countries.

Officers:

E. Bassini	Chairman, President & Chief Investment Officer

Investment Advisor: BEA Associates

Advisory Fee: Quarterly fee at the annual rate of 1.25% of the first $100 mil. of average weekly net assets, 1.125% of the next $100 mil., and 1.00% of any excess.

Administrator: Bear Stearns Funds Management Inc.

Administration Fee: Annual fee of 0.10% of the average weekly net assets of the fund. (BEA Associates also provides certain administrative services for a fee of up to $20,000 per year.)

Capital Structure: *Common stock*: 100 mil. shares authorized, 7,250,000 shares outstanding 6/17/92

Portfolio Highlights: not yet published

Historical Financial Statistics:

	6/17/92
Value of net assets (000)	101,138
NAV	13.95

Special considerations: If, at any time after the second anniversary of the offering, shares trade for a substantial period of time at a substantial discount from the fund's then current net asset value per share, the Board of Directors of the fund will consider, at its next regularly scheduled meeting, taking various actions designed to reduce or eliminate the discount. The fund's Articles of Incorporation contain various anti-takeover provisions including a 75% vote to merge with another entity or liquidate the fund.

The Emerging Mexico Fund, Inc.

1285 Avenue of the Americas, New York, NY 10019

Category: Foreign Equity Fund

Phone: 212-713-2000; 800-553-8080
Listed: MEF, NYSE
Commenced Operations: October, 1990
Cusip: 290891100

1991/mid-1992 Range of Premium/Disc: +13% to -22%
1991/mid-1992 Range of Price: $27 1/4 to $8 3/4
NAV Total Return 1991: +88.88%
Share Price Total Return 1991: +130.26%
Herzfeld Ranking 1991: 4th of 46 foreign equity funds

Investment Objective: Long-term capital appreciation through investment primarily in Mexican equity securities. At least 65% of total assets will be in peso or U.S. denominated fixed income securities.

Officers:

G. de Las Heras   President

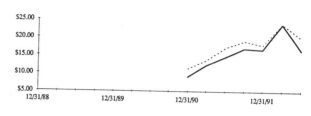

Investment Advisor: Santander Management, Inc.
Sub-Advisor: Acci Worldwide, S.A. de C.V. (See special considerations below.)
Advisory Fee: Monthly fee at the annual rate of 1.00% of average weekly net assets to Santander Management; an annual fee of 0.35% of average weekly net assets is paid by Santander Management to the sub-advisor, Acci Worldwide. Advisory fees for year-ended 12/31/91 were $488,215.
Administrator: Mitchell Hutchins Asset Management, Inc.
Administration Fee: Monthly fee at the annual rate of 0.20% of average weekly net assets up to $50 million, 0.18% of next $25 million, and 0.16% of any excess with a minimum fee of $125,000. Fee for year-ended 12/31/91 was $90,697.
Capital Structure: *Common stock:* 100 mil. shares authorized, 5,009,000 shares outstanding 12/31/91

Portfolio Highlights (as of 12/31/91): Common stocks 98.30%, Mexican government obligations 16.56%, time deposit 0.1%, liabilities in excess of other assets (14.87%). Largest sector concentrations (common stocks): retail 21.61%, construction 19.10%, communications 17.54%, industrial conglomerates 15.15%, food/beverages/tobacco 11.71%. **Largest positions:** Teléfonos de México S.A. de C.V.; Bondes 90-292 16.71-92; Cifra S.A. de C.V. Series ?; Cementos Mexicanos S.A. de C.V.; Empresa Tolteca de México S.A. de C.V. Series B2.

Historical Financial Statistics (fiscal year-end: 6/30/91):

	six months 12/31/91	10/1/90 to 6/30/91
Value of net assets (000)	92,133	86,281
NAV	18.39	17.23
Net investment income	0.03	0.66
Dividends from net investment income	0.32	0.30
Distributions from net realized gains	2.40	0.01
Expense ratio	1.78% ann.*	2.22% ann.
Income ratio	0.39% ann.*	6.86% ann.
Portfolio turnover	22.45%	87.14%

*If a portion of the advisory fee had not been waived, expense ratio would have been 1.84% and income ratio would have been 0.33%.

Special considerations: The fund will distribute net realized capital gains annually. The fund may take action to reduce discounts from net asset value such as repurchasing shares in the open market or making tender offers. The Board of Directors will consider such action on a quarterly basis. The fund's Articles of Incorporation contain various anti-takeover provisions including a 75% vote to merge with another fund, liquidate the fund or convert to an open-end fund. At the May, 1992, annual meeting, shareholders will vote regarding eliminating the sub-advisor, and reducing the advisory fee to an annual rate of 0.90%.

217

Engex, Inc.

44 Wall Street, New York, NY 10005

Category: Equity Fund

Phone: 212-495-4200
Listed: EGX, ASE
Commenced Operations: 1968
Cusip: 292851102

1991/mid-1992 Range of Premium/Disc: est. +10% to -28%
1991/mid-1992 Range of Price: $12 5/8 to $5 5/8
NAV Total Return 1990: -39.07%; **1991**: +53.68%
Share Price Total Return 1990: -38.82%; **1991**: +50.54%
Herzfeld Ranking 1991: 3rd of 15 equity funds

Investment Objective: Capital appreciation through investment in a high-risk portfolio of equity securities.

Officers:

J.M. Davis   Chairman & President

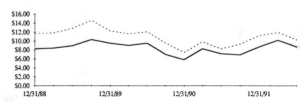

Investment Advisor: D.H. Blair Advisors, Inc.
Advisory Fee: Quarterly fee at annual rate of 1.0% of average weekly net assets. Fee for six months ended 3/31/92 was $58,192.

Capital Structure: *Common stock*: 10 mil. shares authorized; 977,223 shares outstanding 3/31/92

Portfolio Highlights (as of 3/31/92): Common stock 74.46%, U.S. government obligations 9.04%, money market instruments 16.49%. **Largest positions**: Theragenics Corp., Enzo Biochemical Inc., Health Professional Inc., U.S. treasury notes, International Mobile Mach CRP.

Historical Financial Statistics (fiscal year-end: 9/30/91):

	1991	1990	1989	1988	1987	1986
Value of net assets (000)	9,201	9,374	14,478	12,684	17,056	17,670
NAV	9.42	9.59	14.82	12.98	17.45	18.08
Net investment income (loss)	--	(0.10)	0.01	(0.07)	(0.36)	(0.23)
Dividends to shareholders	--	1.36	--	--	--	--
Expense ratio	2.66%	2.34%	2.25%	2.31%	6.68%	4.04%
Income ratio (loss)	(0.03%)	(0.80%)	0.02%	(0.60%)	(1.97%)	(1.27%)
Portfolio turnover	103.91%	34.52%	67.53%	10.65%	49.73%	75.52%

Special considerations: Shareholders over 5%: Mr. J. Morton Davis, 6.0%; Mrs. J. Morton Davis, 22.7%; Thomas J. Herzfeld Advisors, 14.88%.

The Europe Fund, Inc.

780 Third Avenue, New York, NY 10017

Phone: 212-751-8340
Listed: EF, NYSE
Commenced Operations: May, 1990
Cusip: 29874M103

Category: Foreign Equity Fund

1991/mid-1992 Range of Premium/Disc: -3% to -22%
1991/mid-1992 Range of Price: $13 1/2 to $9 5/8
NAV Total Return 1991: +4.81%
Share Price Total Return 1991: +17.94%
Herzfeld Ranking 1991: 31st of 46 foreign equity funds

Investment Objective: Long-term capital appreciation through investment primarily in European equity securities.

Officers:
A.M. Solomon   Chairman
R.P.B. Michaelson   President

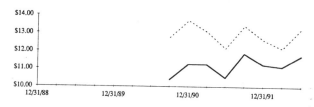

Investment Manager: Warburg Investment Management International (Jersey) Limited
Management Fee: Monthly fee at annual rate of 0.75% of average weekly net assets up to $250 mil., and 0.65% on any excess. Management fees for year-ended 12/31/91 were $825,888.
Investment Advisor: Warburg Investment Management International Ltd.
Advisory Fee (paid by the investment manager): Fee at annual rate of 0.15% of average weekly net assets.
Administrator: Princeton Administrators, Inc.
Administration Fee: Monthly fee at annual rate of 0.25% of average weekly net assets up to $200 mil., and 0.20% on any excess. Fee for year-ended 12/31/91 was $275,297.

Capital Structure: *Common stock*: 100 mil. shares authorized; 8,344,592 shares outstanding 12/31/91

Portfolio Highlights (as of 3/31/92): Common stocks & warrants 93.9%, preferred stocks 2.8%, convertible bonds 0.8%, other assets in excess of liabilities 2.5%. Largest geographic concentrations: United Kingdom 35.1%, Switzerland 14.0%, Germany 13.7%, France 11.0%, Spain 6.2%, Netherlands 4.2%. **Largest positions:** Roche Holding, East German Investment Trust (EGIT), ABAG, Reuters Holdings, GKN.

Historical Financial Statistics (fiscal year-end: 12/31/91):

	1991	5/3/90 to 12/31/90
Value of net assets (000)	105,072	114,600
NAV	12.59	13.73
Net investment income	0.30	0.75
Dividends from net investment income	1.06	--
Distributions from net realized gains	0.55	--
Distributions from paid-in surplus	0.13	--
Operating expense ratio	1.56%	1.00% ann.
Income ratio	2.30%	5.55% ann.
Portfolio turnover	94.63%	25.25% ann.

Special considerations: Annual distributions of at least 7% of net asset value are planned. These distributions will be made from net investment income, net realized capital gains, and from fund assets if needed. During the second quarter of 1995 the board will consider making a tender offer at net asset value; and if not all shares are tendered or the tender offer is not made, the board will be required to submit an open-ending proposal by 1/31/96. Before 4/1/95 an open-ending proposal will require a 75% vote to pass; after that date a majority will be required. The board may also repurchase shares in the open market.

The European Warrant Fund

c/o Julius Baer Securities, Inc.; 330 Madison Avenue,
New York, NY 10017

Category: Foreign Equity Fund

Phone: 617-720-5576; 800-331-1710
Listed: EWF, NYSE
Commenced Operations: July, 1990
Cusip: 298792102

1991/mid-1992 Range of Premium/Disc: 0% to -28%
1991/mid-1992 Range of Price: $9 1/8 to $5 1/4
NAV Total Return 1991: -18.43%
Share Price Total Return 1991: -6.29%
Herzfeld Ranking 1991: 43rd of 46 foreign equity funds

Investment Objective: Enhancement of capital growth by investing primarily in equity warrants of Western European issuers.

Officers:

H. Saurer   Chairman
R.J. Baer   President

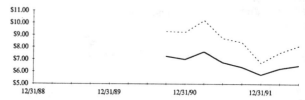

Investment Advisor: Julius Baer Securities, Inc.
Sub-Advisor: James Capel Incorporated
Advisory Fee: Fee at annual rate of 1.25% of average weekly net assets. Sub-advisory fees are paid from the advisory fee at the annual rate of 0.125% of average weekly net assets. Fee for year-ended 3/31/92 was $628,007.
Administrator: The Boston Company Advisors, Inc.
Administration Fee: Fee at annual rate of 0.32% of average weekly net assets, with a minimum of $125,000. Fee for year-ended 3/31/92 was $172,361.

Capital Structure: *Common stock*: 100 mil. shares authorized, 6,040,828 shares outstanding 3/31/92

Portfolio Highlights (as of 3/31/92): Warrants 59.3%, common stock 6.7%, treasury obligation 7.8%, government bonds 4.0%, corporate bonds 2.1%, call options purchased 8.1%, put options purchased 0.4%, time deposit 1.5%, other assets and liabilities 10.1%. Largest geographic concentrations: Germany 31.1%, France 20.4%, Switzerland 13.6%, United Kingdom 6.6%. **Largest positions**: French Treasury bills 9.902-92; Deutsche Bank, expires 6/30/95; RWE Aktiengesellschaft, expires 3/20/96; Viag AG, expires 9/5/97; Roche Bull Spread, expires 5/16/94; Sandoz AG Series A and B, expires 1/11/95.

Historical Financial Statistics (fiscal year-end: 3/31/92):

	1992	7/17/90 to 3/31/91
Value of net assets (000)	45,741	59,377
NAV	7.57	9.88
Net investment income (loss)	(0.07)	0.09
Dividends from net investment income	0.02	--
Distributions from capital	0.42	--
Expense ratio	2.44%	2.36% ann.
Income ratio	(0.79%)	1.35% ann.
Portfolio turnover	100%	248%

Special considerations: The fund will annually distribute its investment company taxable income. The fund's Articles of Incorporation contain various anti-takeover provisions including a 75% vote to merge with another fund, to liquidate, or to approve any shareholder proposal as to specific investment decisions made or to be made with respect to the fund's assets. At 3/31/92 the fund had a capital loss carryforward of $5,841,113 expiring in 2000 and $7,006,679 expiring in 1999.

Excelsior Income Shares, Inc.

114 W. 47th Street, 10th Fl., New York, NY 10036

Category: Bond Fund

Phone: 212-852-3732; 800-257-2356
Listed: EIS, NYSE
Commenced Operations: May, 1973
Cusip: 300723103

1991/mid-1992 Range of Premium/Disc: +1% to -10%
1991/mid-1992 Range of Price: $18 5/8 to $16
NAV Total Return 1990: +7.71%; **1991:** +15.07%
Share Price Total Return 1990: +9.95%; **1991:** +19.69%
Herzfeld Ranking 1991: 71st of 80 bond funds

Investment Objective: Income, with secondary objective of capital appreciation, primarily through investment in U.S. government and corporate debt securities.

Officers:

T. Brown, II   President & CEO

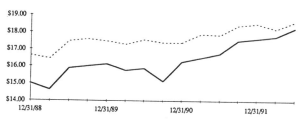

Investment Advisor: United States Trust Company of New York
Advisory Fee: Quarterly fee at annual rate of 0.5% of first $100 mil. of average net assets, 0.4% of assets from $100 mil. to $200 mil., 0.3% of net assets exceeding $200 mil.

Capital Structure: *Common stock:* 15 mil. shares authorized; 2,220,891 shares outstanding 12/31/91

Portfolio Highlights (as of 12/31/91): U.S. government and federal agencies obligations 74.95%, bonds & notes 23.52%, short-term holdings 1.53%. Quality ratings: Aaa 81.94%, Aa1 3.98%, Aa2 6.51%, Aa3 2.63%, B2 4.94%. **Largest issuers:** Government National Mortgage Assn.; U.S. treasury bonds and notes; Small Business Administration gtd. dev. partn. ctfs.; Pennsylvania Power & Light Co. 1st Mtg. 9 1/4-19; Collateralized Mortgage Securities Corp. Ser. 89-2 Cl2-F 9.3-19.

Historical Financial Statistics (fiscal year-end: 12/31/91):

	1991	1990	1989	1988	1987	1986
Value of net assets (000)	41,620	38,867	38,905	36,965	37,392	40,604
NAV	18.74	17.50	17.52	16.64	16.84	18.28
Net investment income	1.44	1.46	1.41	1.27	1.42	1.69
Dividends from net investment income	1.45	1.48	1.39	1.28	1.52	1.78
Expense ratio	0.98%	1.00%	1.03%	1.07%	0.98%	0.93%
Income ratio	8.01%	8.47%	8.20%	7.47%	8.06%	9.25%
Portfolio turnover	65.49%	175.30%	260.45%	469.14%	428.42%	83.94%

The First Australia Fund, Inc.

One Seaport Plaza, New York, NY 10292

Category: Foreign Equity Fund

Phone: 212-214-3334, 800-451-6788
Listed: IAF, ASE
Commenced Operations: December, 1985
Cusip: 318652104

1991/mid-1992 Range of Premium/Disc: 0% to -18%
1991/mid-1992 Range of Price: $10 1/4 to $7
NAV Total Return 1990: -14.79%; **1991:** +28.64%
Share Price Total Return 1990: -12.34%; **1991:** +30.14%
Herzfeld Ranking 1991: 9th of 46 foreign equity funds

Investment Objective: Long-term capital appreciation through investment in equity securities of Australian companies, with a secondary objective of current income, primarily through investment in equity securities listed on the Australian stock exchanges, with current income from Australian corporate and governmental securities.

Officers:
B.M. Sherman   President

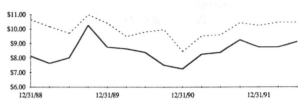

Investment Advisor: EquitiLink Australia Limited (investment manager is EquitiLink International Management Limited)
Consultant: The Prudential Insurance Company of America
Advisory Fee: Advisor and Consultant receive a fee from the Investment Manager, who is paid a monthly fee at an annual rate of 1.10% of first $50 mil. of average weekly net assets, 0.90% of assets between $50 mil. and $100 mil., 0.70% on assets in excess of $100 mil. Fee for year-ended 10/31/91 was $621,262.
Administrator: Prudential Mutual Fund Management Inc.
Administration Fee: Annual fee of the greater of $25,000 or 0.05% of fund's average weekly net assets. Fee for year-ended 10/31/91 was $28,944.

Capital Structure: *Common stock:* 20 mil. shares authorized; 6,019,200 outstanding 1/31/92

Portfolio Highlights (as of 1/31/92): Australian equities 93.0%, long-term interest-bearing securities 5.0-%, cash and short-term interest bearing securities 2.0%. Largest sector concentrations: natural resources 36.2%, diversified industrials 35.1%, services 24.5%, property related 4.2%. **Largest positions:** Broken Hill Proprietary Co. Limited, National Australia Bank Limited, TNT Limited, Western Mining Corporation Holdings Limited, Australian Telecom Commission 13-94.

Historical Financial Statistics (fiscal year-end: 10/31/91; before 10/87 fiscal year-end was 9/30):

	1991	1990	1989	1988	10/30/87*	1987#
Value of net assets (000)	66,374	55,042	63,440	65,976	55,522	99,258
NAV	11.03	9.14	10.56	10.98	9.72	17.38
Net investment income	0.30	0.47	0.53	0.25	0.02	0.20
Dividends from net investment income	0.42	0.59	0.26	0.28	--	0.39
Distributions from net realized gains	0.01	0.03	0.05	0.82	--	--
Total expense ratio	2.54%	2.41%	2.71%	2.81%	2.85% ann.	2.36%
Operating expense ratio	2.25%	2.14%	2.18%	2.30%	2.27% ann.	1.95%
Income ratio	3.11%	4.68%	5.02%	2.58%	2.14% ann.	1.41%
Portfolio turnover	82%	68%	56%	31%	3%	55%

#year-ended 9/30/87   *period from 9/30/87 to 10/31/87

Special considerations: Withholding of U.S. income tax is required on dividends for non-resident aliens. As of 10/31/91 the fund had a capital loss carryforward of approximately $1,415,000 expiring in 1996. No capital gains distributions are expected to be made until net gains have been realized in excess of this carryforward. Semi-annual dividend rate reduced to $0.09 per share.

The First Australia Prime Income Fund, Inc.

One Seaport Plaza, New York, NY 10292   **Category:** Foreign Bond Fund

Phone: 212-214-3334	**1991/mid-1992 Range of Premium/Disc:** +8% to -11%
Listed: FAX, ASE	**1991/mid-1992 Range of Price:** $11 15/16 to $9 1/16
Commenced Operations: April, 1986	**NAV Total Return 1990:** +16.93%; **1991:** +22.55%
Cusip: 318653102	**Share Price Total Return 1990:** +28.45%; **1991:** +32.82%
	Herzfeld Ranking 1991: 1st of 8 foreign bond funds

Investment Objective: Current income through investment primarily in Australian debt securities, and capital appreciation, through investment in Australian dollar-denominated debt securities of Australian issuers and debt securities denominated in Australian or New Zealand dollars, and U.S. treasuries, AA, equivalent or higher rated securities.

Officers:

B.M. Sherman   President

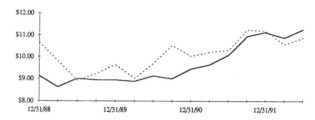

Investment Advisor: EquitiLink Australia Limited

Consultant: The Prudential Insurance Company of America

Advisory Fee: Advisor and Consultant receive a fee from the Investment Manager (EquitiLink International Management Limited), who is paid a monthly fee at the annual rate of 0.65% of first $200 mil. of average weekly net assets, 0.60% of assets between $200 mil. and $500 mil., 0.55% of assets between $500 mil. and $900 mil., and 0.50% on excess. Fee for year-ended 10/31/91 was $6,739,822.

Administrator: Prudential Mutual Fund Management, Inc.

Administration Fee: Annual fee of 0.15% of fund's average weekly net assets and 0.10% of such assets in excess of $900 mil. Fee for year-ended 10/31/91 was $1,710,280.

Capital Structure: *Common stock:* 200 mil. shares authorized; 87,586,727 shares outstanding 1/31/92
                              Auction Market Preferred stock : 100 mil. shares authorized; 3,000 shares outstanding
                              10/31/91, liquidation value $100,000 per share. Dividends reset every 28 days.

Portfolio Highlights (as of 1/31/92): Australian long-term 124.0%, short-term 3.6%, other assets 5.6%, liquidation value of preferred stock (33.2%). Largest sector concentration: government 31%, state and semi-government 50%, corporate 13%, commercial banks 6%. Largest geographic concentrations: Australia 98%, U.S. 2%. **Largest issuers:** Commonwealth of Australia; Australian Telecom Commission; New South Wales Treasury Corporation; Victoria Public Finance Authority; South Australia Finance Authority.

Historical Financial Statistics (fiscal year-end: 10/31/91):

	1991	1990	1989	1988	1987	4/24/86 to 10/31/86
Value of net assets (000)	1,272,569	1,161,379	1,100,166	928,688	751,129	708,012
NAV	11.31	10.02	9.31	10.81	8.74	8.26
Net investment income	1.40	1.49	1.32	0.97	1.02	0.49
Dividends from net investment income to common shares	1.24	1.13	1.08	1.40	1.06	0.08
Dividends from net investment income to preferred shares	0.24	0.30	0.20	--	--	--
Distributions from net realized gains to common shares	--	0.08	0.23	--	--	--
Total expense ratio	2.54%	2.59%	2.70%	2.11%	2.49%	2.64% ann.
Operating expense ratio	1.59%	1.54%	1.35%	1.04%	1.11%	1.09% ann.
Income ratio	11.11%	12.36%	11.39%	9.51%	11.61%	11.75% ann.
Portfolio turnover	83%	80%	46%	60%	52%	13%

Special considerations: At the April, 1991, annual meeting shareholders voted to delete the conditional right of common shareholders to present their shares for payment at net asset value, which was to begin in November, 1991.

First Boston Income Fund, Inc.

Tower 49, 12 East 49th Street, New York, NY 10017   **Category: Bond Fund**

Phone: 215-648-6176	**1991/mid-1992 Range of Premium/Disc**: +3% to -14%
Listed: FBF, NYSE	**1991/mid-1992 Range of Price**: $9 to $6 1/4
Commenced Operations: March, 1987	**NAV Total Return 1990**: -2.98%; **1991**: +27.49%
Cusip: 319338109	**Share Price Total Return 1990**: -7.62%; **1991**: +45.49%
	Herzfeld Ranking 1991: 22nd of 80 bond funds

Investment Objective: Current income consistent with preservation of capital primarily through investment in fixed-income securities, 2/3 of which are rated as investment grade.

Officers:

J.J. Cook, Jr.   President

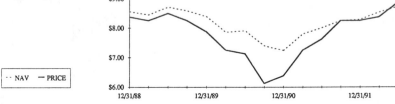

Investment Advisor: First Boston Asset Management Corporation

Advisory Fee: Quarterly fee at annual rate of 0.5% of average weekly net assets. Fee for year-ended 12/31/91 was $914,000.

Administrator: Mutual Funds Service Company

Administration Fee: Quarterly fee at annual rate of 0.15% of first $100 mil. of average weekly net assets, 0.10% of next $300 mil., and 0.05% of excess over $400 mil. Fee for year-ended 12/31/91 was $243,000.

Capital Structure: *Common stock*: 100 mil. shares authorized; 24,127,045 shares outstanding on 3/31/92

Portfolio Highlights (as of 3/31/92): High yield corporates 63.5%, federal agency securities 27.6%, treasuries 6.4%, short-term instruments 2.5%. Largest industry concentrations: manufacturing 22.1%, services 10.4%, retail trade 7.8%, consumer products 6.7%, transportation & communication 5.0%. **Largest issuers**: Federal National Mortgage Association; Federal Home Loan Mortgage Corp.; U.S. treasury note 7.875-01; Dr. Pepper Bottling Co. of Texas; Chrysler Corp. 12-15.

Historical Financial Statistics (fiscal year-end: 12/31/91):

	1991	1990	1989	1988	3/23/87 to 12/31/87
Value of net assets (000)	199,857	175,390	201,297	207,359	209,060
NAV	8.28	7.25	8.32	8.58	8.71
Net investment income	0.89	0.87	0.92	0.87	0.59
Dividends from net investment income	0.90	0.90	0.90	0.90	0.59
Distributions from net realized gains and capital surplus	--	--	--	--	0.07
Expense ratio	0.87%	0.89%	0.92%	0.91%	0.77% ann.
Income ratio	11.12%	11.26%	10.67%	9.96%	9.40% ann.
Portfolio turnover	53.3%	61.4%	95.8%	113.47%	42.02%

Special considerations: The Board of Directors may submit an open-ending proposal after 1/1/93 if it is thought to be advantageous and if certain conditions apply. At the May, 1991, annual meeting shareholders passed on a proposal to limit certain liabilities of the fund's directors and officers and provide for certain rights of indemnification and advancement of expenses. In January, 1992, the Board of Directors eliminated the restrictions on percentage of portfolio's which may be held in junk bonds.

First Boston Strategic Income Fund, Inc.

Tower 49, 12 East 49th Street, New York, NY 10017

Category: Bond Fund

Phone: 215-648-6176
Listed: FBI, NYSE
Commenced Operations: April, 1988
Cusip: 319344107

1991/mid-1992 Range of Premium/Disc: +16% to -11%
1991/mid-1992 Range of Price: $11 5/8 to $7 5/8
NAV Total Return 1990: -2.76%; **1991:** +25.12%
Share Price Total Return 1990: -3.24%; **1991:** +49.35%
Herzfeld Ranking 1991: 24th of 80 bond funds

Investment Objective: High current income with preservation of capital through investment in the following three sectors: U.S. government sector, high yield sector, and international sector.

Officers:

J.J. Cook, Jr.   Chairman & President

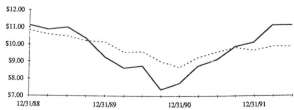

Investment Advisor: First Boston Asset Management Corp.
Advisory Fee: Quarterly fee at annual rate of 0.50% of average weekly net assets. Fee for year-ended 12/31/91 was $378,000.
Administrator: Mutual Funds Service Company
Administration Fee: Quarterly fee at annual rate of 0.15% of first $100 mil. of average net assets, 0.10% on assets in excess of $100 mil. Fee for year-ended 12/31/91 was $120,000.

Capital Structure: *Common stock:* 100 mil. shares authorized; 8,389,642 shares outstanding 3/31/92

Portfolio Highlights (as of 3/31/92): High yield corporates 70.8%, agency securities 17.6% (foreign currency related), foreign currency denominated 8.3%, short-term instruments 3.3%. Largest industry concentrations (corporate obligations): manufacturing 22.3%, services 13.6%, retail trade 12.9%. **Largest issuers:** Federal National Mortgage Association; Student Loan Marketing Association PERL 14.25-94; Government of Australia 10-02; Federal Business Development Bank 13.30-92; Chrysler Corp. 12-15.

Historical Financial Statistics (fiscal year-end: 12/31/91):

	1991	1990	1989	4/8/88 to 12/31/88
Value of net assets (000)	80,606	73,068	84,488	90,775
NAV	9.62	8.70	10.06	10.86
Net investment income	1.16	1.17	1.27	0.82
Dividends from net investment income	1.20	1.20	1.00	0.77
Distributions from capital surplus	--	--	0.31	--
Expense ratio	1.00%	1.00%	1.07%	0.85% ann.
Income ratio	12.13%	12.48%	12.13%	11.17% ann.
Portfolio turnover	48.0%	81.0%	105.5%	112.09% ann.

Special considerations: The Board of Directors may submit an open-ending proposal after 1/1/94 if it is believed to be advantageous, and if certain conditions apply. In January, 1992, the fund announced it intended to increase the investment in junk bonds. Management believes that the additional income and gains realized from this reallocation may compensate for the lower reinvestment rates available to the fund on its mortgage-backed and other securities and increase the possibility for the current dividend rate to be maintained.

The First Commonwealth Fund, Inc.

800 Scudders Mill Road, Plainsboro, NJ 08536

Category: Foreign Bond Fund

Phone: 609-282-4600
Listed: FCO, NYSE
Commenced Operations: February, 1992
Cusip: 31983F102

1991/mid-1992 Range of Premium/Disc: +11% to 0%
1991/mid-1992 Range of Price: $15 1/4 to $14 3/8
NAV Total Return 1991: N/A
Share Price Total Return 1991: N/A
Herzfeld Ranking 1991: N/A

Investment Objective: High current income by investing in high grade fixed income securities denominated in the currencies of Australia, Canada, New Zealand and the United Kingdom. The secondary investment objective is capital appreciation. Under normal circumstances the fund will be invested in debt securities denominated in at least three of these currencies and will not hold more than 50% of its assets in securities denominated in any one Commonwealth currency. At least 75% of assets will be rated at least AA or of equivalent quality.

Officers:

Sir A. R. Cutler   Chairman
L.S. Freedman   President

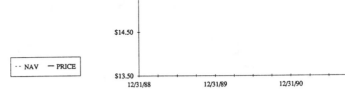

Investment Manager: EquitiLink International Management Limited
Management Fee: Monthly fee at the annual rate of 0.65% of average weekly net assets up to $200 mil., 0.60% of such assets between $200 mil. and $500 mil., and 0.55% of such assets in excess of $500 mil.
Investment Advisor: EquitiLink Australia Limited
Advisory Fee: The investment manager pays the investment advisor a monthly fee at an annual rate of 0.15% of the fund's average weekly net assets with respect to advice relating to overall portfolio structure and at an annual rate of up to 0.10% with respect to the recommendation of specific portfolio securities.
Administrator: Princeton Administrators
Administration Fee: Monthly fee at an annual rate of 0.20% of average weekly net assets subject to a minimum annual payment of $150,000.

Capital Structure: *Common stock*: 300 mil. shares authorized, 7,850,000 shares outstanding 2/20/92
Debt: 100 mil. shares authorized, none outstanding 2/20/92. An offering of preferred shares is planned within six months of common stock offering representing approximately 25% of total assets.

Portfolio Highlights: not yet published

Historical Financial Statistics :

	2/20/92
Value of net assets (000)	110,293
NAV	14.05

Special considerations: During the initial offering of this fund, the initial offering price was reduced (underwriting discount reduced) from $15.00 to $14.85 for single transactions between 2,000 and 6,999 shares, and $14.70 for transactions of greater than 7,000 shares. The board of directors will consider making annual tender offers at net asset value beginning in the third quarter of 1993. The fund will make monthly distributions of net investment income and annual distributions of capital gains. The fund's Articles of Incorporation contain various anti-takeover provisions including a 80% of both classes of stock voting as a single class to, among other things, merge with another fund, open-end, or liquidate the fund. However, only a majority vote is required if 66 2/3% of the directors approve the action. Initial dividend rate $0.105 per month.

First Financial Fund, Inc.

One Seaport Plaza, New York, NY 10292

Phone: 212-214-3334, 800-451-6788
Listed: FF, NYSE
Commenced Operations: May, 1986
Cusip: 320228109

Category: Specialized Equity Fund

1991/mid-1992 Range of Premium/Disc: +22% to -16%
1991/mid-1992 Range of Price: $11 1/8 to $4 3/8
NAV Total Return 1990: -37.96%; **1991**: +89.92%
Share Price Total Return 1990: -41.00%; **1991**: +83.44%
Herzfeld Ranking 1991: 2nd of 18 specialized bond funds

Investment Objective: Long-term capital appreciation, with a secondary objective of current income primarily through investment in savings and banking institutions and their holding companies.

Officers:
R. Wadsworth   President & Treasurer

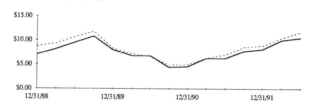

Investment Advisor: Wellington Management Company
Advisory Fee: Quarterly fee computed monthly at annual rate of 0.75% of average month-end net assets up to $50 mil., and 0.625% of excess. Fee for year-ended 3/31/92 was $569,377.
Administrator: Prudential Mutual Fund Management, Inc.
Administration Fee: Quarterly fee computed monthly at annual rate of 0.15% of average month-end net assets. Fee for year-ended 3/31/92 was $121,650.

Capital Structure: *Common stock*: 50 mil. shares authorized; 9,432,623 shares outstanding 3/31/92
Debt: Credit agreement with maximum commitment line of credit of $9 mil., note payable of $9 mil. outstanding 3/31/92 at weighted average interest rate of 6.62%.

Portfolio Highlights (as of 3/31/92): Common stocks 106.7%, bonds 0.8%, short-term investments 5.6%, liabilities in excess of other assets (13.1%). **Largest positions**: Cragin Financial Corp., N S Bancorp Inc., Bankers Corp., Bell Bancorp, Liberty Bancorp Inc., Westcorp Inc.

Historical Financial Statistics (fiscal year-end: 3/31/92):

	1992	1991	1990	1989	1988	5/1/86 to 3/31/87
Value of net assets (000)	99,067	59,979	66,931	83,242	76,707	94,801
NAV	10.50	6.35	7.09	9.32	8.58	10.29
Net investment income	0.11	0.18	0.23	0.21	0.15	
Dividends from net investment income	0.11	0.18	0.26	0.19	0.18	0.12
Distributions from net realized gains	--	--	0.86	--	0.31	--
Distributions from paid-in capital	0.01	0.03	--	--	--	--
Total expense ratio	1.65%	2.14%	1.59%	1.45%	1.46%	1.37% ann.
Expense ratio (excluding loan interest and commitment fees)	1.23%	1.55%	1.42%	1.45%	1.46%	1.37% ann.
Income ratio	1.33%	3.06%	2.40%	2.30%	1.73%	1.95% ann.
Portfolio turnover	89%	42%	58%	41%	69%	51%

Special considerations: Proposals at the 1991 annual meeting included amendments to the Articles of Incorporation to require supermajority voting requirement for open-ending of the fund and to add a 2/3 voting requirement for removal of a director. No action was taken on these proposals. **Shareholders over 5%**: Tiger, 17.9%; Puma 11.1% (These and other entities which Julian H. Robertson, Jr. has a direct or indirect interest in account for 28.92% of outstanding shares.)

The First Iberian Fund, Inc.

One Seaport Plaza, New York, NY 10292

Category: Foreign Equity Fund

Phone: 212-214-3334, 800-451-6788
Listed: IBF, ASE
Commenced Operations: October, 1987
Cusip: 320532104

1991/mid-1992 Range of Premium/Disc: +16% to -22%
1991/mid-1992 Range of Price: $11 5/8 to $6 7/8
NAV Total Return 1990: -10.88%; **1991:** +8.80%
Share Price Total Return 1990: -34.50%; **1991:** +0.32%
Herzfeld Ranking 1991: 26th of 46 foreign equity funds

Investment Objective: Long-term capital appreciation through investment primarily in equity securities traded principally on stock exchanges in Spain or Portugal that derive a majority of their total revenue from goods produced, sales made or services performed in Spain or Portugal, securities organized under the laws of Spain or Portugal, and equity securities of Spanish or Portuguese companies.

Officers:

J.L. Calderon   President

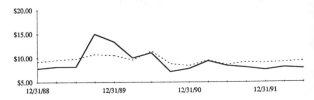

Investment Advisor: Scudder, Stevens & Clark
Advisory Fee: Quarterly fee at annual rate of 1% of average weekly net assets. Fee for year-ended 9/30/91 was $602,777.
Administrator: Prudential Mutual Fund Management, Inc.
Administration Fee: Monthly fee at annual rate of 0.20% of average weekly net assets. Fee for year-ended 9/30/91 was $120,555.

Capital Structure:
Common stock: 200 mil. shares authorized; 6,511,154 shares outstanding 9/30/91
Debt: $2,258,564 loan from Baring Brothers & Co., Limited to be paid in 20 equal quarterly installments at an interest rate of 9.15% as of 9/30/91

Portfolio Highlights (as of 3/31/92): Long-term investments 78.7%, short-term investments 21.4%, liabilities in excess of other assets (0.1%). Geographic distribution: Spanish equities 75.5%, Portuguese equities 3.2%. Largest industry concentrations: utilities 19.3%, banking 15.6%, transportation 12.7%, machinery and equipment 6.2%, building materials & equipment 5.4%. **Largest positions:** Zardoya Otis; S.A.; Banco Popular Español; Autopistas, C.E.S.A.; Europista, C.E.S.A.; Empresa Nacional de Electricidad, S.A.

Historical Financial Statistics (fiscal year-end: 9/30/91):

	1991	1990	1989	4/20/88* to 9/30/88
Value of net assets (000)	60,628	57,330	70,179	56,992
NAV	9.31	8.80	10.78	8.75
Net investment income	0.27	0.16	0.23	0.07
Dividends from net investment income	0.20	0.12	0.25	--
Distributions from net realized gains	0.82	0.13	--	--
Operating expense ratio	2.30%	2.18%	2.08%	2.72% ann.
Total expense ratio	2.93%	3.78%	3.38%	3.87% ann.
Income ratio	2.96%	1.53%	2.32%	1.83% ann.
Portfolio turnover	23%	22%	26%	0%

*commencement of investment operations

Special considerations: Beginning 10/1/92, under certain conditions, the fund will permit quarterly redemption of shares at net asset value. The fund's articles of incorporation contain various anti-takeover provisions. Scudder, Stevens & Clark replaced Iberioncorp Gestion B.V. as investment advisor in 1992.

The First Philippine Fund, Inc.

152 West 57th Street, 25th Fl., New York, NY 10019   **Category:** Foreign Equity Fund

Phone: 212-765-0700	**1991/mid-1992 Range of Premium/Disc:** -8% to -31%
Listed: FPF, NYSE	**1991/mid-1992 Range of Price:** $13 to $6 3/8
Commenced Operations: November, 1989	**NAV Total Return 1990:** -11.70%; **1991:** +28.63%
Cusip: 336100102	**Share Price Total Return 1990:** -48.44%; **1991:** +38.27%
	Herzfeld Ranking 1991: 10th of 46 foreign equity funds

Investment Objective: Long-term capital appreciation through investment primarily in equity securities of Philippine companies.

Officers:

E.B. Espiritu   Chairman
L.C. Clemente   President

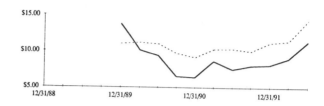

Investment Advisor: Clemente Capital, Inc. (Philippine Advisor: PNB Investments Limited)

Advisory Fee: Monthly fee at the annual rate of 1% of average weekly net assets. (Philippine advisor is paid by the U.S. advisor at the annual rate of 0.35% of average weekly net assets.) Fee for six months ended 12/31/91 was $471,657.

Administrator: Provident Financial Processing Corporation

Administration Fee: Monthly fee at the annual rate of 0.10% of average weekly net assets, subject to a minimum annual fee of $124,800. Fee for six months ended 12/31/91 was $62,740.

Capital Structure: *Common stock:* 25 mil. shares authorized; 8,980,000 shares outstanding 3/31/92

Portfolio Highlights (as of 3/31/92): Common stock 80.1%, bonds 0.2%, time deposits 17.2%, commercial paper 2.1%, call accounts 0.4%. Largest industry concentrations: telecommunications 22.3%, food and beverage 16.6%, investment companies 8.9%, banking 7.9%, real estate development 7.1%. **Largest positions:** Philippine Long Distance Telephone, San Miguel Corp-A and B, Ayala Corp. A and B, Ayala Land Inc.-B, Far East Bank and Trust.

Historical Financial Statistics (fiscal year-end: 6/30/91):

	six months 12/31/91	1991	11/15/89 to 6/30/90
Value of net assets (000)	101,173	92,975	98,467
NAV	11.27	10.35	10.97
Net investment income	0.03	0.40	0.41
Dividends from net investment income	0.19	0.59	0.08
Operating expense ratio	1.95% ann.	1.90%	2.00% ann.
Income ratio	0.64% ann.	3.92%	5.78% ann.
Portfolio turnover	0.37% ann.	1.03%	0%

Special considerations: The fund is taxable as a non-resident corporation; however, as a U.S. corporation it is entitled to preferential tax treatment under the income tax treaty between the Republic of the Philippines and the U.S. Generally, dividend and interest income will be subject to a 15% Philippine withholding tax. The fund's Articles of Incorporation and By-laws contain various anti-takeover provisions.

Fort Dearborn Income Securities, Inc.

70 West Madison, 9th Floor, Chicago, IL 60602

Category: Bond Fund

Phone: 312-346-0676
Listed: FTD, NYSE, MSE
Commenced Operations: September, 1972
Cusip: 347200107

1991/mid-1992 Range of Premium/Disc: +7% to -4%
1991/mid-1992 Range of Price: $16 5/8 to $14 1/2
NAV Total Return 1990: +5.22%; **1991:** +18.06%
Share Price Total Return 1990: +9.22%; **1991:** +18.98%
Herzfeld Ranking 1991: 52nd of 80 bond funds

Investment Objective: Stable stream of current income consistent with external interest rate conditions and total return over time that is above what investors could receive by investing individually in the high quality and long-term maturity sectors of the bond market, primarily by investment in high quality long-term fixed income debt securities.

Officers:

R.M. Burridge   Chairman
G.P. Brinson   President

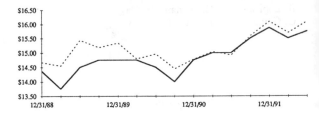

Investment Advisor: Brinson Partners, Inc.
Advisory Fee: Quarterly fee of 0.125% (annual fee of 0.5%) of average weekly net assets up to $100 mil., 0.10% quarterly (annual fee of 0.40%) of assets over $100 mil. Fee for six months ended 3/31/92 was $271,378.

Capital Structure: *Common stock:* 12 mil. shares authorized; 7,031,395 shares outstanding 3/31/92

Portfolio Highlights (as of 3/31/92): U.S. government securities 27.2%, corporate bonds and notes 70.4%, short-term securities 2.4%. Largest industry concentrations (corporate notes): finance 18.9%, industrial 16.2%, transportation 12.0%, international 9.8%. The fund's portfolio had an average market yield of 8.63%, an average Moody's quality ratings of AA3, an average duration of 7.25 years, and an average maturity of 19.0 years. **Largest issuers:** Government National Mortgage Association Pass Thru Mortgage Backed Securities; U.S. treasury bonds; Consolidated Rail Corp. 9.75-20; Resolution Funding Corp. Bonds 8.625-21; Secured Finance Inc. Guaranteed Senior Secured Bonds 9.05-04.

Historical Financial Statistics (fiscal year-end: 9/30/91):

	six months ended 3/31/92	1991	1990	1989	1988	1987
Value of net assets (000)	110,609		109,534	99,998	104,613	102,210	95,339
NAV	15.78	15.63	14.45	15.19	14.84	13.96
Net investment income	0.62	1.28	1.34	1.32	1.27	
Dividends from net investment income	0.62	1.33	1.36	1.36	1.36	1.36
Expense ratio	0.46%	0.81%	0.80%	0.80%	0.80%	0.79%
Income ratio	3.91%	8.53%	8.98%	8.84%	8.61%	8.48%
Portfolio turnover	14.12%	180.5%	190.82%	213.8%	202.4%	155.2%

Special considerations: On 7/25/88 the board authorized a 700,000 share repurchase. Quarterly dividend rate will be reduced from $0.34 per share to $0.31 per share beginning in September, 1991.

The France Growth Fund, Inc.

1230 Avenue of the Americas, New York, NY 10020

Category: Foreign Equity Fund

Phone: 212-408-5671; 800-852-4750
Listed: FRF, NYSE
Commenced Operations: May, 1990
Cusip: 35177K108

1991/mid-1992 Range of Premium/Disc: -7% to -24%
1991/mid-1992 Range of Price: $10 1/2 to $7 1/4
NAV Total Return 1991: +5.33%
Share Price Total Return 1991: +12.19%
Herzfeld Ranking 1991: 29th of 46 foreign equity funds

Investment Objective: Long-term capital appreciation through investment primarily in French equity securities.

Officers:

P.H.R. Daviron Chairman
J.C. Gruffat President

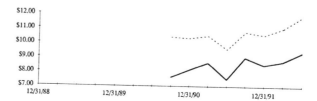

Investment Advisor: Indosuez International Investment Services
Advisory Fee: Monthly fee at the annual rate of 0.90% of average weekly net assets up to $100 mil. and 0.80% on any excess. Fee for year-ended 12/31/91 was $1,060,620.
Administrator: Mitchell Hutchins Asset Management, Inc.
Administration Fee: Monthly fee at the annual rate of 0.20% of average weekly net assets up to $150 mil. and 0.18% of any excess with a minimum annual fee of $150,000. Fee for year-ended 12/31/91 was $238,779.

Capital Structure: *Common stock:* 100 mil. shares authorized; 11,509,000 outstanding as of 12/31/91

Portfolio Highlights (as of 12/31/91): Investments in France 93.75%: common stocks 85.38%, warrants 0.38%, convertible corporate bonds 0.26%, corporate bonds 7.73%; investment in the U.S.: 1.13%: convertible bonds 0.98%, time deposit 0.15%. Largest industry concentrations: food & beverages 12.15%, financial services 8.83%, media & communications services 6.96%, distribution services 6.63%, electrical & electronics 6.07%, consumer non-durables 5.52%. **Largest positions:** Alcatel Alsthom, BSN, Saint-Gobain, L'Oreal, Pechiney.

Historical Financial Statistics (fiscal year-end: 12/31/91):

	1991	5/18/90 to 12/31/90
Value of net assets (000)	123,757	118,832
NAV	10.75	10.33
Net investment income	0.15	0.35
Dividends from net investment income	0.14	0.35
Distributions from net realized foreign exchange gains	0.10	0.17
Expense ratio	2.14%	2.18% ann.
Income ratio	1.46%	5.17% ann.
Portfolio turnover	74.62%	15.88%

Special considerations: The fund distributes substantially all of its net investment income and net realized capital gains at least annually. The fund may repurchase shares in the open market or in private transactions or make tender offers. Such actions will be reviewed by the board of directors on a quarterly basis. If the fund is trading at a discount, the board will consider amending the Articles of Incorporation to provide for conversion to an open-end fund at the next quarterly meeting. The fund's Articles of Incorporation contain various anti-takeover provisions including a 75% voting requirement for merger with another corporation, liquidation of the fund or conversion to an open-end fund.
Shareholders over 5%: Stichting Akzo-Pensionenfonds, Arnhem, 6.1% (not confirmed)

Franklin Multi-Income Trust

777 Mariners Island Blvd., San Mateo, CA 94404

Category: Miscellaneous

Phone: 415-378-2000; 800-DIAL-BEN
Listed: FMI, NYSE
Commenced Operations: October, 1989
Cusip: 354021107

1991/mid-1992 Range of Premium/Disc: +7% to -8%
1991/mid-1992 Range of Price: $10 1/8 to $6 3/4
NAV Total Return 1990: -8.66%; **1991**: +49.83%
Share Price Total Return 1990: -11.21%; **1991**: +45.27%

Investment Objective: High current income consistent with preservation of capital, as well as growth of income through dividend increases and capital appreciation. The fund invests primarily in a portfolio of high yielding, fixed-income corporate securities and dividend-paying stocks of companies engaged in the public utilities industry.

Officers:
H.L. Jamieson — Chairman
C.B. Johnson — President

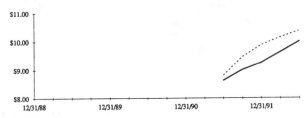

Investment Advisor: Franklin Advisors, Inc.
Administrator: Franklin Advisors, Inc.
Advisory and Administrative Fee: Monthly fee at the annual rate of 0.85% of average weekly net assets. Fee for year-ended 3/31/92 was $607,131.
Corporate Finance Services: Dean Witter Reynolds, Inc.
Fee for Corporate Finance Services (paid by the investment advisor): Annual fee at a rate approximating 0.10% of initial net assets.

Capital Structure: *Common stock*: unlimited number of shares authorized, 5,857,600 shares outstanding 3/31/92
Senior Fixed-Rate Notes: $16,000,000 principal amount, five year notes to mature on 10/15/94 with an annual interest rate of 9.125%. Interest is payable semi-annually. The notes are rated AAA by Standard & Poor's

Portfolio Highlights (as of 3/31/92): Common stocks & warrants 37.9%, preferred stocks 7.0%, bonds 75.9%, foreign government agencies 1.3%, other assets 3.7%, liabilities in excess of other assets (25.8%). Largest industry concentrations: electric utilities 37.0%, cable/cellular system 6.9%, retail 6.2%, grocery/convenience chains 5.0%, hotels/gaming 5.0%, restaurants 5.0%. **Largest positions/issuers**: Central & South West Corp.; Pacific Gas & Electric Co.; RJR Nabisco Holdings Group Inc. S.F. sub. disc. deb. zero coupon to 5/15/94 15-01; Dominion Resources Inc. VA; SCE corp.

Historical Financial Statistics (fiscal year-end: 3/31/92):

	1992	1991	10/24/89 to 3/31/90
Value of net assets (000)	59,470	50,356	50,415
NAV	10.15	8.60	8.61
Net investment income	0.97	1.08	0.43
Dividends from net investment income	0.985	1.0607	0.43
Distributions from capital gain	0.021	--	--
Expense ratio	3.21%	3.43%	3.40% ann.
Income ratio	7.64%	9.79%	8.52% ann.
Portfolio turnover	22.19%	26.07%	4.66%

Special considerations: A meeting will be held during September or October, 1994, to vote on a proposal to open-end the fund. In efforts to reduce any discount which may develop, the fund may repurchase shares in the open market or make tender offers from time to time. Such actions will be reviewed by the Board of Trustees on a regular basis. The monthly dividend was reduced to $0.08 per share due to lower interest rates causing refinancing by high yield issuers and defaults. (3.28% of the fund's portfolio was in default as of 3/31/92.)

Franklin Principal Maturity Trust

777 Mariners Island Blvd., San Mateo, CA 94404

Category: Bond Fund

Phone: 415-378-2000, 800-DIAL-BEN
Listed: FPT, NYSE
Commenced Operations: January, 1989
Cusip: 35459D103

1991/mid-1992 Range of Premium/Disc: +10% to -10%
1991/mid-1992 Range of Price: $8 7/8 to $7 1/8
NAV Total Return 1990: -2.29%; **1991:** +22.72%
Share Price Total Return 1990: -16.92%; **1991:** +23.23%
Herzfeld Ranking 1991: 30th of 80 bond funds

Investment Objective: High monthly income and the return of $10.00 per share to investors on or shortly before 5/31/01, primarily through investment in mortgage-backed securities, zero coupon securities and high income producing debt securities. (Also see Special Considerations below.)

Officers:

H.L. Jamieson — Chairman
C.B. Johnson — President

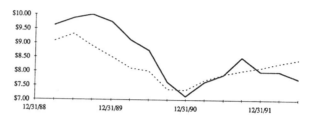

Investment Advisor: Franklin Advisers, Inc.
Administrator: Franklin Advisers, Inc.
Advisory and Administration Fee: Monthly fee computed on average weekly net assets of 0.75% annually through 5/31/93; 0.60% from 6/1/93 to 5/31/97; 0.45% from 6/1/97 to termination of the fund on 5/31/01. Fee for the year-ended 11/30/91 was $1,200,590.
Corporate Finance Services: Paine Webber Incorporated
Fee for Corporate Finance Services: Annual fee not to exceed 0.10% of initial net assets.

Capital Structure: *Shares of beneficial interest:* unlimited number of shares authorized; 20,462,600 shares outstanding 11/30/91
Debt: Interest rate swap agreements of $57,027,000 as of 11/30/91, maturing between 8/93 and 10/93

Portfolio Highlights (as of 11/30/91): Common stocks & warrants 0.4%, preferred stocks 0.2%, convertible preferred stocks 5.1%, senior secured floating rate bank loan 2.0%, corporate bonds 25.1%, foreign government bonds 0.6%, zero coupon bonds 63.4%, U.S. government and its agencies 51.7%, mortgage-backed securities 34.3%, short-term investments 3.3%, liabilities in excess of other assets (34.4%). **Largest issuers:** U.S. treasury strips; FNMA; various Resolution Funding Corp. 8.3-01; Intermountain Power Agency Utah Power Supply Revenue Refunding Series B 7-01; FHLMC REMIC.

Historical Financial Statistics (fiscal year-end: 11/30/91):

	1991	1990	1/19/89 to 11/30/89
Value of net assets (000)	164,994	150,601	175,879
NAV	8.06	7.36	8.60
Net investment income	0.736	0.95	0.839
Dividends from net investment income	0.729	1.002	0.7875
Distributions from paid-in capital	0.064	0.008	--
Expense ratio	4.06%	4.49%	3.60% ann.
Interest expense ratio	3.03%	3.51%	2.51% ann.
Income ratio	9.41%	11.96%	11.25% ann.
Portfolio turnover	49.91%	28.96%	38.73%

Special considerations: The fund may repurchase shares or make tender offers at prices and times it deems advantageous. The fund enters into interest rate swap agreements to hedge for the interest rate exposure on its reverse repurchase agreement transactions. Shareholders approved the following new policies at the 1992 annual meeting: the fund may invest up to 10% of total assets in each of the following: loan participations, convertible debt securities, convertible preferred stocks, preferred stocks, common stocks; and may invest in debt securities which are in default.

Franklin Universal Trust

777 Mariners Island Blvd., San Mateo, CA 94404

Category: Bond Fund

Phone: 415-378-2000, 800-DIAL-BEN
Listed: FT, NYSE
Commenced Operations: September, 1988
Cusip: 355145103

1991/mid-1992 Range of Premium/Disc: +10% to -12%
1991/mid-1992 Range of Price: $8 1/2 to $5 1/4
NAV Total Return 1990: -20.58%; **1991**: +51.39%
Share Price Total Return 1990: -25.48%; **1991**: +62.40%
Herzfeld Ranking 1991: 3rd of 80 bond funds

Investment Objective: High current income consistent with preservation of capital, with the secondary objective of growth of income through dividend increases and capital appreciation. The fund will invest primarily in fixed-income debt securities, dividend paying stocks, and securities of precious metals and natural resource companies.

Officers:

H.L. Jamieson   Chairman
C.B. Johnson   President

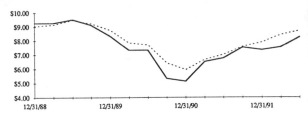

Investment Advisor: Franklin Advisers, Inc.
Administrator: Franklin Advisers, Inc.
Advisory and Administration Fee: Monthly fee at annual rate of 0.75% of average weekly net assets. Fee for six months ended 2/29/92 was $1,061,675.
Corporate Finance Services: Paine Webber Incorporated
Fee for Corporate Finance Services: Annual fee approximating 0.10% of initial net assets.

Capital Structure: *Shares of beneficial interest*: unlimited number of shares authorized; 26,779,333 shares outstanding 2/29/92
Debt: $71.4 mil. of 9.5% Senior Fixed-Rate Notes outstanding payable semi-annually, due 10/1/93

Portfolio Highlights (as of 2/29/92): Common stocks & warrants 27.2%, preferred stocks 9.5%, non-convertible bonds 87.2%, convertible bonds 3.3%, foreign government agencies 3.1%, short-term securities 0.4%, liabilities in excess of other assets (30.7%). High yield corporate bonds represented 68.07% of the portfolio. Largest industry concentrations: utilities 25.5%, paper and forest products 8.5%, conglomerates 6.8%, food 6.7%, beverage 5.4%, retail 5.3%, cable system 4.2%, textiles 4.2%. Largest issuers: Fort Howard Corp.; RJR Nabisco Holdings Capital Corp. S.F. sub. disc. deb. zero coupon 94; Pacific Gas & Electric Co.; Southern Co.; Texas Utilities Co.

Historical Financial Statistics (fiscal year-end: 8/30/91):

	six months 2/29/92	1991	1990	9/23/88 to 8/31/89
Value of net assets (000)	223,053	200,891	186,270	250,049
NAV	8.33	7.50	7.01	9.44
Net investment income	0.35	0.84	1.04	1.14
Dividends from net investment income	0.45	0.934	1.154	0.93
Distributions from paid-in capital	--	0.07	--	--
Expense ratio	3.45% ann.	4.01%	5.47%	4.94% ann.
Interest expense ratio	N/A	N/A	3.99%	3.61% ann.
Income ratio	6.60% ann.	9.04%	12.80%	13.47% ann.
Portfolio turnover	15.91%	38.57%	34.20%	36.56%

Special considerations: Restricted securities represented 7.73% of the fund's net assets 2/29/92, 68.07% of the portfolio was invested in lower-rated, high yielding corporate bonds, and 7.07% of the portfolio holdings were in default. The fund may repurchase shares or make tender offers at net asset value when the board deems it advantageous. An open-ending vote will be held at a shareholders' meeting in 1993. Senior fixed-rate notes carry a AAA S&P rating. At 8/31/91 the fund had capital loss carryovers of $23,224,336 expiring through 1999.

The Future Germany Fund, Inc.

31 West 52nd Street, New York, NY 10019   **Category: Foreign Equity Fund**

Phone: 800-GERMANY, 212-474-7000
Listed: FGF, NYSE
Commenced Operations: February, 1990
Cusip: 360905103

1991/mid-1992 Range of Premium/Disc: -1% to -20%
1991/mid-1992 Range of Price: $14 1/2 to $10 3/8
NAV Total Return 1991: +3.76%
Share Price Total Return 1991: +12.13%
Herzfeld Ranking 1991: 33rd of 46 foreign equity funds

Investment Objective: Capital appreciation through investment primarily in equity and equity-linked securities of companies domiciled in West Germany. The fund will invest in companies which the advisor believes are likely to be positively affected by economic and other reforms in East Germany and in other parts of Eastern Europe.

Officers:

R.E. Breuer   Chairman
C.H. Strenger   President & Chief

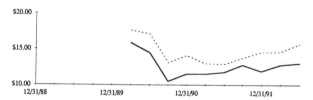

Investment Advisor: DB Capital Management International GmbH
Advisory Fee: Annual fee of 0.35% of average weekly net assets up to $100 mil., and 0.25% of excess. Fee for year-ending 10/31/91 was $535,199.
Investment Manager: Deutsche Bank Capital Corporation
Management Fee: Annual fee of 0.65% of average weekly net assets up to $100 mil., and 0.55% of excess. Fee for year-ending 10/31/91 was $1,057,108.

Capital Structure: *Common stock:* 80 mil. shares authorized, 12,250,706 shares outstanding 10/31/91

Portfolio Highlights (as of 1/31/92): German common stocks 79.1%, German preferred stocks 7.0%, German warrants on common stocks 9.5%, time deposit 7.5%, liabilities in excess of other assets (3.8%). Largest industry concentrations: banking 16.6%, automotive 11.1%, electrical 10.5%, chemical 10.2%, insurance 8.0%, steel-manufacturing 8.3%. **Largest positions:** Siemens, VEBA, Dresdner Bank, Bayer, Commerzbank.

Historical Financial Statistics (fiscal year-end: 10/31/91):

	1991	3/6/90 to 10/31/90
Value of net assets (000)	166,650	185,472
NAV	13.60	14.68
Net investment income	0.18	0.22
Dividends from net investment income	0.22	--
Distributions from net realized gains	0.06	--
Operating expense ratio	1.21%	1.12% ann.
Expense ratio	1.29%	1.46% ann.
Income ratio	1.22%	1.96% ann.
Portfolio turnover	42.84%	8.85%

Special considerations: Annual distributions are made of net investment income and any net realized capital gains. The fund has a staggered board of directors. During the period ended 10/31/91 the fund repurchased 464,700 shares in the open market at a weighted average discount of 15.01%. At the 1991 annual meeting shareholders approved a proposal to allow the fund to write covered call options on portfolio securities and appropriate indices for hedging purposes and to allow the fund to lend portfolio securities.

The Gabelli Equity Trust Inc.

One Corporate Center, Rye, NY 10580-1434

Category: Equity Fund

Phone: 914-921-5070
Listed: GAB, NYSE
Commenced Operations: August, 1986
Cusip: 362397101

1991/mid-1992 Range of Premium/Disc: +8% to -9%
(adjusted for dilution)
1991/mid-1992 Range of Price: $12 1/8 to $8 7/8
NAV Total Return 1990: -12.67%; **1991:** +15.19%
Share Price Total Return 1990: -16.57%; **1991:** +10.81%
Herzfeld Ranking 1991: 14th of 15 equity funds

Investment Objective: Long-term growth of capital primarily through investment in equity securities with a secondary objective of income.

Officers:

M.J. Gabelli   Chairman, President &
                 Chief Investment Officer

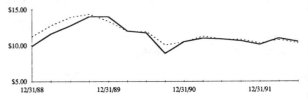

Investment Advisor: Gabelli Funds, Inc.
Advisory Fee: Monthly fee at annual rate of 0.75% of average weekly net assets. Fee for year-ended 12/31/91 was $3,906,289.
Administrator: The Boston Company Advisors, Inc.
Administration Fee: Monthly fee at annual rate of 0.25% of average weekly net assets. Fee for year-ended 12/31/91 was $1,302,429.

Capital Structure: *Shares of beneficial interest:* 100 mil. shares authorized; 56,098,200 shares outstanding 12/31/91

Portfolio Highlights (as of 3/31/92): Common stocks 81.4%, preferred stocks 7.0%, corporate bonds 0.9%, German government bonds 3.5%, treasury bill 4.9%, repurchase agreement 2.2%, other assets and and liabilities 0.1%. Largest industry concentrations: telecommunications 14.6%, broadcasting 11.3%, cable 9.3%, industrial equipment and supplies 7.0%, consumer products 5.9%. **Largest positions/issuers:** Centel Corporation; Time Warner Inc.; Chris-Craft Industries, Inc.; GTE Corporation; Tele-Communications Inc, Class A.

Historical Financial Statistics (fiscal year-end: 12/31/91):

	1991	1990	1989	1988	1987	8/21/86 to 12/31/86
Value of net assets (000)	595,151	479,863	586,990	484,792	429,490	413,759
NAV	10.61	10.49	13.34	11.22	9.82	9.40
Net investment income	0.27	0.44	0.38	0.14	0.16	0.10
Dividends from net investment income	0.27	0.53	0.29	0.21	0.19	--
Distributions from net realized gains	0.14	0.42	1.02	0.78	0.45	--
Distributions from paid-in capital	0.68	0.42	--	--	--	--
Operating expense ratio	1.24%	1.18%	1.18%	1.25%	1.24%	1.24% ann.
Income ratio	2.34%	3.84%	2.82%	1.36%	1.50%	2.89% ann.
Portfolio turnover	11.2%	15.5%	28.1%	51.5%	96.5%	58.8%

Special considerations: The fund has a policy of distributing a minimum of 10% of the net asset value of the fund annually but may retain a portion of net long-term capital gains. The fund may repurchase shares when the fund is trading at a 10% or higher discount from net asset value. The Articles of Incorporation contain various anti-takeover provisions. The fund had a rights offering in October, 1991, to allow shareholders to purchase one additional right for every six rights held; the subscription price was $8.00. At the May, 1992, annual meeting shareholders voted to allow investments in options and futures contracts for hedging purposes.

Gemini II

Vanguard Financial Center, Valley Forge, PA 19482

Category: Dual Purpose Fund

Phone: 800-662-2739
Listed: GMI (capital shares), NYSE
GMI pr (income shares), NYSE
Commenced Operations: February, 1985
Cusip (capital shares): 368904108
Cusip (income shares): 368904207

1991/mid-1992 Range of Premium/Disc:
capital shares: -12% to -25%; income shares: +47% to +18%
1991/mid-1992 Range of Price:
capital shares: $14 1/2 to $8 5/8; income shares: $14 to $11
NAV Total Return GMI 1990: -32.68%; **1991:** +43.42%
NAV Total Return GMIpr 1990: +23.91%; **1991:** +10.55%
Price Total Return GMI 1990: -39.30%; **1991:** +43.68%
Price Total Return GMIpr 1990: -0.69%; **1991:** +35.78%

Investment Objective: Dual objectives of long-term capital appreciation and current and long-term growth of income, primarily through investment in dividend-paying common stocks.

Officers:

J.C. Bogle — Chairman & CEO
J.J. Brennan — President

capital shares

income shares

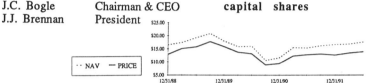

Investment Advisor: Wellington Management Company
Advisory Fee: Quarterly fee at annual rate of 0.35% of first $300 mil. of net assets, 0.275% on excess. The fee will be adjusted up or down by a maximum of 0.10% of net assets based on performance of the fund relative to the S&P 500 Index. Fee for year-ended 12/31/91 was $683,000 (after a reduction of $282,000 performance adjustment).
Administrator: The Vanguard Group
Administration Fee: "At cost" basis, plus minimal charge to cover certain distribution expenses. Fee for year-ended 12/31/91 was $478,000.

Capital Structure:
Common stock: 15 mil. shares authorized; 10,920,550 outstanding 12/31/91
Preferred stock: 15 mil. shares authorized; 10,920,550 outstanding 12/31/91

Portfolio Highlights (as of 3/31/92): Common stocks 56.2%, convertible preferred stocks 13.0%, bonds 8.5%, agency and government securities 17.0%, other securities 0.1%, temporary cash investments 4.9%, other assets and liabilities 0.3%. **Largest positions:** U.S. treasury bonds and notes; Aetna Life & Casualty Co., CIGNA Corp., Commonwealth Edison Co., Chrysler Corp. 10.4-99.

Historical Financial Statistics (fiscal year-end: 12/31/91):

	1991	1990	1989	1988	1987	1986
Value of net assets (000)	279,862	227,684	292,764	283,304	244,310	257,734
NAV capital shares	16.28	11.51	17.44	16.56	12.98	13.87
NAV income shares	0.34	9.34	9.37	9.38	9.39	9.73
Net investment income	1.65	1.63	1.58	1.41	1.38	1.23
Dividends from net investment income (income shares)	1.65	1.66	1.59	1.42	1.72	1.33
Distributions from net realized gains (capital shares)	0.22	0.11	0.19	0.22	0.04	--
Federal taxes paid on behalf of capital shareholders	0.52	0.09	0.33	0.29	1.07	0.74

Special considerations: Income shares will be redeemed in 1997 at initial net asset value of $9.30 plus accumulated and unpaid dividends. The board will then decide if the capital shares should be liquidated or open-ended. The fund retained a portion of the taxable long-term capital gains in the amount of $1.558459 per share for the year-ended 12/31/91. Capital shareholders were able to take a credit on their 1991 tax returns equivalent to $0.529876 per share.

General American Investors Company, Inc.

450 Lexington Avenue, Suite 3300, New York, NY 10017   **Category: Equity Fund**

Phone: 212-916-8400
Listed: GAM, NYSE
Commenced Operations: 1927
Cusip: 368802104

1991/mid-1992 Range of Premium/Disc: +5% to -19%
1991/mid-1992 Range of Price: $29 7/8 to $16
NAV Total Return 1990: +4.62%; **1991:** +60.66%
Share Price Total Return 1990: +7.09%; **1991:** +77.23%
Herzfeld Ranking 1991: 2nd of 15 equity funds

Investment Objective: Long-term capital appreciation with less emphasis on current income. The fund invests primarily in common stocks that management believes have better than average growth potential.

Officers:

A.G. Altschul   Chairman
W.J. Gedale   President

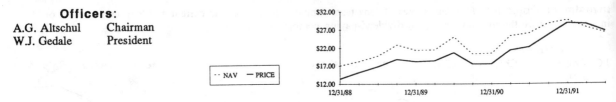

Investment Advisor: Internally managed; affiliate, General American Advisers, Inc., also manages outside accounts
Advisory Fee: Aggregate compensation paid by the company to officers for 1991 was $2,721,530.
Administrator: Internally administered

Capital Structure: *Common stock:* 30 mil. shares authorized; 19,639,386 shares outstanding 3/31/92

Portfolio Highlights (as of 3/31/92): Stocks 97.9%, short-term securities and other assets 2.1%. Largest industry concentrations: retail trade 32.2%, health care 30.0%, consumer products and services 13.7%, finance and insurance 7.5%. **Largest positions:** The Home Depot Inc., Wal-Mart Stores Inc., Glaxo Holdings PLC-ADR, The Limited Inc., Toys R Us Incorporated.

Historical Financial Statistics (fiscal year-end: 12/31/91):

	1991	1990	1989	1988	1987	1986
Value of net assets (000)	587,213	382,234	381,933	301,791	287,142	306,547
NAV	30.60	20.60	21.41	17.03	16.70	19.29
Net investment income	0.09	0.18	0.19	0.28	0.34	0.38
Dividends on common stock	0.105	0.21	0.27	0.25	0.70	0.47
Distributions from realized long-term gains	2.00	1.70	1.46	1.90	1.71	2.84
Expense* ratio	1.02%	1.07%	1.04%	1.14%	1.19%	1.10%
Income ratio	0.37%	0.84%	0.96%	1.60%	1.69%	1.86%
Portfolio turnover	21%	19%	27%	19%	30%	31%

* expenses attributable only to General American Investors Company, Inc., not including expenses of subsidiary.

Special considerations: The fund normally remains fully invested. The fund is internally managed and manages outside accounts. Shareholders approved a proposal to increase the company's authorized common stock from 20 mil. to 30 mil. shares. As of 3/31/92 the fund held $12.2 mil. of restricted securities. During 1990, 333,400 shares of common stock were repurchased at an average discount from net asset value of 16.7%; and during 1991, 277,631 shares were repurchased at an average discount from net asset value of 15.7%.

The Germany Fund, Inc.

31 West 52nd Street, New York, NY 10019

Phone: 800-GERMANY, 212-474-7000
Listed: GER, NYSE
Commenced Operations: July, 1986
Cusip: 374143105

Category: Foreign Equity Fund

1991/mid-1992 Range of Premium/Disc: +23% to -8%
1991/mid-1992 Range of Price: $14 5/8 to $10 1/8
NAV Total Return 1990: -7.24%; **1991:** +1.90%
Share Price Total Return 1990: -40.91%; **1991:** +11.24%
Herzfeld Ranking 1991: 35th of 46 foreign equity funds

Investment Objective: Long-term capital appreciation through investment in equity or equity-linked securities of German companies. The fund may invest, for hedging purposes, in put and call options and bond futures and may write covered call options to generate income.

Officers:
Dr. R-E Breuer   Chairman
H. Risse   President & CEO

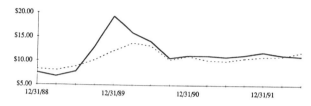

Investment Advisor: Deutsche Asset Management GmbH
Advisory Fee: Monthly fee at annual rate of 0.35% of average weekly net assets up to $100 mil., 0.25% on excess. The fee for 1991 was $453,839.
Manager and Administrator: Deutsche Bank Capital Corporation
Management and Administration Fee: Monthly fee at annual rate of 0.65% of average weekly net assets up to $50 mil., 0.55% on excess. The fee for 1991 was $827,976.

Capital Structure: *Common stock*: 20 mil. shares authorized; 13,222,696 shares outstanding 3/31/92

Portfolio Highlights (as of 3/31/92): Investments in German common stocks 88.0%, investments in German preferred stocks 4.3%, warrants on common stocks 5.0%, rights on common stock 0.3%, short-term investments 21.5%, liabilities in excess of cash and other assets (19.1%). Largest industry concentrations: banking 17.4%, automotive 11.4%, electrical 10.7%, insurance 9.7%, steel/manufacturing 7.8%, utilities 7.7%, chemical 6.9%, pharmaceuticals 5.6%. **Largest positions:** Siemens, VEBA, Allianz Holding, Dresdner Bank, Bayer, Commerzbank.

Historical Financial Statistics (fiscal year-end: 12/31/91):

	1991	1990	1989	12/31/88*	6/30/88**	7/23/86 to 6/30/87
Value of net assets (000)	144,175	144,514	158,497	65,692	60,003	79,931
NAV	10.95	11.05	12.15	8.23	7.32	10.64
Net investment income (loss)	0.13	0.11	0.06	--	0.03	(0.02)
Distributions from net realized gains	--	0.14	0.19	0.01	1.55	--
Distributions from net investment income	0.19	0.11	0.06	0.02	--	--
Distributions from paid-in capital	--	--	--	0.20	--	--
Distributions from other sources	0.06**	--	--	--	--	--
Operating expense ratio	1.39%	1.31%	1.47%	1.75% ann.	1.72%	1.57% ann.
Total expense ratio	1.47%	1.58%	1.77%	2.01% ann.	2.05%	1.57% ann.
Income ratio (loss)	1.17%	0.90%	0.61%	(0.06%) ann.	0.41%	(0.205%) ann.
Portfolio turnover	37%	34%	36%	26%	82%	206%

*fiscal year-end changed from 6/30 to 12/31; figures for six month period from 6/30/88 to 12/31/88
**year-ending 6/30/88

Special considerations: Proposals approved at the 1990 annual meeting increased the number of authorized shares from 20 mil. to 80 mil. and reincorporated the fund under the laws of the State of Maryland. A second public offering on 12/11/89 resulted in the issuance of 4.5 mil. shares for net proceeds to the fund of $53,785,000 and an overallotment resulting in the issuance of 675,000 shares for proceeds to the fund of $8,120,250.

The Global Government Plus Fund, Inc.

One Seaport Plaza, New York, NY 10292

Category: Foreign Bond Fund

Phone: 212-214-3334, 800-451-6788
Listed: GOV, NYSE
Commenced Operations: July, 1987
Cusip: 378907109

1991/mid-1992 Range of Premium/Disc: 0% to -12%
1991/mid-1992 Range of Price: $8 3/8 to $6 5/8
NAV Total Return 1990: +9.47%; **1991:** +9.06%
Share Price Total Return 1990: +9.00%; **1991:** +14.92%
Herzfeld Ranking 1991: 7th of 8 foreign bond funds

Investment Objective: High dividends to shareholders relative to interest and capital appreciation returns generally available from investments in longer-term U.S. government securities, principally by investment in high quality debt securities of governmental entities throughout the world.

Officers:

R.N. Pyle   President

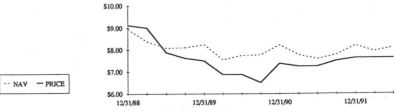

Investment Advisor: The Prudential Investment Corporation
Manager: Prudential Mutual Fund Management, Inc.
Advisory and Management Fee: Monthly fee at annual rate of 0.75% of average weekly net assets up to $1 bil., and 0.70% of excess. Fee for year-ended 12/31/91 was $2,738,186.

Capital Structure: *Common stock:* 200 mil. shares authorized; 45,642,508 shares outstanding 12/31/91
Debt: Note payable with Prudential for $38,000,000 to be repaid in 20 equal payments at the annual rate of 8.73%. $5,700,000 outstanding 12/31/91.

Portfolio Highlights (as of 12/31/91): Long-term investments 91.2%, short-term investments 9.1%, outstanding options purchased 0.5%, liabilities in excess of other assets (0.3%). Largest geographic concentrations (long-term): United States 17.3%, France 14.7%, Canada 13.9%, United Kingdom 13.2%, Australia 8.8%, Spain 6.2%, Denmark 6.1%. **Largest issuers:** U.S. treasury notes and bonds; French government bonds; Canadian government bonds; UK treasury notes; Kingdom of Spain bonds.

Historical Financial Statistics (fiscal year-end: 12/31/91):

	1991	1990	1989	1988	7/31/87 to 12/31/87
Value of net assets (000)	377,911	376,722	434,245	469,141	513,225
NAV	8.28	8.25	8.25	8.95	9.86
Net investment income	0.66	0.59	0.59	0.64	0.25
Dividends from net investment income	0.66	0.59	0.59	0.64	0.25
Distributions from net realized gains	--	--	--	0.32	0.11
Distributions from paid-in capital	0.06	0.21	0.51	0.24	0.05
Operating expense ratio	1.07%	1.09%	1.11%	1.01%	1.12% ann.
Total expense ratio	1.29%	1.47%	1.59%	1.62%	1.83% ann.
Income ratio	8.30%	7.40%	7.00%	6.87%	6.22% ann.
Portfolio turnover	267%	503%	477%	452%	97%

Special considerations: At the April 29, 1992 annual meeting shareholders voted on a shareholder proposal requiring Directors to purchase and maintain a minimum of 2,000 shares of common stock of the fund during his tenure on the board. The proposal passed. The fund has a share repurchase program. Under that program the fund repurchased 7,000,000 shares during 1990 at an average discount of 7.0%. The fund had a capital loss carryforward as of 12/31/91 of approximately $4,211,000 which will expire in 1998.

The Global Health Sciences Fund

7800 E. Union Avenue, Suite 800, Denver, CO 80237

Category: Foreign Equity Fund

Phone: 800-528-8765
Listed: GHS, NYSE
Commenced Operations: January, 1992
Cusip: 37932A102

1991/mid-1992 Range of Premium/Disc: +8% to -13%
1991/mid-1992 Range of Price: $15 1/8 to $11 1/8
NAV Total Return 1991: N/A
Share Price Total Return 1991: N/A
Herzfeld Ranking 1991: N/A

Investment Objective: Capital appreciation by investing substantially all assets in equity and related securities of U.S. and foreign companies principally engaged in the development, production or distribution of products or services relating to the health sciences.

Officers:

C.W. Brady — Chairman
J.J. Kaweske — President

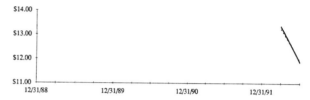

Investment Advisor: INVESCO Trust Company
Advisory Fee: Monthly fee at an annual rate of 1.00% of the fund's ending weekly net assets.
Administrator: Mitchell Hutchins Asset Management Inc.
Administration Fee: Monthly fee by applying the following annual rate to the ending weekly net assets of the fund: 0.20% on assets up to $62.5 mil., 0.18% on assets in excess of 62.5 mil. and up to 125 mil., 0.15% on assets in excess of $125 mil. and up to $250 mil., and 0.10% on assets in excess of $250 mil. The minimum annual fee will be $125,000.

Capital Structure: *Shares of beneficial interest:* Unlimited number of shares authorized, 20,507,200 shares outstanding 4/30/92.

Portfolio Highlights (as of 4/30/92): Common stocks 77.64%, other securities 0.71%, fixed income securities 1.35%, commercial paper 20.30%. Largest geographic concentrations: U.S. 91%, Denmark 2.99%, Sweden 2.91%, Israel 0.98%, United Kingdom 0.79%. Largest industry concentrations: pharmaceuticals 30.57%, health care delivery 21.61%, medical equipment, devices & supplies 14.52%, biotechnology 10.01%. **Largest positions:** Schering-Plough Corp., Baxter International, Bristol-Myers Squibb, Merck & Co., Synergen Inc.

Historical Financial Statistics:

	1/24/92 to 4/30/92
Value of net assets (000)	260,279
NAV	12.692
Net investment income	0.054
Dividends from net investment income	--
Expense ratio	1.37% ann.
Income ratio	1.52% ann.
Portfolio turnover	91%

Special considerations: Up to 25% of assets may be invested in securities for which there is no readily available secondary market. The fund may use hedging transactions, short sales, repurchase agreements and other techniques. The Board of Directors may, from time to time, authorize repurchases or make tender offers for shares to reduce or eliminate market value discounts which may develop. The fund's Declaration of Trust contains various anti-takeover provisions including a 66 2/3% vote of outstanding shares to convert to an open-end fund, liquidate, or merge with another fund.

Global Income Plus Fund, Inc.

1285 Avenue of the Americas, New York, NY 10019   **Category: Foreign Bond Fund**

Phone: 212-713-2710
Listed: GLI, NYSE
Commenced Operations: August, 1988
Cusip: 37933L107

1991/mid-1992 Range of Premium/Disc: +4% to -4%
1991/mid-1992 Range of Price: $10 1/4 to $8 5/8
NAV Total Return 1990: +16.96%; **1991:** +12.16%
Share Price Total Return 1990: +25.97%; **1991:** +19.68%
Herzfeld Ranking 1991: 5th of 8 foreign bond funds

Investment Objective: High level of current income with capital appreciation as a secondary objective. The fund invests primarily in the following: debt securities of certain foreign governments, their agencies, instrumentalities and political subdivisions; U.S. government securities; and debt securities of U.S. and certain foreign issuers.

Officers:
E.G. Bewkes, Jr. Chairman
J.N. Fensterstock President

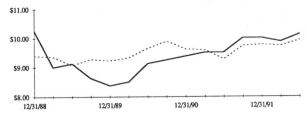

Investment Advisor: Mitchell Hutchins Asset Management Inc.
Administrator: Mitchell Hutchins Asset Management Inc.
Advisory and Administration Fee: Monthly fee at annual rate of 0.85% of average weekly net assets. Fee for year-ended 10/31/91 was $2,023,815.

Capital Structure: *Common stock*: 100 mil. shares authorized; 25,188,538 shares outstanding 10/31/91

Portfolio Highlights (as of 10/31/91): Long-term debt securities 69.54%, short-term debt securities 20.36%, warrants 0.24%, put options purchased 0.03%, repurchase agreements 6.57%, call options written (0.1%), put options written (0.01%), other assets in excess of liabilities 3.28%. Largest sector concentrations: government and other public issuers 51.16%, financial institutions 7.02%. Largest geographic concentrations (long-term positions): U.S. 19.45%, Australia 16.34%, Spain 8.45%, Ireland 7.15%. **Largest issuers:** Republic of Ireland; New South Wales Treasury Corp.; Government of Spain Treasury bonds; Government of France Treasury bonds; New South Wales Treasury Corp.

Historical Financial Statistics (fiscal year-end: 10/31/91):

	1991	1990	1989	8/24/88 to 10/31/88
Value of net assets (000)	242,205	243,171	226,028	229,522
NAV	9.62	9.86	9.16	9.50
Net investment income	0.91	1.00	0.95	0.11
Dividends from net investment income and foreign currency transactions	1.17	0.97	0.99	--
Expense ratio	1.13%	1.27%	1.17%	1.40% ann.
Income ratio	9.50%	10.61%	10.30%	7.53% ann.
Portfolio turnover	53.80%	127.84%	179.70%	30.00%

Special considerations: At the time of purchase all securities will be rated AAA or AA by Standard & Poor's Corporation, Aaa or Aa by Moody's Investors Service, Inc., or if unrated, judged by the fund's investment advisor to be of comparable quality. The fund may invest up to 35% of its total assets in lower rated U.S. and foreign debt and convertible securities. The fund may repurchase shares when prices are below net asset value or make tender offers at net asset value when the board deems it advantageous. On an annual basis, beginning on 11/1/93, under certain circumstances the board will submit an open-ending proposal to shareholders.

The Global Yield Fund, Inc.

One Seaport Plaza, New York, NY 10292   **Category**: Foreign Bond Fund

Phone: 212-214-3338, 800-451-6788
Listed: PGY, NYSE
Commenced Operations: July, 1986
Cusip: 37936L104

1991/mid-1992 Range of Premium/Disc: +2% to -12%
1991/mid-1992 Range of Price: $9 1/2 to $7 5/8
NAV Total Return 1990: +14.59%; **1991**: +7.27%
Share Price Total Return 1990: +14.35%; **1991**: +7.63%
Herzfeld Ranking 1991: 8th of 8 foreign bond funds

Investment Objective: High current yield relative to current yields available from U.S. dollar debt securities primarily through investment in debt securities denominated in other currencies expected to be stable and appreciate versus the U.S. dollar.

Officers:

R.N. Pyle   President

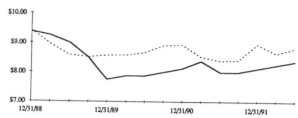

Investment Advisor: The Prudential Investment Corporation
Manager: Prudential Mutual Fund Management, Inc.
Management and Administration Fee: Monthly fee at annual rate of 0.75% of average weekly net assets up to $500 mil., 0.70% on assets between $500 mil. and $1 bil., 0.65% on excess. Fee for year-ended 12/31/91 was $4,264,469.

Capital Structure: *Common stock*: 200 mil. shares authorized; 66,002,123 shares outstanding 12/31/91

Portfolio Highlights (as of 12/31/91): Long-term investments 73.9%, short-term investments 23.0%, outstanding options purchased 0.3%, other assets in excess of other liabilities 3.1%. Largest geographic concentrations (long-term): Australia 11.4%, United Kingdom 9.5%, U.S. 8.3%, Spain 8.0%, Sweden 7.8%, Canada 6.6%, Denmark 6.6%, France 6.6%. **Largest issuers**: United Kingdom treasury notes; U.S. treasury notes; Kingdom of Spain bonds; Kingdom of Denmark bonds; Canadian government bonds.

Historical Financial Statistics (fiscal year-end: 12/31/91):

	1991	1990	1989	1988	1987	7/7/86 to 12/31/86
Value of net assets (000)	593,376	591,339	595,824	638,200	652,461	627,899
NAV	8.99	8.96	8.57	9.41	9.95	9.58
Net investment income	0.84	0.89	0.94	0.99	1.11	0.45
Dividends from net investment income	0.62	0.88	0.94	0.99	1.16	0.41
Distributions from net realized gains and currency gains	--	--	--	0.59	0.79	--
Distributions from paid-in capital	--	--	0.14	--	--	--
Operating expense ratio	0.99%	1.03%	1.07%	1.01%	0.96%	1.01% ann.
Total expense ratio	N/A	1.05%	1.09%	1.08%	1.07%	1.13% ann.
Income ratio	9.69%	10.03%	10.63%	10.00%	10.87%	10.03% ann.
Portfolio turnover	141%	221%	734%	371%	132%	0%

Special considerations: The fund invests at least 65% of total assets in governmental, semi-governmental or government agency securities or in short-term bank securities or deposits. Directors announced a share repurchase program authorizing repurchase of up to 10% of the outstanding shares. During the year-ended 12/31/90 the fund repurchased 3,548,600 shares at a weighted average discount of 6.0%. At 12/31/91 the fund had a capital loss carryforward of $1,996,000. The Board of Directors announced a new distribution policy whereby the fund will pay regular quarterly distributions approximating the fund's net investment income without regard to capital or currency losses. If there are any currency losses during the year, this may result in some distributions being declared a return of capital. This policy follows the omission of the fourth quarter distribution in 1991 due to currency losses.

The Growth Fund of Spain, Inc.
120 South LaSalle Street, Chicago, IL 60603

Category: Foreign Equity Fund

Phone: 312-781-1121; 800-621-1148
Listed: GSP, NYSE
Commenced Operations: February, 1990
Cusip: 399877109

1991/mid-1992 Range of Premium/Disc: +3% to -23%
1991/mid-1992 Range of Price: $12 to $7 3/4
NAV Total Return 1991: +14.24%
Share Price Total Return 1991: +19.06%
Herzfeld Ranking 1991: 19th of 46 foreign equity funds

Investment Objective: Long-term capital appreciation by investment primarily in equity securities of Spanish companies. Investment in investment grade fixed income instruments is also permitted.

Officers:
C.M. Kierscht   Chairman

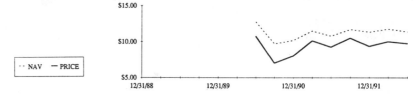

Investment Manager: Kemper Financial Services, Inc.
Management Fee: Fee at the annual rate of 1.0% of average weekly net assets. Fee for year-ended 11/30/91 was $1,958,000.
Spanish Advisor: BSN Gestion de Patrimonios, S.A.
Advisory Fee: Fee paid by the investment manager at annual rate of 0.35% of average weekly net assets.

Capital Structure: *Common stock:* 50 mil. shares authorized; 17,420,000 shares outstanding 11/30/91

Portfolio Highlights (as of 3/31/92): Spanish equities 84%, cash equivalents 16%. Largest industry concentrations: electrical/utilities 19%, banks 16%, telecommunications/motorways 11%, construction/property 10%, food/tobacco 10%, chemicals/textiles 7%. **Largest positions:** Repsol, Banco Intercontinental (Bankinter), Tabacalera, Empresa de Electricidad (ENDESA), Banco Popular Espanol, Autopistas Concesionaria (ACESA), Iberdrola I, Banco Bilbao Vizcaya, Union Electrica Fenosa and Viscofan. Part of the portfolio was hedged against a strengthening of the dollar.

Historical Financial Statistics (fiscal year-end: 11/30/91):

	1991	2/14/90 to 11/30/90
Value of net assets (000)	**192,986**	186,638
NAV	**11.08**	10.71
Net investment income	**0.37**	0.32
Dividends from net investment income	**0.36**	--
Expense ratio	**1.23%**	1.26% ann.
Income ratio	**3.32%**	3.46% ann.
Portfolio turnover	**104%**	19% ann.

Special considerations: The board of directors will consider, on a quarterly basis, repurchasing shares in the open market or making tender offers. If certain conditions are met, the fund may convert to an open-end fund after 12/1/94 with a 3/4 vote of shareholders. The fund's Articles of Incorporation and By-laws contain various anti-takeover provisions. Under current treaties, the fund is subject to certain withholding taxes in Spain. Directors have authorized a 1 million share buyback when shares are trading at less than net asset value, or when directors believe it is in the interest of shareholders. For the year-ended 11/30/90, 578,000 shares were repurchased at a weighted average discount of 17%; and for the year-ended 11/30/91, 11,000 shares were repurchased at a weighted average discount of 14%.
Shareholders over 5%: Stichting Akzo-Pensionenfonds, Arnhem, 5.5%

GT Greater Europe Fund

50 California Street, San Francisco, CA 94111   **Category**: Foreign Equity Fund

Phone: 415-392-6181
Listed: GTF, NYSE
Commenced Operations: March, 1990
Cusip: 362357105

1991/mid-1992 Range of Premium/Disc: 0% to -19%
1991/mid-1992 Range of Price: $11 7/8 to $8 3/4
NAV Total Return 1991: +0.89%
Share Price Total Return 1991: +3.89%
Herzfeld Ranking 1991: 36th of 46 foreign equity funds

Investment Objective: Long-term capital appreciation through investment in issuers and business ventures that are likely to benefit from economic, political and structural and technological changes and developments in Western and Eastern Europe.

Officers:
D.A. Minella   Chairman & President

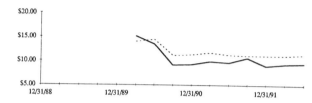

Investment Advisor: G.T. Capital
Advisory Fee: Monthly fee at annualized rate of 1.25% of average weekly adjusted net assets. Advisory and administration fees for year-ended 10/31/91 were $2,769,828.
Administrator: Princeton Administrators, Inc.
Administration Fee: Monthly fee at the annualized rate of 0.25% of average weekly adjusted net assets.

Capital Structure: *Shares of beneficial interest:* unlimited number of shares authorized, 16,007,100 shares outstanding 10/31/91

Portfolio Highlights (as of 10/31/91): Equity investments 89.0%, warrants 0.1%, fixed income investments 3.6%, short-term investments 4.0%, other assets less liabilities 3.3%. Largest geographic concentrations: Germany 24.0%, Netherlands 18.7%, France 14.0%, Switzerland 12.3%, Austria 6.5%. **Largest positions**: Herlitz A.G., Clarins, German City Estates, SMH, Begemann Machinefabriek N.V.

Historical Financial Statistics (fiscal year-end: 10/31/91):

	1991	3/29/90 to 10/31/90
Value of net assets (000)	175,074	191,125
NAV	10.94	11.94
Net investment income	0.02	0.15
Dividends from net investment income	0.15	--
Distributions from net realized gains on currency	0.01	--
Expense ratio	1.87%	1.78% ann.
Income ratio	0.21%	1.82% ann.
Portfolio turnover	47%	41% ann.

Special considerations: Net investment income and net realized capital gains are distributed at least annually. During the second quarter of 1995 the board will determine if a tender offer for all shares is in the best interest of shareholders. If this or subsequent offers are not begun by September 30, 1995, the board will submit an open-ending proposal. Before April 1, 1995, a 75% vote is required for open-ending; after that date only a majority vote will be required. In efforts to reduce any discounts which may develop, the fund may repurchase shares in the open market from time to time.

H&Q Healthcare Investors

50 Rowes Wharf, 4th Fl., Boston, MA 02110

Category: Specialized Equity Fund

Phone: 617-574-0500
Listed: HQH, NYSE
Commenced Operations: April, 1987
Cusip: 404052102

1991/mid-1992 Range of Premium/Disc: +22% to -13%
1991/mid-1992 Range of Price: $30 1/4 to $10 1/8
NAV Total Return 1990: +15.82%; **1991:** +92.93%
Share Price Total Return 1990: +21.38%; **1991:** +132.18%
Herzfeld Ranking 1991: 1st of 18 specialized equity funds

Investment Objective: Long-term capital appreciation through investment primarily in securities of companies in the health services and medical technology industries. Up to 25% of net assets may be invested in venture capital or other restricted securities.

Officers:
A.G. Carr President

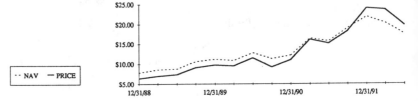

Investment Advisor: Hambrecht & Quist Capital Management Incorporated
Advisory Fee: Monthly fee at annual rate of 2.5% of average net value of venture capital or other restricted securities and 1.0% of all other assets; aggregate fee shall not exceed 1.375% annualized. Fee for six months ended 3/31/92 was $779,313.

Capital Structure: *Shares of beneficial interest* : unlimited number of shares authorized; 5,549,198 shares outstanding 3/31/92

Portfolio Highlights (as of 3/31/92): Convertible securities 11.0%, common stocks 84.5%, temporary cash investments 3.6%, other assets less liabilities 0.9%. Largest sector concentrations: biotechnology 28.5%, managed care 11.1%, pharmaceuticals 10.1%. **Largest positions:** Medco Containment Services 4.64%, U.S. HealthCare 4.03%, Ribi ImmunoChem Research 3.37%, Gensia Pharmaceuticals 3.01%, HealthCare COMPARE 2.88%.

Historical Financial Statistics (fiscal year-end: 9/30/91):

	six months 3/31/92	1991	1990	1989	1988	4/22/87 to 9/30/87
Value of net assets (000)	112,284	106,397	62,661	58,974	44,515	52,367
NAV	20.234	19.207	11.313	10.647	8.036	9.450
Net investment income (loss)	(0.032)	(0.014)	0.014	0.003	(0.019)	0.030
Distributions from income	0.04	0.055	--	--	0.020	--
Distributions from capital gains	0.92	0.78	--	--	--	--
Operating expense ratio	1.71% ann.	1.73%	1.74%	1.89%	1.98%	1.83% ann.
Income ratio (loss)	(0.30%) ann.	(0.10%)	0.12%	0.02%	(0.25%)	0.74% ann.
Portfolio turnover	34.38% ann.	23.04%	47.02%	46.90%	57.42%	17.34% ann.

Special considerations: The fund may repurchase shares if trading at a 10% or greater discount. Up to 25% of net assets may be invested in venture capital or other restricted securities. At 3/31/92, 20.2% of net assets were invested in such securities. The fund may convert to an open-end fund after 1990 if declared advisable by the board and approved by a majority of shareholders. The fund's Declaration of Trust contains various anti-takeover provisions. **Shareholders over 5%:** The fund believes that Cazenove & Co. and Cazenove Unit Trust Management Ltd. hold on behalf of discretionary accounts approximately 11% of the fund's shares.

H&Q Life Sciences Investors

50 Rowes Wharf, 4th Fl., Boston, MA 02110

Category: Specialized Equity Fund

Phone: 617-574-0500, 212-214-3332	**1991/mid-1992 Range of Premium/Disc:** +14% to +7%
Listed: HQL, NYSE	**1991/mid-1992 Range of Price:** $15 3/8 to $14 7/8
Commenced Operations: May, 1992	**NAV Total Return 1991:** N/A
Cusip: 404053100	**Share Price Total Return 1991:** N/A
	Herzfeld Ranking 1991: N/A

Investment Objective: Long-term capital appreciation by investing primarily in equity and related securities of U.S. and foreign companies principally engaged in the development, production or distribution of products or services related to scientific advances in healthcare, agriculture and environmental management.

Officers:

A.G. Carr   President, Principal Executive Officer

Investment Advisor: Hambrecht & Quist Capital Management Incorporated

Advisory Fee: Monthly fee at a rate when annualized of 1.0% of all net assets exclusive of Restricted Securities and 2.5% of all net assets consisting of Restricted Securities. The aggregate fee may not exceed the annualized rate of 1.375% of net assets.

Administrator: Prudential Mutual Fund Management, Inc.

Administration Fee: Monthly fee at a rate when annualized of 0.15% of the trust's average weekly net asset value.

Capital Structure: *Shares of beneficial interest* unlimited number of shares authorized, 3,700,000 shares outstanding 5/1/92

Portfolio Highlights: not yet published

Historical Financial Statistics:

	5/1/92
Value of net assets (000)	51,615
NAV	13.95

Special considerations: The fund emphasizes investment in securities of emerging growth life sciences companies which usually are traded over-the-counter, and may invest up to 25% of net assets in restricted securities. The may only be converted to an open-end fund if declared advisable by the board and approved by 66 2/3% of outstanding shares. Actions may be taken by the board to eliminate discounts from net asset value which may occur, such as repurchasing share or making tender offers. Such actions will be considered at least annually. The fund's Declaration of Trust contains various anti-takeover provisions including a 66 2/3% vote to remove a trustee, and a 75% vote to merge with another entity if that transaction is with a 5% or more holder of the fund.

Hampton Utilities Trust

777 Mariners Island Blvd., San Mateo, CA 94403

Category: Dual Purpose Fund

Phone: 415-378-2000; 800-DIAL-BEN
Listed: HU (capital shares), ASE
HUpr (income shares), ASE
Commenced Operations: March, 1988
Cusip (capital shares): 409528106
Cusip (income shares): 409528205

1991/mid-1992 Range of Premium/Disc:
capital shares: -5% to -18%; income shares: est. +14% to -3%
1991/mid-1992 Range of Price:
capital shares: $13 5/8 to $9 5/8; income shares: $55 3/4 to $47 3/8
NAV Total Return HU **1990:** -1.66%; **1991:** +27.50%
NAV Total Return HUpr **1990:** +4.78%; **1991:** +9.10%
Share Price Total Return HU **1990:** -4.28%; **1991:** +38.25%
Share Price Total Return HUpr **1990:** +4.38%; **1991:** +22.91%

Investment Objective: Cumulative preferred shares seek high after-tax return through income that qualified for the 70% dividends-received deduction and is designed for corporate investors. The capital shares seek long-term capital appreciation. The fund invests primarily in dividend-paying stocks, with at least 65% of total assets in companies engaged in the public utilities industry.

Officers:
W.J. Lippman   President

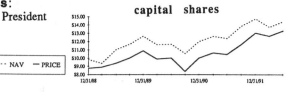

capital shares

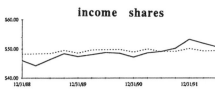

income shares

Investment Advisor: Franklin Advisers, Inc.
Advisory Fee: Monthly fee at annual rate of 0.80% of average weekly net assets. Fee for year-ended 12/31/91 was $186,961.
Capital Structure:
Shares of beneficial interest: unlimited number of shares authorized; 1,032,684 shares outstanding 12/31/91
$4.00 Cumulative Preferred stock: unlimited number of shares authorized; 200,100 shares outstanding 12/31/91. Redemption at $50.00 plus shares appreciation distrubution.

Portfolio Highlights (as of 12/31/91): Common stocks 87.6%, government securities 4.1%, commercial paper 7.3%, receivables from repurchase agreements 3.2%, net liabilities (2.2%). Largest industry concentrations: electric utilities 59.92%, gas distribution 14.79%, telephone 10.98%, U.S. treasury notes 4.03%. **Largest positions:** Carolina Power & Light Co., Interstate Power Co., Pennsylvania Power & Light Co., U.S. treasury notes, Kansas City Power & Light Co., Iowa-Illinois Gas & Electric Co.

Historical Financial Statistics (fiscal year-end: 12/31/91):

	1991	1990	1989	3/7/88 to 12/31/88
Value of net assets (000)	25,370	22,210	22,847	19,777
NAV capital shares	15.02	12.02	12.71	9.80
NAV preferred shares	49.27	48.94	48.61	48.27
Net investment income	1.122	1.203	1.218	0.962
Dividends from net investment income (capital shares)	0.282	0.363	0.379	0.277
Dividends from net investment income (preferred shares)	4.00	4.00	4.00	3.26
Distributions from net realized gains	0.10	--	--	0.015
Distributions from capital in excess of par value (capital shares)	0.068	0.047	0.061	0.053
Expense ratio	1.33%	1.25%	1.45%	1.14% ann.
Income ratio	4.96%	5.72%	5.98%	6.12% ann.
Portfolio turnover	18.82%	5.44%	18.30%	8.66%

Special considerations: The fund maintains at least 75% of total assets in securities of issuers whose long-term debt securities are rated at least "A", or of comparable quality. At a meeting of shareholders in early 1994, the fund will conduct an open-ending vote of capital shareholders. The fund's Declaration of Trust contains various anti-takeover provisions. As of 12/31/91 the fund had loss carryovers of $236,414 expiring through 1999.

Hatteras Income Securities, Inc.

One NCNB Plaza, T09-1, Charlotte, NC 28255

Category: Bond Fund

Phone: 704-386-2458
Listed: HAT, NYSE
Commenced Operations: February, 1973
Cusip: 419025101

1991/mid-1992 Range of Premium/Disc: +16% to -2%
1991/mid-1992 Range of Price: $18 5/8 to $14 1/2
NAV Total Return 1990: +2.63%; **1991:** +18.26%
Share Price Total Return 1990: +6.20%; **1991:** +30.32%
Herzfeld Ranking 1991: 51st of 80 bond funds

Investment Objective: High current income consistent with prudent investment risk, with a secondary objective of capital appreciation.

Officers:
A.M. Walker   Chairman
S.W. Duff   President

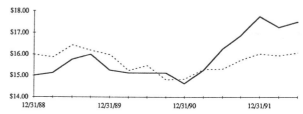

Investment Advisor: NCNB National Bank of North Carolina
Advisory Fee: The sum of 0.45% annually on first $75 mil. of average net assets (scales down), plus 1.5% of gross income accrued. The fee is paid monthly. The fee is reduced if certain expenses exceed 1.5% of the first $30 mil. of average net assets annually and 1% of excess. Fee for year-ended 12/31/91 was $299,165.

Capital Structure: *Common stock:* 5 mil. shares authorized; 3,179,484 shares outstanding 12/31/91

Portfolio Highlights (as of 12/31/91): Long-term debt securities 95.42% , commercial paper 2.49%, cash and other assets less liabilities 2.09%. Largest industry concentrations: public utilities 20.39%, government obligations 16.63%, energy 15.09%, finance 14.58%, manufacturing and distribution 8.37%, food and tobacco 5.42%, retail 5.04%.
Largest Issuers: RGS (AEGCO) Funding Corporation secured lease obligation 9.81-22; Texas Utilities Electric Company secured facilities 10.35-18; Transco Energy Company debs. 9 5/8-00; Barclays, N.A. capital notes 11 5/8-03; Occidental Petroleum sr. debs. 11 3/4-11.

Historical Financial Statistics (fiscal year-end: 12/31/91):

	1991	1990	1989	1988	1987	1986
Value of net assets (000)	50,964	46,559	49,666	49,518	49,377	54,066
NAV	16.03	14.88	15.99	15.99	16.07	17.94
Net investment income	1.54	1.57	1.64	1.61	1.66	1.78
Dividends from net investment income	1.56	1.57	1.63	1.62	2.22	1.80
Expense ratio	0.99%	1.01%	0.97%	1.01%	0.95%	0.93%
Income ratio	9.93%	10.34%	10.15%	9.91%	9.80%	10.01%
Portfolio turnover	27.17%	24.58%	33.49%	58.57%	48.59%	31.09%

Special considerations: At 12/31/91 the fund had a $2,970,085 loss carryforward expiring through 1999. The fund does not plan to distribute any future net realized gains on investments until the capital loss carryforwards are used or expire. As of 12/31/91 the fund held $550,000 of Del Norte Funding Corporation secured lease obligation 11 1/4-14. El Paso Electric Company filed voluntary bankruptcy and had not made its lease payments to Del Norte, therefore interest was not paid on 1/2/92 on this position.

High Income Advantage Trust

Two World Trade Center, 72nd Fl., New York, NY 10048

Category: Bond Fund

Phone: 212-392-2550
Listed: YLD, NYSE
Commenced Operations: October, 1987
Cusip: 429674104

1991/mid-1992 Range of Premium/Disc: +9% to -14%
1991/mid-1992 Range of Price: $5 7/8 to $3 1/2
NAV Total Return 1990: -24.21%; **1991:** +47.17%
Share Price Total Return 1990: -33.45%; **1991:** +55.86%
Herzfeld Ranking 1991: 6th of 80 bond funds

Investment Objective: High level of current income, with a secondary objective of capital appreciation primarily through investment in a diversified portfolio of fixed-income securities rated in the lower categories.

Officers:

C.A. Fiumefreddo Chairman & CEO

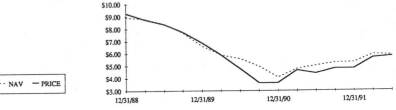

Investment Advisor: Dean Witter Reynolds Inc.

Advisory Fee: Monthly fee at annual rate of 0.75% of average weekly net assets up to $250 mil., 0.60% on assets between $250 mil. and $500 mil., 0.50% on assets between $500 mil. and $750 mil., 0.40% on assets between $750 mil. and $1 bil., and 0.30% on excess. Fee for six months ended 3/31/92 was $636,041.

Capital Structure: *Shares of beneficial interest:* unlimited number of shares authorized; 30,091,951 shares outstanding 3/31/92

Portfolio Highlights (as of 3/31/92): Corporate bonds 95.7%, common stocks 1.1%, other assets in excess of liabilities 3.2%. Largest industry concentrations: entertainment, gaming & lodging 10.7%, retail food chains 10.3%, cable 7.6%, healthcare 6.9%, manufacturing/diversified 5.2%. **Largest issuers:** Auburn Hills Trust 16.875-20 (adjustable rate); Enquirer/Star, Inc. 15-99; Fort Howard Corp. PIK 14.625-04; PA Holdings Corp.; Viacom Arsenal International Inc. 14.75-02.

Historical Financial Statistics (fiscal year-end: 9/30/91):

	six months 3/31/92	1991	1990	1989	10/29/87 to 9/30/88
Value of net assets (000)	177,237	162,002	158,454	247,874	283,967
NAV	5.89	5.23	4.96	7.68	9.19
Net investment income	0.45	0.69	1.07	1.18	1.10
Dividends to shareholders	0.29	0.69	1.13	1.20	1.00
Distributions to shareholders	--	--	--	0.05	--
Expense ratio	1.07% ann.	1.07%	1.01%	0.90%	0.90% ann.
Income ratio	16.02% ann.	14.80%	17.46%	13.60%	13.03% ann.
Portfolio turnover	51%	149%	20%	44%	126%

Special considerations: The trust may repurchase shares to attempt to reduce or eliminate discounts which may develop. During the year-ended 9/30/91 the fund repurchased 1,282,700 shares at a weighted average discount of 14.3%; during the six months ended 3/31/92 the fund repurchased 856,300 shares at a weighted average discount of 6.90%. Trustees intend annually to consider making a tender offer for shares. The Declaration of Trust contains various anti-takeover provisions. As of 9/30/91 the trust had a net capital loss carry-over of approximately $34,453,000 available through 1999. Dividends for the first three months of 1991 were reduced to the monthly rate of $0.065, and for the next three months to $0.045 per month.

High Income Advantage Trust II

Two World Trade Center, 72nd Fl., New York, NY 10048

Category: Bond Fund

Phone: 212-392-2550
Listed: YLT, NYSE
Commenced Operations: September, 1988
Cusip: 429675101

1991/mid-1992 Range of Premium/Disc: -1% to -24%
1991/mid-1992 Range of Price: $6 1/2 to $3 3/8
NAV Total Return 1990: -24.58%; **1991:** +46.29%
Share Price Total Return 1990: -35.14%; **1991:** +59.21%
Herzfeld Ranking 1991: 7th of 80 bond funds

Investment Objective: High level of current income, with a secondary objective of capital appreciation primarily through investment in a diversified portfolio of fixed-income securities rated in the lower categories.

Officers:

A.J. Melton, Jr.   Chairman
C.A. Fiumefreddo   President & CEO

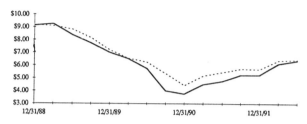

Investment Advisor: Dean Witter Reynolds Inc.

Advisory Fee: Monthly fee at annual rate of 0.75% of average weekly net assets up to $250 mil., 0.60% on assets between $250 mil. and $500 mil., 0.50% on assets between $500 mil. and $750 mil., 0.40% on assets between $750 mil. and $1 bil., and 0.30% on excess. Fee for six months ended 1/31/92 was $810,912.

Capital Structure: *Shares of beneficial interest*: unlimited number of shares authorized; 36,343,307 shares outstanding 1/31/92

Portfolio Highlights (as of 1/31/92): Corporate bonds 94.1%, common stocks 0.6%, short-term investments 2.4%, other assets in excess of liabilities 2.9%. Largest industry concentrations: cable 9.5%, retail/food chains 7.3%, manufacturing/diversified 5.9%, consumer products 5.5%, healthcare 5.3%, entertainment/gaming & lodging 5.2.
Largest Issuers: Fort Howard Corp. 14.625-04; Supermarkets General Holdings Corp. 13.125-03; Adelphia Communications Corp. 16.50-99; TW Food Services Inc.; Kroger Co. 15.5-98.

Historical Financial Statistics (fiscal year-end: 7/31/91):

	six months 1/31/92	1991	1990	9/30/88 to 7/31/89
Value of net assets (000)	223,132	210,595	251,793	343,610
NAV	6.14	5.68	6.44	8.76
Net investment income	0.44	0.77	1.13	0.98
Dividends from net investment income	0.34	0.77	1.19	0.92
Dividends from paid-in capital	--	0.06	--	--
Expense ratio	0.92% ann.	1.07%	0.93%	0.85% ann.
Income ratio	15.13% ann.		15.74%	12.89% ann.
Portfolio turnover	47%		31%	101%

Special considerations: The trust may repurchase shares to attempt to reduce or eliminate discounts which may develop. 733,200 shares were repurchased during the six months ended 1/31/92. Trustees intend annually to consider making a tender offer for shares. The Declaration of Trust contains various anti-takeover provisions. As of 7/31/91 the trust has a capital loss carry-over of approximately $23,221,000 available through 1999. The monthly dividend was increased from $0.05 per share to $0.0525 per share in January, 1992. At the December, 1991 annual meeting, a shareholder proposal to gradually restructure the portfolio over the next five years to a portfolio composition of approximately 55% junk bonds and 45% higher quality securities, from the current 95% junk bond portfolio was defeated.

High Income Advantage Trust III

Two World Trade Center, 72nd Fl., New York, NY 10048

Category: Bond Fund

Phone: 212-392-2550
Listed: YLH, NYSE
Commenced Operations: February, 1989
Cusip: 42967M104

1991/mid-1992 Range of Premium/Disc: 0% to -20%
1991/mid-1992 Range of Price: $7 to $4
NAV Total Return 1990: -22.45%; **1991**: +43.25%
Share Price Total Return 1990: -30.59%; **1991**: +45.25%
Herzfeld Ranking 1991: 10th of 80 bond funds

Investment Objective: High level of current income, with a secondary objective of capital appreciation primarily through investment in a diversified portfolio of fixed-income securities rated in the lower categories.

Officers:

A.J. Melton, Jr.   Chairman
C.A. Fiumefreddo   President & CEO

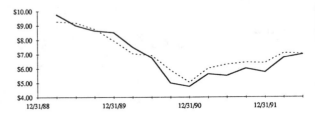

Investment Advisor: Dean Witter Reynolds Inc.
Advisory Fee: Monthly fee at annual rate of 0.75% of average weekly net assets up to $250 mil., 0.60% on assets between $250 mil. and $500 mil., 0.50% on assets between $500 mil. and $750 mil., 0.40% on assets between $750 mil. and $1 bil., and 0.30% on excess. Fee for 1991 was $619,254.

Capital Structure: *Shares of beneficial interest*: unlimited number of shares authorized; 13,046,679 shares outstanding 1/31/92

Portfolio Highlights (as of 1/31/92): Corporate bonds 93.8%, common stocks 0.6%, short-term investment 3.9%, other assets in excess of liabilities 1.7%. Largest industry concentrations: cable 9.4%, retail food chains 7.1%, retail 5.5%, consumer products 5.3%, healthcare 5.3%, forest & paper products 5.2%. **Largest positions:** Fort Howard Corp. 14.625-04; various PA Holdings Corp.; Enquirer/Star Inc. 15-99; Adelphia Communications Corp. 16.5-99; Kroger Co. 15.5-08.

Historical Financial Statistics (fiscal year-end: 1/31/92):

	1992	1991	2/28/89 to 1/31/90
Value of net assets (000)	89,084	68,476	101,102
NAV	6.83	5.18	7.59
Net investment income	0.84	1.11	1.02
Dividends to shareholders	0.77	1.15	0.95
Expense ratio	1.17%	1.05%	0.93% ann.
Income ratio	13.53%	17.39%	12.65% ann.
Portfolio turnover	137%	44%	59%

Special considerations: The trust may repurchase shares to attempt to reduce or eliminate discounts which may develop. During the year-ended 1/31/92 the fund repurchased 255,800 shares. Trustees intend annually to consider making a tender offer for shares. The Declaration of Trust contains various anti-takeover provisions. As of 1/31/91 the trust had a net capital loss carry-over of approximately $15,835,000 which will be available through 1/31/00.

The High Yield Income Fund, Inc.

One Seaport Plaza, New York, NY 10292

Category: Bond Fund

Phone: 212-214-3334	**1991/mid-1992 Range of Premium/Disc:** +18% to -15%
Listed: HYI, NYSE	**1991/mid-1992 Range of Price:** $8 3/4 to $4 3/4
Commenced Operations: November, 1987	**NAV Total Return 1990:** -11.90%; **1991:** +39.01%
Cusip: 429904105	**Share Price Total Return 1990:** -18.03%; **1991:** +53.10%
	Herzfeld Ranking 1991: 14th of 80 bond funds

Investment Objective: High current income by investing in high yielding, lower quality U.S. corporate bonds.

Officers:
L.C. McQuade   President

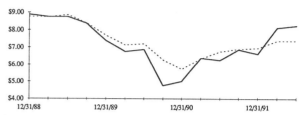

Investment Manager: The Prudential Mutual Fund Management, Inc.

Management Fee: Monthly fee at annual rate of 0.70% of average weekly net assets. Fee for six months ended 2/29/92 was $265,248.

Administrator: Prudential Investment Corporation

Administration Fee: no fee

Capital Structure: *Common stock:* 200 mil. shares authorized; 10,691,962 shares outstanding 2/29/92

Portfolio Highlights (as of 2/29/92): Bonds 94.2%, preferred stocks 1.8%, short-term investments 4.9%, liabilities in excess of other assets (0.9%). Largest industry concentrations: cable & pay TV systems 9.3%, supermarkets 5.3%, grocery chains/major 4.6%, chemicals 4.1%, general industrial 4.0%, automotive parts/equipment 3.8%. **Largest issuers:** SCI Holdings Inc. sr. sub. deb. 15-97; Kroger Co. sub. deb. 13.125-01; Fort Howard Corp. jr. sub. deb. 14.625-04 PIK; E-II Holdings, Inc. sr. sub. notes 12.85-97 (issuer in default on interest payment); Clark Oil & Refining Corp.

Historical Financial Statistics (fiscal year-end: 8/31/91):					
	six months 2/29/92	1991	1990	1989	11/6/87 to 8/31/88
Value of net assets (000)	78,571	73,080	72,494	91,783	97,800
NAV	7.35	6.84	6.79	8.60	9.28
Net investment income	0.44	0.90	0.97	1.17	0.87
Dividends paid to shareholders	0.44	0.90	0.97	1.17	0.87
Distributions from net realized gains	--	--	--	0.09	0.04
Distributions to shareholders from paid-in capital in excess of par	0.01	0.03	0.13	0.02	--
Operating expense ratio	1.21% ann.	1.31%	1.27%	1.15%	1.35% ann.
Total expense ratio	1.21% ann.	1.39%	1.43%	2.10%	1.79% ann.
Income ratio	12.44% ann.	14.23%	12.79%	13.23%	11.29% ann.
Portfolio turnover	40%	72%	27%	105%	50%

Special considerations: The fund may repurchase shares or make tender offers when the Board deems it advantageous. The fund's Articles of Incorporation contain various anti-takeover provisions. On 8/31/91 the fund had a capital loss carryforward of approximately $9,051,000 expiring through 1999.

The High Yield Plus Fund, Inc.

One Seaport Plaza, New York, NY 10292

Category: Bond Fund

Phone: 212-214-3334
Listed: HYP, NYSE
Commenced Operations: April, 1988
Cusip: 429906100

1991/mid-1992 Range of Premium/Disc: +3% to -13%
1991/mid-1992 Range of Price: $8 1/4 to $5 1/4
NAV Total Return 1990: -8.77%; **1991:** +40.73%
Share Price Total Return 1990: -12.93%; **1991:** +43.45%
Herzfeld Ranking 1991: 11th of 80 bond funds

Investment Objective: High level of current income with a secondary objective of capital appreciation, primarily through investment in publicly or privately offered high-yield debt securities rated in the medium to lower categories.

Officers:

E.D. Beach   President
             & Treasurer

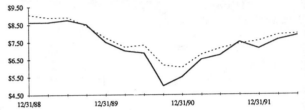

Investment Advisor: Wellington Management Company
Advisory Fee: Monthly fee at annual rate of 0.50% of average weekly net assets. Fee for six months ended 9/30/91 was $193,265.
Administrator: Prudential Mutual Fund Management, Inc.
Administration Fee: Monthly fee at annual rate of 0.20% of average weekly net assets. Fee for six months ended 9/30/91 was $77,306.

Capital Structure: *Common stock:* 100 mil. shares authorized; 10,834,480 shares outstanding 12/31/91
                        Debt: $13,000,000 note payable outstanding 12/31/91 at an average cost of 6%.

Portfolio Highlights (as of 12/31/91): Corporate bonds 109.2%, foreign government obligations 0.7%, preferred stocks 0.8%, common stocks 0.1%, rights 0.1%, warrants 0.2%, short-term investments 3.4%, liabilities in excess of other assets (14.5%). The average quality rating of the fund's securities was B1/B), the portfolio's maturity and duration were 10 and 6 years, respectively. **Largest issuers:** Owens-Illinois, Safeway Stores, RJR Nabisco, Kroger Company, Fort Howard Paper.

Historical Financial Statistics (fiscal year-end: 3/31/92):

	1992	1991	1990	4/5/88 to 3/31/89
Value of net assets (000)	85,742	73,656	78,132	96,259
NAV	7.91	6.80	7.22	8.90
Net investment income	0.87	0.99	1.12	0.93
Dividends from net investment income	0.87	0.99	1.12	0.93
Distributions from paid-in capital in excess of par	--	0.01	--	0.10
Operating expense ratio	1.28%	1.28%	1.30%	1.02% ann.
Total expense ratio	2.26%	2.21%	2.57%	1.44% ann.
Income ratio	11.69%	15.23%	13.68%	10.89% ann.
Portfolio turnover	11.69%	38%	32%	33%

Special considerations: The fund may borrow up to 33 1/3% of total assets for purposes of investment leverage. The fund may invest in privately offered bridge loans and mezzanine debt investments. The fund's Articles of Incorporation contain various anti-takeover provisions.

Hyperion 1999 Term Trust, Inc.

520 Madison Avenue, 10th Floor, New York, NY 10022   **Category: Bond Fund**

Phone: 212-980-8400, 800-497-3746	**1991/mid-1992 Range of Premium/Disc:** +10% to +6%
Listed: HTT, NYSE	**1991/mid-1992 Range of Price:** $10 3/8 to $10
Commenced Operations: June, 1992	**NAV Total Return 1991:** N/A
Cusip: 448913103	**Share Price Total Return 1991:** N/A
	Herzfeld Ranking 1991: N/A

Investment Objective: High level of current income consistent with investing only in securities of the highest credit quality and return of at least $10.00 per share to investors on or shortly before 11/30/99. All securities in which the trust will invest will be either issued or guaranteed by the U.S. government or one of its agencies or instrumentalities, or rated in the highest rating category.

Officers:

K.C. Weiss   Chairman
D.R. Odenath, Jr.   President & Chief Operating Officer

Investment Advisor: Hyperion Capital Management, Inc.
Advisory Fee: Monthly fee at the annual rate of 0.50% of average weekly net assets.
Administrator: Hyperion Capital Management, Inc.
Administration Fee: Fee at the annual rate of 0.17% of the first $100 mil. of average weekly net assets, 0.145% of the next $150 mil., and 0.12% of any excess.
Sub-Administrator: Prudential Mutual Fund Management, Inc.
Sub-Administration Fee: Fee paid out of Hyperion's administrative fee at the annual rate of 0.12% of the first $100 mil. of average weekly net assets, 0.10% of the next $150 mil., and 0.08% of any excess.

Capital Structure: *Common stock*: 50 mil. shares authorized; 55 mil. shares outstanding 6/18/92
Debt: the fund intends to leverage its assets through borrowings and/or the use of reverse repurchase agreements and dollar roll agreements in an amount equal to approximately 30% of the total assets.

Portfolio Highlights: not yet published

Historical Financial Statistics:

	6/18/92
Value of net assets (000)	517,000
NAV	9.40

Special considerations: Beginning twelve months after the offering the trust's Board of Directors will, from time to time, but at least annually, consider open market repurchases of shares or a tender offer at net asset value for all or a portion of the outstanding shares in an attempt to reduce any market price discount from net asset value. The trust's Articles of Incorporation and By-Laws contain various anti-takeover provisions including a 75% vote to remove a director or to amend the Articles of Incorporation, and a staggered board of directors.

Hyperion Total Return Fund, Inc.

520 Madison Avenue, 10th Floor, New York, NY 10022 **Category: Bond Fund**

Phone: 212-980-8400	**1991/mid-1992 Range of Premium/Disc**: +9% to -6%
Listed: HTR, NYSE	**1991/mid-1992 Range of Price**: $12 1/8 to $10
Commenced Operations: August, 1989	**NAV Total Return 1990**: +8.31%; **1991**: +16.21%
Cusip: 449145101	**Share Price Total Return 1990**: +9.40%; **1991**: +23.65%
	Herzfeld Ranking 1991: 65th of 80 bond funds

Investment Objective: To provide shareholders a relatively high level of current income and an investment which will generate superior total returns if interest rates decline substantially and above average returns, over time, regardless of the direction of future interest rates. The fund invests in high-quality mortgage-backed securities and high-yield corporate bonds.

Officers:

L.S. Ranieri Chairman
K.C. Weiss President & Treasurer

Investment Advisor: Hyperion Capital Management, Inc. **Sub-Advisor**: Pacholder Associates, Inc.
Advisory Fee: Monthly fee at the annual rate of 0.65% of average weekly net assets. Fee for year-ended 11/30/91 was $1,764,939. **Sub-Advisory Fee**: (Paid out of advisory fee) Monthly fee at the annual rate of 0.35% of average weekly high yield assets.
Administrator: Princeton Administrators, Inc.
Administration Fee: Monthly fee at the annual fee at the annual rate of 0.20% of average weekly net assets. Fee for year-ended 11/30/91 was $543,058.

Capital Structure: *Common stock*: 50 mil. shares authorized; 24,512,601 shares outstanding 11/30/91
Debt: Average amount of reverse repurchase agreements outstanding during the year-ended 11/30/91 was $2.6 mil., weighted average interest rate 6.60%. Average amount of mortgage dollar rolls outstanding was $115.7 mil., weighted average interest rate 5.98%.

Portfolio Highlights (as of 11/30/91): U.S. government agency mortgage-backed securities 79.9%, stripped mortgage-backed securities 14.1%, asset-backed securities 16.9%, corporate obligations 21.8%, repurchase agreement 10.2%, liabilities in excess of other assets (42.9%). **Largest Issuers**: FHLMC; FNMA; GNMA; Carco Deals Wholesale Trust, FHLMC Trust stripped mortgage-backed securities.

Historical Financial Statistics (fiscal year-end: 11/30/91):

	1991	1990	1989
Value of net assets (000)	**281,898**	262,694	275,160
NAV	**11.50**	10.75	11.09
Net investment income	**1.24**	1.13	0.32
Dividends from net investment income	**1.10**	1.11	0.32
Dividends from net capital gains	**--**	0.12	--
Total operating expense ratio	**1.10%**	1.16%	1.09% ann.
Interest expense ratio	**2.68%**	2.21%	0.34% ann.
Income ratio	**11.14%**	10.38%	9.13% ann.
Portfolio turnover	**65.43%**	200.50%	9.21%

Special considerations: The fund's Board of Directors recently authorized a 1 mil. share buyback at prices below net asset value in an effort to narrow the fund's discount. During the year-ended 11/30/90, the fund repurchased 378,300 shares in the open market at a weighted average discount of 9.37%; and during the year-ended 11/30/91, the fund repurchased 5,000 shares in the open market at a weighted average discount of 8.92%.

INA Investment Securities, Inc.

PO Box 13856, Philadelphia, PA 19101

Category: Bond Fund

Phone: 413-784-0100
Listed: IIS, NYSE
Commenced Operations: January, 1973
Cusip: 449764109

1991/mid-1992 Range of Premium/Disc: -2% to -13%
1991/mid-1992 Range of Price: $18 1/8 to $14 7/8
NAV Total Return 1990: +5.00%; **1991**: +18.30%
Share Price Total Return 1990: -2.21%; **1991**: +28.47%
Herzfeld Ranking 1991: 50th of 80 bond funds

Investment Objective: To generate income with a secondary objective of capital appreciation primarily through investment in fixed-income securities.

Officers:

G.R. Trumbull   Chairman
R.B. Albro   President

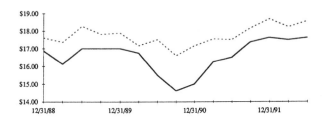

Investment Advisor: CIGNA Investments, Inc.
Advisory Fee: Fee at annual rate of 0.55% of first $75 million of average net assets and 0.40% on excess. Fee for year-ended 12/31/91 was $454,000.

Capital Structure: *Common stock*: 12 mil. shares authorized; 4,792,000 shares outstanding 12/31/91

Portfolio Highlights (as of 12/31/91): Long-term bonds 93.8%, short-term obligations 5.4%. Largest industry concentrations: U.S. government & agencies 31.5%, financial 20.6%, industrial 13.0%, transportation 10.4%, oil & gas 6.2%. Quality ratings: AAA 43.5%, AA 12.2%, A 19.7%, BBB 10.6%, BB 5.1%, B 8.9%. **Largest issuers:** U.S. treasury bonds and notes; Inter-American Development Bank 8.875-09; British Columbia Hydro and Power Authority 15.11; CSX Corp. 9-06; Associations Corp. of N.A. 9.7-97.

Historical Financial Statistics (fiscal year-end: 12/31/91):

	1991	1990	1989	1988	1987	1986
Value of net assets (000)	90,345	82,654	85,719	84,132	85,293	93,216
NAV	18.85	17.25	17.89	17.62	17.86	19.58
Net investment income	1.51	1.66	1.66	1.69	1.67	1.71
Dividends from net investment income	1.52	1.63	1.68	1.75	1.77	1.66
Expense ratio	0.93%	0.96%	1.03%	0.95%	0.88%	0.92%
Income ratio	8.49%	9.60%	9.26%	9.38%	9.02%	8.92%
Portfolio turnover	72%	68%	71%	56%	128%	186%

Special considerations: At the fund's recent annual meeting a proposal to eliminate the investment restriction which prevents the fund from participating in a joint or a joint-and-several basis in a securities transaction passed. As of 12/31/91, the fund had a loss carry-over of $4,404,764 to expire through 1998.

Independence Square Income Securities, Inc.

3 Radnor Corp Ctr., 100 Matsonford Road, Radnor,PA 19087   **Category: Bond Fund**

Phone: 215-964-8882
Listed: ISIS, OTC
Commenced Operations: 1972
Cusip: 453779100

1991/mid-1992 Range of Premium/Disc: 0% to -11%
1991/mid-1992 Range of Price: $17 1/2 to $13 7/8
NAV Total Return 1990: +2.96%; **1991:** +17.34%
Share Price Total Return 1990: +0.09%; **1991:** +20.00%
Herzfeld Ranking 1991: 57th of 80 bond funds

Investment Objective: Income, primarily through investment in a low risk bond portfolio.

Officers:
H.M. Watts, Jr.   Chairman
           & President

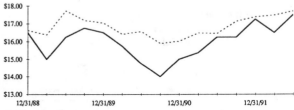

Investment Advisor: Provident Institutional Management Corporation
Advisory Fee: Quarterly fee of 0.05% (0.20% annually) of average net assets and 0.5% (2% annually) of gross income per quarter. If expenses exceed 1 1/2% of first $30 mil. of average net assets and 1% of excess, the advisor will reimburse the fund for the difference. Fee for year-ended 12/31/91 was $120,400.

Capital Structure: *Common stock:* 10 mil. shares authorized; 1,815,000 shares outstanding 3/31/92

Portfolio Highlights (as of 3/31/92): Bonds and other debt obligations 96.82%, short-term obligations 1.52%, other assets less liabilities 1.66%. **Largest issuers:** Arizona Public Service Co.; Detroit Edison Co. 9 7/8-19; Commonwealth Edison Co.; Illinois Power Co.; Texas Utilities Electric.

Historical Financial Statistics (fiscal year-end: 12/31/91):

	1991	1990	1989	1988	1987	1986
Value of net assets (000)	31,424	29,113	30,895	29,895	29,474	31,889
NAV	17.32	16.06	17.05	16.49	16.38	17.83
Net investment income	1.50	1.53	1.57	1.60	1.66	1.82
Dividends from net investment income	1.50	1.51	1.56	1.62	1.93	1.72
Expense ratio	0.90%	1.00%	0.90%	0.91%	0.96%	0.97%
Income ratio	8.97%	9.35%	9.20%	9.67%	10.18%	10.32%
Portfolio turnover	6%	25%	57%	45%	24%	65%

Special considerations: At the latest annual meeting, a proposal to limit certain liabilities of directors and officers and to provide for indemnification was passed, as well as a proposal to require that 25% or greater of the fund's assets be invested in utility companies. As of 12/31/91 the fund had a capital loss carryover of approximately $3,778,000 to expire through 1998.

The India Growth Fund

1285 Avenue of the Americas, New York, NY 10019

Category: Foreign Equity Fund

Phone: 212-713-2000; 800-553-8080
Listed: IGF, NYSE
Commenced Operations: August, 1988
Cusip: 454090101

1991/mid-1992 Range of Premium/Disc: +13% to -25%
1991/mid-1992 Range of Price: $26 to $9 3/4
NAV Total Return 1990: -4.89%; **1991:** +29.33%
Share Price Total Return 1990: -41.04%; **1991:** +34.23%
Herzfeld Ranking 1991: 8th of 46 foreign equity funds

Investment Objective: Long-term capital appreciation through investment primarily in equity securities of Indian companies.

Officers:

S.A. Dave   Chairman & President

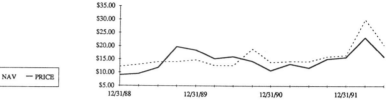

Investment Advisor: Unit Trust of India Investment Advisory Services, Limited
Advisory Fee: Monthly fee at annual rate of 0.75% on first $50 mil. of average weekly net assets, 0.60% on next $50 mil., 0.45% on excess. Fee for six months ended 12/31/91 was $275,002.
Trustee: Unit Trust of India
Trustee Fee: Monthly fee at annual rate of 0.35% on first $50 mil. of average weekly net assets, 0.30% on next $50 mil., and 0.25% on excess.
Administrator: Mitchell Hutchins Asset Management, Inc.
Administration Fee: Monthly fee at annual rate of 0.20% on first $62.5 mil. of average weekly net assets, 0.15% on the next $37.5 mil., 0.10% on any excess, with a minimum annual fee of $125,000. Fee for six months ended 12/31/91 was $131,200.

Capital Structure: *Common stock:* 50 mil. shares authorized; 5,016,362 shares outstanding 12/31/91

Portfolio Highlights (as of 12/31/91): Indian common stocks 91.68%, India rights 1.61%, Indian convertible debentures 7.01%, Indian non-convertible debentures 0.24%, U.S. time deposit 0.84%, liabilities in excess of other assets (1.38%). Largest industry concentrations: textiles 14.83%, automobile & auto ancillaries 11.77%, consumer products 10.33%, paper 7.49%, fertilizers & pesticides 7.28%, steel & steel products 6.49%. **Largest positions:** Century Textiles, TELCO, GSFC, Tata Iron & Steel, I.T.C., Bhadrachalam Paper, I.T.C.

Historical Financial Statistics (fiscal year-end: 6/30/91):

	six months 12/31/91	1991	1990	8/19/88 to 6/30/89
Value of net assets (000)	83,265	70,823	64,462	71,278
NAV	16.60	14.12	12.86	14.23
Net investment income (loss)	(0.10)	(0.13)	0.08	0.29
Dividends from net investment income	--	--	0.37	0.15
Distributions from net realized gains	0.93	0.16	0.73	0.15
Expense ratio*	1.80% ann.	3.00%	2.90%	2.20% ann.
Income ratio (loss)	(0.65%) ann.	(0.86%)	0.56%	2.77% ann.
Portfolio turnover	17.60%	13.50%	19.23%	38.79%

*excluding tax on net investment income

Special considerations: Capital gains and investment income to the trustee (which functions as a financial intermediary) are not subject to Indian tax; remittances from the trustee to the fund are subject to 10% Indian withholding tax (U.S. shareholders may claim a refund with certain limitations). A 75% vote of shareholders is required for, among other things, liquidation of the fund. In 1992 the fund announced that it will use the free market spot rate as the exchange rate for the Indian rupee to the U.S. dollar. **Shareholders over 5%:** United Nations Joint Staff Pension Fund, 10.38%; The Capital Group, Inc., 5.32%; Providence Capital Portfolio Managers Limited, 6.06%

The Indonesia Fund, Inc.

One Citicorp Center, 58th Floor, 153 East 53rd St.,
New York, NY 10022

Category: Foreign Equity Fund

Phone: 212-832-2626
Listed: IF, NYSE
Commenced Operations: March, 1990
Cusip: 455778100

1991/mid-1992 Range of Premium/Disc: +31% to -15%
1991/mid-1992 Range of Price: $12 1/2 to $7 1/4
NAV Total Return 1991: -25.09%
Share Price Total Return 1991: -15.75%
Herzfeld Ranking 1991: 45th of 46 foreign equity funds

Investment Objective: Capital appreciation as a primary objective and income as a secondary objective, primarily through investment in Indonesian securities.

Officers:

E. Bassini   President/Secretary

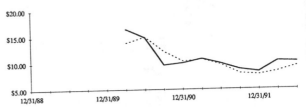

Investment Advisor: BEA Associates
Advisory Fee: Fee at the annual rate of 1.00% of average weekly net assets. Fee for year-ended 12/31/91 was $431,239.
Administrator: Provident Financial Processing Corporation
Administration Fee: Fee at annual rate of 0.10% of average monthly net assets with a minimum. Fee for year-ended 12/31/91 was $75,000.

Capital Structure: *Common stock*: 100 mil. shares authorized; 4,608,968 shares outstanding 12/31/91

Portfolio Highlights (as of 12/31/91): Common stocks 94.31%, United States government securities 5.69%. Of the common stocks: Indonesia 72.39%, Malaysia 0.74%, Pakistan 4.98%, Philippines 8.96%, Singapore 1.07%, Thailand 6.17%. **Largest positions:** Meralco-Manila Electric, Pakuwon Jati, Astra International, Pakistan Growth Fund, Sucaco.

Historical Financial Statistics (fiscal year-end: 12/31/91):

	1991	3/9/90 to 12/31/90
Value of net assets (000)	35,590	47,817
NAV	7.72	10.38
Net investment income	0.04	0.22
Dividends from net investment income	0.05	0.19
Distributions from net realized gains and foreign currency transactions	--	0.53
Expense ratio	2.00%	2.15% ann.
Income ratio	0.49%	2.05% ann.
Portfolio turnover	32.27%	21.73% ann.

Special considerations: The fund makes annual distributions of investment company taxable income plus any net realized long-term capital gains in excess of net realized short-term capital losses. Special risks associated with the fund include: a relatively illiquid secondary trading environment, restrictions on investment by foreigners, and currency exchange risk. The fund's Articles of Incorporation contain various anti-takeover provisions including a 75% voting requirement for, among other things, merger with another fund or liquidation. **Shareholders over 5%:** United Nations Joint Staff Pension Fund, 10.00%; Fiduciary Trust Company International, 12.95%.

The Inefficient-Market Fund, Inc.

1345 Avenue of the Americas, New York, NY 10105

Category: Equity Fund

Phone: 212-698-5367; 800-354-6565	**1991/mid-1992 Range of Premium/Disc:** +4% to -17%
Listed: IMF, ASE	**1991/mid-1992 Range of Price:** $11 1/4 to $7 7/8
Commenced Operations: January, 1990	**NAV Total Return 1991:** +23.27%
Cusip: 456613108	**Share Price Total Return 1991:** +13.70%
	Herzfeld Ranking 1991: 14th of 18 specialized equity funds

Investment Objective: Long-term capital appreciation primarily through investment in equity securities of companies with relatively small market capitalizations that Smith Barney, Harris Upham & Co., Incorporated believes to be inefficiently valued and therefore have good potential for capital appreciation.

Officers:

H.L. Kanev   President

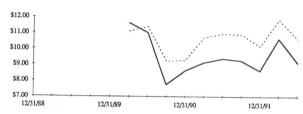

Investment Advisor: Smith Barney, Harris Upham & Co. Incorporated

Advisory Fee: Monthly fee at the annual rate of 0.75% of average daily net assets during the month. Fee for year-ended 12/31/91 was $344,980.

Administrator: Mutual Management Corp.

Administration Fee: Monthly fee at the annual rate of 0.25% of average daily net assets during the month. Fee for year-ended 12/31/91 was $114,993.

Capital Structure: *Common stock:* 100 mil. shares authorized; 4,384,000 outstanding 12/31/91

Portfolio Highlights (as of 12/31/91): Common and preferred stocks 79.1%, short-term investments 20.9%. Largest sector concentrations: manufacturing 15.0%, technology 12.7%, distribution 10.7%, tobacco 9.9%, retail 8.1%.

Largest positions (as of 3/31/92): Grossman's Inc., DH Technology Inc., Oneida Ltd., Helen of Troy Corp., Lillian Vernon Corporation.

Historical Financial Statistics (fiscal year-end: 12/31/91):

	1991	1/23/90 to 12/31/90
Value of net assets (000)	45,335	40,843
NAV	10.34	9.32
Net investment income	0.132	0.375
Dividends from net investment income	0.137	0.37
Distributions from net realized gains	0.795	--
Expense ratio	1.28%	1.32% ann.
Income ratio	1.26%	3.90% ann.
Portfolio turnover	46.77%	26.82%

Special considerations: The fund may borrow up to 33 1/3% of total assets but does not anticipate doing so at present. Distributions are to be made semi-annually. The fund's policy to distribute at least 10% of net asset value was eliminated at the annual meeting in May, 1992. The fund's Articles of Incorporation contain various anti-takeover provisions and allow the directors to reclassify any unissued shares of capital stock and set or change the preferences or other rights of such stock.

InterCapital Income Securities, Inc.

Two World Trade Ctr., 72nd Fl., New York, NY 10048

Category: Bond Fund

Phone: 212-392-2550
Listed: ICB, NYSE
Commenced Operations: April, 1973
Cusip: 458439106

1991/mid-1992 Range of Premium/Disc: +19% to 0%
1991/mid-1992 Range of Price: $22 1/4 to $16 3/4
NAV Total Return 1990: +2.05%; **1991:** +19.41%
Share Price Total Return 1990: -7.90%; **1991:** +31.09%
Herzfeld Ranking 1991: 44th of 80 bond funds

Investment Objective: High current income, primarily through investment in corporate bonds.

Officers:

A.J. Melton, Jr.   Chairman
C.A. Fiumefreddo   President & Chief
                    Executive Officer

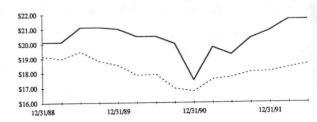

Investment Advisor: Dean Witter Reynolds Inc.
Advisory Fee: Monthly fee at annual rate of 0.50% of average weekly net assets. Fee for six months ended 3/31/92 was $542,246.

Capital Structure: *Common stock:* 15 mil. shares authorized; 12,200,518 shares outstanding 3/31/92

Portfolio Highlights (as of 3/31/92): Corporate bonds 82.7%, taxable municipals 0.2%, foreign government agencies 2.1%, U.S. government agencies & obligations 13.1%, repurchase agreement 1.1%, other assets in excess of liabilities 0.8%. Largest industry concentrations: electric utilities 29.4%, bank holding companies 10.3%, manufacturing 5.7%, oil related 5.3%, insurance & financial services 4.8%, gas utilities 4.3%. **Largest issuers:** U.S. treasury notes; Long Island Lighting Co.; Occidental Petroleum Co. 11.75-11; FNMA Multi Currency; CTC Beaver Valley Funding Corp. 12-17.

Historical Financial Statistics (fiscal year-end: 9/30/91):

	six months 3/31/92	1991	1990	1989	1988	1987
Value of net assets (000)	224,071	218,524	199,519	215,056	213,784	202,101
NAV	18.37	18.03	16.97	18.83	19.28	18.79
Net investment income	0.95	1.94	2.03	2.13	2.10	2.07
Dividends to shareholders	0.96	1.84	2.10	2.10	2.10	2.15
Expense ratio	0.66% ann.	0.72%	0.72%	0.67%	0.72%	0.66%
Income ratio	10.44% ann.	11.11%	11.23%	11.18%	10.93%	10.20%
Portfolio turnover	24%	56%	61%	88%	75%	114%

Special considerations: At 9/30/91 the fund had a capital loss carryover of approximately $20,288,000 available through 1999. Monthly dividend rate reduced to $0.155 per month.

InterCapital Insured Municipal Bond Trust

Two World Trade Ctr., 72nd Fl., New York, NY 10048   **Category:** Municipal Bond Fund

Phone: 212-392-2550; 212-607-3000
Listed: IMB, NYSE
Commenced Operations: February, 1991
Cusip: 45844B100

1991/mid-1992 Range of Premium/Disc: +13% to +2%
1991/mid-1992 Range of Price: $16 3/4 to $14 1/2
NAV Total Return 1991: N/A
Share Price Total Return 1991: N/A
Herzfeld Ranking 1991: N/A

Investment Objective: The fund will seek to provide current income exempt from federal income tax through investment in tax-exempt municipal obligations which are covered by insurance guarantees with respect to timely payment of principal and interest thereon.

Officers:
C.A. Fiumefreddo   Chairman, President & Chief
              Executive Officer

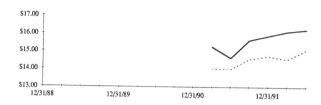

Investment Advisor: Dean Witter Reynolds Inc.

Advisory Fee: Monthly fee at annual rate of 0.35% of average weekly net assets. Fee for six months ended 4/30/92 was $204,678.

Capital Structure: *Shares of beneficial interest:*unlimited number of shares authorized, 5,257,113 shares outstanding 4/30/92
                        Auction Rate Preferred stock 1 mil. shares authorized, 800 shares outstanding 4/30/92, dividend rate ranged from 2.90% to 5.05% during the six months ended 4/30/92. Dividends are set every 7 days by auction.

Portfolio Highlights (as of 4/30/92): Municipal bonds 91.9%, short-term municipal obligations 6.0%. Largest industry concentrations: mortgage revenue/single family 35.6%, hospital revenue 11.4%, industrial development/pollution control revenue 9.8%, transportation facilities revenue 9.3%, water & sewer revenue 9.1%, electric revenue 5.6%. The average maturity was 28 years, and the average call protection of the trust long-term holdings was 8 years.
Largest issuers: Nebraska Investment Finance Authority, GNMA Mortgage-Backed 1990 Ser. 2 RIBS (AMT) 11.662-30; Maine Housing Authority Ser. 1991 A (Bifurcated FSA Insured) 7.40-22; Massachusetts Housing Finance Agency, Ser. 14 (Bifurcated FSA Insured) 7.60-14; Eastern Municipal Water District, California, Water & Sewer Ser. 1991 COPs (FGIC Insured) 6.50-20; Wisconsin Housing & Economic Development Authority, Homeownership 1991 Ser. A Bifurcated FSA Insured) 7.50-17.

Historical Financial Statistics (fiscal year-end: 10/31/91):

	six months 4/30/92	2/28/91 to 10/31/91
Value of net assets (000)	117,238	117,071
NAV	14.69	14.66
Net investment income	0.73	0.86
Dividends to common shareholders	0.53	0.52
Distributions to common shareholders	0.02	--
Expense ratio	0.98% ann.	1.00% ann.
Income ratio	7.92% ann.	7.19%
Portfolio turnover	3%	16%

Special considerations: The fund makes monthly distributions of net investment income and annual distributions of net capital gains. The trustees will consider on an annual basis whether to authorize repurchases in the open-market or tender offers at net asset value. The fund's Declaration of Trust contains various anti-takeover provisions including an 80% vote of each class of shareholders voting separately to, among other things, merge with another corporation. Dividend rate increased to $0.0925 per month in April, 1992.

InterCapital Insured Municipal Trust

Two World Trade Ctr., 72nd Fl., New York, NY 10048

Category: Municipal Bond Fund

Phone: 212-392-2550; 212-607-3000
Listed: IMT, , NYSE
Commenced Operations: February, 1992
Cusip: 45844D106

1991/mid-1992 Range of Premium/Disc: +8% to +2%
1991/mid-1992 Range of Price: $15 1/4 to $14 7/8
NAV Total Return 1991: N/A
Share Price Total Return 1991: N/A
Herzfeld Ranking 1991: N/A

Investment Objective: The fund will seek to provide current income exempt from federal income tax through investment in tax-exempt municipal obligations which are covered by insurance guarantees with respect to timely payment of principal and interest thereon.

Officers:

C.A. Fiumefreddo Chairman, President & Chief
Executive Officer

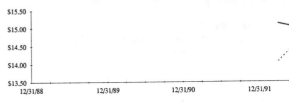

Investment Advisor: Dean Witter Reynolds Inc.
Advisory Fee: Monthly fee at annual rate of 0.35% of average weekly net assets. Fee for period 2/28/92 to 4/30/92 was $230,357.

Capital Structure:

Shares of beneficial interest: unlimited number of shares authorized, 23,507,113 shares outstanding 4/30/92
Auction Rate Preferred stock 1 mil. shares authorized, 3,600 shares outstanding 4/30/92, dividend rate ranged from 3.50% to 4.00% during the period ended 4/30/92. Dividends are set every 7 days by auction.

Portfolio Highlights (as of 4/30/92): Municipal bonds 88.7%, short-term municipal obligations 16.2%, liabilities in excess of cash and other assets (4.9%). Largest industry concentrations: hospital revenue 17.3%, water & sewer revenue 16.4%, industrial development/pollution control revenue 10.7%, electric revenue 10.3%, general obligation 10.0%. **Largest issuers:** South Carolina Public Service Authority, Santee Cooper Ser. D; Wisconsin Health and Educational Facilities Authority; Massachusetts Health and Educational Facilities Authority; Burlington, Kansas, Kansas Gas & Electric Co. Ser. 1991 (MBIA Insured) 7.0-31; Metropolitan Seattle, Washington, Sewer Ser. U (FGIC Insured) 6.6-32.

Historical Financial Statistics:

	2/28/92 to 4/30/92
Value of net assets (000)	509,287
NAV	14.01
Net investment income	0.12
Dividends to common shareholders	--
Expense ratio	0.54% ann.
Income ratio	4.32% ann.
Portfolio turnover	2%

Special considerations: The fund makes monthly distributions of net investment income and annual distributions of net capital gains. The trustees will consider on an annual basis whether to authorize repurchases in the open-market or tender offers at net asset value.

InterCapital Quality Municipal Investment Trust

Two World Trade Ctr., 72nd Fl., New York, NY 10048   **Category:** Municipal Bond Fund

Phone: 212-392-2550; 212-607-3000	**1991/mid-1992 Range of Premium/Disc:**
Listed: IQT, NYSE	**1991/mid-1992 Range of Price:**
Commenced Operations: September, 1991	**NAV Total Return 1991:** N/A
Cusip: 45844F101	**Share Price Total Return 1991:** N/A
	Herzfeld Ranking 1991: N/A

Investment Objective: Current income exempt from federal income tax primarily through investment in long-term municipal securities in the three highest categories by Moody's or S&P or of comparable quality.

Officers:

C.A. Fiumefreddo   Chairman, President & Chief Executive Officer

Investment Advisor: Dean Witter Reynolds Inc.

Advisory Fee: Monthly fee at annual rate of 0.35% of average weekly net assets. Fee for six months ended 4/30/92 was $694,285.

Capital Structure:

Shares of beneficial interest: unlimited number of shares authorized, 18,607,113 shares outstanding 4/30/92

Auction Rate Preferred stock 1 mil. shares authorized, 2,800 shares outstanding 4/30/92, dividends are reset every 7 days through auction. Dividend ranged from 2.93% to 5.75% during the six months ended 4/30/92.

Portfolio Highlights (as of 4/30/92): Municipal bonds 96.7%, short-term municipal obligations 2.3%, cash and other assets in excess of liabilities 1.0%. Larges industry concentrations: mortgage revenue/single family 17.4%, hospital revenue 13.0%, electric revenue 12.0%, industrial development/pollution control revenue 11.7%, transportation facilities revenue 7.9%, mortgage revenue/multi-family 6.4%, water & sewer revenue 6.4%, resource recovery revenue 6.1%. Quality ratings: AAA 24%, AA 31%, A 42%, BBB 3%. **Largest Issuers:** Emmaus General Authority, Pennsylvania, Local Government Ser 1988H (GFIC Insured) 7-18; Dallas-Fort Worth International Airport facilities Improvement Corporation, Texas, American Airlines Inc. Ser. 1990 (AMT) 7.5-25; New Jersey Housing & Mortgage Finance Agency, Presidential Plaza at Newport-FHA Insured Mortgages Refg. 1991 Ser. 1 7-30; California Housing Finance Agency Home 1991 Ser. G (AMT) 7.05-27; Massachusetts Health & Educational Facilities Authority.

Historical Financial Statistics (fiscal year-end: 10/31/91):

	six months 4/30/92	9/27/91 to 10/31/91
Value of net assets (000)	405,696	262,146
NAV	14.28	14.09
Net investment income	0.69	0.06
Dividends to common shareholders	0.42	--
Expense ratio	0.80% ann.	0.49% ann.
Income ratio (common shares)	7.80% ann.	5.01% ann.
Portfolio turnover	4%	0%

Special considerations: The fund pays monthly distributions of net investment income and annual distributions of net capital gains. The trustees will consider on an annual basis whether to authorize repurchases in the open-market or tender offers at net asset value. The fund's Declaration of Trust contains various anti-takeover provisions including an 80% vote of each class of shareholders voting separately to, among other things, merge with another corporation.

The Irish Investment Fund, Inc.

Vanguard Financial Center, PO Box 1102, Valley Forge, PA 19482   **Category: Foreign Equity Fund**

Phone: 800-468-6475
Listed: IRL, NYSE
Commenced Operations: April, 1990
Cusip: 462710104

1991/mid-1992 Range of Premium/Disc: -14% to -27%
1991/mid-1992 Range of Price: $8 5/8 to $6 1/2
NAV Total Return 1991: +11.75%
Share Price Total Return 1991: +19.19%
Herzfeld Ranking 1991: 23rd of 46 foreign equity funds

Investment Objective: Long-term capital appreciation through investment primarily in equity securities of Irish companies.

Officers:

P.J. Hooper   President

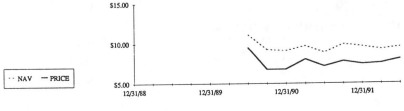

Investment Advisor: Bank of Ireland Asset Management, Limited
Advisory Fee: Monthly fee at the annual rate of 0.75% of average weekly net assets. Fee for year-ended 10/31/91 was $357,000.
Co-Advisor: Salomon Brothers Asset Management, Inc.
Advisory Fee: Monthly fee at the annual rate of 0.25% of average weekly net assets. Fee for year-ended 10/31/91 was $119,000.
Administrator: The Vanguard Group, Inc.
Administration Fee: $100,000 per annum plus an annual fee of 0.08% of the first $50 mil., 0.06% of the second $50 mil., and 0.04% of the remainder of average weekly net assets, payable monthly. Fee for year-ended 10/31/91 was $138,000.

Capital Structure: *Common stock:* 10 mil. shares authorized; 5,009,000 shares outstanding 1/31/92

Portfolio Highlights (as of 1/31/92): Irish common stocks 80.0%, Irish convertible preferred securities 5.6%, United Kingdom common stocks 10.5%, other assets and liabilities 3.9%. **Largest positions:** Smurfit (Jefferson) Group, AIB, CRH, Independent Newspapers, Irish Life.

Historical Financial Statistics (fiscal year-end: 10/31/91):

	1991	3/29/90 to 10/31/90
Value of net assets (000)	48,847	50,299
NAV	9.75	10.04
Net investment income	0.15	0.26
Dividends from net investment income	0.33	--
Expense ratio	2.03%	1.70% ann.
Income ratio	1.55%	4.28% ann.
Portfolio turnover	28%	6%

Special considerations: Net income and net realized capital gains are distributed at least annually. The fund's Articles of Incorporation contain various anti-takeover provisions including a 66 2/3% vote to open-end or liquidate the fund.

The Italy Fund, Inc.

2 World Trade Center, New York, NY 10018

Category: Foreign Equity Fund

Phone: 212-298-6263
Listed: ITA, NYSE
Commenced Operations: February, 1986
Cusip: 465395101

1991/mid-1992 Range of Premium/Disc: -1% to -22%
1991/mid-1992 Range of Price: $12 3/8 to $8 1/8
NAV Total Return 1990: -1.48%; **1991:** +0.44%
Share Price Total Return 1990: -23.10%; **1991:** -4.35%
Herzfeld Ranking 1991: 37th of 46 foreign equity funds

Investment Objective: Long-term capital appreciation primarily through investment in Italian equity securities.

Officers:
H.B. McLendon — Chairman
M. d'Urso — President

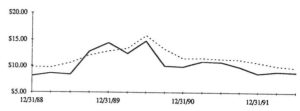

Investment Advisor: Shearson Lehman Global Asset Management Limited
Advisory Fee: Monthly fee at annual rate of 0.75% of average monthly net assets. Fee for year-ended 1/31/92 was $543,755.
Administrator: The Boston Company Advisors, Inc.
Administration Fee: Monthly fee at annual rate of 0.20% of average monthly net assets. Fee for year-ended 1/31/92 was $145,001.

Capital Structure: *Common stock:* 20 mil. shares authorized; 6,334,901 shares outstanding 1/31/92

Portfolio Highlights (as of 1/31/92): Stocks 85.8%, warrants 0.9%, fixed-income investments 11.3%, term deposit 1.4%, other assets and liabilities 0.6%. Largest industry concentrations: insurance 18.8%, communications 13.9%, banks 12.3%, holding companies 10.8%, property/construction & cement 5.7%, retailing 5.3%. **Largest positions:** BTP Italian government bond 12-01; Sirti S.p.A., STET Risp, L.M. Ericsson.

Historical Financial Statistics (fiscal year-end: 1/31/92):

	1992	1991	1990	1989	1988	2/28/86 to 1/31/87
Value of net assets (000)	70,186	72,055	83,902	62,743	57,445	90,793
NAV	11.08	11.37	13.24	9.91	9.07	14.33
Net investment income	0.25	0.32	0.17	0.21	0.12	0.22
Dividends from net investment income	0.25	0.34	0.15	0.19	0.36	--
Distributions from net realized gains	0.24	0.58	--	--	1.37	--
Distributions from capital	0.08	0.26	--	--	--	--
Operating expense ratio	1.53%	1.80%	1.90%	1.99%	1.92%	1.96% ann.
Income ratio	2.17%	2.28%	1.54%	2.23%	1.02%	1.83% ann.
Portfolio turnover	24%	24%	15%	15%	19%	39%

Special considerations: On 1/31/92 the fund had 2.3% of assets in investments restricted as to resale.
Shareholders over 5%: Nomura International Trust Company, 23.8%; The United Nations, 15%; Brown Brothers Harriman & Co., 9.4%; Manufacturers Hanover Trust Co., 5%.

Jakarta Growth Fund, Inc.

180 Maiden Lane, New York, NY 10038

Category: Foreign Equity Fund

Phone: 212-509-7893; 800-833-0018
Listed: JGF, NYSE
Commenced Operations: April, 1990
Cusip: 470120106

1991/mid-1992 Range of Premium/Disc: +23% to -22%
1991/mid-1992 Range of Price: $9 3/8 to $5 3/4
NAV Total Return 1991: -28.05%
Share Price Total Return 1991: -12.15%
Herzfeld Ranking 1991: 46th of 46 foreign equity funds

Investment Objective: Long-term capital appreciation through investment primarily in equity securities of Indonesian companies and non-Indonesian companies that derive a significant proportion of their revenue from Indonesia or that hold a significant proportion of their assets in Indonesia.

Officers:

T. Nakamura   President

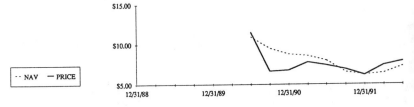

Investment Manager: Nomura Capital Management, Inc.
Management Fee: Monthly fee at annual rate of 1.10% of average weekly net assets. Fee for year-ended 3/31/92 was $392,742.
Investment Advisor: Nomura Investment Management Co., Ltd.
Advisory Fee: Monthly fee (paid by the investment manager) at the annual rate of 0.50% of average weekly net assets.

Capital Structure: *Common stock*: 100 mil. shares authorized; 5,009,000 shares outstanding 3/31/92

Portfolio Highlights (as of 3/31/92): Indonesian stocks 83.9%, cash and equivalents 15.8%, other assets less liabilities 0.3%. Largest industry concentrations: consumer goods/distribution 13.4%, textiles 11.0%, pharmaceuticals 7.1%, food and beverages 6.7%, manufacturing 6.0%, cement 5.6%, industrial 5.4%, finance 5.0%. **Largest positions:** Semen Cibinong 5.6%, Kalbe Farme 5.6%, Procter & Gamble Indonesia 5.3%, International Indorayon Utama 4.7%, Indorama Synthetics 4.3%.

Historical Financial Statistics (fiscal year-end: 3/31/92):

	1992	4/19/90 to 3/31/91
Value of net assets (000)	32,533	42,639
NAV	6.49	8.51
Net investment income	0.05	0.22
Dividends from net investment income	0.12	0.14
Distributions from net realized gains	0.06	--
Expense ratio	2.15%	1.83% ann.
Income ratio	0.63%	2.30% ann.
Portfolio turnover	24.2%	7.00%

Special considerations: At least annually the fund distributes substantially all net investment income and net realized capital gains. Some risks particular to this and many other single country funds include: small size of the market, low trading volume, restrictions on foreign investors, currency risk, political and economic risks. To prevent discounts which may occur, the fund may repurchase shares or make tender offers at net asset value from time to time. Such actions will be considered by the board on a quarterly basis. The fund's Articles of Incorporation contain various anti-takeover provisions including a 75% vote of shareholders to merge with another fund, liquidate, or convert to an open-end fund. As of 3/31/92 the fund had a capital loss carryforward of approximately $1,767,950 expiring through 2000. **Shareholders over 5%:** Allied Dunbar Assurance plc, 6.3%

Japan OTC Equity Fund, Inc.

180 Maiden Lane, New York, NY 10038

Category: Foreign Equity Fund

Phone: 212-509-7893; 800-833-0018
Listed: JOF, NYSE
Commenced Operations: March, 1990
Cusip: 471091108

1991/mid-1992 Range of Premium/Disc: +32 to -16%
1991/mid-1992 Range of Price: $12 7/8 to $6 3/4
NAV Total Return 1991: +16.13%
Share Price Total Return 1991: +28.06%
Herzfeld Ranking 1991: 15th of 46 foreign equity funds

Investment Objective: Long-term capital appreciation primarily through investments in equity securities traded in the Japanese over-the-counter market.

Officers:
T. Nakamura   President

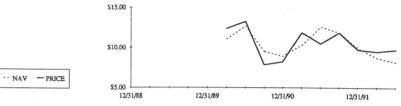

Investment Manager: Nomura Capital Management, Inc.
Management Fee: Monthly fee at annual rate of 1.10% of average weekly net assets up to $50 mil., 1.0% of average weekly net assets between $50 mil. and $100 mil., and 0.90% of any excess. Fee for year-ended 2/29/92 was $997,865.
Investment Advisor: Nomura Investment Management Co., Ltd.
Advisory Fee: Monthly fee (paid by the investment manager) at the annual rate of 0.50% of average weekly net assets up to $50 mil., 0.45% of average weekly net assets between $50 mil. and $100 mil., and 0.40% of any excess.

Capital Structure: *Common stock*: 100 mil. shares authorized; 8,509,000 shares outstanding 2/29/92

Portfolio Highlights (as of 2/29/92): Equity securities 95.5%, short-term securities 4.6%, liabilities in excess of other assets (0.1%). Largest industry concentrations: construction/housing 13.4%, retail/wholesale 13.3%, machinery/machine tools 13.1%, misc. manufacturing 8.4%, restaurant/service 7.6%, real estate/warehouse 7.5%, electronics/electric 6.7%, pharmaceutical/toiletries 5.8%, iron and steel/metals 5.5%. **Largest positions:** Paltac Corporation 4.1%, Sekiwa Real Estate Ltd. 3.9%, Nippon Kanzai Co. Ltd. 3.6%, Ishiguro Homa Corporation 3.5%, Wall Mart Co. Ltd. 3.5%, Aiya & Co. 3.4%, Torii & Co. Ltd. 3.3%, Sanshin Corporation 3.1%, Nishio Rent All Co. Ltd. 3.1%, King Jim Co. Ltd. 3.0%.

Historical Financial Statistics (fiscal year-end: 2/29/92):

	1992	3/21/90 to 2/28/91
Value of net assets (000)	82,196	85,021
NAV	9.66	9.99
Net investment income (loss)	0.06	0.24
Dividends from net investment income	0.19	0.24
Distributions from net realized gains	--	0.46
Expense ratio	1.51%	1.43% ann.
Income ratio	(0.58%)	2.19% ann.
Portfolio turnover	36%	32%

Special considerations: Net investment income and net realized capital gains will be distributed at least annually. To prevent any discounts which may occur, the fund may repurchase shares in the open market from time to time or make tender offers at net asset value from time to time. Such actions will be considered by the board on a quarterly basis. The fund's Articles of Incorporation contain various anti-takeover provisions including a 75% vote of shareholders to merge with another fund, liquidate, or convert to an open-end fund.

John Hancock Income Securities Trust

101 Huntington Avenue, Boston, MA 02199-7603

Category: Bond Fund

Phone: 617-375-1500, 800-843-0090
Listed: JHS, NYSE
Commenced Operations: February, 1973
Cusip: 410123103

1991/mid-1992 Range of Premium/Disc: +8% to -3%
1991/mid-1992 Range of Price: $17 1/2 to $14 3/4
NAV Total Return 1990: +6.53%; **1991:** +16.42%
Share Price Total Return 1990: +5.45%; **1991:** +24.10%
Herzfeld Ranking 1991: 63rd of 80 bond funds

Investment Objective: High level of current income consistent with prudent investment risk, primarily through investment in a diversified portfolio of freely marketable debt securities.

Officers:

E.J. Boudreau, Jr. Chairman & Chieg Executive Officer

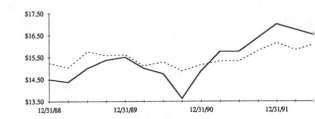

Investment Advisor: John Hancock Advisers, Inc.
Administrator: John Hancock Advisers, Inc.
Advisory Fee: Quarterly fee at annual rate of 0.65% of first $150 mil. of average weekly net assets, 0.375% of next $50 mil., 0.35% of next $100 mil., and 0.30% on excess. The fund also reimburses the advisor for administrative services not to exceed 0.03% of average weekly net assets per year. If normal operating expenses exceed 1.5% of the first $30 mil. of average weekly net assets and 1% of excess, the advisor will reimburse the fund for the difference. Fee for year-ended 12/31/91 was $696,349.
Administration Fee: The trust may pay for administrative services directly as an administration fee or as reimbursement to the advisor for the compensation of the chairman and president, compliance officer, and secretary of the trust who provide administrative services. The amount of such compensation incurred by the trust will not exceed in any fiscal year 0.03% of the average weekly net asset value. Fee for year-ended 12/31/91 was $29,383.

Capital Structure: *Shares of beneficial interest:* 30 mil. shares authorized; 9,846,422 shares outstanding 3/31/92

Portfolio Highlights (as of 3/31/92): Publicly traded bonds 97.48%, short-term investments 1.60%. Largest industry concentrations: utilities 14.35%, U.S. government agencies 13.21%, banks 12.79%, finance 9.88%, U.S. governmental 6.69%, transportation 7.73%, retail 7.52%, oil & gas 5.67%, foreign governmental 5.35%, broadcasting 5.15%. **Largest issuers:** U.S. treasury bonds and notes; Government National Mortgage Association; Financing Corp. bonds; Standard Credit Card Trusts; Hydro-Quebec.

Historical Financial Statistics (fiscal year-end: 12/31/91):

	1991	1990	1989	1988	1987	1986
Value of net assets (000)	159,990	147,764	149,750	144,209	142,981	154,990
NAV	16.25	15.19	15.61	15.24	15.30	16.90
Net investment income	1.44	1.47	1.49	1.46	1.46	1.56
Dividends from net investment income	1.46	1.47	1.47	1.47	1.9025	1.57
Expense ratio	0.74%	0.70%	0.71%	0.71%	0.68%	0.66%
Income ratio	9.28%	9.64%	9.55%	9.39%	9.18%	9.49%
Portfolio turnover	91.97%	84.67%	61.79%	23.95%	35.66%	48.88%

Special considerations: At the April 30, 1992, annual meeting shareholders voted to increase the investment management fee. At the April, 1990, annual meeting shareholders voted to permit the fund to enter into repurchase agreements. As of 12/31/91 the fund had $7,968,571 loss carryforwards available to expire through 1998.

John Hancock Investors Trust

101 Huntington Avenue, Boston, MA 02199-7603

Category: Bond Fund

Phone: 617-375-1500, 800-843-0090
Listed: JHI, NYSE
Commenced Operations: January, 1971
Cusip: 410142103

1991/mid-1992 Range of Premium/Disc: +12% to -3%
1991/mid-1992 Range of Price: $24 1/4 to $19 1/4
NAV Total Return 1990: +5.51%; **1991:** +17.17%
Share Price Total Return 1990: +2.29%; **1991:** +32.97%
Herzfeld Ranking 1991: 59th of 80 bond funds

Investment Objective: Income for distribution to shareholders, with capital appreciation as a secondary objective, primarily through investment in a diversified portfolio of debt securities, some of which may carry equity features. Up to 50% of portfolio may be invested in restricted, direct placement securities.

Officers:

E.J. Boudreau, Jr. Chairman & Chief Executive Officer

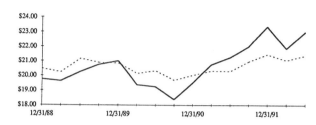

Investment Advisor: John Hancock Advisers, Inc.

Administrator: John Hancock Advisers, Inc.

Advisory Fee: Quarterly fee at annual rate of 0.65% of first $150 mil. of average weekly net assets, 0.375% of next $50 mil., 0.35% of next $100 mil., and 0.30% on excess. The fund also reimburses the advisor for administrative services not to exceed 0.03% of average weekly net assets per year. If normal operating expenses exceed 1.5% of the first $30 mil. of average weekly net assets and 1% of excess, the advisor will reimburse the fund for the difference. Fee for year-ended 12/31/91 was $681,751.

Administration Fee: The trust may pay for administrative services directly as an administration fee or as reimbursement to the advisor for the compensation of the chairman and president, compliance officer, and secretary of the trust who provide administrative services. The amount of such compensation incurred by the trust will not exceed in any fiscal year 0.03% of the average weekly net asset value. Fee for year-ended 12/31/91 was $28,593.

Capital Structure: *Shares of beneficial interest*: 20 mil. shares authorized; 7,220,044 shares outstanding 3/31/92

Portfolio Highlights (as of 3/31/92): Publicly traded bonds 94.0%, direct placement securities 2.77%, short-term investments 1.30%. Largest industry concentrations: banks 14.47%, utilities 14.34%, U.S. government agencies 10.50%, finance 10.33%, retail 7.54%, transportation 5.90%, foreign governmental 5.83%, U.S. governmental 5.82%, broadcasting 5.48%. **Largest issuers:** U.S. treasury bonds & notes; Government National Mortgage Association; Financing Corp. bonds; Standard Credit Card Trust; Hydro-Quebec.

Historical Financial Statistics (fiscal year-end: 12/31/91):

	1991	1990	1989	1988	1987	1986
Value of net assets (000)	156,026	143,334	146,972	142,301	141,486	154,357
NAV	21.61	20.08	20.87	20.46	20.57	22.85
Net investment income	1.92	1.96	2.00	1.99	2.00	2.12
Dividends from net investment income	1.93	1.98	1.99	1.99	2.59	2.11
Expense ratio	0.74%	0.71%	0.71%	0.70%	0.67%	0.65%
Income ratio	9.33%	9.70%	9.58%	9.54%	9.33%	9.58%
Portfolio turnover	81.47%	95.17%	49.61%	15.64%	32.36%	48.10%

Special considerations: At the April 30, 1992, annual meeting shareholders voted to increase the investment management fee. As of 12/31/91 the fund had $5,452,233 loss carryforwards available to expire through 1998.

Jundt Growth Fund, Inc.

1550 Utica Avenue South, Suite 950, Minneapolis, MN 55416

Category: Equity Fund

Phone: 800-543-6217
Listed: JF, NYSE
Commenced Operations: September, 1991
Cusip: 481712107

1991/mid-1992 Range of Premium/Disc: +5% to -10%
1991/mid-1992 Range of Price: $16 5/8 to $12 5/8
NAV Total Return 1991: N/A
Share Price Total Return 1991: N/A
Herzfeld Ranking 1991: N/A

Investment Objective: Long-term capital appreciation primarily through investment in a diversified portfolio of equity securities of companies that are believed by the advisor to have significant potential for growth in revenue and earnings. Income is not a consideration in the selection of investments and is not an investment objective of the fund.

Officers:

J.R. Jundt — Chairman, President & Chief Executive Officer

Investment Advisor: Jundt Associates, Inc.
Advisory Fee: Monthly fee at the annual rate of 1% of the fund's average weekly net assets. Fee for period 9/3/91 to 12/31/91 was $1,479,155.
Administrator: Princeton Administrators, Inc.
Administration Fee: Monthly fee at an annual rate of 0.25% of the fund's average weekly net assets not exceeding $300 mil. and 0.20% of the average weekly net assets in excess of $300 mil. Minimum fee $150,000. Fee for period 9/3/91 to 12/31/91 was $344,998.

Capital Structure: *Common stock*: 1 bil. shares authorized, 32,300,272 shares outstanding 12/31/91

Portfolio Highlights (as of 12/31/91): Common stocks 77.2%, short-term securities 31.8%, liabilities in excess of other assets (9.0%). Largest sector concentrations: drugs 20.6%, retail 17.9%, computer technology 11.3%, financial services 5.4%, medical technology 5.1%. **Largest positions:** Novell Inc., Pfizer Inc., Merck & Company Inc., Home Depot Inc., Microsoft Corp.

Historical Financial Statistics (fiscal year-end: 12/31/91):

	9/3/91 to 12/31/91
Value of net assets (000)	499,319
NAV	15.46
Net investment income	0.11
Dividends from net investment income	0.12
Expense ratio	1.43% ann.
Income ratio	2.45% ann.
Portfolio turnover	2%

Special considerations: During the initial offering of the fund, the share price was reduced from $15.00 to $14.85 for single transactions of between 2,000 and 6,999 shares, and to $14.70 for single transactions of between 7,000 and 70,199 shares. The fund had a concurrent offering of 2 mil. shares at a maximum initial offing price of $14.25 with the minimum purchase of 70,200 shares. The fund was not listed on the NYSE for three months after the initial offering; during that time it was illiquid. Initial shareholders were issued rights to purchase additional shares. The fund's Board of Directors will consider, each third quarter commencing in 1992, making a tender offer. Board meets in July, 1992 to consider the tender. The fund may be converted to an open-end fund by a majority vote of shareholders. The fund may use stock index futures contracts for hedging.

Kemper High Income Trust

120 South LaSalle Street, Chicago, IL 60603

Category: Bond Fund

Phone: 800-621-5027
Listed: KHI, NYSE
Commenced Operations: April, 1988
Cusip: 48841G106

1991/mid-1992 Range of Premium/Disc: +11% to -8%
1991/mid-1992 Range of Price: $9 1/2 to $5 1/2
NAV Total Return 1990: -14.00%; **1991:** +51.79%
Share Price Total Return 1990: -16.67%; **1991:** +61.25%
Herzfeld Ranking 1991: 2nd of 80 bond funds

Investment Objective: Highest current income obtainable consistent with reasonable risk, with a secondary objective of capital gains primarily through investment in a diversified portfolio of income producing securities including: U.S. corporate fixed income securities; debt obligations of the U.S. government, its agencies and instrumentalities; debt obligations of foreign governments, their agencies and instrumentalities.

Officers:
C.M. Kierscht   President

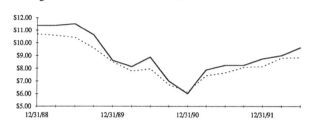

Investment Advisor: Kemper Financial Services, Inc.
Advisory Fee: Annual fee of 0.85% of weekly net assets. Fee for year-ended 11/30/91 was $1,343,000.
Administrator: Mitchell Hutchins Asset Management Inc.
Administration Fee: Annual fee of 0.15% of first $100 mil. of average weekly net assets, 0.14% of excess. Fee for year-ended 11/30/91 was $231,000.

Capital Structure: *Shares of beneficial interest:* unlimited number of shares authorized; 21,522,000 shares outstanding 11/30/91
Note Payable: With Kemper Investors Life Insurance Company equal to underwriting discount and offering costs to be repaid on 5/31/93. Annual interest rate 9.2%.

Portfolio Highlights (as of 3/31/92): High yield corporate securities 98%, U.S. treasury securities 1%, cash equivalents 1%. Quality ratings: Ba 14%, B 58%, Caa 9%, Ca 7%, non-rated 5%, private placements 7%. **Largest Issuers:** RJR Holdings, Storer Communications, Supermarkets General Holdings, Quantum Chemical, K&F Industries. The average maturity was 8 years.

Historical Financial Statistics (fiscal year-end: 11/30/91):

	1991	1990	1989	4/30/88 to 11/30/88
Value of net assets (000)	178,145	131,602	181,023	214,477
NAV	8.28	6.25	8.86	10.84
Net investment income	1.01	1.22	1.29	0.82
Dividends from net investment income	0.94	1.20	1.30	0.69
Dividends from paid-in surplus	0.11	--	0.07	--
Expense ratio	2.22%	2.25%	1.93%	1.28% ann.
Income ratio	13.78%	16.17%	12.92%	12.30% ann.
Portfolio turnover	27%	29%	45%	101%

Special considerations: The fund may repurchase shares or make tender offers from time to time when discounts occur. After 1/1/93, the fund will submit an open-ending proposal each year if certain conditions are met. As of 1/30/91 the fund had a capital loss carryforward of approximately $22,131,000 available through 2000. Dividend rate reduced to $0.08 per month at the beginning of 1992.

Kemper Intermediate Government Trust

120 South LaSalle Street, Chicago, IL 60603

Category: Bond Fund

Phone: 800-621-5027	**1991/mid-1992 Range of Premium/Disc:** +10% to -4%
Listed: KGT, NYSE	**1991/mid-1992 Range of Price:** $10 to $8 5/8
Commenced Operations: July, 1988	**NAV Total Return 1990:** +6.18%; **1991:** +14.20%
Cusip: 488413105	**Share Price Total Return 1990:** +0.26%; **1991:** +9.80%
	Herzfeld Ranking 1991: 73rd of 80 bond funds

Investment Objective: High current income consistent with preservation of capital primarily through investment in U.S. government and foreign government securities, with a dollar-weighted average portfolio maturity of between 3 and 10 years.

Officers:

C.M. Kierscht   President

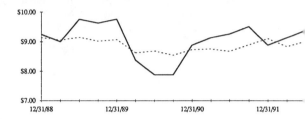

Investment Advisor: Kemper Financial Services, Inc.

Advisory Fee: Annual fee of 0.80% of average weekly net assets. Fee for year-ended 11/30/91 was $2,345,000.

Capital Structure: *Shares of beneficial interest:* unlimited number of shares authorized; 33,579,000 shares outstanding 11/30/91

Portfolio Highlights (as of 3/31/92): U.S. treasury securities 26%, mortgage-backed securities 52%, foreign bonds 11%, money market instruments 11%. Average maturity approx. 6 years. **Largest issuers:** U.S. treasury notes; Government National Mortgage Association Certificates; Federal National Mortgage Association collaterlized mortgage obligations; UK treasury 13.5-92; Kingdom of Spain 12.50-92.

Historical Financial Statistics (fiscal year-end: 11/30/91):

	1991	1990	1989	7/21/88 to 11/30/88
Value of net assets (000)	301,207	288,351	302,142	300,511
NAV	8.97	8.70	9.16	9.30
Net investment income	0.87	0.94	0.97	0.29
Dividends from net investment income	0.88	0.91	0.99	0.25
Distributions from net realized gains	--	--	0.01	--
Expense ratio	0.93%	0.95%	0.95%	0.87% ann.
Income ratio	10.02%	10.85%	10.65%	8.76% ann.
Portfolio turnover	368%	253%	115%	0%

Special considerations: The fund may repurchase shares or make tender offers from time to time when discounts occur. After 1/1/94, the fund will submit an open-ending proposal each year if certain conditions are met. As of 11/30/90, 21,000 shares of the fund had been repurchased at a weighted average discount of 9%. As of 11/30/91 the fund had a capital loss carryforward of approximately $12,273,000 available through 1999.

Kemper Multi-Market Income Trust

120 South LaSalle Street, Chicago, IL 60603

Category: Bond Fund

Phone: 800-621-5027	**1991/mid-1992 Range of Premium/Disc:** +4% to -9%
Listed: KMM, NYSE	**1991/mid-1992 Range of Price:** $11 1/8 to $6 7/8
Commenced Operations: January, 1989	**NAV Total Return 1990:** -10.63%; **1991:** +50.16%
Cusip: 48842B106	**Share Price Total Return 1990:** -10.09%; **1991:** +48.23%
	Herzfeld Ranking 1991: 4th of 80 bond funds

Investment Objective: High current income primarily through investment in a broad range of income-producing securities such as U.S. corporate fixed income securities and debt obligations of foreign governments and their agencies and instrumentalities, denominated in U.S. or foreign currencies.

Officers:
C.M. Kierscht   President

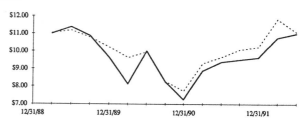

Investment Advisor: Kemper Financial Services, Inc.
Advisory Fee: Monthly fee at annual rate of 0.85% of average adjusted weekly net assets. Fee for year-ended 11/30/91 was $1,568,000.

Capital Structure: *Shares of beneficial interest:* unlimited number of shares authorized; 19,746,000 shares outstanding 11/30/91

Portfolio Highlights (as of 3/31/92): High yield corporates 92%, treasuries 4%, cash equivalents 4%.
Largest Issuers: RJR Holdings, Supermarkets General Holdings, Quantum Chemical, Arkansas Best and American Standard. The average maturity of the portfolio was approximately 8 years. Quality ratings: Baa 2%, Ba 15%, B 59%, Caa 8%, Ca 8%, non-rated 4%, private placement 4%.

Historical Financial Statistics (fiscal year-end: 11/30/91):

	1991	1990	1/23/89 to 11/30/89
Value of net assets (000)	204,509	155,381	203,213
NAV	10.36	7.88	10.33
Net investment income	1.18	1.41	1.05
Dividends from net investment income	1.16	1.40	1.05
Expense ratio	1.00%	1.00%	0.94% ann.
Income ratio	12.60%	15.09%	11.32% ann.
Portfolio turnover	24%	32%	38%

Special considerations: The fund may issue short- or intermediate-term notes and preferred shares for the purpose of leveraging the fund's assets. Trustees will consider repurchasing shares on a quarterly basis. Under certain circumstances the fund will submit an open-ending proposal after 1/1/94. The board may authorize preferred shares; as of 11/30/90 no preferred shares were authorized. As of 11/30/91 the fund had a capital loss carryforward of approximately $5,851,000 available through the year 2000. Dividend rate reduced to $0.09 per month at the beginning of 1992.

Kemper Municipal Income Trust

120 South LaSalle Street, Chicago, IL 60603

Category: Municipal Bond Fund

Phone: 800-621-5027
Listed: KTF, NYSE
Commenced Operations: October, 1988
Cusip: 48842C104

1991/mid-1992 Range of Premium/Disc: +8% to -1%
1991/mid-1992 Range of Price: $13 1/8 to $11 1/8
NAV Total Return 1990: +6.33%; **1991:** +15.69%
Share Price Total Return 1990: +4.26%; **1991:** +18.84%
Herzfeld Ranking 1991: 10th of 51 municipal bond funds

Investment Objective: High level of current income exempt from federal income tax primarily through investment in a diversified portfolio of investment grade tax-exempt municipal securities.

Officers:

C.M. Kierscht   President

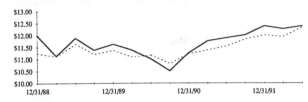

Investment Advisor: Kemper Financial Services, Inc.
Advisory Fee: Annual fee of 0.55% of average weekly net assets. Fee for year-ended 11/30/91 was $3,543,000.

Capital Structure:

Shares of beneficial interest: unlimited number of shares authorized; 36,701,000 shares outstanding 11/30/91
Remarketed Preferred Stock: 10,800 Series A, 10,700 Series B, 10,800 Series C, and 10,700 Series D remarketed preferred shares each at a liquidation value of $5,000 per share. The dividend rate on each series may change every 28 days as set by the remarketing agent.

Portfolio Highlights (as of 3/31/92): Municipal obligations 97.3%, money market instruments 0.4%, cash and other assets less liabilities 2.3%. Quality ratings: AAA 16%, AA 35%, A 29%, BBB 17%, non-rated 3%. **Largest issuers:** New York State Energy Research and Development Authority, Consolidated Edison Company of New York Inc. revenue; Washington Public Power Supply System, Nuclear Project #2, Revenue 7-12; Vermont Housing Finance Agency mortgage purchase revenue 8.1-22; Fairfax County (VA) Economic Development Authority, resource recovery revenue 7.75-11. As of 3/31/92 the average maturity was approximately 25 years, excluding the effects of leveraging. AMT paper represented 63% of the portfolio.

Historical Financial Statistics (fiscal year-end: 11/30/91):

	1991	1990	1989	10/20/88 to 11/30/88
Value of net assets (000)	649,924	623,698	622,989	397,050
NAV	11.85	11.25	11.35	11.13
Net investment income	1.18	1.18	0.92	0.05
Dividends from net investment income	0.87	0.87	0.78	--
Common share equivalent of dividends paid to remarketed preferred shareholders	0.27	0.36	0.13	--
Expense ratio	0.72%	0.66%	0.62%	0.65% ann.
Income ratio	6.76%	6.93%	6.88%	4.31% ann.
Portfolio turnover	4%	15%	38%	13%

Special considerations: The fund may repurchase shares or make tender offers from time to time when discounts occur. After 1/1/94, the fund will submit an open-ending proposal each year if certain conditions are met.

Kemper Strategic Municipal Income Trust

120 South LaSalle Street, Chicago, IL 60603

Category: Municipal Bond Fund

Phone: 800-621-5027
Listed: KSM, NYSE
Commenced Operations: March, 1989
Cusip: 488427105

1991/mid-1992 Range of Premium/Disc: +8% to 0%
1991/mid-1992 Range of Price: $12 3/4 to $11
NAV Total Return 1990: +6.99%; **1991:** +12.16%
Share Price Total Return 1990: +9.63%; **1991:** +12.15%
Herzfeld Ranking 1991: 32nd of 51 municipal bond funds

Investment Objective: High level of current income exempt from federal income tax primarily through investment in a portfolio of tax-exempt municipal securities, at least 50% to be invested in investment grade municipal securities and up to 50% in high-yield municipal securities that are below investment grade.

Officers:
C.M. Kierscht   President

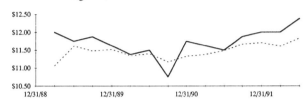

Investment Advisor: Kemper Financial Services, Inc.

Advisory Fee: Monthly fee at annual rate of 0.60% of average weekly net assets. Fee for year-ended 11/30/91 was $701,000.

Capital Structure: *Shares of beneficial interest:* unlimited number of shares authorized; 10,207,000 shares outstanding 11/30/91

Portfolio Highlights (as of 3/31/92): Quality ratings as of 3/31/92: AAA 4%, AA 19%, A 12%, BBB 15%, BB 1%, B 2%, non-rated 47%. Some of the portfolio holdings included: single family housing bonds 19%, senior care bonds 14%, hospital bonds 12%, general obligations 10%. AMT paper represented 40% of the portfolio. 25 states were represented; the average maturity was 22 years. **Largest issuers** (11/30/91): Wyoming Community Development Authority, housing revenue 8.125-20; Nevada Housing Division single family program revenue 7.90-21; New York City general obligation; Industrial Development Authority of the County of Pima single family mortgage revenue 8.2-21; North Dakota Housing Finance Agency, single family mortgage revenue 8.375-21.

Historical Financial Statistics (fiscal year-end: 11/30/91):

	1991	1990	3/22/89 to 11/30/89
Value of net assets (000)	118,864	114,929	115,985
NAV	11.65	11.37	11.55
Net investment income	0.84	0.81	0.52
Dividends from net investment income	0.81	0.85	0.45
Dividends from net realized gains	0.11	0.10	--
Expense ratio	0.77%	0.76%	0.77% ann.
Income ratio	7.31%	7.15%	6.59% ann.
Portfolio turnover	20%	57%	22%

Special considerations: The fund may repurchase shares or make tender offers from time to time when discounts occur. After 1/1/94, the fund will submit an open-ending proposal each year if certain conditions are met. The board may authorize preferred shares; as of 11/30/91 no preferred shares were authorized.

Kleinwort Benson Australian Income Fund, Inc.

200 Park Avenue, 24th Fl. New York, NY 10166   **Category:** Foreign Bond Fund

Phone: 212-687-2515, 800-237-4218	**1991/mid-1992 Range of Premium/Disc:** -1% to -17%
Listed: KBA, NYSE	**1991/mid-1992 Range of Price:** $11 1/4 to $8 3/4
Commenced Operations: November, 1986	**NAV Total Return 1990:** +12.46%; **1991:** +20.87%
Cusip: 498577105	**Share Price Total Return 1990:** +5.55%; **1991:** +34.82%
	Herzfeld Ranking 1991: 2nd of 8 foreign bond funds

Investment Objective: High income through investment primarily in Australian debt securities, with a secondary objective of capital appreciation.

Officers:

R.C. Cotton   Chairman
A. Begg   President

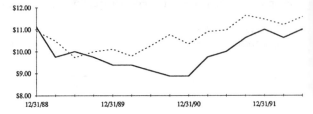

Investment Advisor: Kleinwort Benson International Investment, Limited
Advisory Fee: Monthly fee at annual rate of 0.70% of average weekly net assets. Fee for six months ended 4/30/92 was $250,964.

Capital Structure: *Common stock*: 100 mil. shares authorized; 6,344,756 shares outstanding 4/30/92

Portfolio Highlights (as of 4/30/92): Australian government bonds 21.9%, Australian semi-government bonds 46.2%, Australian dollar denominated Eurobonds 17.0%, New Zealand bonds 4.6%, Australian corporate bonds 4.5%, Australian dollar cash on deposit 6.0%, other assets and liabilities (0.2%). The average life of the portfolio was 5.3 years with a duration of 3.9 years. **Largest issuers:** Commonwealth Government Bonds (Australia); New South Wales Treasury Corp.; South Australian Finance Authority 13-95; General Electric Capital Canada 14.25-95; State Electricity Commission of Queensland 13-96.

Historical Financial Statistics (fiscal year-end: 10/31/91):

	six months 4/30/92	1991	1990	1989	1988	11/28/86 to 10/31/87
Value of net assets (000)	72,092	74,652	65,268	62,669	73,327	59,909
NAV	11.36	11.77	10.29	9.88	11.57	9.45
Net investment income (loss)	0.459	1.044	(1.095)	1.112	1.235	1.057
Dividends from net investment income	0.53	1.01	1.06	0.965	1.262	0.885
Distributions from net realized gains	0.05	--	--	0.580	0.435	0.100
Distributions from paid-in capital	--	--	--	0.200	--	--
Operating expense ratio	1.62% ann.	1.62%	1.61%	1.75%	1.48%	1.54% ann.
Income ratio	8.12% ann.	9.53%	10.86%	10.73%	11.27%	11.32% ann.
Portfolio turnover	35.64%	11.39%	23.78%	11.87%	26.63%	128.90%

Special considerations: The monthly dividend rate was reduced to $0.07 per share because of a weaker Australian dollar and lower Australian interest rates. The fund anticipates making a year-end capital gains distribution for 1992. Dividend rate reduced to $0.07 per month.

The Korea Fund, Inc.

345 Park Avenue, New York, NY 10154

Category: Foreign Equity Fund

Phone: 212-326-6200, 617-330-5602
Listed: KF, NYSE
Commenced Operations: August, 1984
Cusip: 500634100

1991/mid-1992 Range of Premium/Disc: +64% to -7%
1991/mid-1992 Range of Price: $18 to $10 7/8
NAV Total Return 1990: -28.36%; **1991:** +2.07%
Share Price Total Return 1990: -57.60%; **1991:** +5.25%
Herzfeld Ranking 1991: 34th of 46 foreign equity funds

Investment Objective: Long-term capital appreciation primarily through investment in equity securities of Korean companies.

Officers:

J. Padegs   Chairman
N. Bratt   President

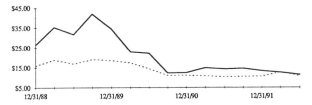

Investment Advisor: Scudder, Stevens & Clark Inc.
Advisory Fee: Monthly fee at annual rate of 1.15% of first $50 mil. of month-end net assets, 1.10% of assets between $50 mil. and $100 mil., 1.00% of excess. Management fee for six months ended 12/31/91 was $1,267,792.
Korean Advisor: Daewoo Capital Management Co., Ltd.
Korean Advisory Fee: (Paid by Scudder, Stevens & Clark Inc.) Monthly fee at annual rate of 0.2875% of first $50 mil., 0.275% of assets between $50 mil. and $100 mil., 0.25% of excess.

Capital Structure:
    Common stock: 50 mil. shares authorized; 22,356,760 shares outstanding 12/31/91
    Debt: The fund had short-term borrowings during the six months ended 12/31/91; the weighted average outstanding daily balance of bank loans was $1,200,000, with a weighted average interest rate of 8.0%. There were no borrowings outstanding on 12/31/91.

Portfolio Highlights (as of 3/31/92): Common stocks 94.4%, preferred stocks 3.0%, corporate bonds 1.4%, short-term investments 1.0%, commercial paper 0.2%. Largest sector concentrations: basic industry 19.9%, consumer cyclical 17.3%, financial 14.1%, consumer nondurable 13.2%, technology 10.8%, utilities 6.7%. **Largest positions**: Korea Long Term Credit Bank, Korea Mobile Telecom, Samsung Electronics Co. Ltd., Hyundai Motor Services Co. Ltd., Han Kook Tire Manufacturing Co. Ltd.

Historical Financial Statistics (fiscal year-end: 6/30/91):

	six months 12/31/91	1991	1990	1989	1988*	1987*
Value of net assets (000)	235,917	228,353	242,261	386,509	265,311	210,230
NAV	10.55	10.27	14.45	16.84	13.97	11.13
Net investment income (loss)	(0.04)	0.09	0.04	0.04	0.11	0.29
Dividends from net investment income	0.06	--	0.08	0.11	0.29	0.01
Distributions from net realized gains	0.34	2.20	1.88	1.74	0.68	0.03
Operating expense ratio	1.50% ann.	1.47%	1.44%	1.54%	1.53%	1.47%
Income ratio (loss)	(0.33%) not ann.	0.83%	0.21%	0.24%	0.92%	3.25%
Portfolio turnover	20.3% ann.	19.2%	17.9%	15.1%	19.7%	4.4%

*per share figures restated to reflect 200% stock dividend paid on 10/11/88

Special considerations: Share price performance presented for 1989 above does not include adjustment for year-end distribution because price was not reduced until payable date in January, 1990. At the 1990 annual meeting shareholders voted to approve a proposal to divide the directors into three classes. A proposal to reclassify the fund as a non-diversified company under the Investment Company Act of 1940 also passed. There was an offering of 1,418,439 shares at $35.25 per share on 8/10/89. **Shareholders over 5%:** Henderson Administration Group, 8.08%

The Korean Investment Fund, Inc.

1345 Avenue of the Americas, New York, NY 10105   **Category: Foreign Equity Fund**

Phone: 800-247-4154	**1991/mid-1992 Range of Premium/Disc:** +16% to -16%
Listed: KIF, NYSE	**1991/mid-1992 Range of Price:** $12 to $9 3/8
Commenced Operations: February, 1992	**NAV Total Return 1991:** N/A
Cusip: 500637103	**Share Price Total Return 1991:** N/A
	Herzfeld Ranking 1991: N/A

Investment Objective: Long-term capital appreciation through investment primarily in equity securities of Korean companies. Under normal circumstances the fund invests at least 65% of its total assets in Korean equity securities, a maximum of 25% in unlisted securities, and a maximum of 35% in non-convertible debt securities. If possible, the fund would consider investing up to 10% of its total assets in North Korean issuers.

Officers:

D.H. Dievler	Chairman
H-G. Yum	President

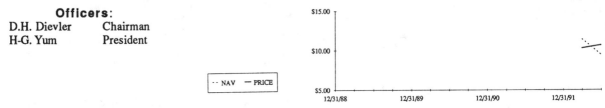

Investment Advisor and Administrator: Alliance Capital Management L.P.
Advisory and Administration Fees: Monthly fee at the annualized rate of 0.75% of the fund's average weekly net assets.
Investment Manager: Orion Asset Management Co., Ltd.
Investment Management Fee: Monthly fee at the annualized rate of 0.50% of the fund's average weekly net assets.

Capital Structure: *Common stock*: 100 mil. shares authorized, 4.2 mil. shares outstanding February, 1992

Portfolio Highlights (as of 4/30/92): Equities 75.2%, cash and short-term 24.8%. Largest industry concentrations: basic industries 22.5%, consumer manufacturing 19.9%, financial services 11.7%, consumer staples 6.7%, healthcare 4.4%. **Largest positions:** Dong Kuk Steel Mill, Hannong, Shinan Investment & Finance, Woo Sung Feedmill, Kisan.

Historical Financial Statistics:

	4/30/92
Value of net assets (000)	46,309
NAV	11.00

Special considerations: The fund has an Investment Strategy Committee which meets quarterly to consider investment strategy for the fund. The fund's Board of Directors will consider from time to time actions to attempt to reduce or eliminate any market value discount from net asset value which may develop. Such actions include open market repurchases or tender offers for the fund's own shares at net asset value. Each quarter the Board will consider making a tender offer. The fund's Articles of Incorporation and Bylaws contain various anti-takeover provisions including a 75% vote for removal of a director, liquidation of the fund or merger with another corporation.

The Latin American Discovery Fund, Inc.

1221 Avenue of the Americas, New York, NY 10020   **Category:** Foreign Equity Fund

Phone: 212-296-7100	**1991/mid-1992 Range of Premium/Disc:** +7% to 0%
Listed: LDF, NYSE	**1991/mid-1992 Range of Price:** $15 1/8 to $14
Commenced Operations: June, 1992	**NAV Total Return 1991:** N/A
Cusip: 51828C106	**Share Price Total Return 1991:** N/A
	Herzfeld Ranking 1991: N/A

Investment Objective: Long-term capital appreciation through investing primarily in equity securities of Latin American issuers and, from time to time, in debt securities issued or guaranteed by a Latin American government or government equity.

Officers:

B.M. Biggs	Chairman
W.J. Olsen	President

Investment Manager: Morgan Stanley Asset Management, Inc.

Management Fee: Monthly fee at the annual rate of 0.75% of the fund's average weekly net assets.

Investment Advisor: Roberts Management S.A. (for the fund's investments in Argentina); Unibanco Consultoria de Investimentos S/C Ltda. (for the fund's investments in Brazil); Bice Chileconsult Finanzas y Servicios Ltda. (for the fund's investments in Chile); Impulsora del Fondo Mexico, S.A. de C.V. (for the fund's investments in Mexico)

Advisory Fee: Each advisor will be paid a monthly fee at the annual rate of 0.125% of the fund's average weekly net assets.

Administrator: United States Trust Company of New York (U.S.); Unibanco-Uniao de Bancos Brasileiros S.A. (Brazil); Bice Chileconsult Agente de Valors S.A. (Chile)

Administration Fee: The U.S. administrator is paid an annual fee of $65,000 plus 0.08% of the average weekly net assets of the Fund. The Brazilian administrator is paid an annual fee of 0.125% of the fund's average weekly net assets invested in Brazil. The Chilean administrator is paid an annual fee equal to the greater of 0.25% of the fund's average weekly net assets invested in Chile or $20,000.

Capital Structure: *Common stock*: 100 mil. shares authorized, 3.3 mil. shares outstanding 6/16/92.

Portfolio Highlights: not yet published

Historical Financial Statistics:

	6/16/92
Value of net assets (000)	46,530
NAV	14.10

Special considerations: At least 55% of the fund's total assets normally will be invested in listed equity securities of Argentine, Brazilian, Chilean and Mexican issuers. The fund plans to invest actively in markets in other Latin American countries such as Columbia, Peru and Venezuela. During the initial offering of the fund at $15.00 per share, there was a concurrent offering with a minimum purchase of 100,000 shares at $14.45 per share. If, at any time following the offering, the average discount from net asset value at which the shares of the fund trade is substantial, the directors, at their next quarterly meeting, will consider taking various actions designed to eliminate the discount including periodic repurchases of shares, tender offers at net asset value or conversion of the fund to an open-end fund.

The Latin American Equity Fund, Inc.

One Citicorp Center, 58th Floor, 153 East 53rd Street,
New York, NY 10022

Category: Foreign Equity Fund

Phone: 212-832-2626
Listed: LAQ, NYSE
Commenced Operations: October, 1991
Cusip: 51827T100

1991/mid-1992 Range of Premium/Disc: +14% to -15%
1991/mid-1992 Range of Price: $19 1/8 to $11 3/4
NAV Total Return 1991: N/A
Share Price Total Return 1991: N/A
Herzfeld Ranking 1991: N/A

Investment Objective: Long-term capital appreciation by investing primarily in Latin American equity securities. Under normal market conditions, the fund invests substantially all, but not less than 80% of its assets in Latin American equity securities.

Officers:

E. Bassini   Chaiman, President & Chief Investment Officer

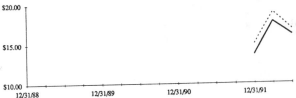

Investment Advisor: BEA Associates
Advisory Fee: Quarterly fee at an annual rate equal to 1.25% of the first $100 mil. of average weekly net assets, 1.15% of the next $50 mil. and 1.05% of any excess. Advisory fees for period 10/30/91 to 12/31/91 were $185,405.
Sub-Advisors: Patrimonio Planejamento Financeira Ltda., Celsius Agente de Valores Limitada, Acci Worldwide, S.A. de C.V., Acciones y Valores de Mexico, S.A. de C.V., and Merchant Bankers Asociados S.A.
Sub-Advisory Fees: Each sub-advisor receives out of BEA Associates' advisory fee, fees payable quarterly at an annual rate equal to 0.25% of the fund's average weekly net assets invested in Argentina, Brazil, Chile and Mexico, respectively.
Administrator: Provident Financial Processing Corp. (in U.S.); Administradora de Fondos de Inversion de Capital Extranjero S.A. (in Chile); Banco Bradesco de Investmento S.A. (in Brazil)
Administration Fee: Provident Financial Processing Corp. is paid a fee at the annual rate of 0.10% of the value of the fund's average weekly net assets, subject to a minimum annual fee of $75,000. The Chilean administrator is paid an annual fee equal to the greater of 2,000 U.F. (approx. $44,000 U.S.) or 0.10% of the fund's average weekly net assets. Administrative fees for period 10/30/91 to 12/31/91 were $36,679.

Capital Structure: *Common stock:* 100 mil. shares authorized, 6,007,169 shares outstanding 12/31/91.

Portfolio Highlights (as of 12/31/91): Common stock 79.92%, bonds 9.77%, short-term 10.31%. Largest geographic concentrations: Mexico 33.6%, Brazil 18.6%, Argentina 16.8%, Chile 8.2%, Venezuela 2.1%. **Largest positions:** Telebras, Telmex L, Petrobas, Cementos Mexicana A, Republic of Venezuela-Series DL 7.375%.

Historical Financial Statistics (fiscal year-end: 12/31/91):

	10/30/91 to 12/31/91
Value of net assets (000)	92,751
NAV	15.44
Net investment income	0.06
Dividends from net investment income	0.06
Distributions from net realized gains and currency transactions	0.01
Expense ratio	2.35% ann.
Income ratio	2.46% ann.
Portfolio turnover	69.50% ann.

Special considerations: Annual distributions are made from net investment income and net realized short-term capital gains. The fund's Articles of Incorporation and Bylaws contain various anti-takeover provisions including a 75% vote of shareholders to merge with another fund, or liquidate. **Shareholders over 5%:** Newberger & Berman, 10.6%

The Latin American Investment Fund, Inc.

One Citicorp Center, 58th Floor, 153 East 53rd Street
New York, NY 10022

Category: Foreign Equity Fund

Phone: 212-832-2626
Listed: LAM, NYSE
Commenced Operations: August, 1990
Cusip: 518279104

1991/mid-1992 Range of Premium/Disc: +17% to -23%
1991/mid-1992 Range of Price: $34 7/8 to $10 5/8
NAV Total Return 1991: +112.97%
Share Price Total Return 1991: +178.78%
Herzfeld Ranking 1991: 2nd of 46 foreign equity funds

Investment Objective: Long-term capital appreciation primarily through investment in Latin American equity and debt securities. Under normal conditions 65% of assets will be invested in Brazilian, Chilean and Mexican issuers, and not more than 10% in any one other Latin American country.

Officers:

E. Bassini — Chairman, President & Chief Investment Officer

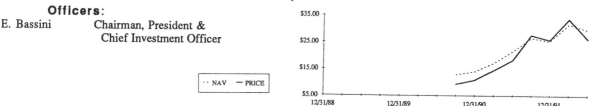

Investment Advisor: BEA Associates; Salomon Brothers Asset Management Inc. (sovereign debt portfolio only)

Advisory Fee: To BEA Associates: annual fee calculated monthly and paid quarterly, equal to 0.8125% of the first $100 mil. av. net assets, $0.07475% of the next $50 mil., and $0.6825% of any excess. To Salomon Brothers Asset Management: annual fee calculated monthly and paid quarterly, equal to 0.4375% of first $100 mil. of av. weekly net assets, 0.4025% of next $50 mil., and 0.3675% of any excess. Fee for 1991 was $1,082,325.

Sub-Advisors: Patrimonio Planejamento Financeira Ltda., Celsius Agente de Valores Limitada, Acci Worldwide, S.A. de C.V. and Merchant Bankers Asociados S.A.

Sub-Advisory Fees: Patrimontio, Celsius and Acci paid out of advisory fees paid to BEA and Salomon at annual rate of 0.05% of average weekly net assets. Merchant Bankers receives an annual fee of 0.02% of average weekly net assets.

Administrator: Provident Financial Processing Corp. (in U.S.); Administradora de Fondos de Inversion de Capital Extranjero S.A. (in Chile); Banco Bradesco de Investmento S.A. (in Brazil)

Administration Fee: Each administrator: quarterly fee at annual rate of 0.10% of average weekly net assets with a minimum annual fee. Fee for 1991 was $209,712.

Capital Structure: *Common stock*: 100 mil. shares authorized, 4,009,701 shares outstanding 12/31/91

Portfolio Highlights (as of 12/31/91): Common stock 86.66%, U.S. government securities 0.21%, short-term investments 13.13%. Largest geographic concentrations: Mexico 34.6%, Chile 18.1%, Brazil 14.6%, Argentina 15.5%, Venezuela 2.4%. **Largest positions**: Telemex Nominative A & L; Cifra B & C; Cementos Mexicana A & B; Telebras PN INT; Sidek A & B.

Historical Financial Statistics (fiscal year-end: 12/31/91):

	1991	8/1/90 to 12/31/90
Value of net assets (000)	104,435	57,081
NAV	26.05	14.24
Net investment income	0.61	0.29
Dividends from net investment income	0.63	0.27
Distributions from net realized gains and foreign currency transactions	2.83	--
Expense ratio	2.30%	3.27% ann.
Income ratio	2.85%	5.10% ann.
Portfolio turnover	82.39%	125.97% ann.

Special considerations: At the 1992 annual meeting, shareholders approved a proposal to allow for rights offerings at prices below net asset value, such rights offerings would result in a dilution of the fund's net asset value. The fund pays quarterly distributions of net investment income and may pay annual distributions of net realized short-term capital gains and net realized long-term capital gains. The fund's Articles of Incorporation and Bylaws contain various anti-takeover provisions including a 75% vote of shareholders to merge with another fund or liquidate.

Liberty All-Star Equity Fund

Federal Reserve Plaza, 600 Atlantic Avenue, 24th Floor, Boston, MA 02210 **Category: Equity Fund**

Phone: 800-542-3863	**1991/mid-1992 Range of Premium/Disc:** +2% to -16%
Listed: USA, NYSE	**1991/mid-1992 Range of Price:** $11 1/2 to $7 3/8
Commenced Operations: November, 1986	**NAV Total Return 1990:** +1.98%; **1991:** +38.22%
Cusip: 530158104	**Share Price Total Return 1990:** +4.85%; **1991:** +51.87%
	Herzfeld Ranking 1991: 5th of 15 equity funds

Investment Objective: Total investment return, comprised of long-term capital appreciation and current income primarily though investment in a diversified portfolio of equity securities. The fund uses a multi-manager approach, with 5 investment managers currently managing the portfolio.

Officers:

R.I. Roberts   President

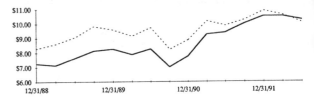

Investment Advisor: Liberty Asset Management Company

Advisory Fee: Annual fee of 0.80% of average weekly net assets up to $400 mil. and 0.72% on any excess. Fee for year-ended 12/31/91 was $4,152,182.

Portfolio Managers' Fees: (Paid by investment advisor from advisory fee) Annual fee of 0.40% of average weekly net assets up to $400 mil., and 0.36% on any excess.

Administrator: Liberty Asset Management Company

Administration Fee: Annual fee of 0.20% of average weekly net assets up to $400 mil., and 0.18% of any excess. Fee for year-ended 12/31/91 was $1,054,978.

Capital Structure: *Common stock:* 56,410,000 shares authorized; 54,641,672 shares outstanding 3/31/92

Portfolio Highlights (as of 3/31/92): Common stocks 97.1%, commercial paper 1.8%, U.S. government securities 1.5%, repurchase agreements 1.5%, other assets and liabilities (2.0%). Largest industry concentrations: drugs & health care 14.0%, retail trade 9.3%, computers & business equipment 7.2%, insurance 6.3%, oil & gas 6.3%.

Largest positions: Philip Morris Companies Inc. 2.3%, Home Depot Inc. 2.2%, Wal-Mart Stores Inc. 2.0%, Royal Dutch Petroleum Co. 1.9%, Exxon Corp. 1.9%.

Historical Financial Statistics (fiscal year-end: 12/31/91):

	1991	1990	1989	1988	1987	11/3/86 to 12/31/86
Value of net assets (000)	601,219	478,715	514,173	444,796	423,821	552,939
NAV	11.20	8.92	9.58	8.29	7.90	9.80
Net investment income	0.17	0.18	0.19	0.16	0.08	0.03
Dividends from net investment income	0.15	0.20	0.20	0.16	0.15	--
Distributions from net realized gains	0.87	0.47	0.31	--	0.65	--
Distributions from paid-in capital	--	0.23	0.44	0.48	0.38	--
Operating & management expense ratio	1.16%	1.23%	1.25%	1.33%	1.92%	2.77% ann.
Income ratio	1.66%	1.98%	2.07%	1.96%	0.80%	1.81% ann.
Portfolio turnover	72.12%	67.57%	69.89%	72.58%	72.48%	0%

Special considerations: The fund has a policy to distribute 10% of net asset value annually, payable quarterly at a rate of 2 1/2%. The fund may repurchase shares when the fund trades at a 10% or greater discount to net asset value. The fund's Declaration of Trust contains various anti-takeover provisions. In 1993 a vote will be taken regarding open-ending the fund. A shareholder proposal to replace Liberty Asset Management with The Vanguard Group was defeated. As part of the settlement of a lawsuit, the fund will rebate some of its management fee. During 1992 the fund had a rights offering, allowing shareholders to subscribe for one additional share for every 10 shares held. A total of 5,464,168 shares were subscribed for at a price of $10.05 per share. **Shareholders over 5%:** Liberty Mutual Insurance Company and Liberty Mutual Fire Insurance Company, 12.7%

Liberty Term Trust, Inc.--1999

Federated Investors Tower, Pittsburgh, PA 15222

Category: Bond Fund

Phone: 412-288-1900	**1991/mid-1992 Range of Premium/Disc**: +7% to 0%
Listed: LTT, NYSE	**1991/mid-1992 Range of Price**: $10 1/4 to $9 1/2
Commenced Operations: March, 1992	**NAV Total Return 1991**: N/A
Cusip: 531282101	**Share Price Total Return 1991**: N/A
	Herzfeld Ranking 1991: N/A

Investment Objective: To return at least $10 per share to investors on or shortly before 12/31/99 while providing high monthly income. The trust invests in high-quality debt securities, primarily mortgage-backed securities issued or guaranteed by the U.S. government, its agencies or instrumentalities.

Officers:

J.F. Donahue	Chairman
R.B. Fisher	President

Investment Advisor: Federated Advisers Co.

Advisory Fee: Weekly fee based on the trust's average weekly net asset value, computed at the per annum rate of 0.50% of the trust average weekly net asset value through 12/31/93, and 0.45% from that date until termination of the trust.

Administrator: Federated Administrative Services, Inc.

Administration Fee: The trust will reimburse the administrator for the approximate cost of the administrative services provided by it to the trust.

Capital Structure: *Common stock*: 1 bil. shares authorized, 5 mil. shares outstanding 3/27/92.

Portfolio Highlights (as of 5/31/92): Municipal bonds 4.22%, U.S. treasury notes 18.61%, fixed rate mortgage-backed securities 58.19%, Floating Rate Mortgage-Backed securities 18.98%.

Historical Financial Statistics:

	3/27/92
Value of net assets (000)	47,500
NAV	9.50

Special considerations: The trust may use various investments techniques designed to hedge interest rate risk (short sales, selling covered call options, mortgage dollar rolls, etc.) The fund will make monthly distributions of net investment income starting June, 1992, including all or a portion of net short-term capital gains, and annual distributions of net long-term capital gains. The trust currently intends to retain, until the final liquidating distribution, the tax-exempt income attributable to its investment in municipal securities, but in no event greater than 10% of the trust's income per year. The Board of Directors may consider tender offers and open market share repurchases to seek to reduce discounts to trust's net asset value, which may develop. The fund's Articles of Incorporation and By-Laws contain various anti-takeover provisions including a 75% vote to remove a director or convert to an open-end fund. S&P assigned a AAAf rating to the fund, the highest rating available. Initial dividend rate $0.05 per month, May, 1992 dividend $0.068 per share.

Lincoln National Convertible Securities Fund, Inc.

1300 South Clinton Street, Fort Wayne, IN 46801

Category: Convertible Fund

Phone: 219-455-2210
Listed: LNV, NYSE
Commenced Operations: June, 1986
Cusip: 534183108

1991/mid-1992 Range of Premium/Disc: -6% to -16%
1991/mid-1992 Range of Price: $17 3/8 to $11 1/2
NAV Total Return 1990: -4.14%; **1991:** +39.01%
Share Price Total Return 1990: -5.46%; **1991:** +40.04%
Herzfeld Ranking 1991: 2nd of 8 convertible funds

Investment Objective: High level of total return through both capital appreciation and current income, primarily through investment in convertible securities, including direct placement.

Officers:

C.G. Freund   Chairman
J.A. Boscia   President

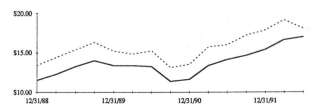

Investment Advisor: Lincoln National Investment Management Company
Sub-Advisor: Lynch & Mayer, Inc.
Advisory Fee: Quarterly fee at annual rate of 0.6% of average monthly net assets. If annual expenses (excluding taxes and interest) exceed 1.5% of average net assets up to $30 mil., the manager will reimburse the fund for the difference. Fee for year-ended 12/31/91 was $619,993.

Capital Structure: *Common stock*: 20 mil. shares authorized; 6,286,361 shares outstanding 12/31/92

Portfolio Highlights (as of 3/31/92): Public debt securities 41.9%, direct placement securities 17.5%, convertible preferred stocks 8.1%, common stock and warrants-public issues 5.2%, short-term investments 3.1%, excess of other assets over liabilities 1.2%. Largest industry concentrations: automotive 14.5%, banking 12.5%, electronics 6.1%. **Largest Issuers:** Tyco Toys Inc., Magna International Inc., International Shipholding Corporation, Ford Motor Company, CUC International Inc.

Historical Financial Statistics (fiscal year-end: 12/31/91):

	1991	1990	1989	1988	1987	6/26/86 to 12/31/86
Value of net assets (000)	113,398	85,434	95,656	91,607	87,304	99,460
NAV	18.04	13.59	15.21	13.41	12.62	14.38
Net investment income	0.97	1.03	1.53	0.95	0.92	0.43
Dividends from net investment income	1.02	1.02	1.07	0.95	1.13	0.20
Distributions from net realized gains	--	--	0.50	--	--	--
Operating expense ratio	0.89%	0.97%	0.94%	0.96%	0.88%	0.38%
Income ratio	5.96%	7.21%	6.64%	6.90%	6.43%	3.08%
Portfolio turnover	132.99%	134.64%	147.31%	110.70%	73.41%	34.00%

Special considerations: The fund may borrow to invest in securities for possible capital appreciation. It may also issue commercial paper, bonds, debentures or notes as determined by the Board of Directors. At the upcoming annual meeting, the shareholders will vote on a shareholder proposal by Grace Brothers, Ltd. to urge the board to take steps necessary for shareholders to receive full net asset value. The actions proposed include but are not limited to: liquidating the fund, open-ending the fund, or merging with an open-end fund. The fund retained a portion of the taxable long-term capital gains in 1989 in the amount of $0.4258 per share for the year-ended 12/31/89. Shareholders were able to take a credit on their 1989 tax returns equivalent to $0.1448 per share. There were no retained capital gains in 1990. The fund retained a portion of the taxable long-term capital gains in 1991 in the amount of $0.3832 per share for the year-ended 12/31/91. Shareholders were able to take a credit on their 1991 tax returns equivalent to $0.1303 per share.

Lincoln National Income Fund, Inc.

(formerly Lincoln National Direct Placement Fund)
1300 South Clinton Street, Fort Wayne, IN 46801

Category: Bond Fund

Phone: 219-455-2210
Listed: LND, NYSE
Commenced Operations: 1972
Cusip: 534217104

1991/mid-1992 Range of Premium/Disc: 0% to -11%
1991/mid-1992 Range of Price: $29 1/4 to $23 3/4
NAV Total Return 1990: +0.66%; **1991:** +19.54%
Share Price Total Return 1990: +1.35%; **1991:** +25.30%
Herzfeld Ranking 1991: 43rd of 80 bond funds

Investment Objective: High level of current income from interest on fixed-income securities, with a secondary objective of additional income through capital appreciation.

Officers:

J.A. Boscia   President

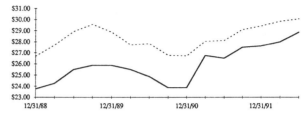

Investment Advisor: Lincoln National Investment Management Company

Advisory Fee: Quarterly fee of 0.125% of net asset value on the last day of the quarter (0.5% annual rate), plus 1.5% of net cash dividends and interest earned. If certain expenses exceed 1.5% of average net assets up to $30 mil., or 1.0% of excess, the manager will reimburse the fund for the excess. Fee for year-ended 12/31/91 was $447,714.

Capital Structure:

Common stock: 10 mil. shares authorized; 2,449,853 shares outstanding 3/31/92
Debt: Term loan of $5 mil. with Morgan Guaranty Trust Company of New York, interest rate 5.21% as of 12/31/91.

Portfolio Highlights (as of 3/31/92): Public debt securities 84.9%, direct placement securities 12.5%, common stocks-public issues 2.4%, convertible preferred stocks-public issues 3.6%, short-term investments 1.4%, excess of liabilities over other assets (54.8%). Largest industry concentrations: finance 23.5%, public utility 16.3%, energy 10.6%, government/government agency 10.1%, banking 6.4%, transportation 5.2%. **Largest positions:** Federal National Mortgage Association, Dow Chemical Company, International Shipholding Corporation, NCNB Corp., Transamerica Financial Corporation. Quality ratings (as of 12/31/91): direct placement equities & short-term 20.0%, Aaa 19.3%, Aa 12.0%, A 19.8%, Baa 20.9%, Ba 3.1%, B 4.9%.

Historical Financial Statistics (fiscal year-end: 12/31/91):

	1991	1990	1989	1988	1987	1986
Value of net assets (000)	72,752	65,652	70,598	65,383	62,870	67,031
NAV	29.70	26.80	28.88	26.69	25.66	27.36
Net investment income	2.29	2.34	2.31	2.32	2.41	2.41
Dividends from net investment income	2.29	2.35	2.32	2.31	3.04	2.34
Distributions from net realized gains	--	--	0.02	0.15	--	--
Operating expense ratio	0.97%	0.97%	0.96%	0.97%	0.93%	0.91%
Income ratio	8.05%	8.49%	8.04%	8.43%	8.93%	8.90%
Portfolio turnover	15.07%	28.85%	44.46%	62.69%	46.71%	29.68%

Special considerations: The fund may borrow up to 20% of net assets to purchase securities. The fund retained a portion of the taxable long-term capital gains in 1989 in the amount of $0.1063 per share for the year-ended 12/31/89. Shareholders were able to take a credit on their 1989 tax returns equivalent to $0.0361 per share. There were no retained long-term capital gains in 1990 or 1991. Shareholders approved the issuance of preferred shares at the April, 1992 annual meeting.

The Malaysia Fund, Inc.

1221 Avenue of the Americas, New York, NY 10020

Category: Foreign Equity Fund

Phone: 215-669-8503; 800-221-6726
Listed: MF, NYSE
Commenced Operations: May, 1987
Cusip: 560905101

1991/mid-1992 Range of Premium/Disc: +13% to -17%
1991/mid-1992 Range of Price: $14 7/8 to $10 1/8
NAV Total Return 1990: -8.56%; **1991:** +9.20%
Share Price Total Return 1990: -40.21%; **1991:** +7.45%
Herzfeld Ranking 1991: 25th of 46 foreign equity funds

Investment Objective: Long-term capital appreciation through investment in equity securities of Malaysian companies.

Officers:

R.A. Debs   Chairman
W.J. Olsen   President & Secretary

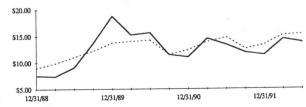

Investment Advisor: Morgan Stanley Asset Management, Inc.
Advisory Fee: Monthly fee at annual rate of 0.90% on first $50 mil. of average weekly net assets, 0.70% of next $50 mil., 0.50% on excess. Fee for year-ended 12/31/91 was $781,000.
Sub-Advisor: Arab-Malaysian Consultant Sdn Bhd
Sub-Advisory Fee: Monthly fee at annual rate of 0.25% on first $50 mil. of average weekly net assets, 0.15% of excess. Fee for year-ended 12/31/91 was $196,000.
Administrator: The Vanguard Group, Inc.
Administration Fee: Quarterly fee at annual rate of 0.20% on first $50 mil. of average weekly net assets, 0.15% on next $50 mil., 0.10% on excess. Fee for year-ended 12/31/91 was $171,000.

Capital Structure: *Common stock:* 20 mil. shares authorized; 7,259,336 shares outstanding 3/31/92

Portfolio Highlights (as of 3/31/92): Malaysia common stocks 94.8%, foreign currency on deposit 3.9%, temporary cash investment 0.8%, other assets & liabilities 0.5%. Largest sector concentrations: commercial & industrial 68.2%, finance companies 10.8%, palm oil plantations 4.2%. **Largest positions:** Genting Bhd, Malaysia International Shipping Bhd, Sime Darby Bhd, Malayan Banking Bhd, Telekom Malaysia.

Historical Financial Statistics (fiscal year-end: 12/31/91):

	1991	1990	1989	1988	5/4/87 to 12/31/87
Value of net assets (000)	98,338	90,104	99,942	65,186	53,831
NAV	13.55	12.41	13.77	8.98	7.42
Net investment income	0.10	0.14	0.10	0.20	0.16
Dividends from net investment income	0.07	0.21	0.11	0.17	0.15
Expense ratio	1.70%	1.93%	1.95%	2.29%	1.80% ann.
Income ratio	0.77%	1.07%	0.88%	2.30%	2.43% ann.
Portfolio turnover	14.9%	17.8%	30.2%	13.68%	4.77% ann.

Special considerations: At last year's annual meeting the authorized number of shares was increased from 10 mil. to 20 mil. At 12/31/91 the fund had net capital loss carryforward of approximately $194,000 expiring through 1997.
Shareholders over 5%: Fiduciary Trust Company International, 6.92%; United Nations Joint Staff Pension Fund, 6.88%

MassMutual Corporate Investors

1295 State Street, Springfield, MA 01111

Category: Bond Fund

Phone: 413-788-8411	**1991/mid-1992 Range of Premium/Disc:** +1% to -21%
Listed: MCI, NYSE	**1991/mid-1992 Range of Price:** $29 5/8 to $20 3/8
Commenced Operations: September, 1971	**NAV Total Return 1990:** +0.20%; **1991:** +17.99%
Cusip: 576292106	**Share Price Total Return 1990:** -4.28%; **1991:** +44.94%
	Herzfeld Ranking 1991: 53rd of 80 bond funds

Investment Objective: Current income and an opportunity for capital gains primarily through investment in long-term corporate debt obligations with equity features purchased directly from issuers.

Officers:

R.G. Dooley   Chairman
G.E. Wendlandt   President

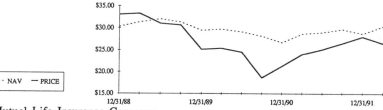

Investment Advisor: Massachusetts Mutual Life Insurance Company

Advisory Fee: Quarterly fee of 5/16 of 1% of net assets, equal to approximately 1.25% annually with a performance adjustment of up to 0.25% annually. Fee for year-ended 12/31/91 was $1,236,105.

Capital Structure: *Shares of beneficial interest:* unlimited number of shares authorized; 4,256,724 shares outstanding 12/31/91

Senior Floating Rate Convertible Notes: $20 mil. of notes due 5/15/95. Interest on notes are adjusted quarterly to a rate equal to 0.65% over the bond equivalent of the three month U.S. treasury bill rate subject to a maximum annual rate of 15% and minimum of 7%. Notes were at a rate of 7.00% on 12/31/91

Portfolio Highlights (as of 3/31/92): Restricted securities 60.4%: straight debt 33.5%, convertible debt 20.0%, equity issues 6.9%; public securities 39.6%: corporate bonds 22.7%, short-term 7.5%, equity issues 5.7%, convertible bonds 3.7%. Largest industry concentrations: electrical equipment/electronics 8.18%, manufacturing/industrial and consumer products 7.59%, retailing 6.48%, auto parts 6.44%, services 6.32%, health care 5.87%. **Largest issuers:** DeVry Inc./Keller Graduate School of Management Inc., Nichols Institute, Stuart Hall Company Inc., American Exploration Company, Davis Wire Corporation.

Historical Financial Statistics (fiscal year-end: 12/31/91):

	1991	1990	1989	1988	1987	six months 12/31/86
Value of net assets (000)	122,326	113,797	125,443	127,844	129,494	142,545
NAV	28.74	26.73	29.47	30.29	31.16	34.77
Net investment income	2.79	2.69	2.77	3.09	3.00	1.43
Dividends from net investment income	2.80	2.64	2.77	3.11	4.31	1.43
Distributions from net realized gains	--	0.16	0.53	0.71	0.29	0.51
Expense ratio	2.77%	2.90%	2.70%	2.43%	1.95%	1.05%
Income ratio	9.70%	9.33%	8.90%	9.87%	8.77%	9.25%
Portfolio turnover	45.96%	23.74%	20.00%	28.18%	39.95%	31.26%

Special considerations: Massachusetts Mutual Life Insurance Company invests concurrently with the trust in private placements; as of 12/31/91, private placements comprised 63.0% of the trust's portfolio. The fund retained a portion of the taxable long-term capital gains in the amount of $0.2303 per share for the year-ended 12/31/90. Shareholders were able to take a credit on their 1990 tax returns equivalent to $0.0783 per share. No capital gains were retained in 1991. As of 12/31/91 the fund had a capital loss carryforward of $162,377 expiring through 1999. Management announced in April, 1992, that the dividend rate could be reduced as "the current dividend level is probably not sustainable."

MassMutual Participation Investors

1295 State Street, Springfield, MA 01111

Category: Bond Fund

Phone: 413-788-8411
Listed: MPV, NYSE
Commenced Operations: October, 1988
Cusip: 576299101

1991/mid-1992 Range of Premium/Disc: +2% to -24%
1991/mid-1992 Range of Price: $9 to $6 3/8
NAV Total Return 1990: +0.33%; **1991:** +14.66%
Share Price Total Return 1990: -9.03%; **1991:** +43.47%
Herzfeld Ranking 1991: 72nd of 80 bond funds

Investment Objective: Maximum total return by providing a high level of income, the potential for growth of such income and capital appreciation primarily through investment in privately placed fixed-income securities, at least half of which include equity features.

Officers:

R.G. Dooley   Chairman
G.E. Wendlandt   President

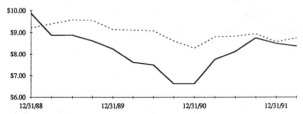

Investment Advisor: Massachusetts Mutual Life Insurance Company
Administrator: Massachusetts Mutual Life Insurance Company
Advisory and Administration Fee: Quarterly fee equal to 0.225% of net assets as of the last business day of each fiscal quarter, equal to about 0.90% annually. Fee for year-ended 12/31/91 was $724,581.
Sub-Administrator: Dean Witter Reynolds
Sub-Administration Fee: Quarterly fee paid by Massachusetts Mutual Life Insurance of 0.15% of net assets.

Capital Structure: *Shares of beneficial interest*: unlimited number of shares authorized; 9,181,705 shares outstanding 12/31/91

Portfolio Highlights (as of 3/31/92): Restricted securities 68.0%, public securities 32.0%. Straight debt 47.1%, debt with warrants 13.7%, convertible bonds 12.0%, corporate bonds 10.4%, convertible debt 5.1%, equity issues 6.7%, short-term 5.0%. Largest industry concentrations: retailing 12.88%, manufacturing 10.37%, electrical equipment/electronics 6.37%, oil and gas service 5.47%, . **Largest issuers:** Super Rite Food, Inc., Intelligent Electronics, Telex Communications Inc., A.T.-Sentinel Inc., J. Baker Inc., J. Baker Inc. The overall credit quality of the portfolio (as of 12/31/91) included 57.7% of investment grade securities. Weighted average maturity of fixed income issues was 6.83 years.

Historical Financial Statistics (fiscal year-end: 12/31/91):

	1991	1990	1989	10/6/88 to 12/31/88
Value of net assets (000)	78,763	75,821	83,584	84,149
NAV	8.58	8.29	9.14	9.21
Net investment income	0.82	0.87	0.86	0.12
Dividends from net investment income	0.82	0.88	0.84	0.12
Distributions from net realized gains	0.06	--	0.04	0.02
Expense ratio	1.28%	1.23%	1.27%	0.27%
Income ratio	9.50%	9.79%	9.18%	1.73%
Portfolio turnover	32.98%	16.25%	77.84%	27.96%

Special considerations: Massachusetts Mutual Life Insurance Company invests concurrently with the trust in private placements; as of 12/31/91 private placements comprised 69.4% of the fund's portfolio. The trust retained a portion of the taxable long-term capital gains in 1989 in the amount of $0.0339 per share, shareholders were able to take a credit on their 1989 tax returns equivalent to $0.0115 per share. The trust retained no capital gains in 1990 or 1991. At 12/31/91 the trust had a capital loss carryforward of $323,339 expiring through 1998. Management announced in April, 1992, that the dividend rate could be reduced as "the current dividend level is probably not sustainable."

The Mexico Equity and Income Fund, Inc.

200 Liberty Street, New York, NY 10291

Category: Foreign Equity Fund

Phone: 212-667-5018
Listed: MXE, NYSE
Commenced Operations: August, 1990
Cusip: 592834105

1991/mid-1992 Range of Premium/Disc: +20% to -21%
1991/mid-1992 Range of Price: $21 7/8 to $9 1/8
NAV Total Return 1991: +43.84%
Share Price Total Return 1991: +40.20%
Herzfeld Ranking 1991: 7th of 46 foreign equity funds

Investment Objective: High total return from capital appreciation and current income primarily through investment in convertible debt securities issued by Mexican companies.

Officers:

A.S. Fernandez   Chairman
A. Rappaport   President

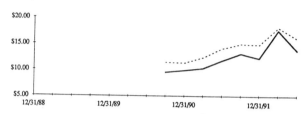

Mexican Investment Advisor: Acci Worldwide S.A. de C.V.
Advisory Fee: Monthly fee at annual rate of 0.60% of average monthly net assets. Fee for six months ended 1/31/92 was $435,288.
U.S. Co-Advisor: Advantage Advisers, Inc.
Co-Advisory Fee: Monthly fee at annual rate of 0.40% of average monthly net assets.
Administrator: Oppenheimer & Co., Inc.; sub-advisor: Provident Financial Processing Corporation
Administration Fee: Monthly fee at annual rate of 0.20% of average monthly net assets. Fee for six months ended 1/31/92 was $97,161.

Capital Structure: *Common stock:* 100 mil. shares authorized, 6,311,792 shares outstanding 1/31/92

Portfolio Highlights (as of 1/31/92): Common stock 65.6%, government bonds 19.0%, promissory notes 3.3%, Mexican convertible debt 11.5%, U.S. money market funds 0.3%, other assets in excess of liabilities 0.3%.
Largest positions: various Cetes (Mexican government bonds); Teléfonos de México S.A. de C.V.; Cifra S.A. de C.V.; Apasco S.A. de C.V. 9.63-97; Kimberly Clark de Mexico S.A. de C.V.

Historical Financial Statistics (fiscal year-end: 7/31/91):

	six months 1/31/92	8/21/90 to 7/31/91
Value of net assets (000)	102,481	94,741
NAV	16.24	15.08
Net investment income	0.36	1.13
Dividends from net investment income	0.96	0.58
Dividends from capital gains	0.01	--
Expense ratio	1.57% ann.	1.98% ann.
Income ratio	4.61% ann.	9.71% ann.
Portfolio turnover	24.03%	8.65%

Special considerations: The fund annually distributes its investment company taxable income and determines annually whether to distribute any net realized long-term capital gains. The fund's Articles of Incorporation and by-laws contain various anti-takeover provisions, including a 75% vote to merge with another corporation or convert to an open-end fund.

The Mexico Fund, Inc.

77 Aristoteles Street, 3rd Floor, Polanco 11560 México DF Mexico

Category: Foreign Equity Fund

Phone: 212-750-4200; 525-280-1636 (Mexico); 212-440-9862
Listed: MXF, NYSE
Commenced Operations: June, 1981
Cusip: 592835102

1991/mid-1992 Range of Premium/Disc: +9% to -23% (adjusted for dilution)
1991/mid-1992 Range of Price: $34 to $11 7/8
NAV Total Return 1990: +28.02%; **1991:** +75.91%
Share Price Total Return 1990: +15.38%; **1991:** +79.98%
Herzfeld Ranking 1991: 5th of 46 foreign equity funds

Investment Objective: Long-term capital appreciation primarily through investment in equity securities listed on the Mexican Stock Exchange.

Officers:

J. Gallardo T. — Chairman
J.L. Gómez Pimienta — President

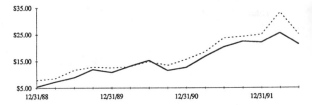

Investment Advisor: Impulsora del Fondo Mexico, S.A. de C.V.
Advisory Fee: Monthly fee at annual rate of 0.85% of first $200 mil. of average daily net assets, 0.70% of excess. Fee for year-ended 10/31/91 was $1,486,931.
Administrator (Trustee): Fiduciary Department of Nacional Financiera, S.N.C.
Administration Fee: Quarterly fee at annual rate of 0.25% of first $75 mil. average daily net assets and 0.20% of excess. Fee for year-ended 10/31/91 was $205,454.

Capital Structure: *Common stock:* 50 mil. shares authorized; 26,291,939 shares outstanding 4/92

Portfolio Highlights (as of 1/31/92): Common stock 97.15%, short-term securities 2.77%, other assets in excess of liabilities 0.08%. Largest industry concentrations: retail trade 19.80%, development companies 15.56%, construction 14.44%, communications 12.96%, banks 11.04%, consumer goods 9.56%, paper 6.09%. **Largest positions:** CIFRA S.A. de C.V., Teléfonos de México S.A. de C.V., Cemex S.A. Series A, Kimberly-Clark de México S.A. de C.V. Series A, Grupo Industrial Bimbo S.A. de C.V.

Historical Financial Statistics (fiscal year-end: 5/31/91):	eight months 1/31/92	1991	1990	1989	1988	1987
Value of net assets (000)	555,348	474,667	303,286	202,389	145,287	196,108
NAV	28.16	24.07	15.38	10.26	7.37	9.84
Net investment income (loss)	(0.01)	0.45	0.53	0.62	0.18	0.25
Dividends from net investment income	0.08	0.36	0.56	0.45	0.15	0.31
Dividend from net realized gains on investments	1.03	--	--	--	--	--
Operating expense ratio	1.22*	1.37%	1.60%	1.77%	1.74%	1.74%
Income ratio	(0.16%)*	2.75%	4.21%	7.81%	4.44%	4.77%
Portfolio turnover	32.59%*	12.53%	8.88%	10.54%	19.58%	34.83%

*quarter ended 1/31/92 annualized

Special considerations: This fund is listed on the New York Stock Exchange, the International Stock Market of the United Kingdom and the Republic of Ireland, Ltd., and on the Third Section of the Stuttgart Stock Exchange in West Germany. In 1989 shareholders voted to approve an amendment to the Articles of Incorporation limiting certain liabilities of directors and officers. The fund has a stock repurchase program. A rights offering in 1992 added 6.6 mil. shares to the capitalization and caused a real dilution to net asset value of approximately 0.73%. For comparison purposes, prices prior to the fund's rights offering in March - April, 1992 must be multiplied by 0.9167, NAV's must be multiplied by 0.89383. **Shareholders over 5%:** United Nations Joint Staff Pension Fund

MFS Charter Income Trust

500 Boylston Street, Boston, MA 02116

Category: Bond Fund

Phone: 617-954-5000
Listed: MCR, NYSE
Commenced Operations: July, 1989
Cusip: 552727109

1991/mid-1992 Range of Premium/Disc: +4% to -14%
1991/mid-1992 Range of Price: $11 to $8 5/8
NAV Total Return 1990: +4.23%; **1991**: +23.83%
Share Price Total Return 1990: +2.56%; **1991**: +30.69%
Herzfeld Ranking 1991: 27th of 80 bond funds

Investment Objective: Maximum current income through equal investment in the following three sectors of the fixed income securities markets: securities issued or guaranteed as to principal and interest by the U.S. government, its agencies, authorities or instrumentalities and related options; debt securities issued by foreign governments, their political subdivisions and other foreign issuers; and high yielding corporate fixed income securities.

Officers:

A.K. Brodkin   Chairman & President

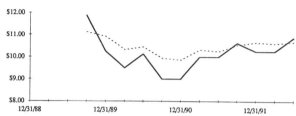

Investment Advisor: Massachusetts Financial Services Company

Advisory Fee (includes administration services): Fee at annual rate of 0.32% of average daily net assets plus 4.57% of gross income; total fee will not exceed 0.60% of average daily net assets. Fee for year-ended 11/30/91 was $7,509,320.

Capital Structure: *Shares of beneficial interest:* unlimited number of shares authorized; 87,226,000 shares outstanding 11/30/91
Debt: line of credit with a bank established on 9/29/89 and available to MFS funds allows the funds to borrow up to $300 mil. collectively. Commitment fee for 1991 was $16,505. No loan made during year-end 11/30/91.

Portfolio Highlights (as of 2/3/92): Foreign securities 31%, high-yield corporates 33%, U.S. treasury bonds 32%, short-term 4%. Foreign: Spain 8%, Australia 7%, Sweden 8%, Italy 5%, Canada 2%, Finland 1%. 47% of the U.S. treasuries had call options sold against them. Average maturity of the portfolio was 10.8 years. **Largest issuers** (as of 11/30/91): U.S. treasury; Government of Spain; Swedish Mortgage Bonds; RJR Nabisco, Government of Italy.

Historical Financial Statistics (fiscal year-end: 11/30/91):

	1991	1990	7/21/89 to 11/30/89
Value of net assets (000)	923,287	864,254	977,875
NAV	10.59	9.93	11.00
Net investment income	1.06	1.17	0.43
Dividends from net investment income	1.06	1.2243	0.378
Dividends from net realized gains	--	0.0703	--
Distributions from paid-in capital	0.44	0.2174	--
Expense ratio	1.02%	1.08%*	0.74% ann.*
Income ratio	10.34%	11.32%*	11.32% ann.*
Portfolio turnover	416%	184%	480% ann.

a portion of the advisory fee was waived

Special considerations: The trust may borrow money and issue senior securities. In June, 1990, the trustees announced a plan to repurchase up to 5% of the fund's shares when trading at a discount of at least 3% below net asset value. Under certain circumstances, during the third quarter of 1992 the fund will make a tender offer at net asset value; and in the third quarter of 1994, if certain conditions exist, the fund will submit an open-ending proposal at the 1995 annual meeting. A majority vote of shareholders would be required for open-ending at that time. The Declaration of Trust contains various anti-takeover provisions.

MFS Government Markets Income Trust

500 Boylston Street, Boston, MA 02116

Category: Bond Fund

Phone: 617-954-5000
Listed: MGF, NYSE
Commenced Operations: May, 1987
Cusip: 552939100

1991/mid-1992 Range of Premium/Disc: +9% to -7%
1991/mid-1992 Range of Price: $9 to $7
NAV Total Return 1990: +7.73%; **1991:** +12.34%
Share Price Total Return 1990: -8.34%; **1991:** +14.62%
Herzfeld Ranking 1991: 77th of 80 bond funds

Investment Objective: High current income primarily through investment in U.S. government securities and by engaging in transactions involving related options. Up to 40% of total assets may be invested in foreign government securities.

Officers:

A.K. Brodkin   Chairman & President

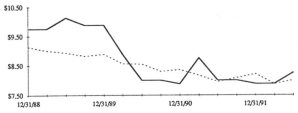

Investment Advisor: Massachusetts Financial Services Company
Advisory Fee (includes administration services): Monthly fee at annual rate of 0.32% of average daily net assets plus 5.33% of daily gross income. Fee for year-ended 11/30/91 was $6,511,018.

Capital Structure: *Shares of beneficial interest:* unlimited number of shares authorized; 97,303,000 shares outstanding 11/30/91
Debt: line of credit with a bank established on 9/29/89 and available to MFS funds allows the funds to borrow up to $300 mil. collectively. Commitment fee for 1991 was $10,991. No loan made during year-end 11/30/91

Portfolio Highlights (as of 11/30/91): Bonds 96.9%, call options written (0.1%), other assets less liabilities 3.2%. Portfolio breakdown: U.S. dollar denominated 63.1%, foreign non-U.S. dollar denominated 33.8%. **Largest Issuers:** U.S. treasury obligations; Government National Mortgage Association 9%/1997-2021; Government of Spain; Government of Canada 9.75-21; Tasmanian Public Finance Corp.

Historical Financial Statistics (fiscal year-end: 11/30/91):

	1991	1990	1989	1988	5/28/87 to 11/30/87
Value of net assets (000)	785,992	813,978	857,252	873,503	879,686
NAV	8.08	8.41	8.92	9.18	9.33
Net investment income	0.69	0.78	0.82	0.94	0.45
Dividends from net investment income	0.64	0.6769	0.83597	0.9085	0.4530
Distributions from net realized gains	--	--	--	0.2086	0.0370
Distributions from paid-in capital	0.54	0.4991	0.34207	0.0966	--
Expense ratio	1.04%	1.05%*	1.08%	1.11%	1.01% ann.
Income ratio	8.38%	9.16%*	9.23%	9.87%	9.91% ann.
Portfolio turnover	805%	535%	640%	307%	88%

*a portion of the advisory fee was waived

Special considerations: In June, 1990, the trustees announced a plan to repurchase up to 5% of the fund's shares when trading at a discount of at least 3% below net asset value. The program began in the third quarter of 1990. The fund's Declaration of Trust contains various anti-takeover provisions.

MFS Intermediate Income Trust

500 Boylston Street, Boston, MA 02116　　　　　　　　　**Category: Bond Fund**

Phone: 617-954-5000
Listed: MIN, NYSE
Commenced Operations: March, 1988
Cusip: 55273C107

1991/mid-1992 Range of Premium/Disc: +2% to -12%
1991/mid-1992 Range of Price: $9 to $7
NAV Total Return 1990: +6.64%; **1991:** +11.64%
Share Price Total Return 1990: +5.15%; **1991:** +16.52%
Herzfeld Ranking 1991: 79th of 80 bond funds

Investment Objective: Preservation of capital and high current income primarily through investment in U.S. and foreign government securities. Average maturity of portfolio will be approximately seven years or less.

Officers:

A.K. Brodkin　　　Chairman & President

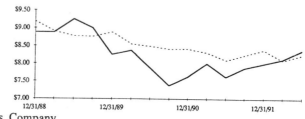

Investment Advisor: Massachusetts Financial Services Company
Advisory Fee (includes administration services): Monthly fee at annual rate of 0.32% of average daily net assets plus 5.65% of daily gross income. Fee for year-ended 10/31/91 was $13,817,006.

Capital Structure:　　*Shares of beneficial interest:* unlimited number of shares authorized; 199,553,000 shares outstanding 10/31/91
　　Debt: line of credit with a bank established on 9/29/89 and available to MFS funds allows the funds to borrow up to $300 mil. collectively. Commitment fee for 1991 was $39,798. No loan made during year-end 10/30/91

Portfolio Highlights (as of 10/31/91): Bonds 95.0%, short-term obligations 2.4%, call options written (0.2%), other assets less liabilities 2.8%. Portfolio breakdown: U.S. dollar denominated (treasury obligation 72.3%), foreign non-U.S. dollar denominated 23.7%. **Largest issuers:** U.S. treasury notes; Government of Spain; Swedish National Housing Finance Corporation; Government of Canada; South Australian Government Finance Authority.

Historical Financial Statistics (fiscal year-end: 10/31/91):

	1991	1990	1989	3/18/88 to 10/31/88
Value of net assets (000)	1,643,701	1,695,382	1,790,697	1,836,746
NAV	8.24	8.45	8.87	9.16
Net investment income	0.67	0.75	0.83	0.48
Dividends from net investment income	0.62	0.6263	0.919	0.3922
Distributions from paid-in capital	0.43	0.4237	0.1310	0.1328
Expense ratio	1.00%	1.01%*	1.10%	0.99% ann.
Income ratio	8.10%	8.74%*	9.34%	8.49% ann.
Portfolio turnover	1,004%	554%	546%	206%

*a portion of the advisory fee was waived

Special considerations: In June, 1990, the trustees announced a plan to repurchase up to 5% of the fund's shares when trading at a discount of at least 3% below net asset value. The program began in the third quarter of 1990. The fund's Declaration of Trust contains various anti-takeover provisions.

MFS Multimarket Income Trust

500 Boylston Street, Boston, MA 02116

Category: Bond Fund

Phone: 617-954-5000
Listed: MMT, NYSE
Commenced Operations: March, 1987
Cusip: 552737108

1991/mid-1992 Range of Premium/Disc: +10% to -11%
1991/mid-1992 Range of Price: $8 3/4 to $6 5/8
NAV Total Return 1990: +2.08%; **1991:** +22.18%
Share Price Total Return 1990: -7.37%; **1991:** +24.42%
Herzfeld Ranking 1991: 33rd of 80 bond funds

Investment Objective: High current income through investment in fixed income securities.

Officers:
A.K. Brodkin   Chairman & President

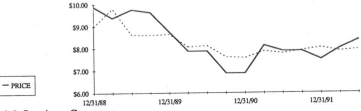

Investment Advisor: Massachusetts Financial Services Company
Advisory Fee (includes administration services): Monthly fee at annual rate of 0.34% of average daily net assets plus 5.4% of daily gross income. Fee for year-ended 10/31/91 was $8,576,469.

Capital Structure:

Shares of beneficial interest: unlimited number of shares authorized, 122,160,843 shares outstanding 10/31/91

Debt: line of credit with a bank established on 9/29/89 and available to MFS funds allows the funds to borrow up to $200 mil. collectively. Commitment fee for 1991 was $439,093. During the year-ended 10/31/91 the maximum amount outstanding was $90 mil. at a weighted average interest of 6.97%; no loan was outstanding on 10/31/91.

Portfolio Highlights (as of 10/31/91): Bonds 91.1%, preferred stocks 0.4%, repurchase agreement 7.6%, short-term obligation 1.9%, call options written (0.1%)., other assets less liabilities (0.9%). Portfolio breakdown: U.S. dollar denominated 69.3%, foreign non-U.S. dollar denominated 21.7%. **Largest issuers:** U.S. treasury notes; Swedish National Housing Finance Corp. 13-95; Government of Spain; RJR Nabisco Group; Government of Canada.

Historical Financial Statistics (fiscal year-end: 10/31/91):

	1991	1990	1989	1988	3/12/87 to 10/31/87
Value of net assets (000)	968,813	917,522	1,056,536	1,086,399	1,052,274
NAV	7.93	7.54	8.66	9.01	8.81
Net investment income	0.72	0.86	0.94	0.90	0.57
Dividends from net investment income	0.70	0.7949	1.113	0.0391	0.4593
Distributions from net realized gains	--	--	--	0.2893	0.1353
Distributions from paid-in capital	0.53	0.4351	0.1167	0.4909	0.0199
Expense ratio	1.11%*	1.19%*	1.23%	1.12%	1.08% ann.
Interest expense ratio	0.23%	0.45%	--	--	--
Income ratio	9.22%*	10.61%*	10.90%	9.96%	9.94% ann.
Portfolio turnover	740%	365%	423%	159%	58%

*a portion of the advisory fee was waived

Special considerations: In June, 1990, the trustees announced a plan to repurchase up to 5% of the fund's shares when trading at a discount of at least 3% below net asset value. The program began in the third quarter of 1990; 437,100 and 942,600 shares were purchased by the trust during the year-ended 10/31/91 and 10/31/90, respectively at an average discount of 8.51% and 10.67% per share. The fund's Declaration of Trust contains various anti-takeover provisions.

MFS Municipal Income Trust

500 Boylston Street, Boston, MA 02116   **Category: Municipal Bond Fund**

Phone: 617-954-5000
Listed: MFM, NYSE
Commenced Operations: November, 1986
Cusip: 552738106

1991/mid-1992 Range of Premium/Disc: +10% to -7%
1991/mid-1992 Range of Price: $9 3/4 to $8
NAV Total Return 1990: +2.51%; **1991:** +8.46%
Share Price Total Return 1990: -8.79%; **1991:** +14.64%
Herzfeld Ranking 1991: 47th of 51 municipal bond funds

Investment Objective: High current income exempt from federal income taxes through investment primarily in medium and lower quality municipal bonds and notes.

Officers:

R.B. Bailey   Chairman
A.K. Brodkin   President

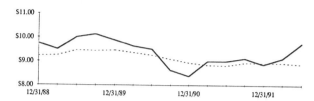

Investment Advisor: Massachusetts Financial Services Company

Advisory Fee (includes administration services): Monthly fee at annual rate of 0.40% of average weekly net assets and 6.32% of gross income. Fee for year-ended 10/31/91 was $3,140,757.

Capital Structure:

Shares of beneficial interest: unlimited number of shares authorized; 36,373,045 shares outstanding 10/31/91

Debt: line of credit with a bank established on 9/29/89 and available to MFS funds allows the funds to borrow up to $300 mil. collectively. Commitment fee allocated to the trust was $4,420. No loan made during year-end 10/31/91

Portfolio Highlights (as of 10/31/91): Municipal bonds 97.5%, other assets less liabilities 2.5%. Largest sector concentrations: health care revenue 30.3%, industrial revenue (corporate guarantee) 20.7%, single family mortgage revenue 15.2%, multi-family housing revenue 5.6%, airport and port revenue 5.3%. **Largest issuers:** Salt River Pima-Maricopa Indian Community, AZ (Phoenix Cement Co.) 10 3/4-07; East Chicago, IL, Pollution Control Rev. (Inland Steel Co.) 10-11; Dade County, FL, Housing Finance Authority 10 1/4-02; El Paso, TX, Industrial Development Authority (Popular Dry Goods Co.) 9 7/8-16; Maine Health & High Education Facilities Authority (D'Youville Pavillion) 10-17.

Historical Financial Statistics (fiscal year-end: 10/31/91):

	1991	1990	1989	1988	11/25/86 to 10/31/87
Value of net assets (000)	325,077	325,767	338,461	327,193	305,118
NAV	8.94	9.02	9.44	9.22	8.67
Net investment income	0.70	0.75	0.76	0.75	0.65
Dividends from net investment income	0.73	0.763	0.759	0.7440	0.5875
Expense ratio	1.27%	1.21%	1.28%	1.25%	1.04% ann.
Income ratio	7.79%	8.07%	8.15%	8.35%	7.62% ann.
Portfolio turnover	21%	19%	16%	37%	58%

The advisor waived $55,614 of the $3,195,514 fee during the year ended 10/31/88

Special considerations: In June, 1990, the trustees announced a plan to repurchase up to 5% of the fund's shares when trading at a discount of at least 3% below net asset value. The program began in the third quarter of 1990. The fund repurchased 48,800 shares during the year-ended 10/31/90 at a weighted average discount of 6.76%, and 6,700 shares during the year-ended 10/31/91 at a weighted average discount of 6.80%. Under normal conditions, the fund will invest at least 75% of assets in tax-exempt securities rated in the lower rating categories or unrated. The fund's Declaration of Trust contains various anti-takeover provisions.

MFS Special Value Trust

500 Boylston Street, Boston, MA 02116

Category: Bond Fund

Phone: 617-954-5000
Listed: MFV, NYSE
Commenced Operations: November, 1989
Cusip: 55274E102

1991/mid-1992 Range of Premium/Disc: +9% to -11%
1991/mid-1992 Range of Price: $16 3/8 to $10 5/8
NAV Total Return 1990: +0.53%; **1991**: +38.35%
Share Price Total Return 1990: -14.57%; **1991**: +54.60%
Herzfeld Ranking 1991: 15th of 80 bond funds

Investment Objective: Maintain an annual distributions rate of 11%, based on the original offering price ($15.00), while seeking opportunities for capital appreciation through investment in securities issued or guaranteed by the U.S. government, its agencies, authorities and instrumentalities and, when appropriate, related options.

Officers:

A.K. Brodkin   Chairman & President

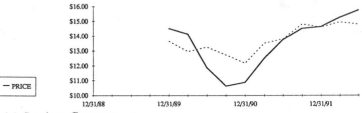

Investment Advisor: Massachusetts Financial Services Company
Advisory Fee (includes administration services): Monthly fee at annual rate of 0.68% of average daily net assets and 3.40% of daily gross income. Fee for year-ended 10/31/91 was $742,923.

Capital Structure:

Shares of beneficial interest: unlimited number of shares authorized; 5,770,555 shares outstanding 10/31/91
Debt: line of credit with a bank established on 9/29/89 and available to MFS funds allows the funds to borrow up to $300 mil. collectively. Commitment fee allocated to the trust was $1,373. No loan made during year-end 10/31/91

Portfolio Highlights (as of 10/31/91): Bonds 72.7%, common stocks 22.7%, repurchase agreement 3.9%, other assets less liabilities 0.7%. **Largest issuers**: U.S. treasury notes and bonds; Harcourt Brace Jovanovich, Inc. 14 3/4-02; Federated Department Stores Inc.; Goldriver Finance Corp. 13 7/8-97; Adams Russell Co. 16 3/4-97.

Historical Financial Statistics (fiscal year-end: 10/31/91):

	1991	1990
Value of net assets (000)	85,978	69,393
NAV	14.90	11.66
Net investment income	0.90	1.04
Dividends from net investment income	0.90	1.0373
Distributions from net realized gains	0.75	--
Distributions from paid-in capital	--	0.3377
Expense ratio	1.37%	1.40% ann.
Income ratio	7.97%	8.65% ann.
Portfolio turnover	327%	237%

Special considerations: Distributions are to be made monthly at 0.916% of the initial public offering price of $15.00. If the distributions can not be met from net investment income and short-term capital gains, the difference will be paid as a return of capital. An annual distribution of any excess income, short-term capital gains and long-term capital gains will be made. Under certain circumstances, during the fourth quarter of 1992, the fund will make a tender offer for all or a portion of outstanding shares at net asset value. In June, 1990, the trustees announced a plan to repurchase up to 5% of the fund's shares when trading at a discount of at least 3% below net asset value. The program began in the third quarter of 1990. 178,600 shares and 78,000 shares were repurchased by the trust during the years ended 10/31/91 and 10/31/90, respectively, at an average discount of 5.1% and 10.8% per share. The fund's Declaration of Trust contains various anti-takeover provisions.

Minnesota Municipal Term Trust Inc.

222 South Ninth Street, Minneapolis, MN 55502   **Category: Municipal Bond Fund**

Phone: 800-333-6000 (x6387)	**1991/mid-1992 Range of Premium/Disc**: +11% to -1%
Listed: MNA, NYSE	**1991/mid-1992 Range of Price**: $10 7/8 to $9 1/2
Commenced Operations: September, 1991	**NAV Total Return 1991**: N/A
Cusip: 604065102	**Share Price Total Return 1991**: N/A
	Herzfeld Ranking 1991: N/A

Investment Objective: High current income exempt from both regular federal income tax and State of Minnesota personal income tax and return of $10 per share to the holders of common stock outstanding upon termination of the Trust, expected to occur on or shortly before 4/15/02 (although termination may be extended to a date no later than 4/15/07). The trust will invest in investment grade, tax-exempt Minnesota Municipal Obligations, including Municipal Zero Coupon Securities. At least 65% of total assets will be invested in municipal obligations rated A or better.

Officers:

E.J. Kohler   Chairman
R.R. Reuss   President

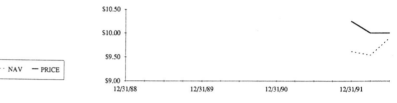

Investment Advisor: Piper Capital Management Incorporated
Advisory Fee: Monthly fee at the annual rate of 0.25% of average weekly net assets. Fee for period 9/26/91 to 12/31/91 was $42,974.
Administrator: Piper Capital Management Incorporated
Administration Fee: Monthly fee at the annual rate of 0.15% of average weekly net assets. Fee for period 9/26/91 to 12/31/91 was $25,784.

Capital Structure: *Common stock*: 200 mil. shares authorized, 5,732,710 outstanding 12/31/91
Remarketed preferred stock: 1 mil. shares authorized, 576 shares outstanding 12/31/91 with liquidation preference of $50,000. The dividend rate is adjusted every seven days as determined by the remarketing agent; rate on 12/31/91 was 5.10%.

Portfolio Highlights (3/31/92): Fixed-rate Minnesota municipals 92.9%, Minnesota municipal zeros 7.1%. Quality ratings: AAA 40.0%, AA 28.7%, A 30.3%, BBB 1.0%. Implied duration, 7.9 years. Call protection extends to nearly the expected life of the fund. **Largest issuers** (as of 12/31/91): Minnesota PFA Water Revenue; St. Louis Park Hospital Facilities 7.25-15; Minnesota State general obligations; Minneapolis Multi-Family, Churchill Apts. 7.05-22; Northern Municipal Power.

Historical Financial Statistics (fiscal year-end: 12/31/91):

	9/26/91 to 12/31/91
Value of net assets (000)	84,304
NAV	9.68
Net investment income	0.17
Dividends from net investment income to common shareholders	0.10
Dividends from net investment income to preferred shareholders	0.02
Expense ratio	0.55% ann.
Income ratio	5.66% ann.
Portfolio turnover	23%

Special considerations: Standard & Poor's has rated the fund A$_f$. The fund makes monthly distributions of net investment income and annual distributions of net realized capital gains. The Board of Directors will quarterly consider making tender offers or repurchasing shares in the open market to reduce discounts from net asset value which may develop. As of 12/31/91 the fund had a capital loss carryover of $22,292 expiring in 1999.

Minnesota Municipal Term Trust Inc.--II

222 South Ninth Street, Minneapolis, MN 55502

Category: Municipal Bond Fund

Phone: 800-333-6000 (x6387)	**1991/mid-1992 Range of Premium/Disc:** +9% to +2%
Listed: MNB, NYSE	**1991/mid-1992 Range of Price:** $10 1/8 to $9 7/8
Commenced Operations: April, 1992	**NAV Total Return 1991:** N/A
Cusip: 604066100	**Share Price Total Return 1991:** N/A
	Herzfeld Ranking 1991: N/A

Investment Objective: High current income exempt from both regular federal income tax and State of Minnesota personal income tax and return of $10 per share to the holders of common stock outstanding upon termination of the Trust, expected to occur on or shortly before 4/15/03 (although termination may be extended to a date no later than 4/15/08). The trust will invest in investment grade, tax-exempt Minnesota Municipal Obligations, including Municipal Zero Coupon Securities. At least 65% of total assets will be invested in municipal obligations rated A or better.

Officers:

E.J. Kohler	Chairman
R.R. Reuss	President

Investment Advisor: Piper Capital Management Incorporated
Advisory Fee: Monthly fee at the annual rate of 0.25% of average weekly net assets.
Administrator: Piper Capital Management Incorporated
Administration Fee: Monthly fee at the annual rate of 0.15% of average weekly net assets.

Capital Structure: *Common stock:* 200 mil. shares authorized, 3,011,000 outstanding
Preferred Stock: 1 mil. shares authorized, within 12 months of common stock offering, the trust intends to offer preferred stock representing in the aggregate up to 35% of the trust's capital after the preferred stock issuance.

Portfolio Highlights: not yet published

Historical Financial Statistics:

	4/30/92
Value of net assets (000)	28,362
NAV	9.42

Special considerations: The fund will make monthly distributions of net investment income and will make annual distributions of net realized capital gains. The Board of Directors will quarterly consider making tender offers or repurchasing shares in the open market to reduce discounts from net asset value which may develop.

Montgomery Street Income Securities, Inc.

101 California St., Suite 4100, San Francisco, CA 94111

Category: Bond Fund

Phone: 415-981-8191
Listed: MTS, NYSE
Commenced Operations: February, 1973
Cusip: 614115103

1991/mid-1992 Range of Premium/Disc: +11% o -3%
1991/mid-1992 Range of Price: $20 7/8 to $17
NAV Total Return 1990: +5.51%; **1991:** +21.54%
Share Price Total Return 1990: +6.00%; **1991:** +20.48%
Herzfeld Ranking 1991: 36th of 80 bond funds

Investment Objective: As high a level of current income as is consistent with prudent investment risks from a diversified portfolio primarily of debt securities; secondary objective is capital appreciation.

Officers:

J.C. Van Horne   Chairman
J.T. Packard   President

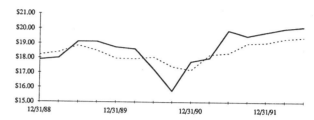

Investment Advisor: Scudder, Stevens & Clark Inc.

Advisory Fee: Monthly fee at annual rate of 0.50% of first $150 mil. of net assets and 0.45% of excess. This agreement began October, 1988, and for the first, second and third years, 75%, 50%, and 25%, respectively, of the fee will not be imposed. Fee for year-ended 12/31/91 was $607,597.

Capital Structure: *Common stock*: 15 mil. shares authorized; 8,193,386 shares outstanding 12/31/91

Portfolio Highlights (as of 12/31/91): Long-term bonds 79.8%, intermediate bonds 16.5%, short-term investments 1.7%, other assets and liabilities 2.0%. Largest sector concentrations: financial 27.3%, utilities 18.5%, U.S. treasury & agency 14.2%, consumer non-durables 7.6%. **Largest issuers:** Federal National Mortgage Association; Federal Home Loan Mortgage Corp.; Government National Mortgage Association II; GG1A Funding Corp. secured lease obligation bond 11.5-14; Ryland Acceptance Corp. REMIC series 97, collateralized mortgage bond floating rate 15.912-21.

Historical Financial Statistics (fiscal year-end: 12/31/91):

	1991	1990	1989	1988	1987	1986
Value of net assets (000)	157,060	139,844	144,776	145,772	147,639	159,504
NAV	19.17	17.21	17.97	18.21	18.44	19.93
Net investment income	1.75	1.79	1.84	1.87	1.94	1.98
Dividends from net						
investment income	1.76	1.78	1.85	1.84	2.14	2.00
Operating expense ratio	0.69%	0.57%	0.52%	0.86%	0.80%	0.82%
Income ratio	9.60%	10.20%	10.00%	9.98%	10.13%	10.02%
Portfolio turnover	72.0%	69.1%	97.08%	160.0%	57.7%	76.5%

Special considerations: Scudder, Stevens & Clark became investment advisor to the fund in October, 1988. The fund may invest up to 15% of total assets in privately placed debt. A rights offering allowing shareholders to purchase one additional share of common stock for every five shares owned expired on May 18, 1992, subscription price was 10% the average net asset value following the expiration of the offering; $17.42 per share. As of 12/31/91 the fund had a capital loss carryforward of approximately $18,781,587 available through 1999.

Morgan Grenfell SMALLCap Fund, Inc.

855 Third Avenue, Ste. 1740, New York, NY 10022   **Category: Specialized Equity Fund**

Phone: 212-230-2600
Listed: MGC, NYSE
Commenced Operations: May, 1987
Cusip: 617357108

1991/mid-1992 Range of Premium/Disc: +12% to -11%
1991/mid-1992 Range of Price: $14 1/4 to $8 1/4
NAV Total Return 1990: -14.17%; **1991:** +56.61%
Share Price Total Return 1990: -2.34%; **1991:** +58.23%
Herzfeld Ranking 1991: 3rd of 18 specialized equity funds

Investment Objective: Long-term capital appreciation principally by investment in common stocks and securities convertible into common stock; secondary investment objective is current income.

Officers:

M. Bullock	Chairman
R.E. Kern, Jr.	President

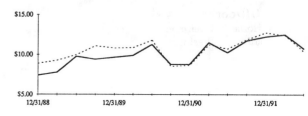

Investment Advisor: Morgan Grenfell Capital Management
Advisory Fee: Fee at annual rate of 1% of average daily net assets. Fee for year-ended 12/31/91 was $590,802.

Capital Structure: *Common stock:* 150 mil. shares authorized; 5,240,424 shares outstanding 12/31/91

Portfolio Highlights (as of 12/31/91): Common stocks 98.9%, commercial paper 1.1%. Largest sector concentrations: technology 25.1%, consumer 24.3%, health care 22.4%, service companies 12.3%, energy 6.9%.
Largest positions: Legent Corp., Xilinx Inc., Duty Free International Inc., Babbages Inc., Circon Corp.

Historical Financial Statistics (fiscal year-end: 12/31/91):

	1991	1990	1989	1988	5/6/87 to 12/31/87
Value of net assets (000)	64,461	45,581	54,136	44,462	37,316
NAV	12.30	8.70	10.80	8.87	7.45
Net investment income (loss)	0.10	0.11	0.11	0.11	0.16
Expense ratio	1.79%	2.01%	2.13%	2.56%	4.32% ann.
Income ratio (loss)	(0.85%)	(1.05%)	(1.10%)	(1.30%)	(1.80% ann.)
Portfolio turnover	74%	78%	90%	84%	106% ann.

Special considerations: An open-ending vote will be held in 1994. The fund's charter and bylaws contain various anti-takeover provisions. The fund repaid a loan payable to Morgan Grenfell Capital Management during 1992.
Shareholders over 5%: Yale University, 8.22%

Morgan Stanley Emerging Markets

1221 Avenue of the Americas, New York, NY 10020

Category: Foreign Equity Fund

Phone: 212-296-7100
Listed: MSF, NYSE
Commenced Operations: November, 1991
Cusip: 61744G107

1991/mid-1992 Range of Premium/Disc: +18% to -9%
1991/mid-1992 Range of Price: $19 to $13 3/8
NAV Total Return 1991: N/A
Share Price Total Return 1991: N/A
Herzfeld Ranking 1991: N/A

Investment Objective: Long-term capital appreciation through investment primarily in emerging country equity securities.

Officers:
B.M. Biggs   Chairman
W.J. Olsen   President

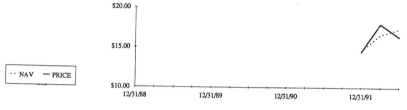

Investment Advisor: Morgan Stanley Asset Management Inc.
Advisory Fee: Monthly fee at the annual rate of 1.25% of the fund's average weekly net assets. Fee for period ended 12/31/91 was $304,986.
Administrator: United States Trust Company of New York
Administration Fee: Monthly fee at the annual rate of $65,000 plus 0.08% of the fund's average weekly net assets, plus reimbursement for certain out-of-pocket expenses. Fee for period ended 12/31/91 was $30,352.

Capital Structure: *Common stock*: 100 mil. shares authorized, 10,567,192 shares outstanding 3/31/92

Portfolio Highlights (as of 3/31/92): Common stocks 92.5%, rights 0.4%, foreign currencies 0.5%, short-term investments 7.4%, other assets and liabilities (0.8%). . Largest geographic concentrations (common stocks): Indonesia 14.1%, Thailand 12.6%, Malaysia 9.3%, Brazil 8.6%, Hong Kong 7.2%, India 7.2%, Mexico 7.2%, Argentina 7.0%, Korea 5.8%. **Largest positions:** India Magnum Fund Class 'A' and Class 'B' Shares; Telebras Bre Preferred Regd., Pabrik Ketras Tjiwi Kima, Chile Fund, Indocement Tunggal.

Historical Financial Statistics (fiscal year-end: 12/31/91):

	10/91 to 12/31/91
Value of net assets (000)	155,321
NAV	14.71
Dividends from net investment income	0.04
Expense ratio	2.25% ann.
Income ratio	2.32% ann.
Portfolio turnover	2.33%

Special considerations: There was a concurrent offering by Morgan Stanley & Co. Incorporated of 6 mil. shares, with a minimum purchase of 100,000 shares at a price of $14.45 (regular offering price was $15.00). The fund makes distributions of substantially all of its net investment income from dividends and interest earnings and net realized capital gains at least annually. The fund's Articles of Incorporation contain various anti-takeover provisions including a 75% voting requirement for conversion to an open-end fund or liquidation of the fund.

Municipal High Income Fund, Inc.

2 World Trade Center, 100th Floor, New York, NY 10048   **Category: Municipal Bond Fund**

Phone: 212-298-6266; 212-767-3833
           212-298-7162; 212-298-7163
Listed: MHF, NYSE
Commenced Operations: November, 1988
Cusip: 626214100

1991/mid-1992 Range of Premium/Disc: +2% to -4%
1991/mid-1992 Range of Price: $9 3/4 to $8 3/4
NAV Total Return 1990: +5.46%; **1991:** +10.12%
Share Price Total Return 1990: +1.30%; **1991:** +9.61%
Herzfeld Ranking 1991: 42nd of 51 municipal bond funds

Investment Objective: High tax-exempt current income by investing primarily in a variety of obligations issued by or on behalf of states, territories and possessions of the United States and the District of Columbia and their political subdivisions, agencies and instrumentalities or multistate agencies or authorities.

Officers:

T.A. Belshé   Chairman
H.B. McLendon   President

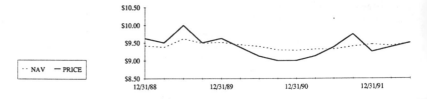

Investment Advisor: Shearson Lehman Advisors
Advisory Fee: Fee at annual rate of 0.40% of average monthly net assets. Fee for year-ended 10/31/91 was $674,407.
Sub-Investment Advisor and Administrator: The Boston Company Advisors, Inc.
Sub-Investment Advisory and Administration Fee: Fee at annual rate of 0.20% of average monthly net assets. Fee for year-ended 10/31/91 was $337,204.

Capital Structure: *Common stock:* 500 mil. shares authorized; 18,445,264 shares outstanding 1/31/92

Portfolio Highlights (as of 1/31/92): Municipal bonds and notes 98.2%, short-term tax-exempt investments 0.4%, other assets and liabilities 1.4%. Quality ratings: AAA 2%, AA 13%, A 11%, BBB 41%, not-rated 33%. Largest geographic concentrations: Texas 15.8%, Massachusetts 9.5%, Pennsylvania 8.5%, Florida 7.8%, Illinois 6.0%.
Largest issuers: Commonwealth of Massachusetts Industrial Finance Agency; New Hampshire State Industrial Development Authority; Port Corpus Christi, Texas, Industrial Development Corporation Revenue; Montgomery County, Pennsylvania, Industrial Development Authority, Pollution Control Revenue (Philadelphia Electric Company) Series A 10.5-15; Port New Orleans, Louisiana, Industrial Development Revenue.

Historical Financial Statistics (fiscal year-end: 10/31/91):

	1991	1990	11/28/88 to 10/31/89
Value of net assets (000)	173,290	164,531	164,221
NAV	9.42	9.28	9.52
Net investment income	0.74	0.75	0.66
Dividends from net investment income	0.75	0.76	0.64
Expense ratio	0.90%	0.87%	0.86% ann.*
Income ratio	7.90%	8.00%	7.54% ann.
Portfolio turnover	22%	11.21%	15.92%

*portion of fees waived by investment advisor

Special considerations: The fund may repurchase shares when the board deems it advisable. The fund's Articles of Incorporation contain various anti-takeover provisions. At 10/31/91 the fund had capital loss carryforwards of $244,407 expiring in 1998.

MuniEnhanced Fund, Inc.

Box 9011, Princeton, NJ 08543

Category: Municipal Bond Fund

Phone: 609-282-2800
Listed: MEN, NYSE
Commenced Operations: March, 1989
Cusip: 626243109

1991/mid-1992 Range of Premium/Disc: +11% to -4%
1991/mid-1992 Range of Price: $13 1/4 to $10 3/4
NAV Total Return 1990: +5.89%; **1991:** +15.06%
Share Price Total Return 1990: +6.05%; **1991:** +28.66%
Herzfeld Ranking 1991: 13th of 51 municipal bond funds

Investment Objective: High level of current income exempt from federal income taxes primarily through investment in long-term, investment-grade municipal obligations, the interest on which is exempt from federal income taxes.

Officers:

A. Zeikel   President

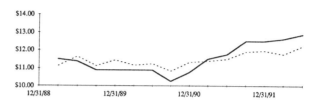

Investment Advisor: Fund Asset Management, Inc.

Advisory Fee: Monthly fee at annual rate of 0.50% of average weekly net assets. Fee for year-ended 1/31/92 was $2,373,385.

Capital Structure:

Common stock: 200 mil. shares authorized; 28,032,318 shares outstanding 1/31/92
Preferred stock: 500 Series A, 500 Series B, and 500 Series C AMPS. Liquidation preference is $100,000 per shares, plus accumulated and unpaid dividends. The yields in effect at 1/31/92 were: Series A, 2.992%; Series B, 3.375%; and Series C, 2.92%.

Portfolio Highlights (as of 1/31/92): Investments 99.3%, other assets less liabilities 0.7%. Largest geographic concentrations: New York 11.9%, Texas 9.3%, California 8.2%, Illinois 8.1%, Florida 6.2%. **Largest issuers:** New Jersey State Housing and Mortgage Finance Agency Revenue Bonds AMT; New York City, NY general obligation; Chicago, Illinois, Public Building Commission, Building Revenue Bonds (Chicago Board of Education) Series A 7.75-06; New York City, NY, Municipal Water Finance Authority, Water and Sewer System Revenue Bonds; Metropolitan Nashville Airport Authority, Tennessee, Airport Revenue Bonds Series B.

Historical Financial Statistics (fiscal year-end: 1/31/92):

	1992	1991	3/2/89 to 1/31/90
Value of net assets (000)	485,268	463,765	455,633
NAV	11.96	11.45	11.15
Net investment income	1.09	1.12	0.90
Dividends from net investment income	0.84	0.79	0.64
Expense ratio	0.70%	0.71%	0.63%* ann.
Income ratio	6.41%	6.68%	6.67% ann.
Portfolio turnover	70.17%	116.42%	30.44%

*the investment advisor waived $113,105 of the $1,847,134 fee for the period ended 1/31/90

Special considerations: During the first quarter of 1992, the fund made a tender offer at net asset value for all outstanding shares as per provisions in its prospectus. 204,326 shares were tendered at $11.77 per share. The Board will submit an open-ending proposal no later than 10/92. The fund's Articles of Incorporation contain various anti-takeover provisions.

MuniInsured Fund, Inc.

Box 9011, Princeton, NJ 08543

Category: Municipal Bond Fund

Phone: 609-282-2800
Listed: MIF, ASE
Commenced Operations: October, 1987
Cusip: 626245104

1991/mid-1992 Range of Premium/Disc: +6% to -4%
1991/mid-1992 Range of Price: $10 1/2 to $9 1/2
NAV Total Return 1990: +6.24%; **1991**: +12.66%
Share Price Total Return 1990: +8.80%; **1991**: +16.96%
Herzfeld Ranking 1991: 29th of 51 municipal bond funds

Investment Objective: High level of current income exempt from federal income taxes primarily through investment in a portfolio of long-term, investment grade municipal obligations, the interest on which is exempt from federal income taxes.

Officers:

A. Zeikel   President

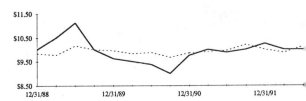

Investment Advisor: Fund Asset Management, Inc.
Advisory Fee: Fee at annual rate of 0.50% of average weekly net assets. Fee for six months ended 3/31/92 was $196,193.

Capital Structure: *Common stock*: 150 mil. shares authorized; 7,820,022 shares outstanding 3/31/92

Portfolio Highlights (as of 3/31/92): Municipal investments 101.4%, liabilities in excess of other assets (1.4%). Largest geographic concentrations: California 14.4%, Texas 10.0%, Florida 8.5%, Kentucky 8.5%, New Jersey 7.6%, Wisconsin 6.8%, Ohio 6.0%. **Largest issuers**: Louisville and Jefferson County, Kentucky, Regional Airport Authority, Airport System Revenue Bonds AMT, Series A. 8.5-17; San Antonio, Texas, Electric and Gas Improvement Revenue Bonds 8-16; Reedy Creek, Florida, Improvement District, Utility Revenue Bonds AMT, Series 1 9-07; New Jersey Health Care Facilities and Financing Authority Health Care Revenue Bonds (Saint Peter's Medical Center) Series C 8.6-17.

Historical Financial Statistics (fiscal year-end: 9/30/91):

	six months 3/31/92	1991	1990	1989	10/27/87 to 9/30/88
Value of net assets (000)	77,313	79,033	74,293	76,606	74,317
NAV	9.89	10.21	9.68	10.00	9.87
Net investment income	0.31	0.64	0.65	0.66	0.63
Dividends from net investment income	0.31	0.63	0.64	0.67	0.59
Distributions from net realized gains	0.39	0.08	0.22	0.15	--
Expense ratio	0.88% ann.	0.89%	0.91%	0.88%	0.76% ann.
Income ratio	6.18% ann.	6.47%	6.57%	6.70%	7.12% ann.
Portfolio turnover	55.15%	92.07%	132.60%	76.62%	91.84%

Special considerations: The directors serve for staggered terms. The fund will consider making a tender offer at n asset value quarterly. The fund's Articles of Incorporation contain various anti-takeover provisions.

MuniVest Fund, Inc.

Box 9011, Princeton, NJ 06543

Category: Municipal Bond Fund

Phone: 609-282-2800
Listed: MVF, ASE
Commenced Operations: September, 1988
Cusip: 626295109

1991/mid-1992 Range of Premium/Disc: +14% to -1%
1991/mid-1992 Range of Price: $11 1/4 to $9 1/4
NAV Total Return 1990: +5.85%; **1991**: +14.98%
Share Price Total Return 1990: +4.81%; **1991**: +25.70%
Herzfeld Ranking 1991: 15th of 51 municipal bond funds

Investment Objective: High level of current income exempt from federal income taxes primarily through investment in long-term, investment-grade municipal obligations, the interest on which is exempt from federal income taxes.

Officers:

A. Zeikel   President

 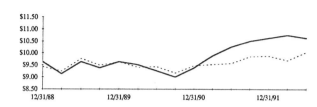

Investment Advisor: Fund Asset Management, Inc.

Advisory Fee: Monthly fee at annual rate of 0.50% of average weekly net assets. Fee for six months ended 2/29/92 was $2,107,910.

Capital Structure:

Shares of beneficial interest: 150 mil. shares authorized; 58,467,199 shares outstanding 2/29/92

Preferred stock: 500 Series A, 500 Series B, 500 Series C, 500 Series D, and 750 Series E AMPS. Liquidation preference is $100,000 per shares, plus accumulated and unpaid dividends. The yields in effect at 2/29/92 were: Series A, 3.10%; Series B, 3.09%; Series C, 3.10%; Series D, 3.127%; and Series E, 3.01%.

Portfolio Highlights (as of 2/29/92): Municipal securities 97.2%, other assets less liabilities 2.8%. Largest geographic concentrations: Texas 16.7%, New York 8.9%, Washington 8.6%, Florida 6.8%, Massachusetts 6.8%, Illinois 6.5%. 88% of the portfolio was rated A or better. **Largest issuers**: Austin, Texas, Utility System Revenue bonds; Massachusetts general obligation consolidated loans; New York City, New York general obligation; Chicago, Illinois, O'Hare International Airport, Airport Revenue Bonds, Series A 8.75-16; Ohio HFA, S/F Mortgage Revenue Bonds AMT.

Historical Financial Statistics (fiscal year-end: 8/31/91):

	six months 2/29/92	1991	1990	9/29/88 to 8/31/89
Value of net assets (000)	847,881	838,867	802,574	811,950
NAV	9.80	9.76	9.28	9.58
Net investment income	0.48	0.96	1.02	0.88
Dividends from net investment income	0.38	0.73	0.71	0.58
Distributions from net realized gains	0.16	--	0.05	--
Expense ratio	0.65% ann.	0.66%	0.67%	0.61% ann.
Income ratio	6.59% ann.	6.84%	7.05%	7.14% ann.
Portfolio turnover	53.48%	129.73%	112.81%	52.63%

*for period ended 8/31/89 $179,544 of $3,428,398 advisory fee was waived

Special considerations: The fund's Articles of Incorporation contain various anti-takeover provisions. As of 8/31/91 the fund had a capital loss carryforward of $51,000 expiring in 1998.

MuniYield California Fund, Inc.

800 Scudders Mill Road, Plainsboro, NJ 08536

Category: Municipal Bond Fund

Phone: 609-282-2800
Listed: MYC, NYSE
Commenced Operations: February, 1992
Cusip: 626296107

1991/mid-1992 Range of Premium/Disc: +8% to -4%
1991/mid-1992 Range of Price: $15 1/4 to $13 7/8
NAV Total Return 1991: N/A
Share Price Total Return 1991: N/A
Herzfeld Ranking 1991: N/A

Investment Objective: High level of current income exempt from federal and California income taxes primarily through investment in a portfolio of longer-term municipal obligations, the interest on which is exempt from federal and California income taxes. Investments will be investment grade or of comparable quality.

Officers:
A. Zeikel   President

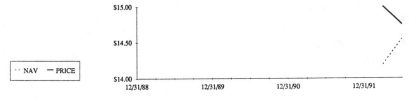

Investment Advisor: Fund Asset Management, Inc.
Advisory Fee: Monthly fee at the annual rate of 0.50% of average weekly net assets.

Capital Structure: *Common stock*: 200 mil. shares authorized, 14,750,000 shares outstanding 2/28/92. *Preferred shares*: The fund intends to offer preferred stock representing approximately 35% of the fund's capital immediately after the issuance within approximately 3 months of the common stock offering.

Portfolio Highlights: not yet published

Historical Financial Statistics:

	2/28/92
Value of net assets (000)	208,991
NAV	14.16

Special considerations: During the initial offering, shares were offered at prices ranging $15.00 down to $14.70 for larger transactions. The fund was not listed on the NYSE for an initial period, during which time shares were illiquid. Initial investors in the fund have the right to reinvest the net proceeds from the sale of these shares in Class A initial shares of certain Merrill Lynch-sponsored open-end mutual funds at their net asset value without the imposition of the initial sales charge under certain conditions. The fund will make monthly distributions of substantially all net investment income and annual distributions of net capital gains. The fund's Articles of Incorporation contain various anti-takeover provisions including a 66 2/3% vote to merge with another fund or liquidate. Initial dividend was $0.14095 payable in May, 1992; June dividend was $0.08463 per share.

MuniYield Florida Fund, Inc.

800 Scudders Mill Road, Plainsboro, NJ 08536

Category: Municipal Bond Fund

Phone: 609-282-2800
Listed: MYF, NYSE
Commenced Operations: February, 1992
Cusip: 626297105

1991/mid-1992 Range of Premium/Disc: +12% to +3%
1991/mid-1992 Range of Price: $16 to $14 7/8
NAV Total Return 1991: N/A
Share Price Total Return 1991: N/A
Herzfeld Ranking 1991: N/A

Investment Objective: High level of current income exempt from federal income taxes and exempt from Florida intangible personal property taxes primarily through investment in a portfolio of longer-term municipal obligations, the interest on which is exempt from federal income taxes and from Florida intangible personal property taxes. Investments will be investment grade or of comparable quality.

Officers:
A. Zeikel   President

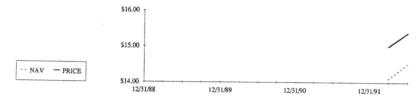

Investment Advisor: Fund Asset Management, Inc.
Advisory Fee: Monthly fee at the annual rate of 0.50% of average weekly net assets.

Capital Structure:

Common stock: unlimited number of shares authorized, 7,000,000 shares outstanding 2/28/92.

Preferred shares: The fund intends to offer preferred stock representing approximately 35% of the fund's capital immediately after the issuance within approximately 3 months of the common stock offering.

Portfolio Highlights: not yet published

Historical Financial Statistics:

	2/28/92
Value of net assets (000)	99,143
NAV	14.15

Special considerations: During the initial offering, shares were offered at prices ranging $15.00 down to $14.70 for larger transactions. The fund was not listed on the NYSE for an initial period, during which time shares were illiquid. Initial investors in the fund have the right to reinvest the net proceeds from the sale of these shares in Class A initial shares of certain Merrill Lynch-sponsored open-end mutual funds at their net asset value without the imposition of the initial sales charge under certain conditions. The fund will make monthly distributions of substantially all net investment income, and annual distributions of net capital gains. The fund's Articles of Incorporation contain various anti-takeover provisions including a 66 2/3% vote to merge with another fund or liquidate. Initial dividend was $0.13519 payable in May, 1992; June dividend was $0.08556 per share.

MuniYield Fund, Inc.

800 Scudders Mill Road, Plainsboro, NJ 08536

Category: Municipal Bond Fund

Phone: 609-282-2800	**1991/mid-1992 Range of Premium/Disc**: +7% to 0%
Listed: MYD, NYSE	**1991/mid-1992 Range of Price**: $15 7/8 to $14 3/8
Commenced Operations: November, 1991	**NAV Total Return 1991**: N/A
Cusip: 626299101	**Share Price Total Return 1991**: N/A
	Herzfeld Ranking 1991: N/A

Investment Objective: High level of current income exempt from federal income taxes primarily through investment in a portfolio of longer-term municipal obligations, the interest on which is exempt from federal income taxes. Investments will be investment grade or of comparable quality. The fund may invest up to 25% of assets in municipal obligations which are rated below investment grade or, if unrated, are of comparable quality.

Officers:

A. Zeikel   President

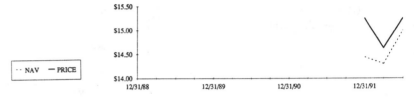

Investment Advisor: Fund Asset Management, Inc.

Advisory Fee: Monthly fee at the annual rate of 0.50% of average weekly net assets. Fee for period 11/29/92 to 4/30/92 was $1,465,874.

Capital Structure: *Common stock*: 200 mil. shares authorized, 35,160,507 shares outstanding 4/30/92
Preferred shares: 5,000 shares of unissued capital stock reclassified as AMPS; 5,000 shares outstanding with a liquidation preference of $50,000. Dividends vary by dividend period and ranged from 3.20% to 3.95% on 4/30/92 for various Series.

Portfolio Highlights (as of 4/30/92): Municipal investments 99.1%, other assets less liabilities 0.9%. Largest geographic concentrations: Texas 16.0%, New York 12.9%, Illinois 6.3%, Washington 5.6%, New Jersey 5.2%.
Largest issuers: Texas National Research Laboratory, Community Financing Corporation, Lease Revenue Bonds (Superconducting Super Collider Project); Washington State Public Power Supply Systems Revenue Refunding Bonds; New York City New York general obligation; New York State Environmental Facilities Corporation, PCR, Series E 6.875-10; Valdez, Alaska, Marine Terminal Revenue Refunding Bonds.

Historical Financial Statistics:

	11/29/91 to 4/30/92
Value of net assets (000)	758,339
NAV	14.46
Net investment income	0.51
Dividends from net investment income to common shareholders	0.34
Expense ratio	0.51% ann.*
Income ratio	6.29% ann.*
Portfolio turnover	35.85%

*net of reimbursement of various expenses

Special considerations: During the initial offering, shares were offered at prices ranging $15.00 down to $14.70 for larger transactions. The fund was not listed on the NYSE for an initial period, during which time shares were illiquid. Initial investors in the fund have the right to reinvest the net proceeds from the sale of these shares in Class A initial shares of certain Merrill Lynch-sponsored open-end mutual funds at their net asset value without the imposition of the initial sales charge under certain conditions. The fund will make monthly distributions of substantially all net investment income and annual distributions of net capital gains. The fund's Articles of Incorporation contain various anti-takeover provisions including a 66 2/3% vote to merge with another fund or liquidate.

MuniYield Insured Fund, Inc.

800 Scudders Mill Road, Plainsboro, NJ 08536   **Category:** Municipal Bond Fund

Phone: 609-282-2800	**1991/mid-1992 Range of Premium/Disc:** +5% to 0%
Listed: MYI, NYSE	**1991/mid-1992 Range of Price:** $15 1/8 to $14 3/8
Commenced Operations: March, 1992	**NAV Total Return 1991:** N/A
Cusip: 63630E107	**Share Price Total Return 1991:** N/A
	Herzfeld Ranking 1991: N/A

Investment Objective: High level of current income exempt from federal income taxes as consistent with its investment policies and prudent investment management. The fund invests primarily in a portfolio of long-term, investment-grade municipal obligations the interest on which is exempt from federal income taxes. Under normal circumstances, at least 80% of the fund's assets are invested in municipal obligations with remaining maturities of one year or more which are covered by insurance guaranteeing the timely payment of principal at maturity and interest.

Officers:

A. Zeikel   President

Investment Advisor: Fund Asset Management, Inc.
Advisory Fee: Monthly fee at the annual rate of 0.50% of average weekly net assets.

Capital Structure: *Common stock*: 200 mil. shares authorized, 38,333,333 shares outstanding 3/27/92
Preferred shares: The fund intends to offer preferred stock representing approximately 35% of the fund's capital immediately after the issuance within approximately 3 months of the common stock offering.

Portfolio Highlights: not yet published

Historical Financial Statistics:

	3/27/92
Value of net assets (000)	542,815
NAV	14.16

Special considerations: During the initial offering, shares were offered at prices ranging from $15.00 down to $14.70 for larger transactions. The fund was not listed on the NYSE for an initial period, during which time shares were illiquid. Initial investors in the fund have the right to reinvest the net proceeds from the sale of these shares in Class A initial shares of certain Merrill Lynch-sponsored open-end mutual funds at their net asset value without the imposition of the initial sales charge under certain conditions. The fund will make monthly distributions of substantially all net investment income and annual distributions of net capital gains. The fund's Articles of Incorporation contain various anti-takeover provisions, including a 66 2/3% vote to merge with another fund or liquidate. Initial dividend was $0.14622 payable in June, 1992.

MuniYield Michigan Fund, Inc.
800 Scudders Mill Road, Plainsboro, NJ 08536

Category: Municipal Bond Fund

Phone: 609-282-2800
Listed: MYM, NYSE
Commenced Operations: February, 1992
Cusip: 626300107

1991/mid-1992 Range of Premium/Disc: +7% to +2%
1991/mid-1992 Range of Price: $15 1/2 to $14 5/8
NAV Total Return 1991: N/A
Share Price Total Return 1991: N/A
Herzfeld Ranking 1991: N/A

Investment Objective: High level of current income exempt from federal and Michigan income taxes primarily through investment in a portfolio of longer-term municipal obligations, the interest on which is exempt from federal and New Jersey income taxes. Investments will be investment grade or of comparable quality.

Officers:
A. Zeikel   President

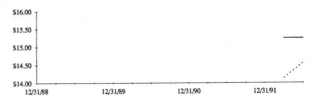

Investment Advisor: Fund Asset Management, Inc.
Advisory Fee: Monthly fee at the annual rate of 0.50% of average weekly net assets.

Capital Structure: *Common stock*: 200 mil. shares authorized, 6,750,000 shares outstanding 2/28/92.
Preferred shares: The fund intends to offer preferred stock representing approximately 35% of the fund's capital immediately after the issuance within approximately 3 months of the common stock offering.

Portfolio Highlights: not yet published

Historical Financial Statistics:

	2/28/92
Value of net assets (000)	95,663
NAV	14.16

Special considerations: During the initial offering, shares were offered at prices ranging $15.00 down to $14.70 for larger transactions. The fund was not listed on the NYSE for an initial period, during which time shares were illiquid. Initial investors in the fund have the right to reinvest the net proceeds from the sale of these shares in Class A initial shares of certain Merrill Lynch-sponsored open-end mutual funds at their net asset value without the imposition of the initial sales charge under certain conditions. The fund will make monthly distributions of substantially all net investment income and annual distributions of net capital gains. The fund's Articles of Incorporation contain various anti-takeover provisions including a 66 2/3% vote to merge with another fund or liquidate. Initial dividend was $0.13846 payable in May, 1992; June dividend was $0.08638 per share.

MuniYield New Jersey Fund, Inc.

800 Scudders Mill Road, Plainsboro, NJ 08536

Category: Municipal Bond Fund

Phone: 609-282-2800
Listed: MYJ, NYSE
Commenced Operations: May, 1992
Cusip: 62630L101

1991/mid-1992 Range of Premium/Disc: +9% to +4%
1991/mid-1992 Range of Price: $15 3/4 to $14 7/8
NAV Total Return 1991: N/A
Share Price Total Return 1991: N/A
Herzfeld Ranking 1991: N/A

Investment Objective: High level of current income exempt from federal and New Jersey income taxes primarily through investment in a portfolio of longer-term municipal obligations, the interest on which is exempt from federal and Michigan income taxes. Investments will be investment grade or of comparable quality.

Officers:

A. Zeikel   President

Investment Advisor: Fund Asset Management, Inc.
Advisory Fee: Monthly fee at the annual rate of 0.50% of average weekly net assets.

Capital Structure: *Common stock:* 200 mil. shares authorized, 7,400,000 shares outstanding 5/8/92
Preferred shares: The fund intends to offer preferred stock representing approximately 35% of the fund's capital immediately after the issuance within approximately 3 months of the common stock offering.

Portfolio Highlights: not yet published

Historical Financial Statistics:

	5/8/92
Value of net assets (000)	119,542
NAV	14.20

Special considerations: During the initial offering, shares were offered at prices ranging from $15.00 down to $14.70 for larger transactions. The fund was not listed on the NYSE for an initial period, during which time shares were illiquid. Initial investors in the fund have the right to reinvest the net proceeds from the sale of these shares in Class A initial shares of certain Merrill Lynch-sponsored open-end mutual funds at their net asset value without the imposition of the initial sales charge under certain conditions. The fund will make monthly distributions of substantially all net investment income and annual distributions of net capital gains. The fund's Articles of Incorporation contain various anti-takeover provisions, including a 66 2/3% vote to merge with another fund or liquidate.

MuniYield New York Insured Fund, Inc.

800 Scudders Mill Road, Plainsboro, NJ 08536

Category: Municipal Bond Fund

Phone: 609-282-2800
Listed: MYN, NYSE
Commenced Operations: February, 1992
Cusip: 626301105

1991/mid-1992 Range of Premium/Disc: +10% to +1%
1991/mid-1992 Range of Price: $15 1/2 to $14 3/4
NAV Total Return 1991: N/A
Share Price Total Return 1991: N/A
Herzfeld Ranking 1991: N/A

Investment Objective: High level of current income exempt from federal, New York income taxes and New York City income taxes primarily through investment in a portfolio of longer-term municipal obligations, the interest on which is exempt from federal, New York income taxes and New York City income taxes. Investments will be investment grade or of comparable quality.

Officers:

A. Zeikel   President

Investment Advisor: Fund Asset Management, Inc.
Advisory Fee: Monthly fee at the annual rate of 0.50% of average weekly net assets.

Capital Structure: *Common stock:* 200 mil. shares authorized, 10,250,000 shares outstanding 2/28/92. *Preferred shares:* The fund intends to offer preferred stock representing approximately 35% of the fund's capital immediately after the issuance within approximately 3 months of the common stock offering.

Portfolio Highlights: not yet published

Historical Financial Statistics:

	2/28/92
Value of net assets (000)	145,156
NAV	14.15

Special considerations: During the initial offering, shares were offered at prices ranging $15.00 down to $14.70 for larger transactions. The fund was not listed on the NYSE for an initial period, during which time shares were illiquid. Initial investors in the fund have the right to reinvest the net proceeds from the sale of these shares in Class A initial shares of certain Merrill Lynch-sponsored open-end mutual funds at their net asset value without the imposition of the initial sales charge under certain conditions. The fund will make monthly distributions of substantially all net investment income and annual distributions of net capital gains. The fund's Articles of Incorporation contain various anti-takeover provisions including a 66 2/3% vote to merge with another fund or liquidate. Initial dividend was $0.13048 payable in May, 1992; June dividend was $0.0841 per share.

Mutual of Omaha Interest Shares, Inc.

10235 Regency Circle, Omaha, NB 68114

Category: Bond Fund

Phone: 402-397-8555
Listed: MUO, NYSE
Commenced Operations: 1972
Cusip: 628316101

1991/mid-1992 Range of Premium/Disc: +8% to -6%
1991/mid-1992 Range of Price: $15 1/8 to $12 1/2
NAV Total Return 1990: +5.57%; **1991**: +15.14%
Share Price Total Return 1990: +1.56%; **1991**: +20.94%
Herzfeld Ranking 1991: 70th of 80 bond funds

Investment Objective: Interest income by investing in a diversified portfolio of debt obligations.

Officers:
J.M. Delich   President

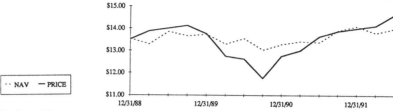

Investment Advisor and Administrator: Mutual of Omaha Fund Management Company.
Advisory and Administration Fee: Annual fee of 0.625% of average monthly net assets up to $50 mil., and 0.50% on excess. The advisor must reimburse the fund for various expenses if in excess of 1 1/2% of first $30 mil. of average monthly net assets, 1% of next $100 mil. and 0.75% of excess. Fee for year-ended 12/31/91 was $541,615.

Capital Structure: *Common stock*: 50 mil shares authorized, 7,051,440 shares outstanding 12/31/91

Portfolio Highlights (as of 12/31/91): Bonds 97.3%, short-term securities 2.5%, cash and other assets less liabilities 0.2%. Largest sector concentrations: utilities/electric 21.7%, utilities/gas 13.1%, electric power 12.8%, telecommunications 8.9%, oil 8.7%, utilities/diversified 6.6%. **Largest issuers**: Rural Electric Cooperating (Deseret) 10.11-17; Big Rivers Electric Corp. 10.70-17; Barclay's N.A. Capital Corp. 10.50-17; South Central Bell Telephone Co. 10.375-25; Colorado Interstate Gas Co. 10-05.

Historical Financial Statistics (fiscal year-end: 12/31/91):

	1991	1990	1989	1988	1987	1986
Value of net assets (000)	99,798	93,386	95,383	92,179	90,150	92,625
NAV	14.15	13.34	13.73	13.53	13.48	14.09
Net investment income	1.17	1.22	1.27	1.37	1.43	1.47
Dividends from net investment income	1.17	1.22	1.26	1.39	1.44	1.44
Distributions from net realized gains	--	--	--	0.18	--	--
Expense ratio	0.82%	0.84%	0.85%	0.85%	0.83%	0.80%
Income ratio	8.63%	9.16%	9.30%	10.21%	10.47%	10.46%
Portfolio turnover	39.5%	32.3%	62.0%	82.1%	119.2%	75.4%

Special considerations: As of 12/31/91, the fund had a capital loss carry-forward of $6,425,778 expiring through 1999. Quarterly dividend, payable in July, 1992 was $0.29 per share.

The New America High Income Fund, Inc.

200 State Street, Boston, MA 02109

Category: Bond Fund

Phone: 617-951-5762
Listed: HYB, NYSE
Commenced Operations: February, 1988
Cusip: 641876107

1991/mid-1992 Range of Premium/Disc: -8% to -27%
1991/mid-1992 Range of Price: $4 3/4 to $2 1/2
NAV Total Return 1990: -34.19%; **1991**: +28.11%
Share Price Total Return 1990: -45.79%; **1991**: +67.46%
Herzfeld Ranking 1991: 20th of 80 bond funds

Investment Objective: High current income while seeking to preserve shareholders' capital primarily through investment in a professionally managed, diversified portfolio of "high yield" fixed-income securities, principally lower or non-rated fixed-income securities.

Officers:
Robert Birch   President

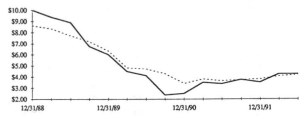

Investment Advisor: Wellington Management Company
Advisory Fee: Annual fee of 0.50% of average weekly net assets. Fee for year-ended 12/31/91 was $430,000.

Capital Structure:

Common stock: 200 mil. shares authorized; 24,586,875 shares outstanding 12/31/91
Preferred stock: 350 shares outstanding, cumulative dividends paid at a rate reset every 30 days by an auction. Stock is redeemable at the option of the fund at a redemption price of $100,000 plus accumulated and unpaid dividends. 235 shares of preferred stock were redeemed during 1990
Senior Extendible Notes: $45,490,000 notes outstanding, initially due in 1993 and extendible for one or more periods of 1, 2 or 3 years until 1998. Notes bear interest at the rate of 9% per annum through 2/14/93. $2,400,000 of note redeemed during 1991

Portfolio Highlights (as of 12/31/91): Corporate debt securities 76.18%, U.S. government agencies and instrumentalities 5.44%, preferred stock 2.08%, common stock 1.52%, warrants 1.79%, partnership interest 0.01%, short-term investments 9.67%. Largest sector concentrations: broadcasting 5.27%, electronics 4.60%, textiles/apparel 4.56%. **Largest positions**: U.S. treasury notes; WorldCorp. Inc. sub. notes 13.875-97; Magma Copper Company sr. sub. reset notes 14.60-98; Adelphia Communications Corp. sr. sub. notes 13-96; Anacomp Inc. sr. sub. notes 14-00.

Historical Financial Statistics (fiscal year-end: 12/31/91):

	1991	1990	1989	2/26/88 to 12/31/88
Value of net assets (000)	128,227	118,813	210,656	281,363
NAV	3.79	3.42	6.23	8.60
Net investment income	0.65	0.92	1.54	1.42
Dividends to preferred shares	0.10	0.16	0.30	0.23
Dividends from net investment income to common shares	0.56	0.75	1.25	1.18
Distributions from paid-in capital to common shares	--	--	0.10	--
Expense ratio	5.22%	5.89%	4.49%	4.22% ann.
Operating expense ratio*	1.97%	1.72%	0.93%	0.93% ann.
Income ratio	12.62%	14.50%	20.28%	15.5% ann.
Portfolio turnover	121.15%	49.98%	65.39%	149%

*excludes interest expense

Special considerations: In 1992 shareholders approved a new advisory agreement with Wellington Management to replace Ostrander Capital Management, L.P. Portfolio investments are primarily rated BB or lower by S&P or non-rated. The fund may repurchase common shares or make tender offers for common shares; and in 1993 may submit an open-ending proposal to shareholders. As of 12/31/91 the fund had a loss carryforward of $112,437,000 expiring through 1999. The fund held defaulted securities representing 4.10% of the fund's total assets as of 12/31/91.

The New Germany Fund, Inc.

31 West 52nd Street, New York, NY 10019

Category: Foreign Equity Fund

Phone: 212-474-7000, NAV info. 212-474-7483
Listed: GF, NYSE
Commenced Operations: January, 1990
Cusip: 644465106

1991/mid-1992 Range of Premium/Disc: 0% to -22%
1991/mid-1992 Range of Price: $13 1/2 to $8 7/8
NAV Total Return 1991: -0.24%
Share Price Total Return 1991: -4.88%
Herzfeld Ranking 1991: 38th of 46 foreign equity funds

Investment Objective: Capital appreciation by investing primarily in equity and equity-linked securities of companies that are likely, in the opinion of the fund's investment advisor and manager, to be positively affected by economic and other reforms in East Germany and in other parts of Eastern Europe. The fund may invest, for hedging purposes, in put and call options and bond futures and may write covered call options to generate income.

Officers:
R.E. Breuer — Chairman
H. Risse — President & CEO

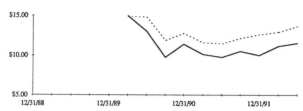

Investment Advisor: Deutsche Asset Management GmbH
Advisory Fee: Annual fee of 0.35% of average weekly net assets up to $100 mil. and 0.25% of excess. Fee for 1991 was $950,358.
Manager: Deutsche Bank Capital Corporation
Management Fee: Annual fee of 0.65% of average weekly net assets up to $100 mil. and 0.55% of excess. Fee for 1991 was $1,970,457.

Capital Structure: *Common stock:* 80 mil. shares authorized; 27,271,538 outstanding 12/31/91

Portfolio Highlights (as of 3/31/92): Investments in German common stocks 73.0%, investments in German preferred stocks 8.4%, investments in warrants on German common stocks 9.9%, investments in French common stock 1.4%, investment in Norway common stock 1.5%, investments in Switzerland common stocks 2.1%, repurchase agreements 10.9%, time deposit 0.7%, liabilities in excess of cash and other assets (7.9%). Largest sector concentrations: banking 13.4%, electrical 12.9%, engineering-specialists 7.9%, pharmaceuticals 6.9%. **Largest positions:** Siemens, Deutsche Pfandbrief-und Hypothekenbank, SAP, Münchener Rückversicherung, Schering.

Historical Financial Statistics (fiscal year-end: 12/31/91):

	1991	1/30/90 to 12/31/90
Value of net assets (000)	344,569	358,421
NAV	12.63	12.76
Net investment income	0.13	0.21
Dividends from net investment income	--	0.21
Distributions from net realized gains	0.07	0.05
Expense ratio	1.13%	1.21% ann.
Operating expense ratio	1.05%	0.98% ann.
Income ratio	1.02%	1.65% ann.
Portfolio turnover	48.97%	36.02%

Special considerations: The fund intends to distribute all net investment income and net realized capital gains at least annually with the option to receive such distributions in cash or stock. During the period ended 12/31/90 the fund purchased 659,800 shares of common stock on the open market at an average discount of 16.0%.

317

The New York Tax-Exempt Income Fund, Inc.

500 West Madison Street, Suite. 3000, Chicago, IL 60606   **Category: Municipal Bond Fund**

Phone: 800-426-5523
Listed: XTX, ASE
Commenced Operations: October, 1987
Cusip: 650081102

1991/mid-1992 Range of Premium/Disc: +6% to -7%
1991/mid-1992 Range of Price: $10 7/8 to $9 1/8
NAV Total Return 1990: +6.01%; **1991**: +10.99%
Share Price Total Return 1990: +8.46%; **1991**: +13.27%
Herzfeld Ranking 1991: 37th of 51 municipal bond funds

Investment Objective: Current income exempt from federal income tax and exempt from New York State and New York City income taxes, also preservation and enhancement of net asset value through professional management of assets of the fund. The fund invests primarily in tax-exempt New York Municipal Securities.

Officers:

J.C. Swain	Chairman & Chief Executive Officer
J.S. Fossel	President

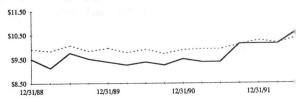

Investment Advisor: Oppenheimer Management Corporation
Advisory Fee: Annual fee of 0.50% of average weekly net assets. Management fees for six months ended 4/30/92 wat $58,951.
Sub-Investment Advisor: Clayton Brown Investment Management, Inc.
Sub-Advisory Fee: Annual fee of 0.20% of average weekly net assets.

Capital Structure: *Common stock*: 250 mil. shares authorized; 2,327,074 shares outstanding 4/30/92

Portfolio Highlights (as of 4/30/92): Municipal bonds & notes 97.9%, other assets net of liabilities 2.1%.
Largest issuers: City of New York general obligation bonds; New York State Medical Care Facilities Finance Agency; Triborough Bridge and Tunnel Authority of New York Revenue Bonds Series K 8.24-17; New York State Urban Development Corp. Correctional Facilities Revenue Refunding Bonds 8-06; New York State Power Authority Revenue Bonds.

	Historical Financial Statistics (fiscal year-end: 10/31/91):					
	six months 4/30/92	1991	1990*	1989	1988	10/22/87 to 11/30/87
Value of net assets (000)	23,839	23,713	22,705	23,203	23,004	21,973
NAV	10.24	10.22	9.78	10.00	9.92	9.51
Net investment income	0.32	0.64	0.57	0.62	0.61	0.04
Dividends from net investment income	0.32	0.64	0.56	0.63	0.59	--
Distributions from net realized gains	--	0.03	0.11	0.06	0.08	--
Expense ratio	1.03% ann.	0.97%	1.12% ann.	1.34%	1.53%	1.46% ann.
Income ratio	6.28% ann.	6.43%	6.33% ann.	6.57%	6.27%	4.02% ann.
Portfolio turnover	5%	2%	4%	24%	45%	35% ann.

*11 months ended 10/31/90; fiscal year-end changed from 11/30

Special considerations: The fund's Articles of Incorporation contain various anti-takeover provisions. Shareholders approved a change of investment advisor from Clayton Brown Advisors, Inc. to Oppenheimer Managemen Corporation.

Niagara Share Corporation
344 Delaware Avenue, Buffalo, NY 14202

Category: Equity Fund

Phone: 716-856-2600; 800-225-5163
800-225-5021
Listed: NGS, NYSE
Commenced Operations: 1929
Cusip: 653556100

1990/mid-1991 Range of Premium/Disc: -2% to -18%
1990/mid-1991 Range of Price: $15 1/2 to $11 1/2
NAV Total Return 1990: -8.69%; **1991:** +19.63%
Share Price Total Return 1990: -4.74%; **1991:** +34.39%
Herzfeld Ranking 1991: 13th of 15 equity funds

Investment Objective: Overall rate of return which compares favorably over the long-term with results of the broad market averages through both income and capital appreciation. The fund invests primarily in common stocks throughout the world.

Officers:
P.A. Schoellkopf Chairman
R.J.A. Irwin   President & CEO

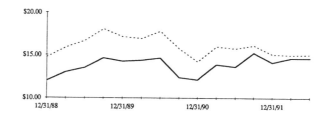

Investment Advisor: Internally managed
Advisory Fee: Salaries to corporate officers were $837,696 during 1991.

Capital Structure: *Common stock:* 21 mil. shares authorized; 14,100,897 shares outstanding 12/31/91

Portfolio Highlights (as of 12/31/91): Portfolio investments 53.0%, short-term securities 47.4%, cash and other (0.4%). Largest industry concentrations: utilities 8.9%, chemicals 8.2%, electronic and data processing 5.9%, petroleum and natural gas 5.4%. Largest holdings: Archer-Daniels-Midland, Great Lakes Chemical Corporation, Corning Incorporated, Philip Morris Companies Inc., Crompton & Knowles Corporation.

Historical Financial Statistics (fiscal year-end: 12/31/91):

	1991	1990	1989	1988	1987	1986
Value of net assets (000)	215,766	201,975	229,762	191,238	169,111	176,051
NAV	15.30	14.32	17.15	14.77	14.34	16.22
Net investment income	0.33	0.36	0.40	0.39	0.28	0.27
Dividends from net investment income	0.35	0.39	0.413	0.398	0.365	0.30
Distributions from net realized gains	1.32	1.06	1.057	1.052	1.785	2.91
Expense ratio	1.22%	1.13%	1.08%	1.25%	1.00%	1.04%
Income ratio	2.12%	2.20%	2.35%	2.55%	1.66%	1.52%
Portfolio turnover	0%	13.73%	24.83%	15.28%	21.03%	27.61%

Special considerations: Niagara Share Corp. was incorporated in 1929 and was originally oriented in great part to special investments with an emphasis on public utilities. It became a Diversified Investment Company in 1952 and a Regulated Investment Company for tax purposes in 1955. At the fund's 1989 annual meeting, shareholders voted to increase the number of authorized shares to 21 mil. from 16 mil. and to limit certain liabilities of directors and officers. During the year-ended 12/31/90 the fund purchased 85,200 shares at an average discount of 16.4%. In July, 1991, the Board announced that it would dissolve the fund; however in November, 1991, they announced they would explore other alternatives. The fund has reached a definitive agreement with Scudder, Stevens and Clark to have Scudder Growth and Income Fund (an open-end series fund) acquire the assets of Niagara Share in a tax-free transaction. Shareholders of both funds approved the agreement and the fund has been merged with Scudder Growth and Income Fund **Shareholders over 5%:** Paul A. Schoellkopf, 8.54%

Nuveen California Investment Quality Municipal Fund, Inc.

333 West Wacker Drive, Chicago, IL 60606   **Category: Municipal Bond Fund**

Phone: 312-917-7810; 800-323-5063
Listed: NQC, NYSE
Commenced Operations: November, 1990
Cusip: 67062A101

1991/mid-1992 Range of Premium/Disc: +10% to 0%
1991/mid-1992 Range of Price: $15 7/8 to $14 5/8
NAV Total Return 1991: +12.55%
Share Price Total Return 1991: +7.89%
Herzfeld Ranking 1991: 30th of 51 municipal bond funds

Investment Objective: Current income exempt from federal and California income taxes with a secondary objective of enhancement of portfolio value relative to the California municipal bond market through investment in a portfolio of tax-exempt California municipal obligations.

Officers:

R.J. Franke   Chairman
D.E. Sveen   President

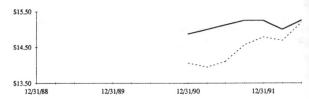

Investment Advisor: Nuveen Advisory Co.
Advisory Fee: Fee of 0.60% of average net asset value of the fund up to $500 mil., 0.575% on next $500 mil., and 0.55% on any excess. Fee for period 11/30/90 to 10/31/91 was $1,329,496.

Capital Structure: *Common stock*: 200 mil. shares authorized, 12,695,819 shares outstanding 10/31/91
Municipal Auction Rate Preferred stock: 1 mil. shares authorized, 1,800 outstanding 10/31/91, with $50,000 stated value per share.

Portfolio Highlights (as of 10/31/91): Municipal investments 98.2%, other assets less liabilities 1.8%. Quality ratings: AAA 37%, AA+/AA/AA- 35%, A+ 12%, A/A- 9%, BBB+/BBB/BBB- 7%. Largest industry concentrations: health care facilities 20%, electric utilities 18%, housing facilities 17%, lease rental facilities 13%, educational facilities 9%. 19% of long-term and intermediate-term investments are covered by insurance issued by several private issuers. **Largest issuers:** California Health Facilities Financing Authority; California Educational Facilities Authority; California Housing Finance Agency home mortgage; Fontana Public Financing Authority tax allocation 7.75-20; Los Angeles Department of Water & Power Electric Plant.

Historical Financial Statistics (fiscal year-end: 10/31/91):

	11/30/90 to 10/31/91
Value of net assets (000)	276,571
NAV	14.70
Net investment income	1.022
Dividends from net investment income to common shares	0.756
Common stock equivalent of dividends to preferred shares	0.188
Expense ratio	0.78% ann.
Income ratio	5.85% ann.
Portfolio turnover	19% ann.

Special considerations: The fund makes monthly distributions to reflect the past and projected performance of the fund that will result in distribution of all net investment income and makes annual distributions of net capital gains. On an annual basis, the board will consider repurchasing shares, making a tender offer or open-ending the fund on an annual basis. The fund's Articles of Incorporation contain various anti-takeover provisions. Open-ending of the fund would require a shareholder vote with both classes of stock voting together and the preferred shareholders voting as a separate class.

Nuveen California Municipal Income Fund, Inc.

333 West Wacker Drive, Chicago, IL 60606

Category: Municipal Bond Fund

Phone: 312-917-7810; 800-323-5063
Listed: NCM, NYSE
Commenced Operations: April, 1988
Cusip: 67062B109

1991/mid-1992 Range of Premium/Disc: +10% to 0%
1991/mid-1992 Range of Price: $13 1/8 to $11 3/4
NAV Total Return 1990: +6.64%; **1991:** +9.35%
Share Price Total Return 1990: +7.93%; **1991:** +12.18%
Herzfeld Ranking 1991: 45th of 51 municipal bond funds

Investment Objective: High level of current income exempt from federal and California income taxes primarily through investment in a diversified portfolio of tax-exempt California municipal obligations.

Officers:

R.J. Franke   Chairman
D.E. Sveen   President

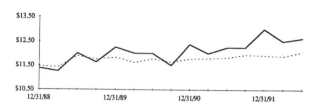

Investment Advisor: Nuveen Advisory Co.
Advisory Fee: Fee of 0.50% of average net asset value of the fund. Fee for year-ended 11/30/91 was $300,329.

Capital Structure: *Common stock:* 200 mil. shares authorized; 5,080,789 shares outstanding 11/30/91

Portfolio Highlights (as of 11/30/91): Municipal investments 97.9%, other assets less liabilities 2.1%. Quality ratings: AAA 13%, AA+/AA/AA- 34%, A+ 17%, A/A- 9%, BBB+/BBB/BBB- 9%, non-rated 18%. Largest industry concentrations: electric utilities 23%, housing facilities 19%, health care facilities 15%, pollution control facilities 7%. **Largest issuers:** California Housing Finance Agency Revenue; California State Department of Water Resources (Central Valley Project) Power Facilities 8-16; Los Angeles Department of Water and Power Electric Plant; California Health Facilities; Sacramento Municipal Utility District 8.75-00; Lassen Municipal Utility District Certificates of Participation 8.25-98.

Historical Financial Statistics (fiscal year-end: 11/30/91*):

	1991	10/31/90*	1989	4/20/88 to 10/31/88
Value of net assets (000)	60,964	59,091	59,363	58,298
NAV	12.00	11.71	11.81	11.64
Net investment income	0.80	0.797	0.813	0.282
Dividends from net investment income	0.786	0.797	0.813	0.282
Distributions from net realized gains	--	0.081	0.006	--
Expense ratio	0.73%	0.76%	0.72%	0.74% ann.
Income ratio	6.75%	6.77%	6.89%	6.13% ann.
Portfolio turnover	9%	7%	23%	21%

*fiscal year end changed to 11/30; value of net assets as of 11/30/90, $59,503,000; NAV, 11.79

Special considerations: On an annual basis, the board will consider repurchasing shares, making a tender offer or open-ending the fund. The fund's Articles of Incorporation contain various anti-takeover provisions.

Nuveen California Municipal Market Opportunity Fund, Inc.

333 West Wacker Drive, Chicago, IL 60606   **Category: Municipal Bond Fund**

Phone: 312-917-7810; 800-323-5063
Listed: NCO, NYSE
Commenced Operations: May, 1990
Cusip: 67062U107

1991/mid-1992 Range of Premium/Disc: +11% to 0%
1991/mid-1992 Range of Price: $16 to $14 5/8
NAV Total Return 1991: +14.67%
Share Price Total Return 1991: +9.38%
Herzfeld Ranking 1991: 18th of 51 municipal bond funds

Investment Objective: Current income exempt from both regular federal and California income taxes, and a secondary objective of enhancement of portfolio value relative to the California municipal bond market through investments in tax-exempt California municipal obligations that, in the opinion of the fund's investment advisor, are underrated or undervalued or represent municipal market sectors that are undervalued. Substantially all investment will be made in municipal obligations rated within the four highest grades.

Officers:

R.J. Franke   Chairman
D.E. Sveen   President

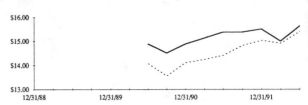

Investment Advisor: Nuveen Advisory Co.
Advisory Fee: Fee of 0.60% of average net asset value of the fund up to $500 mil., 0.575% on next $500 mil., and 0.55% on any excess. Fee for year-ended 10/31/91 was $990,115.

Capital Structure: *Common stock*: 200 mil. shares authorized; 7,663,960 shares outstanding 10/31/91 *Municipal Auction Rate Preferred stock*: 1 mil. shares authorized, 1,100 shares Series W outstanding 10/31/91, liquidation value $50,000 per share. The dividend rate is set every 7 days by auction.

Portfolio Highlights (as of 10/31/91): Municipal investments 97.9%, temporary municipal investments 0.6%, other assets 1.5%. Quality ratings: AAA 31%, AA+/AA/AA- 27%, A+ 13%, A/A- 21%, BBB+/BBB/BBB- 8%. Largest industry concentrations: housing facilities revenue bonds 18%, health care facilities 16%, water/sewer facilities 12%, educational facilities 11%, electric utilities 10%. **Largest issuers:** CA Housing Finance Agency, Home Mtg. Rev. AMT; CA Edl. Facilities Auth. (University of San Diego Projects) 9.125-10; Santa Ana Community Redev. Tax Alloc. 7.5-16; San Diego Redev. Agency (Marina Redev. Project) 8.75-08; Los Angeles Wastewater System Rev. 7.15-20.

Historical Financial Statistics (fiscal year-end: 10/31/91):

	1991	5/17/90 to 10/31/90
Value of net assets (000)	169,554	159,753
NAV	14.95	13.76
Net investment income	1.35	0.442
Dividends from net investment income	1.02	0.255
Common stock equivalent of dividends paid to preferred shareholders	0.328	0.109
Expense ratio	0.80%	0.83% ann.
Income ratio	6.25%	5.63% ann.
Portfolio turnover	0%	38% ann.

Special considerations: The fund makes regular monthly cash distributions from net investment income remaining after payment of preferred dividends and at least annual distributions of net capital gains, if any. On an annual basis, the board will consider repurchasing shares, making a tender offer or open-ending the fund. The fund's Articles of Incorporation contain various anti-takeover provisions. As of 10/31/91 the fund had a capital loss carryforward of $384,451 available through 1999.

Nuveen California Municipal Value Fund, Inc.

333 West Wacker Drive, Chicago, IL 60606

Category: Municipal Bond Fund

Phone: 312-917-7810; 800-323-5063
Listed: NCA, NYSE
Commenced Operations: October, 1987
Cusip: 67062C107

1991/mid-1992 Range of Premium/Disc: +8% to -1%
1991/mid-1992 Range of Price: $11 1/4 to $10 1/8
NAV Total Return 1990: +6.16%; **1991:** +10.05%
Share Price Total Return 1990: +7.79%; **1991:** +13.98%
Herzfeld Ranking 1991: 43rd of 51 municipal bond funds

Investment Objective: Current income exempt from federal and California income taxes with a secondary objective of enhancement of portfolio value, primarily through investment in tax-exempt California municipal obligations.

Officers:
R.J. Franke   Chairman
D.E. Sveen   President

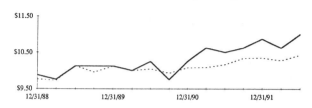

Investment Advisor: Nuveen Advisory Co.

Advisory Fee: Fee of 0.40% of average net asset value of the fund plus 4.75% of the gross interest income for the first $50 mil., 4.625 of the gross interest income for the next $50 mil., and 4.5% of the gross interest income for any excess, not to exceed in the aggregate 1% of average weekly net asset value. Fee for six months ended 1/31/92 was $680,300.

Capital Structure: *Common stock:* 250 mil. shares authorized; 18,458,532 shares outstanding 1/31/92

Portfolio Highlights (as of 1/31/92): Municipal investments 98.4%, temporary investments in short-term municipal securities 0.2%. Quality ratings: AAA 35%, AA+/AA/AA- 23%, A+ 2%, A/A- 16%, BBB+/BBB/BBB- 6%, non-rated 18%. Largest industry concentrations: escrowed bonds 38%, housing facilities revenue 16%, health care facilities revenue 14%, water/sewer facilities revenue 27%. **Largest issuers:** Los Angeles Convention and Exhibition Center Certificates of Participation 9-20 (pre-refunded to 12/1/05); Orange County Public Facilities Corporation Certificates of Participation 8.25-18 (pre-refunded to 12/1/97); Los Angeles Wastewater System 8.125-17 (pre-refunded to 11/1/97); California Housing Finance Agency, Home Mortgage Revenue, 8.2-17; Upland Hospital (San Antonio Community Hospital) 7.125-11.

Historical Financial Statistics (fiscal year-end: 7/31/91):

	six months 1/31/92	1991	1990	1989	10/7/87 to 7/31/88
Value of net assets (000)	191,430	188,370	184,888	185,116	174,645
NAV	10.37	10.25	10.12	10.19	9.67
Net investment income	0.335	0.667	0.664	0.664	0.482
Dividends from net investment income	0.331	0.66	0.666	0.67	0.421
Distributions from net realized gains	0.023	--	0.031	0.076	--
Expense ratio	0.83% ann.	0.88%	0.91%	0.94%	0.94% ann.
Income ratio	6.43% ann.	6.62%	6.62%	6.75%	6.29% ann.
Portfolio turnover	8% ann.	5%	2%	27%	35%

Special considerations: The fund may repurchase shares in the open market when the board deems it advantageous. The fund's Articles of Incorporation contain various anti-takeover provisions.

Nuveen California Performance Plus Municipal Fund, Inc.

333 West Wacker Drive, Chicago IL 60606   **Category: Municipal Bond Fund**

Phone: 312-917-7810; 800-323-5063
Listed: NCP, NYSE
Commenced Operations: November, 1989
Cusip: 67062Q106

1991/mid-1992 Range of Premium/Disc: +7% to 0%
1991/mid-1992 Range of Price: $16 to $14 5/8
NAV Total Return 1990: +6.53%; **1991:** +13.78%
Share Price Total Return 1990: +6.29%; **1991:** +10.22%
Herzfeld Ranking 1991: 21st of 80 municipal bond funds

Investment Objective: Current income exempt from both regular federal and California income taxes and a secondary objective of enhancement of portfolio value relative to the California municipal bond market through investment in tax-exempt California municipal obligations that, in the opinion of the fund's investment advisor, are underrated or undervalued or represent municipal market sectors that are undervalued.

Officers:

R.J. Franke   Chairman
D.E. Sveen   President

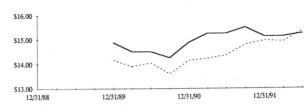

Investment Advisor: Nuveen Advisory Corp.
Advisory Fee: Annual fee equal to 0.60% of average net asset value of the fund up to $500 mil., 0.575% on next $500 mil., and 0.55% of any excess. Fee for year-ended 10/31/91 was $1,580,788.

Capital Structure: *Common stock:* 200 mil. shares authorized; 12,089,051 shares outstanding 10/31/91
Money Market Preferred Stock: 1 mil. shares authorized, 1,800 shares (900 shares Series T, 900 shares Series F) outstanding 10/31/91, liquidation value $50,000 per share. Dividend rate is set every 7 days by auction.

Portfolio Highlights (as of 10/31/91): California municipal investments 96.0%, temporary investments in short-term municipal securities 1.0%, other assets less liabilities 3.0%. Largest industry concentrations: health care facilities 22%, water/sewer facilities 18%, housing facilities 16%, transportation 10%, electric utilities 9%. Quality ratings: AAA 31%, AA+/AA/AA- 32%, A+ 11%, B/B- 20%, BBB+/BBB/BBB- 4%, non-rated 2%. **Largest issuers:** California Health Facilities Financing Authority; California Housing Finance Agency; Pleasanton Limited Obligation Improvement (North Pleasanton Assessment District No. 3); Los Angeles Wastewater System; California Educational Facilities Authority.

Historical Financial Statistics (fiscal year-end: 10/31/91):

	1991	11/15/89 to 10/31/90
Value of net assets (000)	269,890	255,862
NAV	14.88	13.82
Net investment income	1.372	1.095
Dividends from net investment income	1.02	0.765
Common stock equivalent of dividends paid to preferred shareholders	0.336	0.269
Expense ratio	0.78%	0.79% ann.
Income ratio	6.28%	6.18% ann.
Portfolio turnover	6%	30% ann.

Special considerations: Investments are rated BBB or higher; however up to 20% of assets may be invested in unrated California municipal obligations that the advisor feels are of comparable quality. The fund's Articles of Incorporation contain various anti-takeover provisions including a 66 2/3% voting requirement for converting to an open-end fund, merger with another corporation, or liquidation of the fund.

Nuveen California Quality Income Municipal Fund, Inc.

333 West Wacker Drive, Chicago IL 60606

Category: Municipal Bond Fund

Phone: 312-917-7810; 800-323-5063
Listed: NUC, NYSE
Commenced Operations: November, 1991
Cusip: 670985100

1991/mid-1992 Range of Premium/Disc: +7% to -3%
1991/mid-1992 Range of Price: $15 1/8 to $13 5/8
NAV Total Return 1991: N/A
Share Price Total Return 1991: N/A
Herzfeld Ranking 1991: N/A

Investment Objective: Current income exempt from both regular federal income taxes and California personal income taxes, with a secondary investment objective of enhancement of portfolio value relative to the California municipal boned market through investments in tax-exempt California municipal obligations rated in the four highest categories, or unrated securities that the fund's advisor believes to be of investment-grade quality.

Officers:

R.J. Franke	Chairman
D.E. Sveen	President

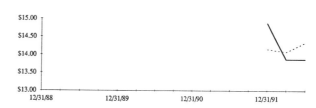

Investment Advisor: Nuveen Advisory Corp.

Advisory Fee: Annual fee equal to 0.65% of average net asset value of the fund up to $500 mil., 0.625% on next $500 mil., and 0.60% of any excess.

Capital Structure:

Common stock: 21,227,199 shares outstanding 5/31/92
Municipal Auction Rate: 1 mil. shares authorized, 3,000 shares outstanding 5/31/92, liquidation preference $50,000 per share, interest rate reset every 7 days.

Portfolio Highlights: not yet published

Historical Financial Statistics:

	6/19/92
Value of net assets (000)	496,925
NAV	14.24

Special considerations: At least annually the fund's directors will consider taking any action to reduce any discounts which may be present, including such remedies as repurchasing shares in the open market, making tender offers or converting to an open-end fund. The fund's Declaration of Trust contains various anti-takeover provisions including a 66 2/3% vote to convert to an open-end fund, merger with another corporation, or termination of the trust. Mid-1992 dividend rate $0.075 per share.

Nuveen California Select Quality Municipal Fund, Inc.

333 West Wacker Drive, Chicago IL 60606

Category: Municipal Bond Fund

Phone: 312-917-7810; 800-323-5063
Listed: NVC, NYSE
Commenced Operations: May, 1991
Cusip: 670975101

1991/mid-1992 Range of Premium/Disc: +7% to -3%
1991/mid-1992 Range of Price: $15 3/8 to $14 1/8
NAV Total Return 1991: N/A
Share Price Total Return 1991: N/A
Herzfeld Ranking 1991: N/A

Investment Objective: Current income exempt from both regular federal and California income taxes, with a secondary investment objective of enhancement of portfolio value relative to the California municipal bond market through investments in tax-exempt California municipal obligations that the advisor feels are underrated or undervalued or represent municipal market sectors that are undervalued.

Officers:
R.J. Franke   Chairman
D.E. Sveen   President

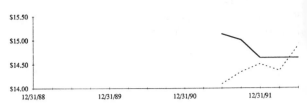

Investment Advisor: Nuveen Advisory Corp.
Advisory Fee: Annual fee equal to 0.65% of average net asset value of the fund up to $500 mil., 0.625% on next $500 mil., and 0.60% of any excess. Fee for year-ended 10/31/91 was $950,199.

Capital Structure: *Common stock:* 200 mil. shares authorized, 22,025,728 shares outstanding 10/31/91
Preferred stock: 1 mil. shares authorized, 3,000 shares outstanding as of 10/31/91 with a $50,000 stated value per share.

Portfolio Highlights (as of 10/31/91): Municipal investments 85.9%, temporary investments 16.8%, other assets less liabilities (2.7%). Quality ratings: AAA 34%, AA+/AA/AA- 11%, A+ 14%, A/A- 33%, BBB+/BBB/BBB- 5%, non-rated 3%. Largest industry concentrations: lease rental facilities 24%, health care facilities 19%, housing facilities 12%, electric facilities 11%. **Largest issuers:** California Health Facilities Financing Authority; California Housing Finance Agency; Loma Linda (Loma Linda University Medical Center); Northern California Power Agency Hydroelectric Project Number One 7.15-24; Santa Ana Community Redevelopment Agency tax allocation 6.75-19.

Historical Financial Statistics (fiscal year-end: 10/31/91):

	5/22/92 to 10/31/91
Value of net assets (000)	467,392
NAV	14.41
Net investment income	0.341
Dividends from net investment income	0.243
Common stock equivalent of dividends paid to preferred shareholders	0.029
Expense ratio	0.75% ann.
Income ratio	5.13% ann.
Portfolio turnover	6% ann.

Special considerations: Investments are rated BBB or higher; however, up to 20% of assets may be invested in unrated California municipal obligations that the advisor feels are of comparable quality. The fund's Articles of Incorporation contain various anti-takeover provisions including a 66 2/3% voting requirement for converting to an open-end fund, merger with another corporation, or liquidation of the fund.

Nuveen Florida Investment Quality Municipal Fund, Inc.

333 West Wacker Drive, Chicago IL 60606   **Category: Municipal Bond Fund**

Phone: 312-917-7810; 800-323-5063
Listed: NQF, NYSE
Commenced Operations: February, 1991
Cusip: 670970102

1991/mid-1992 Range of Premium/Disc: +10% to +3%
1991/mid-1992 Range of Price: $16 1/2 to $14 1/2
NAV Total Return 1991: N/A
Share Price Total Return 1991: N/A
Herzfeld Ranking 1991: N/A

Investment Objective: The fund seeks current income exempt from regular federal income taxes with a secondary objective of enhancement of portfolio value relative to the Florida municipal bond market through investments in tax-exempt Florida municipal obligations. Investments will be made in municipal securities rated BBB or better; 20% of investments may be in unrated securities which in the opinion of the advisor are of comparable quality.

Officers:

R.J. Franke	Chairman
D.E. Sveen	President

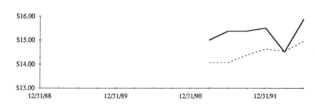

Investment Advisor: Nuveen Advisory Corp.
Advisory Fee: Annual fee equal to 0.60% of average net asset value of the fund up to $500 mil., 0.575% on next $500 mil., and 0.55% of any excess. Fee for period from 2/21/91 to 10/31/91 was $1,156,130.

Capital Structure: *Common stock*: unlimited number of shares authorized, 15,719,104 shares outstanding 10/31/91
Preferred Shares: unlimited number of shares authorized, 2,200 shares outstanding 10/31/91, $50,000 stated value per share.

Portfolio Highlights (as of 10/31/91): Florida municipal investments 98.7%, temporary investments 3.3%, other assets less liabilities (2.0%). Quality ratings: AAA 60%, AA+/AA/AA- 28%, A+ 2%, A/A- 2%, BBB+/BBB/BBB-8%. Largest industry concentrations: health care facilities 21%, electric utilities 19%, housing facilities 15%, transportation 10%, water/sewer facilities 9%. **Largest issuers**: Jacksonville Electric Authority; Hernando County (Criminal Justice Complex); Orange County Housing Finance Authority; GNMA Collateralized Mortgage AMT: Orlando and Orange County Expressway Authority 7.5-16; Palm Beach County Health Facilities Authority (JFK Medical Center) 8.875-18.

Historical Financial Statistics (fiscal year-end: 10/31/91):

	2/21/91 to 10/31/91
Value of net assets (000)	337,834
NAV	14.49
Net investment income	0.671
Dividends from net investment income	0.495
Common stock equivalent of dividends paid to preferred shareholders	0.122
Expense ratio	0.76% ann.
Income ratio	5.47% ann.
Portfolio turnover	0%

Special considerations: At least annually the fund's directors will consider taking any action to reduce any discounts which may be present, including such remedies as repurchasing shares in the open market, making tender offers or converting to an open-end fund. The fund's Declaration of Trust contains various anti-takeover provisions including a 66 2/3% vote to convert to an open-end fund, merge with another corporation, or terminate of the trust.

Nuveen Florida Quality Income Municipal Fund, Inc.

333 West Wacker Drive, Chicago IL 60606

Category: Municipal Bond Fund

Phone: 312-917-7810; 800-323-5063
Listed: NUF, NYSE
Commenced Operations: October, 1991
Cusip: 670978105

1991/mid-1992 Range of Premium/Disc: +7% to 0%
1991/mid-1992 Range of Price: $15 1/4 to $14
NAV Total Return 1991: N/A
Share Price Total Return 1991: N/A
Herzfeld Ranking 1991: N/A

Investment Objective: Current income exempt from regular federal income taxes, with a secondary objective of enhancement of portfolio value, relative to the municipal bond market, through investment of substantially all of the fund's assets in municipal bonds rated in the four highest categories or unrated securities that the fund's advisor believes to be of investment-grade quality.

Officers:

R.J. Franke   Chairman
D.E. Sveen   President

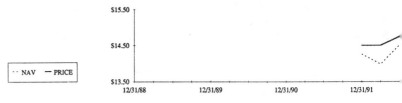

Investment Advisor: Nuveen Advisory Corp.
Advisory Fee: Annual fee equal to 0.65% of average net asset value of the fund up to $500 mil., 0.625% on next $500 mil., and 0.60% of any excess. Fee for period from 10/17/91 to 12/31/91 was $197,105.

Capital Structure:

Common stock: unlimited number of shares authorized, 11,752,090 shares outstanding 12/31/91
Municipal Auction Rate Preferred stock: unlimited number of shares authorized, 850 shares Series M and 850 shares Series TH outstanding 2/18/92, liquidation preference $50,000 per share.

Portfolio Highlights (as of 12/31/91): Florida municipal investments 65.4%, temporary investments in short-term municipal securities 36.0%, other assets less liabilities (1.4%). Largest industry concentrations: electric utilities 19%, transportation 18%, housing facilities 17%, pollution control facilities 14%, general obligation bonds 12%, health care facilities 9%. Quality ratings: AAA 53%, AA+/AA/AA- 29%, A/A- 6%, BBB+/BBB/BBB- 12%. **Largest issuers:** Jacksonville Electric Authority; Florida Housing Finance Agency; Palm Beach County Airport Authority 7.75-10; Florida State Board of Education 6.7-22; Dade County (Miami International Airport), alternative minimum tax 6.75-06.

Historical Financial Statistics:

	10/17/91 to 12/31/91
Value of net assets (000)	168,206
NAV	14.31
Net investment income	0.111
Dividends from net investment income	--
Expense ratio	0.79% ann.
Income ratio	4.28% ann.
Portfolio turnover	0%

Special considerations: At least annually the fund's directors will consider taking any action to reduce any discounts which may be present, including such remedies as repurchasing shares in the open market, making tender offer or converting to an open-end fund. The fund's Declaration of Trust contains various anti-takeover provisions including a 66 2/3% vote to convert to an open-end fund, merger with another corporation, or termination of the trust. Mid-1992 dividend rate $0.076 per share.

Nuveen Insured California Select Tax-Free Income Portfolio

333 West Wacker Drive, Chicago IL 60606   **Category: Municipal Bond Fund**

Phone: 312-917-7810; 800-323-5063	**1991/mid-1992 Range of Premium/Disc:** +6% to +5%
Listed: NXC, NYSE	**1991/mid-1992 Range of Price:** $15 1/8 to $15
Commenced Operations: June, 1992	**NAV Total Return 1991:** N/A
Cusip: 67063R103	**Share Price Total Return 1991:** N/A
	Herzfeld Ranking 1991: N/A

Investment Objective: Stable dividends exempt from both regular federal income tax and California personal income tax, consistent with preservation of capital The fund invests in a diversified portfolio of long-term California municipal obligations which are either covered by insurance guaranteeing the timely payment of principal and interest thereon or backed by an escrow or trust account containing sufficient U.S. government or U.S. government agency securities to ensure timely payment of principal and interest. The fund will terminate in approximately 20-25 years after the offering (6/19/92) but not later than June 30, 2017 unless extended. The portfolio will be fixed.

Officers:

R.J. Franke	Chairman
D.E. Sveen	President

Investment Advisor and Administrator: Nuveen Advisory Corp.

Advisory and Administration Fee: One-time Portfolio Structuring Fee of 0.95% of the net proceeds of the offering; plus an advisory fee for ongoing administration, surveillance and management of the portfolio equal to 0.35% of the fund's average daily net asset value of the fund up to $500 mil., reduced to 0.275% of average daily net assets between $500 mil. and $1 bil., and to 0.25% of any excess.

Capital Structure: *Common stock*: unlimited number of shares authorized, 5,750,000 shares outstanding as of 6/19/92

Portfolio Highlights: not yet published

Historical Financial Statistics:

	6/19/92
Value of net assets (000)	81,363
NAV	14.15

Special considerations: At least annually the fund's directors will consider taking any action to reduce any discounts which may be present, including such remedies as repurchasing shares in the open market, making tender offers or converting to an open-end fund. The fund's Declaration of Trust contains various anti-takeover provisions including a 66 2/3% vote to convert to an open-end fund, merge with another corporation, or terminate the trust.

Nuveen Insured Municipal Opportunity Fund, Inc.

333 West Wacker Drive, Chicago IL 60606

Category: Municipal Bond Fund

Phone: 312-917-7810; 800-323-5063
Listed: NIO, NYSE
Commenced Operations: September, 1991
Cusip: 670984103

1991/mid-1992 Range of Premium/Disc: +8% to -2%
1991/mid-1992 Range of Price: $15 1/8 to $13 7/8
NAV Total Return 1991: N/A
Share Price Total Return 1991: N/A
Herzfeld Ranking 1991: N/A

Investment Objective: Current income exempt from regular federal income taxes, with a secondary objective of enhancement of portfolio value, relative to the municipal bond market, through investment of substantially all of the fund's assets in municipal bonds whose timely payment of principal and interest is guaranteed by AAA rated insurers or backed by escrow accounts containing U.S. government or U.S. government agency securities.

Officers:

R.J. Franke   Chairman
D.E. Sveen   President

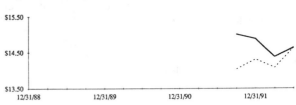

Investment Advisor: Nuveen Advisory Corp.
Advisory Fee: Annual fee equal to 0.65% of average net asset value of the fund up to $500 mil., 0.625% on next $500 mil., and 0.60% of any excess. Fee for period from 9/19/91 to 10/31/91 was $652,642.

Capital Structure: *Common stock*: 200 mil. shares authorized, 79,007,118 shares outstanding 10/31/91. *Municipal Auction Rate Cumulative Preferred Stock*: 1 mil. shares authorized, $600 mil. of preferred shares outstanding 10/31/91. 2,000 shares each Series M, Series T and Series TH1 with a liquidation preference of $50,000 per share issued in December, 1991; and 2,000 shares each Series W and TH2 with a liquidation preference of $50,000 per share issued in February, 1992.

Portfolio Highlights (as of 10/31/91): Municipal investments 44.1%, temporary investments in short-term municipal securities 66.6%, other assets less liabilities (10.7%). Quality ratings: AAA 85%, AA+/AA/AA- 11%, A+ 3%, A/A- 1%. Largest industry concentrations: general obligations bonds 18%, housing facilities 17%, health care utilities 16%, pollution control facilities 6%, transportation 5%. Largest geographic concentrations: Oklahoma 5.5%, Michigan 5.0%, Washington 5.0%. **Largest issuers**: Oklahoma Housing Finance Agency, GNMA Collateralized Single Family Mortgage AMT 7.997-18; Municipality of Metropolitan Seattle, Limited Sales Tax General Obligation; Detroit Sewage Disposal System Revenue 6.625-21; Detroit Economic Development Corporation, Resource Recovery AMT 6.875-09; Michigan Strategic Fund (The Detroit Edison Company) 6.875-21.

Historical Financial Statistics (fiscal year-end: 10/31/91):

	9/19/91 to 10/31/91
Value of net assets (000)	1,116,736
NAV	14.13
Net investment income	0.052
Dividends from net investment income	--
Expense ratio	0.77% ann.
Income ratio	4.00% ann.
Portfolio turnover	0%

Special considerations: At least annually the fund's directors will consider taking any action to reduce any discounts which may be present, including such remedies as repurchasing shares in the open market, making tender offers or converting to an open-end fund. The fund's Declaration of Trust contains various anti-takeover provisions including a 66 2/3% vote to convert to an open-end fund, merger with another corporation, or termination of the trust.

Nuveen Insured New York Select Tax-Free Income Portfolio

333 West Wacker Drive, Chicago IL 60606

Category: Municipal Bond Fund

Phone: 312-917-7810; 800-323-5063
Listed: NXN, NYSE
Commenced Operations: June, 1992
Cusip: 67063X100

1991/mid-1992 Range of Premium/Disc: +6% to +6%
1991/mid-1992 Range of Price: $15 to $15
NAV Total Return 1991: N/A
Share Price Total Return 1991: N/A
Herzfeld Ranking 1991: N/A

Investment Objective: Stable dividends exempt from both regular federal income tax as well as New York State and New York City personal income tax, consistent with preservation of capital The fund invests in a diversified portfolio of long-term New York municipal obligations which are either covered by insurance guaranteeing the timely payment of principal and interest thereon or backed by an escrow or trust account containing sufficient U.S. government or U.S. government agency securities to ensure timely payment of principal and interest. The fund will terminate in approximately 20-25 years after the offering (6/19/92) but not later than June 30, 2017, unless extended. The portfolio will be fixed.

Officers:

R.J. Franke   Chairman
D.E. Sveen   President

Investment Advisor and Administrator: Nuveen Advisory Corp.
Advisory and Administration Fee: One-time Portfolio Structuring Fee of 0.95% of the net proceeds of the offering; plus an advisory fee for ongoing administration, surveillance and management of the portfolio equal to 0.35% of the fund's average daily net asset value of the fund up to $500 mil., reduced to 0.275% of average daily net assets between $500 mil. and $1 bil., and to 0.25% of any excess.

Capital Structure: *Common stock*: unlimited number of shares authorized, 3,500,000 shares outstanding as of 6/19/92

Portfolio Highlights: not yet published

Historical Financial Statistics:

	6/19/92
Value of net assets (000)	49,525
NAV	14.15

Special considerations: At least annually the fund's directors will consider taking any action to reduce any discounts which may be present, including such remedies as repurchasing shares in the open market, making tender offers or converting to an open-end fund. The fund's Declaration of Trust contains various anti-takeover provisions including a 6 2/3% vote to convert to an open-end fund, merge with another corporation, or terminate the trust.

Nuveen Insured Quality Municipal Fund, Inc.

333 West Wacker Drive, Chicago IL 60606

Category: Municipal Bond Fund

Phone: 312-917-7810; 800-323-5063
Listed: NQI, NYSE
Commenced Operations: December, 1990
Cusip: 67062N103

1991/mid-1992 Range of Premium/Disc: +10% to +2%
1991/mid-1992 Range of Price: $16 1/2 to $14 5/8
NAV Total Return 1991: +13.85%
Share Price Total Return 1991: +11.73%
Herzfeld Ranking 1991: 19th of 51 municipal bond funds

Investment Objective: The fund seeks current income exempt from regular federal income taxes with a secondary objective of enhancement of portfolio value relative to the municipal bond market through investments in tax-exempt municipal obligations. Investments will be made in municipal securities which are either covered by insurance guaranteeing timely payment of principal and interest or backed by an escrow or trust account.

Officers:

R.J. Franke — Chairman
D.E. Sveen — President

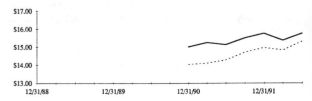

Investment Advisor: Nuveen Advisory Corp.

Advisory Fee: Annual fee equal to 0.60% of average net asset value of the fund up to $500 mil., 0.575% on next $500 mil., and 0.55% of any excess. Fee for period 12/19/90 to 10/31/91 was $3,514,799.

Capital Structure:

Common stock: unlimited number of shares authorized, 36,440,232 shares outstanding 10/31/91

Municipal Auction Rate Cumulative Preferred Stock: 1 mil. shares authorized, 1,300 shares outstanding each of Series F, M, T, and W; liquidation value $50,000 per share. Dividend rate is set every 7 days by auction.

Portfolio Highlights (as of 10/31/91): Municipal investments 98.3%, other assets 1.7%. Largest geographic concentrations: NY 12.0%, TX 9.8%, IN 6.6%, AZ 5.3%, CO 5.3%, AK 5.2%. Quality ratings: AAA 82%. AA+/AA/AA- 14%, A+ 2%, A/A- 1%, BBB+/BBB/BBB- 1%. Largest industry concentrations: housing facilities revenue 28%, health care facilities 14%, transportation 26%, escrowed and collateralized bonds 12%, general obligation bonds 10%. All of the long-term and intermediate-term investments in revenue and general obligation bonds were covered by insurance.

Largest Issuers: AK Housing Finance Corp. insured mtg. program 7.8-30; RI Depositors Economic Protection Corp. special obl.; NY State Medical Care Facilities Finance Agency (St. Luke's-Roosevelt Hospital Ctr.) FHA-Insured Mtg. Rev. 7.45-29; Minneapolis/St. Paul Housing Finance Board single family mtg. 8.3-21; DC general obl..

Historical Financial Statistics (fiscal year-end: 10/31/91):

	12/19/90 to 10/31/91
Value of net assets (000)	801,050
NAV	14.85
Net investment income	1.004
Dividends from net investment income	0.684
Common stock equivalent of dividends paid to preferred shareholders	0.19
Expense ratio	0.77% ann.
Income ratio	6.14% ann.
Portfolio turnover	39% ann.

Special considerations: The fund will pay monthly distributions of projected net investment income and annual distributions of any net capital gains. At least annually the fund's directors will consider taking any action to reduce any discounts which may be present, including such remedies as repurchasing shares in the open market, making tender offer, or converting to an open-end fund. The fund's Declaration of Trust contains various anti-takeover provisions including a 66 2/3% vote for converting to an open-end fund, merger with another corporation, or liquidation of the fund.

Nuveen Investment Quality Municipal Fund, Inc.

333 West Wacker Drive, Chicago IL 60606

Category: Municipal Bond Fund

Phone: 312-917-7810; 800-323-5063
Listed: NQM, NYSE
Commenced Operations: June, 1990
Cusip: 67062E103

1991/mid-1992 Range of Premium/Disc: +10% to 0%
1991/mid-1992 Range of Price: $17 to $14 5/8
NAV Total Return 1991: +15.71%
Share Price Total Return 1991: +15.83%
Herzfeld Ranking 1991: 9th of 51 municipal bond funds

Investment Objective: Current income exempt from regular federal income tax, with a secondary objective of enhancement of portfolio value relative to the municipal bond market through investments in tax-exempt municipal obligations that, in the opinion of the fund's investment advisor, are underrated or undervalued or represent municipal market sectors that are undervalued.

Officers:
R.J. Franke — Chairman
D.E. Sveen — President

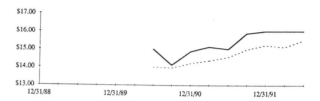

Investment Advisor: Nuveen Advisory Corp.

Advisory Fee: Annual fee equal to 0.60% of average weekly net assets up to $500 mil., 0.575% on next $500 mil., and 0.55% of any excess. Fee for year-ended 10/31/91 was $4,423,704.

Capital Structure: *Common stock*: 200 mil. shares authorized, 34,360,140 shares outstanding 10/31/91
Municipal Auction Rate Preferred Stock: 1 mil. shares authorized, 1,250 shares outstanding each Series M,T,W, and F; liquidation value $50,000. Dividend rate is set every 7 days by auction.

Portfolio Highlights (as of 10/31/91): Municipal investments 97.9%, temporary investments in short-term municipal securities 0.2%, other assets 1.9%. Largest geographic concentrations: NY 17.0%, FL 8.9%, TX 8.4%, MA 7.8%, GA 6.3%, WA 5.9%, IL 5.9%, LA 5.5%. Quality ratings: AAA 26%, AA=/AA/AA- 29%, A+ 11%, A/A- 18%, BBB+/BBB/BBB- 15%, non-rated 1%. Largest industry concentrations: housing facilities revenue 25%, health care facilities 15%, electric utilities 14%. 21% of the long-term and intermediate-term investments are covered by insurance.

Largest Issuers: AZ Municipal Financial Program; Hernando Cty., FL, Criminal Justice Complex Financing Program 8.0-15 (Mandatory put 7/1/15): Jacksonville, FL, Health Fac. Auth. (Daughters of Charity Health Sys.-St. Vincent) 7.5-15; LA Public Facilities Auth. (West Jefferson Medical Ctr.) 7.9-15; Orange Cty., FL, Housing Fin. Auth.

Historical Financial Statistics (fiscal year-end: 10/31/91):

	1991	6/21/90 to 10/31/90
Value of net assets (000)	769,837	724,011
NAV	15.13	13.93
Net investment income	1.457	0.318
Dividends from net investment income (common)	1.092	0.178
Common stock equivalent of dividends paid to preferred shares	0.350	0.034
Expense ratio	0.75%	0.72% ann.
Income ratio	6.67%	6.06% ann.
Portfolio turnover	3%	0% ann.

Special considerations: Monthly distributions are made from net investment income remaining after payment of preferred dividends, and annual distributions are made of net capital gains. At least annually the board of directors will consider various actions to reduce discounts including: repurchases of shares in the open market or in private transactions, tender offers, or converting to an open-end fund. The fund's Articles of Incorporation contain various anti-takeover provisions including a 66 2/3% shareholder vote of both classes of stock voting together to convert to an open-end fund, merge with another corporation, or liquidate the fund.

Nuveen Michigan Quality Income Municipal Fund, Inc.

333 West Wacker Drive, Chicago IL 60606

Category: Municipal Bond Fund

Phone: 312-917-7810; 800-323-5063	**1991/mid-1992 Range of Premium/Disc:** +10% to 0%
Listed: NUM, NYSE	**1991/mid-1992 Range of Price:** $15 1/2 to $14 1/4
Commenced Operations: October, 1991	**NAV Total Return 1991:** N/A
Cusip: 670979103	**Share Price Total Return 1991:** N/A
	Herzfeld Ranking 1991: N/A

Investment Objective: Current income exempt from regular federal and Michigan State income taxes, with a secondary objective of enhancement of portfolio value, relative to the municipal bonds market, through investment of substantially all of the fund's assets in municipal bonds rated in the four highest categories or unrated securities that the fund's advisor believes to be of investment-grade quality.

Officers:
R.J. Franke — Chairman
D.E. Sveen — President

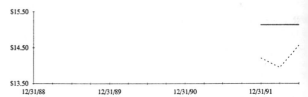

Investment Advisor: Nuveen Advisory Corp.

Advisory Fee: Annual fee equal to 0.65% of average net asset value of the fund up to $500 mil., 0.625% on next $500 mil., and 0.60% of any excess. Fee for period from 10/17/91 to 11/30/91 was $94,501.

Capital Structure: *Common stock:* 200 mil. shares authorized, 10,770,434 shares outstanding 11/30/91 *Municipal Auction Rate Preferred stock:* 1 mil. shares authorized, 1,600 shares Series TH with liquidation preference $50,000 issued in February, 1992.

Portfolio Highlights (as of 11/30/91): Michigan municipal investments 30.4%, temporary investments in short-term municipal securities 80.5%, other assets less liabilities (10.9%). Quality ratings: AAA 55%, AA+/AA/AA-40%, A/A- 5%. Largest industry concentrations: health care facilities 34%, general obligation bonds 24%, electric utilities 19%, pollution control facilities 16%, housing facilities 7%. 55% of the long-term and intermediate-term investments were covered by insurance. **Largest issuers:** Detroit Economic Development Corporation, Resource recovery, alternative minimum tax 6.875-09; Michigan State Hospital Finance Authority; Michigan Strategic Fund (The Detroit Edison Company) 6.875-21; Royal Oak Hospital Finance Authority (William Beaumont Hospital) 6.75-20; Detroit Sewage Disposal System 6.625-21.

Historical Financial Statistics:

	10/17/91 to 11/30/91
Value of net assets (000)	151,447
NAV	14.06
Net investment income	--
Dividends from net investment income	--
Expense ratio	0.79% ann.
Income ratio	3.59% ann.
Portfolio turnover	0%

Special considerations: At least annually the fund's directors will consider taking any action to reduce any discounts which may be present, including such remedies as repurchasing shares in the open market, making tender offers or converting to an open-end fund. The fund's Declaration of Trust contains various anti-takeover provisions including a 66 2/3% vote to convert to an open-end fund, merger with another corporation, or termination of the trust. Mid-1992 dividend rate $0.0755 per month.

Nuveen Municipal Advantage Fund, Inc.

333 West Wacker Drive, Chicago IL 60606

Category: Municipal Bond Fund

Phone: 312-917-7810; 800-323-5063
Listed: NMA, NYSE
Commenced Operations: December, 1989
Cusip: 67062H106

1991/mid-1992 Range of Premium/Disc: +7% to 0%
1991/mid-1992 Range of Price: $16 3/8 to $14 3/8
NAV Total Return 1990: +6.53%; **1991:** +15.40%
Share Price Total Return 1990: +2.63%; **1991:** +17.05%
Herzfeld Ranking 1991: 11th of 51 municipal bond funds

Investment Objective: Current income exempt from regular federal income tax, with a secondary objective of enhancement of portfolio value relative to the municipal bond market through investments in tax-exempt municipal obligations that, in the opinion of the fund's investment advisor, are underrated or undervalued or that represent municipal market sectors that are undervalued. The fund invests substantially all its assets in a diversified portfolio of tax-exempt municipal obligations within the four highest grades, except that up to 20% of the fund's assets may be invested in unrated municipal obligations.

Officers:

R.J. Franke — Chairman
D.E. Sveen — President

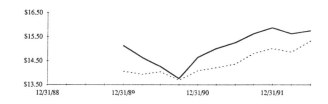

Investment Advisor: Nuveen Advisory Corp.

Advisory Fee: Annual fee equal to 0.60% of average weekly net assets up to $500 mil., 0.575% on next $500 mil., and 0.55% of any excess. Fee for year-ended 10/31/91 was $5,206,968.

Capital Structure: *Common stock:* 200 mil. shares authorized; 40,765,716 shares outstanding 10/31/91 *Municipal Auction Rate Preferred stock:* 1 mil. shares authorized, 1,500 shares outstanding each of Series M, T, W, and F; liquidation value $50,000 per share. Dividend rate is set every 7 days by auction

Portfolio Highlights (as of 10/31/91): Municipal investments 97.4%, short-term municipal securities 0.8%, other assets 1.8%. Quality ratings: AAA 20%, AA+/AA/AA- 36%, A+ 5%, A/A- 22%, BBB+/BBB/BBB- 15%, non-rated 2%. Largest industry concentrations: housing fac. rev. 28%, health care fac. rev. 18%, electric util. 15%. 11% of the long-term and intermediate-term investments were covered by insurance. **Largest Issuers:** Dormitory Auth. of the State of NY; Piedmont (SC) Municipal Power Agency; NY State Medical Care Facilities Fin. Agency; Washington Public Power Supply System Nuclear Project No. 1; NY State Housing Finance Agency health finance rev. (New York City) 8-08.

Historical Financial Statistics (fiscal year-end: 10/31/91):

	1991	12/19/89 to 10/31/90
Value of net assets (000)	909,345	856,867
NAV	14.95	13.78
Net investment income	1.458	1.088
Dividends from net investment income (common)	1.098	0.716
Common stock equivalent of dividends paid to preferred shares	0.355	0.287
Expense ratio	0.76%	0.75% ann.
Income ratio	6.70%	6.65% ann.
Portfolio turnover	5%	3% ann.

Special considerations: The fund makes monthly distributions of net investment income and annual distributions of realized capital gains. At least annually the board will consider actions to reduce discounts which may develop, including repurchasing shares in the open market, tender offers, and converting to an open-end fund. The fund's Articles of Incorporation contain various anti-takeover provisions including a 2/3 vote of common and preferred shareholders voting together as a single class for, among other things, converting to an open-end fund, merger with another corporation, or liquidation of the fund.

Nuveen Municipal Income Fund, Inc.

333 West Wacker Drive, Chicago, IL 60606   **Category: Municipal Bond Fund**

Phone: 312-917-7810; 800-323-5063
Listed: NMI, NYSE
Commenced Operations: April, 1988
Cusip: 67062J102

1991/mid-1992 Range of Premium/Disc: +9% to 0%
1991/mid-1992 Range of Price: $13 1/4 to $11 5/8
NAV Total Return 1990: +6.21%; **1991:** +11.77%
Share Price Total Return 1990: +5.90%; **1991:** +14.80%
Herzfeld Ranking 1991: 33rd of 51 municipal bond funds

Investment Objective: High level of current income exempt from federal income taxes primarily through investment in a diversified portfolio of tax-exempt municipal obligations.

Officers:

R.J. Franke   Chairman
D.E. Sveen   President

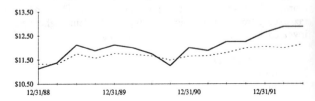

Investment Advisor: Nuveen Advisory Co.
Advisory Fee: Fee of 0.50% of average net asset value of the fund. Fee for six months ended 1/31/92 was $225,287.

Capital Structure: *Common stock*: 200 mil. shares authorized; 7,472,833 shares outstanding 1/31/92

Portfolio Highlights (as of 1/31/92): Municipal investments 97.6%, temporary investments in short-term municipal securities 2.2%, other assets less liabilities 0.2%. Quality ratings: AAA 9%, AA+/AA/AA- 16%, A+ 2%, A/A- 22%, BBB+/BBB/BBB- 30%, non-rated 21%. Largest industry concentrations: housing facilities revenue 20%, health care facilities revenue 20%, transportation revenue 17%, pollution control facilities revenue 16%, electric utilities revenue 13%. Largest geographic concentrations: Texas 15.4%, Florida 9.1%, Oklahoma 6.3%, New York 6.1%, Illinois 5.5%, Massachusetts 5.1%. **Largest issuers:** Brownsville (TX) Utilities System 8-14; Illinois Health Facilities Authority; Sacramento (CA) Municipal Utility District 9-09; Brazos River (TX) Authority (Houston Lighting and Power Company) AMT 7.875-18; Comanche County (OK) Hospital Authority 8.05-16.

Historical Financial Statistics (fiscal year-end: 7/31/91):

	six months 1/31/92	1991	1990	1989	4/20/88 to 7/31/88
Value of net assets (000)	89,912	88,384	86,359	86,535	81,375
NAV	12.03	11.90	11.71	11.81	11.15
Net investment income	0.425	0.855	0.842	0.828	0.151
Dividends from net investment income	0.426	0.841	0.842	0.817	0.095
Distributions from net realized gains	0.055	--	--	--	--
Expense ratio	0.72% ann.	0.69%	0.72%	0.73%	0.73% ann.
Income ratio	7.03% ann.	7.33%	7.24%	7.25%	5.21% ann.
Portfolio turnover	4% ann.	3%	7%	35%	0%

Special considerations: The board will consider repurchasing shares, making a tender offer or open-ending the fund on an annual basis. The fund's Articles of Incorporation contain various anti-takeover provisions.

Nuveen Municipal Market Opportunity Fund, Inc.

333 West Wacker Drive, Chicago, IL 60606

Category: Municipal Bond Fund

Phone: 312-917-7810; 800-323-5063
Listed: NMO, NYSE
Commenced Operations: March, 1990
Cusip: 67062W103

1991/mid-1992 Range of Premium/Disc: +8% to 0%
1991/mid-1992 Range of Price: $16 5/8 to $14 1/4
NAV Total Return 1991: +15.75%
Share Price Total Return 1991: +20.16%
Herzfeld Ranking 1991: 7th of 51 municipal bond funds

Investment Objective: Current income exempt from regular federal income tax. Its secondary investment objective is the enhancement of portfolio value relative to the municipal bond market through investments in tax-exempt municipal obligations that, in the opinion of the fund's investment advisor, are underrated or undervalued or represent municipal market sectors that are undervalued. The fund will seek to achieve its investment objectives by investing substantially all of its assets in a diversified portfolio of tax-exempt municipal obligations rated within the four highest grades, except that up to 20% of the fund's assets may be invested in unrated municipal obligations.

Officers:

R.J. Franke   Chairman
D.E. Sveen   President

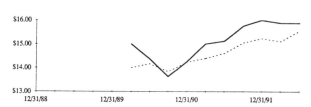

Investment Advisor: Nuveen Advisory Co.

Advisory Fee: Fee of 0.60% of average net asset value of the fund up to $500 mil., 0.575% on next $500 mil., and $0.55% on any excess. Fee for year-ended 10/31/91 was $5,477,593.

Capital Structure: *Common stock:* 200 mil. shares authorized, 42,963,400 shares outstanding 10/31/91
Municipal Auction Rate Preferred stock: 1 mil. shares authorized, 2,000 shares outstanding each Series M,T, and F; liquidation value $50,000 per share. Dividend rate is set every 7 days by auction.

Portfolio Highlights (as of 10/31/91): Municipal investments 98.2%, other assets 1.8%. Quality ratings: AAA 21%, AA+/AA/AA- 32%, A+ 8%, A/A- 25%, BBB+/BBB/BBB- 13%, non-rated 1%. Largest industry concentrations: housing facilities revenue 30%, electric utilities revenue 19%, health care facilities revenue 15%, transportation revenue 8%. Largest geographic concentrations: New York 18.0%, Washington 10.0%, Massachusetts 7.9%, Texas 7.6%, Illinois 7.4%, Florida 5.3%. **Largest issues:** Washington Public Power Supply System Nuclear Proj. No. 1, 2, and 3; Municipal Electric Auth. of GA; Arizona Municipal Financing Program; Dormitory Auth. of the State of NY (City University Sys.); NYC Municipal Water Fin. Auth.

Historical Financial Statistics (fiscal year-end: 10/31/91)

	1991	3/21/90 to 10/31/90
Value of net assets (000)	958,781	901,754
NAV	15.16	13.98
Net investment income	1.442	0.718
Dividends from net investment income (common)	1.104	0.45
Common stock equivalent of dividends paid to preferred shares	0.337	0.184
Expense ratio	0.75%	0.73% ann.
Income ratio	6.70%	6.31% ann.
Portfolio turnover	7%	3% ann.

Special considerations: The fund makes regular monthly cash distributions to common shareholders at a level rate that reflects the past and projected performance of the fund and will result in the distribution of all net investment income of the fund and will make at least annual distributions of net capital gains. The fund's Articles of Incorporation contain various anti-takeover provisions including a 66 2/3% vote to convert to an open-end fund, merge with another corporation or liquidate the fund.

Nuveen Municipal Value Fund, Inc.
333 West Wacker Drive, Chicago, IL 60606

Category: Municipal Bond Fund

Phone: 312-917-7810; 800-323-5063
Listed: NUV, NYSE
Commenced Operations: June, 1987
Cusip: 670928100

1991/mid-1992 Range of Premium/Disc: +9% to 0%
1991/mid-1992 Range of Price: $11 7/8 to $9 1/2
NAV Total Return 1990: +6.36%; **1991**: +11.44%
Share Price Total Return 1990: +8.42%; **1991**: +14.80%
Herzfeld Ranking 1991: 34th of 51 municipal bond funds

Investment Objective: Current income exempt from federal income taxes with a secondary objective of enhancement of portfolio value, primarily through investment in tax-exempt municipal obligations.

Officers:
R.J. Franke   Chairman
D.E. Sveen   President

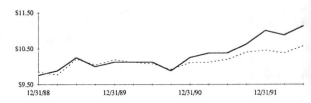

Investment Advisor: Nuveen Advisory Co.
Advisory Fee: Fee of 0.40% of the first $500 mil. of average net asset value of the fund, 0.375% of next $500 mil., and 0.35% of excess; plus 4.75% of the gross interest income on the first $50 mil., 4.625% of gross interest income on the next $50 mil. and 4.5% on any excess; the fee shall not exceed in the aggregate 1% of average weekly net asset value. Fee for year-ended 11/30/91 was $11,763,579.

Capital Structure: *Common stock*: 350 mil. shares authorized; 162,145,046 shares outstanding 11/30/91

Portfolio Highlights (as of 11/30/91): Municipal investments 97.8%, temporary investments 0.2%, other assets less liabilities 2.0%. Quality ratings: AAA 11%, AA+/AA/AA- 24%, A+ 8%, A/A- 24%, BBB+/BBB/BBB- 27%, BB+/BB 2%, B 1%, non-rated 3%. Largest industry concentrations: electric utilities 36%, health care facilities 19%, housing facilities 11%, pollution control facilities 8%. **Largest issuers**: (UT) Intermountain Power Agency; North Carolina Eastern Municipal Power Agency; North Carolina Municipal Power Agency No. 1 (Catawba); Piedmont (SC) Municipal Power Agency; Massachusetts Municipal Wholesale Electric Company.

Historical Financial Statistics (fiscal year-end: 11/30/91*):

	11/30/91	10/30/90	1989	10/88	6/17/87 to 10/31/87
Value of net assets (000)	**1,686,936**	1,595,189	1,613,404	1,572,110	1,445,069
NAV	**10.40**	9.97	10.14	9.94	9.14
Net investment income	**0.715**	0.714	0.714	0.682	0.162
Dividends from net investment income	**0.714**	0.714	0.717	0.682	0.131
Distributions from net realized gains	--	0.030	0.025	--	--
Expense ratio	**0.83%**	0.86%	0.89%	0.94%	0.80% ann.
Income ratio	**6.98%**	7.10%	7.13%	7.12%	4.99% ann.
Portfolio turnover	**7%**	5%	7%	42%	1%

*fiscal year-end changed to 11/30; value of net assets as of 11/30/90, $1,617,486,719; NAV 10.10

Special considerations: The fund may repurchase shares in the open market when the board deems it advantageous. The fund's Articles of Incorporation contain various anti-takeover provisions. Dividend rate lowered to $0.059 per month beginning with February, 1992 dividend.

Nuveen New Jersey Investment Quality Municipal Fund, Inc.

333 West Wacker Drive, Chicago, IL 60606   **Category:** Municipal Bond Fund

Phone: 312-917-7810; 800-323-5063
Listed: NQJ, NYSE
Commenced Operations: February, 1991
Cusip: 670971100

1991/mid-1992 Range of Premium/Disc: +12% to +2%
1991/mid-1992 Range of Price: $16 to $14 5/8
NAV Total Return 1991: N/A
Share Price Total Return 1991: N/A
Herzfeld Ranking 1991: N/A

Investment Objective: The fund seeks current income exempt from both regular federal and New Jersey income taxes with a secondary objective of enhancement of portfolio value relative to the New Jersey municipal bond market through investments in tax-exempt New Jersey municipal obligations. Investments will be made in municipal securities rated BBB or better; 20% of investments may be in unrated securities which in the opinion of the advisor are of comparable quality.

Officers:

R.J. Franke   Chairman
D.E. Sveen   President

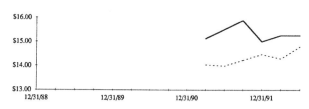

Investment Advisor: Nuveen Advisory Co.

Advisory Fee: Fee of 0.60% of average net asset value of the fund up to $500 mil., 0.575% on next $500 mil., and $0.55% on any excess. Fee for year-ended 10/31/91 was $853,045.

Capital Structure: *Common stock*: unlimited number of shares authorized, 11,742,712 shares outstanding 10/31/91
Municipal Auction Rate Cumulative Preferred Stock: 1 mil. shares authorized, 1,600 shares outstanding; liquidation value $50,000 per share. Dividend rate is set every 7 days by auction.

Portfolio Highlights (as of 10/31/91): Municipal investments 98.0%, short-term municipal securities 0.5%, other assets 1.5%. Quality ratings: AAA 52%, AA+/AA/AA- 21%, A+ 3%, A/A- 18%, non-rated 6%. Largest industry concentrations: transportation revenue 22%, housing facilities 16%, health care facilities 13%, general obligation bonds 12%, escrowed bonds 8%, water/sewer facilities 7%. 38% of the long-term and intermediate-term investments are covered by insurance. **Largest Issuers:** NJ Turnpike Auth. 7.2-18; Port Auth. of NY and NJ consolidated bonds AMT 8.25-23; NJ Housing and Mtg. Fin. Agency 7.0-20; NJ Highway Auth. (Garden State Pkwy.) 7.25-16.

Historical Financial Statistics (fiscal year-end: 10/31/91):

	1991
Value of net assets (000)	248,154
NAV	14.32
Net investment income	0.614
Dividends from net investment income	0.49
Common stock equivalent of dividends paid to preferred shareholders	0.116
Expense ratio	0.76% ann.
Income ratio	5.06% ann.
Portfolio turnover	2% ann.

Special considerations: The fund makes monthly distributions of projected net investment income and annual distributions of any net capital gains. At least annually the fund's directors will consider taking action to reduce any discounts which may be present, including such remedies as repurchasing shares in the open market, making tender offers or converting to an open-end fund. The fund's Articles of Incorporation contain various anti-takeover provisions including a 66 2/3% vote to convert to an open-end fund, merge with another corporation, or liquidate the fund.

Nuveen New Jersey Quality Income Municipal Fund, Inc.

333 West Wacker Drive, Chicago, IL 60606   **Category: Municipal Bond Fund**

Phone: 312-917-7810; 800-323-5063	**1991/mid-1992 Range of Premium/Disc:** +7% to 0%
Listed: NUJ, NYSE	**1991/mid-1992 Range of Price:** $15 1/8 to $14 1/4
Commenced Operations: October, 1991	**NAV Total Return 1991:** N/A
Cusip: 670982107	**Share Price Total Return 1991:** N/A
	Herzfeld Ranking 1991: N/A

Investment Objective: Current income exempt from regular federal and New Jersey State income taxes, with a secondary objective of enhancement of portfolio value, relative to the municipal bond market, through investment of substantially all of the fund's assets in municipal bonds rated in the four highest categories, or unrated securities that the fund's advisor believes to be of investment-grade quality.

Officers:

R.J. Franke   Chairman
D.E. Sveen   President

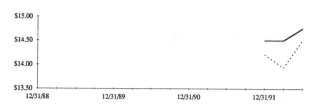

Investment Advisor: Nuveen Advisory Corp.
Advisory Fee: Annual fee equal to 0.65% of average net asset value of the fund up to $500 mil., 0.625% on next $500 mil., and 0.60% of any excess. Fee for period from 10/17/91 to 12/31/91 was $119,220.

Capital Structure: *Common stock:* 200 mil. shares authorized, 7,007,118 shares outstanding 12/31/91
Municipal Auction Rate Preferred stock: 1 mil. shares authorized, none outstanding 12/31/91

Portfolio Highlights (as of 12/31/91): New Jersey municipal investments 84.8%, temporary investments in short-term municipal securities 18.1%, other assets less liabilities (2.9%). Quality ratings: AAA 36%, AA+/AA/AA-32%, A+ 3%, A/A- 16%, BBB+/BBB/BBB- 7%, non-rated 6%. Largest industry concentrations: general obligation bonds 27%, pollution control facilities 17%, transportation 16%, escrowed bonds 13%, housing facilities 8%. 15% of the long-term and intermediate-term investments are covered by insurance. **Largest issuers:** New Jersey Economic Development Authority; New Jersey Health Care Facilities Financing Authority; Port Authority of New York and New Jersey consolidated bonds AMT 8.24-23; Salem County Pollution Control Authority (EI duPont-Chambers Works Project) 6.5-21; Ocean County Utilities Authority, Wastewater System 8.375-18 (pre-refunded to 1/1/97).

Historical Financial Statistics (fiscal year-end: 6/30/92):

	10/17/91 to 12/31/91
Value of net assets (000)	99,859
NAV	14.25
Net investment income	0.112
Dividends from net investment income	--
Expense ratio	0.86% ann.
Income ratio	4.28% ann.
Portfolio turnover	0%

Special considerations: At least annually the fund's directors will consider taking any action to reduce any discounts which may be present, including such remedies as repurchasing shares in the open market, making tender offers or converting to an open-end fund. The fund's Articles of Incorporation contain various anti-takeover provisions including a 66 2/3% vote to convert to an open-end fund, merge with another corporation, or liquidate the fund. Mid-1992 dividend rate $0.074 per share.

Nuveen New York Investment Quality Municipal Fund, Inc.

333 West Wacker Drive, Chicago, IL 60606

Category: Municipal Bond Fund

Phone: 312-917-7810; 800-323-5063
Listed: NQN, NYSE
Commenced Operations: November, 1990
Cusip: 67062X101

1991/mid-1992 Range of Premium/Disc: +10% to 0%
1991/mid-1992 Range of Price: $16 3/4 to $14 7/8
NAV Total Return 1991: +15.08%
Share Price Total Return 1991: +9.57%
Herzfeld Ranking 1991: 12th of 51 municipal bond funds

Investment Objective: Current income exempt from regular federal as well as New York State and New York City income taxes, with a secondary objective of enhancement of portfolio value relative to the New York municipal bond market through investments in tax-exempt New York municipal obligations that the advisor feels are underrated or undervalued.

Officers:

R.J. Franke   Chairman
D.E. Sveen   President

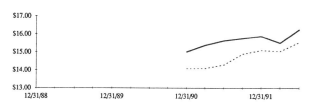

Investment Advisor: Nuveen Advisory Co.

Advisory Fee: Fee of 0.60% of average net asset value of the fund up to $500 mil., 0.575% on next $500 mil., and $0.55% on any excess. Fee for six months ended 3/31/92 was $923,948.

Capital Structure: *Common stock:* 200 mil. shares authorized, 16,652,930 shares outstanding 3/31/92
Municipal Auction Rate Cumulative Preferred Stock: 1 mil. shares authorized, 1,200 shares outstanding each Series T and F; liquidation value $50,000 per share. Dividend rate is set every 7 days by auction.

Portfolio Highlights (as of 3/31/92): Municipal investments 98.3%, temporary investments 0.1%, other assets less liabilities 1.6%. Quality ratings: AAA 87%, AA+/AA/AA- 11%, A/A- 1%, BBB+/BBB/BBB- 1%. Largest industry concentrations: transportation 21%, housing facilities 15%, general obligation bonds 14%, educational facilities 11%, health care facilities 10%. **Largest issuers:** New York State Medical Care Facilities Finance; Dormitory Authority of the State of New York; Triborough Bridge and Tunnel Authority general purpose revenue; New York State Energy Research and Development Authority; New York City general obligation.

Historical Financial Statistics (fiscal year-end: 10/31/91):

	six months 3/31/92	11/20/90 to 10/31/91
Value of net assets (000)	371,093	368,269
NAV	15.08	14.98
Net investment income	0.558	1.071
Dividends from net investment income	0.433	0.773
Common stock equivalent of dividends paid to preferred shareholders	0.107	0.20
Expense ratio	0.79% ann.	0.80% ann.
Income ratio	6.02% ann.	6.03% ann.
Portfolio turnover	0%	10% ann.

Special considerations: The fund makes regular monthly cash distributions to common shareholders at a level rate that reflects the past and projected performance of the fund and will result in the distribution of all net investment income of the fund and makes at least annual distributions of net capital gains. The fund's Articles of Incorporation contain various anti-takeover provisions including a 66 2/3% vote to convert to an open-end fund, merge with another corporation or liquidate the fund. At least annually the board of directors will consider actions which may reduce a discount from net asset value such as repurchasing shares in the open market, making a tender offer, or converting to an open-end fund.

Nuveen New York Municipal Income Fund, Inc.

333 West Wacker Drive, Chicago, IL 60606

Category: Municipal Bond Fund

Phone: 312-917-7810; 800-323-5063
Listed: NNM, ASE
Commenced Operations: April, 1988
Cusip: 67062L107

1991/mid-1992 Range of Premium/Disc: +8% to -3%
1991/mid-1992 Range of Price: $12 3/4 to $11 1/4
NAV Total Return 1990: +4.65%; **1991:** +12.78%
Share Price Total Return 1990: +7.04%; **1991:** +9.34%
Herzfeld Ranking 1991: 27th of 51 municipal bond funds

Investment Objective: High level of current income exempt from federal, New York state and New York City income taxes primarily through investment in a diversified portfolio of tax-exempt New York municipal obligations.

Officers:
R.J. Franke — Chairman
D.E. Sveen — President

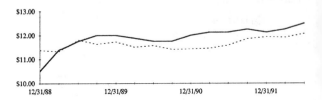

Investment Advisor: Nuveen Advisory Co.
Advisory Fee: Fee of 0.50% of average net asset value of the fund. Fee for six months ended 3/31/92 was $48,696.

Capital Structure: *Common stock*: 200 mil. shares authorized; 2,452,946 shares outstanding 3/31/92

Portfolio Highlights (as of 3/31/92): Municipal investments 97.8%, other assets less liabilities 2.2%. Quality ratings: AAA 8%, AA+/AA/AA- 21%, A/A- 15%, BBB+/BBB/BBB- 42%, non-rated 14%. Largest sector concentrations: pollution control facilities 18%, housing facilities 17%, lease rental facilities 8%, transportation 8%. **Largest issuers:** New York State Energy Research and Development Authority; New York State Housing Finance Agency; Babylon Industrial Development Agency resource recovery revenue 8.5-19; New York City Industrial Development Agency; Metropolitan Transportation Authority, Transit Facilities.

Historical Financial Statistics (fiscal year-end: 11/30/91*):

	six months 3/31/92	11/30/91	10/31/90	1989	4/20/88 to 10/31/88
Value of net assets (000)	29,160	29,187	27,564	28,177	27,689
NAV	11.89	11.94	11.37	11.71	11.53
Net investment income	0.27	0.795	0.806	0.806	0.358
Dividends from net investment income	0.262	0.802	0.810	0.808	0.282
Distributions from net realized gains	0.071	--	0.070	0.028	--
Expense ratio	0.80% ann.	0.92%	0.86%	0.90%	0.94% ann.
Income ratio	6.79% ann.	6.84%	6.99%	6.95%	6.21% ann.
Portfolio turnover	0%	14%	11%	36%	39% ann.

*fiscal year end changed to 11/30; value of net assets as of 11/30/90, $27,735,546; NAV, 11.43

Special considerations: On an annual basis, the board will consider repurchasing shares, making a tender offer or open-ending the fund. The fund's Articles of Incorporation contain various anti-takeover provisions.

Nuveen New York Municipal Market Opportunity Fund, Inc.

333 West Wacker Drive, Chicago, IL 60606   **Category: Municipal Bond Fund**

Phone: 312-917-7810; 800-323-5063   **1991/mid-1992 Range of Premium/Disc:** +10% to -1%
Listed: NNO, NYSE   **1991/mid-1992 Range of Price:** $17 to $13 7/8
Commenced Operations: May, 1990   **NAV Total Return 1991:** +18.85%
Cusip: 67062V105   **Share Price Total Return 1991:** +18.22%
     Herzfeld Ranking 1991: 1st of 51 municipal bond funds

Investment Objective: Current income exempt from both regular federal and New York State and New York City income taxes, with a secondary objective of enhancement of portfolio value relative to the New York municipal bond market through investments in tax-exempt New York municipal obligations that, in the opinion of the fund's investment advisor, are underrated or undervalued or that represent municipal market sectors that are undervalued. Substantially all investments will be made in municipal obligations rated within the four highest grades.

Officers:

R.J. Franke   Chairman
D.E. Sveen   President

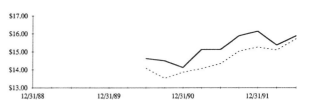

Investment Advisor: Nuveen Advisory Co.
Advisory Fee: Fee of 0.60% of average net asset value of the fund up to $500 mil., 0.575% on next $500 mil., and 0.55% on any excess. Fee for six months ended 3/31/92 was $314,015.

Capital Structure: *Common stock:* 200 mil. shares authorized, 5,675,573 shares outstanding 3/31/92
Municipal Auction Rate Preferred stock: 1 mil. shares authorized, 800 shares outstanding of Series M; liquidation value $50,000 per share. Dividend rate is set every 7 days by auction.

Portfolio Highlights (as of 3/31/92): Municipal investments 98.2%, temporary investments in short-term municipal securities 0.2%, other assets less liabilities 1.6%. Quality ratings: AAA 25%, AA+/AA/AA- 24%, A/A- 16%, BBB+/BBB/BBB- 35%. Largest industry concentrations: housing facilities revenue 20%, general obligation bonds 16%, educational facilities 15%, transportation 14%, water/sewer facilities 9%, pollution control facilities 8%, escrowed bonds 6%. 17% of long-term and intermediate-term investments were covered by insurance. **Largest issuers:** Dormitory Auth. of the State of NY; NY State Medical Care Facilities Fin. Agency; NY State Urban Dev. Corp.; NY State Mtg. Agency, Homeowner Mortgage Rev. AMT; Metropolitan Trans. Auth., Transit Fac.

Historical Financial Statistics (fiscal year-end: 10/31/91):

	six months 3/31/92	1991	5/17/90 to 10/31/90
Value of net assets (000)	125,900	126,027	115,726
NAV	15.14	15.23	13.54
Net investment income	0.583	1.409	0.475
Dividends from net investment income (common)	0.45	1.058	0.263
Common stock equivalent of dividends paid to preferred shares	0.106	0.331	0.108
Expense ratio	0.83% ann.	0.84%	0.87% ann.
Income ratio	6.31% ann.	6.57%	6.12% ann.
Portfolio turnover	2% ann.	29%	12% ann.

Special considerations: The fund makes regular monthly cash distributions from net investment income remaining after payment of preferred dividends and at least annual distributions of net capital gains if any. On an annual basis, the board will consider repurchasing shares, making a tender offer or open-ending the fund. The fund's Articles of Incorporation contain various anti-takeover provisions.

Nuveen New York Municipal Value Fund, Inc.

333 West Wacker Drive, Chicago, IL 60606   **Category: Municipal Bond Fund**

Phone: 312-917-7810; 800-323-5063
Listed: NNY, NYSE
Commenced Operations: October, 1987
Cusip: 67062M105

1991/mid-1992 Range of Premium/Disc: +7% to 0%
1991/mid-1992 Range of Price: $11 1/4 to $10 1/8
NAV Total Return 1990: +4.53%; **1991**: +13.36%
Share Price Total Return 1990: +2.08%; **1991**: +13.92%
Herzfeld Ranking 1991: 23rd of 51 municipal bond funds

Investment Objective: Current income exempt from federal , New York state and New York City income taxes with a secondary objective of enhancement of portfolio value, primarily through investment in tax-exempt New York municipal obligations.

Officers:

R.J. Franke   Chairman
D.E. Sveen   President

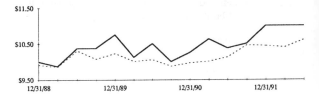

Investment Advisor: Nuveen Advisory Co.

Advisory Fee: Fee of 0.40% of average net asset value of the fund plus 4.75% of the first $50 mil. of gross interest income, 4.625% of the next $50 mil. of gross interest income, and 4.50% on any excess; annual fee not to exceed in the aggregate 1% of average weekly net asset value. Fee for six months ended 1/31/92 was $425,576.

Capital Structure: *Common stock*: 250 mil. shares authorized; 11,398,766 shares outstanding 1/31/92

Portfolio Highlights (as of 1/31/92): Municipal investments 97.7%, other assets less liabilities 2.3%. Quality ratings: AAA 17%, AA+/AA/AA- 35%, A/A- 18%, BBB+/BBB/BBB- 28% non-rated 2%. Largest industry concentrations: housing facilities revenue 28%, escrowed bonds 14%, lease rental facilities revenue 13%, general obligation bonds 13%, transportation revenue 12%, pollution control revenue 7%. **Largest issuers**: New York State Medical Care Facilities Finance Agency; Dormitory Authority of the State of New York; New York State Energy Research and Development Authority, Pollution Control Revenue; New York State Mortgage Agency, Homeowner Mortgage Revenue, AMT; New York City Municipal Water Finance Authority, water and sewer system revenue.

Historical Financial Statistics (fiscal year-end: 7/31/91):

	six months 1/31/92	1991	1990	1989	10/7/87 to 7/31/88
Value of net assets (000)	**118,926**	116,236	114,368	115,379	109,750
NAV	**10.43**	10.27	10.20	10.37	9.95
Net investment income	**0.338**	0.679	0-.677	0.675	0.514
Dividends from net investment income	**0.338**	0.676	0.676	0.679	0.455
Distributions from net realized gains	**0.127**	0.048	0.044	0.235	--
Expense ratio	**0.91% ann.**	0.96%	0.98%	1.03%	0.99% ann.
Income ratio	**6.44% ann.**	6.77%	6.70%	6.75%	6.54% ann.
Portfolio turnover	**6% ann.**	14%	16%	24%	58%

Special considerations: The fund may repurchase shares in the open market when the board deems it advantageous. The fund's Articles of Incorporation contain various anti-takeover provisions.

Nuveen New York Performance Plus Municipal Fund, Inc.

333 West Wacker Drive, Chicago, IL 60606 **Category:** Municipal Bond Fund

Phone: 312-917-7810; 800-323-5063
Listed: NNP, NYSE
Commenced Operations: November, 1989
Cusip: 67062R104

1991/mid-1992 Range of Premium/Disc: +12% to 0%
1991/mid-1992 Range of Price: $16 1/4 to $14 1/2
NAV Total Return 1990: +2.90%; **1991:** +18.18%
Share Price Total Return 1990: +6.47%; **1991:** +12.97%
Herzfeld Ranking 1991: 2nd of 51 municipal bond funds

Investment Objective: Current income exempt from regular federal as well as New York state and New York City income taxes, with a secondary objective of enhancement of portfolio value relative to the New York municipal bond market through investment in tax-exempt New York municipal obligations that, in the opinion of the fund's investment advisor, are underrated or undervalued or represent municipal market sectors that are undervalued. The fund will invest substantially all of the assets in a diversified portfolio of tax-exempt New York municipal obligations rated within the four highest grades, except that up to 20% of the fund's assets may be invested in unrated New York municipal obligations which, in the opinion of the fund's investment advisor, are of comparable quality to those so rated.

Officers:
R.J. Franke — Chairman
D.E. Sveen — President

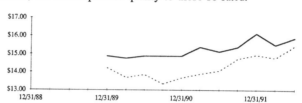

Investment Advisor: Nuveen Advisory Co.
Advisory Fee: Fee of 0.60% on the first $500 mil. of average net asset value of the fund, 0.575% of the next $500 mil., and 0.55% of any excess. Fee for five months ended 3/31/92 was $382,013.

Capital Structure: *Common stock:* 200 mil. shares authorized; 6,953,170 shares outstanding 3/31/92
Money Market Preferred stock: 1 mil. shares authorized, 1,000 shares outstanding; liquidation value $50,000. Dividend set every 7 days by auction.

Portfolio Highlights (as of 3/31/92): Municipal investments 98.0%, temporary investments 0.2%, other assets less liabilities 1.8%. Quality ratings: AAA 18%, AA+/AA/AA- 30%, A/A- 22%, BBB+/BBB/BBB- 30%. Largest industry concentrations: housing facilities revenue 30%, transportation 13%, educational facilities 13%, general obligation bonds 12%, lease rental facilities 10%, pollution control facilities 10%. 13% of the long-term and intermediate-term investments are covered by insurance. **Largest issuers:** Dormitory Authority of the State of New York; New York State Medical Care Facilities Finance Agency; New York State Mortgage Agency, Homeowner Mortgage Revenue AMT; Metropolitan Transportation Authority; Ne York State Energy Research and Development Authority, Electric Facilities Revenue (Consolidated Edison Company) AMT.

Historical Financial Statistics (fiscal year-end: 10/31/91):

	five months 3/31/92	1991	11/15/89 to 10/31/90
Value of net assets (000)	153,147	153,310	142,169
NAV	14.83	14.93	13.44
Net investment income	0.583	1.394	1.138
Dividends from net investment income	0.443	1.053	0.788
Common stock equivalent of dividends paid to preferred shares	0.111	0.335	0.263
Expense ratio	0.81% ann.	0.84%	0.83% ann.
Income ratio	6.35% ann.	6.53%	6.54% ann.
Portfolio turnover	1% ann.	46%	72% ann.

Nuveen New York Quality Income Municipal Fund, Inc.

333 West Wacker Drive, Chicago, IL 60606

Category: Municipal Bond Fund

Phone: 312-917-7810; 800-323-5063
Listed: NUN, NYSE
Commenced Operations: November, 1991
Cusip: 670986108

1991/mid-1992 Range of Premium/Disc: +7% to -2%
1991/mid-1992 Range of Price: $15 1/8 to $13 3/4
NAV Total Return 1991: N/A
Share Price Total Return 1991: N/A
Herzfeld Ranking 1991: N/A

Investment Objective: Current income exempt from regular federal income taxes as well as New York State and New York City personal income taxes, with a secondary objective of enhancement of portfolio value relative to the New York municipal bond market through investments in tax-exempt New York municipal obligations. Under normal circumstances, investments will be made in a diversified portfolio of tax-exempt New York Municipal obligations which are either covered by insurance guaranteeing the timely payment of principal and interest thereon or backed by an escrow or trust account.

Officers:

R.J. Franke — Chairman
D.E. Sveen — President

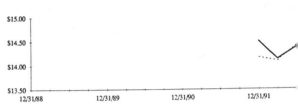

Investment Advisor: Nuveen Advisory Corp.
Advisory Fee: Annual fee equal to 0.65% of average net asset value of the fund up to $500 mil., 0.625% on next $500 mil., and 0.60% of any excess. Fee for period from 11/20/91 to 3/31/92 was 684,848.

Capital Structure: *Common stock*: 200 mil. shares authorized, 23,223,942 shares outstanding 3/31/92
Municipal Auction Rate Preferred Stock: 1 mil. shares authorized, none outstanding 3/31/92

Portfolio Highlights (as of 3/31/92): Municipal investments 98.4%, temporary investments in short-term municipal securities 4.0%, other assets less liabilities (2.4%). Quality ratings: AAA 96%, AA+/AA/AA- 4%. Largest industry concentrations: transportation revenue bonds 31%, general obligation bonds 19%, educational facilities revenue bonds 12%, housing facilities revenue bonds 10%, pollution control facilities revenue bonds 10%. **Largest issuers:** New York State Urban Development Corporation, Correctional Facilities Revenue; New York State Medical Care Facilities Finance Agency; New York City Municipal Water Finance Authority, Water and Sewer System Revenue; New York City general obligation; Triborough Bridge and Tunnel Authority, special obligation, 6.875-15.

Historical Financial Statistics:

	11/20/91 to 3/31/92
Value of net assets (000)	328,048
NAV	14.13
Net investment income	0.205
Dividends from net investment income	0.148
Expense ratio	0.73% ann.
Income ratio	4.51% ann.
Portfolio turnover	51% ann.

Special considerations: At least annually the fund's directors will consider taking any action to reduce any discounts which may be present, including such remedies as repurchasing shares in the open market, making tender offer or converting to an open-end fund. The fund's Declaration of Trust contains various anti-takeover provisions including a 66 2/3% vote to convert to an open-end fund, merge with another corporation, or terminate the trust. Mid-1992 dividend rate $0.0738 per month.

Nuveen New York Select Quality Municipal Fund, Inc.

333 West Wacker Drive, Chicago IL 60606   **Category:** Municipal Bond Fund

Phone: 312-917-7810; 800-323-5063
Listed: NVN, NYSE
Commenced Operations: May, 1991
Cusip: 670976109

1991/mid-1992 Range of Premium/Disc: +8% to -2%
1991/mid-1992 Range of Price: $15 3/8 to $14 3/8
NAV Total Return 1991: N/A
Share Price Total Return 1991: N/A
Herzfeld Ranking 1991: N/A

Investment Objective: Current income exempt from both regular federal and New York income taxes, with a secondary investment objective of enhancement of portfolio value relative to the New York municipal bond market through investments in tax-exempt New York municipal obligations that the advisor feels are underrated or undervalued or represent municipal market sectors that are undervalued.

Officers:

R.J. Franke   Chairman
D.E. Sveen   President

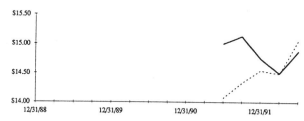

Investment Advisor: Nuveen Advisory Corp.
Advisory Fee: Annual fee equal to 0.65% of average net asset value of the fund up to $500 mil., 0.625% on next $500 mil., and 0.60% of any excess. Fee for five months ended 3/31/92 was $1,272,102.

Capital Structure: *Common stock:* 200 mil. shares authorized, 22,158,072 shares outstanding 3/31/92
     Preferred stock: 1 mil. shares authorized, 3,000 shares outstanding; liquidation value $50,000 per share. Dividend rate is set every 7 days by auction.

Portfolio Highlights (as of 3/31/92): Municipal investments 98.4%, temporary investments 0.1%, other assets less liabilities 1.5%. Quality ratings: AAA 89%, AA+/AA/AA- 10%, BBB+/BBB/BBB- 1%. Largest industry concentrations: transportation revenue 21%, educational facilities 20%, general obligation bonds 15%, housing facilities 13%, pollution control facilities 8%. 98% of the long-term and intermediate-term investments are covered by insurance. **Largest issuers:** Dormitory Authority of the State of New York; Triborough Bridge and Tunnel Authority; New York State Medical Care Facilities Finance Agency; New York State Energy Research and Development Authority; New York City Municipal Water Finance Authority, Water and Sewer System Revenue.

Historical Financial Statistics (fiscal year-end: 10/31/91):

	five months 3/31/92	1991
Value of net assets (000)	472,116	467,181
NAV	14.54	14.39
Net investment income	0.509	0.347
Dividends from net investment income	0.398	0.239
Common stock equivalent of dividends paid to preferred shares	0.103	0.030
Expense ratio	0.82% ann.	0.79% ann.
Income ratio	5.75% ann.	5.22% ann.
Portfolio turnover	24% ann.	5% ann.

Special considerations: The fund's Articles of Incorporation contain various anti-takeover provisions including a 66 2/3% voting requirement for converting to an open-end fund, merger with another corporation, or liquidation of the fund.

Nuveen Ohio Quality Income Municipal Fund, Inc.

333 West Wacker Drive, Chicago IL 60606 — **Category: Municipal Bond Fund**

Phone: 312-917-7810; 800-323-5063
Listed: NUO, NYSE
Commenced Operations: October, 1991
Cusip: 670980101

1991/mid-1992 Range of Premium/Disc: +9% to +3%
1991/mid-1992 Range of Price: $15 7/8 to $14 1/2
NAV Total Return 1991: N/A
Share Price Total Return 1991: N/A
Herzfeld Ranking 1991: N/A

Investment Objective: Current income exempt from regular federal and Ohio state income taxes, with a secondary objective of enhancement of portfolio value, relative to the municipal bond market, through investment of substantially all of the fund's assets in municipal bonds rated in the four highest categories or unrated securities that the fund's advisor believes to be of investment-grade quality.

Officers:

R.J. Franke — Chairman
D.E. Sveen — President

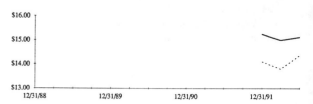

Investment Advisor: Nuveen Advisory Corp.
Advisory Fee: Annual fee equal to 0.65% of average net asset value of the fund up to $500 mil., 0.625% on next $500 mil., and 0.60% of any excess. Fee for period from 10/17/91 to 11/30/91 was $37,707.

Capital Structure: *Common stock:* 200 mil. shares authorized, 4,357,118 shares outstanding 11/30/91
Preferred stock 1 mil. shares authorized, 700 shares Series TH, with liquidation preference of $50,000 outstanding 2/18/92.

Portfolio Highlights (as of 10/31/91): Investments in Ohio municipal securities 31.9%, temporary investments 92.3%, other assets less liabilities (4.2%). Quality ratings: AAA 50%, AA+/AA/AA- 8%, A+ 23%, A/A- 4%, BBB+/BBB/BBB- 15%. Largest industry concentrations: health care facilities 37%, escrowed bonds 17%, pollution control facilities 15%, housing facilities 14%, water/sewer facilities 12%. 33% of the long-term and intermediate-term investments are covered by insurance. **Largest issuers:** Ohio Water Development Authority; Ohio Housing Finance Agency, Single Family Mortgage (GNMA) AMT 7.65-29; Cuyahoga County (Meridia Health System) 7-23; Clermont County Waterworks System 6.625-14; Carroll County (Timken Mercy Medical Center) 7.125-18.

Historical Financial Statistics (fiscal year-end: 6/30/92):

	10/17/91 to 11/30/91
Value of net assets (000)	60,882
NAV	13.97
Net investment income	0.047
Dividends from net investment income	--
Expense ratio	0.89% ann.
Income ratio	3.52% ann.
Portfolio turnover	0%

Special considerations: At least annually the fund's directors will consider taking any action to reduce any discounts which may be present, including such remedies as repurchasing shares in the open market, making tender offers or converting to an open-end fund. The fund's Declaration of Trust contains various anti-takeover provisions including a 66 2/3% vote to convert to an open-end fund, merger with another corporation, or termination of the trust. Mid-1992 dividend rate $0.073 per month.

Nuveen Pennsylvania Investment Quality Municipal Fund

333 West Wacker Drive, Chicago IL 60606   **Category**: Municipal Bond Fund

Phone: 312-917-7810; 800-323-5063	**1991/mid-1992 Range of Premium/Disc**: +12% to +2%
Listed: NQP, NYSE	**1991/mid-1992 Range of Price**: $16 5/8 to $15
Commenced Operations: February, 1991	**NAV Total Return 1991**: N/A
Cusip: 670972108	**Share Price Total Return 1991**: N/A
	Herzfeld Ranking 1991: N/A

Investment Objective: The fund seeks current income exempt from regular federal and Pennsylvania income taxes with a secondary objective of enhancement of portfolio value relative to the Pennsylvania municipal bond market through investments in tax-exempt Pennsylvania municipal obligations. Investments will be made in municipal securities rated BBB or better; 20% of investments may be in unrated securities which in the opinion of the advisor are of comparable quality.

Officers:

R.J. Franke	Chairman
D.E. Sveen	President

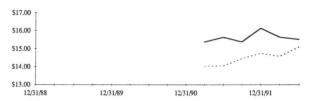

Investment Advisor: Nuveen Advisory Corp.

Advisory Fee: Annual fee equal to 0.60% of average net asset value of the fund up to $500 mil., 0.575% on next $500 mil., and 0.55% of any excess. Fee for period 2/21/91 to 10/31/91 was $611,598.

Capital Structure: *Common stock*: unlimited number of shares authorized, 8,235,228 shares outstanding 10/31/91

Preferred Shares: unlimited number of shares authorized, 1,200 shares outstanding, with liquidation value of $50,000 per share. Dividend rate is set every 7 days by auction.

Portfolio Highlights (as of 10/31/91): Pennsylvania municipal securities 98.3%, temporary investments 4.2%, other assets less liabilities (2.5%). Quality ratings: AAA 46%, AA+/AA/AA- 23%, A+ 2%, A/A- 9%, BBB+/BBB/BBB- 20%. Largest industry concentrations: educational facilities 18%, health care facilities 15%, housing facilities 13%, transportation 9%, general obligation bonds 8%. 48% of the long-term and intermediate-term investments are covered by insurance. **Largest issuers**: Montgomery County Industrial Dev. Auth.; PA Higher Education Facilities Authority; Allegheny Cty. (Greater Pittsburgh Int'l Airport) AMT 8.2-08; PA Hospitals and Higher Educational Facilities Auth. (St. Agnes Medical Ctr.) 7.25-31; Somerset Cty. General Auth., Commonwealth Lease 7-13.

Historical Financial Statistics (fiscal year-end: 10/31/91):

	2/17/91 to 10/31/91	
Value of net assets (000)	180,203	
NAV	14.60	
Net investment income	0.682	
Dividends from net investment income	0.498	
Common stock equivalent of dividends paid to preferred shares	0.123	
Expense ratio	0.81%	ann.
Income ratio	5.50%	ann.
Portfolio turnover	0%	

Special considerations: At least annually the fund's directors will consider taking any action to reduce any discounts which may be present, including such remedies as repurchasing shares in the open market, making tender offers or converting to an open-end fund. The fund's Declaration of Trust contains various anti-takeover provisions including a 66 2/3% vote to convert to an open-end fund, merge with another corporation, or terminate the trust.

Nuveen Pennsylvania Quality Income Municipal Fund, Inc.

333 West Wacker Drive, Chicago IL 60606   **Category: Municipal Bond Fund**

Phone: 312-917-7810; 800-323-5063
Listed: NUP, NYSE
Commenced Operations: October, 1991
Cusip: 670981109

1991/mid-1992 Range of Premium/Disc: +8% to -1%
1991/mid-1992 Range of Price: $15 3/8 to $14 1/4
NAV Total Return 1991: N/A
Share Price Total Return 1991: N/A
Herzfeld Ranking 1991: N/A

Investment Objective: Current income exempt from regular federal and Pennsylvania State income taxes, with a secondary objective of enhancement of portfolio value, relative to the municipal bond market, through investment of substantially all of the fund's assets in municipal bonds rated in the four highest categories, or in unrated securities that the fund's advisor believes to be of investment-grade quality.

Officers:

R.J. Franke   Chairman
D.E. Sveen   President

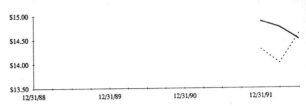

Investment Advisor: Nuveen Advisory Corp.
Advisory Fee: Annual fee equal to 0.65% of average net asset value of the fund up to $500 mil., 0.625% on next $500 mil., and 0.60% of any excess. Fee for period from 10/17/91 to 12/31/91 was $114,090.

Capital Structure: *Common stock*: unlimited number of shares authorized, 6,985,289 shares outstanding 12/31/91
Preferred stock unlimited number of shares authorized, 1,000 shares Series TH with liquidation preference of $50,000 outstanding 2/18/92.

Portfolio Highlights (as of 12/31/91): Pennsylvania municipal investments 100.5%, temporary investments 16.6%, other assets less liabilities (17.1%). Quality ratings: AAA 53%, AA+/AA/AA- 15%, A+ 4%, A/A- 4%, BBB+/BBB/BBB- 24%. Largest industry concentrations: water/sewer facilities 28%, general obligation bonds 23%, health care facilities 14%, pollution control facilities 8%, educational facilities 7%, transportation 6%. 48% of the long-term and intermediate-term investments were covered by insurance. **Largest issuers:** Philadelphia Water and Sewer; Bethlehem Authority, Water System; Pennsylvania Higher Educational Facilities Authority (Thomas Jefferson University) 6.0-19; Allegheny County (Greater Pittsburgh International Airport), AMT 7.75-19; Butler County Hospital Authority (North Hills Passavant Hospital) 7-22.

Historical Financial Statistics (fiscal year-end: 6/30/92):

	10/17/91 to 12/31/91
Value of net assets (000)	100,406
NAV	14.37
Net investment income	0.104
Dividends from net investment income	- -
Expense ratio	0.86% ann.
Income ratio	4.13% ann.
Portfolio turnover	0%

Special considerations: At least annually the fund's directors will consider taking any action to reduce any discounts which may be present, including such remedies as repurchasing shares in the open market, making tender offers or converting to an open-end fund. The fund's Declaration of Trust contains various anti-takeover provisions including a 66 2/3% vote to convert to an open-end fund, merger with another corporation, or termination of the trust. Mid-1992 dividend rate $0.0765 per month.

Nuveen Performance Plus Municipal Fund, Inc.

333 West Wacker Drive, Chicago, IL 60606   **Category**: Municipal Bond Fund

Phone: 312-917-7810; 800-323-5063
Listed: NPP, NYSE
Commenced Operations: June, 1989
Cusip: 67062P108

1991/mid-1992 Range of Premium/Disc: +5% to -1%
1991/mid-1992 Range of Price: $15 5/8 to $13 5/8
NAV Total Return 1990: +5.45%; **1991**: +15.74%
Share Price Total Return 1990: +5.63%; **1991**: +17.51%
Herzfeld Ranking 1991: 8th of 51 municipal bond funds

Investment Objective: Current income exempt from regular federal income tax, with a secondary investment objective of enhancement of portfolio value relative to the municipal market through investments in tax-exempt municipal obligations that, in the opinion of the fund's investment advisor, are underrated or undervalued or represent municipal market sectors that are undervalued. The fund will invest substantially all of its assets in a diversified portfolio of tax-exempt municipal obligations rated within the four highest grades. Up to 20% of the fund's assets may be invested in unrated municipal obligations which, in the opinion of the fund's investment advisor, are of comparable quality.

Officers:
R.J. Franke   Chairman
D.E. Sveen   President

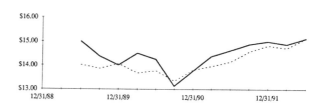

Investment Advisor: Nuveen Advisory Co.
Advisory Fee: Fee of 0.60% on the first $500 mil. of average net asset value of the fund, 0.575% of the next $500 mil., and 0.55% of any excess. Fee for six months ended 11/30/91 was $3,539,170.

Capital Structure: *Common stock*: 200 mil. shares authorized; 56,632,303 shares outstanding 11/30/91
Money Market Preferred stock: 1 mil. shares authorized; 1,000 shares each of Series M, T, W and F $100,000 stated value Money Market Preferred Stock. The dividend rates on each series will change every 7 days as set by the Auction Agent.

Portfolio Highlights (as of 11/30/91): Municipal investments 97.9%, other assets less liabilities 2.1%. Quality ratings: AAA 28%, AA+/AA/AA- 37%, A+ 5%, A/A- 20%, BBB+/BBB/BBB- 8%, non-rated 2%. Largest industry concentrations: housing facilities 29%, electric utilities 17%, health care facilities 16%, pollution control facilities 13%. 12% of the long-term and intermediate-term investments are covered by insurance. Largest geographic concentrations: Texas 13.4%, Georgia 9.4%, New York 8.2%, South Carolina 6.6%, Massachusetts 6.3%, California 5.3%, Florida 5.3%, Illinois 5.1%. **Largest issuers**: Washington Public Power Supply System, Nuclear Project No. 1; (UT) Intermountain Power Agency; (GA) Burke County Development Authority, Pollution Control (Ogelthorpe Power Corporation-Vogte Project); Alaska Housing Finance Corporation; Nebraska Investment Finance Authority, Single Family Mortgage AMT 8.125-38.

Historical Financial Statistics (fiscal year-end: 5/31/91):

	six months 11/30/91	1991	6/22/89 to 5/31/90
Value of net assets (000)	1,229,035	1,204,809	1,166,027
NAV	14.64	14.28	13.68
Net investment income	0.696	1.387	1.032
Dividends from net investment income to common shares	0.52	1.025	0.700
Common stock equivalent of dividends paid to preferred stock	0.155	0.39	0.265
Expense ratio	0.74% ann.	0.75%	0.71% ann.
Income ratio	6.46% ann.	6.63%	6.57% ann.
Portfolio turnover	8%	14%	24% ann.

Nuveen Premier Insured Municipal Income Fund, Inc.

333 West Wacker Drive, Chicago, IL 60606

Category: Municipal Bond Fund

Phone: 312-917-7810; 800-323-5063	**1991/mid-1992 Range of Premium/Disc**: +7% to -1%
Listed: NIF, NYSE	**1991/mid-1992 Range of Price**: $15 1/8 to $13 3/4
Commenced Operations: December, 1991	**NAV Total Return 1990: 1991**: N/A
Cusip: 670987106	**Share Price Total Return 1990: 1991**: N/A
	Herzfeld Ranking 1991: N/A

Investment Objective: Current income exempt from regular federal income tax, and a secondary objective of enhancement of portfolio value relative to the municipal bond market through investments in tax-exempt municipal obligations that, in the opinion of the fund's advisor, are underrated or undervalued or that represent municipal market sectors that are undervalued. Investments will be in municipal obligations which are either covered by insurance guaranteeing the timely payment of principal and interest or backed by an escrow or trust account.

Officers:

R.J. Franke	Chairman
D.E. Sveen	President

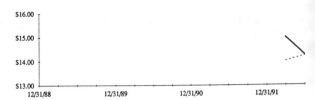

Investment Advisor: Nuveen Advisory Co.

Advisory Fee: Fee of 0.65% on the first $500 mil. of average net asset value of the fund, 0.625% of the next $500 mil., and 0.60% of any excess.

Capital Structure:

Common stock: 200 mil. shares authorized; 19,017,334 shares outstanding 4/30/92
Preferred stock an offering is planned for 1992

Portfolio Highlights: not yet published

Historical Financial Statistics:

	4/30/92
Value of net assets (000)	267,940
NAV	14.09

Special considerations: The fund's directors will annually consider measures to reduce or eliminate material discounts which may develop; such measures may include repurchase of shares in the open market, tender offers at net asset value or converting to an open-end fund. The fund's Declaration of Trust contains various anti-takeover provisions including a 66 2/3% vote to convert to an open-end fund, merge with another corporation, or terminate the trust. Mid-1992 dividend rate $0.075 per month.

Nuveen Premier Municipal Income Fund, Inc.

333 West Wacker Drive, Chicago, IL 60606

Category: Municipal Bond Fund

Phone: 312-917-7810; 800-323-5063	**1991/mid-1992 Range of Premium/Disc:** +7% to -1%
Listed: NPF, NYSE	**1991/mid-1992 Range of Price:** $15 1/8 to $13 3/4
Commenced Operations: December, 1991	**NAV Total Return 1991:** N/A
Cusip: 670988104	**Share Price Total Return 1991:** N/A
	Herzfeld Ranking 1991: N/A

Investment Objective: Current income exempt from regular federal income tax, with a secondary objective of enhancement of portfolio value relative to the municipal bond market through investments in tax-exempt municipal obligations that, in the opinion of the fund's advisor are underrated or undervalued or that represent municipal market sectors that are undervalued. Investments are in the four highest grades; 20% may be invested in unrated securities which the fund's advisor believes to be investment-grade.

Officers:

R.J. Franke	Chairman
D.E. Sveen	President

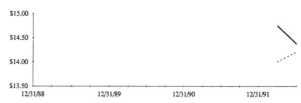

Investment Advisor: Nuveen Advisory Co.

Advisory Fee: Fee of 0.65% on the first $500 mil. of average net asset value of the fund, 0.625% of the next $500 mil., and 0.60% of any excess.

Capital Structure:
Common stock: 200 mil. shares authorized; 19,517,745 shares outstanding 4/30/92
Preferred stock 1 mil. shares authorized; 1,400 shares each Series T and Series TH with liquidation preference $50,000 outstanding 5/18/92.

Portfolio Highlights: not yet published

Historical Financial Statistics:

	4/30/92
Value of net assets (000)	274,709
NAV	14.07

Special considerations: The fund's directors will annually consider measures to reduce or eliminate material discounts which may develop; such measures may include repurchase of shares in the open market, tender offers at net asset value or converting to an open-end fund. The fund's Declaration of Trust contains various anti-takeover provisions including a 66 2/3% vote to convert to an open-end fund, merge with another corporation, or terminate the trust. Mid-1992 dividend rate $0.08 per month.

Nuveen Premium Income Municipal Fund, Inc.

333 West Wacker Drive, Chicago, IL 60606   **Category: Municipal Bond Fund**

Phone: 312-917-7810; 800-323-5063
Listed: NPI, NYSE
Commenced Operations: July, 1988
Cusip: 67062T100

1991/mid-1992 Range of Premium/Disc: +8% to 0%
1991/mid-1992 Range of Price: $17 to $14 7/8
NAV Total Return 1990: +6.26%; **1991:** +14.90%
Share Price Total Return 1990: +7.20%; **1991:** +19.90%
Herzfeld Ranking 1991: 16th of 51 municipal bond funds

Investment Objective: High level of current income exempt from federal income tax, consistent with preservation of capital, primarily through investment in a diversified portfolio of investment grade tax-exempt municipal obligations.

Officers:
R.J. Franke   Chairman
D.E. Sveen   President

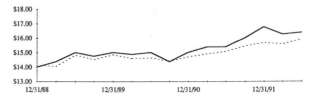

Investment Advisor: Nuveen Advisory Corp.
Advisory Fee: Fee equal to 0.50% of the first $500 mil. of net asset value of the fund, 0.475% on next $500 mil., and 0.45% on any excess. Fee for six months ended 11/30/91 was $2,751,034.

Capital Structure: *Common stock:* 200 mil. shares authorized; 51,515,931 shares outstanding 11/30/91
Remarketed Preferred stock: 1 mil. shares authorized; 3,500 shares outstanding Remarketed Preferred stock; liquidation value $100,000 par value. Dividend rate on Series A-D set every 28 days, dividend rate of Series E set every 7 days.

Portfolio Highlights (as of 11/30/91): Municipal investments 97.2%, temporary investments 0.5%, other assets less liabilities 2.3%. Quality ratings: AAA 24%, AA+/AA/AA- 32%, A+ 8%, A/A- 19%, BBB+/BBB/BBB- 16%, non-rated 1%. Largest industry concentrations: housing facilities 24%, pollution control facilities 17%, health care facilities 14%, electric utilities 13%, escrowed bonds 11%. Largest geographic concentrations: Texas 14.6%, Georgia 12.7%, Florida 6.8%, North Carolina 6.1%, Washington 5.2%. **Largest issuers:** Wisconsin Housing and Economic Development Authority AMT; Burke County (GA) Development Authority, Pollution Control (Georgia Power Company); (UT) Intermountain Power Agency; Monroe County (GA) Development Authority, Pollution Control (Georgia Power Company); Harris County (TX) Health Facilities Development Corporation 7.375-25 (mandatory put 12/1/98).

Historical Financial Statistics (fiscal year-end: 5/31/91):

	six months 11/30/91	1991	1990	7/18/88 to 5/31/89
Value of net assets (000)	1,148,040	1,127,103	1,090,365	1,089,152
NAV	15.49	15.18	14.60	14.72
Net investment income	0.748	1.504	1.508	1.101
Dividends from net investment income	0.565	1.080	1.08	0.75
Common stock equivalent of dividends paid to preferred shares	0.149	0.376	0.433	0.27
Expense ratio	0.65% ann.	0.65%	0.65%	0.62% ann.
Income ratio	6.76% ann.	6.97%	6.98%	6.92% ann.
Portfolio turnover	1% ann.	1%	4%	9%

Special considerations: The fund's directors will annually consider measures to reduce or eliminate material discounts which may develop; such measures may include repurchase of shares in the open market, tender offers at net asset value or converting to an open-end fund.

Nuveen Quality Income Municipal Fund, Inc.

333 West Wacker Drive, Chicago, IL 60606

Category: Municipal Bond Fund

Phone: 312-917-7810; 800-323-5063
Listed: NQU, NYSE
Commenced Operations: June, 1991
Cusip: 670977107

1991/mid-1992 Range of Premium/Disc: +7% to -2%
1991/mid-1992 Range of Price: $15 1/8 to $14 1/8
NAV Total Return 1991: N/A
Share Price Total Return 1991: N/A
Herzfeld Ranking 1991: N/A

Investment Objective: Current income exempt from regular federal income taxes, with a secondary objective of enhancement of portfolio value, relative to the municipal bond market, through investment of substantially all of the fund's assets in municipal bonds rated in the four highest categories, or in unrated securities that the fund's advisor believes to be of investment grade quality.

Officers:
R.J. Franke   Chairman
D.E. Sveen   President

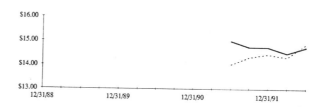

Investment Advisor: Nuveen Advisory Corp.

Advisory Fee: Fee equal to 0.50% of the first $500 mil. of net asset value of the fund, 0.475% on next $500 mil., and 0.45% on any excess. Fee for the period 6/19/91 to 10/31/91 was $1,798,609.

Capital Structure: *Common stock:* 200 mil. shares authorized; 52,276,825 shares outstanding 10/31/91 *Municipal Auction Rate Preferred stock:* 1 mil. shares authorized; 8,000 shares outstanding Remarketed Preferred stock; liquidation value $50,000 par value. Dividend rate is set every 7 days by auction.

Portfolio Highlights (as of 11/30/91): Municipal investments 74.4%, temporary investments 31.5%, other assets less liabilities (5.9%). Quality ratings: AAA 36%, AA+/AA/AA- 27%, A+ 5%, A/A- 18%, BBB+/BBB/BBB- 9%, non-rated 5%. Largest geographic concentrations: FL 6.6%, OK 6.4%, TX 6.0%, WA 5.6%, IL 5.5%. Largest industry concentrations: housing facilities 28%, health care facilities 16%, transportation 8%, electric utilities 7%. 21% of the long-term and intermediate-term investments are covered by insurance. **Largest issuers:** City and County of Denver Airport System AMT; Oklahoma County Home Finance Authority single family mortgage 8.75-12; Washington Public Power Supply System; Piedmont Municipal Power Agency; Illinois Health Facilities Authority.

Historical Financial Statistics (fiscal year-end: 10/31/91):

	6/19/91 to 10/31/91
Value of net assets (000)	1,146,962
NAV	14.29
Net investment income	0.276
Dividends from net investment income	0.168
Common stock equivalent of dividends to preferred shares	0.021
Expense ratio	0.74% ann.
Income ratio	5.13% ann.
Portfolio turnover	0%

Special considerations: The fund makes monthly distributions to common shareholders at a level that reflects the past and projected performance of the fund, which over time will result in the distribution of all net investment income, and distributes any net capital gains annually. The fund's directors will annually consider measures to reduce or eliminate material discounts which may develop; such measures may include repurchase of shares in the open market, tender offers at net asset value or converting to an open-end fund.

Nuveen Select Quality Municipal Fund, Inc.

333 West Wacker Drive, Chicago, IL 60606

Category: Municipal Bond Fund

Phone: 312-917-7810; 800-323-5063
Listed: NQS, NYSE
Commenced Operations: March, 1991
Cusip: 670973106

1991/mid-1992 Range of Premium/Disc: +7% to -2%
1991/mid-1992 Range of Price: $15 1/2 to $14 3/8
NAV Total Return 1991: N/A
Share Price Total Return 1991: N/A
Herzfeld Ranking 1991: N/A

Investment Objective: Current income exempt from regular federal income tax with a secondary objective of enhancement of portfolio value relative to the municipal bond market through investments in tax-exempt municipal obligations that the advisor feels are underrated or undervalued.

Officers:

R.J. Franke   Chairman
D.E. Sveen   President

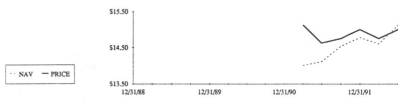

Investment Advisor: Nuveen Advisory Corp.
Advisory Fee: Fee equal to 0.65% of the first $500 mil. of net asset value of the fund, 0.625% on next $500 mil., and 0.60% on any excess. Fee for period 3/21/91 to 10/31/91 was $2,334,518.

Capital Structure: *Common stock*: 200 mil. shares authorized, 32,344,399 shares outstanding 10/31/91
    Preferred Shares: 1 mil. shares authorized, 4,800 shares outstanding, $50,000 liquidation value per share. Dividend rate is set every 7 days by auction.

Portfolio Highlights (as of 10/31/91): Municipal investments 97.2%, temporary investments 0.7%. Largest geographic concentrations: Texas 11.9%, Massachusetts 7.4%, Utah 5.8%, New York 5.5%, Washington 5.2%, Georgia 5.0%. Quality ratings: AAA 22%, AA+/AA/AA- 30%, A+ 8%, A/A- 26%, BBB+/BBB/BBB- 10%. Largest industry concentrations: housing facilities revenue 32%, electric utilities 17%, escrowed bonds 13%, transportation 10%, health care facilities 8%, general obligation bonds 4%. **Largest issuers**: (UT) Intermountain Power Agency; Oklahoma County Home Finance Authority, Single Family Mortgage; Georgia Municipal Electric Authority; Washington Public Power Supply System, Nuclear Project No. 3 7.25-15; Piedmont (SC) Municipal Power Agency.

Historical Financial Statistics (fiscal year-end: 10/31/91):

	3/21/91 to 10/31/91
Value of net assets (000)	713,377
NAV	14.64
Net investment income	0.653
Dividends from net investment income	0.425
Common stock equivalent of dividends paid to preferred shares	0.124
Expense ratio	0.79% ann.
Income ratio	5.81% ann.
Portfolio turnover	1% ann.

Special considerations: At least annually the fund's directors will consider taking action to reduce any discounts which may be present, including such remedies as repurchasing shares in the open market, making tender offers or converting to an open-end fund. The fund's Declaration of Trust contains various anti-takeover provisions including a 66 2/3% vote to convert to an open-end fund, merge with another corporation, or terminate the trust.

Nuveen Select Tax-Free Income Portfolio

333 West Wacker Drive, Chicago, IL 60606

Category: Municipal Bond Fund

Phone: 312-917-7810; 800-323-5063
Listed: NXP, NYSE
Commenced Operations: March, 1992
Cusip: 67062F100

1991/mid-1992 Range of Premium/Disc: +9% to -2%
1991/mid-1992 Range of Price: $15 1/8 to $13 3/4
NAV Total Return 1991: N/A
Share Price Total Return 1991: N/A
Herzfeld Ranking 1991: N/A

Investment Objective: To provide stable dividends exempt from regular federal income tax, consistent with preservation of capital. The trust invests substantially all of its assets in a diversified portfolio of long-term investment-grade quality municipal obligations which are judged by the advisor to represent the best long-term values among those municipal obligations that satisfy the trust's credit quality standards. Investments will be rated within the four highest grades; up to 20% of assets may be invested in unrated municipal obligations which the advisor feels are of comparable quality. The trust will liquidate approximately 20-25 years after the offering (3/19/92) but not later than March 31, 2017 unless extended. The portfolio will be fixed.

Officers:

R.J. Franke	Chairman
D.E. Sveen	President

Investment Advisor: Nuveen Advisory Corp.

Advisory Fee: Annual fee equal to 0.25% of the fund's average daily net asset value of the fund.

Capital Structure: *Common stock*: unlimited number of shares authorized, 16,378,097 shares outstanding as of 4/30/92

Portfolio Highlights: not yet published

Historical Financial Statistics:

	4/30/92
Value of net assets (000)	229,793
NAV	14.03

Special considerations: At least annually the fund's directors will consider taking action to reduce any discounts which may be present, including such remedies as repurchasing shares in the open market, making tender offers or converting to an open-end fund. The fund's Declaration of Trust contains various anti-takeover provisions including a 66 2/3% vote to convert to an open-end fund, merge with another corporation, or terminate the trust. Initial monthly dividend $0.079 payable in July, 1992.

Nuveen Select Tax-Free Income Portfolio 2

333 West Wacker Drive, Chicago, IL 60606   **Category: Municipal Bond Fund**

Phone: 312-917-7810; 800-323-5063	**1991/mid-1992 Range of Premium/Disc:** +8% to +4%
Listed: NXQ, NYSE	**1991/mid-1992 Range of Price:** $15 1/8 to $14 3/4
Commenced Operations: May, 1992	**NAV Total Return 1991:** N/A
Cusip: 67063C106	**Share Price Total Return 1991:** N/A
	Herzfeld Ranking 1991: N/A

Investment Objective: To provide stable dividends exempt from regular federal income tax, consistent with preservation of capital. The trust invests substantially all of its assets in a diversified portfolio of long-term investment-grade quality municipal obligations which are judged by the advisor to represent the best long-term values among those municipal obligations that satisfy the trust's credit quality standards. Investments will be rated within the four highest grades, up to 20% of assets may be invested in unrated municipal obligations which the advisor feels are of comparable quality. The trust will liquidate approximately 20-25 years after the offering (5/21/92) but not later than June 30, 2017, unless extended. The portfolio will be fixed.

Officers:

R.J. Franke	Chairman
D.E. Sveen	President

Investment Advisor: Nuveen Advisory Corp.

Advisory Fee: One-time Portfolio Structuring Fee of 0.95% of the net proceeds of the offering; plus an advisory fee for ongoing administration, surveillance and management of the portfolio equal to 0.30% of average daily net assets, reduced to 0.275% on amounts in excess of $500 mil., and to 0.25% in excess of $1 billion.

Capital Structure: *Common stock*: unlimited number of shares authorized, 16,500,000 as of 5/26/92

Portfolio Highlights: not yet published

Historical Financial Statistics:

	6/19/92
Value of net assets (000)	296,239
NAV	14.07

Special considerations: At least annually the fund's directors will consider taking action to reduce any discounts which may be present, including such remedies as repurchasing shares in the open market, making tender offers or converting to an open-end fund. The fund's Declaration of Trust contains various anti-takeover provisions including a 66 2/3% vote to convert to an open-end fund, merge with another corporation, or terminate the trust.

Nuveen Texas Quality Income Municipal Fund, Inc.

333 West Wacker Drive, Chicago, IL 60606

Category: Municipal Bond Fund

Phone: 312-917-7810; 800-323-5063
Listed: NTX, NYSE
Commenced Operations: October, 1991
Cusip: 670983105

1991/mid-1992 Range of Premium/Disc: +10% to -2%
1991/mid-1992 Range of Price: $16 3/4 to $13 5/8
NAV Total Return 1991: N/A
Share Price Total Return 1991: N/A
Herzfeld Ranking 1991: N/A

Investment Objective: Current income exempt from regular federal income taxes, with a secondary objective of enhancement of portfolio value, relative to the municipal bond market, through investment of substantially all the fund's assets in municipal bonds rated in the four highest categories, or in unrated securities that the fund's advisor believes to be of investment-grade quality.

Officers:

R.J. Franke   Chairman
D.E. Sveen   President

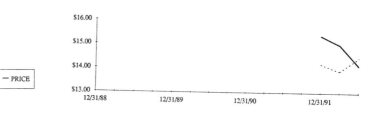

Investment Advisor: Nuveen Advisory Corp.

Advisory Fee: Annual fee equal to 0.65% of average net asset value of the fund up to $500 mil., 0.625% on next $500 mil., and 0.60% of any excess. Fee for period from 10/17/91 to 11/30/91 was $59,611.

Capital Structure: *Common stock*: unlimited number of shares authorized, 7,007,118 shares outstanding 11/30/91

Preferred stock unlimited number of shares authorized, 1,000 shares Series TH with liquidation preference of $50,000 outstanding 2/18/92.

Portfolio Highlights (as of 11/30/91): Texas municipal investments 32.4%, temporary investments 78.8%, other assets less liabilities (11.2%). Quality ratings: AAA 47%, AA+/AA/AA- 14%, A/A- 33%, BBB+/BBB/BBB- 6%. Largest industry concentrations: housing facilities 28%, health care facilities 26%, pollution control facilities 18%, water/sewer facilities 12%, escrowed bonds 10%. 38% of the long-term and intermediate-term investments are covered by insurance. **Largest Issuers:** Brazos River Authority, Collateralized Recenue Refunding Bonds (Houston Lighting & Power) 7.75-15; State of Texas, Veterans' Land Board 8.3-15; Bexar County Health Facilities Development Corporation, Hospital Revenue Bonds (Southwest Texas Methodist Hospital) 6.75-21; Harris COunty Health Facilities (Texas Children's Hospital) 7-19; Houston Water and Sewer System, Junior Lien 6.375-17.

Historical Financial Statistics (fiscal year-end: 11/30/91):

	10/17/91 to 11/30/91
Value of net assets (000)	98,310
NAV	14.03
Net Investment income	0.047
Dividends from net investment income	---
Expense ratio	0.87% ann.
Income ratio	3.58% ann.
Portfolio turnover	0%

Special considerations: At least annually the fund's directors will consider taking any action to reduce any discounts which may be present, including such remedies as repurchasing shares in the open market, making tender offers or converting to an open-end fund. The fund's Declaration of Trust contains various anti-takeover provisions including a 66 2/3% vote to convert to an open-end fund, merger with another corporation, or termination of the trust.

Oppenheimer Multi-Government Trust

Two World Trade Center, New York, NY 10048-0302

Category: Bond Fund

Phone: 800-426-5523
Listed: OGT, NYSE
Commenced Operations: November, 1988
Cusip: 683939102

1991/mid-1992 Range of Premium/Disc: +12% to -5%
1991/mid-1992 Range of Price: $11 to $8 1/8
NAV Total Return 1990: +6.13%; **1991:** +15.66%
Share Price Total Return 1990: +5.66%; **1991:** +26.01%
Herzfeld Ranking 1991: 67th of 80 bond funds

Investment Objective: High current income consistent with preservation of capital, secondary objective of capital appreciation. The fund invests primarily in debt instruments issued or guaranteed by the U.S. government, its agencies or instrumentalities, or by foreign governments or their political subdivisions, agencies or instrumentalities.

Officers:

L. Levy   Chairman
D.W. Spiro   President

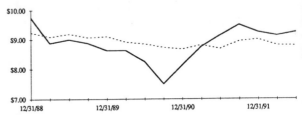

Investment Advisor: Oppenheimer Management Corporation
Advisory Fee: Annual fee of 0.65% of weekly net assets. Fee for year-ended 10/31/91 was $363,531.
Administrator: Mitchell Hutchins Asset Management, Inc.
Administration Fee: Annual fee of 0.20% of weekly net assets. Fee for year-ended 10/31/91 was $110,589.

Capital Structure: *Shares of beneficial interest:* unlimited number of shares authorized; 6,378,202 shares outstanding 10/31/91

Portfolio Highlights (as of 10/31/91): U.S. government obligations 49.0%, corporate bonds, notes, stocks and warrants 29.8%, foreign fixed-income securities 18.6%, short-term money market instruments 0.4%. **Largest issuers:** Federal National Mortgage Association mortgage-backed certificates 14-13; Federal Home Loan Mortgage Corp. mortgage-backed certificates; Canadian treasury bonds & notes; U.S. treasury bonds & notes; Banque Paribas 6.50% Lira/Deutsche Mark Indexed Certificate of Deposit 5/22/92.

Historical Financial Statistics (fiscal year-end: 10/31/91):

	1991	1990	11/30/88 to 10/31/89
Value of net assets (000)	57,208	54,676	57,418
NAV	8.97	8.66	9.12
Net investment income	0.97	0.96	0.82
Dividends from net investment income	0.99	0.94	0.80
Distributions from net realized gains	--	0.05	0.04
Expense ratio	1.21%	1.22%	1.34% ann.
Income ratio	11.06%	10.83%	9.85% ann.
Portfolio turnover	59.9%	95.3%	98.7%

Special considerations: The fund may repurchase shares or make tender offers for shares when the Board deems it advantageous. After 11/1/89, if certain conditions are met, the Board may propose conversion to an open-end fund. The fund's Declaration of Trust and By-Laws contain various anti-takeover provisions. Dividend rate reduced to $0.066 in May, 1992.

Oppenheimer Multi-Sector Income Trust

Two World Trade Center, New York, NY 10048-0302   **Category**: Bond Fund

Phone: 800-426-5523	**1991/mid-1992 Range of Premium/Disc**: +10% to -6%
Listed: OMS, NYSE	**1991/mid-1992 Range of Price**: $11 5/8 to $9 3/8
Commenced Operations: March, 1988	**NAV Total Return 1990**: +5.43%; **1991**: +19.20%
Cusip: 683933105	**Share Price Total Return 1990**: +7.67%; **1991**: +28.04%
	Herzfeld Ranking 1991: 46th of 80 bond funds

Investment Objective: High current income consistent with preservation of capital, with a secondary objective of capital appreciation through the allocation of assets among the following sectors of the fixed-income securities market: U.S. government (maximum 90% of assets), corporate, international, mortgage-backed, municipal, convertible and money market.

Officers:

L. Levy	Chairman
D.W. Spiro	President

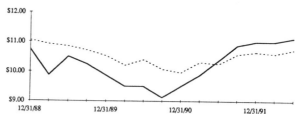

Investment Advisor: Oppenheimer Management Corporation

Advisory Fee: Annual fee of 0.65% of weekly net assets. Fee for year-ended 10/31/91 was $1,883,550.

Administrator: Mitchell Hutchins Asset Management, Inc.

Administration Fee: Annual fee of 0.20% of weekly net assets. Fee for year-ended 10/31/91 was $579,576.

Capital Structure: *Shares of beneficial interest*: unlimited number of shares authorized; 28,347,068 shares outstanding 10/31/91

Portfolio Highlights (as of 10/31/91): U.S. treasury securities 14.1%, corporate bonds, notes and stocks 39.3%, mortgage-backed securities 18.3%, foreign fixed-income securities 18.2%, convertible securities 4.9%, municipal bonds 1.9%, short-term money market instruments 0.3%. **Largest issuers**: U.S. treasury bonds & notes: Canadian treasury notes; Government National Mortgage Association; Federal National Mortgage Association; Banque Paribas 6.5% Lira/Deutsche Mark Indexed Certificate of Deposit 5/22/92.

Historical Financial Statistics (fiscal year-end: 10/31/91):

	1991	1990	1989	3/31/88 to 10/31/88
Value of net assets (000)	**301,568**	278,511	299,673	314,656
NAV	**10.64**	9.88	10.63	11.17
Net investment income	**1.11**	1.15	1.12	0.64
Dividends from net investment income	**1.07**	1.10	1.132	0.59
Distributions from net realized gains	**0.10**	0.02	0.01	0.06
Expense ratio	**1.16%**	1.03%	1.03%	1.01% ann.
Income ratio	**10.80%**	11.16%	10.28%	9.80% ann.
Portfolio turnover	**59.7%**	85.7%	162.0%	60.1%

Special considerations: The fund may repurchase shares or make tender offers for shares when the Board deems it advantageous. After 11/1/93, if certain conditions are met, the Board may propose conversion to an open-end fund. The fund's Declaration of Trust and By-Laws contain various anti-takeover provisions.

Pacific American Income Shares, Inc.

117 E. Colorado Blvd., Pasadena, CA 91105

Category: Bond Fund

Phone: 818-584-4300
Listed: PAI, NYSE
Commenced Operations: March, 1973
Cusip: 693796104

1991/mid-1992 Range of Premium/Disc: +5% to -9%
1991/mid-1992 Range of Price: $16 1/2 to $13 1/4
NAV Total Return 1990: +5.60%; **1991**: +19.15%
Share Price Total Return 1990: -2.70%; **1991**: +27.48%
Herzfeld Ranking 1991: 47th of 80 bond funds

Investment Objective: High level of current income through investment in a diversified portfolio of debt securities. The company's fundamental investment policies provide that its assets be invested as follows: at least 75% in debt securities rated within the four highest grades, and in government securities, bank debt, commercial paper, cash or cash equivalents; up to 25% in other fixed income securities, convertible bonds, convertible preferred and preferred stock; not more than 25% in securities restricted as to resale.

Officers:

N. Barker, Jr.   Chairman
W.C. Livingston, III   President

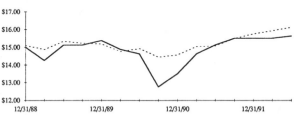

Investment Advisor and Administrator: Western Asset Management Company
Advisory and Administration Fee: Monthly fee at annual rate of 0.7% of average monthly net assets up to $60 mil. and 0.4% of excess. If certain expenses in any fiscal year exceed 1 1/2% of average net assets up to $30 mil. and 1% of net assets over $30 mil., advisor will reimburse the fund for any such excess. Fee for 1991 was $589,622.

Capital Structure: *Common stock*: 10 mil. shares authorized; 6,708,248 shares outstanding 12/31/91
Convertible Extendible Notes: $5,000,000 5-year convertible extendible extended to 10/15/93 at an annual interest rate of 9.25%. Notes may be converted to common stock at $13.73 per share.

Portfolio Highlights (as of 12/31/91): Debt securities 101.7%, short-term securities 4.8%. Largest industry concentrations: industrials & misc. 29.15%, utilities/gas & electric 23.92%, mortgage-backed pass-throughs 16.50%, financial & leasing 13.67%, U.S. government & agencies 9.16%, foreign & international 2.12%, convertibles 0.95%. Quality ratings: Aaa 25.46%, Aa 3.81%, A 11.73%, Baa 33.22%, Ba 14.01%, B 6.43%, not rated 0.81%, short-term investments 4.53%. **Largest issuers**: Federal Home Loan Mortgage Corp.; Government National Mortgage Association; U.S. treasury bonds & notes; Occidental Petroleum sr. notes.; Systems Energy Resources Inc. 1st mtg. 14-94.

Historical Financial Statistics (fiscal year-end: 12/31/91):

	1991	1990	1989	1988	1987	1986
Value of net assets (000)	107,735	98,102	102,240	101,675	88,118	96,875
NAV	16.06	14.62	15.24	15.16	15.39	16.92
Net investment income	1.47	1.47	1.53	1.51	1.52	
Dividends paid	1.46	1.46	1.53	1.54	1.91	1.54
Expense ratio*	0.84%	0.89%	0.88%	0.94%	0.91%	0.91%
Income ratio*	9.60%	10.02%	10.04%	9.79%	9.44%	9.24%
Portfolio turnover	41.52%	48.48%	60.01%	35.85%	75.20%	76.16%

*excludes expenses relating to convertible notes

Special considerations: The quarterly dividend rate was reduced to $0.35 per share beginning with the March, 1992, dividend. A proposal to require directors to own 2000 shares of common stock did not pass at the 1990 annual meeting. **Shareholders over 5%**: The Guardian Life Insurance Company of America, 14.66%

Pacific-European Growth Fund, Inc.

222 South Ninth Street, Minneapolis, MN 55402-3804

Category: Foreign Equity Fund

Phone: 800-866-7778 x6384 or x6223
Listed: PEF, ASE
Commenced Operations: April, 1990
Cusip: 694237108

1991/mid-1992 Range of Premium/Disc: +7% to -20%
1991/mid-1992 Range of Price: $11 to $7 3/8
NAV Total Return 1991: +10.83%
Share Price Total Return 1991: +12.32%
Herzfeld Ranking 1991: 24th of 46 foreign equity funds

Investment Objective: Long-term capital appreciation with current income incidental to this objective. The fund will invest primarily in equity securities of companies in the Pacific Basin or in Europe.

Officers:

E.J. Kohler   Chairman & President

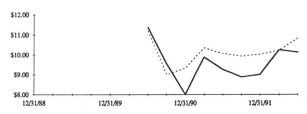

Investment Advisor: Piper Capital Management Incorporated
Advisory Fee: Monthly fee at the annual rate of 1.00% of average weekly net assets up to $100 mil., 0.875% of next $100 mil., and 0.75% of any excess. The fee will be increased or decreased depending on the fund's performance relative to the Morgan Stanley Capital International EAFE Index after 3/31/91. Fee for year-ended 2/29/92 was $345,337.
Sub-Advisor: Edinburgh Fund Managers plc
Sub-Advisory Fee: Will be paid by the investment advisor
Administrator: Piper Capital Management Incorporated
Administration Fee: Monthly fee at the annual rate of 0.25% of average weekly net assets. Fee for year-ended 2/29/92 was $86,633.

Capital Structure: *Common stock:* 1 bil. shares authorized; 3,388,334 outstanding 2/29/92

Portfolio Highlights (as of 2/29/92): Common stocks 99.2%, short-term securities 1.5%. Largest geographic concentrations: Japan 28.1%, Hong Kong 22.7%, Singapore 8.9%, Thailand 8.1%, Malaysia 6.9%. **Largest positions:** HSBC Holdings 3.5%, Good Peak Batteries 2.4%, Malaysian International Shipping Corporation 2.4%, Bangkok Rubber Footwear 2.3%, Genting Berhad 2.3%.

Historical Financial Statistics (fiscal year-end: 2/29/92):

	1992	4/27/91 to 2/28/91
Value of net assets (000)	35,680	34,492
NAV	10.53	10.18
Net investment income	0.06	0.20
Dividends from net investment income	0.06	0.20
Distributions from other sources	0.02	--
Expense ratio	1.92%	1.77% ann.
Income ratio	0.60%	2.36% ann.
Portfolio turnover	69%	10%

Special considerations: Annual distributions are made from net investment income and net realized capital gains. In efforts to reduce any discount which may develop, the fund will consider, on a quarterly basis, tender offers or repurchase of shares in the open market. The fund's Articles of Incorporation contain various anti-takeover provisions, including a 66 2/3% vote of shareholders to open-end the fund. At the June, 1992, annual meeting, shareholders will vote on an open-ending proposal. Management recommends voting in favor of the proposal; however, a 2/3 affirmative vote of shareholders is required.

Patriot Premium Dividend Fund I

101 Huntington Avenue, Boston, MA 02199-7603

Category: Specialized Equity Fund

Phone: 617-375-1500, 800-843-0090
Listed: PDF, NYSE
Commenced Operations: October, 1988
Cusip: 70336K103

1991/mid-1992 Range of Premium/Disc: +3% to -10%
1991/mid-1992 Range of Price: $10 to $7 1.2
NAV Total Return 1990: -2.79%; **1991:** +29.70%
Share Price Total Return 1990: -19.46%; **1991:** +34.32%
Herzfeld Ranking 1991: 9th of 18 specialized equity funds

Investment Objective: High current income qualifying for the Dividends Received Deduction, consistent with modest growth of capital for shareholders of common stock, primarily through investment in a diversified portfolio of dividend-paying (investment grade) preferred and common equity securities.

Officers:

E.J. Boudreau, Jr. Chairman & Chief Executive Officer
R.G. Freedman   President & Chief Investment Officer

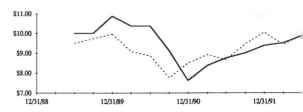

Investment Advisor: John Hancock Advisors, Inc.
Advisory Fee: Monthly fee at annual fee of 0.5% of average weekly net assets plus 5% of the fund's weekly gross income, limited to a maximum of 1% annually of the fund's average weekly net assets. Fee for six months ended 3/31/92 was $900,801.

Capital Structure: *Common stock:* 99,998,000 shares authorized; 14,434,715 shares outstanding 3/31/92 *Dutch Auction Rate Transferable Securities Preferred Stock:* 2,000 shares authorized; 685 shares outstanding, liquidation preference of $100,000 per share. Dividends are cumulative at a rate which was established at the offering of the DARTS and has been reset every 49 days thereafter by auction. Dividend rates ranged from 3.249% to 4.60% during the six months ended 3/31/92.

Portfolio Highlights (as of 3/31/92): Common stocks 48.7%, preferred stocks 14.2%, U.S. government obligations 29.8%, short-term investment 6.3%, other net assets 1.0%. Largest industry concentration: utilities 59.4%
Largest positions: U.S. treasury notes, Pacific Gas & Electric Co., Southern Co., New England Electric Systems, DPL Inc.

Historical Financial Statistics (fiscal year-end: 9/30/91):

	six months 3/31/92	1991	1990	10/28/88 to 9/30/89
Value of net assets (000)	205,169	205,847	179,984	206,025
NAV	9.47	9.54	7.77	9.74
Net investment income	0.48	1.00	1.06	1.31
Dividends from net investment income to common shares	0.40	0.65	0.82	1.05
Distributions from net realized short-term gains to common shares	--	0.19	0.22	0.10
Distributions to common shares from capital in excess of par	--	--	0.16	--
Dividends to DARTS shareholders	0.08	0.25	0.24	0.26
Operating expense ratio	1.41% ann.	1.48%	1.34%	1.39% ann.
Income ratio	6.90% ann.	7.53%	8.31%	10.69% ann.
Portfolio turnover	135.70% ann.	100.82%	123.84	196.88% ann.

Special considerations: The fund may repurchase shares on the open market or make a tender offer. On 9/18/90 the fund approved a reorganization plan as a Massachusetts business trust. John Hancock Advisors became investment advisor and administrator in April, 1992.

Patriot Premium Dividend Fund II

101 Huntington Avenue, Boston, MA 02199-7603   **Category:** Specialized Equity Fund

Phone: 617-375-1500, 800-843-0090
Listed: PDT, NYSE
Commenced Operations: December, 1989
Cusip: 70336L101

1991/mid-1992 Range of Premium/Disc: 0% to -13%
1991/mid-1992 Range of Price: $11 5/8 to $8 5/8
NAV Total Return 1990: +1.82%; **1991:** +31.71%
Share Price Total Return 1990: -19.46%; **1991:** +45.22%
Herzfeld Ranking 1991: 8th of 18 specialized equity funds

Investment Objective: High current income consistent with modest growth of capital for common shareholders. The fund invests in investment grade preferred and comparable quality dividend-paying common stocks.

Officers:

E.J. Boudreau, Jr.   Chairman & Chief Executive Officer
R.G. Freedman   President & Chief Investment Officer

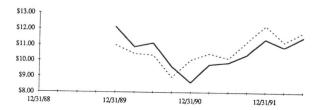

Investment Advisor: John Hancock Advisors, Inc.
Advisory Fee: Monthly fee at annual fee of 0.5% of average weekly net assets plus 5% of the fund's weekly gross income, limited to a maximum of 1% annually of the fund's average weekly net assets. Fee for year-ended 10/31/91 was $2,523,709.

Capital Structure: *Shares of beneficial interest:* unlimited number of shares; 15,002,724 shares outstanding 10/31/91
Dutch Auction Rate Transferable Securities Preferred Stock: 500 Series A and 50 Series B outstanding, liquidation preference of $100,000 per share. Dividends set every 49 days by auction. (98 shares of each series retired during the year-ended 10/31/91.)

Portfolio Highlights (as of 10/31/91): Common stocks 50.7%, preferred stocks 14.2%, U.S. government obligations 30.4%, short-term investments 4.5%, other net assets 0.2%. **Largest issuers:** U.S. treasury notes; Pacific Gas & Electric Co.; Southern Co.; Texas Utilities Co.; Commonwealth Edison Co.

Historical Financial Statistics (fiscal year-end: 10/31/91):

	1991	12/21/89 to 10/31/90
Value of net assets (000)	270,701	245,378
NAV	11.38	9.69
Net investment income	1.28	1.20
Dividends from net investment income	0.90	0.89
Distributions to common shares from capital in excess of par	--	0.10
Dividends to DART shareholders	0.28	0.31
Operating expense ratio	1.38%	1.39% ann.
Income ratio	8.13%	8.83% ann.
Portfolio turnover	157.38%	288.46% ann.

Special considerations: The fund makes annual distributions of capital gains. In efforts to reduce any discounts which may occur, the fund may repurchase shares or make tender offers. The fund intends to invest more than 65% of assets in the utilities industry. The fund's Declaration of Trust and Bylaws contain various anti-takeover provisions including a 67% vote of each class of shares, voting separately for, among other things, merger or consolidation of the fund, liquidation, or sale of substantially all assets. John Hancock Advisors became investment advisor and administrator in April, 1992.

Patriot Select Dividend Trust

101 Huntington Avenue, Boston, MA 02199-7603

Category: Specialized Equity Fund

Phone: 617-375-1500, 800-843-0090
Listed: DIV, NYSE
Commenced Operations: July, 1990
Cusip: 70336P102

1991/mid-1992 Range of Premium/Disc: +11% to -9%
1991/mid-1992 Range of Price: $17 1/2 to $12 5/8
NAV Total Return 1991: +28.73%
Share Price Total Return 1991: +37.31%
Herzfeld Ranking 1991: 11th of 18 specialized equity funds

Investment Objective: High current income consistent with modest growth of capital for common shares. The fund will invest in a diversified portfolio of dividend-paying preferred and common equity securities, and to maximize income qualifying for the Dividends Received Deduction. Preferred stocks are rated at least BBB or of comparable quality.

Officers:

E.J. Boudreau, Jr. Chairman & Chief Executive Officer
R.G. Freedman   President & Chief Investment Officer

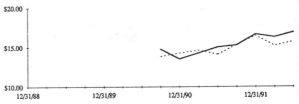

Investment Advisor and Administrator: John Hancock Advisers, Inc.
Advisory and Administrative Fee: Annual fee of 0.80% of average weekly net assets, plus an annual administrative fee of 0.20% of average weekly net assets. Advisory and sub-advisory fees for six months ended 10/31/91 were $1,090,132.
Sub-Advisor: InterCapital Division of Dean Witter
Sub-Advisory Fee: Annual fee of 0.20% of average weekly net assets.

Capital Structure: *Shares of beneficial interest:* unlimited number of shares authorized, 9,651,525 shares outstanding 12/31/91
Auction Market Preferred shares: 700 shares outstanding, dividend rate set every 49 days by auction. Dividend rates ranged from 4.00% to 4.61% during period ended 12/31/91; redemption at option of the trust at $100,000 per share

Portfolio Highlights (as of 12/31/91): Common stocks 44.8%, preferred stocks 19.6%, U.S. government obligations 32.5%, short-term investments 2.7%, other net assets 0.4%. Largest sector concentrations: utility 62.6%, governments 32.5%. **Largest positions:** U.S. treasury bonds and notes; Commonwealth Edison Co., Southern Co., DPL Inc., Consolidated Edison Co. of NY Inc.

Historical Financial Statistics (fiscal year-end: 6/30/91):

	six months 12/31/91	7/31/90 to 6/30/91
Value of net assets (000)	231,180	205,781
NAV	16.70	14.08
Net investment income	0.773	1.2467
Dividends to common from net investment income	0.9625	0.8480
Dividends to common from net realized short-term capital gains	--	0.3895
Dividends to AMPS shareholders	0.1396	0.2828
Operating expense ratio	1.46% ann.	1.39% ann.
Income ratio	7.19% ann.	7.16% ann.
Portfolio turnover	111.48% ann.	208.80% ann.

Special considerations: The trust makes monthly distributions of substantially all net investment income to common shares after paying AMPS dividends. Distributions of net capital gains are made annually. In efforts to reduce any discounts which may occur, the fund may repurchase shares or make tender offers. The fund's Declaration of Trust and Bylaws contain various anti-takeover provisions including a 67% vote of each class of shares voting separately for, among other things, merger or consolidation of the fund, liquidation, or sale of substantially all assets. John Hancock Advisers became investment advisor and administrator in April, 1992.

Petroleum & Resources Corporation

7 St. Paul Street, Ste 1140, Baltimore, MD 21202 **Category:** Specialized Equity Fund

Phone: 410-752-5900, 800-638-2479
Listed: PEO, NYSE
Commenced Operations: January, 1929
Cusip: 716549100

1991/mid-1992 Range of Premium/Disc: +2% to -11%
1991/mid-1992 Range of Price: $29 to $24 1/4
NAV Total Return 1990: -0.93%; **1991:** +6.81%
Share Price Total Return 1990: +2.22%; **1991:** +11.49%
Herzfeld Ranking 1991: 16th of 18 specialized equity funds

Investment Objective: Preservation of capital, attainment of reasonable and dependable investment income and capital appreciation. The fund invests at least 80% of assets in securities of companies engaged in petroleum or natural resources industries or in related industries, and at least 25% of assets in securities of companies engaged in the petroleum industry or related industries or in petroleum properties.

Officers:
D.G. Ober   Chairman & CEO
R.F. Koloski   President

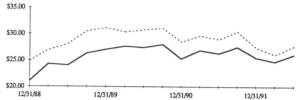

Investment Advisor: Internally managed
Advisory Fee: Officers' and directors' remuneration for year ended 12/31/91, $807,346.
Administrator: Internally administered
Administration Fee: Administration and operations expenses for year ended 12/31/91, $397,974.

Capital Structure: *Common stock:* 15 mil. shares authorized; 11,185,572 shares outstanding 3/31/92. *$1.575 Convertible preferred stock:* 2 mil. shares authorized; 1,993,000 shares outstanding 3/31/92.

Portfolio Highlights (as of 3/31/92): Stocks and convertible securities 89.4%, short-term investments 10.3%. Largest sector concentrations: energy 69.3%, basic industries 21.1%. **Largest positions:** Royal Dutch Petroleum Co., Atlantic Richfield Co., Mobil Corp., Exxon Corp., Chevron Corp.

Historical Financial Statistics (fiscal year-end: 12/31/91):

	1991	1990	1989	1988	1987	1986
Value of net assets (000)	343,919	338,495	322,866	278,267	263,972	276,048
NAV	28.07	28.59	31.09	24.84	24.29	27.40
Net investment income	1.20	1.35	1.48	1.28	1.43	1.62
Dividends from net investment income	0.92	1.10	1.20	0.92	1.67	1.45
Distributions from net realized gains	1.23	1.25	1.20	1.20	2.31	2.89
Dividends on preferred stock	0.29	0.30	0.31	0.32	0.34	0.35
Expense ratio	0.59%	0.57%	0.66%	0.68%	0.58%	0.66%
Income ratio	3.06%	3.44%	4.11%	3.72%	3.62%	4.75%
Portfolio turnover	11.41%	18.41%	18.68%	14.35%	27.87%	32.70%

Special considerations: Convertible preferred shares are convertible into common stock at any time at a ratio of 0.4704 of common stock for each preferred share. The preferred stock is redeemable at the option of the corporation; the current redemption price is $15.00 per share. **Shareholders over 5%:** Adams Express Co., 9.7%

Pilgrim Prime Rate Trust

10100 Santa Monica Blvd., Los Angeles, CA 90067

Category: Miscellaneous

Phone: 800-331-1080
Listed: PPR, NYSE
Commenced Operations: May, 1988
Cusip: 72146M105

1991/mid-1992 Range of Premium/Disc: -7% to -21%
1991/mid-1992 Range of Price: $9 1/4 to $7 7/8
NAV Total Return 1991: N/A
Share Price Total Return 1991: N/A
Herzfeld Ranking 1991: N/A

Investment Objective: High level of current income consistent with the preservation of capital. The trust invests in Senior Collateralized Corporate Loans, the interest rates on which reset periodically at various spreads above established short-term lending rates. Since the loan's rates reset to current market rates, the principal value does not change when interest rates rise or fall. The collateral of each borrower is reviewed in detail to provide a "second way out" source of repayment in the event unforeseeable problems adversely impact the borrower's cash flow.

Officers:

P. Weingarten   Chairman & President

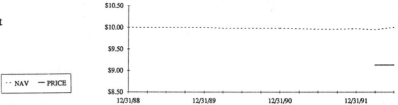

Investment Manager: Pilgrim Management Corporation
Management Fee: Monthly fee at the annual rate of 0.85% of average daily net assets, reduced to 0.75% on average net assets in excess of $700 mil. (This reduction was a voluntary reduction by the manager). Fee for year-ended 2/29/92 was $8,294,729.
Administrator: Pilgrim Group Inc.
Administration Fee: Monthly fee at the annual rate of 0.25% of average daily net assets. Fee for year-ended 2/29/92 was $2,462,455.

Capital Structure: *Shares of beneficial interest*: unlimited number of shares authorized, 87,782,506 shares outstanding 2/29/92

Portfolio Highlights (as of 2/29/92): Senior collateralized loan participations 94.1%, common stock, preferred stock and other 0.5%, short-term investments 5.1%, cash and other assets in excess of liabilities 0.3%. Largest industry concentrations: health care services 13.0%, transportation 12.0%, food stores 8.2%, paper products 6.0%, restaurants 5.8%, electronic equipment 5.6%, specialty retailing 5.5%. **Largest loan holdings:** Hospital Corporation of America; Jefferson Smurfit Corporation/Container Corporation of America; Lin Cellular Network; American Medical Inc.; T.W. Services Inc.

Historical Financial Statistics (fiscal year-end: 2/29/92):

	1992	1991	1990	5/12/88 to 2/28/89
Value of net assets (000)	874,104	1,156,224	1,036,470	N/A
NAV	9.96	9.97	10.00	10.00
Net investment income	0.76	0.98	1.06	0.72
Dividends from net investment income	0.75	0.96	1.06	0.72
Expense ratio	1.42%*	1.38%	1.46%*	1.18% ann.*
Income ratio	7.62%**	9.71%	10.32%**	9.68% ann.**
Portfolio turnover	53%	55%	100%	49%

*prior to the waiver of expenses the expense ratios would have been: 1992, 1.44%; 1990, 1.48%; 1989, 1.95%.
**prior to the waiver of expenses the income ratios would have been: 1992, 7.61%; 1990, 10.29%; 1989, 8.91%.

Special considerations: The fund commenced operations in 1988 and conducted quarterly tender offers as a way for shareholders to sell their positions; the fund was not listed on the New York Stock Exchange until March, 1992. After the fund began trading at discounts of 10% to 12%, the trust commenced a tender offer for 7.5 mil. shares at net asset value.

Pilgrim Regional BankShares

10100 Santa Monica Blvd., Los Angeles, CA 90067

Category: Specialized Equity Fund

Phone: 800-331-1080
Listed: PBS, NYSE
Commenced Operations: January, 1986
Cusip: 721464105

1991/mid-1992 Range of Premium/Disc: +8% to -11%
1991/mid-1992 Range of Price: $12 to $6 3/4
NAV Total Return 1990: -18.62%; **1991:** +48.19%
Share Price Total Return 1990: -13.64%; **1991:** +49.00%
Herzfeld Ranking 1991: 5th of 18 specialized equity funds

Investment Objective: Long-term capital appreciation with a secondary objective of income, primarily through investment in equity securities of regional banks and bank holding companies of such banks.

Officers:

P. Weingarten   Chairman & CEO
R. Grunburg   President

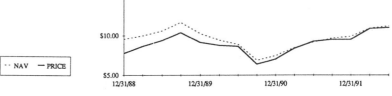

Investment Advisor and Administrator: Pilgrim Management Corporation
Advisory and Administration Fee: Monthly fee at annual rate of 1% of the first $30 mil. of average weekly net assets and 0.75% of excess. Fee for year-ended 12/31/91 was $762,159.

Capital Structure: *Common stock:* 50 mil. shares authorized; 9,985,028 shares outstanding 12/31/91

Portfolio Highlights (as of 3/31/92): Common stocks 97.4%, convertible bonds 0.6%, commercial paper 2.9%, liabilities in excess of other assets (0.9%). Largest sector concentrations: regional banks 80.8%, community banks 12.0%, thrifts 4.6%. **Largest positions:** Manufacturers National Corp. (MI), First Security Corp (UT); Commerce Bancshares Inc. (MO), Security Bankcorp Inc. (MI), Mercantile Bankshares Corp. (MD).

Historical Financial Statistics (fiscal year-end: 12/31/91):

	1991	1990	1989	1988	1987	1/17/86 to 12/31/86
Value of net assets (000)	101,092	74,855	102,553	95,696	82,162	91,452
NAV	10.12	7.49	10.26	9.54	8.17	9.09
Net income	0.24	0.31	0.30	0.31	0.22	0.24
Dividends from net investment income	0.24	0.31	0.31	0.37	0.22	0.17
Distributions from net realized gains	--	--	0.44	--	0.05	--
Distributions from paid-in capital	0.70	0.57	0.33	--	--	--
Expense ratio	1.31%	1.29%	1.26%	1.18%	1.13%	1.04% ann.
Income ratio	2.68%	3.59%	4.15%	3.28%	2.31%	2.59% ann.
Portfolio turnover	31%	46%	63%	43%	76%	33% ann.

Special considerations: The Board of Directors may classify or reclassify any unissued shares of the fund. In the first quarter of 1989 the Board approved an annual payout rate of 10%, which was reduced to 7% in 1992. Each quarter the fund will distribute 1.75% of net asset value. During the year-ended 12/31/91 the fund repurchased 212.779 shares of common stock at an average discount of 2.5%. There will be a rights offering in 1992 whereby shareholders will receive one non-transferable right for each share held. One additional common share may be purchased for every three rights held at a price per share that will be about a 10% discount from the closing net asset value of the offering. **Shareholders over 5%:** Sovran Capital Management Corporation, 8.41%

The Portugal Fund, Inc.
153 East 53rd Street, New York, NY 10022

Category: Foreign Equity Fund

Phone: 212-832-2626
Listed: PGF, NYSE
Commenced Operations: November, 1989
Cusip: 737265108

1991/mid-1992 Range of Premium/Disc: +18% to -23%
1991/mid-1992 Range of Price: $13 1/4 to $8 1/2
NAV Total Return 1990: -20.49%; **1991**: -0.57%
Share Price Total Return 1990: -44.98%; **1991**: +5.48%
Herzfeld Ranking 1991: 39th of 46 foreign equity funds

Investment Objective: Total return consisting of capital appreciation and current income by investing primarily in Portuguese securities.

Officers:
E. Bassini   Chairman, President, Chief Investment

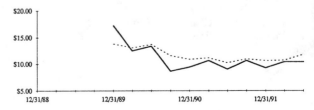

Investment Advisor: BEA Associates
Advisory Fee: Annual fee of 1.20% of the first U.S. $50 mil. of average monthly net assets, 1.15% of the next $50 mil., and 1.10% of the excess. Fee for year-ended 12/31/91 was $689,331.
Sub-Advisor: Socifa & Beta, S.A.
Advisory Fee: (paid by BEA Associates) Annual fee of 0.20% of the first U.S. $50 mil. of average monthly net assets, 0.15% of the next $50 mil., and 0.10% of the excess.
Administrator: Provident Financial Processing Corporation
Administration Fee: Annual fee of 0.10% of average monthly net assets with a minimum annual fee. Fee for year-ended 12/31/91 was $76,672.

Capital Structure: *Common stock*: 100 mil. shares authorized; 5,297,253 shares outstanding 12/31/91

Portfolio Highlights (as of 12/31/91): Common stocks 85.72%, convertible bonds 2.63%, U.S. treasury bills 11.65%. Largest industry concentrations: banks 15.91%, construction and public works 8.72%, chemicals and petroleum products 7.31%, retail trade 6.90%. **Largest positions**: Banco Commercial Portuguese (registered); Filmes Lusomundo; Jeronimo Martins; Continente SA, Modelo Hipermercados; Marconi (bearer & registered).

Historical Financial Statistics (fiscal year-end: 12/31/91):

	1991	1990	11/9/89 to 12/31/89
Value of net assets (000)	57,036	58,084	73,023
NAV	10.77	10.96	13.79
Net investment income	0.13	0.16	0.04
Dividends from net investment income	0.11	0.12	0.04
Distributions in excess of net investment income	--	--	0.04
Expense ratio	1.96%	2.04%	2.26% ann.
Income ratio	1.20%	1.38%	2.03% ann.
Portfolio turnover	13.31%	10.09%	0%

Special considerations: Distributions are made annually. The fund's Articles of Incorporation and Bylaws contain various anti-takeover provisions. The fund is subject to Portuguese corporate income taxes on dividends from Portuguese resident corporations. **Shareholders over 5%**: Ardsley Advisory Partners, 16.1%

Preferred Income Fund Incorporated

301 E. Colorado Blvd., Pasadena, CA 91101

Category: Specialized Equity Fund

Phone: 818-795-7300
Listed: PFD, NYSE
Commenced Operations: January, 1991
Cusip: 74037G106

1991/mid-1992 Range of Premium/Disc: +12% to 0%
1991/mid-1992 Range of Price: $19 1/8 to $15
NAV Total Return 1991: N/A
Share Price Total Return 1991: N/A
Herzfeld Ranking 1991: N/A

Investment Objective: The fund seeks high current income for holders of its common stock consistent with preservation of capital. The fund's portfolio will be managed with a view to maximizing income eligible for the Dividend Received Deduction through investment in a professionally managed, diversified portfolio of preferred stocks that, under current market conditions, will consist principally of adjustable rate, investment grade preferred stocks. The fund will concentrate on investments in the utilities and banking industries.

Officers:

R.T. Flaherty   Chairman & President

Investment Advisor: Flaherty & Crumrine Incorporated
Advisory Fee: Monthly fee at the annual rate of 0.625% of average monthly net assets up to $100 mil., and 0.50% of excess. Fee for period 1/31/91 to 11/30/91 was $781,306.
Administrator and Economic Consultant: The Boston Company Economic Advisors, Inc.
Administration and Consulting Fee: Monthly fee at annual rate of 0.25% of average monthly net assets, plus annual consulting fee of $75,000. Administrative fee for period 1/31/91 to 11/30/91 was $310,472; consulting fee was $62,500.

Capital Structure: *Common stock:* 250 mil. shares authorized, 8,245,700 shares outstanding 5/31/92
Money Market Cumulative Preferred stock: 10 mil. shares authorized, 575 shares outstanding 5/31/92 at the rate of 3.17%. Redemption price $100,000.

Portfolio Highlights: (as of 2/29/92): Adjustable rate preferred stocks 65.3%, fixed rate preferred stocks 33.2%, short-term investments 0.4%, other assets and liabilities 1.1%. Largest industry concentrations: 53.3%, banking 38.0%. **Largest Issuers** (as of 11/30/91): Bank of New York; First Chicago Corporation; First Bank System; Chemical Bank Corporation, New York; First Interstate Bancorp.

Historical Financial Statistics (fiscal year-end: 11/30/91):

	1/31/91 to 11/30/91
Value of net assets (000)	187,928
NAV common shares	16.56
NAV preferred shares	100,540.46
Net investment income	1.43
Dividends from net investment income common shares	0.99
Operating expense ratio	1.67% ann.
Income ratio	9.18% ann.
Portfolio turnover	90%

Special considerations: The fund makes monthly dividends of net investment income after payment of accumulated dividends on preferred shares and annual distributions of net realized capital gains. After the third year following the offering, if the shares trade at a significant discount for a substantial period of time, the Board of Directors will consider various actions to reduce the discount. Open-ending would require an 80% vote of the Board, 80% vote of shareholders, and possibly an 80% vote of preferred shareholders. Under certain circumstances only a majority vote of common and preferred shareholders (voting separately) would be required. The fund's Articles of Incorporation contain various anti-takeover provisions including an 80% vote for liquidating of the fund.

Preferred Income Opportunity Fund Incorporated

301 E. Colorado Blvd., Pasadena, CA 91101   **Category:** Specialized Equity Fund

Phone: 818-795-7300	**1991/mid-1992 Range of Premium/Disc:** +10% to +2%
Listed: PFO, NYSE	**1991/mid-1992 Range of Price:** $13 5/8 to $12 1/4
Commenced Operations: February, 1992	**NAV Total Return 1991:** N/A
Cusip: 74037H104	**Share Price Total Return 1991:** N/A
	Herzfeld Ranking 1991: N/A

Investment Objective: The fund seeks high current income for holders of its common stock consistent with preservation of capital. The fund's advisor will pursue strategies that it expects generally to result in the fund's income increasing as interest rates rise while being relatively resistant to the impact of declining interest rates. The fund's portfolio will be managed with a view to maximizing income eligible for the Dividend Received Deduction. The fund invests primarily in investment grade preferred stocks. The fund will concentrate on investments in the utilities and banking industries, with no more than 25% invested in the banking industry.

Officers:

R.T. Flaherty   Chairman, President & CEO

Investment Advisor: Flaherty & Crumrine, Incorporated

Advisory Fee: Monthly fee at the annual rate of 0.625% of average monthly net assets up to $100 mil., and 0.50% of excess.

Administrator and Economic Consultant: The Boston Company Economic Advisors, Inc.

Administration and Consulting Fee: Monthly fee at annual rate of 0.25% of average monthly net assets, plus annual consulting fee of $75,000.

Capital Structure: *Common stock:* 250 mil. shares authorized, 10,008,603 shares outstanding 2/27/92
Auction Rate Preferred stock: 10 mil. shares authorized; 700 shares outstanding, $100,000 par value per share at rate of 3.45%.

Portfolio Highlights: not yet published

Historical Financial Statistics:

	5/31/92
Value of net assets (000)	123,765
NAV	12.37

Special considerations: The fund will pay monthly dividends of substantially all net investment income after payment of accumulated dividends on preferred shares and will make annual distributions of net realized capital gains. The fund's Board of Directors at least once a year may consider repurchasing shares in the open market or in private transactions or tendering for shares in an attempt to reduce or eliminate a market value discount to net asset value. At any time after the third year after the initial offering, if the fund is trading at a significant discount to net asset value, the board may consider various actions to reduce or eliminate the discount including open-ending the fund. Open-ending would require an 80% vote of the Board of Directors, 80% vote of shareholders, and possibly an 80% vote of preferred shareholders. Under certain circumstances only a majority vote of common and preferred shareholders (voting separately) would be required. The fund's Articles of Incorporation contain various anti-takeover provisions including an 80% vote for liquidating of the fund or amending the fund's Articles of Incorporation. The fund began paying dividends in May, 1992 at the monthly rate of $0.0825 per share.

Prospect Street High Income Portfolio Inc.

Exchange Place, 37th Fl., Boston, MA 02109   **Category: Bond Fund**

Phone: 617-742-3800
Listed: PHY, NYSE
Commenced Operations: November, 1988
Cusip: 743586109

1991/mid-1992 Range of Premium/Disc: +5% to -21%
1991/mid-1992 Range of Price: $4 1/8 to $2 3/8
NAV Total Return 1990: -40.57%; **1991**: +40.07%
Share Price Total Return 1990: -47.15%; **1991**: +52.00%
Herzfeld Ranking 1991: 13th of 80 bond funds

Investment Objective: High current income, while seeking to preserve shareholders' capital through investment in a professionally managed, diversified portfolio of "high yield" securities (primarily in the lower rating categories).

Officers:
R.E. Omohundro, Jr.   President

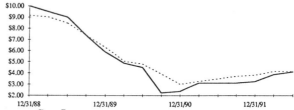

Investment Advisor: Prospect Street Investment Management Co., Inc.
Advisory Fee: Monthly fee at annual rate of 0.50% of weekly net assets. Fee for year-ended 10/31/91 was $407,397.

Capital Structure: *Common stock*: 100 mil. shares authorized; 13,647,220 shares outstanding 10/31/91 *Senior extendible notes*: $5 mil. outstanding initially due in 1993 and extendible for one or more periods of 1, 2 or 3 years until 1998. The notes bear interest at the rate of 10.28% per annum through 11/30/93 and are subject to repurchase by the fund at the option of any holder beginning on 11/30/93 and 30 days following each interest period thereafter. *Redeemable preferred stock*: 300 shares outstanding, redeemable at the option of the fund at a redemption price equal to $100,000 per share plus accumulated and unpaid dividends. Dividends are cumulative at a rate which was established at the offering and which has been and will continue to be reset every month by auction.

Portfolio Highlights (as of 10/31/91): Fixed income 82.88%, common stocks and warrants 2.09%, short-term 9.65%, other assets 5.39%. Largest sector concentrations: insurance companies 9.92%, general and specialty retail 7.38%, healthcare/drugs/hospital supplies 6.94%, automobile/auto parts/truck manufacturing 5.87%. **Largest issuers**: Reliance Group Holdings; Horace Mann Educators Corp. sub. deb. 15-01; Hospital Corp. of America s.f. deb. 11.25-15; Jordan Industries Inc. ser. A. sr. sub. notes 13.875-98; U.S. Air.

Historical Financial Statistics (fiscal year-end: 10/31/91):

	1991	1990	12/5/88 to 10/31/89
Value of net assets (000)	83,040	75,028	122,487
NAV	3.89	3.30	6.82
Net investment income	0.55	0.98	1.31
Dividends to preferred shares	0.16	0.22	0.19
Dividends from net investment income to common shares	0.36	0.76	1.12
Dividends from paid-in capital to common shares	--	0.09	0.01
Expense ratio (incl. interest)	2.93%	6.15%	3.62% ann.
Operating expense ratio (excl. interest)	2.23%	2.60%	1.279% ann.
Income ratio	9.24%	13.23%	10.09% ann.
Portfolio turnover	114%	63.50%	89.70%

Special considerations: Notes and preference shares carry a rating of AAA/Aaa. The fund entered an insurance agreement with Financial Security Assurance, Inc. which has unconditionally and irrevocably guaranteed dividend, redemption and liquidation payments to preferred shareholders. The fund may repurchase common shares when the Board deems it advantageous or make tender offers for common stock. After 1993, the board may submit an open-ending proposal (notes and preferred shares would have to be redeemed for open-ending to take place).

Putnam Dividend Income Fund

One Post Office Square, Boston, MA 01209

Category: Specialized Equity Fund

Phone: 617-292-1000
Listed: PDI, NYSE
Commenced Operations: September, 1989
Cusip: 746706100

1991/mid-1992 Range of Premium/Disc: +10% to -5%
1991/mid-1992 Range of Price: $12 1/2 to $9 1/2
NAV Total Return 1990: -3.37%; **1991:** +28.11%
Share Price Total Return 1990: -13.24%; **1991:** +28.90%
Herzfeld Ranking 1991: 12th of 18 specialized equity funds

Investment Objective: High current income eligible for the Dividends Received Deduction, consistent with preservation of capital. The fund invests in a portfolio of preferred and common equity securities that pay dividends eligible for the Dividends Received Deduction. The fund will invest in investment grade preferred stocks and in common stocks whose outstanding debt securities are rated investment grade, or of comparable quality.

Executive Officers:

G. Putnam   President & Chairman

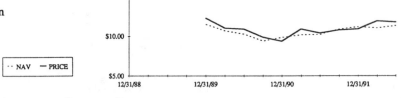

Investment Advisor: The Putnam Management Company, Inc.
Advisory Fee: Quarterly fee at the annual rate of 0.85% of average weekly net assets, subject to reduction to the extent that certain expenses exceed 2.5% of the first $30 mil. of average net assets, 2% of next $70 mil, and 1.5% of any excess over $100 mil. Fee for six months ended 12/31/91 was $716,952.
Administrator: Goldman Sachs Asset Management
Administration Fee: fee paid by Putnam Management Company, Inc. Fee for six months ended 12/31/91 was $5,997.

Capital Structure: *Common stock*: unlimited number of shares authorized; 10,608,295 shares outstanding 12/31/91
Remarketed preferred shares: 740 shares outstanding, liquidation preference of $100,000.

Portfolio Highlights (as of 3/31/92): Preferred stocks 65.0%, common stocks 26.8%, conv. preferred stocks 1.5%, short-term 9.3%. Largest industry concentrations: electric utilities 43.8%, combined utilities 16.8%, banks 12.3%. **Largest issuers:** Public Service Electric & Gas; Texas Utilities Electric; Alabama Power, Baltimore Gas & Electric; Commonwealth Edison.

Historical Financial Statistics (fiscal year-end: 6/30/91):

	six months 12/31/91	1991	9/28/89 to 6/30/90
Value of net assets (000)	194,779	182,003	180,338
NAV	11.35	10.21	10.26
Net investment income	0.50	1.16	1.01
Dividends from net investment income (common shares)	0.60	1.25	0.92
Dividends from paid-in capital	--	0.04	--
Dividends declared to remarketed preferred shares	0.13	0.49	0.35
Expense ratio	0.82% not ann.	2.02%	1.48% not ann.
Income ratio	3.58% not ann.	9.64%	7.63% not ann.
Portfolio turnover	30.16% not ann.	197.57%	201.55% not ann.

Special considerations: The trust may repurchase shares in the open market from time to time to reduce discounts. In the second quarter of 1995 and every fifth fiscal year thereafter, the trustees will consider making a tender offer at net asset value. Beginning in 1992 and each fiscal year thereafter, if certain conditions are met, the trustees will consider making a tender offer at net asset value. The fund may convert to an open-end fund by a 2/3 vote of each class of shares voting separately (or majority vote if approved by 2/3 of trustees).

Putnam High Income Convertible and Bond Fund

One Post Office Square, Boston, MA 02109   **Category:** Convertible Fund

Phone: 617-292-1000
Listed: PCF, NYSE
Commenced Operations: July, 1987
Cusip: 746779107

1991/mid-1992 Range of Premium/Disc: +13% to -7%
1991/mid-1992 Range of Price: $8 3/4q¤ to $5
NAV Total Return 1990: -9.38%; **1991:** +41.49%
Share Price Total Return 1990: -11.59%; **1991:** +73.84%
Herzfeld Ranking 1991: 1st of 8 convertible bond funds

Investment Objective: High current income through a portfolio of convertible and high-yield securities with potential for capital appreciation.

Executive Officers:

G. Putnam   Chairman &President

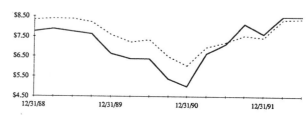

Investment Advisor: The Putnam Management Company, Inc.

Advisory Fee: Quarterly fee at annual rate of 0.75% on the first $500 mil., 0.65% on next $500 mil., 0.60% on next $500 mil., and 0.55% on any excess over $1.5 billion, minus certain brokerage commissions and fees received by affiliates of the manager on the fund's portfolio transactions. Fee for six months ended 2/29/92 was $364,801.

Investor Servicing Agent: Putnam Investor Services, Inc.

Capital Structure: *Shares of beneficial interest*: unlimited number of shares authorized; 12,757,161 shares outstanding 2/29/92

Portfolio Highlights (as of 2/28/92): Convertibles 48.0%, high yield bonds 44.1%, stocks 4.2%, cash and equivalents 3.5%. Largest industry concentrations: electronics 6.0%, computers 5.2%, oils 3.7%, conglomerates 2.9%, banking 2.8%. **Largest holdings**: American Standard Inc.; Auburn Hills Trust gtd. exch. certif. 16 7/8-20; Quantum Chemical Corp.; McCaw Cellular; Horsehead Industries Inc.; TW Food Services Inc.

Historical Financial Statistics (fiscal year-end: 8/31/91):

	six months 2/28/92	1991	1990	1989	1988	7/9/87 to 8/31/87
Value of net assets (000)	105,635	95,770	87,866	105,304	105,304	116,691
NAV	8.28	7.56	6.94	8.37	8.32	9.24
Net investment income	0.45	0.83	0.83	0.93	0.88	0.09
Dividends from net investment income	0.52	0.85	0.92	0.85	0.85	0.07
Distributions from net realized gains	--	0.01	0.02	--	--	--
Expense ratio	0.57% not ann.	1.31%	1.26%	1.15%	1.18%	0.18%*
Income ratio	5.78% not ann.	12.35%	11.07%	11.00%	10.52%	1.07%*
Portfolio turnover	31.41% not ann.	68.36%	53.30%	69.68%	85.34%	12.90%*

*not annualized

Special considerations: Beginning in 1992 and annually thereafter, if certain conditions exist, the fund will submit an open-ending proposal. The fund's Declaration of Trust contains various anti-takeover provisions. At 8/31/90 the fund had a capital loss carryforward of $15,168,000 expiring through 1998. At the 1991 annual meeting shareholders approved a proposed change in the advisory fee to: 0.75% on the first $500 mil., 0.65% on next $500 mil., 0.60% on next $500 mil., and 0.55% on any excess over $1.5 billion from an annual fee of 0.085% of average net assets. At the 1992 annual meeting shareholders approved a proposal to allow up to 15% of the value of the fund's net assets in restricted securities that the Trustees have determined to be readily marketable.

Putnam High Yield Municipal Trust

One Post Office Square, Boston, MA 02109
Category: Municipal Bond Fund

Phone: 617-292-1000
Listed: PYM, NYSE
Commenced Operations: May, 1989
Cusip: 746781103

1991/mid-1992 Range of Premium/Disc: +11% to -8%
1991/mid-1992 Range of Price: $10 1/4 to $8 1/8
NAV Total Return 1990: +3.92%; **1991:** +10.29%
Share Price Total Return 1990: -2.22%; **1991:** +29.97%
Herzfeld Ranking 1991: 41st of 51 municipal bond funds

Investment Objective: High current income exempt from federal income tax primarily through investment in high yielding tax-exempt municipal securities (Baa or lower by Moody's or BBB or lower by S&P).

Officers:

G. Putnam   Chairman & President

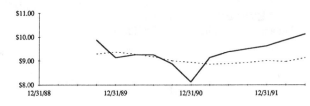

Investment Advisor: The Putnam Management Company, Inc.
Advisory Fee: Quarterly fee at annual rate of 0.70% of average net assets, subject to reduction in any year to the extent that certain expenses of the fund exceed 2.5% of the first $30 mil. of average net assets, 2% of the next $70 mil., and 1.5% of any excess. Fee for year-ended 3/31/92 was $1,500,545.

Capital Structure: *Shares of beneficial interest:* unlimited number of shares authorized; 20,436,551 shares outstanding 3/31/92
Remarketed preferred stock: 900 shares outstanding 3/31/92, redemption price $50,000 per share.

Portfolio Highlights (as of 3/31/92): Municipal bonds and notes 97.5%. Largest geographic concentrations: Illinois 8.4%, Michigan 7.9%, Ohio 7.3%, Pennsylvania 7.1%, Georgia 7.1%, Massachusetts 7.0%, Florida 5.6%, Texas 5.1%. Quality ratings: AAA 13.1%, AA 2.4%, A 8.6%, BBB 33.5%, BB 13.6%, B 24.7%, CCC 0.8%, D 0.8%. Largest industry concentrations: health care 25.3%, pollution control 17.9%, ports/airports 17.7%. **Largest issuers:** (GA) Burke County Development Authority Poll. Control Rev. Bonds; Denver City & County Airport Revenue Bonds Ser. A 8 1/2-23; (MI) Greater Detroit Resource Recovery Auth. Rev. Bonds; NH State Indl. Development Authority Pollution Control Revenue Bonds (United Illuminating Co.) Ser. B.; IA Fin. Auth. Health Care Fac. Revenue Bonds (Mercy Health Initiatives Project) 9.95-19.

Historical Financial Statistics (fiscal year-end: 3/31/92):

	1992	1991	5/25/89 to 3/31/90
Value of net assets (000)	228,735	178,871	186,520
NAV	8.99	8.85	9.28
Net investment income	0.78	0.78	0.66
Dividends from net investment income	0.81	0.81	0.59
Expense ratio	1.13%	0.90%	0.70%*
Income ratio	8.77%	8.55%	7.08%*
Portfolio turnover	62.28%	19.69%	48.90%*

*not annualized

Special considerations: The fund may repurchase shares or make tender offers when the Trustees deem it advantageous. Beginning in 1994, with a 2/3 vote of each class of shareholders, the fund may convert to an open-end fund.

Putnam Intermediate Government Income Trust

One Post Office Square, Boston, MA 02109

Category: Bond Fund

Phone: 617-292-1000
Listed: PGT, NYSE
Commenced Operations: June, 1988
Cusip: 746798107

1991/mid-1992 Range of Premium/Disc: +6% to -4%
1991/mid-1992 Range of Price: $10 to $8 1/4
NAV Total Return 1990: +9.52%; **1991:** +14.13%
Share Price Total Return 1990: +7.91%; **1991:** +14.14%
Herzfeld Ranking 1991: 73rd of 80 bond funds

Investment Objective: High current income and relative stability of net asset value through a portfolio of U.S. government and foreign government securities with limited maturities.

Executive Officers:

G. Putnam   Chairman & President

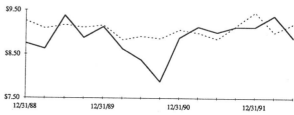

Investment Advisor: The Putnam Management Company, Inc.

Advisory Fee: Quarterly fee at annual rate of 0.75% on the first $500 mil., 0.65% on next $500 mil., 0.60% on next $500 mil., and 0.55% on any excess over $1.5 billion.. Fee for year-ended 11/30/91 was $4,574,404.

Capital Structure: *Shares of beneficial interest:* unlimited number of shares authorized; 63,598,496 shares outstanding 11/30/91

Portfolio Highlights (as of 2/28/92): U.S. government and agency obligations 69.8%, foreign bonds and notes 7.6%, short-term investments 5.0%. **Largest issuers:** U.S. treasury notes and stripped coupon securities; Federal Home Loan Mortgage Corp., Federal National Mortgage Association; Resolution Funding Corp.; Government National Mortgage Association.

Historical Financial Statistics (fiscal year-end: 11/30/91):

	1991	1990	1989	6/27/88 to 11/30/88
Value of net assets (000)	585,650	567,117	562,115	569,990
NAV	9.21	9.08	9.11	9.38
Net investment income	0.68	0.73	0.79	0.35
Dividends from net investment income	0.68	0.73	0.79	0.34
Distributions from net realized gains	0.05	0.08	0.22	--
Distributions from paid-in capital	0.16	0.17	--	--
Expense ratio	1.01%	1.02%	1.00%	0.42% not ann.
Income ratio	7.51%	8.19%	8.43%	3.71% not ann.
Portfolio turnover	255.49%	268.42%	174.57%	34.74% not ann.

Special considerations: Beginning in 1993 and each year thereafter, if certain conditions are met, the fund will submit an open-ending proposal. The fund may repurchase shares when the Board deems it advantageous. The fund's Declaration of Trust contains various anti-takeover provisions.

Putnam Investment Grade Municipal Trust

One Post Office Square, Boston, MA 02109

Category: Municipal Bond Fund

Phone: 617-292-1000	**1991/mid-1992 Range of Premium/Disc:** +9% to -2%
Listed: PGM, NYSE	**1991/mid-1992 Range of Price:** $12 3/4 to $11
Commenced Operations: October, 1989	**NAV Total Return 1990:** +5.71%; **1991:** +16.05%
Cusip: 746805100	**Share Price Total Return 1990:** +12.98%; **1991:** +20.34%
	Herzfeld Ranking 1991: 5th of 51 municipal bond funds

Investment Objective: Current income free from federal income tax, primarily through investment in investment-grade municipal securities.

Officers:

G. Putnam   Chairman & President

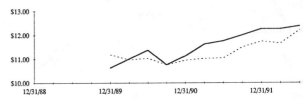

Investment Advisor: The Putnam Management Company, Inc.

Advisory Fee: Quarterly fee at annual rate of 0.70% of average net assets, subject to reduction to the extent that certain expenses exceed 2.5% of the first $30 mil. average net assets, 2% of the next $70 mil., and 1.5% of the excess over $100 mil. of average net assets. Fee for year-ended 11/30/91 was 2,342,080.

Capital Structure: outstanding 11/30/91

Shares of beneficial interest: unlimited number of shares authorized; 19,371,673

Remarketed Preferred shares: unlimited number of shares authorized; 1,400 shares outstanding 11/30/91, redemption price $100,000 per share. 2000 Serial Remarketed Preferred shares authorized, none outstanding 11/30/91.

Portfolio Highlights (as of 11/30/91): Municipal bonds and notes 99.5%. Largest industry concentrations: utilities 24.1%, health care 13.5%, ports/airports 13.1%, housing 11.1%. Largest geographic concentrations: Texas 12.0%, Massachusetts 11.7%, New York 9.5%, Washington 8.5%, California 8.4%, Pennsylvania 5.4%. **Largest issuers**: MA State Cons. Loan general obligation bonds; New York City general obligation bonds; Washington State Public Power Supply System Revenue Bonds; N. Central Texas Health Fac. Dev. Corp.; Dallas-Fort Worth International Airport Fac. Impt. Corp. Rev. Bonds (American Airlines, Inc.) 7 1/2-25.

Historical Financial Statistics (fiscal year-end: 11/30/91):

	1991	1990	10/26/89 to 11/30/89
Value of net assets (000)	362,974	311,731	213,924
NAV	11.51	11.03	11.19
Net investment income	0.98	0.91	0.07
Dividends from net investment income	0.89	0.87	--
Distributions from net realized gains	--	0.01	--
Expense ratio	1.46%	1.21%	0.12% not ann.
Income ratio	7.26%	7.69%	1.09% not ann.
Portfolio turnover	72.49%	89.65%	13.17% not ann.

Special considerations: Monthly dividends will be paid to common shareholders from net investment income remaining after payment of preferred dividends. Before 1994, conversion to an open-end fund will require a 2/3 vote of each class of shares voting separately; after that year a majority will be required. If certain circumstances are met after 1994, the trustees will submit an open-ending proposal at the following annual meeting. At the 1991 annual meeting shareholders voted in favor of a proposal to amend the fund's investment restriction concerning pledging its assets.

Putnam Managed Municipal Income Trust

One Post Office Square, Boston, MA 02109

Category: Municipal Bond Fund

Phone: 617-292-1000
Listed: PMM, NYSE
Commenced Operations: February, 1989
Cusip: 746823103

1991/mid-1992 Range of Premium/Disc: +9% to 0%
1991/mid-1992 Range of Price: $10 1/2 to $8 7/8
NAV Total Return 1990: +5.12%; **1991:** +14.85%
Share Price Total Return 1990: +2.71%; **1991:** +19.58%
Herzfeld Ranking 1991: 17th of 51 municipal bond funds

Investment Objective: High level of current income exempt from federal income tax. The fund invests in a diversified portfolio of tax-exempt municipal securities.

Executive Officers:

G. Putnam   Chairman & President

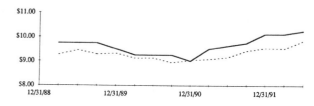

Investment Advisor: The Putnam Management Company, Inc.

Advisory Fee: Quarterly fee at annual rate of 0.70% of average net asset. Fee for year-ended 10/31/91 was $3,974,042.

Capital Structure:

Shares of beneficial interest: unlimited number of shares authorized; 42,951,118 outstanding 10/31/91

Remarketed Preferred shares: unlimited number of shares authorized; 1,750 shares outstanding; redemption price $100,000.

Portfolio Highlights (as of 1/31/92): Municipal bonds and notes 99.0%. Quality ratings (including unrated securities of comparable quality): AAA 24.1%, AA 15.1%, A 26.6%, BBB 17.7%, BB 6.0%, B 8.5%, CCC 0.5%, D 0.2%. Largest geographic concentrations: Georgia 11.4%, Florida 8.5%, California 8.4%, Texas 7.3%, New York 6.7%, Illinois 5.8%. **Largest issuers:** Burke County (GA) Dev. Auth. Poll. Control Rev. Bonds; New York City General Obligation Bonds; UT State School Dist. Rev. Bonds (Financing Pool) 8 3/8 various maturities; Chicago Single Family Mortgage Revenue Bonds; Denver City & County Airport Revenue Bonds.

Historical Financial Statistics (fiscal year-end 10/31/91):

	1991	1990	2/24/89 to 10/31/89
Value of net assets (000)	580,495	555,583	567,749
NAV	9.44	8.94	9.31
Net investment income avail. to common shares	0.82	0.77	0.52
Dividends from net investment income	0.76	0.76	0.47
Distributions from net realized gains	--	0.02	--
Expense ratio	1.33%	1.29%	0.62%*
Income ratio	7.69%	7.69%	5.76%*
Portfolio turnover	49.62%	41.48%	107.11%*

*not annualized

Special considerations: Before 1994, conversion to an open-end fund will require a 2/3 vote of each class of shares voting separately; after that year a majority will be required. If certain circumstances are met after 1994, the trustees will submit an open-ending proposal at the following annual meeting.

Putnam Master Income Trust

One Post Office Square, Boston, MA 02109

Category: Bond Fund

Phone: 617-292-1000
Listed: PMT, NYSE
Commenced Operations: December, 1987
Cusip: 74683K104

1991/mid-1992 Range of Premium/Disc: +1% to -13%
1991/mid-1992 Range of Price: $9 7/8 to $7
NAV Total Return 1990: +3.23%; **1991:** +22.99%
Share Price Total Return 1990: +2.84%; **1991:** +28.84%
Herzfeld Ranking 1991: 29th of 80 bond funds

Investment Objective: High current income consistent with preservation of capital. The fund invests primarily in fixed income and debt securities of the following three sectors: U.S. government, high yield, and international.

Executive Officers:

G. Putnam   Chairman & President

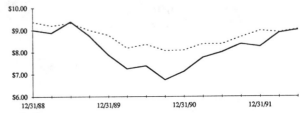

Investment Advisor: The Putnam Management Company, Inc.
Advisory Fee: Fee at the annual rate of 0.75% on the first $500 mil., 0.65% on next $500 mil., 0.60% on next $500 mil., and 0.55% on any excess over $1.5 billion. Fee for year-ended 10/30/91 was $3,648,829.

Capital Structure: *Shares of beneficial interest*: unlimited number of shs. authorized; 53,207,901 shares outstanding 10/31/91

Portfolio Highlights (as of 1/31/92): Corporate bonds and notes 32.8%, foreign bonds and notes 30.7%, U.S. government and agency obligations 28.7%, preferred stocks 1.4%, short-term investments 6.8%. **Largest issuers:** U.S. treasury notes; Government of France bonds; Government of Spain 12 1/4-00; Federal National Mortgage Association; Bundesobligationen.

Historical Financial Statistics (fiscal year-end: 10/31/91):

	1991	1990	1989	12/28/87 to 10/31/88
Value of net assets (000)	468,234	428,862	482,494	515,253
NAV	8.80	8.01	8.86	9.50
Net investment income	0.82	0.84	0.95	0.81
Dividends from net investment income	0.82	0.84	0.96	0.80
Distributions from net realized gains	--	0.01	0.19	0.03
Distributions from paid-in capital	0.11	0.15	--	--
Expense ratio	1.08%	1.08%	1.06%	0.85% not ann.
Income ratio	9.74%	10.07%	10.21%	8.54% not ann.
Portfolio turnover	323.27%	125.33%	323.44%	117.10% not ann.

Special considerations: The fund may repurchase shares when selling below net asset value. Beginning 11/1/92 and each year thereafter, under certain conditions, the fund will submit an open-ending proposal. The fund's Declaration of Trust contains various anti-takeover provisions. The fund has commenced a 3 million share repurchase program. During the year-ended 10/31/90 the fund repurchased 951,000 shares at an average discount of 14.7%; and during the year-ended 10/31/91 the fund repurchased 313,000 shares at an average discount of 12.25%.

Putnam Master Intermediate Income Trust

One Post Office Square, Boston, MA 02109

Category: Bond Fund

Phone: 617-292-1000
Listed: PIM, NYSE
Commenced Operations: April, 1988
Cusip: 746909100

1991/mid-1992 Range of Premium/Disc: 0% to -13%
1991/mid-1992 Range of Price: $9 1/4 to $6 1/2
NAV Total Return 1990: +1.54%; **1991:** +21.78%
Share Price Total Return 1990: +0.45%; **1991:** +27.63%
Herzfeld Ranking 1991: 35th of 80 bond funds

Investment Objective: High current income and relative stability of net asset value through investment in U.S. government, high yield, and international fixed income securities with limited maturities.

Officers:

G. Putnam   Chairman & President

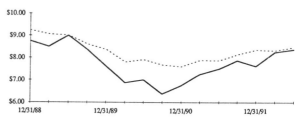

Investment Advisor: The Putnam Management Company, Inc.
Advisory Fee: Fee at the annual rate of 0.75% of the first $500 mil. of average weekly net assets, 0.65% of next $500 mil., 0.60% of next $500 mil. and 0.55% of any excess. Fee for six months ended 3/31/92 was $1,215,460.

Capital Structure: *Shares of beneficial interest*: unlimited number of shares authorized; 38,960,119 shares outstanding 3/31/92

Portfolio Highlights (as of 3/31/92): Corporate bonds and notes 34.7%, U.S. government and agency obligations 30.6%, foreign bonds and notes 30.1%, preferred stocks 1.0%, warrants 0.1%. Largest industry concentrations (corporate bonds): recreation 5.3%, conglomerates 5.3%. **Largest Issuers:** U.S. treasury notes; Federal Home Loan Mortgage Corporation; Government of France; Government of Canada; Government National Mortgage Association.

Historical Financial Statistics (fiscal year-end: 9/30/91):

	six months 3/31/92	1991	1990	1989	4/29/88 to 9/30/88
Value of net assets (000)	325,170	317,747	301,613	345,931	371,282
NAV	8.35	8.16	7.60	8.62	9.27
Net investment income	0.37	0.76	0.84	0.97	0.38
Dividends from net investment income	0.37	0.76	0.85	0.99	0.34
Distributions from net realized gains	0.04	--	0.08	0.08	--
Distributions from paid-in capital	0.01	0.11	0.02	--	--
Expense ratio	0.49%*	1.08%	1.04%	1.04%	0.39%*
Income ratio	4.42%*	9.65%	10.40%	10.61%	4.13%*
Portfolio turnover	67.65%*	204.31%	211.22%	202.47%	33.18%*

*not annualized

Special considerations: The fund may repurchase shares when selling below net asset value. The fund repurchased 724,000 shares during the six months ended 3/31/91 at an average discount of 12.88%. Beginning in 1993 and each year thereafter, under certain conditions, the fund will submit an open-ending proposal. The fund's Declaration of Trust contains various anti-takeover provisions. The fund has commenced a 2 million share repurchase program. During the six months ended 3/31/92, the fund repurchased no shares; during the year-ended 9/30/91 the fund repurchased 724,000 shares at a weighted average discount of 12.88%.

Putnam Premier Income Trust

One Post Office Square, Boston, MA 02109

Category: Bond Fund

Phone: 617-292-1000
Listed: PPT, NYSE
Commenced Operations: February, 1988
Cusip: 746853100

1991/mid-1992 Range of Premium/Disc: 0% to -12%
1991/mid-1992 Range of Price: $9 3/8 to $6 7/8
NAV Total Return 1990: +3.65%; **1991:** +18.46%
Share Price Total Return 1990: +2.95%; **1991:** +21.47%
Herzfeld Ranking 1991: 49th of 80 bond funds

Investment Objective: High current income primarily through investment in fixed income and debt securities among the following three sectors: U.S. government, high yield, and international.

Officers:

G. Putnam   President & Chairman

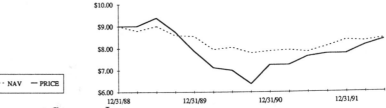

Investment Advisor: The Putnam Management Company, Inc.
Advisory Fee: Quarterly fee at annual rate of 0.75% on the first $500 mil., 0.65% on next $500 mil., 0.60% on next $500 mil., and 0.55% on any excess over $1.5 billion. Fee for six months ended 1/31/92 was $3,972,525.

Capital Structure: *Shares of beneficial interest*: unlimited number of shares authorized; 140,143,436 shares outstanding 1/31/92

Portfolio Highlights (as of 1/31/92): U.S. government and agency obligations 33.5%, corporate bonds and notes 31.3%, foreign bonds and notes 31.0%, preferred stocks 1.2%, convertible bonds 0.1%, common stocks 0.1%, short-term investments 5.6%. **Largest issuers:** U.S. treasury bonds and notes; Government National Mortgage Association; Federal National Mortgage Association; World Bank bonds 6 3/4-00; Government of Canada bonds.

Historical Financial Statistics (fiscal year-end: 7/31/91):

	six months 1/31/92	1991	1990	1989	2/29/88 to 7/31/88
Value of net assets (000)	1,173,624	1,106,772	1,169,007	1,278,922	1,255,520
NAV	8.37	7.90	8.20	8.98	8.95
Net investment income	0.39	0.75	0.75	0.85	0.35
Dividends from net investment income	0.38	0.75	0.75	0.88	0.33
Distributions from net realized gains	--	--	0.02	0.27	0.05
Distributions from paid-in capital	0.05	0.18	0.30	--	--
Expense ratio	0.44% not ann.	1.06%	1.02%	0.99%	0.40% not ann.
Income ratio	4.78% not ann.	9.41%	9.03%	9.54%	3.82% not ann.
Portfolio turnover	106.59%	350.45%	165.97%	249.07%	41.74% not ann.

Special considerations: The fund may repurchase shares when selling below net asset value. Beginning in 1993 and each year thereafter, under certain conditions, the fund will submit an open-ending proposal. The fund's Declaration of Trust contains various anti-takeover provisions. The fund has commenced a 7 million share repurchase program. During the six months ended 1/31/91 the fund repurchased 2,502,000 shares at an average discount of 14.44%; no additional shares were repurchased through 1/31/92. At the 1992 annual meeting shareholders approved a proposal to allow up to 15% of the value of the fund's net assets in restricted securities which the Trustees have determined to be readily marketable.

Putnam Tax-Free Health Care Fund

One Post Office Square, Boston, MA 02109

Category: Municipal Bond Fund

Phone: 617-292-1000	**1991/mid-1992 Range of Premium/Disc:** +8% to +8%
Listed: PMH, NYSE	**1991/mid-1992 Range of Price:** $15 1/4 to $15
Commenced Operations: June, 1992	**NAV Total Return 1991:** N/A
Cusip: 746920107	**Share Price Total Return 1991:** N/A
	Herzfeld Ranking 1991: N/A

Investment Objective: High level of current income exempt from federal income tax as the fund's investment manager believes is consistent with preservation of capital. The fund invests primarily in a diversified portfolio of tax exempt securities in the health care sector of the tax exempt securities market. At least 70% of total assets will be rated BBB or higher.

Officers:

G. Putnam   President & Chairman

Investment Advisor: The Putnam Management Company, Inc.

Advisory Fee: Quarterly fee at annual rate of 0.70% of average weekly net assets of the fund. The fee is waived for the first six months after the offering.

Capital Structure: *Common stock*: unlimited number of shares authorized, 12 mil. shares outstanding 6/23/92

Portfolio Highlights: not yet published

Historical Financial Statistics:

	6/29/92
Value of net assets (000)	180,000
NAV	14.04

Special considerations: The fund may from time to time take action to repurchase shares in the open market or to tender for its shares to reduce any market discount. The fund's Declaration of Trust includes provisions that could limit the ability of other persons or entities to acquire control of the fund including a 2/3 vote of outstanding shares to merge with another corporation or convert to an open-end fund.

Quest for Value Dual Purpose Fund, Inc.

Oppenheimer Tower, World Financial Center, New York, NY 10281   **Category: Dual Purpose Fund**

Phone: 800-232-FUND; 800-525-1103
Listed: KFV (capital shares), NYSE
            KFVpr (income shares), NYSE
Commenced Operations: February, 1987
Cusip (capital shares): 748343209
Cusip (income shares): 748343100

1991/mid-1992 Range of Premium/Disc:
capital shares: -17% to -33%; income shares: +20% to +9%
1991/mid-1992 Range of Price:
capital shares: $20 3/4 to $10 1/2; income shares: $13 3/4 to $12 5/8
NAV Total Return capital shs. **1990**: -6.08%; **1991**: +34.47%
NAV Total Return income shs. **1990**: +13.44%; **1991**: +12.06%
Price Total Return capital shs. **1990**: -14.50%; **1991**: +48.54%
Price Total Return income shs. **1990**: +4.38%; **1991**: +15.63%

Investment Objective: Both long-term capital appreciation with preservation of capital and current income and long-term growth of income. The fund invests primarily in dividend-paying common stocks and interest-bearing securities of a wide range of both domestic and foreign companies.

Officers:
J.M. La Motta   President

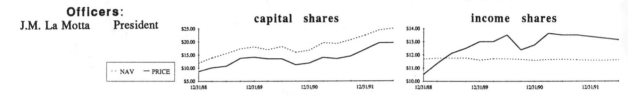

Investment Advisor: Quest for Value Advisors
Advisory Fee: Monthly fee at annual rate of 0.75% of first $200 mil. net assets, 0.50% on excess. Fee for year-ended 12/31/91 was $3,309,558.
Administrator: Oppenheimer Capital
Administration Fee: Monthly fee at annual rate of 0.10% of average weekly net assets. Fee for year-ended 12/31/91 was $561,912.

Capital Structure: *Common stock*: 20 mil. shares authorized; 18,004,302 shares outstanding 3/31/92
                       Preferred stock: 20 mil. shares authorized; 18,004,302 shares outstanding 3/31/92

Portfolio Highlights (as of 3/31/92): Common stocks 61.2%, conv. preferred stocks 15.0%, corporate notes & bonds 6.0%, conv. corporate bonds 3.7%, short-term 10.4%, other assets 1.0%. Largest sector concentrations: insurance 17.9%, textiles 7.5%, banking 6.7%, tobacco/beverage/food products 6.1%. **Largest positions**: Fruit of The Loom, Inc. Class A; Progressive Corp., Ohio; Transamerica Corp.; Honeywell; Freeport McMorRan

Historical Financial Statistics (fiscal year-end 12/31/91):

	1991	1990	1989	1988	11/1/87 to 12/31/87	2/13/87 to 10/31/87
Value of net assets (000)	**615,727**	504,739	533,994	425,376	365,781	
NAV capital shares	**22.59**	16.43	18.05	11.93	8.70	9.41
NAV income shares	**11.60**	11.60	11.61	11.69	11.62	11.86
Net investment income	**1.37**	1.57	1.41	1.12	0.08	0.64
Dividends from net investment income (income shares)	**1.37**	1.58	1.49	1.05	0.32	0.41
Distributions from net realized gains (capital shares)	**0.01**	0.20	--	--	0.77	--
Operating expense ratio	**0.77%**	0.81%	0.83%	0.86%	1.06% ann.	0.77% ann.
Income ratio	**4.39%**	5.50%	5.17%	5.04%	2.37% ann.	3.80% ann.
Portfolio turnover	**62%**	78%	76%	155%	25%	137%

Special considerations: The fund may repurchase equal numbers of shares of each class of stock when the Board deems it advantageous. On 1/31/97 the income shares will be redeemed at the initial net asset value per share ($11.60) plus accumulated and unpaid dividends and the board will decide whether to liquidate the capital shares or submit an open-ending proposal. The fund retained a portion of the taxable long-term capital gains of $1.7367 per share for the year-ended 12/31/91. Capital shareholders were able to take a credit on their 1991 tax returns equivalent to $0.5905 per share.

RAC Income Fund, Inc.

10221 Wincopin Circle, Columbia, MD 21044

Category: Bond Fund

Phone: 301-730-6851
Listed: RMF, NYSE
Commenced Operations: January, 1989
Cusip: 749208104

1991/mid-1992 Range of Premium/Disc: +15% to -4%
1991/mid-1992 Range of Price: $13 1/8 to $10 5/8
NAV Total Return 1990: +10.64%; **1991**: +16.68%
Share Price Total Return 1990: +14.57%; **1991**: +23.35%
Herzfeld Ranking 1991: 60th of 80 bond funds

Investment Objective: High monthly income, consistent with preservation of capital, by investing in a portfolio of fixed income securities, mainly mortgage-backed securities and other mortgage related securities (the average life of the portfolio is expected to be between 7 and 10 years). The fund seeks to distribute monthly income in excess of that obtainable on an annualized basis by investment in U.S. Treasury securities with the same maturity.

Officers:

W. Edwards   Chairman
C.W. Grant   President

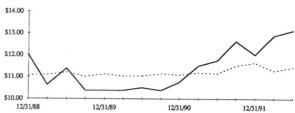

Investment Advisor: Ryland Acceptance Advisers, Inc.
Advisory Fee: Monthly fee at annual rate of 0.65% of average weekly net assets. Fee for year-ended 10/31/91 was $744,158.
Administrator: Ryland Acceptance Advisers, Inc.
Administration Fee: (for administration, custodian and transfer agent services) Monthly fee at annual rate of 0.20% of average weekly net assets. Fee for year-ended 10/31/91 was $114,459.

Capital Structure: *Common stock*: 200 mil. shares authorized; 10,374,048 shares outstanding 10/31/91
Debt: $30,485,000 reverse repurchase agreements outstanding 10/31/91. Average daily balance for the year-ended 10/31/91 was approximately $29.7 mil, at a weighted average interest rate of 6.68%.

Portfolio Highlights (as of 10/31/91): Adjustable rate mortgage-backed securities 32.3%, fixed rate single class mortgage-backed securities 24.9%, fixed rate multiple class collateralized mortgage obligations 19.9%, residual interests 15.2%, interest-only securities 7.7%. Quality ratings: AAA and government-backed mortgage securities 49.5%, AA 35.3%, private placements equivalent to AA 15.2%. **Largest issuers**: Federal National Mortgage Association; Resolution Trust Corporation; General Mortgage Securities; California Federal ARM; Glendale Federal Savings & Loan ARM.

Historical Financial Statistics (fiscal year-end: 10/31/91):

	1991	1990	12/20/88 to 10/31/89
Value of net assets (000)	120,051	112,425	112,144
NAV	11.57	11.12	11.09
Net investment income	1.32	1.21	0.89
Dividends from net investment income	1.26	1.27	0.85
Operating expense ratio	1.17%	1.28%	1.37% ann.
Total expense ratio	2.90%	4.42%	2.22% ann.
Income ratio	11.79%	10.94%	9.61% ann.
Portfolio turnover	132.44%	155.40%	241.81% ann.

Special considerations: The fund may repurchase shares when trading below net asset value. During the last quarter of 1991, under certain circumstances, the fund will make a tender offer for all shares at net asset value. The Board is not required to purchase shares pursuant to the tender offer. If all shares have not been tendered by 3/31/92, the board will submit a proposal to convert to an open-end fund. The fund's Articles of Incorporation contain various anti-takeover provisions. At 10/31/91 the fund had $16.9 mil. of dollar roll agreements.

Real Estate Securities Income Fund

757 Third Avenue, 16th Fl., New York, NY 10017

Category: Specialized Equity Fund

Phone: 212-832-3232
Listed: RIF, ASE
Commenced Operations: August, 1988
Cusip: 756008108

1991/mid-1992 Range of Premium/Disc: +20% to -14%
1991/mid-1992 Range of Price: $8 1/2 to $4 5/8
NAV Total Return 1990: -19.44%; **1991:** +52.76%
Share Price Total Return 1990: -18.37%; **1991:** +64.32%
Herzfeld Ranking 1991: 4th of 18 specialized equity funds

Investment Objective: High current income and capital appreciation through investment in publicly traded real estate securities.

Officers:
R.H. Steers   Chairman
M. Cohen   President

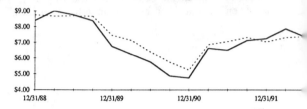

Investment Advisor: Cohen & Steers Capital Management, Inc.
Advisory Fee: Monthly fee at annual rate of 0.65% of average weekly net assets. Fee for 1991 was $123,316.
Administrator: Mutual Funds Service Company
Administration Fee: Monthly fee at annual rate of 0.20% of average weekly net assets. Fee for 1991 was $37,942.

Capital Structure: *Common stock:* 50 mil. shares authorized; 2,772,556 shares outstanding 12/31/91

Portfolio Highlights (as of 3/31/92): Equities 82.42%, fixed income 17.51%, other assets less liabilities 0.07%. Largest industry concentrations (equities): shopping centers 36.54%, health care 34.65%, office/industrial 6.42%. **Largest positions:** Health Equity Properties, Health Care REIT, Sizeler Property Investors, REIT of California, Illinois Central Railroad 14.125-01.

Historical Financial Statistics (fiscal year-end: 12/31/91):

	1991	1990	1989	8/30/88 to 12/31/88
Value of net assets (000)	20,379	14,776	20,692	23,856
NAV	7.35	5.33	7.46	8.75
Net investment income	0.64	0.72	0.99	0.32
Dividends from net investment income	0.64	0.72	1.00	0.33
Distributions from paid-in capital	0.04	0.04	--	--
Expense ratio	1.66%	1.88%	1.29%	2.90% ann.
Income ratio	9.26%	11.24%	11.88%	10.87% ann.
Portfolio turnover	77.62%	103.11%	163.40%	79.35%

Special considerations: The fund may repurchase shares at prices below net asset value. After 1/1/93, under certain circumstances, the fund can be converted to an open-end fund with a 2/3 vote of shareholders. The fund's Articles of Incorporation contain various anti-takeover provisions. At 12/31/91 capital loss carryforwards were $1,143,048, $5,771,906 and $277,200 and expiring in 1997, 1998 and 1999, respectively.

The R.O.C. Taiwan Fund

100 East Pratt Street, Baltimore, MD 21202   **Category: Foreign Equity Fund**

Phone: 800-343-9567; 410-752-2880
Listed: ROC, NYSE
Commenced Operations: May, 1989
Cusip: 749651105

1991/mid-1992 Range of Premium/Disc: +25% to -23%
1991/mid-1992 Range of Price: $13 5/8 to $6 7/8
NAV Total Return 1990: -34.91%; **1991**: +12.47%
Share Price Total Return 1990: -39.28%; **1991**: +41.94%
Herzfeld Ranking 1991: 21st of 46 foreign equity funds

Investment Objective: Long-term capital appreciation through investment primarily in publicly traded equity securities of Republic of China (R.O.C.) issuers.

Officers: T.S.S. Cheng — Chairman
D. Chan — President &Portfolio MGR

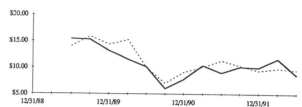

Investment Manager: International Investment Trust Company, Limited
Management Fee: Monthly fee in New Taiwan Dollars at the annual rate of 1.5% of the net asset value of the total assets held under the investment contract. Fee for 1991 was $3,681,409.
U.S. Administrator: T. Rowe Price Associates, Inc.
Administration Fee: Fee at the annual rate of 0.1% of the trust's average weekly net asset value up to $250 mil., 0.075% on the next $250 mil., and 0.05% on any excess. Fees for 1991 were $259,602.

Capital Structure: *Common stock*: unlimited number of shares authorized; 25,612,932 shares outstanding 1 12/31/91

Portfolio Highlights (as of 3/31/92): Common and preferred stocks 87.23%, bonds 3.09%, short-term investments 4.64%, other assets 4.42%. Largest industry concentrations: electrical and electronics 15.50%, textiles 12.07%, plastics 8.11%, steel and other metals 7.03%, cement 7.01%, banking 6.79%, food 6.11%, construction 5.55%. **Largest positions**: various R.O.C. government bonds, Teco Electric and Machinery Co. Ltd., United Microelectronics Corporation, President Enterprise Corporation, Cathay Life Insurance Co. Ltd.

Historical Financial Statistics (fiscal year-end: 12/31/91):

	1991	1990	1989	1988	1987	1986
Value of net assets (000)	244,073	235,736	370,693	185,908	247,730	125,242*
NAV	9.53	9.15	14.38	8.58	4.74	2.29
Net investment income (loss) (after reorganization expense)	(0.01)	0.08	(0.21)	(0.08)	(0.01)	??
Dividends from net investment income and realized gains	0.75	0.22	0.43	0.01	0.02	0.02
Expense ratio	2.11%	2.03%	1.93%	1.77%	1.76%	1.79%
Income ratio (loss)	(0.15%)	0.69%	(0.51%)	(0.38%)	(0.13%)	0.70%
Portfolio turnover	35%	27%	30%	38%	46%	41%

*unaudited

Special considerations: Established in October, 1983, The Taiwan (R.O.C.) Fund (which became this fund) was the largest and oldest investment fund organized for investment in securities of the Republic of China. On May 19, 1989, the trust acquired entire beneficial interest in the net assets of The Taiwan (R.O.C.) Fund in exchange for approximately 21,656,000 newly issued shares and issued an additional 6,407 shares to International Investment Trust Company Limited in respect to its initial investment. A public offering of 4,112,626 shares at $14.55 per share was also completed on that date. There was a change in ownership of the investment advisor in 1990. The fund repurchased 70,200 shares during 1991 under a plan announced in June, 1991. Additional shares may be repurchased when selling at a discount to the net asset value. In April, 1992 the fund had an offering of 2 mil. shares priced at $10 1/8.
Shareholders over 5%: Kuwait Investment Office, 9.4%

Royce Value Trust

1414 Avenue of the Americas, New York, NY 10019

Category: Equity Fund

Phone: 212-355-7311
Listed: RVT, NYSE
Commenced Operations: November, 1986
Cusip: 780910105

1991/mid-1992 Range of Premium/Disc: +5% to -13%
1991/mid-1992 Range of Price: $12 to $7 1/2
NAV Total Return 1990: -14.98%; **1991:** +39.39%
Share Price Total Return 1990: -11.11%; **1991:** +35.20%
Herzfeld Ranking 1991: 4th of 15 equity funds

Investment Objective: Long-term investment returns using a value-oriented style with small to mid-sized companies.

Officers:

C.M. Royce   President
                & Treasurer

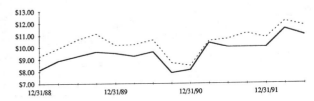

Investment Advisor: Quest Advisory Corp.
Advisory Fee: Monthly fee equal to annual rate of 1% of the average total net assets of the fund at the end of each month, subject to increase or decrease determined by performance of the fund relative to the S&P 500 index. Fee for year-ended 12/31/91 was $647,493.

Capital Structure: *Common stock:* 150 mil. shares authorized; 15,426,004 shares outstanding 3/31/92

Portfolio Highlights (as of 12/31/91): Common stocks 101.49%, preferred stocks 1.32%, corporate bonds 1.32%, repurchase agreement 1.80%, liabilities less cash and other assets (5.93%). Largest sector concentrations: business and industrial products 28.72%, financial intermediaries and services 21.50%, business and industrial services 15.84%, consumer products 11.49%, consumer services 8.64%. **Largest positions** (3/31/92): Alleghany Corporation, Avatar Moldings Inc., Quaker Chemical Corporation, Puerto Rican Cement Company Inc., Midwest Grain Products Inc.

Historical Financial Statistics (fiscal year-end: 12/31/91):

	1991	1990	1989	1988	1987	11/26/86 to 12/31/86
Value of net assets (000)	166,550	118,308	130,502	107,315	90,326	
NAV	11.23	8.58	10.35	9.25	7.98	9.29
Net investment income	0.17	0.17	0.15	0.13	0.28	0.03
Dividends from net investment income	0.17	0.17	0.17	0.06	0.36	--
Distributions from net realized gains	0.44	0.15	0.35	0.45	0.16	--
Expense ratio	0.79%	0.94%	0.95%	1.09%	0.40%	1.79% ann.
Income ratio	1.52%	1.78%	1.48%	1.42%	2.92%	3.45% ann.
Portfolio turnover	34.01%	28.16%	36.06%	29.26%	65.82%	12.76% ann.

Special considerations: Distributions are reinvested at market price. The fund has been authorized to repurchase up to 50,000 shares of common stock at prices less than NAV and not in excess of current market price. The fund completed a rights offering of 706,352 shares at a subscription price of $9.625 in August, 1991. One right was issued for every share held and shareholders had the right to purchase one additional share for every 20 rights. **Shareholders over 5%:** Bartlett & Co. 6.83%, Yale University 5.47%

The Salomon Brothers Fund, Inc.

(formerly The Lehman Corporation)

7 World Trade Center, New York, NY 10048

Category: Equity Fund

Phone: 212-783-1301, 800-725-6666
Listed: SBF, NYSE
Commenced Operations: September, 1929
Cusip: 795477108

1991/mid-1992 Range of Premium/Disc: -7% to -19%
1991/mid-1992 Range of Price: $14 1/4 to $10 3/8
NAV Total Return 1990: -7.99%; **1991:** +29.80%
Share Price Total Return 1990: -8.31%; **1991:** +42.39%
Herzfeld Ranking 1991: 8th of 15 equity funds

Investment Objective: Provide investors with a means of participating in a professionally managed and continuously supervised common stock portfolio of companies which the management believes will grow and prosper. As a general rule, the fund invests for the longer term.

Officers:

R. Salomon, Jr.   Chairman & President

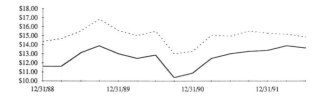

Investment Advisor: Salomon Brothers Asset Management Inc.
Advisory Fee: Quarterly fee at annual rate of 0% on first $25 mil. of average daily net assets, 0.50% of next $325 mil., 0.30% of next $150 mil., 0.25% of next $250 mil., and 0.20% of excess. Fee for 1991 was $3,254,442.

Capital Structure: *Common stock:* 75 mil. shares authorized; 71,229,661 shares outstanding 3/31/92

Portfolio Highlights (as of 3/31/92): Common stocks 98.6%, repurchase agreement 1.3%. Largest industry concentrations: basic industries 17.6%, consumer products & services 13.2%, energy 12.3%, health care 11.9%, financial services 10.7%, telecommunications 9.6%. **Largest positions:** Federal National Mortgage Association, Consolidated Rail, J.P. Morgan, Pfizer, Union Pacific.

Historical Financial Statistics (fiscal year-end: 12/31/91):

	1991	1990	1989	1988	1987	1986
Value of net assets (000)	1,115,174	906,022	1,027,117	885,368	801,483	851,765
NAV	15.66	13.33	15.58	14.37	13.26	15.42
Net investment income	0.45	0.46	0.60	0.49	0.47	0.50
Dividends from net investment income	0.47	0.485	0.59	0.505	0.49	0.515
Distributions from net realized gains	1.14	0.71	1.515	0.49	1.88	3.085
Expense ratio	0.43%	0.46%	0.44%	0.47%	0.44%	0.43%
Income ratio	3.01%	3.21%	3.83%	3.44%	2.81%	2.95%
Portfolio turnover	14%	15%	30%	49%	54%	58%

Special considerations: At the 1992 annual meeting, a stockholder proposal recommending that the board consider converting the fund to an open-end fund was defeated.

Scudder New Asia Fund, Inc.

345 Park Avenue, New York, NY 10154

Category: Foreign Equity Fund

Phone: 212-326-6200; 617-330-5602
Listed: SAF, NYSE
Commenced Operations: June, 1987
Cusip: 811183102

1991/mid-1992 Range of Premium/Disc: +11% to -12%
1991/mid-1992 Range of Price: $17 1/2 to $11 5/8
NAV Total Return 1990: -3.91%; **1991:** +12.38%
Share Price Total Return 1990: -9.83%; **1991:** +26.27%
Herzfeld Ranking 1991: 22nd of 46 foreign equity funds

Investment Objective: Long-term capital appreciation primarily through investment in equity securities of Asian companies including, in particular, smaller Japanese companies.

Officers:

E.D. Villani   Chairman
N. Bratt   President

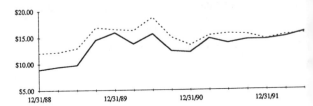

Investment Advisor: Scudder, Stevens & Clark Inc.
Advisory Fee: Monthly fee at annual rate of 1.15% of first $50 mil. month-end net assets, 1.10% of assets between $50 mil. and $100 mil., 1.00% of excess. Fee for 1991 was $1,209,394.

Capital Structure: *Common stock:* 50 mil. shares authorized; 7,064,096 shares outstanding 12/31/91
                       Note Payable: Note outstanding from its custodian for $1,050,000 on 12/31/91

Portfolio Highlights (as of 3/31/92): Common stocks 87.1%, convertible bonds 5.8%, limited partnership 0.7%, preferred stock 0.1%, commercial paper 6.3%. Largest geographic concentrations: Japan 24.3%, Hong Kong 15.7%, Thailand 11.2%, Malaysia 10.4%, Korea 8.5%, India 5.3%, Indonesia 5.2%. **Largest positions:** Freeport McMoRan Copper and Gold Inc. "A"; Federation of Malaysia (convertible into Telecom Malaysia) 6-01; The India Fund; Henderson Land Development Co. Ltd.; Cable and Wireless PLC; Chiyoda Co. Ltd.

Historical Financial Statistics (fiscal year-end: 12/31/91):

	1991	1990	1989	1988	6/25/87 to 12/31/87
Value of net assets (000)	105,517	94,458	114,681	84,362	75,749
NAV	14.94	13.44	16.36	12.04	10.81
Net investment income (loss)	0.08	0.08	(0.02)	(0.08)	0.04
Dividends from net investment income	0.08	0.08	--	0.05	0.02
Distributions from net realized gains	0.11	2.11	1.38	--	--
Operating expense ratio	1.79%	1.77%	1.88%	1.90%	1.74% ann.
Interest expense ratio	--	0.02%	0.44%	0.64%	0.75% ann.
Income ratio (loss)	0.54%	0.46%	(0.14%)	(0.68%)	0.64% ann.
Portfolio turnover	12.3%	24.1%	61.1%	37.2%	62.9% ann.

Special considerations: The fund's Articles of Incorporation contain various anti-takeover provisions. A proposal to limit the liability of and indemnify officers and directors was passed at the July, 1990, annual meeting.

Scudder New Europe Fund, Inc.

345 Park Avenue, New York, NY 10154

Category: Foreign Equity Fund

Phone: 212-326-6200; 617-330-5602
Listed: NEF, NYSE
Commenced Operations: February, 1990
Cusip: 810905109

1991/mid-1992 Range of Premium/Disc: -7% to -21%
1991/mid-1992 Range of Price: $10 3/8 to $7 5/8
NAV Total Return 1991: -2.09%
Share Price Total Return 1991: +3.58%
Herzfeld Ranking 1991: 40th of 46 foreign equity funds

Investment Objective: Long-term capital appreciation through investment primarily in equity securities of companies traded on smaller or emerging European securities markets and companies that, in the opinion of the fund's investment manager, are likely to benefit from economic, political, structural and technological changes and developments in Western and Eastern Europe.

Officers:

D. Pierce	Chairman
N. Bratt	President

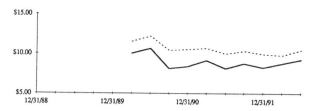

Investment Advisor: Scudder, Stevens & Clark Inc.
Administrator: Scudder, Stevens & Clark Inc.
Advisory and Administration Fee: Monthly fee at annual rate of 1.25% of average weekly net assets up to $75 mil., 1.15% on the next $125 mil., and 1.10% of any excess. Fee for year-ended 10/31/91 was $2,016,713. Economic advisory fees for same period were $190,000.

Capital Structure: *Common stock*: 100 mil. shares authorized; 16,022,606 shares outstanding 10/31/91

Portfolio Highlights (as of 1/31/92): Common stocks 84.3%, preferred stocks 8.1%, bonds 5.4%, repurchase agreement 2.2%. Largest geographic concentrations: Germany 25.0%, France 15.6%, Netherlands 9.9%, United Kingdom 9.6%, Switzerland 9.2%, Spain 6.8%. **Largest positions:** Federal Republic of Germany 6-93; Alcatel Alsthom; Compañía Telefónica Nacional de España SA; Computer 2000; Banco Pastor SA.

Historical Financial Statistics (fiscal year-end: 10/31/91):

	1991	2/16/90 to 10/31/90
Value of net assets (000)	162,117	176,285
NAV	10.12	11.01
Net investment income	0.19	0.42
Dividends from net investment income	0.47	--
Distributions from net realized gains	0.20	--
Operating expense ratio	1.85%	1.84% ann.
Income ratio	1.74%	5.07% ann.
Portfolio turnover	31.7%	104.5% ann.

Special considerations: An advisory board, maintained separately from the investment manager, consults with the Board of Directors regarding smaller or emerging European securities markets and economic and political developments. Up to 25% of assets may be invested in illiquid securities. The fund's Articles of Incorporation contain various anti-takeover provisions, including a 75% voting requirement for conversion to an open-end fund. Mid-1992 dividend rate, $0.0782 per month.

Seligman Quality Municipal Fund, Inc.

130 Liberty Street, New York, NY 10006

Category: Municipal Bond Fund

Phone: 800-221-2450, 212-488-0200
Listed: SQF, NYSE
Commenced Operations: November, 1991
Cusip: 816343107

1991/mid-1992 Range of Premium/Disc: +10% to -4%
1991/mid-1992 Range of Price: $15 1/8 to $13 1/2
NAV Total Return 1991: N/A
Share Price Total Return 1991: N/A
Herzfeld Ranking 1991: N/A

Investment Objective: High level of current income exempt from federal income taxes consistent with the preservation of capital and with consideration given to opportunities for capital gain. The fund will invest in a portfolio of municipal obligations, at least 80% of which will be rated AAA or covered by insurance guaranteeing the timely repayment of both principal and interest.

Officers:

W.C. Morris   Chairman
T.G. Moles   President & Portfolio Manager

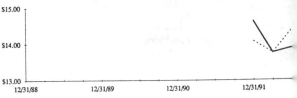

Investment Advisor: J. & W. Seligman & Co. Incorporated
Advisory Fee: Monthly fee at the annual rate of 0.65% of average daily net assets up to $500 mil., 0.625% of average daily net assets in excess of $500 mil. but less than $1 bil., and 0.60% of average daily net assets of $1 bil. or more. A portion of the management fee will be waived if the regular monthly dividend is less than $0.0656 per share. Fee for period 11/29/91 to 4/30/92 was $48,282.
Administrator: The Boston Company Advisors, Inc.
Administration Fee: Monthly fee at the annual rate of 0.07% of the fund's average daily net assets.

Capital Structure: *Common stock:* 50 mil. shares authorized, 4,627,575 outstanding as of 4/30/92
Auction Rate Preferred Stock: 1,000 shares authorized, 672 shares outstanding with liquidation preference of $50,000 per share. Dividend rate reset every 7 days by auction. Dividends rates ranged from 3.09% to 4.20% during the period ended 4/30/92.

Portfolio Highlights (as of 4/30/92): Municipal bonds 96.8%, variable rate demand notes 1.2%, other assets less liabilities 2.0%. Largest geographic concentrations: Illinois 9.2%, Massachusetts 8.9%, South Carolina 8.6%, New York 6.2%, California 6.0%, Washington 5.6%, Montana 5.5%. 80% of assets carried a AAA rating **Largest issuers** Massachusetts Health & Educational Facilities Authority Revenue; Hawaii State Airports System Rev.; South Carolina State Ports Authority Rev. 6 3/4-21; Allegheny County Airport Rev. (Greater Pittsburgh International Airport); Henderson Health Care Facilities Rev. (Catholic Health Care West) 7-20.

Historical Financial Statistics:

	11/29/91 to 4/30/92	
Value of net assets (000)	97,782	
NAV	13.87	
Net investment income	0.38	
Dividends paid to common shares	0.23	
Expense ratio	0.55%	ann.
Income ratio	5.77%	ann.
Portfolio turnover	4.41%	

Special considerations: Dividends are paid monthly from net investment income while net capital gains are distributed annually. In efforts to reduce any discounts which may develop, the Board of Directors may repurchase share make tender offers at net asset value, or propose conversion to an open-end fund.

Seligman Select Municipal Fund, Inc.

130 Liberty Street, New York, NY 10006

Category: Municipal Bond Fund

Phone: 800-221-2450, 212-488-0200
Listed: SEL, NYSE
Commenced Operations: February, 1990
Cusip: 816344105

1991/mid-1992 Range of Premium/Disc: +5% to 0%
1991/mid-1992 Range of Price: $12 1/2 to $11 1/8
NAV Total Return 1991: +14.99%
Share Price Total Return 1991: +17.66%
Herzfeld Ranking 1991: 14th of 51 municipal bond funds

Investment Objective: High level of current income exempt from federal income taxes consistent with the preservation of capital and with consideration given to opportunities for capital gain. The fund will invest in a portfolio of municipal obligations, at least 80% of which will be rated AAA or covered by insurance guaranteeing the timely repayment of both principal and interest.

Officers:

W.C. Morris — Chairman
T.G. Moles — President

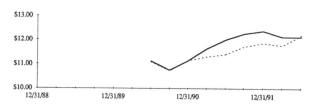

Investment Advisor: J. & W. Seligman & Co. Incorporated
Advisory Fee: Monthly fee at the annual rate of 0.55% of average daily net assets. Fee for 1991 was $1,224,166.
Stockholder Service Agency: Union Data Service Center, Inc.

Capital Structure: *Common stock*: 50 mil. shares authorized; 12,848,826 shares outstanding 12/31/91
Remarketed Preferred Stock: 375 Class A and 375 Class B remarketed preferred shares each at a liquidation value of $100,000 per share. The dividend rate on each class may change every 28 days as set by the remarketing agent. Dividend rates ranged from 3.92% to 6.80% during the period ended 12/31/91.

Portfolio Highlights (as of 12/31/91): Municipal bonds 96.4%, short-term holdings 1.7%, other assets less liabilities 1.9%. Largest geographic concentrations: Texas 9.3%, District of Columbia 8.0%, Massachusetts 7.9%, Florida 7.8%, New York 7.6%, New Hampshire 6.6%. **Largest Issuers:** New York State Energy Research & Development Authority Electric Facilities Rev. (Consolidated Edison Co. NY Inc. Project) 7.5-26; Louisiana Public Facilities Authority Hospital Rev. (Southern Baptist Hospitals, Inc. Project) 8-12; Alaska Housing Finance Corp. (Collateralized Home Mortgage Rev.) 7.65-24; South Dakota Student Loan Corporation Student Loan Rev. 7 5/8-06; Metropolitan Washington D.C. Airports Authority Airport System Rev. 7.60-14.

Historical Financial Statistics (fiscal year-end: 12/31/91):

	1991	2/15/90 to 12/31/90
Value of net assets (000)	228,501	217,385
NAV	12.25	11.25
Net investment income	1.10	0.92
Dividends on common stock	0.84	0.63
Expense ratio	0.90%	0.78% ann.
Income ratio	6.33%	6.58% ann.
Portfolio turnover	7.36%	10.75%

Special considerations: Dividends are paid monthly from net investment income while net capital gains are distributed annually. In efforts to reduce any discounts which may develop, the Board of Directors may repurchase shares, make tender offers at net asset value, or propose conversion to an open-end fund. The fund has elected to retain the remainder of its capital gains realized in 1991 and to pay the tax thereon.

The Singapore Fund, Inc.
c/o Daiwa Securities Trust Company
One Evertrust Plaza, 9th Fl., Jersey City, NJ 07302

Category: Foreign Equity Fund

Phone: 800-933-3440; 201-915-3020	**1991/mid-1992 Range of Premium/Disc:** +5% to -23%
Listed: SGF, NYSE	**1991/mid-1992 Range of Price:** $12 to $8 3/8
Commenced Operations: July, 1990	**NAV Total Return 1991:** +16.02%
Cusip: 82929L109	**Share Price Total Return 1991:** +24.01%
	Herzfeld Ranking 1991: 16th of 46 foreign equity funds

Investment Objective: Long-term capital appreciation through investment primarily in Singapore equity securities.

Officers:

K. Yoneyama	Chairman
Gan K. Kok	President

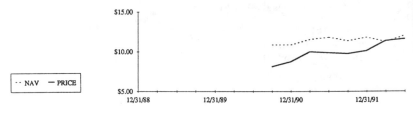

Investment Manager: DBS Asset Management (United States) Pte. Ltd.

Management Fee: Monthly fee at the annual rate of 0.80% of the first $50 mil. of average weekly net assets and 0.66% of any excess. Management fee and applicable expenses for year-ended 10/31/91 were $464,246.

Investment Advisor: Daiwa International Capital Management (Singapore) Limited

Advisory Fee: Monthly fee at the annual rate of 0.40% of the first $50 mil. of average weekly net assets and 0.34% of any excess. Advisory fee and applicable expenses for year-ended 10/31/91 were $228,901.

Administrator: Daiwa Securities Trust Company

Administration Fee: Monthly fee at the annual rate of 0.20% of average weekly net assets, with a minimum annual fee of $150,000. Administrative fee for year-ended 10/31/91 was $150,000.

Capital Structure: *Common stock:* 100 mil. shares authorized, 5,068,502 shares outstanding 10/31/91

Portfolio Highlights (as of 10/31/91): Common stocks 80.82%, convertible bonds 3.56%, time deposits 19.94%, liabilities in excess of other assets (4.32%). Largest geographic concentrations: Singapore 81.66%, Malaysia 7.71%, U.S. dollar time deposits 14.95%. Largest sector concentrations: shipyards 13.86%, banks 11.49%, commercial & industrial 10.22%, property development 8.39%, transportation--marine 8.06%, construction materials 7.74%.

Largest positions: Oversea-Chinese Banking Corporation Ltd. (foreign shares), Singapore Press Holdings Ltd. (foreign shares), Natsteel Ltd., Far East Levingston Shipbuilding Ltd., Singapore Airlines Ltd. (foreign shares)

Historical Financial Statistics (fiscal year-end: 10/31/91):

	1991	7/31/90 to 10/31/90
Value of net assets (000)	59,379	55,698
NAV	11.72	11.12
Net investment income	0.17	0.12
Dividends from net investment income and realized gains	0.21	--
Expense ratio	2.56%	2.83% ann.
Income ratio	1.47%	4.25% ann.
Portfolio turnover	29.53%	--

Special considerations: The Board of Directors will consider making repurchases or tender offers on a quarterly basis to reduce or eliminate discounts which may develop. The Board of Directors may also consider whether to submit an open-end conversion proposal to shareholders. The fund's Articles of Incorporation and By-Laws contain various anti-takeover provisions including a 75% voting requirement to, among other things, merge with another corporation, liquidate or convert to an open-end fund.

Smith Barney Intermediate Municipal Fund, Inc.

1345 Avenue of the Americas, New York, NY 10105   **Category:** Municipal Bond Fund

Phone: 212-698-5349	**1991/mid-1992 Range of Premium/Disc:** +6% to -5%
Listed: SBI, ASE	**1991/mid-1992 Range of Price:** $10 1/2 to $7 1/8
Commenced Operations: February, 1992	**NAV Total Return 1991:** N/A
Cusip: 831802103	**Share Price Total Return 1991:** N/A
	Herzfeld Ranking 1991: N/A

Investment Objective: High level of current income exempt from federal income taxes consistent with prudent investing. The fund will invest only in municipal securities rated investment grade and at least two thirds of total assets in municipal securities rated A or better. At least 80% of total assets will be invested in municipal securities with remaining maturities of less than fifteen years, and the fund will maintain a dollar-weighted average maturity of the entire portfolio of not less than three, but not more than ten years.

Officers:

S.J. Treadway   President

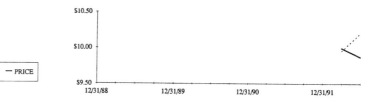

Investment Advisor: Mutual Management Corp.

Advisory Fee: Monthly fee in arrears equal to 0.60% annually of the fund's average daily net assets during the month.

Capital Structure: *Common stock*: 100 mil. shares authorized, 7 mil. shares outstanding 2/27/92.

Portfolio Highlights: not yet published

Historical Financial Statistics:

	2/27/92
Value of net assets (000)	70,000
NAV	10.00

Special considerations: The fund was brought to market as a no-load closed-end fund (no underwriting discount). The fund may use various hedging transactions to protect the value of the portfolio against declines resulting from interest rate changes. The fund makes monthly distributions from net investment income, and annual distributions from net realized capital gains. The Board of Directors may take certain actions to reduce or eliminate discounts to net asset value such as tender offers, share repurchases, or conversion to an open-end fund. The fund's Articles of Incorporation and By-laws contain various anti-takeover provisions including a 75% voting requirement for merger with another fund or liquidation of the fund.

Source Capital Inc.

11400 West Olympic Blvd., Suite 1200, Los Angeles, CA 90064   **Category: Equity Fund**

Phone: 310-996-5406
Listed: SOR, NYSE
Commenced Operations: June, 1968
Cusip: 836144105

1991/mid-1992 Range of Premium/Disc: +13% to 0%
1991/mid-1992 Range of Price: $47 1/2 to $36 1/2
NAV Total Return 1990: -3.72%; **1991**: +22.23%
Share Price Total Return 1990: -4.47%; **1991**: +29.32%
Herzfeld Ranking 1991: 12th of 15 equity funds

Investment Objective: Maximum total return for common shareholders from both capital appreciation and investment income to the extent consistent with protection of invested capital and provision for sufficient income to meet the dividend requirements of preferred shareholders.

Officers:
G.H. Michaelis   President

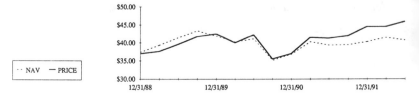

Investment Advisor: First Pacific Advisors, Inc.

Advisory Fee: Monthly fee at annual rate of 0.725% of first $100 mil. of total net assets, 0.700% of next $100 mil., and 0.675% of excess. The fee is reduced to the extent necessary to reimburse the company for any annual expenses (excluding various expenses) in excess of 1 1/2% of first $30 mil. and 1% of remaining average total assets. Fee for 1991 was $2,141,005.

Capital Structure: *Common stock*: 12 mil. shares authorized; 6,392,934 shares outstanding 12/31/91
$2.40 Cumulative Preferred Stock: 3 mil. shares authorized; 1,969,212 shares outstanding 12/31/91, $27.50 per share liquidation value plus accrued dividends

Portfolio Highlights (as of 12/31/91): Common stocks 54.0%, convertible securities 9.57%, non-convertible securities 24.41%. Largest industry concentrations: producer durable goods 13.78%, materials 9.69%, multi-industry 8.50%, consumer services-retail 8.47%, communications & information 6.91%. **Largest positions**: SCI Holdings, Inc. 0-92; Melville Corporation, Lubrizol Corporation; Minnesota Mining and Manufacturing Company, Tennessee Valley Authority 8 1/8-99; First National Bank of Anchorage, American Home Products Corporation.

Historical Financial Statistics (fiscal year-end: 12/31/91):

	1991	1990	1989	1988	1987	1986
Value of net assets (000)	317,715	286,467	313,724	284,583	268,912	285,508
NAV	41.23	36.94	41.95	37.38	35.16	38.04
Net investment income	2.04	2.40	2.51	2.36	2.20	2.28
Dividends from net investment income (common shares)	1.21	1.69	1.63	1.70	1.53	1.64
Distributions from net realized gains (common shares)	2.39	1.91	1.95	1.69	1.95	1.74
Distributions from paid in capital (common)	--	--	--	0.11	--	--
Dividends to preferred shares	0.75	0.76	0.76	0.77	0.77	0.78
Expense ratio	0.97%	0.97%	0.96%	1.00%	0.96%	0.97%
Income ratio	4.22%	5.10%	5.01%	5.07%	4.51%	4.70%
Portfolio turnover	41.48%	42.87%	36.17%	42.52%	75.55%	81.93%

Special considerations: The fund has had a 10% payout policy for many years. The fund retained a portion of the taxable long-term capital gains in the amount of $1.54414 per share for the year-ended 12/31/89. Shareholders were able to take a credit on the 1989 tax returns equivalent to $0.52501 per share. There were no retained capital gains for the year-ended 1990 or 1991. United Asset Management Corp. acquired First Pacific Advisors, Inc. in 1991. The advisor continues to operate under its own name and investment philosophy.

The Southeastern Thrift and Bank Fund, Inc.
(formerly The Southeastern Savings Institutions Fund)
One Beacon Street, Boston, MA 02108

Category: Specialized Equity Fund

Phone: 800-225-6258
Listed: STBF, OTC
Commenced Operations: July, 1989
Cusip: 841901101

1991/mid-1992 Range of Premium/Disc: -8% to -22%
1991/mid-1992 Range of Price: $11 1/2 to $4 5/8
NAV Total Return 1990: -31.72%; **1991:** +44.60%
Share Price Total Return 1990: -49.95%; **1991:** +57.38%
Herzfeld Ranking 1991: 7th of 18 specialized equity funds

Investment Objective: Long-term capital appreciation principally through investment in equity securities issued by Southeastern savings and loan institutions and savings and loan holding companies and, to a lesser extent, Southeastern banking institutions and bank holding companies.

Officers:
F.C. Golden   President

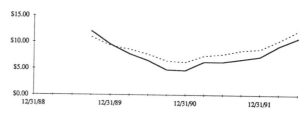

Investment Advisor: John Hancock Advisers
Advisory Fee: Monthly fee at an annual rate of 0.65% of the fund's average net assets or a flat annual fee of $50,000, whichever is higher. If the fund's expenses exceed 2% in any one year, the fund may require the advisor to reimburse the fund for such excess, subject to a minimum fee of $50,000. Fee for six months ended 12/31/91 was $54,999.
Administrator: John Hancock Advisers
Administration Fee: Monthly fee at the annual rate of 0.15% of average weekly net assets or a flat annual fee of $22,000, whichever is higher. Fee for six months ended 12/31/91 was $6,507.

Capital Structure: *Common stock:* 50 mil. shares authorized; 1,992,483 shares outstanding 12/31/91

Portfolio Highlights (as of 12/31/91): Common stocks 97.49%, convertible debentures 0.37%, cash equivalents 0.55%, other assets and liabilities 1.15%. Geographic concentrations: Southeastern savings & loans 58.52%, other savings & loans 13.25%, banks 25.72%. **Largest positions:** Cumberland Federal Bancorporation KY; United Financial Corp. of SC Inc.; Omni Capital Group Inc.; Farm & Home Financial Corp. MO; South Carolina Federal Corp.

Historical Financial Statistics (fiscal year-end: 6/30/91):			
	six months 12/31/91	1991	7/3/89 to 6/30/90
Value of net assets (000)	17,623	15,371	15,605
NAV	8.84	7.71	7.73
Net investment income	0.06	0.13	0.18
Dividends from net investment income	0.07	0.17	0.13
Expense ratio	1.98% ann.	2.76%	1.73%
Income ratio	1.49% ann.	1.84%	2.22%
Portfolio turnover	21.80%	18.48%	16.33%

Special considerations: The fund changed its name from The Southeastern Savings Institutions Fund, Inc. in 1991. At the same time, shareholders voted to allow the fund to invest a larger percentage of assets in equity-related securities of banks and bank holding companies. From time to time, the fund may make open market repurchases of its shares in order to attempt to reduce or eliminate the amount of any discount or to increase the net asset value of its shares. The fund will dissolve on 6/30/97 unless the Board of Directors extends the duration of the fund for up to three years. Shareholders may vote to open-end the fund after 6/30/94. During the six months ended 12/31/90, the fund repurchased 5,850 shares of capital stock at an average discount of 16.4%; there were no repurchases in 1991. **Shareholders over 5%:** David Ware & Associates, 10.5%.

The Spain Fund, Inc.

1345 Avenue of the Americas, New York, NY 10105   **Category: Foreign Equity Fund**

Phone: 800-247-4154
Listed: SNF, NYSE
Commenced Operations: June, 1988
Cusip: 846330108

1991/mid-1992 Range of Premium/Disc: +41% to -17%
1991/mid-1992 Range of Price: $17 1/4 to $9 3/4
NAV Total Return 1990: -14.40%; **1991**: +15.09%
Share Price Total Return 1990: -61.69%; **1991**: +22.94%
Herzfeld Ranking 1991: 18th of 46 foreign equity funds

Investment Objective: Long-term capital appreciation primarily through investment in equity securities of Spanish companies.

Officers:

D.H. Williams   Chairman
D.H. Dievler   President

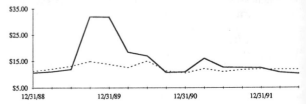

Investment Advisor: Alliance Capital Management, L.P.
Advisory Fee: Monthly fee at annual rate of 1.10% of average weekly net assets up to $50 mil., 1.00% of next $50 mil., and 0.90% of excess. Fee for year-ended 11/30/91 was $1,191,447.

Capital Structure: *Common stock*: 100 mil. shares authorized; 10,0116,957 shares outstanding 11/30/91

Portfolio Highlights (as of 2/29/92): Common stocks and other investments 90.3%, convertible bonds 3.1%, time deposit 0.1%, currency call accounts 5.7%, other assets less liabilities 0.8%. Largest industry concentrations: food/tobacco 20.5%, banks/financial 14.3%, electric utilities 10.8%, telecom & motorways 8.2%, oil & chemicals 7.7%, metals/engineering 5.0%. **Largest positions**: Antena 3 Television S.A., Viscofan Envolturas, Compania Telefonica Nacional De Espana S.A., Iberdrola I S.A., Repsol S.A.

Historical Financial Statistics (fiscal year-end: 11/30/91):

	1991	1990	1989	6/28/88 to 11/30/88
Value of net assets (000)	116,665	122,685	144,146	117,217
NAV	11.65	12.26	14.40	11.71
Net investment income	0.15	0.15	0.15	0.11
Dividends from net investment income	0.14	0.13	0.14	--
Distributions from net realized gains	1.15	0.85	0.02	--
Expense ratio	1.98%	2.22%	1.93%	1.90% ann.
Income ratio	1.33%	1.14%	1.11%	2.27% ann.
Portfolio turnover	35%	41%	32%	3.00%

Special considerations: The fund may repurchase shares or make tender offers when the board deems it advantageous. If certain conditions are met, after 1/1/94 the fund may convert to an open-end fund. The fund's Articles of Incorporation contain various anti-takeover provisions. Spanish investment advisors resigned in 1990. As of 11/30/9 the fund held 13.2% of assets in restricted securities.

State Mutual Securities Trust

440 Lincoln Street, Worcester, MA 01605

Category: Bond Fund

Phone: 508-855-1000; 508-855-3195
Listed: SMS, NYSE
Commenced Operations: 1972
Cusip: 857119101

1991/mid-1992 Range of Premium/Disc: +1% to -7%
1991/mid-1992 Range of Price: $11 3/8 to $9 3/8
NAV Total Return 1990: +4.12%; **1991**: +19.35%
Share Price Total Return 1990: -4.23%; **1991**: +20.47%
Herzfeld Ranking 1991: 45th of 80 bond funds

Investment Objective: High rate of current income with capital appreciation as a secondary objective, primarily through investment in fixed income securities. Up to 50% of assets may be invested in restricted securities through direct placements.

Officers:
J.F. O'Brien — Chairman
R.M. Reilly — President

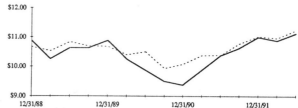

Investment Advisor: State Mutual Life Assurance Company of America

Advisory Fee: Monthly fee at annual rate of 0.3% of average weekly net assets plus 2 1/2% of interest dividend income. If certain expenses exceed 1.5% of first $30 mil. of average weekly net assets and 1% of excess, advisor will bear such excess expenses. Fee for 1991 was $490,348.

Capital Structure: *Share of beneficial interest*: 10 mil. shares authorized; 8,442,388 shares outstanding 12/31/91

Portfolio Highlights (as of 3/31/92): Corporate bonds 74.75%, U.S. government and U.S. government agencies 19.41%, foreign government obligations 5.82%, money market fund shares 0.02%. Quality ratings: AAA 19.0%, AA 7.9%, A 13.6%, Baa 29.8%, Ba 6.0%, B 12.3%, private placements 9.2%, short-term 2.2%. Maturity distribution: under 1 year 1.8%, 1-5 years 11.1%, 5-10 years 46.9%, 10-20 years 20.2%, 20 and over 20.0%. Largest industry concentrations (corporate bonds): utilities 12.98%, consumer & retail services 13.92%, manufacturing 11.09%, transportation 8.93%, banks 7.79%, financial 7.18%. **Largest issuers**: Government National Mortgage Association obligations; U.S. treasury notes; Province of Ontario deb. 9.875-09; Federal National Mortgage Association obligations; Kroger Co. sub. note 13.125-01.

Historical Financial Statistics (fiscal year-end: 12/31/91):

	1991	1990	1989	1988	1987	1986
Value of net assets (000)	93,571	85,350	89,594	89,474	89,704	96,064
NAV	11.084	10.11	10.68	10.67	10.85	11.70
??Net investment income	0.98	1.03	1.084	1.139	1.134	1.17
Dividends from net investment income	0.97	1.04	1.09	1.13	1.20	1.20
Expense ratio	0.77%	0.82%	0.84%	0.81%	0.81%	0.90%
Income ratio	9.29%	10.00%	10.14%	10.50%	10.11%	10.11%
Portfolio turnover	43%	39%	31%	10%	21%	52%

Special considerations: At the April, 1992 annual meeting, shareholders approved a proposal which eliminated the requirement that State Mutual provide pricing and bookkeeping services to the fund, and approved 440 Financial Group for such services.

Sterling Capital Corporation

635 Madison Avenue, New York, NY 10022

Phone: 212-980-3360
Listed: SPR, ASE
Commenced Operations: February, 1968
Cusip: 859160103

1991/mid-1992 Range of Premium/Disc: N/A
1991/mid-1992 Range of Price: $6 3/4 to $3 1/2
NAV Total Return 1990: N/A; **1991:** N/A
Share Price Total Return 1990: N/A; **1991:** N/A
Herzfeld Ranking 1991: N/A

Investment Objective: Capital gains.

Officers:

W. Scheuer   Chairman
E. Robbins   President

Investment Advisor: internally managed
Advisory Fee: Officers' salaries for year ended 12/31/91 were $431,254.

Capital Structure: *Common stock*: 10 mil. shares authorized; 2,500,000 shares outstanding 12/31/91

Portfolio Highlights (as of 12/31/91): Common and preferred stocks and common stock warrants 44.20%, U.S. treasury notes 10.90%, corporate bonds and notes 16.98%. Largest industry concentrations (common and preferred stocks): consumer goods 7.15%, telephone, telecommunication and cable companies 5.66%, health care products 4.96%, financial services and insurance 4.19%, transportation services 3.90%, oil and oil services 3.61%. **Largest positions:** U.S. treasury notes, Viacom International Inc. sr. sub. notes 10.25-01, American Greetings Corp. class A, Stolt Tankers & Terminals Holdings SA, Rhone Poulence Preferred Class A SA ADRs.

Historical Financial Statistics (fiscal year-end: 12/31/91):

	1991	1990	1989	1988	1987	1986
Value of net assets (000)	18,378	17,328	17,983	17,504	16,990	18,735
NAV	7.35	6.93	7.19	7.00	6.80	7.49
Net investment income (loss)	(0.02)	(0.10)	(0.03)	0.07	(0.12)	(0.50)
Dividends from net realized gains	1.23	--	0.66	0.30	1.36	--
Expense ratio	4.7%	6.8%	5.8%	6.0%	5.7%	8.0%
Income ratio (loss)	(0.3%)	(1.4%)	(0.3%)	1.0%	(1.5%)	(6.0%)
Portfolio turnover	158%	161%	123%	143%	250%	246%

Special considerations: The fund was previously known as Value Line Development Capital Corporation.

Strategic Global Income Fund, Inc.

1285 Avenue of the Americas, New York, NY 10019

Category: Foreign Bond Fund

Phone: 212-713-2000	**1991/mid-1992 Range of Premium/Disc:** +9% to -3%
Listed: SGL, NYSE	**1991/mid-1992 Range of Price:** $15 1/4 to $13 1/2
Commenced Operations: January, 1992	**NAV Total Return 1991:** N/A
Cusip: 862719101	**Share Price Total Return 1991:** N/A
	Herzfeld Ranking 1991: N/A

Investment Objective: High level of current income with capital appreciation as a secondary objective in the selection of investments. The fund invests in a combination of debt securities of the U.S. government, foreign governments, and their respective agencies, instrumentalities and political subdivisions, and debt and other fixed income securities of other U.S. and foreign issuers. Up to 35% of total assets may be invested in securities rated below BBB and comparable unrated U.S. and foreign debt and other fixed income securities.

Officers:

E.G. Bewkes, Jr.   Chairman
J.N. Fensterstock President

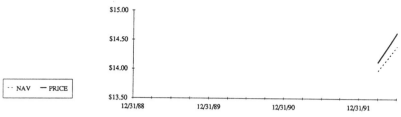

Investment Advisor and Administrator: Mitchell Hutchins Asset Management Inc.
Advisory and Administration Fee: Monthly fee at the annual rate of 1.00% of the fund's average weekly net assets.
Latin American Debt Advisor: BEA Associates
Latin American Advisory Fee: (paid by Mitchell Hutchins) Monthly fee at the annual rate of 0.25% of the fund's average weekly net assets.

Capital Structure: *Common stock:*100 mil. shares authorized, 19,000,000 shares outstanding 1/24/92.
Debt: the fund may borrow up to 33 1/3% of total assets.

Portfolio Highlights: not yet published

Historical Financial Statistics:

	1/24/92
Value of net assets (000)	266,570
NAV	14.03

Special considerations: The fund makes quarterly distributions of interest and dividend income. The fund may (but is not required to) distribute, with its first three quarterly dividends in each fiscal year, all or a portion of any net realized gains from foreign currency transactions. Net capital gains and short-term capital gains will be distributed with the fourth quarterly dividend. From time to time, the Board of Directors will consider share repurchases, tender offers at net asset value and conversion of the fund to an open-end fund. The fund's Articles of Incorporation contain various anti-takeover provisions including 66 2/3% voting requirements for various actions. Initial dividend rate $0.16, payable April, 1992.

The Swiss Helvetia Fund, Inc.
(formerly The Helvetia Fund)
521 Fifth Avenue, New York, NY 10175

Category: Foreign Equity Fund

Phone: 212-867-7660; NAV 212-661-1507
Listed: SWZ, NYSE
Commenced Operations: August, 1987
Cusip: 870875101

1991/mid-1992 Range of Premium/Disc: +10% to -12%
1991/mid-1992 Range of Price: $15 to $11 1/2
NAV Total Return 1990: +1.23%; **1991**: +5.09%
Share Price Total Return 1990: -21.16%; **1991**: +11.83%
Herzfeld Ranking 1991: 30th of 46 foreign equity funds

Investment Objective: Long-term capital appreciation through investment in equity and equity-linked securities of Swiss companies.

Officers:
P. Hottinger — Chairman
D.M. Wilkinson, Jr. — President

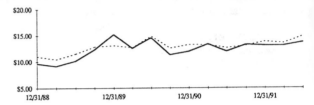

Investment Advisor: Helvetia Capital Corp.
Advisory Fee: Monthly fee at annual rate of 1.0% of first $60 mil. average monthly net assets, 0.90% on assets between $60 mil. and $100 mil., and 0.80% of excess. Fee for year-ended 12/31/91 was $995,613.
Administrator: Alex. Brown & Sons Incorporated
Administration Fee: Monthly fee at annual rate of 0.20% of first $100 mil. of average monthly net assets, 0.15% of excess. Fee for year-ended 12/31/91 was $208,978.

Capital Structure: *Common stock*: 50 mil. shares authorized; 8,007,859 shares outstanding 3/31/92

Portfolio Highlights (as of 3/31/92): Common stocks and warrants 98.6%, other assets in excess of liabilities 1.4%. Largest industry concentrations: pharmaceuticals 21.3%, banks 18.8%, food/beverages 16.7%, machinery and metals 11.9%, insurance 6.9%, chemicals 6.1%. **Largest positions**: Nestlé AG registered shares, Roche Holding AG, Schweizerische Bankgesellschaft, (Union Bank of Switzerland bearer shares, Ciba-Geiby AG registered shares, Compagnie Financière Richemont bearer shares.

Historical Financial Statistics (fiscal year-end: 12/31/91):

	1991	1990	1989	1988	8/27/87 to 12/31/87
Value of net assets (000)	110,500	105,439	104,433	87,993	98,792
NAV	13.80	13.17	13.04	10.99	12.34
Net investment income	0.01	0.07	0.01	(0.01)	0.02
Dividends from net investment income	0.03	0.05	--	0.02	--
Expense ratio	1.85%	1.77%	1.80%	1.83%	1.85% ann.
Income ratio (loss)	0.07%	0.49%	0.07%	(0.14%)	0.39% ann.
Portfolio turnover	41.08%	43.83%	30.46%	63.64%	28.10%

Special considerations: The fund may repurchase shares when trading at a discount to net asset value. Under certain circumstances, if the fund has been trading at a discount wider than 10%, after the fifth fiscal year of the fund, the fund may submit a proposal that shares may be exchanged on a quarterly basis at net asset value. The fund's Articles of Incorporation contain various anti-takeover provisions. At the fund's 1990 annual meeting shareholders voted to increase the number of authorized shares from 20 mil. to 50 mil., and to change the name of the fund to The Swiss Helvetia Fund, Inc. A proposal to reincorporate in Maryland was defeated. The fund's rights offering in mid-1992 was fully subscribed; 800,786 shares were subscribed for at 90% of the average closing price of the fund for 5 days following the closing date. Shareholders could purchase one additional share for every 10 shares held.

The Taiwan Fund, Inc.

82 Devonshire Street, Boston, MA 02109

Category: Foreign Equity Fund

Phone: 800-334-9393, 800-544-4774
Listed: TWN, ASE
Commenced Operations: December, 1986
Cusip: 874036106

1991/mid-1992 Range of Premium/Disc: +54% to -11%
1991/mid-1992 Range of Price: $30 7/8 to $18 1/8
NAV Total Return 1990: -15.77%; **1991:** +26.47%
Share Price Total Return 1990: -23.08%; **1991:** +15.88%
Herzfeld Ranking 1991: 11th of 46 foreign equity funds

Investment Objective: Long-term capital appreciation through investment primarily in equity securities listed on the Taiwan Stock Exchange.

Officers:

G.R. Moreno — Chairman
B.T. Hu — President

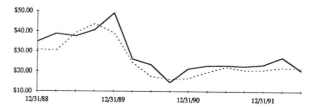

Investment Advisor: China Securities Investment Trust Corporation

Advisory Fee: Monthly fee at annual rate of 1.50% of average daily net assets, subject to a performance adjustment based on the fund's performance relative to the Taiwan Stock Exchange Index. Management fees for six months ended 2/29/92 were $1,126,327, plus a performance adjustment of $375,443.

Sub-Advisor: Fidelity International Investment Advisors Limited

Sub-Advisory Fee: China Securities Investment Trust Corporation pays Fidelity International Investment Advisors Limited a monthly fee at annual rate of 0.75% of daily net assets up to $50 mil., 0.65% on assets between $50 mil. and $100 mil., and 0.50% on excess, subject to the same performance adjustments.

Administrator: Fidelity International Limited

Administration Fee: Annual fee equal to the greater of $40,000 or 0.10% of the fund's average daily net assets in excess of $10 mil., to $80 mil., 0.085% on the next $20 mil. of net assets, and 0.07% on any excess.

Capital Structure: *Common stock*: 20 mil. shares authorized; 8,037,350 shares outstanding 2/29/92

Portfolio Highlights (as of 2/29/92): Common stocks 59.5%, government obligations 13.7%, short-term investments 26.8%. Largest industry concentrations: paper and forest products 12.4%, textiles and apparel 9.4%, building materials 9.0%, autos/tires and accessories 5.5%, construction 3.9%. **Largest positions:** Shing Kong Spinning Co. 4.8%, Yue Loong Motor 4.2%, Kuo Chan Development and Construction Co. 4.1%, Taiwan Agriculture and Forestry 3.7%, Yuen Foong Yu Paper Manufacturing 3.4%.

Historical Financial Statistics (fiscal year-end: 8/31/91; fiscal year-end changed from 12/31 in 1991):

	six months 2/29/92	eight months 8/31/91	12/31 90	12/31 89	12/31 88	12/31 87
Value of net assets (000)	**185,061**	124,974	69,597	66,914	66,040	41,178
NAV	**23.03**	19.67	16.51	22.345	22.230	17.315
Net investment income (loss)	**(0.08)**	(0.10)	0.56	(0.24)	(0.36)	(0.39)
Dividends from net investment income	**- -**	--	0.53	--	--	--
Dividends from net realized gains	**- -**	--	1.16	14.75	10.35	7.260
Expense ratio	**3.10% ann.**	3.47% ann.	2.34%	2.11%	2.50%	3.75%
Income ratio (loss)	**(0.78%) ann.**	(0.79%) ann.	2.80%	(0.69%)	(1.31%)	(2.03%)
Portfolio turnover	**150% ann.**	298% ann.	103.00%	169.00%	141.06%	203.13%

Special considerations: The fund had an offering of 1,860,963 shares in June, 1991, at $23 3/8 per share, and an offering of 2,682,682 shares in November, 1991, at $21.75 per share.

Taurus MuniCalifornia Holdings

Box 9011, Princeton, NJ 08543

Category: Municipal Bond Fund

Phone: 609-282-2800
Listed: MCF, NYSE
Commenced Operations: February, 1990
Cusip: 87670H108

1991/mid-1992 Range of Premium/Disc: +13% to -3%
1991/mid-1992 Range of Price: $13 1/8 to $10 3/4
NAV Total Return 1991: +13.05%
Share Price Total Return 1991: +18.31%
Herzfeld Ranking 1991: 25th of 51 municipal bond funds

Investment Objective: High level of current income exempt from federal and California income taxes as is consistent with its investment policies and prudent investment management, primarily through investment in a portfolio of long-term, investment-grade municipal obligations, the interest on which is exempt from federal and California income taxes.

Officers:

A. Zeikel   President

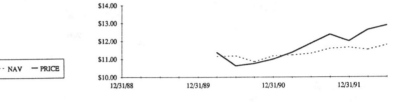

Investment Advisor: Fund Asset Management, Inc.
Advisory Fee: Monthly fee at annual rate of 0.50% of average weekly net assets. Fee for year-ended 10/31/91 was $382,239.

Capital Structure:

Common stock: 200 mil. shares authorized, 5,022,277 shares outstanding 10/31/91
Preferred stock: 400 Auction Market Preferred Stock ("AMPS") authorized, 400 shares outstanding at $50,000 per share as of 10/31/91. The yield in effect at 10/31/91 was 4.10%.

Portfolio Highlights (as of 1/31/92): Distribution by market sector: other revenue bonds 40.2%, general obligations & tax revenue bonds 33.2%, pre-refunded bonds 13.9%, utility revenue bonds 12.7%. Quality ratings: AAA 36%, AA 29%, A 27%, BBB 7%, other 1%. **Largest issuers** (as of 10/31/91): California Health Facilities Financing Authority Revenue Bonds; California HFA Home Mortgage Revenue Bonds; Los Angeles, California, Convention and Exhibition Center Authority, COP 11.5-96; Los Angeles, California, Department of Water and Power, Electric Plant Revenue Bonds.

Historical Financial Statistics (fiscal year-end: 10/31/91):

	1991	2/1/90 to 10/31/90
Value of net assets (000)	78,543	74,500
NAV	11.66	11.05
Net investment income	1.01	0.67
Dividends from net investment income	0.82	0.49
Distributions from net realized gains	0.01	--
Expense ratio	0.91%	0.97% ann.
Expense ratio, net of reimbursement	0.91%	0.82% ann.
Income ratio	6.60%	6.65% ann.
Portfolio turnover	27.89%	85.91%

Taurus MuniNew York Holdings

Box 9011, Princeton, NJ 08543

Category: Municipal Bond Fund

Phone: 609-282-2800
Listed: MNY, NYSE
Commenced Operations: February, 1990
Cusip: 876700105

1991/mid-1992 Range of Premium/Disc: +14% to -4%
1991/mid-1992 Range of Price: $13 3/8 to $10 1/4
NAV Total Return 1991: +16.20%
Share Price Total Return 1991: +18.03%
Herzfeld Ranking 1991: 3rd of 51 municipal bond funds

Investment Objective: High level of current income exempt from federal and New York income taxes as is consistent with its investment policies and prudent investment management, primarily through investment in a portfolio of long-term, investment-grade municipal obligations, the interest on which is exempt from federal and New York income taxes.

Officers:

A. Zeikel   President

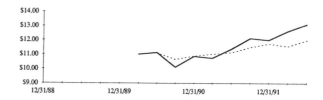

Investment Advisor: Fund Asset Management, Inc.
Advisory Fee: Monthly fee at annual rate of 0.50% of average weekly net assets. Fee for year-ended 10/31/91 was $499,297.

Capital Structure:

Common stock: 200 mil. shares authorized; 6,334,971 shares outstanding 10/31/91
Preferred stock: 600 Auction Market Preferred Stock ("AMPS") authorized, 600 shares outstanding at $50,000 per share as of 10/31/91. The yield in effect at 10/31/91 was 4.39%.

Portfolio Highlights (as of 1/31/92): Distribution by market sector: general obligations & tax revenue bonds 36.7%, other revenue bonds 29.1%, pre-refunded bonds 27.3%, utility revenue bonds 6.9%. Quality ratings: AAA 39%, AA 17%, A 18%, BBB 24%, other 2%.

Historical Financial Statistics (fiscal year-end: 10/31/91):

	1991	2/1/90 to 10/31/90
Value of net assets (000)	103,721	96,711
NAV	11.64	10.76
Net investment income	1.06	0.72
Dividends from net investment income	0.83	0.52
Total expense ratio	0.86%	0.88% ann.
Expense ratio, net of reimbursement	0.86%	0.75% ann.
Income ratio	6.70%	6.90% ann.
Portfolio turnover	35.80%	59.18%

Special considerations: At 10/31/91 the fund had a net capital loss carryforward of $447,000 expiring through 1999.

TCW Convertible Securities Fund, Inc.

865 S. Figeroa, Los Angeles, CA 90017   **Category:** Convertible Fund

Phone: 213-244-0000
Listed: CVT, NYSE
Commenced Operations: March, 1987
Cusip: 872340104

1991/mid-1992 Range of Premium/Disc: +14% to -8%
1991/mid-1992 Range of Price: $9 1/4 to $7 3/8
NAV Total Return 1990: -8.17%; **1991:** +31.91%
Share Price Total Return 1990: -0.44%; **1991:** +34.60%
Herzfeld Ranking 1991: 3rd of 8 convertible funds

Investment Objective: Total investment return comprised of current income and capital appreciation primarily through investment in convertible securities.

Officers:

E.O. Ellison   President

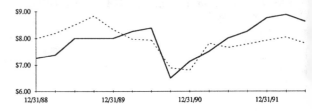

Investment Advisor: TCW Funds Management, Inc.
Advisory Fee: Monthly fee at annual rate of 0.75% of first $100 mil. average net assets and 0.50% of excess, plus accounting costs. Fee for year-ended 12/31/91 was $1,048,461.

Capital Structure: *Common stock*: 50 mil. shares authorized; 21,295,156 shares outstanding 12/31/91

Portfolio Highlights (as of 12/31/91): Total investments 103.8%, liabilities in excess of other assets (3.8%). Largest sector concentrations: consumer staples 51.7%, basic industries 20.8%, capital goods 11.9%, credit sensitive 9.7%, consumer cyclicals 6.8%. **Largest issuers:** RJR Nabisco Holdings Corp.; Time Warner Inc.; Comcast Corp.; Waste Management Inc.; Eastman Kodak Company 0-11; WR Grace & Company.

Historical Financial Statistics (fiscal year-end: 12/31/91):

	1991	1990	1989	1988	3/5/87 to 12/31/87
Value of net assets (000)	172,331	144,593	175,732	167,797	162,989
NAV	8.09	6.85	8.36	7.99	7.76
Net investment income	0.43	0.46	0.50	0.55	0.46
Distributions	0.84	0.84	0.84	0.76	0.44
Expense ratio	0.94%	0.94%	0.95%	0.94%	0.83% ann.
Income ratio	5.68%	5.93%	5.90%	6.6%	6.21% ann.
Portfolio turnover	114.13%	99.53%	84.17%	70.62%	76.91%

Special considerations: Under certain circumstances, the fund may repurchase shares. Beginning 1/1/90, if certain conditions exist, the fund may convert to an open-end fund with a 2/3 vote of shareholders. The fund's Articles of Incorporation contain various anti-takeover provisions. Restricted securities accounted for 1.5% of net assets at 12/31/91. As of 12/31/91 the fund had net realized loss carryforward of $13,555,151 to expire through 1998. The fund announced a rights offering in 1992 whereby shareholders could purchase one additional share for every 5 held at the net asset value of the fund after the offer expires (7/13/92); record date, 6/15/92. **Shareholders over 5%:** Trust Company of the West, 8.3%

Templeton Emerging Markets Fund, Inc.

700 Central Avenue, St. Petersburg, FL 33701

Category: Foreign Equity Fund

Phone: 813-823-8712
Listed: EMF, NYSE
Commenced Operations: March, 1987
Cusip: 880191101

1991/mid-1992 Range of Premium/Disc: +37% to -5%
1991/mid-1992 Range of Price: est. $25 7/8 to $11 1/2
NAV Total Return 1990: +2.38%; **1991:** +72.92%
Share Price Total Return 1990: -1.61%; **1991:** +98.10%
Herzfeld Ranking 1991: 6th of 46 foreign equity funds

Investment Objective: Long-term capital appreciation primarily through investment in emerging country equity securities.

Officers:

J.M. Templeton, Jr. Chairman
J.M. Mobius   President

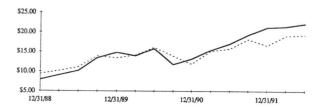

Investment Advisor: Templeton, Galbraith & Hansberger Ltd.

Advisory Fee: Monthly fee at annual rate of 1.25% of average weekly net assets. Investment management fees for six months ended 2/29/92 were $1,331,702; administrative fees were $159,804.

Business Manager (administrative services): Templeton Fund Management, Inc.

Business Management Fee: Monthly fee at annual rate of 0.15% of average weekly net assets.

Capital Structure: *Common stock:* 30 mil. shares authorized; 12,977,871 shares outstanding 2/29/92

Portfolio Highlights (as of 2/29/92): Common stocks 69.2%, preferred stocks 14.0%, short-term obligations 14.9%. Largest geographic concentrations: Brazil 15.5%, Hong Kong 14.5%, Philippines 9.0%, Turkey 6.8%, Mexico 6.2%, Thailand 5.6%, Argentina 5.2%, Singapore 4.8%. Largest industry concentrations: telecommunications 11.1%, banking 10.5%, multi-industries 7.2%, real estate 6.7%. **Largest positions:** Compania Naviera Perez Companc S.A.; Philippine Long Distance Telephone Co. NY shares; Telebras-Telecomunicacoes Brasileiras S.A.; Telefonos de Mexico S.A. de C.V. L (ADR); Cia Vale do Rio Doce PN.

Historical Financial Statistics (fiscal year-end: 8/31/91):

	six months 2/29/92	1991	1990	1989	1988	3/5/87 to 8/31/87
Value of net assets (000)	247,416	210,579	177,372	143,206	104,557	118,793
NAV	19.06	18.16	15.40	12.44	9.08	10.32
Net investment income	0.02	0.21	0.24	0.15	0.15	0.15
Dividends from net investment income	0.07	0.24	0.16	0.14	0.20	--
Distributions from net realized gains	3.96	1.64	0.17	0.18	0.10	--
Expense ratio	1.85% ann.	1.91%	1.89%	2.03%	2.07%	1.67% ann.
Income ratio	0.38% ann.	1.43%	1.67%	1.44%	1.73%	3.16% ann.
Portfolio turnover	21.38%	33.53%	23.53%	13.15%	12.31%	11.66%

Special considerations: The fund's Board of Directors will regularly consider repurchase of shares and conversion of the fund to an open-end fund. The fund's Articles of Incorporation contain various anti-takeover provisions including a staggered board of directors. At the 1990 annual meeting, a proposal to limit the liabilities of directors and officers passed.

Templeton Global Governments Income Trust

700 Central Avenue, St. Petersburg, FL 33701   **Category: Foreign Bond Fund**

Phone: 813-823-8712
Listed: TGG, NYSE
Commenced Operations: November, 1988
Cusip: 879929107

1991/mid-1992 Range of Premium/Disc: +10% to -2%
1991/mid-1992 Range of Price: $9 3/4 to $8 3/8
NAV Total Return 1990: +10.15%; **1991**: +13.44%
Share Price Total Return 1990: +17.24%; **1991**: +13.37%
Herzfeld Ranking 1991: 4th of 8 foreign bond funds

Investment Objective: High level of current income consistent with preservation of capital primarily through investment in debt securities issued or guaranteed by governments, government agencies, supranational entities, political subdivisions and other government entities of various nations throughout the world. Remaining assets are invested in U.S. and foreign corporate debt and preferred equity securities.

Officers:
J.M. Templeton, Jr.   Chairman
T.L. Hansberger   President

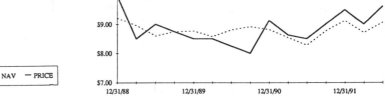

Investment Advisor: Templeton, Galbraith & Hansberger Ltd.
Advisory Fee: Monthly fee at annual rate of 0.55% of average daily net assets up to $200 mil., 0.50% of excess. Advisory fees for six months ended 2/29/92 were $530,287.
Sub-Advisor: Templeton Investment Counsel Inc.
Sub-Advisory Fee: (paid by investment advisor) Fee at annual rate of 0.40% of average daily net assets
Business Manager: Templeton Funds Management, Inc.
Sub-Management Fee: Monthly fee at annual rate of 0.25% of daily net assets
Sub-Administration Fee: Dean Witter Reynolds, Inc.
Sub-Administration Fee: (Paid by Templeton Funds Management, Inc.) Monthly fee at annual rate of 0.15% of average weekly net assets. Administrative fees for six months ended 2/29/92 were $241,040.

Capital Structure: *Shares of beneficial interest*: unlimited number of shares authorized; 21,925,552 shares outstanding 2/29/92

Portfolio Highlights (as of 2/29/92): Bonds/government & government agencies 73.0%, corporate bonds 17.7%, short-term obligations 8.0%, outstanding put options purchased 2.4%, equity in foreign exchange contracts (0.5%), other assets less liabilities (0.6%). Largest geographic concentrations: U.S. 14.7%, UK 12.2%, Sweden 10.3%, Spain 9.7%, Australia 9.5%, France 9.4%, Italy 9.2%, Denmark 5.8%. **Largest issuers**: UK treasury; Bonos del Estado; Republic of Italy; Swedish National Housing Finance Authority; Government of Denmark.

Historical Financial Statistics (fiscal year-end: 8/31/91):

	six months 2/29/92	1991	1990	11/30/88 to 8/31/89
Value of net assets (000)	193,740	184,720	188,604	179,911
NAV	8.84	8.54	8.92	8.67
Net investment income	0.42	0.86	0.95	0.74
Dividends from net investment income	0.42	0.86	0.93	0.70
Distributions from net realized gains	--	0.04	--	--
Expense ratio	1.09% ann.	1.11%	1.14%	1.18% ann.
Income ratio	9.37% ann.	9.85%	10.90%	11.14% ann.
Portfolio turnover	157.73%	135.10%	112.55%	91.60%

Special considerations: The fund may repurchase shares. Under certain conditions, in the fourth calendar quarter of 1993 the Trustees will submit an open-ending proposal. The fund's Declaration of Trust contains various anti-takeover provisions.

Templeton Global Income Fund, Inc.

700 Central Avenue, St. Petersburg, FL 33701

Phone: 813-823-8712
Listed: GIM, NYSE
Commenced Operations: March, 1988
Cusip: 880198106

Category: Foreign Bond Fund

1991/mid-1992 Range of Premium/Disc: +8% to -7%
1991/mid-1992 Range of Price: $9 3/8 to $7 7/8
NAV Total Return 1990: +11.03%; **1991:** +14.14%
Share Price Total Return 1990: +10.24%; **1991:** +16.18%
Herzfeld Ranking 1991: 3rd of 8 foreign bond funds

Investment Objective: High current income with a secondary objective of capital appreciation primarily through investment in debt securities of U.S. and/or foreign issuers.

Officers:
J.M. Templeton, Jr. Chairman
T.L. Hansberger   President

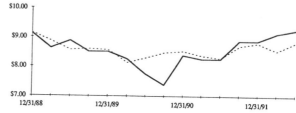

Investment Advisor: Templeton, Galbraith & Hansberger, Ltd.
Advisory Fee: Monthly fee at annual rate of 0.55% of average daily net assets up to $200 mil., 0.50% of excess. Advisory fees for six months ended 2/29/92 were $2,589,356.
Sub-Advisor: Templeton Investment Counsel, Inc.
Sub-Advisory Fee: (paid by investment advisor) Fee at annual rate of 0.40% of average daily net assets.
Business Manager: Templeton Funds Management, Inc.
Sub-Management Fee: Monthly fee at annual rate of 0.15% of daily net assets reduced to 0.135% on net assets in excess of $200 mil. Fee for six months ended 2/29/92 was $644,675.

Capital Structure: *Common stock:* 200 mil. shares authorized; 117,906,754 shares outstanding 2/29/92

Portfolio Highlights (as of 2/29/92): Corporate bonds 25.1%, government & government agency bonds 67.5%, short-term obligations 3.0%, outstanding put and call options purchased 1.5%, equity in foreign exchange contracts (0.1%), other assets less liabilities 3.0%. Largest geographic concentrations: Australia 13.1%, U.S. 12.8%, Canada 11.5%, Sweden 9.4%, Spain 8.9%, Mexico 6.8%, New Zealand 6.5%, Italy 6.3%, Denmark 6.1%. Largest issuers: Bonos del Estado; Swedish National Housing Finance Authority; Republic of Italy; Government of Denmark; United Mexican States bonds.

Historical Financial Statistics (fiscal year-end: 8/31/91):

	six months 2/29/92	1991	1990	1989	3/24/88 to 8/31/88
Value of net assets (000)	1,017,663	991,042	992,555	994,872	993,346
NAV	8.63	8.48	8.51	8.62	8.92
Net investment income	0.42	0.86	0.97	1.02	0.37
Dividends from net investment income	0.42	0.86	0.96	0.98	0.34
Dividends from net realized gains	--	0.09	--	--	--
Expense ratio	0.81% ann.	0.82%	0.81%	0.81%	0.78% ann.
Income ratio	9.75% ann.	10.12%	11.60%	11.44%	8.97% ann.
Portfolio turnover	98.82%	257.11%	130.40%	78.73%	20.08%

Special considerations: The fund may repurchase shares and its Board of Directors will regularly consider making tender offers and conversion of the fund to an open-end fund. The fund's Articles of Incorporation contain various anti-takeover provisions including a staggered board of directors. A proposal to limit the liabilities of directors and officers passed at the recent annual meeting. Sir John Templeton, a director of the fund, announced that he intends to buy $1 million of the fund's stock. As of 8/31/91 the fund had a capital loss carryfoward of $75,196,602 expiring through 1999.

Templeton Global Utilities, Inc.

700 Central Avenue, St. Petersburg, FL 33701

Category: Foreign Equity Fund

Phone: 813-823-8712
Listed: TGU, ASE
Commenced Operations: May, 1990
Cusip: 879932101

1991/mid-1992 Range of Premium/Disc: +8% to -9%
1991/mid-1992 Range of Price: $14 to $10 3/8
NAV Total Return 1991: +24.49%
Share Price Total Return 1991: +16.91%
Herzfeld Ranking 1991: 12th of 46 foreign equity funds

Investment Objective: High level of total return, without incurring undue risk, through investment of at least 65% of total assets in securities issued by domestic and foreign companies in the utility industries.

Officers:

J.M. Templeton, Jr. Chairman
T.L. Hansberger   President

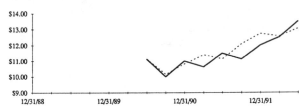

Investment Manager: Templeton, Galbraith & Hansberger, Ltd.
Management Fee: Monthly fee at annual rate of 0.60% of average daily net assets. Advisory fees for six months ended 2/29/92 were $111,496.
Sub-Advisor: Templeton Investment Counsel, Inc.
Sub-Advisory Fee: (Paid by investment manager) Fee at annual rate of 0.25% of average daily net assets.
Business Manager: Templeton Funds Management, Inc.
Sub-Management Fee: Monthly fee at annual rate of 0.15% of daily net assets up to $200 mil., 0.135% on net assets between $200 mil. and $700 mil, and 0.075% on any excess. Administrative fees for six months ended 2/29/92 were $27,874.

Capital Structure: *Common stock:* 100 mil. shares authorized, 3,025,382 shares outstanding as of 2/29/92

Portfolio Highlights (as of 2/29/92): Common stocks 63.3%, preferred stock 1.4%, bonds 33.4%, short-term obligations 0.7%, other assets less liabilities 1.2%. Largest industry concentrations: electrical & gas 47.1%, telecommunications 13.1%. Largest geographic concentrations: U.S. 61.8%, UK 8.8%, Spain 8.0%, Hong Kong 4.3%, Mexico 3.8%. **Largest positions:** Hongkong Electric Holdings Ltd., Regional Electric Companies England & Wales ADR, Telefonos de Mexico SA L. ADR, Southern Co., Compania de Telephonos de Chile SA ADR.

Historical Financial Statistics (fiscal year-end: 8/30/91):

	six months 2/29/92	1991	5/23/90 to 8/31/90
Value of net assets (000)	38,785	35,855	31,889
NAV	12.82	11.85	10.60
Net investment income	0.31	0.61	0.16
Dividends from net investment income	0.31	0.68	0.06
Expense ratio	1.45% ann.	1.55%	1.29% ann.
Income ratio	4.98% ann.	5.46%	4.52% ann.
Portfolio turnover	8.60%	19.85%	0.47%

Special considerations: Monthly distributions from net investments income, short-term capital gains, and net realized gains from currency transactions will be made. Long-term capital gains and any remaining short-term capital gains will be paid annually. Beginning 8/31/91 and each year thereafter until 1995, if the fund's shares have traded at an average discount from NAV of 2% or more for the previous fiscal quarter, the fund will submit an open-ending proposal which would require a majority vote of shareholders for passage. The fund may repurchase shares in the open market from time to time. Various anti-takeover provisions are included in the fund's Articles of Incorporation and Bylaws. As of 8/31/91 the fund had a capital loss carryforward of $721,210 expiring through 1999.

The Thai Capital Fund, Inc.

c/o Daiwa Securities Trust Company
One Evertrust Plaza, 9th Fl. Jersey City, NJ 07302

Phone: 201-915-3020; 800-933-3440
Listed: TC, NYSE
Commenced Operations: May, 1990
Cusip: 882905102

Category: Foreign Equity Fund

1991/mid-1992 Range of Premium/Disc: +10% to -25%
1991/mid-1992 Range of Price: $11 1/4 to $6 1/8
NAV Total Return 1991: +13.05%
Share Price Total Return 1991: +38.89%
Herzfeld Ranking 1991: 20th of 46 foreign equity funds

Investment Objective: Long-term capital appreciation primarily through investment in Thai companies.

Officers:
K. Yoneyama   Chairman
U. Vichayabhai   President

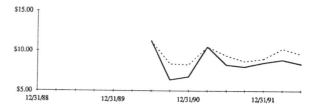

Investment Manager: The Mutual Fund Co., Ltd.
Management Fee: Monthly fee at the annual rate of 0.60% of the investment plan's average weekly net assets. Fee and applicable expenses for 1991 were $341,483.
Investment Advisor: Daiwa International Capital Management (H.K.), Ltd.
Advisory Fee: Monthly fee at the annual rate of 0.60% of the fund's average weekly net assets. Fee and applicable expenses for 1991 were $311,378.
Administrator: Daiwa Securities Trust Company
Administration Fee: Monthly fee at the annual rate of 0.20% of the fund's average weekly net assets, with a minimum annual fee of $150,000. Fee for 1991 was $152,867.

Capital Structure: *Common stock:* 100 mil. shares authorized; 6,158,961 shares outstanding 12/31/91

Portfolio Highlights (as of 12/31/91): Thai common stocks 88.07%, short-term investments 13.53%. Largest industry concentrations: banks 19.13%, building 14.71%, finance & securities 14.52%, property development 5.98%. **Largest positions:** The Siam Cement Company Ltd., The Siam Commercial Bank Ltd., Bangkok Bank Ltd., The Thai Farmers Bank Ltd., The Siam City Cement Co. Ltd.

Historical Financial Statistics (fiscal year-end: 12/31/91):

	1991	5/30/90 to 12/31/90
Value of net assets (000)	55,963	50,242
NAV	9.09	8.16
Net investment income	0.10	0.19
Dividends from net investment income	0.21	--
Dividends from net realized gains on investments and foreign currency transactions	0.07	--
Expense ratio**	2.70%*	2.06% ann.
Income ratio	1.36%*	3.31% ann.
Portfolio turnover	78.83%	10.19%

*includes non-recurring expense related to listing on Osaka Securities Exchange of 0.19%.   **excludes taxes

Special considerations: Annual distributions of net income from dividends and interest and annual distributions of capital gains are paid. In efforts to reduce or eliminate any discounts which may develop, the board of directors will consider on a quarterly basis repurchasing shares in the open market, making tender offers, or converting the fund to an open-end fund. The fund's Articles of Incorporation and By-laws contain various anti-takeover provisions including a 5% shareholder vote for merger with another corporation, liquidation of the fund, or conversion to an open-end fund.

The Thai Fund, Inc.

126 High Street, Boston, MA 02110

Category: Foreign Equity Fund

Phone: 800-221-6726
Listed: TTF, NYSE
Commenced Operations: February, 1988
Cusip: 882904105

1991/mid-1992 Range of Premium/Disc: +23% to -20%
1991/mid-1992 Range of Price: $22 3/8 to $13 3/4
NAV Total Return 1990: -20.33%; **1991**: +23.39%
Share Price Total Return 1990: -46.47%; **1991**: +10.11%
Herzfeld Ranking 1991: 13th of 46 foreign equity funds

Investment Objective: Long-term capital appreciation through investment primarily in equity securities of companies organized under the laws of the Kingdom of Thailand.

Officers:

F.B. Whitlemore   Chairman
W.J. Olsen   President

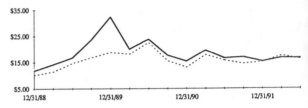

U.S. Investment Advisor: Morgan Stanley Asset Management, Inc.
U.S. Advisory Fee: Fee at annual rate of 0.90% of first $50 mil. average weekly net assets, 0.70% of next $50 mil., and 0.50% of excess. Fee for year-ended 12/31/91 was $1,073,000.
Thai Investment Advisor: The Mutual Fund Company, Limited
Thai Advisory Fee: Monthly fee at annual rate of 0.40% of first $50 mil. average weekly net assets, 0.25% of next $50 mil., 0.20% of excess. Fee for year-ended 12/31/91 was $463,000.
Administrator: Morgan Stanley Asset Management, Inc.
Administration Fee: Fee calculated as a percentage of average weekly net asset. For 1989 the fee represented 0.12% of average weekly net assets. Fee for year-ended 12/31/91 was $177,000

Capital Structure: *Common stock*: 30 mil. shares authorized; 10,015,326 shares outstanding 3/31/92

Portfolio Highlights (as of 3/31/92): Thai common stocks 97.5%, foreign currency on deposit 0.2%, repurchase agreement 2.3%. Largest industry concentrations: financial 42.1%, construction material 18.7%, commercial 13.0%. **Largest positions**: Siam Cement Co. Ltd., Bangkok Bank Ltd., The Thai Farmers Bank Ltd., The Siam Commercial Bank Ltd., National Finance & Securities Co. Ltd.

Historical Financial Statistics (fiscal year-end: 12/31/91):

	1991	1990	1989	2/16/88 to 12/31/88
Value of net assets (000)	154,344	128,676	181,187	98,199
NAV	15.41	13.08	18.88	10.24
Net investment income	0.38	0.34	0.34	0.28
Dividends from net investment income	0.21	0.21	0.36	0.29
Distributions from net realized gains	0.47	1.68	2.09	--
Operating expense ratio	1.44%	1.35%	1.51%	1.50% ann.
Expense ratio	1.69%	1.78%	1.51%	1.50% ann.
Income ratio	2.45%	1.89%	2.32%	2.88% ann.
Portfolio turnover	9.6%	17.6%	51.1%	0.89% ann.

Special considerations: The fund has an "opt-out" Dividend Reinvestment Plan and an optional Cash Purchase Plan whereby shareholders may have all distributions automatically reinvested in additional shares.

Transamerica Income Shares, Inc.

1150 S. Olive Street, Los Angeles, CA 90015

Category: Bond Fund

Phone: 213-742-4141
Listed: TAI, NYSE
Commenced Operations: February, 1972
Cusip: 893506105

1991/mid-1992 Range of Premium/Disc: +10% to -5%
1991/mid-1992 Range of Price: $26 1/2 to $21 1/2
NAV Total Return 1990: +7.28%; **1991:** +17.51%
Share Price Total Return 1990: +3.31%; **1991:** +25.85%
Herzfeld Ranking 1991: 55th of 80 bond funds

Investment Objective: High level of current income with capital appreciation as a secondary objective. The fund invests primarily in debt securities.

Officers:

G.U. Rolle   President & Chairman

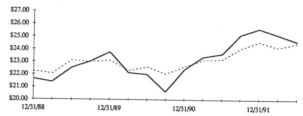

Investment Advisor: Transamerica Investment Services, Inc.
Advisory Fee: Fee at annual rate of 0.05% of weekly net assets. Fee for year-ended 3/31/92 was $628,559.

Capital Structure: *Common stock:* 20 mil. shares authorized; 5,265,643 shares outstanding 3/31/92

Portfolio Highlights (as of 3/31/92): Bonds & debentures 97.6%, convertible debentures 0.8%, short-term investments 1.5%, receivables and other assets less liabilities (0.1%). Largest industry concentrations: electric utilities 23.2%, industrials 18.4%, financial 16.4%, petroleum 9.0%, telephones 7.5%, media 5.8%, governments 5.2%. Quality ratings: AAA 4.0%, AA 10.9%, A 28.9%, BBB 48.3%, lower or non-rated 7.9%. **Largest issuers:** Occidental Petroleum; GG1A Funding Corp. 11 1/2-14; General Telephone & Electronics; Long Island Lighting; Texas Utilities Electric.

Historical Financial Statistics (fiscal year-end: 3/31/92):

	1992	1991	1990	1989	1988	1987
Value of net assets (000)	126,361	121,798	117,411	116,100	117,833	126,660
NAV	24.00	23.13	22.30	22.05	22.37	24.05
Net investment income	2.13	2.15	2.18	2.21	2.21	2.28
Dividends from net investment income	2.16	2.16	2.16	2.23	2.48	2.28
Expense ratio	0.68%	0.69%	0.71%	0.68%	0.67%	0.66%
Income ratio	8.98%	9.58%	9.53%	9.93%	9.86%	9.45%
Portfolio turnover	30%	17%	30%	15%	38%	167%

Special considerations: At 3/31/92 the fund had a capital loss carryforward of $4,586,002 expiring through 1997. Dividend rate reduced to $0.1675 per month beginning in May, 1992.

413

Tri-Continental Corporation

130 Liberty Street, New York, NY 10006 **Category: Equity Fund**

Phone: 800-221-2450
Listed: TY, NYSE
Commenced Operations: December, 1929
Cusip: 895436103

1991/mid-1992 Range of Premium/Disc: +1% to -13%
1991/mid-1992 Range of Price: $28 5/8 to $20 3/8
NAV Total Return 1990: (.20); **1991:** +27.04%
Share Price Total Return 1990: +3.54%; **1991:** +42.98%
Herzfeld Ranking 1991: 9th of 15 equity funds

Investment Objective: Future growth of both capital and income while providing reasonable current income primarily through investment in common stocks.

Officers:
W.C. Morris   Chairman
R.T. Schroeder   President

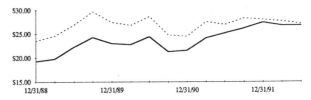

Investment Advisor: J. & W. Seligman & Co. Incorporated
Advisory Fee: Monthly fee at annual rate of 0.45% of first $4 billion net assets of all investment companies managed by the manager plus certain accounts advised or managed by the manager, ranging down to 0.375% over $8 billion. For 1991 fee was equal to 0.42% of average net assets and was $7,143,772.

Capital Structure:

Common stock: 75 mil. shares authorized; 64,192,086 shares outstanding 12/31/91
$2.50 Cumulative Preferred stock: 1 mil. shares authorized; 752,740 shares outstanding 12/31/91; $50 par value
Warrants: Entitle holder to purchase 9.69 shares of common stock at $2.32 per share; 21,374 warrants outstanding 12/31/91

Portfolio Highlights (as of 3/31/92): Common stocks 81.0%, U.S. government securities 7.3%, foreign government securities 1.1%, corporate bonds 1.9%, convertible issues 5.1%, private placement holdings 0.6%, short-term holdings 1.5%, other assets less liabilities 1.5%. Largest industry concentrations: consumer goods and services 11.1%, drugs and health care 10.1%, finance and insurance 9.3%, communications 6.9%, energy 6.4%, basic materials 5.6%, industrial equipment 5.2%. **Largest positions:** U.S. treasury bonds and notes; Philip Morris Companies Inc.; General Electric Company; Schering-Plough Corporation; Pfizer Inc.; Dillard Department Stores Class "A".

Historical Financial Statistics (fiscal year-end:12/31/91):

	1991	1990	1989	1988	1987	1986
Value of net assets (000)	1,871,301	1,537,918	1,632,142	1,301,485	1,274,728	1,317,355
NAV	28.57	24.60	27.44	23.55	23.94	27.94
Net investment income	0.81	0.81	0.88	0.84	0.86	1.02
Dividends on preferred shares	0.03	0.03	0.04	0.04	0.04	0.04
Dividends on common shares investment income	0.78	0.86	0.84	0.81	0.89	0.97
Distributions from net realized gain	1.80	1.60	2.55	1.25	3.73	6.96
Expense ratio	0.67%	0.56%	0.55%	0.57%	0.53%	0.53%
Income ratio	2.90%	3.01%	3.19%	3.33%	2.66%	3.14%
Portfolio turnover	49.02%	41.23%	59.87%	67.39%	78.99%	51.46%

Special considerations: At the 1991 annual meeting shareholders approved a proposal to increase the management fee. At the May, 1992, annual meeting, shareholders will vote on a proposal to eliminate the requirement that 75% of directors be non-interested.

The Turkish Investment Fund, Inc.

Vanguard Financial Center, P.O. Box 1102, Valley Forge, PA 19482   **Category:** Foreign Equity Fund

Phone: 215-669-8503
Listed: TKF, NYSE
Commenced Operations: December, 1989
Cusip: 900145103

1991/mid-1992 Range of Premium/Disc: +42% to -25%
1991/mid-1992 Range of Price: $13 1/4 to $6
NAV Total Return 1990: -36.05%; **1991:** -5.45%
Share Price Total Return 1990: -43.17%; **1991:** +16.52%
Herzfeld Ranking 1991: 42nd of 46 foreign equity funds

Investment Objective: Long-term capital appreciation through investment primarily in equity securities of Turkish corporations.

Officers:

B.M. Biggs   Chairman
W.J. Olsen   President

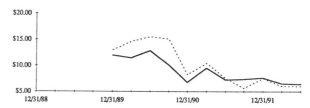

Investment Advisor: Morgan Stanley Asset Management, Inc.
Advisory Fee: Monthly fee at annual rate of 0.95% of the first $50 mil. of net assets, 0.75% on next $50 mil., 0.55% on any excess. Fee for year-ended 10/31/91 was $549,000.
Turkish Investment Advisor: TEB Ekonomi, Arastirmalari, A.S.
Advisory Fee: Monthly fee at annual rate of 0.20% of the first $50 mil. of net assets, 0.10% on next $50 mil., 0.05% on any excess. Fee for year-ended 10/31/91 was $108,000.
Administrator: The Vanguard Group, Inc.
Administration Fee: $130,000 annually plus a monthly fee at the annual rate of 0.08% of average weekly net assets of the fund. Fee for year-ended 10/31/91 was $178,000.

Capital Structure: *Common stock:* 30 mil. shares authorized; 7,023,431 shares outstanding 1/31/91

Portfolio Highlights (as of 10/31/91): Turkish common stocks 97.0%, foreign currency on deposit 2.0%, U.S. short-term securities 2.8%, other assets and liabilities (1.8%). Largest sector concentrations: food and beverage 17.4%, iron and steel 11.7%, electronics 12.0%, financial 7.7%, cement 7.0%, cable and wire 6.4%, building materials 6.0%.
Largest positions: Eregil Demir Celik, Arcelik, Maret, Petkim, Guney Bairacilik.

Historical Financial Statistics (fiscal year-end: 10/31/91):

	1991	1990
Value of net assets (000)	36,255	89,754
NAV	5.16	12.78
Net investment income	0.28	0.12
Dividends from net investment income	--	0.03
Expense ratio	2.42%	1.65% ann.
Income ratio	3.28%	0.86% ann.
Portfolio turnover	45%	1%

Special considerations: The fund will annually distribute substantially all net income from dividends and interest payments and net realized capital gains. For the year 1991, the fund retained a portion of its long-term capital gains in the amount of $0.36605. Shareholders were able to take a credit on their 1991 tax returns equivalent to $0.12446 per share.

Tyler Cabot Mortgage Securities
(formerly Lomas Mortgage Securities Fund)
2001 Bryan Tower, Suite 3600, Dallas TX 75201

Category: Bond Fund

Phone: 214-746-7406
Listed: TMF, NYSE
Commenced Operations: December, 1988
Cusip: 902175108

1991/mid-1992 Range of Premium/Disc: +15% to -3%
1991/mid-1992 Range of Price: $12 3/4 to $10 3/4
NAV Total Return 1990: +9.71%; **1991**: +16.68%
Share Price Total Return 1990: +14.05%; **1991**: +22.64%
Herzfeld Ranking 1991: 61st of 80 bond funds

Investment Objective: Investment in a balanced portfolio of highest quality mortgage securities such as GNMAs, FNMAs, Freddie Macs, Collateralized Mortgage Obligations, Real Estate Mortgage Investment Conduits and other mortgage securities.

Officers:
J. Hay   Chairman
R.K. Lytle   President

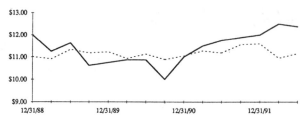

Investment Advisor: Tyler Cabot Securities Advisers, Inc.
Advisory Fee: Fee payable monthly at annual rate of 0.65% of average weekly net assets. Fee for six months ended 4/30/92 was $1,026,114.
Administrator: Princeton Administrators, Inc.
Administration Fee: Fee payable monthly at annual rate of 0.20% of average weekly net assets. Fee for six months ended 4/30/92 was $326,547.

Capital Structure: *Common stock*: 200 mil. shares authorized; 28,789,710 shares outstanding 10/31/91
Debt: $176,827,886 dollar reverse repurchase agreements and reverse repurchase agreements outstanding 10/31/91. Weighted average interest rate for the year-ended 10/31/91 was 6.06% and 5.52%, respectively.

Portfolio Highlights (as of 10/31/91): U.S. government agency mortgage-backed obligations 140.5%, CMO residuals 10.0%, options written (0.8%). **Largest issuers**: Federal Home Loan Mortgage Corporation; Federal National Mortgage Association; Government National Mortgage Association 9.0% coupon; Federal National Mortgage Association REMIC Trust CMO residuals; Federal Home Loan Mortgage Corporation REMIC Series 22.

Historical Financial Statistics (fiscal year-end: 10/31/91):

	1991	1990	12/1/88 to 10/31/89
Value of net assets (000)	331,976	320,572	330,205
NAV	11.53	10.92	11.33
Net investment income	1.09	1.16	0.99
Dividends from net investment income	0.92	1.22	0.96
Dividends from net realized gain on investments	0.33	0.04	0.08
Operating expense ratio	1.13%	1.12%	1.03% ann.
Income ratio	9.71%	10.01%	9.73% ann.
Portfolio turnover	332.35%	148.46%	196.03%

Special considerations: The fund reached an agreement with Capstead Mortgage Corporation (CMO, NYSE) to merge the funds. Under the proposed agreement, each share of Tyler Cabot common stock would be converted into one newly issued share of Capstead $1.26 Cumulative Convertible Preferred Stock, Series B. Directors of the two companies have approved the merger, shareholders will vote on the proposal. Tyler Cabot Mortgage Securities Fund stated that if the merger is not consummated, the decline in interest rates will require a reduction of the monthly dividend beginning in November, 1992.

The United Kingdom Fund, Inc.

245 Park Avenue, 13th Fl., New York, NY 10167

Category: Foreign Equity Fund

Phone: 212-272-6404, 800-524-4458	**1991/mid-1992 Range of Premium/Disc:** -4% to -18%
Listed: UKM, NYSE	**1991/mid-1992 Range of Price:** $11 7/8 to $8 1/2
Commenced Operations: August, 1987	**NAV Total Return 1990:** -1.37%; **1991:** +4.55%
Cusip: 910766104	**Share Price Total Return 1990:** -9.49%; **1991:** +10.61%
	Herzfeld Ranking 1991: 32nd of 46 foreign equity funds

Investment Objective: Long-term capital appreciation, primarily through investment in equity securities of United Kingdom companies.

Officers:

S.A. Zimmerman   President

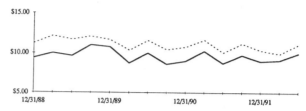

Investment Manager: Warburg Investment Management International (Jersey) Limited

Advisory Fee: Monthly fee at annual rate of 0.75% of average weekly net assets up to $150 mil. and 0.065% of excess. Fee for year-ended 3/31/92 was $337,894.

Investment Advisor: Warburg Investment Management International, Ltd.

Administrator: Bear Stearns Funds Management, Inc.

Administration Fee: Fee at annual rate of 0.15% of average weekly net assets up to $200 mil. and 0.10% of excess. Fee for year-ended 3/31/92 was $67,579.

Capital Structure: *Common stock*: 15 mil. shares authorized; 4,008,602 shares outstanding 3/31/92

Portfolio Highlights (as of 3/31/92): Investments in United Kingdom common stocks 96.5%, investments in U.S. securities 0.3%, cash and other assets in excess of liabilities 3.2%. Largest industry concentrations: oil & gas 12.8%, food manufacturing 10.1%, banks 7.2%, brewers & distillers 6.5%, stores 6.2%, chemicals 5.5%, telephone networks 5.4%, electronics 5.3%, health & household 5.1%. **Largest positions:** Midland Bank plc. ord., Great Universal Stores plc Class A ord. (non-voting), B.A.T. Industries plc. ord., Cadbury-Schweppes, Imperial Chem. Industries ord.

Historical Financial Statistics (fiscal year-end: 3/31/92):

	1992	1991	1990	1989	8/14/87 to 3/31/88
Value of net assets (000)	39,823	46,775	41,609	48,707	43,864
NAV	9.93	11.67	10.38	12.15	10.94
Net investment income	0.40	0.38	0.36	0.25	0.20
Dividends from net investment income	0.45	--	0.35	0.22	0.13
Distributions from net realized gains	0.38	0.73	0.25	0.43	0.22
Expense ratio	1.74%	2.19%	1.92%	1.89%	1.99% ann.
Income ratio	3.73%	3.34%	3.06%	4.10%	3.01% ann.
Portfolio turnover	47.30%	36.37%	22.07%	40.91%	22.15%

Special considerations: The fund may repurchase shares or make tender offers when the Board deems it advantageous. The fund's Charter and By-Laws contain various anti-takeover provisions. Under certain circumstances, beginning 3/31/90, the fund will submit an open-ending proposal. Those conditions were met for the period ending 3/31/90, and an open-end proposal was voted on at the 1990 annual meeting. The proposal did not pass. A similar proposal will be voted on at the 1992 annual meeting, as the conditions were met once again. As of 3/31/92 the fund had capital loss carryforwards of $2,406,170 available through 1999. Dividend rate for June, 1992 dividend, $0.09 per share, consisting of $0.0389 income and $0.0511 long-term capital gains. **Shareholders over 5%:** Mercury Asset Management, Ltd. (an affiliate of the advisor), 22.6%; Stichting Philips Pension Funds, 7.1%

USF&G Pacholder Fund, Inc.

Towers of Kenwood, 8044 Montgomery Road, Suite 382, Cincinnati, OH 45236 **Category: Bond Fund**

Phone: 513-985-3200	**1991/mid-1992 Range of Premium/Disc**: +3% to -19%
Listed: PHF, ASE	**1991/mid-1992 Range of Price**: $20 to $12
Commenced Operations: November, 1988	**NAV Total Return 1990**: -0.42%; **1991**: +32.63%
Cusip: 903291102	**Share Price Total Return 1990**: -10.16%; **1991**: +59.92%
	Herzfeld Ranking 1991: 17th of 80 bond funds

Investment Objective: High level of total return through current income and capital appreciation primarily through investment in a diversified portfolio of very high-yield, low-rated or non-rated fixed income securities of domestic companies which are generally trading at a significant discount to face value.

Officers:

A.O. Pacholder Chairman & President

Investment Advisor: Pacholder & Company

Advisory Fee: Quarterly fee at annual rate of 1.2% of total net assets if investment performance equals The First Boston High Yield Index plus 3 percentage points. The fee is increased or decreased by 8% of the amount by which the fund's investment performance exceeds or is less than this measure, with a maximum fee of 2.0%, and a minimum fee of 0.4%. Fee for 1991 was $122,894.

Administrator: Alex. Brown & Sons, Incorporated

Administration Fee: Monthly fee at annual rate of 0.20% of average net assets up to $100 mil., and 0.15% of excess. Fee for 1991 was $61,437.

Capital Structure: *Common stock*: 50 mil. shares authorized; 1,823,850 shares outstanding 12/31/91
8.60% Cumulative Preferred Stock: 10,000 shares outstanding 6/8/92

Portfolio Highlights (as of 3/31/92): Corporate debt securities 86.4%, commercial paper 7.8%, common stock 1.7%, other assets in excess of liabilities 4.1%. Largest industry concentrations: chemicals 7.2%, conglomerate 7.1%, grocery 6.0%, health care 5.8%, hotels/motels/inns 5.5%, industrial equipment 5.3%, oil & gas 5.3%, finance 5.1%

Largest Issuers: RJR Holdings Capital Corp., Nortek Inc., Integrated Resources Inc., Grow Group Inc., Morningstar Foods.

Historical Financial Statistics (fiscal year-end: 12/31/91):

	1991	1990	1989	11/11/88 to 12/31/88
Value of net assets (000)	31,678	26,432	30,246	33,036
NAV	17.37	14.49	16.58	18.21
Net investment income	2.18	1.79	1.88	0.16
Dividends to shareholders	2.14	1.80	2.10	0.18
Expense ratio	1.37%	2.34%	2.15%	2.10% ann.
Income ratio	12.94%	10.91%	10.41%	8.20% ann.
Portfolio turnover	48.34%	33.08%	101.71%	0%

Special considerations: The fund may repurchase shares or make tender offers when it deems it advantageous. After the fund is in existence for 5 years, the Directors will consider making tender offers. The fund's Articles of Incorporation contain various anti-takeover provisions. Authorized unissued shares may be reclassified by the Board of Directors as preferred shares. **Shareholders over 5%**: USF&G Corporation and its affiliates (including their employee benefit plans, 14.74%.

USLife Income Fund, Inc.

125 Maiden Lane, New York, NY 10038

Category: Bond Fund

Phone: 212-709-6000
Listed: UIF, NYSE
Commenced Operations: October, 1972
Cusip: 917324105

1991/mid-1992 Range of Premium/Disc: +3% to -11%
1991/mid-1992 Range of Price: $10 1/4 to $7 3/8
NAV Total Return 1990: +2.29%; **1991:** +23.05%
Share Price Total Return 1990: -7.62%; **1991:** +33.93%
Herzfeld Ranking 1991: 28th of 80 bond funds

Investment Objective: High level of current income through a diversified portfolio composed predominantly of marketable fixed income securities.

Officers:

G.E. Crosby, Jr.   Chairman
R.J. Chouinard   President & CEO

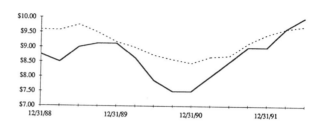

Investment Advisor: USLIFE Advisers, Inc.
Advisory Fee: Fee of 0.04167% of net asset value plus 2 1/2% of net investment income. Fee for six months ended 12/31/91 was $186,934.

Capital Structure: *Common stock:* 10 mil. shares authorized; 5,356,668 shares outstanding 12/31/91

Portfolio Highlights (as of 12/31/91): Corporate obligations 96.1%, short-term obligations 1.8%. **Largest issuers:** Olympia & York Corp. Euro Notes 10 3/8-95; Westinghouse Electric Corp. notes 8 7/8-01; Loral Corp. debs. 10 1/2-17; Oryx Energy Co. debs. 10 3/8-18; ACF Industries Inc. sr. debs. 15 1/4-96.

Historical Financial Statistics (fiscal year-end: 6/30/91):

	six months 12/31/91	1991	1990	1989	1988	1987
Value of net assets (000)	50,552	46,674	46,742	52,265	50,983	52,421
NAV	9.44	8.71	8.73	9.76	9.52	9.79
Net investment income	0.47	0.95	0.94	0.98	0.91	1.07
Dividends from net investment income	0.46	0.93	0.93	0.92	0.94	1.20
Expense ratio	0.66%	1.38%	1.37%	1.32%	1.35%	1.29%
Income ratio	5.13%	10.97%	10.17%	10.19%	9.58%	10.51%
Portfolio turnover	11.41%	59.73%	36.53%	41.97%	72.72%	116.91%

Special considerations: At the October, 1991, annual meeting, shareholders approved an amendment to the fund's Articles of Incorporation to limit the personal liability and require indemnification of directors and officers.

Van Kampen Merritt California Municipal Income Trust

One Parkview Plaza, Oakbrook Terrace, IL 60181   **Category: Municipal Bond Fund**

Phone: 800-225-2222; 708-684-6000
          800-341-2929
Listed: VKC, ASE
Commenced Operations: November, 1988
Cusip: 920910106

1991/mid-1992 Range of Premium/Disc: +6% to -3%
1991/mid-1992 Range of Price: $10 1/2 to $9 1/8
NAV Total Return 1990: +7.46%; **1991:** +13.23%
Share Price Total Return 1990: +11.06%; **1991:** +8.31%
Herzfeld Ranking 1991: 24th of 51 municipal bond funds

Investment Objective: High level of current income exempt from federal and California income taxes with safety of principal primarily through investment in a diversified portfolio of investment grade tax-exempt California municipal securities.

Officers:

J.C. Merritt   Chairman
D.J. McDonnell   President

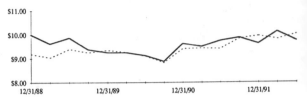

Investment Advisor: Van Kampen Merritt Investment Advisory Corp.
Advisory Fee: Monthly fee of 0.60% of average weekly net assets. Fee for six months ended 12/31/91 was $153,151.

Capital Structure: *Shares of beneficial interest:* unlimited number of shares authorized; 3,136,011 shares outstanding 12/31/91
                      Remarketed preferred stock: 1 mil. shares authorized; 400 shares outstanding 12/31/91, liquidation preference of $50,000. Dividend rate is set by auction every 28 days; rate in effect on 12/31/91 was 4.81%.

Portfolio Highlights (as of 12/31/91): Long-term investments 93.0%, short-term investments 0.8%, other assets in excess of liabilities 6.2%. **Largest Issuers:** California Housing Fin. Agy. Rev. Home Mtg. Ser. D. 0-20; Desert Hosp. Dist. CA Hosp. Rev. Ctfs. Partn. 8.1-20; California Health Fac. Fin. Auth. Rev. Insd. Hlth. Fac. Eskaton Pptys. 7.5-20; Los Angeles CA Univ. Sch. Dist. Ctfs. Partn. Ser. B. Sr. High Sch. Ambassador Site 7.8-13; Emeryville CA Pub. Fin. Auth. Rev. Hsg. Increment Sub. Lien A 7.875-15.

Historical Financial Statistics (fiscal year-end: 6/30/91):

	six months 12/31/91	1991	1990	11/1/88 to 6/30/89
Value of net assets (000)	51,256	49,566	48,372	29,314
NAV	9.967	9.408	9.095	9.416
Net investment income	0.474	0.975	0.719	0.385
Dividends from net investment income to common shareholders	0.324	0.648	0.648	0.385
Common share equivalent of distributions paid to preferred shares	0.136	0.327	0.071	--
Distributions from net realized gains	0.027	--	--	--
Expense ratio	2.26%	1.88%	0.50%	0.87% ann.*
Income ratio	6.91%	6.98%	7.01%	6.26% ann.*
Portfolio turnover	20.38%	99.43%	99.54%	57.06%

*for three periods presented above, certain expenses were assumed by the advisor; expense ratio would have been 1.96% ann., 1.31% and 1.09% ann., respectively; and income ratio would have been 6.66% ann., 6.21%, and 6.04% ann., respectively.

Special considerations: The fund may repurchase or make tender offers for shares; Trustees will consider these options on a quarterly basis. The fund's Declaration of Trust contains various anti-takeover provisions. Dividend rate increased to $0.055 per month at the beginning of 1992.

Van Kampen Merritt California Quality Municipal Trust

One Parkview Plaza, Oakbrook Terrace, IL 60181   **Category**: Municipal Bond Fund

Phone: 800-225-2222; 708-684-6000   **1991/mid-1992 Range of Premium/Disc**: 0% to -6%
         800-341-2929   **1991/mid-1992 Range of Price**: $15 to $14 1/8
Listed: VQC, NYSE   **NAV Total Return 1991**: N/A
Commenced Operations: September, 1991   **Share Price Total Return 1991**: N/A
Cusip: 920920105   **Herzfeld Ranking 1991**: N/A

Investment Objective: High level of current income exempt from federal and California income taxes with safety of principal primarily through investment in a diversified portfolio of investment grade tax-exempt California municipal securities.

Officers:

J.C. Merritt   Chairman
D.J. McDonnell   President

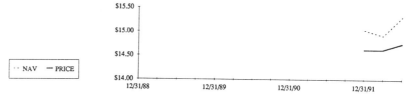

Investment Advisor: Van Kampen Merritt Investment Advisory Corp.
Advisory Fee: Monthly fee of 0.70% of average weekly net assets. Fee for period 9/27/91 to 2/29/92 was $526,835.

Capital Structure: *Shares of beneficial interest*: unlimited number of shares authorized; 9,623,295 shares outstanding 2/29/92
         Auction Preferred Shares: 1,500 shares outstanding 2/29/92 at an offering price of $50,000. Rate is reset every 28 days; rate in effect on 2/29/92 was 3.25%.

Portfolio Highlights (as of 2/29/92): Municipal securities 100.8%, short-term investments 0.5%, liabilities in excess of other assets (1.3%). **Largest issuers**: California Health Fac. Fin. Auth. Rev.; Los Angeles, CA, Dept. Water & Power Elec. Plt. Rev. Rfdg. 6.0-28; Sacramento, CA, City Fin. Auth. Rev. 6.8-20; Clovis, CA Uni. School Dist. Ctfs. Partn. Buchanan High School Construction Project 6.65-23; Los Angeles County, CA Tran. Comm. Sales Tax Rev. Ser. A 6.75-20.

Historical Financial Statistics:

	9/27/91 to 2/29/92
Value of net assets (000)	218,385
NAV	14.90
Net investment income	0.376
Dividends from net investment income	0.228
Common share equivalent of distributions paid to preferred shares	0.065
Expense ratio	1.57% ann.
Income ratio	5.20% ann.
Portfolio turnover	34.48%

Special considerations: The fund was brought to market as a no-load closed-end fund. The fund makes monthly distributions of net investment income and annual distributions of net realized capital gains. The fund's Declaration of Trust contains various anti-takeover provisions. Conversion to an open-end fund would require approval by a majority of the trustees, majority vote of outstanding common and preferred shares voting as a class, or 67% vote of each of the common and preferred shares voting as a class in which more than 50% of the outstanding shares of each class are present in person or by proxy. After the initial offering, the shares were offered through a continuous offering before being listed on the stock exchange. In order to reduce or eliminate discount to net asset value, the Board of Trustees may authorize repurchases of common stock in the open market or tender offers at net asset value.

421

Van Kampen Merritt Florida Quality Municipal Trust

One Parkview Plaza, Oakbrook Terrace, IL 60181 **Category: Municipal Bond Fund**

Phone: 800-225-2222; 708-684-6000	**1991/mid-1992 Range of Premium/Disc**: +1% to -3%
800-341-2929	**1991/mid-1992 Range of Price**: $15 1/2 to $14 5/8
Listed: VFM, NYSE	**NAV Total Return 1991**: N/A
Commenced Operations: September, 1991	**Share Price Total Return 1991**: N/A
Cusip: 920921103	**Herzfeld Ranking 1991**: N/A

Investment Objective: High level of current income exempt from federal income taxes and exempt from Florida intangible personal taxes, consistent with preservation of capital. The fund will invest in Florida municipal securities rated investment grade. Up to 20% of total assets may be invested in unrated Florida municipal securities of comparable quality.

Officers:

J.C. Merritt   Chairman
D.J. McDonnell   President

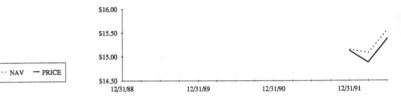

Investment Advisor: Van Kampen Merritt Investment Advisory Corp.

Advisory Fee: Monthly fee at an annual rate of 0.70% of the average daily managed assets of the fund. Fee for period 9/17/91 to 2/29/92 was $3,018,932.

Administrator: Van Kampen Merritt Inc.

Administration Fee: Monthly fee at the annual rate of 0.20% of average daily managed assets of the fund. Fee for period 9/17/91 to 2/29/92 was $98,422.

Capital Structure: *Common stock*: unlimited number of shares authorized, 6,428,084 shares outstanding 2/29/92
Auction Preferred Shares: 1,000 shares outstanding 2/29/92 at an offering price of $50,000. Rate is reset every 28 days; rate in effect on 2/29/92 was 3.25%.

Portfolio Highlights (as of 2/29/92): Long-term Florida municipal investments 97.8%, short-term investments 0.7%, other assets 1.5%. **Largest issuers**: Reedy Creek, FL Impt. Dist. FL Utility Rev.; Polk County, FL Indl. Dev. Authority Indl. Dev. Rev. IMC Fertilizer Inc. Ser. A 7.25-15; Florida Housing Finance Agency Home Ownership Mtg. 8.595-18; Jacksonville, FL Electric Auth. Revenue; Palm Beach County, FL Arpt. Sys. Revenue Refunding 7.75-10.

Historical Financial Statistics:

	9/27/91 to 2/29/92
Value of net assets (000)	147,394
NAV	15.167
Net investment income	0.37
Dividends from net investment income	0.243
Common share equivalent of distributions paid to preferred shares	0.064
Expense ratio	1.66% ann.
Income ratio	5.25% ann.
Portfolio turnover	15.37%

Special considerations: The fund was brought to market as a no-load closed-end fund. The fund makes monthly distributions of net investment income and annual distributions of net realized capital gains. The fund's Declaration of Trust contains various anti-takeover provisions. Conversion to an open-end fund would require approval by a majority of the trustees, majority vote of outstanding common and preferred shares voting as a class, or 67% vote of each of the common and preferred shares voting as a class at which more than 50% of the outstanding shares of each class are present in person or by proxy. In order to reduce or eliminate discounts to net asset value, the Board of Trustees may authorize repurchases of common stock in the open market, or tender offers at net asset value.

Van Kampen Merritt Intermediate Term High Income Trust

One Parkview Plaza, Oakbrook Terrace, IL 60181

Category: Bond Fund

Phone: 800-225-2222; 708-684-6000	**1991/mid-1992 Range of Premium/Disc:** +28% to -15%
800-341-2929	**1991/mid-1992 Range of Price:** $8 1/8 to $3 7/8
Listed: VIT, NYSE	**NAV Total Return 1990:** -24.13%; **1991:** +47.83%
Commenced Operations: January, 1989	**Share Price Total Return 1990:** -31.08%; **1991:** +92.88%
Cusip: 920911104	**Herzfeld Ranking 1991:** 5th of 80 bond funds

Investment Objective: High current income while seeking to preserve shareholders' capital primarily through investment in a professionally managed, diversified portfolio of high yield fixed-income securities. Investments will be mainly from medium and lower ratings categories, with a dollar-weighted average maturity of approximately 10 years.

Officers:

R.C. Merritt	Chairman
D.J. McDonnell	President

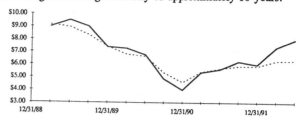

Investment Advisor: Van Kampen Merritt Investment Advisory Corp.

Advisory Fee: Monthly fee at annual rate of 0.75% of average weekly net assets. Fee for 1991 was $1,011,181.

Capital Structure:

Shares of beneficial interest: unlimited number of shares authorized; 13,710,760 shares outstanding 12/31/91

Auction Market Preferred stock : 1 mil. shares authorized; 588 shares outstanding at $100,000 per share. Dividends are cumulative and rate is reset through an auction process every 28 days. The AMPS rate in effect on 12/31/91 was 5.92%; rates ranged from 4.899% to 9.25%.

Portfolio Highlights (as of 12/31/91): Bonds 95.6%, warrants 0.1%, repurchase agreement at amortized cost 5.0%, liabilities in excess of other assets (0.7%). Largest industry concentrations: grocery 8.4%, automotive 8.1%, containers and packaging 8.1%, diversified conglomerate 7.9%, chemicals and plastics 7.4%, printing/publishing and broadcasting 7.3%, hotel/motel/inns and gaming 7.1%, oil and gas 6.0%. **Largest positions:** SCI Holdings Inc. 15-97; PA Holdings Corp. 15-98; Mark IV Industries Inc. 13.375-99; Fruit of the Loom Inc. 10.75-95; Kelsey Hayes Co. 13.25-94.

Historical Financial Statistics (fiscal year-end: 12/31/91):

	1991	1990	1/26/89 to 12/31/89
Value of net assets (000)	140,025	121,910	187,660
NAV	5.924	4.603	7.488
Net investment income	1.14	1.566	1.387
Dividends from net investment income to common shareholders	0.84	1.083	1.02
Common share equivalent of distributions to preferred shareholders	0.271	0.502	0.328
Expense ratio	2.51%	2.10%	1.56% ann.
Income ratio	15.86%	17.24%	13.20% ann.
Portfolio turnover	78.37%	57.49%	33.12%

Special considerations: The fund may repurchase or make tender offers for shares; Trustees will consider these options on a quarterly basis. The fund's Declaration of Trust contains various anti-takeover provisions. Mid-1992 dividend rate $0.0725 per month.

Van Kampen Merritt Investment Grade Municipal Trust

One Parkview Plaza, Oakbrook Terrace, IL 60181
Category: Municipal Bond Fund

Phone: 800-225-2222; 708-684-6000
       800-341-2929
Listed: VIG, NYSE
Commenced Operations: November, 1989
Cusip: 920915105

1991/mid-1992 Range of Premium/Disc: +14% to 0%
1991/mid-1992 Range of Price: $13 1/4 to $10 3/8
NAV Total Return 1990: +6.94%; **1991:** +13.83%
Share Price Total Return 1990: -0.04%; **1991:** +17.92%
Herzfeld Ranking 1991: 20th of 51 municipal bond funds

Investment Objective: High level of current income exempt from federal income tax, consistent with preservation of capital. The fund will invest at least 80% of total assets in tax-exempt municipal securities rated investment grade at the time of investment.

Officers:

J.C. Merritt   Chairman
D.J. McDonnell President

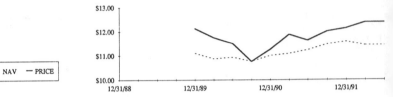

Investment Advisor: Van Kampen Merritt Investment Advisory Corp.
Advisory Fee: Monthly fee at annual rate of 0.60% of average weekly net assets. Fee for year-ended 10/31/91 was $475,359.

Capital Structure: *Shares of beneficial interest*: unlimited number of shares authorized; 4,839,000 shares outstanding 10/31/91.
    Remarketed preferred stock : 100 mil. shares authorized; 250 shares outstanding 10/31/91 at $100,000 per share. Dividends are cumulative and rate is reset through an auction process every 28 days. The dividend rate in effect on 10/31/91 was 3.99%.

Portfolio Highlights (as of 10/31/91): Long-term investments 97.9%, short-term investments 0.2%, other assets in excess of liabilities 1.9%. Largest geographic concentrations: Illinois 25.8%, Florida 10.7%, Colorado 8.7%, Montana 5.0%. **Largest Issuers:** Chicago, IL O'Hare Intl. Arpt. Special Fac. Rev.; Forsyth, MT Pollution Ctl. Rev. Rfdg. Puget Sound Power & Light Ser. B 7.24-21; Denver, CO City & Cnty. Arpt. Revenue Ser. A 8.3-23; Kasaan, AK Lease Rev. 8.0-10; Idaho Hsg. Agy. Single Family Mtg. Ser. B 7.5-24.

Historical Financial Statistics (fiscal year-end: 10/31/91):

	1991	11/30/89 to 10/31/90
Value of net assets (000)	80,660	77,414
NAV	11.502	10.832
Net investment income	1.153	1.001
Dividends from net investment income to common shareholders	0.886	0.725
Common share equivalent of distributions to preferred shareholders	0.244	0.230
Expense ratio	1.53%	1.41% ann.
Income ratio	8.12%	7.75% ann.
Portfolio turnover	52.20%	133.73%

Special considerations: The fund may repurchase or make tender offers for shares. Trustees will consider these options on a quarterly basis. The fund's Declaration of Trust contains various anti-takeover provisions. Dividend rate increased to $0.085 per month in June, 1992.

Van Kampen Merritt Limited Term High Income Trust

One Parkview Plaza, Oakbrook Terrace, IL 60181   **Category**: Bond Fund

Phone: 800-225-2222; 708-684-6000	**1991/mid-1992 Range of Premium/Disc**: +5% to -20%
800-341-2929	**1991/mid-1992 Range of Price**: $8 3/4 to $4 3/4
Listed: VLT, NYSE	**NAV Total Return 1990**: -23.36%; **1991**: +46.09%
Commenced Operations: April, 1989	**Share Price Total Return 1990**: -29.11%; **1991**: +64.29%
Cusip: 920913100	**Herzfeld Ranking 1991**: 8th of 80 bond funds

Investment Objective: High current income, while seeking to preserve shareholders' capital, through investment in a professionally managed, diversified portfolio of high income producing fixed-income securities.

Officers:
J.C. Merritt   Chairman
D.J. McDonnell   President

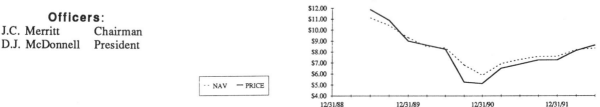

Investment Advisor: Van Kampen Merritt Investment Advisory Corp.

Advisory Fee: Monthly fee at annual rate of 0.75% of average weekly net assets. Fee for 1991 was $781,770.

Capital Structure:

Shares of beneficial interest: unlimited number of shares authorized; 8,109,000 shares outstanding 12/31/91

9.50% Cumulative Preferred stock : 1,855,500 shares outstanding at $25 per share, redeemable at the option of the trust at various prices between 7/1/90 and 7/1/94.

Portfolio Highlights (as of 12/31/91): Bonds 97.3%, warrants 0.1%, repurchase agreement at amortized cost 1.6%, other assets in excess of liabilities 1.0%. Largest industry concentrations: containers and packaging 8.6%, grocery 7.7%, printing/publishing and broadcasting 7.6%, hotel/motel/inns and gaming 7.3%, beverage, food and tobacco 7.1%, chemicals and plastics 6.1%, automotive 6.1%, retail 5.9%, personal/food and misc. services 5.8%, diversified conglomerate 5.3%, oil and gas 5.1%. **Largest issuers**: Foodmaker Inc.; Eagle Industries Inc. 13-98; Jones Intercable Inc. 13-00; Container Corp. 14-01; Marley Co. 13-98.

Historical Financial Statistics (fiscal year-end: 12/31/91):

	1991	1990	4/28/89 to 12/31/89
Value of net assets (000)	108,173	94,098	135,474
NAV	7.619	5.884	9.307
Net investment income	1.512	1.908	1.283
Dividends from net investment income to common shareholders	0.92	1.238	0.909
Common share equivalent of distributions to preferred shares	0.543	0.666	0.371
Expense ratio	2.73%	2.12%	1.57% ann.
Income ratio	13.59%	15.99%	12.91% ann.
Portfolio turnover	96.79%	64.64%	31.04%

Special considerations: The fund may repurchase or make tender offers for shares. Trustees will consider these options on a quarterly basis. The fund's Declaration of Trust contains various anti-takeover provisions. At 12/31/91 the trust had an accumulated capital loss carryforward of $29,128,815 to expire through 1999. Dividend rate for common shares reduced to $0.075 per month in March, 1992.

Van Kampen Merritt Municipal Income Trust

One Parkview Plaza, Oakbrook Terrace, IL 60181   **Category: Municipal Bond Fund**

Phone: 800-225-2222; 708-684-6000
        800-341-2929
Listed: VMT, NYSE
Commenced Operations: August, 1988
Cusip: 920909108

1991/mid-1992 Range of Premium/Disc: +10% to -1%
1991/mid-1992 Range of Price: $11 3/8 to $9 1/2
NAV Total Return 1990: +5.96%; **1991:** +15.81%
Share Price Total Return 1990: +13.14%; **1991:** +20.60%
Herzfeld Ranking 1991: 6th of 51 municipal bond funds

Investment Objective: High level of current income exempt from federal income taxes with safety of principal, primarily through investment in a diversified portfolio of investment grade tax-exempt municipal securities.

Officers:

J.C. Merritt   Chairman
D.J. McDonnell   President

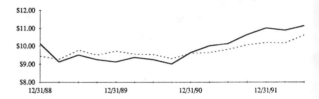

Investment Advisor: Van Kampen Merritt Investment Advisory Corp.
Advisory Fee: Monthly fee at annual rate of 0.60% of average weekly net assets. Fee for six months ended 12/31/91 was $1,309,022.

Capital Structure: *Shares of beneficial interest*: unlimited number of shares authorized; 26,778,157 shares outstanding 12/31/91
Rate Adjusted Tax-Exempt Shares: (RATES) 1 mil. shares authorized; 330 shares outstanding at $500,000 per share on 12/31/91. Dividends are cumulative and are reset every 28 days through a reauction process. For the six months ended 12/31/91 dividends ranged from 3.00% to 5.05%; as of 12/31/91 the average dividend rate was 4.308%.

Portfolio Highlights (as of 12/31/91): Long-term investments 98.1%, short-term investments 0.4%, other assets in excess of liabilities 1.5%. Largest geographic concentrations: Illinois 18.4%, Florida 9.9%, New York 8.4%, Pennsylvania 7.3%, Texas 6.0%, Colorado 5.0%. **Largest issuers:** Chicago, IL O'Hare International Arpt. Spl. Fac. Rev.; Illinois Health Fac. Auth. Rev.; Denver, CO City & Cnty. Arpt. Rev. Ser. A; Palm Beach Cnty., FL Health Fac. Auth. Rev. Rfdg. Hosp. JFK Med. Cent. Inc. Proj. 8.875-18; Nebraska Invt. Fin. Auth. Single Family Mortgage Ribs. Ser B. 10.223-22.

Historical Financial Statistics (fiscal year-end: 6/30/91):

	six months 12/31/91	1991	1990	8/26/88 to 6/30/89
Value of net assets (000)	439,223	426,680	418,330	424,373
NAV	10.241	9.805	9.534	9.767
Net investment income	0.546	1.093	1.07	0.766
Dividends from net investment income to common shares	0.389	0.725	0.685	0.501
Common share equivalent of distributions to preferred shares	0.136	0.337	0.389	0.237
Distributions from net realized gains	0.031	0.055	--	--
Expense ratio	1.44% ann.	1.46%	1.43%	0.92% ann.*
Income ratio	8.16% ann.	7.88%	7.11%	6.15% ann*
Portfolio turnover	19.55%	68.76%	116.21%	89.63%

*for the year-ended 6/30/89 presented above, certain expenses were assumed by the advisor: expense ratio would have been 1.07% ann.; and income ratio would have been 5.99% ann.

Special considerations: The fund may repurchase or make tender offers for shares. Trustees will consider these options on a quarterly basis. The fund's Declaration of Trust contains various anti-takeover provisions. Dividend rate increased to $0.067 per month at the beginning of 1992.

Van Kampen Merritt Municipal Opportunity Trust

One Parkview Plaza, Oakbrook Terrace, IL 60181   **Category: Municipal Bond Fund**

Phone: 800-225-2222; 708-684-6000	**1991/mid-1992 Range of Premium/Disc:** -2% to -6%
800-341-2929	**1991/mid-1992 Range of Price:** $15 to $14 1/2
Listed: VMO, NYSE	**NAV Total Return 1991:** N/A
Commenced Operations: June, 1992	**Share Price Total Return 1991:** N/A
Cusip: 920935103	**Herzfeld Ranking 1991:** N/A

Investment Objective: High level of current income exempt from federal income tax, consistent with preservation of capital through investment in municipal securities rated investment grade at the time of investments.

Officers:

J.C. Merritt	Chairman
D.J. McDonnell	President

Investment Advisor: Van Kampen Merritt Investment Advisory Corp.
Advisory Fee: Monthly fee of 0.65% of average weekly net assets.
Administrator: Van Kampen Merritt Inc.
Administration Fee: Monthly fee of 0.20% of average weekly net assets.

Capital Structure: *Common stock:* unlimited number of shares authorized, 15,352,891 shares outstanding 6/26/92
                Preferred stock $150 mil. of preferred stock outstanding

Portfolio Highlights: not yet published

Historical Financial Statistics:

	6/26/92
Value of net assets (000)	387,900
NAV	15.50

Special considerations: The fund was brought to market as a no-load closed-end fund. The fund makes monthly distributions of net investment income, and annual distributions of net realized capital gains. The fund's Declaration of Trust contains various anti-takeover provisions. Conversion to an open-end fund would require approval by a majority of the trustees, majority vote of outstanding common and preferred shares voting as a class, or 67% vote of each of the common and preferred shares voting as a class at which more than 50% of the outstanding shares of each class are present in person or by proxy. After the initial offering, the shares were offered through a continuous offering before being listed on the stock exchange. In order to reduce or eliminate discount to net asset value, the Board of Trustees may authorize repurchases of common stock in the open market, or tender offers at net asset value. The Board has authorized a repurchase of up to 5% of outstanding shares.

Van Kampen Merritt Municipal Trust

One Parkview Plaza, Oakbrook Terrace, IL 60181   **Category: Municipal Bond Fund**

Phone: 800-225-2222; 708-684-6000	**1991/mid-1992 Range of Premium/Disc:** +2% to -3%
800-341-2929	**1991/mid-1992 Range of Price:** $15 5/8 to $14 5/8
Listed: VKQ, NYSE	**NAV Total Return 1991:** N/A
Commenced Operations: September, 1991	**Share Price Total Return 1991:** N/A
Cusip: 920919107	**Herzfeld Ranking 1991:** N/A

Investment Objective: High level of current income exempt from federal income taxes, consistent with preservation of capital. The fund will invest in municipal securities rated investment grade. Up to 20% of total assets may be invested in unrated municipal securities of comparable quality.

Officers:

J.C. Merritt   Chairman
D.J. McDonnell   President & Chief Executive Officer

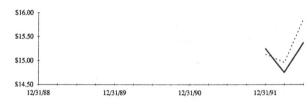

Investment Advisor: Van Kampen Merritt Investment Advisory Corp.

Advisory Fee: Monthly fee at an annual rate of 0.70% of the average daily managed assets of the fund. Fee for period 9/17/91 to 2/29/92 was $2,023,116.

Administrator: Van Kampen Merritt Inc.

Administration Fee: Monthly fee at the annual rate of 0.20% of average daily managed assets of the fund. Fee for period 9/27/91 to 2/29/92 was $578,033.

Capital Structure: *Common stock:* unlimited number of shares authorized, 36,207,467 shares outstanding 2/29/92

Auction Preferred Shares: four series with 1,500 shares each at an offering price of $50,000 per share. Dividends are cumulative and reset every 7 days for Series A and C and every 28 days for Series B and D through a reauction process. The average rate in effect of 2/29/92 was 3.183%.

Portfolio Highlights (as of 2/29/92): Long-term investments 97.8%, short-term investments 0.9%, other assets 1.3%. Largest geographic concentrations: NY 17.7%, IL 9.9%, CO 9.3%, NJ 7.6%, TX 6.5%. **Largest issuers:** NY St. Urban Dev. Corp. Rev.; NY St. Dorm. Auth. Rev.; Hawaii St. Arpt. Sys. Rev. Ser. 2 7-18; NH St. Indl. Dev. Auth. Rev. Pollution Control Pub. Svc. Co. NH Proj.; Camden Cty., NJ, Pollution Ctl. Fin. Auth. Solid Waste Res. Recovery Rev. Ser. B. 7.5-09.

Historical Financial Statistics:

	9/27/91 to 2/29/92
Value of net assets (000)	849,480
NAV	15.176
Net investment income	0.44
Dividends from net investment income to common shares	0.266
Common share equivalent of distributions to preferred shares	0.068
Expense ratio	1.49% ann.
Income ratio	6.16% ann.
Portfolio turnover	67.12%

Special considerations: The fund was brought to market as a no-load closed-end fund. The fund makes monthly distributions of net investment income and annual distributions of net realized capital gains. The fund's Declaration of Trust contains various anti-takeover provisions. Conversion to an open-end fund would require approval by a majority o the trustees, majority vote of outstanding common and preferred shares voting as a class, or 67% vote of each of the common and preferred shares voting as a class. In order to reduce or eliminate discounts to net asset value, the Board of Trustees may authorize open market repurchases of common stock or tender offers at net asset value.

Van Kampen Merritt New York Quality Municipal Trust

One Parkview Plaza, Oakbrook Terrace, IL 60181   **Category: Municipal Bond Fund**

Phone: 800-225-2222; 708-684-6000	**1991/mid-1992 Range of Premium/Disc**: +1% to -5%
800-341-2929	**1991/mid-1992 Range of Price**: $15 1/4 to $14 1/2
Listed: VNM, NYSE	**NAV Total Return 1991**: N/A
Commenced Operations: September, 1991	**Share Price Total Return 1991**: N/A
Cusip: 920922101	**Herzfeld Ranking 1991**: N/A

Investment Objective: High level of current income exempt from federal income taxes, New York State and New York City income taxes, consistent with preservation of capital. The fund will invest in New York municipal securities rated investment grade. Up to 20% of total assets may be invested in unrated New York municipal securities of comparable quality.

Officers:

J.C. Merritt   Chairman
D.J. McDonnell   President

Investment Advisor: Van Kampen Merritt Investment Advisory Corp.

Advisory Fee: Monthly fee at an annual rate of 0.70% of the average daily managed assets of the fund. Fee for period 9/27/91 to 2/29/92 was $308,213.

Administrator: Van Kampen Merritt, Inc.

Administration Fee: Monthly fee at the annual rate of 0.20% of average daily managed assets of the fund. Fee for period 9/27/91 to 2/29/92 was $88,061.

Capital Structure: *Common stock*: unlimited number of shares authorized, 5,643,496 shares outstanding 2/29/92

Auction Preferred Shares: 900 shares outstanding 2/29/92 at an offering price of $50,000. Rate is reset every 28 days; rate in effect on 2/29/92 was 3.12%.

Portfolio Highlights (as of 2/29/92): Long-term New York municipal investments 84.5%, long-term Puerto Rico municipal investments 3.2%, short-term investments 0.1%, other assets in excess of liabilities 12.2%. **Largest Issuers**: New York State Dorm. Auth. Revenue; Metropolitan Trans. Auth. NY Svcs. Contract Refunding Tran. Fac. Ser. ;; New York City Ser. C Subser. C-1; New York State Energy Res. & Dev. Authority Electric Fac. Revenue Consolidated Edison Project; Port Authority NY 7 NJ Cons.

Historical Financial Statistics:

	9/27/91 to 2/29/92
Value of net assets (000)	128,882
NAV	14.864
Net investment income	0.396
Dividends from net investment income	0.243
Common share equivalent of distributions paid to preferred shares	0.066
Expense ratio	1.73% ann.
Income ratio	5.58% ann.
Portfolio turnover	40.96%

Special considerations: The fund was brought to market as a no-load closed-end fund. The fund makes monthly distributions of net investment income and annual distributions of net realized capital gains. The fund's Declaration of Trust contains various anti-takeover provisions. Conversion to an open-end fund would require approval by a majority of the trustees, majority vote of outstanding common and preferred shares voting as a class, or 67% vote of each of the common and preferred shares voting as a class. In order to reduce or eliminate discount to net asset value, the Board of Trustees may authorize repurchases of common stock in the open market or tender offers at net asset value.

Van Kampen Merritt Ohio Quality Municipal Trust

One Parkview Plaza, Oakbrook Terrace, IL 60181   **Category: Municipal Bond Fund**

Phone: 800-225-2222; 708-684-6000
         800-341-2929
Listed: VOQ, NYSE
Commenced Operations: September, 1991
Cusip: 920923109

1991/mid-1992 Range of Premium/Disc: +7% to -2%
1991/mid-1992 Range of Price: $16 1/4 to $14 3/4
NAV Total Return 1991: N/A
Share Price Total Return 1991: N/A
Herzfeld Ranking 1991: N/A

Investment Objective: High level of current income exempt from federal income taxes and Ohio income taxes, consistent with preservation of capital. The fund will invest in Ohio municipal securities rated investment grade. Up to 20% of total assets may be invested in unrated Ohio municipal securities of comparable quality.

Officers:

J.C. Merritt	Chairman
D.J. McDonnell	President & Chief Executive Officer

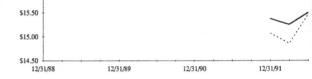

Investment Advisor: Van Kampen Merritt Investment Advisory Corp.

Advisory Fee: Monthly fee at an annual rate of 0.70% of the average daily managed assets of the fund. Fee for period 9/27/91 to 2/29/92 was $227,468.

Administrator: Van Kampen Merritt Inc.

Administration Fee: Monthly fee at the annual rate of 0.20% of average daily managed assets of the fund. Fee for period 9/27/91 to 2/29/92 was $64,991.

Capital Structure: *Common stock*: unlimited number of shares authorized, 4,158,139 shares outstanding 2/29/92

Auction Preferred shares 1 mil. shares authorized, 700 shares outstanding, offering price $50,000. Dividends are cumulative and are reset every 28 days through a reauction process. The rate in effect on 2/29/92 was 3.12%.

Portfolio Highlights (as of 2/29/92): Ohio municipal investments 89.1%, Puerto Rico municipal investments 15.6%, liabilities in excess of other assets (4.7%). **Largest Issuers**: Puerto Rico Commonwealth Rfdg. Pub. Impt. 3.0-06; Gateway Economic Dev. Corp. Gtr. Cleveland, OH Excise Tax Rev. Sr. Lien A 6.875-05; Puerto Rico Electric Power Auth. Power Revenue; Akron Bath Copley Ohio St. Twp. Hosp. Dist Rev. Akron General Medical Center Project.

Historical Financial Statistics:

	9/27/91 to 2/29/92	
Value of net assets (000)	97,328	
NAV	14.989	
Net investment income	0.345	
Dividends from net investment income	0.240	
Common share equivalent of distributions paid to preferred shares	0.073	
Expense ratio	1.84%	ann.
Income ratio	4.45%	ann.
Portfolio turnover	7.41%	

Special considerations: The fund was brought to market as a no-load closed-end fund. The fund makes monthly distributions of net investment income and annual distributions of net realized capital gains. The fund's Declaration of Trust contains various anti-takeover provisions. Conversion to an open-end fund would require approval by a majority the trustees, majority vote of outstanding common and preferred shares voting as a class, or 67% vote of each of the common and preferred shares voting as a class. In order to reduce or eliminate discount to net asset value, the Board of Trustees may authorize repurchases of common stock in the open market or tender offers at net asset value.

Van Kampen Merritt Pennsylvania Quality Municipal Trust

One Parkview Plaza, Oakbrook Terrace, IL 60181

Category: Municipal Bond Fund

Phone: 800-225-2222; 708-684-6000
      800-341-2929
Listed: VPQ, NYSE
Commenced Operations: September, 1991
Cusip: 920924107

1991/mid-1992 Range of Premium/Disc: +4% to -2%
1991/mid-1992 Range of Price: $15 7/8 to $14 3/4
NAV Total Return 1991: N/A
Share Price Total Return 1991: N/A
Herzfeld Ranking 1991: N/A

Investment Objective: High level of current income exempt from federal income taxes, Pennsylvania income taxes, and where possible under local law, local income and personal property taxes, consistent with preservation of capital. The fund will invest in Pennsylvania municipal securities rated investment grade. Up to 20% of total assets may be invested in unrated Pennsylvania municipal securities of comparable quality.

Officers:
A.C. Merritt   Chairman
D.J. McDonnell   President & Chief Executive Officer

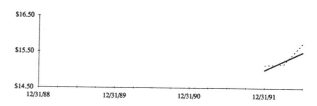

Investment Advisor: Van Kampen Merritt Investment Advisory Corp.

Advisory Fee: Monthly fee at an annual rate of 0.70% of the average daily managed assets of the fund. Fee for period 9/27/91 to 2/29/92 was $459,822.

Administrator: Van Kampen Merritt, Inc.

Administration Fee: Monthly fee at the annual rate of 0.20% of average daily managed assets of the fund. Fee for period 9/27/91 to 2/29/92 was $131,378.

Capital Structure: *Common stock:* unlimited number of shares authorized, 8,045,664 shares outstanding 2/29/92

Auction Preferred shares 1 mil. shares authorized, 1,300 shares outstanding, offering price $50,000. Dividends are cumulative and are reset every 28 days through a reauction process. The rate in effect on 2/29/92 was 3.20%.

Portfolio Highlights (as of 2/29/92): Pennsylvania municipal securities 95.6%, Puerto Rico municipal securities 3.4%, short-term 0.3%, other assets 0.7%. **Largest Issuers:** PA St. Higher Edl. Assistance Agy. Student Loan Rev. Ser. A. 7.05-16; Emmaus, PA General Auth. Rev. Loc. Govt. Pool 7-18; Phil., PA Hospital & Higher Edl. Fac. Auth. Hosp. Rev.; PA St. Higher Edl. Fac. Auth. Rev. Red. College PA Ser. A; Phil., PA Water & Sewer Rev. Ser. 16.

Historical Financial Statistics:

	9/27/91 to 2/29/92
Value of net assets (000)	187,754
NAV	15.257
Net investment income	0.405
Dividends from net investment income	0.248
Common share equivalent of distributions paid to preferred shares	0.066
Expense ratio	1.61% ann.
Income ratio	5.40% ann.
Portfolio turnover	52.03%

Special considerations: The fund was brought to market as a no-load closed-end fund. The fund makes monthly distributions of net investment income and annual distributions of net realized capital gains. The fund's Declaration of Trust contains various anti-takeover provisions. Conversion to an open-end fund would require approval by a majority of the trustees, majority vote of outstanding common and preferred shares voting as a class, or 67% vote of each of the common and preferred shares voting as a class. In order to reduce or eliminate discount to net asset value, the Board of Trustees may authorize repurchases of common stock in the open market or tender offers at net asset value.

Van Kampen Merritt Trust for Insured Municipals

One Parkview Plaza, Oakbrook Terrace, IL 60181   **Category: Municipal Bond Fund**

Phone: 800-225-2222; 708-684-6000
         800-341-2929
Listed: VIM, NYSE
Commenced Operations: January, 1992
Cusip: 920928108

1991/mid-1992 Range of Premium/Disc: 0% to -5%
1991/mid-1992 Range of Price: $15 to $14 1/4
NAV Total Return 1991: N/A
Share Price Total Return 1991: N/A
Herzfeld Ranking 1991: N/A

Investment Objective: High level of current income exempt from federal income tax, consistent with preservation of capital. The fund will invest substantially all of its total assets in municipal securities which are covered by insurance with respect to the timely payment of principal and interest thereon from an entity with claims-paying ability rating of AAA at the time of investment. Up to 20% of total assets may be invested in municipal securities backed by an escrow or trust account containing sufficient U.S. government or U.S. government agency securities to ensure timely payment of principal and interest or municipal securities that are guaranteed as to the timely payment of principal and interest by an entity which has a credit rating of AAA at the time of investment.

Officers:

J.C. Merritt   Chairman
D.J. McDonnell   President & Chief Executive Officer

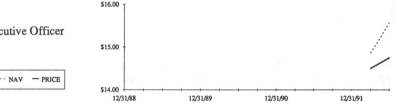

Investment Advisor: Van Kampen Merritt Investment Advisory Corp.
Advisory Fee: Monthly fee at the annual rate of 0.60% of average daily managed assets of the fund.
Administrator: Van Kampen Merritt Inc.
Administration Fee: Monthly fee at the annual rate of 0.20% of average daily managed assets of the fund.

Capital Structure: *Common stock*: unlimited number of shares authorized, 9,619,286 shares outstanding 6/26/92
                     Auction Preferred stock $90 mil. of preferred shock outstanding

Portfolio Highlights: not yet published

Historical Financial Statistics:

	6/26/92
Value of net assets (000)	239,888
NAV	15.58

Special considerations: The fund was brought to market as a no-load closed-end fund. The fund makes monthly distributions of net investment income and annual distributions of net realized capital gains. The fund's Declaration of Trust contains various anti-takeover provisions. Conversion to an open-end fund would require approval by a majority of the trustees, majority vote of outstanding common and preferred shares voting as a class, or 67% vote of each of the common and preferred shares voting as a class in which more than 50% of the outstanding shares of each class are present in person or by proxy. After the initial offering, the shares were offered through a continuous offering before being listed on the stock exchange. In order to reduce or eliminate discount to net asset value, the Board of Trustees may authorize repurchases of common stock in the open market or tender offers at net asset value. The fund's board authorized a 5% repurchase in the open market from time to time. Mid-1992 dividend rate, $0.075 per month.

Van Kampen Merritt Trust for Investment Grade California Municipals

One Parkview Plaza, Oakbrook Terrace, IL 60181   **Category: Municipal Bond Fund**

Phone: 800-225-2222; 708-684-6000   **1991/mid-1992 Range of Premium/Disc:** -1% to -4%
           800-341-2929   **1991/mid-1992 Range of Price:** $15 to $14 3/8
Listed: VIC, NYSE   **NAV Total Return 1991:** N/A
Commenced Operations: March, 1992   **Share Price Total Return 1991:** N/A
Cusip: 920930104   **Herzfeld Ranking 1991:** N/A

Investment Objective: High level of current income exempt from federal and California income taxes, consistent with preservation of capital. The fund invests primarily in California municipal securities rated investment grade.

Officers:

J.C. Merritt   Chairman
D.J. McDonnell   President & Chief Executive Officer

Investment Advisor: Van Kampen Merritt Investment Advisory Corp.
Advisory Fee: Monthly fee at the annual rate of 0.65% of average daily managed assets of the fund.
Administrator: Van Kampen Merritt Inc.
Administration Fee: Monthly fee at the annual rate of 0.20% of average daily managed assets of the fund.

Capital Structure: *Common stock*: unlimited number of shares authorized, 4,619,242 shares outstanding 6/26/92
                 Auction Preferred stock: $45 mil. of preferred stock outstanding

Portfolio Highlights: not yet published

Historical Financial Statistics:

	6/26/92
Value of net assets (000)	114,620
NAV	15.07

Special considerations: The fund was brought to market as a no-load closed-end fund. The fund makes monthly distributions of net investment income and annual distributions of net realized capital gains. The fund's Declaration of Trust contains various anti-takeover provisions. Conversion to an open-end fund would require approval by a majority of the trustees, majority vote of outstanding common and preferred shares voting as a class, or 67% vote of each of the common and preferred shares voting as a class at which more than 50% of the outstanding shares of each class are present in person or by proxy. After the initial offering, the shares were offered through a continuous offering before being listed on the stock exchange. In order to reduce or eliminate discount to net asset value, the Board of Trustees may authorize repurchases of common stock in the open market or tender offers at net asset value. The fund's board has authorized a 5% repurchase in the open market from time to time. Initial dividend, $0.077 per shares, June, 1992.

Van Kampen Merritt Trust for Investment Grade Florida Municipals

One Parkview Plaza, Oakbrook Terrace, IL 60181   **Category: Municipal Bond Fund**

Phone: 800-225-2222; 708-684-6000	**1991/mid-1992 Range of Premium/Disc:** 0% to -4%
800-341-2929	**1991/mid-1992 Range of Price:** $15 1/8 to $14 1/2
Listed: VTF, NYSE	**NAV Total Return 1991:** N/A
Commenced Operations: March, 1992	**Share Price Total Return 1991:** N/A
Cusip: 920932100	**Herzfeld Ranking 1991:** N/A

Investment Objective: High level of current income exempt from federal income taxes, consistent with preservation of capital. The fund also seeks to offer its shareholders the opportunity to own securities exempt from Florida intangible personal property taxes. The fund invests primarily in Florida municipal securities rated investment grade.

Officers:

J.C. Merritt	Chairman
D.J. McDonnell	President & Chief Executive Officer

Investment Advisor: Van Kampen Merritt Investment Advisory Corp.
Advisory Fee: Monthly fee at the annual rate of 0.65% of average daily managed assets of the fund.
Administrator: Van Kampen Merritt Inc.
Administration Fee: Monthly fee at the annual rate of 0.20% of average daily managed assets of the fund.

Capital Structure: *Common stock*: unlimited number of shares authorized, 4,135,802 shares outstanding 6/26/92
Auction Preferred stock: $40 mil. of preferred stock outstanding

Portfolio Highlights: not yet published

Historical Financial Statistics:

	6/26/92
Value of net assets (000)	102,887
NAV	15.21

Special considerations: The fund was brought to market as a no-load closed-end fund. The fund makes monthly distributions of net investment income and annual distributions of net realized capital gains. The fund's Declaration of Trust contains various anti-takeover provisions. Conversion to an open-end fund would require approval by a majority of the trustees, majority vote of outstanding common and preferred shares voting as a class, or 67% vote of each of the common and preferred shares voting as a class in which more than 50% of the outstanding shares of each class are present in person or by proxy. After the initial offering, the shares were offered through a continuous offering before being listed on the stock exchange. In order to reduce or eliminate discount to net asset value, the Board of Trustees may authorize repurchases of common stock in the open market or tender offers at net asset value. The fund's board had authorized a 5% repurchase in the open market from time to time. Initial dividend, $0.078 per shares, June, 1992.

Van Kampen Merritt Trust for Investment Grade Municipals

One Parkview Plaza, Oakbrook Terrace, IL 60181   **Category:** Municipal Bond Fund

Phone: 800-225-2222; 708-684-6000	**1991/mid-1992 Range of Premium/Disc:** 0% to -5%
800-341-2929	**1991/mid-1992 Range of Price:** $15 1/8 to $14 3/8
Listed: VGM, NYSE	**NAV Total Return 1991:** N/A
Commenced Operations: January, 1992	**Share Price Total Return 1991:** N/A
Cusip: 920929106	**Herzfeld Ranking 1991:** N/A

Investment Objective: High level of current income exempt from federal income tax, consistent with preservation of capital. The fund will invest substantially all of its total assets in municipal securities rated investment grade; the fund does not invest in unrated municipal securities.

Officers:

J.C. Merritt	Chairman
D.J. McDonnell	President & Chief Executive Officer

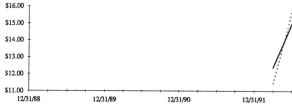

Investment Advisor: Van Kampen Merritt Investment Advisory Corp.
Advisory Fee: Monthly fee at the annual rate of 0.65% of average daily managed assets of the fund.
Administrator: Van Kampen Merritt Inc.
Administration Fee: Monthly fee at the annual rate of 0.20% of average daily managed assets of the fund.

Capital Structure: *Common stock:* unlimited number of shares authorized, 27,013,149 shares outstanding 6/26/92
Auction Preferred stock: $265 mil. of preferred stock outstanding

Portfolio Highlights: not yet published

Historical Financial Statistics:

	6/26/92
Value of net assets (000)	690,741
NAV	15.76

Special considerations: The fund was brought to market as a no-load closed-end fund. The fund makes monthly distributions of net investment income and annual distributions of net realized capital gains. The fund's Declaration of Trust contains various anti-takeover provisions. Conversion to an open-end fund would require approval by a majority of the trustees, majority vote of outstanding common and preferred shares voting as a class, or 67% vote of each of the common and preferred shares voting as a class in which more than 50% of the outstanding shares of each class are present in person or by proxy. After the initial offering, the shares were offered through a continuous offering before being listed on the stock exchange. In order to reduce or eliminate discount to net asset value, the Board of Trustees may authorize repurchases of common stock in the open market or tender offers at net asset value. The fund's board has authorized a 5% repurchase in the open market from time to time. Initial dividend, $0.0775 per shares, June, 1992.

Van Kampen Merritt Trust for Investment Grade New Jersey Municipals

One Parkview Plaza, Oakbrook Terrace, IL 60181 **Category: Municipal Bond Fund**

Phone: 800-225-2222; 708-684-6000	**1991/mid-1992 Range of Premium/Disc:** +2% to -2%
800-341-2929	**1991/mid-1992 Range of Price:** $15 1/4 to $14 5/8
Listed: VTJ, NYSE	**NAV Total Return 1991:** N/A
Commenced Operations: March, 1992	**Share Price Total Return 1991:** N/A
Cusip: 920933108	**Herzfeld Ranking 1991:** N/A

Investment Objective: High level of current income exempt from federal income taxes and New Jersey gross income taxes, consistent with preservation of capital. The fund invests primarily in New Jersey municipal securities rated investment grade.

Officers:

J.C. Merritt   Chairman
D.J. McDonnell   President & Chief Executive Officer

Investment Advisor: Van Kampen Merritt Investment Advisory Corp.
Advisory Fee: Monthly fee at the annual rate of 0.65% of average daily managed assets of the fund.
Administrator: Van Kampen Merritt Inc.
Administration Fee: Monthly fee at the annual rate of 0.20% of average daily managed assets of the fund.

Capital Structure: *Common stock:* unlimited number of shares authorized, 3,922,264 shares outstanding 6/26/92
Auction Preferred stock: $40 mil. of preferred stock outstanding

Portfolio Highlights: not yet published

Historical Financial Statistics:

	6/26/92
Value of net assets (000)	99,252
NAV	15.11

Special considerations: The fund was brought to market as a no-load closed-end fund. The fund makes monthly distributions of net investment income and annual distributions of net realized capital gains. The fund's Declaration of Trust contains various anti-takeover provisions. Conversion to an open-end fund would require approval by a majority of the trustees, majority vote of outstanding common and preferred shares voting as a class, or 67% vote of each of the common and preferred shares voting as a class in which more than 50% of the outstanding shares of each class are present in person or by proxy. After the initial offering, the shares were offered through a continuous offering before being listed on the stock exchange. In order to reduce or eliminate discount to net asset value, the Board of Trustees may authorize repurchases of common stock in the open market or tender offers at net asset value. The fund's board has authorized a 5% repurchase in the open market from time to time. Initial dividend, $0.077 per shares, June, 1992.

Van Kampen Merritt Trust for Investment Grade New York Municipals

One Parkview Plaza, Oakbrook Terrace, IL 60181   **Category: Municipal Bond Fund**

Phone: 800-225-2222; 708-684-6000	**1991/mid-1992 Range of Premium/Disc:** +2% to -2%
800-341-2929	**1991/mid-1992 Range of Price:** $15 1/2 to $14 1/2
Listed: VTN, NYSE	**NAV Total Return 1991:** N/A
Commenced Operations: March, 1992	**Share Price Total Return 1991:** N/A
Cusip: 920931102	**Herzfeld Ranking 1991:** N/A

Investment Objective: High level of current income exempt from federal as well as from New York State and New York City income taxes, consistent with preservation of capital. The fund invests primarily in New York municipal securities rated investment grade.

Officers:

J.C. Merritt	Chairman
D.J. McDonnell	President, Chief Executive Officer

Investment Advisor: Van Kampen Merritt Investment Advisory Corp.
Advisory Fee: Monthly fee at the annual rate of 0.65% of average daily managed assets of the fund.
Administrator: Van Kampen Merritt, Inc.
Administration Fee: Monthly fee at the annual rate of 0.20% of average daily managed assets of the fund.

Capital Structure: *Common stock*: unlimited number of shares authorized, 6,193,214 shares outstanding 6/26/92
                                Auction Preferred stock: $60 mil. of preferred stock outstanding

Portfolio Highlights: not yet published

Historical Financial Statistics:

	6/26/92
Value of net assets (000)	153,801
NAV	15.15

Special considerations: The fund was brought to market as a no-load closed-end fund. The fund makes monthly distributions of net investment income and annual distributions of net realized capital gains. The fund's Declaration of Trust contains various anti-takeover provisions. Conversion to an open-end fund would require approval by a majority of the trustees, majority vote of outstanding common and preferred shares voting as a class, or 67% vote of each of the common and preferred shares voting as a class in which more than 50% of the outstanding shares of each class are present in person or by proxy. After the initial offering, the shares were offered through a continuous offering before being listed on the stock exchange. In order to reduce or eliminate discount to net asset value, the Board of Trustees may authorize repurchases of common stock in the open market or tender offers at net asset value. The fund's board has authorized a 5% repurchase in the open market from time to time. Initial dividend, $0.085 per shares, June, 1992.

Van Kampen Merritt Trust for Investment Grade Pennsylvania Municipals

One Parkview Plaza, Oakbrook Terrace, IL 60181   **Category: Municipal Bond Fund**

Phone: 800-225-2222; 708-684-6000	**1991/mid-1992 Range of Premium/Disc:** +2% to -2%
800-341-2929	**1991/mid-1992 Range of Price:** $15 3/8 to $14 3/4
Listed: VTP, NYSE	**NAV Total Return 1991:** N/A
Commenced Operations: March, 1992	**Share Price Total Return 1991:** N/A
Cusip: 920934106	**Herzfeld Ranking 1991:** N/A

Investment Objective: High level of current income exempt from federal and Pennsylvania income taxes, and where possible under local law, local income and personal property taxes; consistent with preservation of capital. The fund invests primarily in Pennsylvania municipal securities rated investment grade.

Officers:

J.C. Merritt	Chairman
D.J. McDonnell	President & Chief Executive Officer

Investment Advisor: Van Kampen Merritt Investment Advisory Corp.
Advisory Fee: Monthly fee at the annual rate of 0.65% of average daily managed assets of the fund.
Administrator: Van Kampen Merritt Inc.
Administration Fee: Monthly fee at the annual rate of 0.20% of average daily managed assets of the fund.

Capital Structure: *Common stock:* unlimited number of shares authorized, 7,399,760 shares outstanding 6/26/92
                              Auction Preferred stock $70 mil. of preferred stock outstanding

Portfolio Highlights: not yet published

Historical Financial Statistics:

	6/26/92
Value of net assets (000)	182,432
NAV	15.19

Special considerations: The fund was brought to market as a no-load closed-end fund. The fund makes monthly distributions of net investment income and annual distributions of net realized capital gains. The fund's Declaration of Trust contains various anti-takeover provisions. Conversion to an open-end fund would require approval by a majority of the trustees, majority vote of outstanding common and preferred shares voting as a class, or 67% vote of each of the common and preferred shares voting as a class in which more than 50% of the outstanding shares of each class are present in person or by proxy. After the initial offering, the shares were offered through a continuous offering before being listed on the stock exchange. In order to reduce or eliminate discount to net asset value, the Board of Trustees may authorize repurchases of common stock in the open market or tender offers at net asset value. The fund's board has authorized a 5% repurchase in the open market from time to time. Initial dividend, $0.083 per shares, June, 1992.

Vestaur Securities, Inc.

Centre Square West, 11th Fl., PO Box 7558, Philadelphia, PA 19101-7558   **Category**: Bond Fund

Phone: 215-567-3969	**1991/mid-1992 Range of Premium/Disc**: +1% to -5%
Listed: VES, NYSE	**1991/mid-1992 Range of Price**: $15 1/8 to $13 1/4
Commenced Operations: November, 1972	**NAV Total Return 1990**: +6.56%; **1991**: +17.39%
Cusip: 925464019	**Share Price Total Return 1990**: +9.04%; **1991**: +20.22%
	Herzfeld Ranking 1991: 56th of 80 bond funds

Investment Objective: Generation of a high level of income, with capital appreciation as a secondary objective. The fund invests primarily in investment grade debt securities.

Officers:
S.T. Saunders, Jr. Chairman
D.T. Walker   President

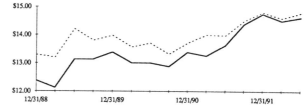

Investment Advisor: CoreStates Investment Advisors, Inc.

Advisory Fee: Monthly fee of 0.5% of average net assets plus 2 1/2% of net amount of interest and dividend income after deducting interest on borrowed funds. Fee for year-ended 11/30/91 was $673,248.

Capital Structure: *Common stock*: 10 mil. shares authorized; 6,463,000 shares outstanding 11/30/91

Portfolio Highlights (as of 11/30/91): Bonds and long-term notes 96.4%, short-term notes 3.6%. Largest industry concentrations: industrial and conglomerate 39.6%, public utilities 31.0%, U.S. government agencies 20.6%. **Largest issuers**: GNMA; Chiquita Brands Int'l. sub. deb.; RJR Holdings Capital Corp.; Bell Telephone of PA; Southern Bell Telephone Co.

Historical Financial Statistics (fiscal year-end:11/30/91):

	1991	1990	1989	1988	1987	1986
Value of net assets (000)	95,492	87,934	91,575	87,506	85,239	94,031
NAV	14.78	13.75	14.32	13.68	13.36	14.74
Net investment income	1.20	1.21	1.21	1.22	1.23	1.25
Dividends from net investment income	1.21	1.21	1.22	1.23	1.25	1.26
Operating expense ratio	0.9%	1.0%	1.0%	1.0%	1.0%	0.9%
Income ratio	8.5%	8.8%	8.8%	9.0%	8.8%	9.0%
Portfolio turnover	43.0%	25.5%	26.0%	11.8%	9.5%	168.1%

Special considerations: The fund had a capital loss carry-forward of $1,810,000 on 11/30/91 expiring through 1998. Orion Capital Corp. submitted an open-ending proposal at the September, 1989, annual meeting; but the proposal did not pass. A proposal to amend the certificate of incorporation to require a 70% vote of outstanding shares to directly or indirectly convert the fund to an open-end fund was passed at that meeting.

Voyageur Minnesota Municipal Income Fund, Inc.

100 South Fifth Street, Suite 2200, Minneapolis, MN 55402   **Category: Municipal Bond Fund**

Phone: 612-376-7000
Listed: VMN, ASE
Commenced Operations: April, 1992
Cusip: 928922103

1991/mid-1992 Range of Premium/Disc: +11% to +5%
1991/mid-1992 Range of Price: $15 5/8 to $15
NAV Total Return 1991: N/A
Share Price Total Return 1991: N/A
Herzfeld Ranking 1991: N/A

Investment Objective: To provide current income exempt from both regular federal income tax and Minnesota state personal income tax, consistent with the preservation of capital. The fund invests substantially all of its net assets in tax-exempt Minnesota municipal obligations rated investment grade at the time of investment.

Officers:

K.E. Dawkins, C.F.A.   President & Chairman

Investment Advisor: Voyageur Fund Managers
Advisory Fee: Monthly fee at the annual rate of 0.40% of the fund's average weekly net assets.
Administrator: Mitchell Hutchins Asset Management Inc.
Administration Fee: Monthly fee at the annual rate of 0.15% of the fund's average weekly net assets.

Capital Structure: *Common stock:* 200 mil. shares authorized, 2,250,000 shares outstanding 4/23/92.
Debt: The fund will issue preferred securities approximately 3 to 6 months after the common stock offering.

Portfolio Highlights: not yet published

Historical Financial Statistics:
	4/23/92
Value of net assets (000)	31,388
NAV	13.95

Special considerations: The fund may invest up to 20% of its assets in unrated Minnesota municipal obligations. Up to 20% of the securities owned by the fund may generate interest that is subject to federal and Minnesota alternative minimum tax. The fund makes monthly distributions of net investment income. Net realized capital gains if any will be paid at least annually. At least annually, the board of directors will consider actions to reduce any discounts which may occur including tender offers and open market repurchases. The fund's Articles of Incorporation contain various anti-takeover provisions including a 66 2/3% vote to convert to an open-end fund or liquidate the fund.

Worldwide Value Fund, Inc.

PO Box 1476, 111 South Calvert Street, Baltimore, MD 21202

Category: Foreign Equity Fund

Phone: 410-539-0000
Listed: VLU, NYSE
Commenced Operations: August, 1986
Cusip: 981599103

1991/mid-1992 Range of Premium/Disc: -11% to -20%
1991/mid-1992 Range of Price: $15 to $11 1/2
NAV Total Return 1990: -20.74%; **1991:** +6.63%
Share Price Total Return 1990: -28.92%; **1991:** +4.82%
Herzfeld Ranking 1991: 27th of 46 foreign equity funds

Investment Objective: Long-term growth of capital, primarily through investment in equity securities of foreign and domestic issuers which the investment advisor believes are undervalued.

Officers:
C.J. Swindells   Chairman
P.E.F. Newbald   President

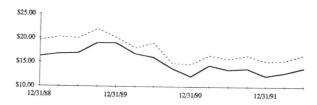

Investment Advisor: Lombard Odier International Portfolio Management Limited
Advisory Fee: Monthly fee at annual rate of 1.00% month-end net assets up to $100 mil., 0.875 of assets between $100 mil. and $150 mil., and 0.80% of excess. Fee for year-ended 12/31/91 was $485,487.
Administrator: Legg Mason Fund Advisor, Inc.
Administration Fee: Monthly fee at annual rate of 0.20% of month-end net assets up to $100 mil., 0.175% month-end assets between $100 mil. and $150 mil., and 0.15% of excess. Fee for year-ended 12/31/91 was $97,097.

Capital Structure: *Common stock:* 50 mil. shares authorized; 3,005,000 shares outstanding 12/31/91

Portfolio Highlights (as of 3/31/92): Common stocks, rights, warrants and options 95.2%, preferred stocks 4.1%, other assets less liabilities 0.7%. Largest geographic concentrations: United Kingdom 34.2%, France 17.8%, Germany 12.2%, Switzerland 7.9%, Netherlands 6.2%, Spain 5.5%, Italy 5.3%. Largest industry concentrations: Food/beverage/tobacco 12.4%, banking 8.5%, insurance 7.4%, construction materials 6.4%, pharmaceuticals and health care 6.3%, multi-industry 6.0%, electrical equipment 5.1%. **Largest positions:** P.S. Delhaize le Lion, Bons Brown Boveri & Cie, Great Universal Stores Ltd. (Series A) non-vot., Grand Metropolitan P.L.C., Compagnie de Saint-Gobain S.A.

Historical Financial Statistics (fiscal year-end: 12/31/91):

	1991	1990	1989	1988	6/30/87 to 12/31/87	8/19/86 to 6/30/87
Value of net assets (000)	46,405	44,026	60,522	58,684	49,463	66,040
NAV	15.44	14.65	20.14	19.53	16.46	21.98
Net investment income	0.08	0.19	0.03	0.03	--	0.16
Dividends from net investment income	0.21	0.31	0.19	--	0.09	--
Distributions from net realized gains	--	0.62	1.42	1.00	1.02	--
Distributions from paid-in capital	--	0.45	--	--	--	--
Expense ratio	2.3%	2.4%	2.2%	2.2%	2.1% ann.	2.2% ann.
Income ratio	0.5%	1.1%	0.1%	0.20%	--	0.90% ann.
Portfolio turnover	91.9%	84.3%	121.5%	95.6%	110.5%	117.0% ann.

Shareholders over 5%: Lazard Frères & Co., 16%

Zenix Income Fund, Inc.

2 World Trade Center, 100th Floor, New York, NY 10048

Category: Bond Fund

Phone: 212-298-6266
Listed: ZIF, NYSE
Commenced Operations: April, 1988
Cusip: 989414107

1991/mid-1992 Range of Premium/Disc: +13% to -11%
1991/mid-1992 Range of Price: $7 1/8 to $4 3/8
NAV Total Return 1990: -13.55%; **1991:** +38.35%
Share Price Total Return 1990: -15.59%; **1991:** +46.79%
Herzfeld Ranking 1991: 16th of 80 bond funds

Investment Objective: High current income primarily through investment in a professionally managed portfolio of fixed-income securities rated in the lower categories.

Officers:

H.B. McLendon   Chairman
T.A. Belshé   President

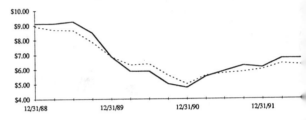

Investment Advisor: Shearson Lehman Advisors
Advisory Fee: Monthly fee at annual rate of 0.50% of average weekly net assets. Fee for year-ended 3/31/92 was $615,564.
Sub-Investment Advisor and Administrator: The Boston Company Advisors, Inc.
Sub-Investment Advisory and Administration Fee: Monthly fee at annual rate of 0.20% average weekly net assets. Fee for year-ended 12/31/91 was $246,225.

Capital Structure: *Common stock:* 250 mil. shares authorized; 11,856,419 shares outstanding 3/31/92
9.67% Cumulative Preferred stock: 250,000 shares authorized; 28,750 shares outstanding, redeemable on 4/15/93 at $1,000 per share.
Senior Money Market Notes: $25,800,000 outstanding, due 1995. Interest rate is set by auction every 28 days; during the year ended 3/31/92 the interest rates ranged from 4.19% to 6.80%.

Portfolio Highlights (as of 3/31/92): Corporate bonds and notes 112.0%, U.S. treasury obligations 8.6%, senior money market notes due 1995 (24.4%), other assets and liabilities 3.8%. Largest industry concentrations: food 14.8%, packaging and containers 14.0%, health care 10.5%, retail 10.3%, publishing 7.9%, chemicals 7.0%, building and construction 6.8%, conglomerate 6.4%. **Largest issuers:** U.S. treasury bills and notes; various Big Bear Stores; Hospital Corporation of America sub. deb. 9.0-16; Anacomp Inc. sr. sub. note 15-00; Unisys Corporation Credit Sensitive Notes 15-97; Snyder General Corporation gtd. sr. deb. 14.25-00.

Historical Financial Statistics (fiscal year-end: 3/31/92):

	1992	1991	1990	4/27/88 to 3/31/89
Value of net assets (000)	105,842	92,543	99,253	120,063
NAV	6.39	5.58	6.30	8.71
NAV preferred shares	1,044.32	1,044.32	1,044.32	1,044.32
Net investment income	1.08	1.17	1.42	1.29
Dividends from net investment income	0.85	0.90	1.20	1.01
Dividends to preferred shares	96.70	96.70	96.70	46.20
Operating expense ratio	2.15%	2.47%	2.32%	2.04% ann.
Interest expense ratio	2.10%	4.18%	5.16%	4.61% ann.
Income ratio	14.16%	16.12%	15.11%	13.84% ann.
Portfolio turnover	86%	68%	81%	105%

Special considerations: The fund may repurchase shares or make tender offers for shares. At 3/31/92 the fund had capital loss carryforward of $35,804,737 expiring through 2000. Monthly dividend rate reduced to $0.06 per share in June, 1992.

Z-Seven Fund, Inc.

2302 W. Monterey Circle, Mesa, AZ 85202

Phone: 602-897-6214
Listed: ZSEV, OTC, Pacific
Commenced Operations: 1983
Cusip: 988789103

Category: Specialized Equity Fund

1991/mid-1992 Range of Premium/Disc: +22% to -3%
1991/mid-1992 Range of Price: $21 1/2 to $11 1/2
NAV Total Return 1990: -7.72%; **1991**: +46.85%
Share Price Total Return 1990: -0.92%; **1991**: +67.35%
Herzfeld Ranking 1991: 6th of 18 specialized equity funds

Investment Objective: Long-term capital appreciation primarily through investment in common stocks. Portfolio securities are selected using the advisor's analysis of the following seven criteria: consistency, magnitude, working capital, corporate liquidity, accounting procedures, owner diversification, price/earnings multiple.

Officers:
B. Ziskin   President

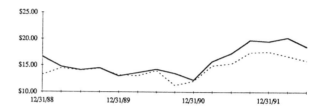

Investment Advisor: TOP Fund Management, Inc.

Advisory Fee: Base annual rate of 1.25%, plus or minus a performance fee bonus or penalty of up to 2.5% per quarter of average daily net assets. Fee for year-ended 12/31/91 was $252,110; performance bonus was $190,718.

Capital Structure: *Common stock*: 5 mil. shares authorized; 1,285,324 shares outstanding 12/31/91

Portfolio Highlights (as of 12/31/91): Common stocks 108.4%, cash, receivables & other assets less liabilities (8.40%). Largest industry concentrations: air travel & leisure 19.91%, data processing services 12.70%, alcohol and tobacco 9.85%, transportation 8.27%, food and household products 7.08%, electronics 6.89%, fluid control equipment 6.66%. Geographic breakdown: UK 66.41%, U.S. 21.34%, Western Europe 12.25%. **Largest positions**: Airtours PLC, Geodynamics Inc., Boston Acoustics Inc., Kewill Systems PLC, Arnold Industries Inc.

Historical Financial Statistics (fiscal year-end: 12/31/91):

	1991	1990	1989	1988	1987	1986
Value of net assets (000)	22,687	15,756	18,231	21,083	22,827	24,210
NAV	17.65	12.16	13.25	14.33	15.23	16.09
Net investment income (loss)	0.18	0.15	0.45	0.01	(0.14)	(0.35)
Dividends from net investment income	--	0.13	0.45	--	--	--
Expense ratio	4.33%	2.63%	1.16%	2.73%	3.23%	4.42%
Income ratio (after performance adjustment) (loss)	(0.15%)	1.44%	3.33%	0.04%	(0.74%)	(2.30%)
Portfolio turnover	44.12%	42.82%	87.29%	4.73%	23.34%	30.56%

Special considerations: Performance figures after taking into consideration taxes paid on behalf of shareholders are: NAV total return 1989, -3.14%; price total return 1989, -18.02%. The fund's president has stated that he will continue to increase his holdings in the fund. He also advocates the theory that well managed closed-end funds are worth higher P/E multiples. The fund retained a portion of the taxable long-term capital gains in the amount of $0.53763 per share for the year-ended 12/31/89. Shareholders were able to take a credit on the 1989 tax returns equivalent to $0.18279 per share. The fund did not retain any long-term capital gains for 1991. During 1991 the fund repurchasd 10,600 shares in the open market, and during the six years ended 12/31/91 over 260,000 shares were repurchased. **Shareholders over 5%**: Barry Ziskin, 23%

The Zweig Fund, Inc.
900 Third Avenue, New York, NY 10022

Phone: 212-755-9860
Listed: ZF, NYSE
Commenced Operations: October, 1986
Cusip: 989834106

Category: Specialized Equity Fund

1991/mid-1992 Range of Premium/Disc: +17% to +2%
1991/mid-1992 Range of Price: $14 1/8 to $10 1/4
NAV Total Return 1990: +1.66%; **1991**: +29.60%
Share Price Total Return 1990: -0.57%; **1991**: +33.66%
Herzfeld Ranking 1991: 10th of 18 specialized equity funds

Investment Objective: Capital appreciation, primarily through investment in equity securities, consistent with the preservation of capital and elimination of unnecessary risk.

Officers:
M.E. Zweig, Ph.D.   Chairman & President

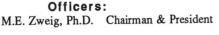

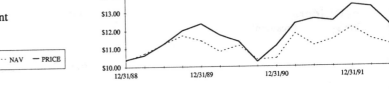

Investment Advisor: Zweig Advisors, Inc.
Advisory Fee: Monthly fee at annual rate of 0.85% of average daily net assets. Fee for year-ended 12/31/91 was $3,746,556.
Administrator: Zweig/Glaser Advisors
Administration Fee: Monthly fee at annual rate of 0.15% of average daily net assets. Fee for year-ended 12/31/91 was $661,157.

Capital Structure: *Common stock*: 100 mil. shares authorized; 42,800,451 shares outstanding 3/31/92

Portfolio Highlights (as of 3/31/92): Common stock 57.96%, long-term U.S. government obligations 9.63%, short-term money market instruments 31.49%, cash and other assets less liabilities 0.92%. Largest industry concentrations: computer software 7.78%, retail trade & services 5.36%, biotechnology 4.79%. **Largest positions**: U.S. treasury bonds & notes; Allied-Signal Inc.; Chiron Corp. Hasbro Inc.; Novell Inc., Amgen Inc.

Historical Financial Statistics (fiscal year-end: 12/31/91):

	1991	1990	1989	1988	1987	10/2/86 to 12/31/86
Value of net assets (000)	526,252	389,816	408,864	356,775	329,335	316,503
NAV	12.40	10.48	11.43	10.35	9.73	9.31
Net investment income	0.26	0.47	0.52	0.33	0.22	0.10
Dividends from net investment income	0.30	0.49	0.52	0.25	0.28	--
Distributions from net realized gains	0.82	0.69	0.60	0.79	0.64	--
Expense ratio	1.28%	1.27%	1.31%	1.39%	1.51%	1.16% ann.
Income ratio	2.37%	4.39%	4.68%	3.38%	2.21%	4.15% ann.
Portfolio turnover	144.3%	201.8%	183.6%	205.74%	281.78%	55.90%

Special considerations: The fund may repurchase shares when trading at a 10% discount to net asset value. The fund has a policy to distribute at least 2.5% of net asset value per quarter. The fund's Articles of Incorporation contain various anti-takeover provisions. The fund had a rights offering in August, 1991, whereby shareholders could acquire one new share for every 5 owned at a price of $11.71 per share.

The Zweig Total Return Fund

900 Third Avenue, New York, NY 10022

Category: Miscellaneous

Phone: 212-755-9860	**1991/mid-1992 Range of Premium/Disc:** +16% to -4%
Listed: ZTR, NYSE	**1991/mid-1992 Range of Price:** $11 3/4 to $8
Commenced Operations: September, 1988	**NAV Total Return 1990:** +4.17%; **1991:** +19.49%
Cusip: 989837109	**Share Price Total Return 1990:** -1.18%; **1991:** +35.77%

Investment Objective: Highest total return, consisting of capital appreciation and current income, consistent with the preservation of capital. Under normal circumstances the fund will invest 50% to 65% of total assets in U.S. government securities.

Officers:

M.E. Zweig, Ph.D.   Chairman & President

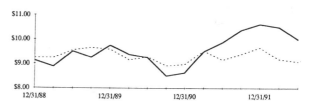

Investment Advisor: Zweig Total Return Advisors, Inc.

Advisory Fee: Monthly fee at annual rate of 0.70% of average daily net assets. Fee for year-ended 12/31/91 was $4,235,571.

Administrator: The Boston Company Advisors, Inc.

Administration Fee: Monthly fee at annual rate of 0.25% of average daily net assets plus certain out-of-pocket expenses. Fee for year-ended 12/31/91 was $1,210,163.

Capital Structure: *Common stock*: 500 mil. shares authorized; 66,912,643 shares outstanding 3/31/92

Portfolio Highlights (as of 3/31/92): Common stock 25.64%, corporate bonds 3.00%, foreign bonds 2.27%, Yankee 1.12%, U.S. government and other agency obligations 28.86%, short-term money market instruments 38.65%, other assets less liabilities 1.58%. **Largest positions:** U.S. treasury notes and bonds; Philip Morris Companies Inc., Pfizer Inc., Deutsche Bank of Finance 9.375-99, KFW International Finance Inc. 7.625-04.

Historical Financial Statistics (fiscal year-end: 12/31/91):

	1991	1990	1989	9/30/88 to 12/31/88
Value of net assets (000)	648,118	573,782	596,508	564,330
NAV	9.79	9.02	9.59	9.24
Net investment income	0.44	0.56	0.68	0.25
Dividends from net investment income	0.43	0.60	0.73	0.16
Distributions from net realized gains	0.53	0.04	0.23	--
Distributions from capital	--	0.29	--	--
Expense ratio	1.11%	1.09%	1.14%	1.19% ann.
Income ratio	4.74%	6.14%	7.18%	11.19% ann.
Portfolio turnover	148.60%	145.16%	192.73%	112.56%

Special considerations: The fund may repurchase shares when trading at a discount to net asset value or make tender offers when the Board deems it advantageous. Such actions will be considered by the Board on a quarterly basis. Under certain circumstances, beginning 1/1/90, the fund may be required to submit an open-ending proposal. The fund has a policy to distribute at least 0.83% of net asset value per month (10% annually). The fund's Articles of Incorporation contain various anti-takeover provisions.

Inactive or Small Closed-End Funds
Abbreviated Coverage

Capital Investments, Inc.
744 N. Fourth Street, Milwaukee, WI 53203   **Category:** Miscellaneous

Phone: 414-273-6560
Listed: OTC

Investment Objective: The company provides venture capital and long-term financing to qualified small business concerns. These investments are structured to generate current income and provide the opportunity to participate in the capital appreciation of growing businesses.

Historical Financial Statistics (fiscal year-end: 12/31/91):

	1991	1990	1989	1988	1987
Value of net assets (000)	4,795	5,427	5,006	5,556	5,272
NAV	8.73	9.88	9.12	10.26	9.73

Special considerations: A tender offer for 51% of outstanding shares during 1988 was not successful. Officers and directors own 88.9% of outstanding shares.

Combined Penny Stock Fund, Inc.
2055 Anglo Drive, Suite 202, Colorado Springs, CO 80918   **Category:** Specialized Equity Fund

Phone: 719-636-1511
Listed: OTC

Investment Objective: Capital appreciation primarily through investment in common stocks whose total market capitalization is $75 million or less, however investments may be made in slightly larger, more stable and somewhat less speculative companies.

Historical Financial Statistics (fiscal year-end: 9/30/91):

	six months 3/31/92	1991	1990	1989	1988	1987
Value of net assets (000)	863	673	691	1,270	1,350	
NAV	0.01	0.01	0.01	0.018	0.019	0.024

Special considerations: In 1991 the shareholders approved a proposal to allow the fund to invest a larger portion of net assets in slightly larger, more stable and somewhat less speculative companies. The fund will invest at least 80% of assets in common stocks of companies whose total market capitalization is $75 million or less. As of 3/31/92 the fund's investments in restricted securities and bridge loans comprised 9.5% of the value of its total assets.

Redwood MicroCap Fund, Inc.
(formerly Infinity Speculative Fund, Inc.)
2616 W. Colorado Ave., Colorado Springs, CO 80904

Category: Specialized Equity Fund

Phone: 719-636-1511
Listed: OTC

Investment Objective: Capital appreciation primarily through investment in common stocks whose total market capitalization is $50 million or less.

Historical Financial Statistics (fiscal year-end: 3/31/92):

	1992	1991	1990	1989	1988
Value of net assets (000)	739	336	476	801	607
NAV	0.374	0.168	0.234	0.379	0.318

Special considerations: The shareholders approved a proposal to allow the fund to invest a larger portion of net assets in slightly larger, more stable and somewhat less speculative companies. The fund will invest at least 80% of assets in common stocks of companies whose total market capitalization is $50 million or less. At the 1991 annual meeting shareholder approved a name change to Redwood MicroCap Fund, Inc. because the name Infinity Speculative Fund, Inc. is similar to that of a mutual fund. The fund had a loss carryforward as of 3/31/92 of approximately $830,000, available through 2007.

Jupiter Industries, Inc.
(formerly Greater Washington Investors, Inc.)
5454 Wisconsin Avenue, Chevy Chase, MD 20815

Category: Miscellaneous

Phone: 301-656-4053
Listed: JPI, ASE

Investment Objective: The fund seeks above-average capital appreciation on venture capital investments and takes commensurate risks to achieve this objective. The fund favors ventures associated with new or emerging technologies because it believes that such companies, when they are successful, generate proportionately higher returns for investors. It also participates in the financings of later-stage companies and leveraged buy-outs in a broad range of industry segments with the objective of achieving a current return as well as above-average, long-term capital appreciation.

Historical Financial Statistics (fiscal year-end: 12/31/91):

	1991	1990	1989	1988	1987	1986
Value of net assets (000)	20,029	18,129	20,716	26,193	24,818	30,863
NAV	19.56*	4.43	5.06	6.40	6.06	7.00

*after reverse stock split, one-for-four

Special considerations: Shareholders approved a proposal that effectively will reverse-split the common stock on a one-for-four basis. Johnston Industries, Inc. owns 36.9% and Research Industries Incorporated owns 10.8% of outstanding shares. Officers and directors own 38.9% of outstanding shares.

PMC Capital, Inc.
(formerly Pro-Med Capital, Inc.)
18301 Biscayne Blvd., 2nd Floor, N. Miami Beach, FL 33160   **Category: Specialized Equity Fund**
Phone: 305-933-5858
Listed: PMC, ASE

Investment Objective: The fund primarily makes loans under certain programs established by the Small Business Administration through three of its wholly owned subsidiaries.

Historical Financial Statistics (fiscal year-end: 12/31/91):

	1991	1990	1989	1988	1987
Value of net assets (000)	25,143	16,751	10,961	9,636	8,007
NAV	3.53	2.87	2.46	2.45	2.39

Special considerations: The fund completed a private placement at the end of 1988. Shareholders approved a proposal to allow an increase in the percentage of loans collateralized by real estate, equipment, and other tangible and/or intangible assets to individuals outside of the health-care industry and to change the name of the fund to PMC Capital, Inc. from Pro-Med Capital, Inc.

Rand Capital Corporation
1300 Rand Building, Buffalo, NY 14203   **Category: Miscellaneous**
Phone: 716-853-0802
Listed: RAND, OTC

Investment Objective: Rand Capital Corporation is a registered closed-end management investment company, and its wholly-owned subsidiary, Rand SBIC Inc., is a small business investment company chartered under the investment regulations of the U.S. Small Business Administration. They invest in the securities of small businesses which offer unique opportunities for growth.

Historical Financial Statistics (fiscal year-end: 12/31/91):

	1991	1990	1989	1988	1987
Value of net assets (000)	7,139	6,956	8,486	8,181	6,951
NAV	5.19	5.06	6.17	5.95	5.06

Special considerations: Officers and directors own 41.2% of outstanding shares. The following are shareholders with greater than a 5% stake: Jayne Kathryn Rand, 18.0%; Reginald B. Newman II, 13.9%; Francesca W. Rand, 6.5%; George F. Rand IV, 6.5%; Brederica Rand Zuerner, 5.8%.

Special considerations: The fund paid a 25% stock dividend on 6/5/92. At the July 14, 1992 annual meeting shareholders will consider a proposal to increase the authorized shares to 4.4 mil. from 2.2 mil.

Spectra Fund, Inc.

75 Maiden Lane, New York, NY 10038

Category: Specialized Equity Fund

Phone: 212-806-8800
Listed: OTC

Investment Objective: The fund invests in U.S. equity securities.

Historical Financial Statistics (fiscal year-end: 6/30/91):

	six months 12/31/91	1991	1990	1989	1988	1987
Value of net assets (000)	5,257	5,006	4,805	3,881	3,525	6,021
NAV	20.48	19.50	18.72	15.12	13.73	23.45

Index

About the Authors

THOMAS J. HERZFELD is chairman and president of Thomas J. Herzfeld & Co., Inc., a stock brokerage firm, and Thomas J. Herzfeld Advisors, Inc., an investment advisory firm; both specializing in closed-end funds. The world's leading expert on closed-end funds, he has been a featured guest on *Your Portfolio (CNBC)*, *The Nightly Business Report*, and *Wall $treet Week with Louis Rukeyser*. He is the coauthor, with Robert Drach, of *High-Return, Low-Risk Investment*, Second Edition. In addition, Mr. Herzfeld publishes his own monthly research report on closed-end funds, *The Investor's Guide to Closed-End Funds*. He has written numerous articles for *Barrons* on the subject of closed-end funds.

CECILIA L. GONDOR is Executive Vice President of Thomas J. Herzfeld & Co., Inc., and Thomas J. Herzfeld Advisors, Inc., both specializing in the field of closed-end funds. Ms. Gondor is registered with the National Association of Securities Dealers as a Financial and Operations Principal, Options Principal, and Registered Representative. She is Deputy Editor of *The Thomas J. Herzfeld Encyclopedia of Closed-End Funds*, an annual reference volume, and coordinates preparation and publication of the monthly research report on closed-end funds.